# A-Z GREAT BRITAIN NORTHERN IRELAND
## Handy Road Atlas

Reference and Tourist Information.............................. 2-3

Road Maps at 5 miles to 1" (1:316,800).....................4-169

Outer Hebrides at 10 miles to 1" (1:633,600)........ 170-171

Northern Isles at 10 miles to 1" (1:633,600)..........172-173

Northern Ireland at 12 miles to 1" (1:760,320).......174-175

Route Planning Maps.............................................176-179

Index to Towns, Villages & Hamlets......................180-256

Mileage Chart.........................................Inside Back Cover

EDITION 29 2021
Copyright © Geographers' A-Z Map Company Ltd.

Contains OS data © Crown copyright and database rights 2020

Northern Ireland: This is Based upon Crown Copyright and is reproduced with the permission of Land & Property Services under delegated authority from the Controller of Her Majesty's Stationery Office, © Crown copyright and database right 2020 PMLPA No 100508. The inclusion of parts or all of the Republic of Ireland is by permission of the Government of Ireland who retain copyright in the data used. © Ordnance Survey Ireland and Government of Ireland.

registered trade marks of
Geographers' A-Z Map Company Ltd

Land & Property Services
Paper Map Licensed Partner

This is a registered Trade Mark of
Department of Finance and Personnel.

www./az.co.uk

**Motorway**
Autoroute
Autobahn
≣M1≣

**Motorway Under Construction**
Autoroute en construction
Autobahn im Bau

**Motorway Proposed**
Autoroute prévue
Geplante Autobahn

**Motorway Junctions with Numbers**
Autoroute échangeur numéroté
Beschränkter Fahrtrichtungswechsel

Unlimited Interchange **4**
Echangeur complet
Autobahnanschlußstelle mit Nummer

Limited Interchange **5**
Echangeur partiel
Unbeschränkter Fahrtrichtungswechsel

**Motorway Service Area**
with access from one carriageway only
Ⓢ
Aire de services d'autoroute
accessible d'un seul côté
Rastplatz oder Raststätte
Einbahn
Ⓢ

**Major Road Service Areas** with 24 hour facilities
Aire de services sur route prioritaire ouverte 24h sur 24
Raststätte durchgehend geöffnet

Primary Route ≡Ⓢ≡
Route à grande circulation
Hauptverkehrsstraße

Class A Road ≡Ⓢ≡
Route de type A
A- Straße

**Truckstop** (selection of)
Sélection d'aire pour poids lourds
Auswahl von Fernfahrerrastplatz
⬤Ⓣ⬤

**Major Road Junctions**
Jonctions grands routiers
Hauptverkehrsstrasse Kreuzungen

Other Autre Andere

**Primary Route**
Route à grande circulation
Hauptverkehrsstraße
A40

**Primary Route Junction with Number**
Echangeur numéroté
Hauptverkehrsstraßenkreuzung mit Nummer
⬤4⬤

**Primary Route Destination**
Route prioritaire
Hauptverkehrsstraße Richtung
DOVER

**Dual Carriageways** (A & B roads)
Route à double chaussées séparées (route A & B)
Zweispurige Schnellstraße (A- und B- Straßen)

**Class A Road**
Route de type A
A-Straße
A129

**Class B Road**
Route de type B
B-Straße
B177

**Narrow Major Road** (passing places)
Route prioritaire étroite (possibilité de dépassement)
Schmale Hauptverkehrsstraße (mit Überholmöglichkeit)

**Major Roads Under Construction**
Route prioritaire en construction
Hauptverkehrsstraße im Bau

**Major Roads Proposed**
Route prioritaire prévue
Geplante Hauptverkehrsstaße

**Gradient 1:7** (14%) **& steeper**
(Descent in direction of arrow)
≫
Pente égale ou supérieure à 14% (dans le sens de la descente)
14% Steigung und steiler (in Pfeilrichtung)

**Toll**
Barrière de péage
Gebührenpflichtig
Toll

**Dart Charge**
www.gov.uk/pay-dartford-crossing-charge
Ⓖ

**Park & Ride**
Parking avec Service Navette
Parken und Reisen
P+R

**Mileage between markers**
Distence en miles entre les flèches
Strecke zwischen Markierungen in Meilen
8

**Airport**
Aéroport
Flughafen
✈

**Railway and Station**
Voie ferrée et gare
Eisenbahnlinie und Bahnhof

**Level Crossing and Tunnel**
Passage à niveau et tunnel
Bahnübergang und Tunnel

**River or Canal**
Rivière ou canal
Fluß oder Kanal

**County or Unitary Authority Boundary**
Limite de comté ou de division administrative
Grafschafts- oder Verwaltungsbezirksgrenze

**National Boundary**
Frontière nationale
Landesgrenze

**Built-up Area**
Agglomération
Geschloßene Ortschaft

**Town, Village or Hamlet**
Ville, Village ou hameau
Stadt, Dorf oder Weiler
○

**Wooded Area**
Zone boisée
Waldgebiet

**Spot Height in Feet**
Altitude (en pieds)
Höhe in Fuß
· 813

**Height Above Sea Level**   1,400'-2000'  427m-610m
Altitude par rapport au niveau de la mer  2000'+  610m+
Höhe über Meeresspiegel

**National Grid Reference** (kilometres)
Coordonnées géographiques nationales (Kilomètres)
Nationale geographische Koordinaten (Kilometer)
¹00

**Page Continuation**
Suite à la page indiquée
Seitenfortsetzung
24

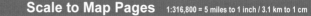

# Scale to Map Pages  1:316,800 = 5 miles to 1 inch / 3.1 km to 1 cm

0  1  2  3  4  5          10          15          20 Miles

0  1  2  3  4  5      10      15      20      25      30 Kilometres

| | | | | |
|---|---|---|---|---|
| **Airfield** <br> Terrain d'aviation <br> Flugplatz | ✈ | | **Horse Racecourse** <br> Hippodrome <br> Pferderennbahn | 🐎 |
| **Heliport** <br> Héliport <br> Hubschrauberlandeplatz | Ⓗ | | **Industrial Monument** <br> Monument Industrielle <br> Industriedenkmal | ✸ |
| **Abbey, Church, Friary, Priory** <br> Abbaye, église, monastère, prieuré <br> Abtei, Kirche, Mönchskloster, Kloster | † | | **Leisure Park, Leisure Pool** <br> Parc d'Attraction, Loisirs Piscine <br> Freizeitpark, Freizeit pool | ⅅ |
| **Animal Collection** <br> Ménagerie <br> Tiersammlung | ⚘ | | **Lighthouse** <br> Phare <br> Leuchtturm | 🛆 |
| **Aquarium** <br> Aquarium <br> Aquarium | ⬭ | | **Mine, Cave** <br> Mine, Grotte <br> Bergwerk, Höhle | ⛏ |
| **Arboretum, Botanical Garden** <br> Jardin Botanique <br> Botanischer Garten | ♣ | | **Monument** <br> Monument <br> Denkmal | ⓘ |
| **Aviary, Bird Garden** <br> Volière <br> Voliere | 🐦 | | **Motor Racing Circuit** <br> Circuit Automobile <br> Automobilrennbahn | 🏎 |
| **Battle Site and Date** <br> Champ de bataille et date <br> Schlachtfeld und Datum | ⚔ <br> *1066* | | **Museum, Art Gallery** <br> Musée <br> Museum, Galerie | Ⓜ |
| **Blue Flag Beach** <br> Plage Pavillon Bleu <br> Blaue Flagge Strand | 🏖 | | **National Park** <br> Parc national <br> Nationalpark | ▥ |
| **Bridge** <br> Pont <br> Brücke | ⌂ | | **National Trust Property** <br> National Trust Property <br> National Trust- Eigentum | ⋰ |
| **Castle** (open to public) <br> Château (ouvert au public) <br> Schloß / Burg (für die Öffentlichkeit zugänglich) | 🏰 | | **Natural Attraction** <br> Attraction Naturelle <br> Natürliche Anziehung | ★ |
| **Castle with Garden** (open to public) <br> Château avec parc (ouvert au public) <br> Schloß mit Garten (für die Öffentlichkeit zugänglich) | Ⓜ | | **Nature Reserve or Bird Sanctuary** <br> Réserve naturelle botanique ou ornithologique <br> Natur- oder Vogelschutzgebiet | 🐦 |
| **Cathedral** <br> Cathédrale <br> Kathedrale | ✛ | | **Nature Trail or Forest Walk** <br> Chemin forestier, piste verte <br> Naturpfad oder Waldweg | 🍃 |
| **Cidermaker** <br> Cidrerie (fabrication) <br> Apfelwein Hersteller | 🍶 | | **Place of Interest**        *Craft Centre* • <br> Site, curiosité <br> Sehenswürdigkeit | |
| **Country Park** <br> Parc régional <br> Landschaftspark | 🌳 | | **Prehistoric Monument** <br> Monument Préhistorique <br> Prähistorische Denkmal | ⛩ |
| **Distillery** <br> Distillerie <br> Brennerei | ⚗ | | **Railway, Steam or Narrow Gauge** <br> Chemin de fer, à vapeur ou à voie étroite <br> Eisenbahn, Dampf- oder Schmalspurbahn | 🚂 |
| **Farm Park, Open Farm** <br> Park Animalier <br> Bauernhof Park | 🐖 | | **Roman Remains** <br> Vestiges Romains <br> Römischen Ruinen | ⚱ |
| **Ferry** (vehicular, sea) <br>      (vehicular, river) <br>      (foot only) <br> Bac (véhicules, mer) <br>      (véhicules, rivière) <br>      (piétons) <br> Fähre (auto, meer) <br>      (auto, fluß) <br>      (nur für Personen) | ⛴ <br> ⛴ <br> 🚶 | | **Theme Park** <br> Centre de loisirs <br> Vergnügungspark | 🎡 |
| | | | **Tourist Information Centre** <br> Office de Tourisme <br> Touristeninformationen | ⅈ |
| **Fortress, Hill Fort** <br> Château Fort <br> Festung | ✻ | | **Viewpoint**   (180 degrees)     (360 degrees) <br> Vue panoramique (180 degrés)    (360 degrés) <br> Aussichtspunkt (180 Grade)      (360 Grade) | ⧫   ⧫ |
| **Garden** (open to public) <br> Jardin (ouvert au public) <br> Garten (für die Öffentlichkeit zugänglich) | ❀ | | **Vineyard** <br> Vignoble <br> Weinberg | ⚜ |
| **Golf Course** <br> Terrain de golf <br> Golfplatz | ⚑ | | **Visitor Information Centre** <br> Centre d'information touristique <br> Besucherzentrum | Ⅴ |
| **Historic Building** (open to public) <br> Monument historique (ouvert au public) <br> Historisches Gebäude (für die Öffentlichkeit zugänglich) | 🏛 | | **Wildlife Park** <br> Réserve de faune <br> Wildpark | ⚘ |
| **Historic Building with Garden** (open to public) <br> Monument historique avec jardin (ouvert au public) <br> Historisches Gebäude mit Garten (für die Öffentlichkeit zugänglich) | 🏛 | | **Windmill** <br> Moulin à vent <br> Windmühle | ✗ |
| | | | **Zoo or Safari Park** <br> Parc ou réserve zoologique <br> Zoo oder Safari-Park | 🐘 |

*Please note: symbols have been enlarged for clarity*

**4**

# ISLES OF SCILLY

Round Island
White Island
St Helen's
Piper's Hole
King Charles's Castle
Day Mark
**BRYHER** Lower Town Middle Town
Cromwell's Castle Tean
The Town New Grimsby ST MARTIN'S
Gweal Figurehead Collection Old Grimsby Higher Town
Valhalla Ships Abbey Halangy
**TRESCO**
Maiden Bower Samson Bant's Down EASTERN ISLES
Mincarlo Crow Innisidgen Burial Ground
The Road
Harry's Walls Porth Hellick Down Burial Chamber
Maypole
**Hugh Town** ST MARY'S
**ISLES OF SCILLY** Garrison ISLES OF SCILLY
Walls Old Town Giant's (St Mary's) Castle

Crim Rocks
Annet Troy Town Maze
Broad Sound North West Passage
St Mary's Sound
Gugh
Nag's Punch Bowl
Head
Western Rocks
Bishop Rock **ST AGNES**

Hugh Town to Penzance 2hrs. 40mins. (Seasonal)

The Isles of Scilly lie 28 miles WSW of Land's End

---

Godrevy Island
Navax Point
Crane Islands
**Portreath**
Hell's Mouth
Illogan
Tehidy
Park Bottom
The Carracks
Gwithian
Kehelland
**CAMBORNE**
Tuckingmill
St Ives Bay
B3301
Treswithian
Brea
Barbara Hepworth
Tate
Lifeboat Station
**St Ives** The Towans Phillack
Connor Downs
Roseworthy Penponds
B3306 Hellesveor Carbis Bay Angarrack
Penbeagle
Gurnard's Head Towednack Halsetown Knill's Lelant Downs
Trencrom Hill Carnhell Green
Zennor Cripplesease Connor Downs Praze-an-Beeble
Cam Galver Engine House Treen Porthmeor B3311 Canonstown Wall
Zennor Quoit Mutfra Quoit Nancledra Gwinear
**Pendeen Watch** 9 Maidens Stone Circle Fraddam
Levant Mine & Higher Morvah Ancient Village New Mill Leedstown Crowan
Beam Engine Chysauster Ludgvan Releath
Geevor Men-an-Tol **Pendeen** Ding Dong Lanyon Quoit
Tin Mine Chun Castle Engine House Boswarthen **COR**
Trewellard Quoit Great Bosullow Boswarthen Crowlas St Hilary Godolphin
**Carnyorth** Standing Stone Relubbus Townshend Godolphin
Botallack Count House **Madron** Trevarrack Gulval Cross
Tregeseal Newbridge Heamoor Longrock Crowntown
**St Just** Trengwainton **Marazion** Rosudgeon
**Cape Cornwall** Drift Trereife A30
The Brisons Ballowall Barrow Chyandour Germoe **HELSTON**
Kelynack B3306 736 **Sancreed** St Michael's Mount Trew
Carn Euny **Perranuthnoe**
Ancient Village Brane Drift Tredavoe **Newlyn** Kenneggy Ashton
Whitesand Bay Crows-an-wra **PENZANCE** Downs A394
Sennen Cove Lifeboat A30 Kerris Pengersick Breage
**Sennen** Boscawen-un Stone Circle B3283 Paul Mousehole Cudden Point Praa Sands Rinsey Wheal Prosper Engine House
Longships Maen Castle Trevescan Pipers Standing St Clement's Isle Wheal Trewavas
Land's End Treville Trewoofe Isle B3315 Engine House **Porthleven**
**LAND'S END** B3315 St Buryan Lamorna Trewavas Head Loe Bar Loe Pool & Bar
Telegraph Tregiffian Burial Chamber Merry Maidens Stone Circle Berepper
Porthcurno Treen Penberth
Gwennap Head St Minack Theatre Logan Rock **MOUNT'S BAY** Poldhu Point
Porthgwarra Levan Cribba Head Marconi Monument
Mullion Cove
Runnel Stone Penzance to Hugh Town 2hrs. 40mins. (Seasonal) Mullion Island Mullion Cove

Vellan Head

Wolf Rock
**Wolf Rock** Kynance

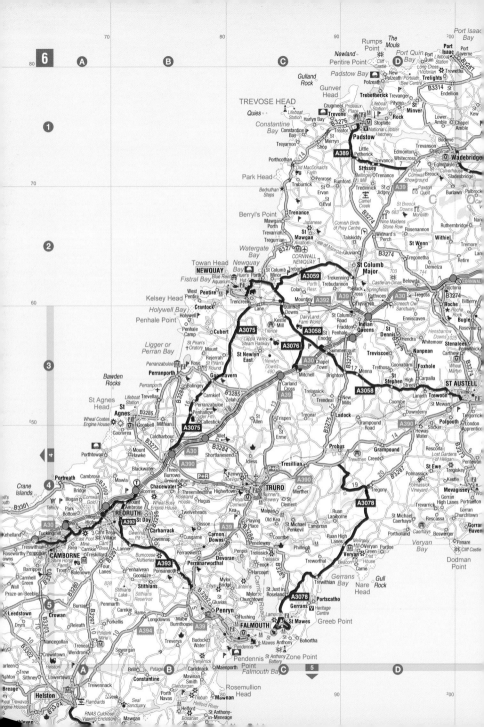

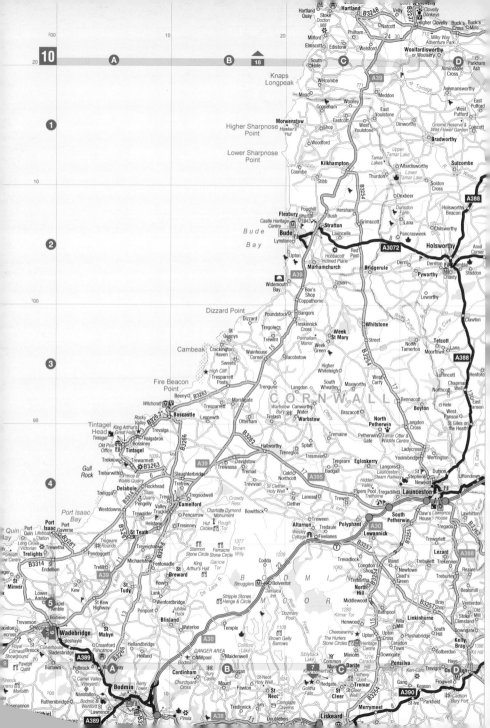

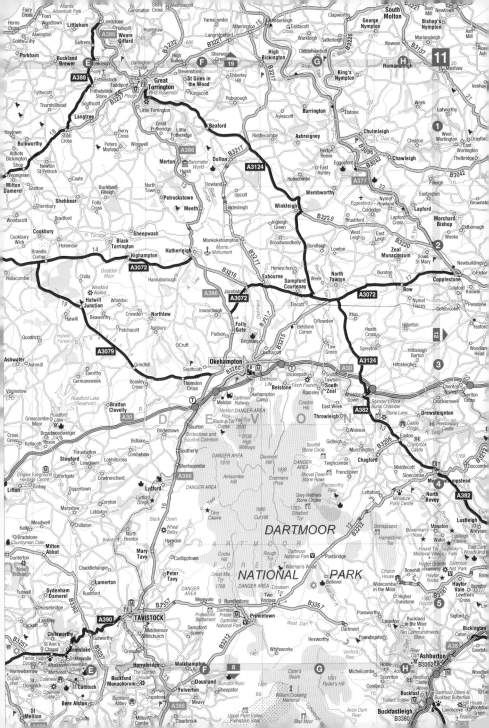

Poole to:
Cherbourg 4hrs. 30mins.
Guernsey 3hrs.
(Fast Ferry, Seasonal)
Jersey 4hrs. 30mins.
(Fast Ferry, Seasonal)
St Malo 6hrs.
(Fast Ferry, Seasonal)

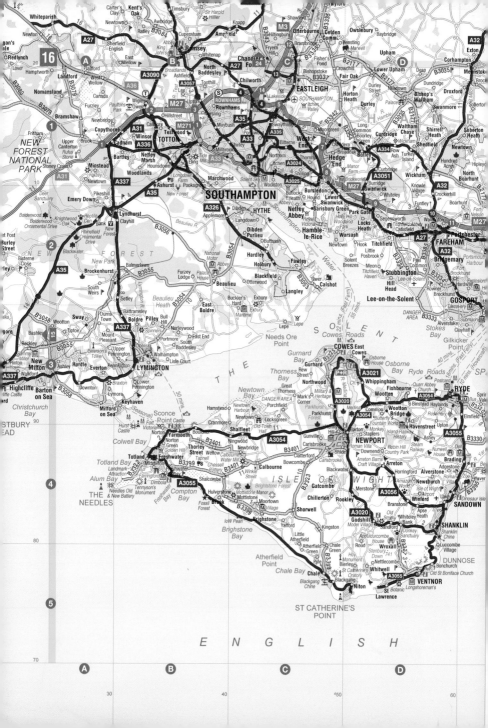

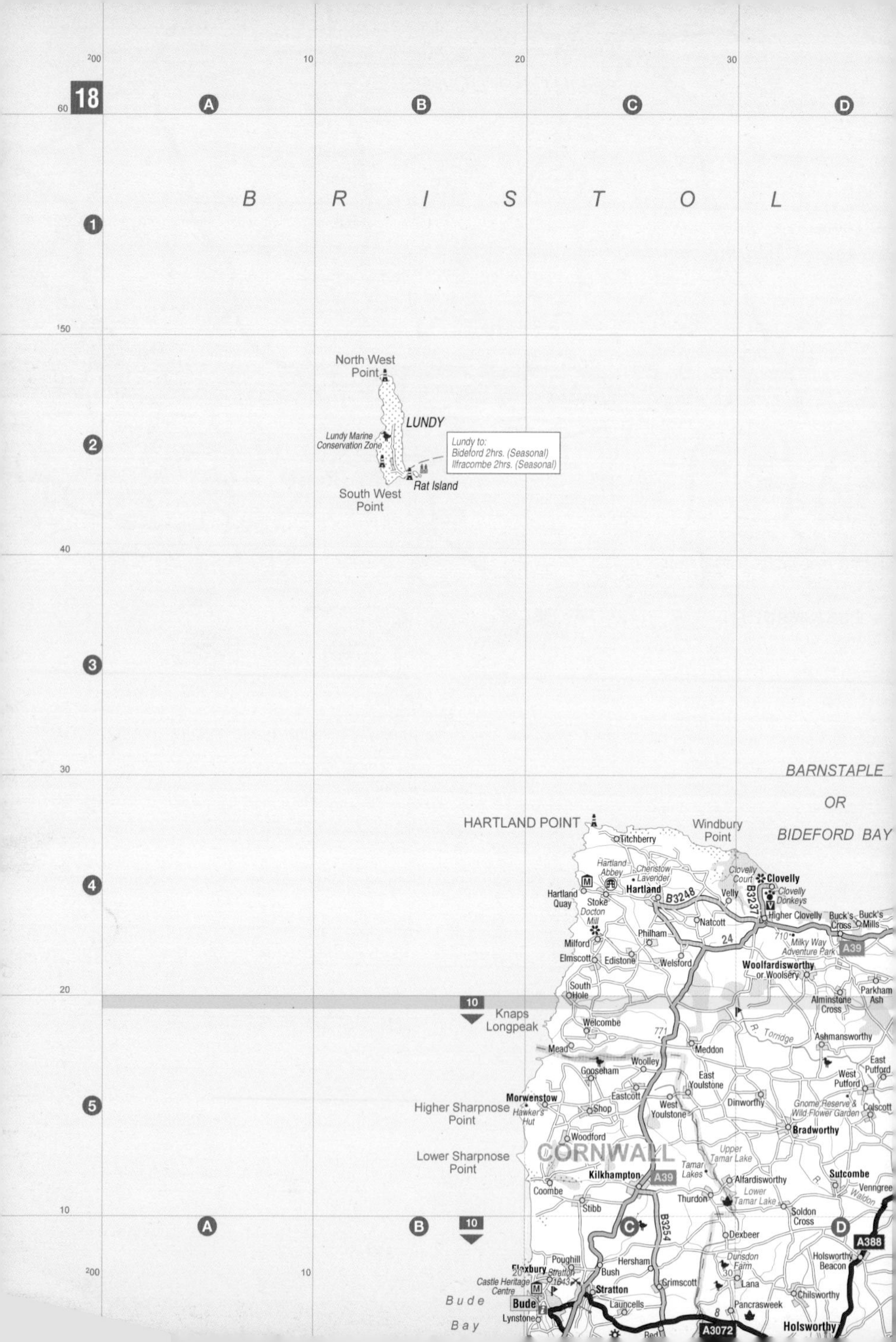

200    10    20    30

60 ⒶⒷⒸⒹ

*B   R   I   S   T   O   L*

**1**

¹50

North West
Point

**2**    Lundy Marine
Conservation Zone

*LUNDY*

Lundy to:
Bideford 2hrs. (Seasonal)
Ilfracombe 2hrs. (Seasonal)

Rat Island

South West
Point

40

**3**

30

BARNSTAPLE

OR

BIDEFORD BAY

**4**    HARTLAND POINT    Windbury
Point

○Titchberry
Hartland    Cheriston
Abbey    Lavender
Ⓜ    **Hartland**    ○Velly    Clovelly
Court    ⚘ **Clovelly**
Hartland    B3248    Clovelly
Quay    Stoke    B3237    Donkeys
○Docton    Higher Clovelly    Buck's    Buck's
Mill    Cross    Mills
Milford    ○Philham    ○Natcott    710⚘ Milky Way    ○
○Elmscott    24    Adventure Park    A39
○Edistone    Welsford    **Woolfardisworthy**
South    or Woolsery
20    Ⓞhole
**10**    Welcombe    Almsminster    Parkham
Knaps    Cross    Ash
Longpeak    771    R Torridge
Mead    ○Woolley    Meddon    Ashmansworthy
Gooseham    East    West
**5**    Morwenstow    ○Eastcott    Youlstone    Putford
Higher Sharpnose    Hawker's    ○Shop    West    Dinworthy    Gnome Reserve &    ○Colscott
Point    Hut    Youlstone    Wild Flower Garden    ○
Woodford    **Bradworthy**
Lower Sharpnose    **CORNWALL**    Upper    **Sutcombe**
Point    Tamar Lake    ○
Tamar    Alfardisworthy    R    Vennigree
10    **Kilkhampton**    A39    Lakes    Lower    Soldon    Waldon
Coombe    ○    Thurdon    Tamar Lake    Cross    ○
○Stibb    B3254    Dexbeer    Holsworthy
ⒶⒷ    ⒸⒹ    Beacon
**10**    Dunsdon    A388
200    10    Poughill    Farm    Lana    ○Chilsworthy
○Flexbury    ○Bush    ○Hersham    30    ○Pancrasweek    **Holsworthy**
Castle Heritage    ○Grimscott    8    R Waldon
Centre    **Stratton**    Launcells
*Bude*    **Bude**    A3072
*Bay*    Lynstone    Red P

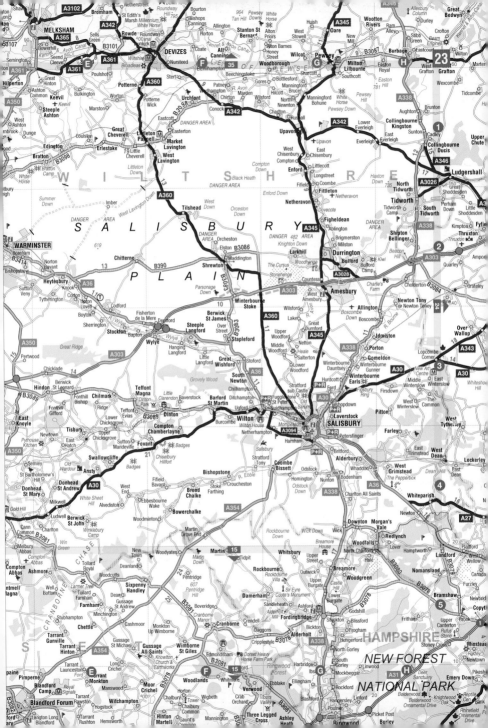

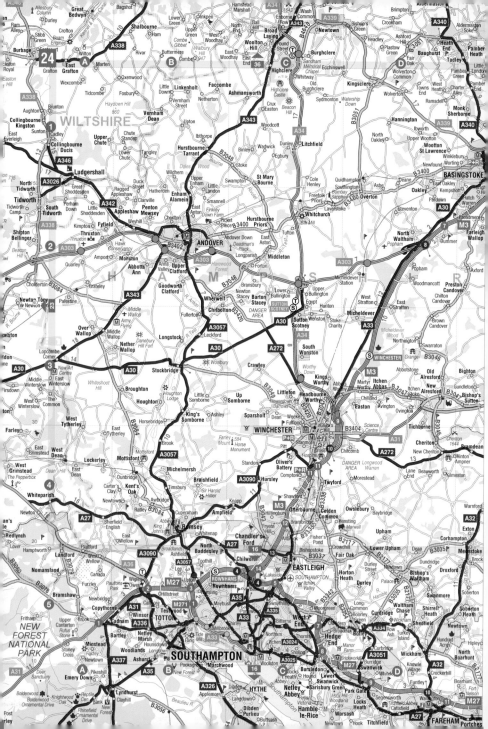

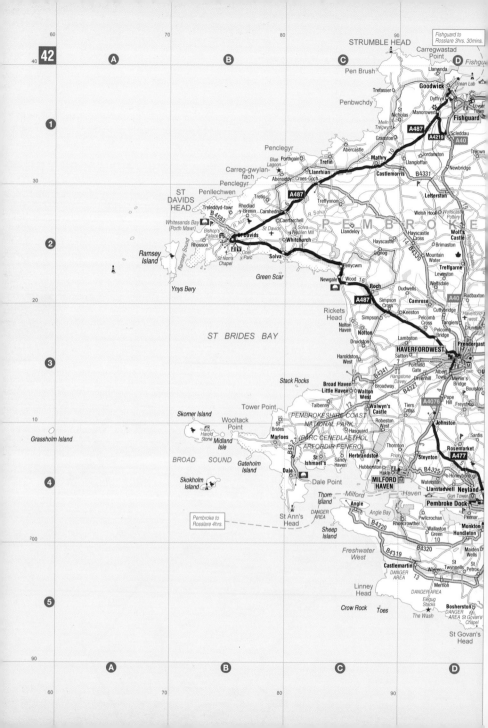

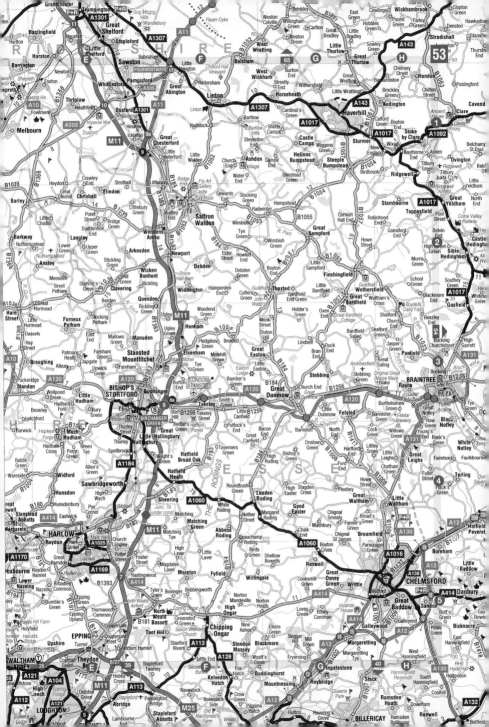

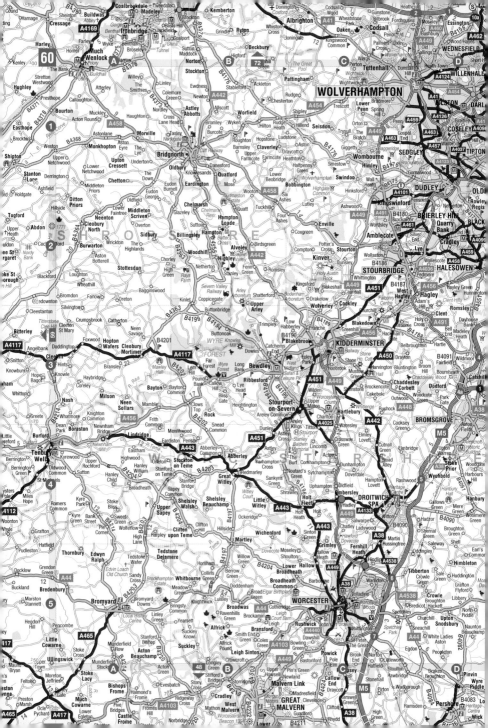

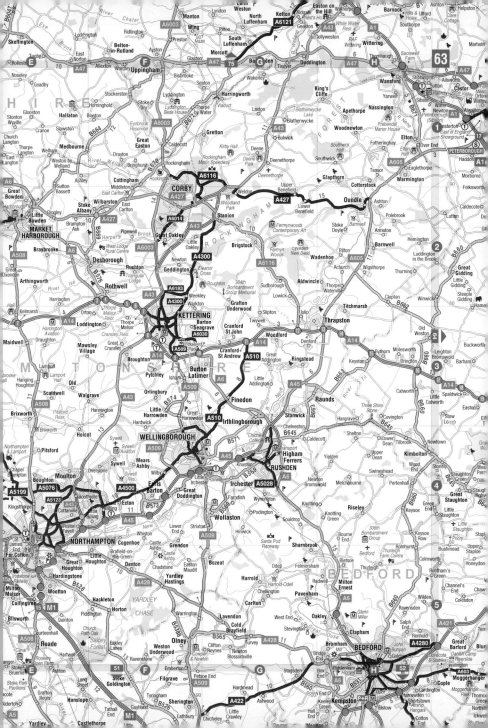

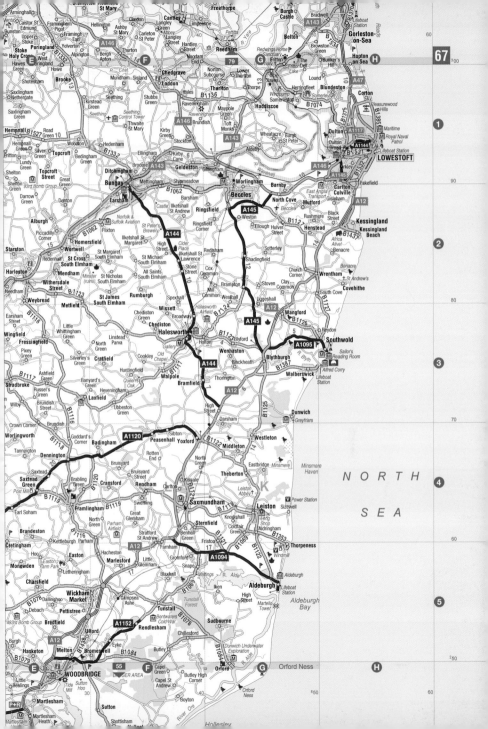

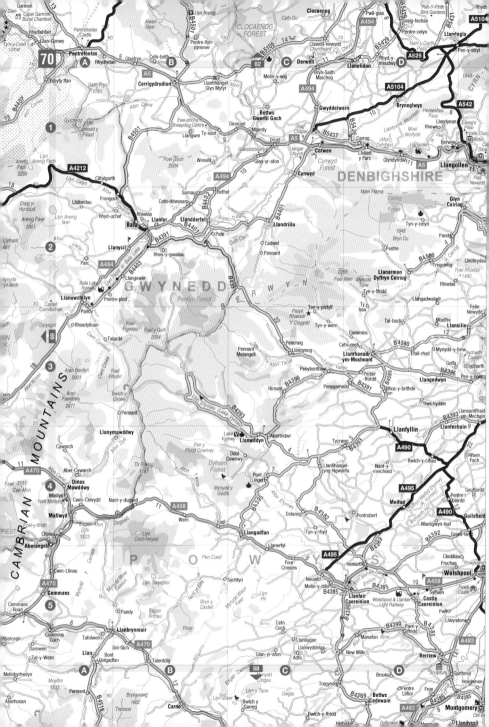

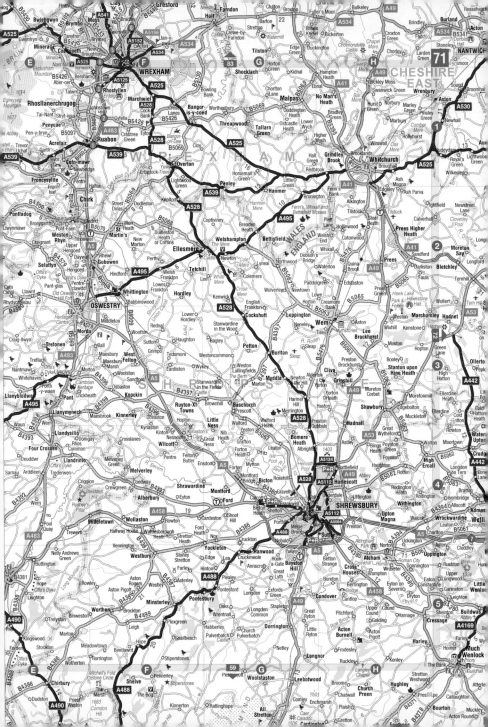

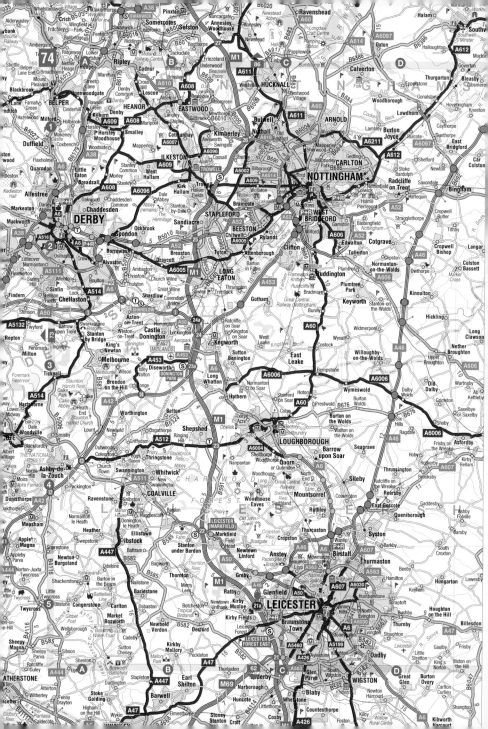

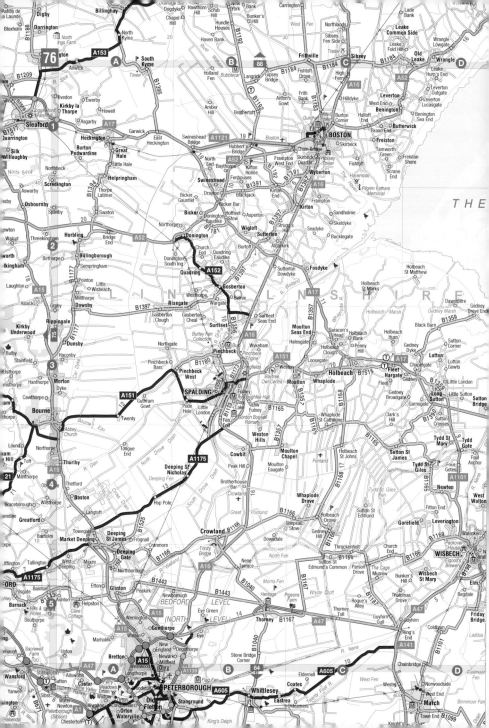

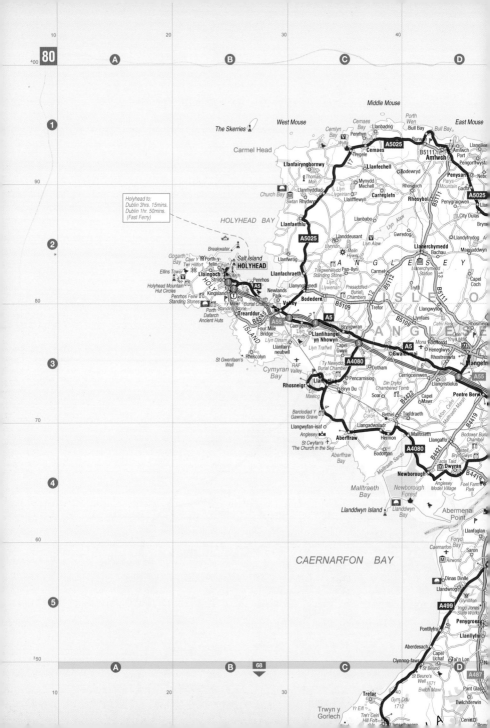

Middle Mouse

West Mouse

Porth
Wen
Bull Bay

East Mouse

The Skerries

Cemaes
Bay

Cemlyn
Bay

Llanbadrig

Bull Bay

Llaneilian

Carmel Head

Penrhyn

Wylfa

**Cemaes**

Tregele

Burwen

**Amlwch**

Amlwch
Port

Pengorffwysfa

Nebo

**Llanfairynghornwy**

**Llanfechell**

Bodewryd

B5111

**Penysarn**

Parys
Mountain

Gadfa

Thomas
Môn

Mynydd
Mechell

Rhosgoch

**Carreglefn**

**Rhosybol**

Penygraigwen

**A5025**

Church Bay

Llanrhyddlad

Llanfflewyn

City Dulas

Swtan Rhydwyn

Llanbabo

Llandyfrydog
Bachau

Brynr

HOLYHEAD BAY

**Llanfaethlu**

Llanddeusant

Llyn Alaw

Gwredog

Llanerchymedd

Maenaddwyn

Melin
Hywel

**A5025**

Llynfon

Llanfwrog

Llannerch-y-medd
Station

Capel
Coch

Gogarth
Bay

Breakwater

Caer Y
Twr Hillfort

Salt Island

**HOLYHEAD**

Trewgewheilydd
Standing Stone

A N G L E S E Y

Carmel

Tryfil

Ellins Tower

Porth-y-
felin Fort

**Llanfachraeth**

Penrhos

Llanynghenedl

Presaddfed
Burial
Chambers

Llangwyllog

Holyhead Mountain
Hut Circles

Llaingoch

Stryd

Arch

Newlands
Park

**Bodedern**

B5109

Trefor

B5110

Llynfaes

Rhosmis

Penrhos Feilw
Standing Stones

Kingsland

Ty Mawr
Standing Stone

Trefignath
Burial Chamber

Valley

I S L E  O

Porth
Dafarch
Ancient Huts

**Trearddur**

A5

Caergeiliog

A5

B5112

L A N G L E S E

Four Mile
Bridge

Llyn Dinam

Bryngwran

Heneglwys

Mona

Bodffordd

Rhostrehwfa

**Gwalchmai**

A5

Llyn
Penrhyn

**Llanfihangel
yn Nhowyn**

Capel
Gwyn

Ynys Môn

Llangefn

St Gwenfaen's
Well

Llanfair-
neubwll

Llyn Traffwll

Cerrigceinwen

**Llangristiolus**

A55

**Pentre Berw**

Cymyran
Bay

RAF
Valley

Rhoscolyn

Ty Newydd
Burial Chamber

Pencarnisiog

Din Dryfol
Chambered Tomb

Soar

**Llanfaelog**

A4080

Bryn Du

Dothan

B4422

Capel
Mawr

Bethel

Trefdraeth

Abon Cefni

Bodowyr Burial
Chamber

**Rhosneigr**

Llyn
Maelog

Llangaffo

Castell
Bryn Gwyn

Barclodiad Y
Gawres Grave

Llyn
Coron

Llangwyfan-isaf

Llangadwaladr

Hermon

Maltraeth Marsh

Bryn
Celli
Ddu

Acia Taid

**Dwyran**

Anglesey
'The Church in the Sea'

**Aberffraw**

St Cwyfan's

Bodorgan

Malltraeth

B4421

Foel Farm
Park

B4419

Aberffraw
Bay

Maltraeth Sands

A4080

**Newborough**

Anglesey
Model Village

Malltraeth
Bay

Newborough
Forest

Llanddwyn
Bay

**Abermenai
Point**

Llanddwyn Island

Llanfaglan

Foryd
Bay

Llanfair

CAERNARFON BAY

Caernarfon

Saron

Airworld

Dinas Dinlle

Llandwrog

Yr
Glynllifon
Ingo Jones
Slate Works

A499

**Penygroes**

Pontllyfni

**Llanllyfni**

Aberdesach

Capel
Uchaf

Clynnog-fawr

Tai'r Lôn

St Beuno

St Beuno's
Well  1671

Capel
Glas

Pant Glas

**Trefor**

Gyrn Ddu
1712

Bwlch Mawr

Bwichderwin

Trwyn y
Gorlech

Yr Eifl

Tre'r Ceiri
Hill Fort

Holyhead to:
Dublin 3hrs. 15mins.
Dublin 1hr. 50mins.
(Fast Ferry)

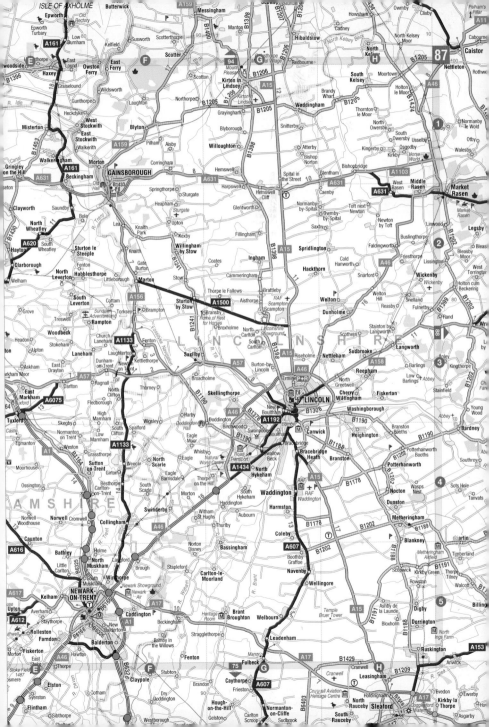

NORTH

SEA

Theddlethorpe
St Helen
Seal Sanctuary
& Wildlife Centre
Meers
Bridge
Lifeboat
Station
**Mablethorpe**
Ye Olde
Curiosity
**Trusthorpe**
A1104
Thorpe
**Sutton on Sea**
altby
Marsh
Sandilands
A1111
Hannah
A52
Markby
Huttoft
Anderby
Creek
Thurlby
Anderby
Drainage
B1449
Mumby
Farlesthorpe
13
On Your Marques
Cumberworth
Authorpe
Row
Bonthorpe
Helsey
Chapel St
Leonards
Willoughby
**Hogsthorpe**
Slothby
Ashley's
Field
A52
Hardys
Animal Farm
Hasthorpe
Slackholme
End
Addlethorpe
**Ingoldmells**
Ingoldmells
Point
Orby
Skegness
(Ingoldmells)
Butlin's
Orby
Marsh
Water
Leisure Park
A158
**Seathorne**
Winthorpe
Natureland
Seal Sanctuary
Burgh le
Marsh
Church
Farm
Bottons
Pleasure
Beach
**SKEGNESS**
Croft
Model
Village
Thorpe
St Peter
A52
Seacroft
Croft Marsh
Bateman's
Brewery
Magdalen
**Wainfleet
All Saints**
Gibraltar
Wainfleet
St Mary
Key's Toft
Gibraltar
Point

DANGER AREA

Deeps

Boston

Sco... Head Island

Holkham Ba

Holme
Dunes
Brancaster Bay

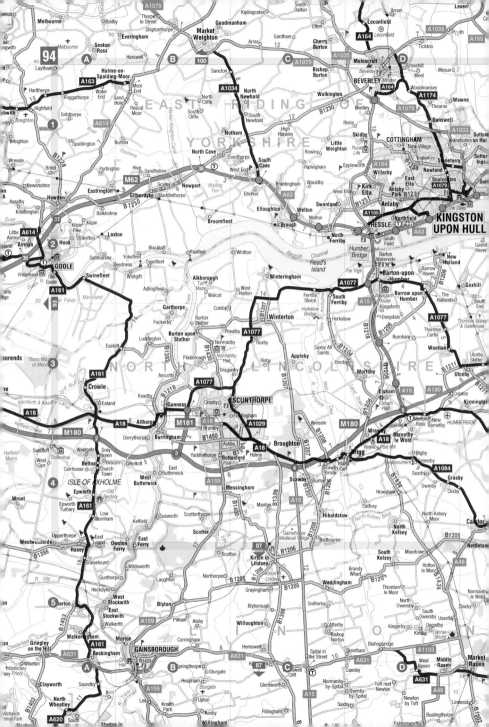

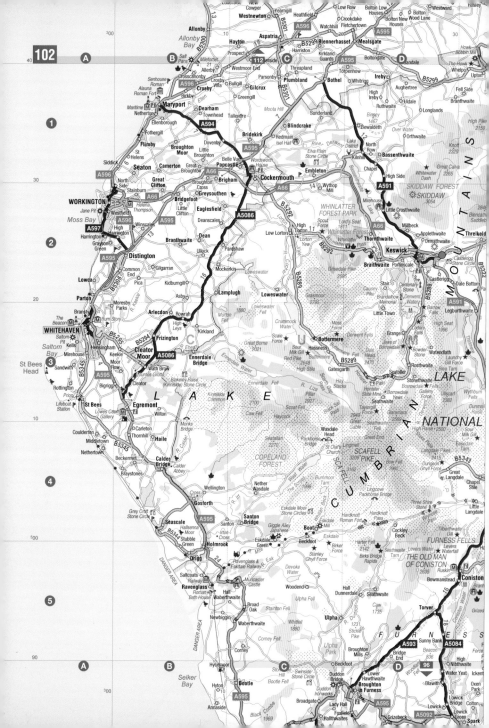

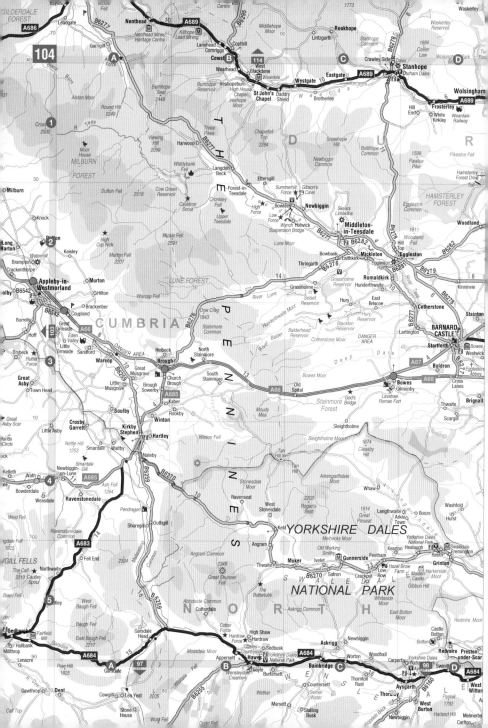

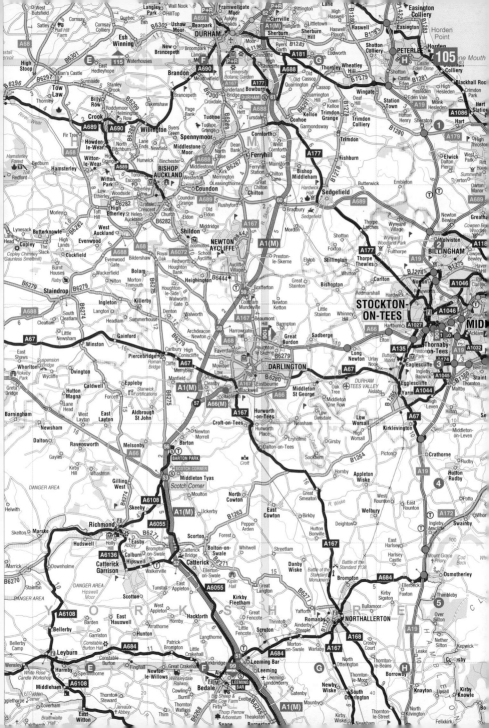

POINT OF AYRE

Rue Point

The Ayres

A16

The Ayres

Cranstal

The Lhen

A10

B6

Dhoon

A10  A17  Bride

A10  B13  A19  B3  Andreas  A10  Shellag Point

Jurby Head  Jurby West  Jurby  Crosses  B7

Jurby East  A9

Ballasalla  B5  Sandygate  Regaby

The Cronk  St Judes  Civil War Fort  Dhoon Grove  Ramsey Bay

A13  A17  A14  Sulby  B14  A13

Orrisdale  Caraghyn  B8  Churchtown  Ramsey  Lhergy Frissel  Manx Electric Railway

Orrisdale Head  Ballaugh  T.T. Course  Glen Auldyn  Elfin Glen  Port e Vullen

A3  Ravensdale  Bishopscourt Glen  A15  Lewaigue  Maughold  Crosses

Glen Wyllin  Kirk Michael  Tholt-y-Will Glen  A14  North Barrule  A18  Ballajora  B19  Maughold Head

Glen Mooar  Ballaleigh  Sleau Dhoo 1601  SNAEFELL 2036  Clagh Ouyr  Corrany  A2  Port Mooar

Ballacarnane Beg  Barregarrow  21  Glen Mona  Cornaa  Cashtal Yn'Ard  Port Cornaa

Gob y Deigan  Cronk-y-Voddy  Sulby Resr.  14  Snaefell Mountain  Dhoon  Dhoon Glen  Bulgham Bay

A4  Rhenass Waterfall  B10  B10  Great Laxey  Laxey Wheel Lady Isabella

Knocksharry  Lambfell Moar  Glen Helen  Colden 1599  Injebreck Resr.  Laxey Glen  Laxey Mines  Old Laxey Head

St Patrick's Isle  Leece  Ballagyr  Laxey  Old Laxey

House of Manannan  ISLE  Ballaragh  Ballacannell

Peel  A20  A1  Tynwald Hill  Greeba Castle  B12  B12  Laxey Bay

Contrary Head  Patrick  St John's  Sleau Ruy 1570  OF  Baldrine

A30  Ballig  Baldwin  Clay Head

Glen Maye  Lower Foxdale  Crosby  A23  MAN  A2  A20  A11

Dalby Point  A27  Dalby  T.T. Course  A1  Glen Vine  A22  Hillberry  B11  Groudle

Niarbyl  Foxdale  Eairy  Strang  Onchan  Groudle Glen  Port Groudle

Niarbyl Bay  A36  South Barrule  A24  Garth  B32  A1  Union Mills  A6  Onchan Head  A11

Stroin Vuigh  Hill 1586 Fort  B36  B35  Braaid  A24  Spring Valley  Kewaigue  DOUGLAS  Manx  Onchan Head

Fleshwick Bay  A36  A27  Ballamodha  B31  A5  Quine's Hill  B80  Douglas Bay

Lingague  Ronague  Grenaby  St Mark's Newtown  A26  Kerristal  Douglas Head

Bradda Head Bradda  Surby  B42  Ballabeg  A3  A25  Port Soderick  Little Ness

Bradda Glen  Colby  Rushen Abbey  Isle of Man Steam

Port Erin  A7  Ballasalla  B25  Santon Head

Railway  A5  ISLE OF MAN  Derby Fort

Chambered Cairn  The Nowe  Ship Roads  Castletown  A12  St Michael's Island

The Sound  Cregneash  Port St Mary  Nautical  Derbyhaven

Kitterland  A31  B18  Scarlett  Rushen  St Michael's Island

National Folk  Keys

SPANISH HEAD

Calf of Man  Dreswick Point

Douglas to:
Belfast 2hrs.45mins.
(Fast Ferry, Seasonal)
Birkenhead 4hrs. 15mins.
(Seasonal)
Heysham 3hrs. 30mins.
Dublin 2hrs. 45mins.
(Fast Ferry, Seasonal)
Liverpool 2hrs. 30mins.
(Fast Ferry, Seasonal)

PAGE NOT CONTINUED

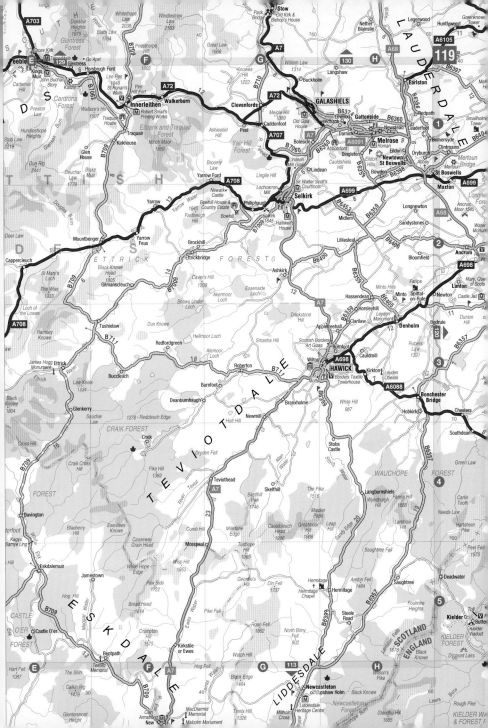

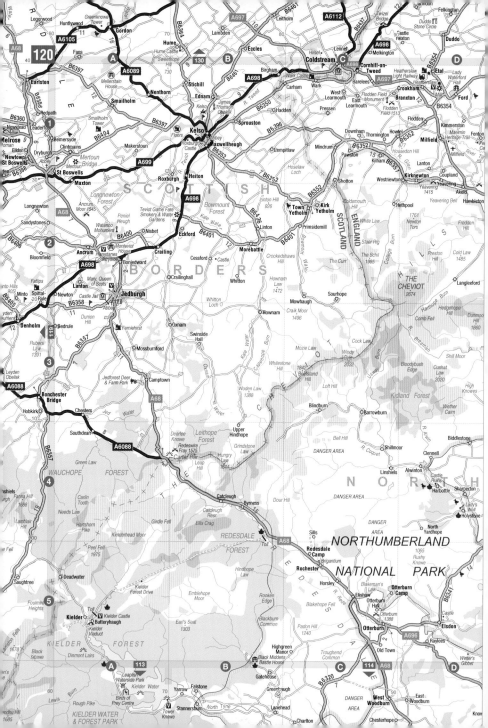

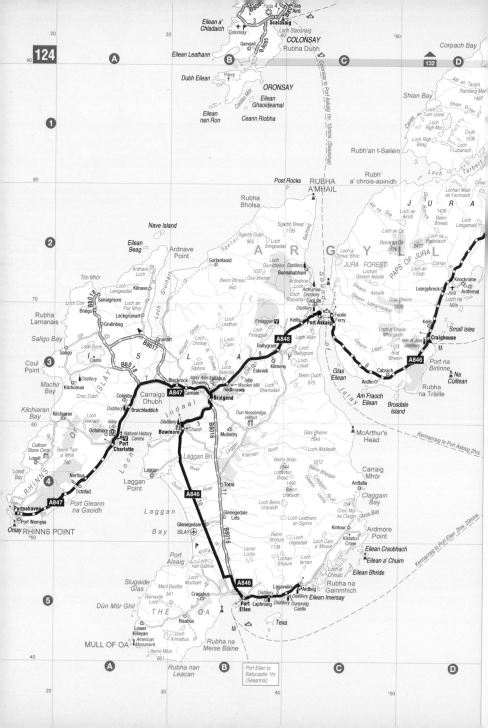

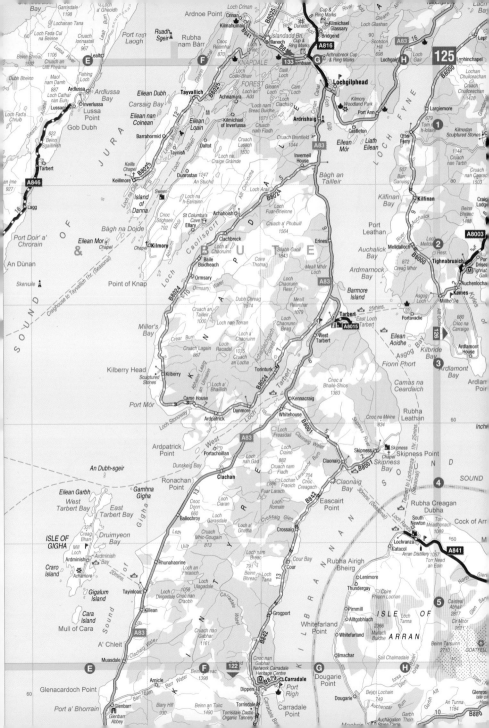

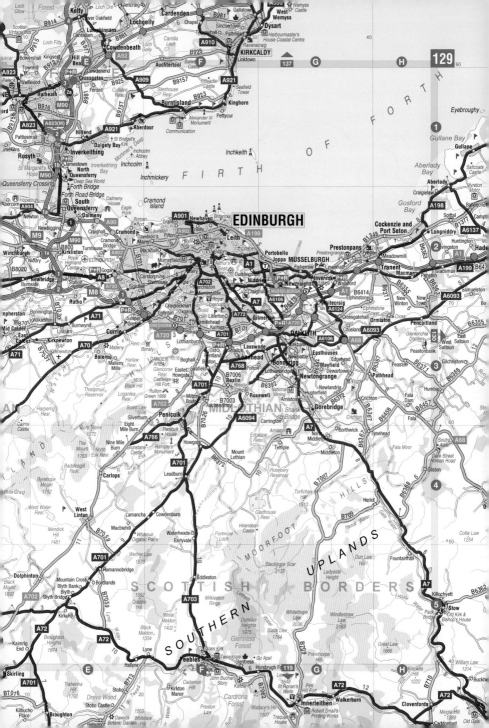

NORTH      SEA

Fast Castle
Head
Point                    Fast
                        Castle
        Telegraph
        Hill    Lumsdaine          ST ABB'S HEAD
               Cross Law
               744
        Coldingham Moor        St Abbs
A1107          11        B6438   Lifeboat
                                 Station
        Houndwood        Coldingham      Priory   Coldingham
                                                  Bay   Lifeboat
                                                        Station
        Eye                     Eyemouth        Gunsgreen
        Water                                   House
859  Horseley        Reston          Gunsgreenhill
     Hill                    18   Ayton          A1107
B6438          Auchencrow              Burnmouth
B6438   B6437                          Ross

Lintlaw
        B6355   Chirnside      12   B6355        A1
Chirnsidebridge                        Lamberton        Marshall
Duns-                                          Meadows
Arch          Whiteadder   Water   Foulden        Heddon
Edrom                                             Hill  1333        Bell
A6105          Allanton                A6105               Tower
        B6437                                              Cell Block
B6460          Hutton              Paxton        Castle    A1167
        B6461                      B6461        BERWICK-UPON-TWEED
Whitsome        B6461    Union              Tweedmouth
                        Bridge   Tweed              Lifeboat Station
               Fishwick   Loanend        Spittal
        Horndean        Chain Bridge   East Ord   A1167
               Honey Farm        A698        Poho-
Ladykirk        Horncliffe              Doodle Do   Redshin
        Norham              Murton              Cove
Swinton        B6470        Thornton        Scremerston
        B6470              West
Simprim                    Allerdean      Cheswick
A6112          Upsettlington   Grindon        Goswick
        Twizel              Felkington              Haggerston
        Bridge   Duddo        B6354   Berrington        LINDISFARNE
A698   Castle   Stone Circle            Law        HOLY ISLAND
        Heaton   Duddo              Berrington   Beal        Keel
               Bowsden                                 Head
A698   Melkington                          A1   Lindisfarne   Holy
Cornhill-on-        NORTHUMBERLAND   B6353   West        Centre   Island
A697   Tweed   Heatherslaw        Barmoor   Kyloe   Fenwick        Lindisfarne
        Light Railway   Etal           Lowick   Kyloe        121   Priory
West   Crookham   Heatherslaw              Hills
Learmouth   Cranxton   Hall   Ford           Buckton
        Flodden Field   Ford              Holburn   Elwick   Ross
        Monument        B6354        14        St Cuthbert's   Detchant
Pressen        Flodden Field 1513              Cave        Bamburgh
Flodden              Kimmerston              Hetton        Middleton   Waren

Staple
Sound   FARN
Chapel   ISLAN
Inner
Budle
Bay

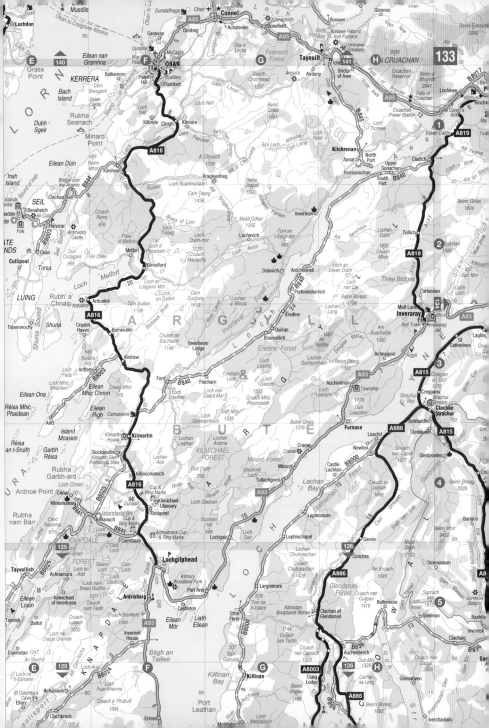

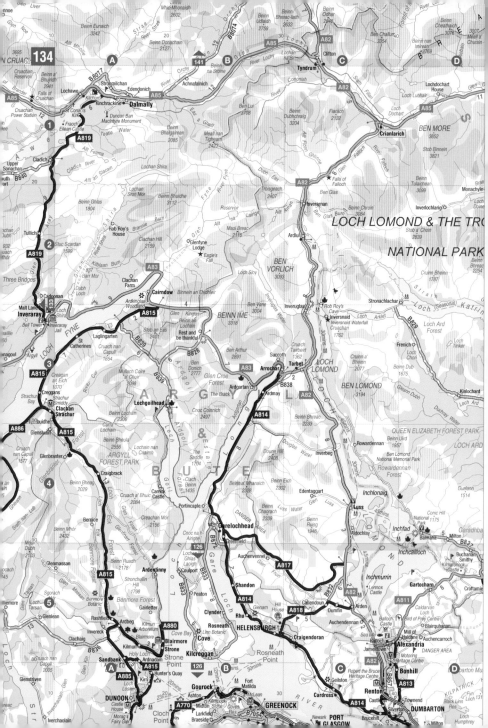

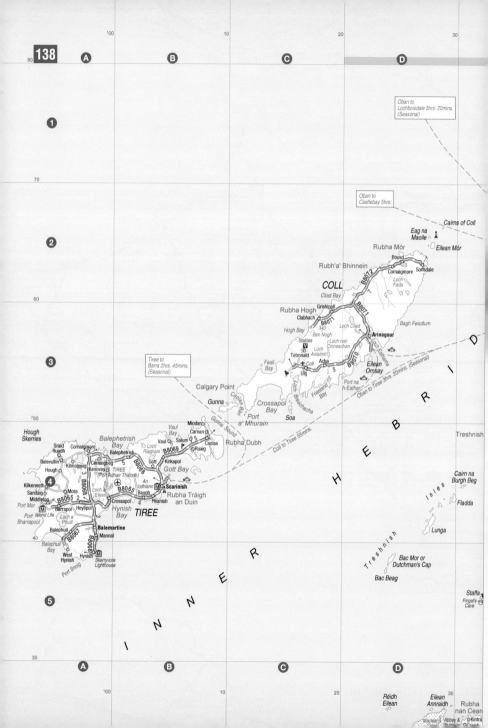

A    B    C    D

100    10    20    30

80

**1**

Oban to
Lochboisdale 5hrs, 20mins.
(Seasonal)

70

Oban to
Castlebay 5hrs.

Cairns of Coll

**2**

Eag na
Maoile

Eilean Mór

Rubha Mór

Bousd

Cornaigmore    Sorisdale

**COLL**

B8072

Loch
Fada

60

Cliad Bay

Rubha Hogh    Grishipoll

Clabhach    B8071    B8071

Bagh Feisdlum

Hogh Bay    340    Ben Nogh    Loch Cliad

Arinagour

**3**

Stables    Loch nan    Cinneachan

Totronald    Loch    Anlaimh

Coll

Acha

Eilean
Omsay

750    Feall
Bay    Uig    5

Oban to Tiree 3hrs 20mins (Seasonal)

Tiree to
Barra 2hrs, 45mins.
(Seasonal)

Calgary Point

Port na
h-Eathar

Gunna    Caolas Bàn

Crossapol
Bay

Loch Breachacha

Friesland
Bay

Port
a' Mhurain    Soa

Coll to Tiree 55mins.

Rubha Dubh

Vaul
Bay

Miodar

Carnan

Hough
Skerries

Balephetrish
Bay

Salum

Loch
Riaghain    Ruaig

Caolas

Treshnish

Sràid
Ruadh    Cornaigmore

Balephetrish

Balevullin    Cornaigbeg    B8069

Kilmoluaig    Kenovay    TIREE    Gott    Kirkapol

Gott Bay

Hough    (Port Adhair Thioodh)

An
Iodhann

Cairn na
Burgh Beg

Kilkenneth

**4**    Moss    Baugh

Vaul

Sandaig    Crossapol    Heanish

Scarinish

Fladda

Middleton    B8065    B8065    B8065    Heylipol

Port Mor

Barrapol    Hynish
Bay

Rubha Tràigh
an Duin

Island Life    Loch a'
Phuill    **TIREE**

Lunga

Port
Bharrapol

Balephuil

**Balemartine**    Mannal

Isles

B8067    B8065

Balephuil
Bay    West
Hynish    Hynish

Bac Mor or
Dutchman's Cap

Port Snoig    Skerryvore
Lighthouse

Bac Beag

**5**

Staffa
Fingal's
Cave

**I    N    N    E    R**

H    E    B    R    I    D    E    S

Treshnish

40

30

100    10    20    30

A    B    C    D

Réidh
Eilean

Eilean
Annraidh

Rubha
nan Cean

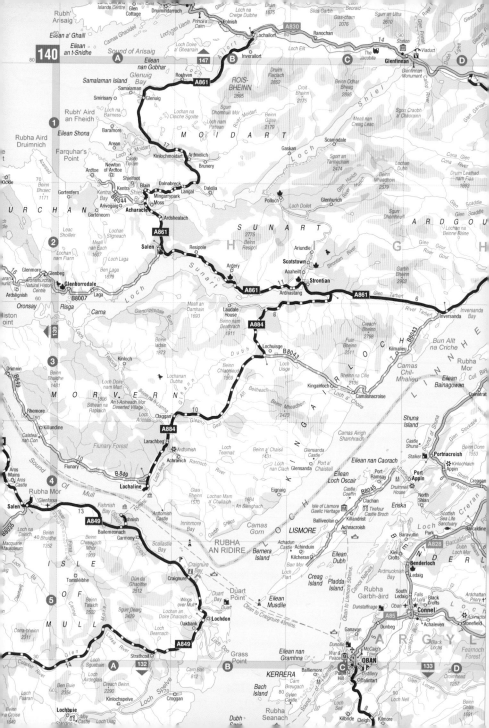

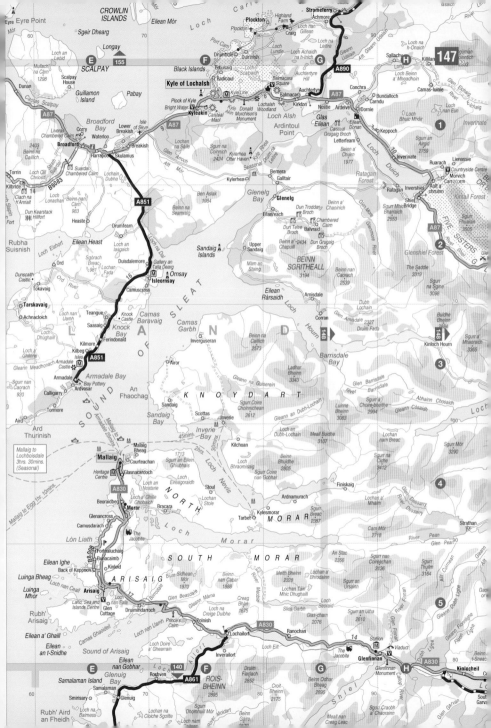

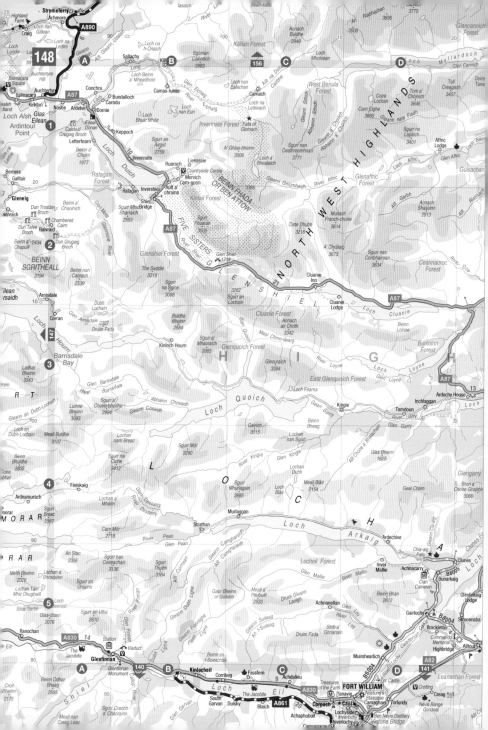

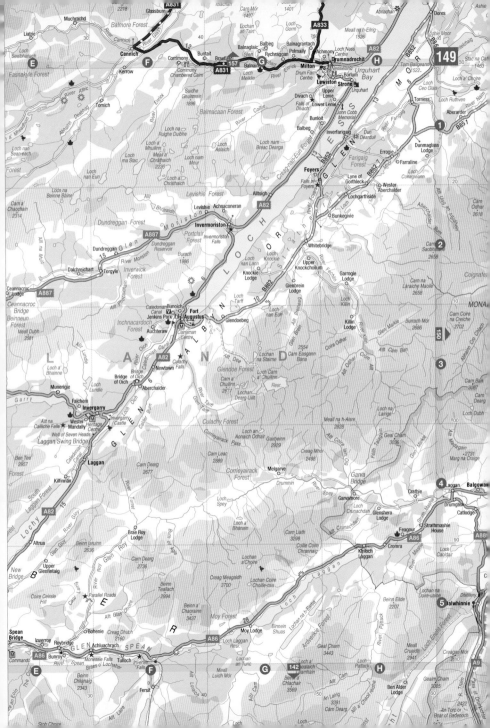

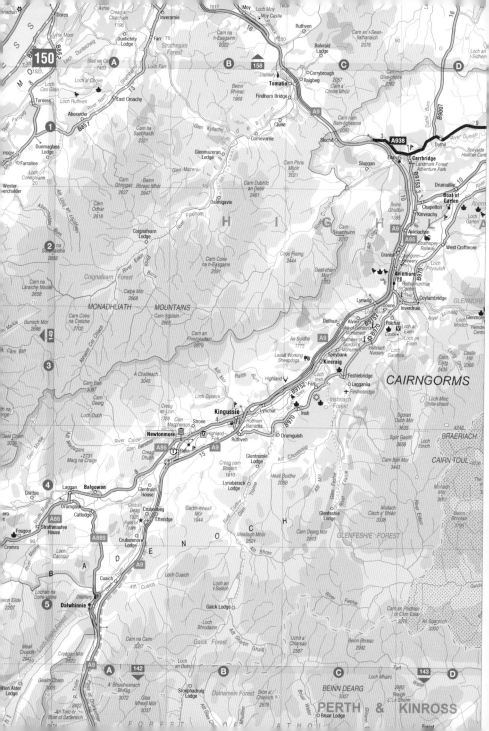

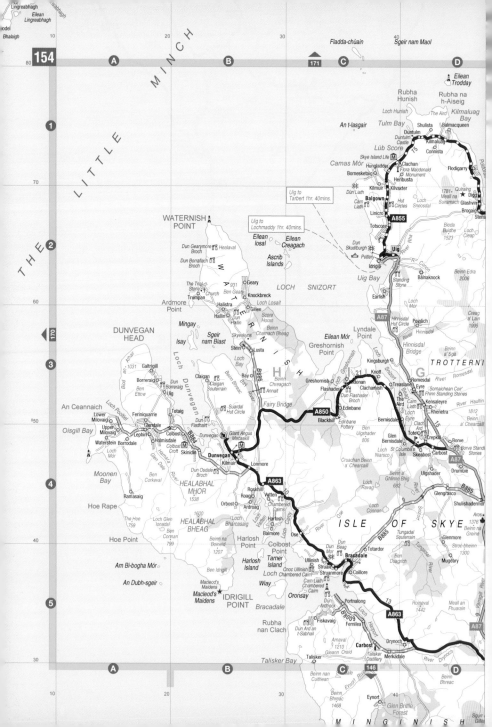

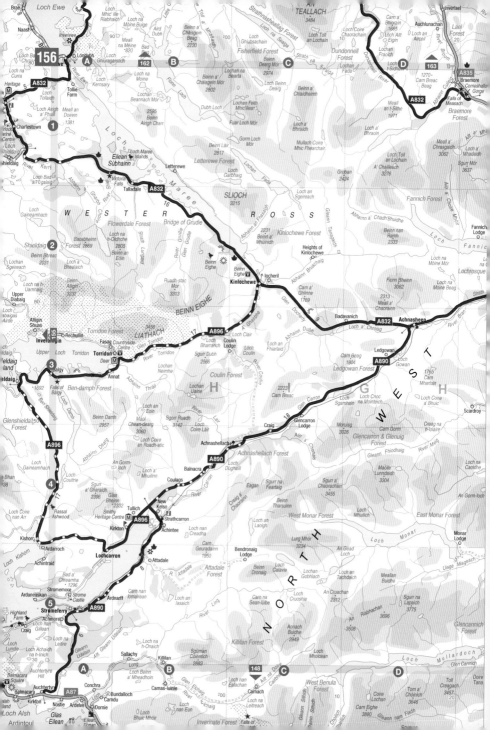

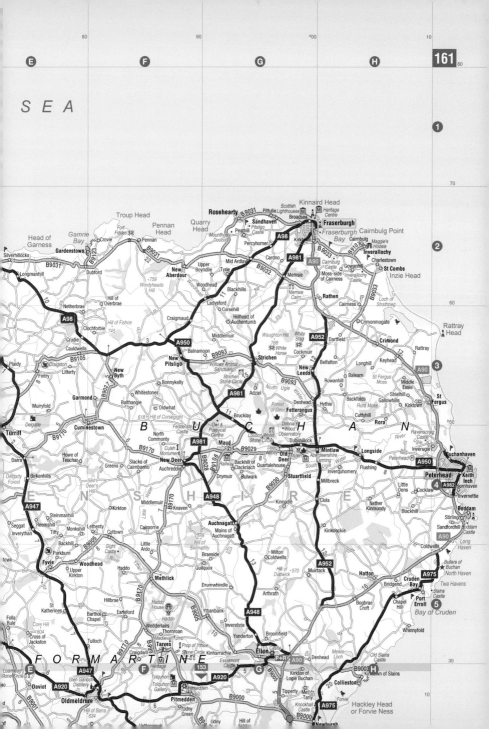

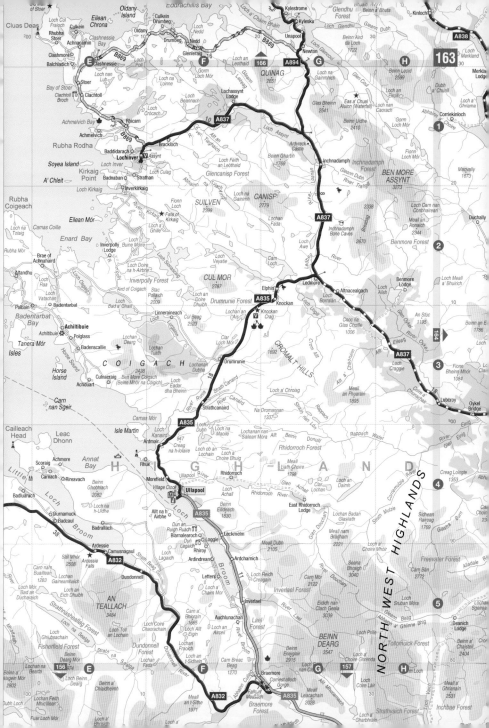

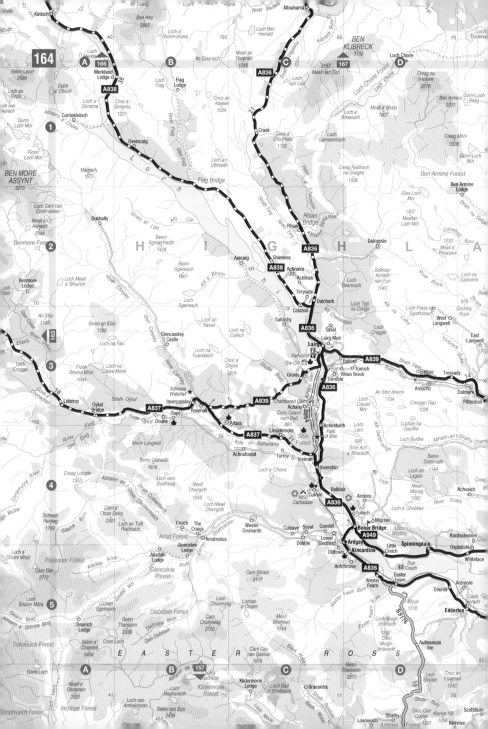

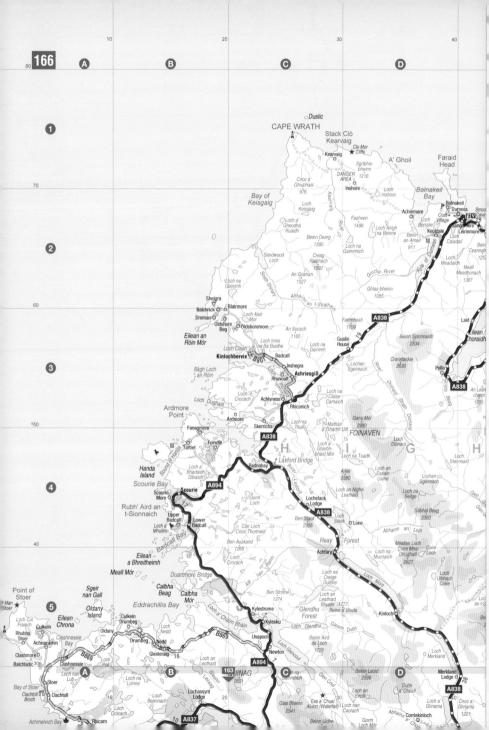

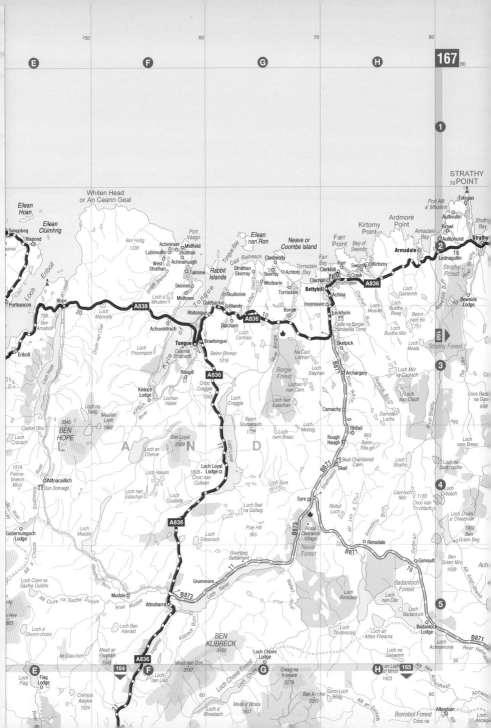

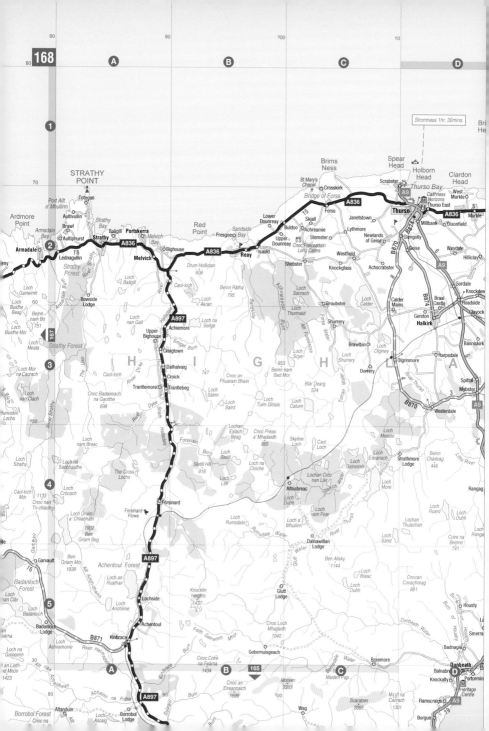

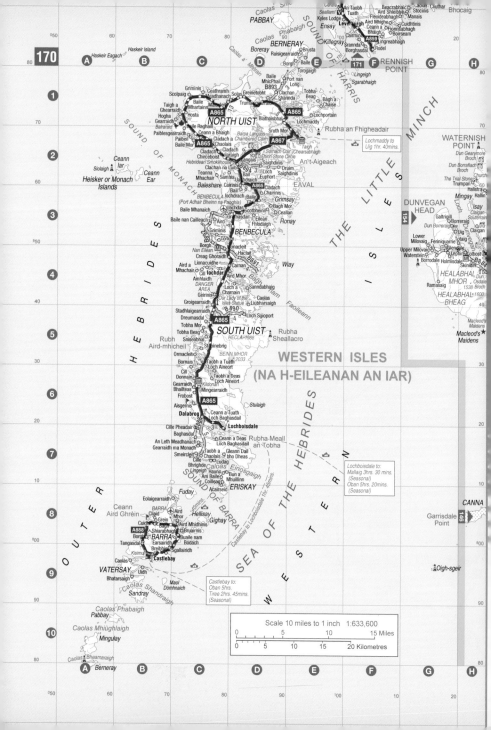

ORKNEY ISLANDS
ORKNEY ISLANDS
Fair Isle lies approx. 27 miles ENE of North Ronaldsay
FAIR ISLE
Fair Isle
Skroo
Stonybreck
Leogh
SHETLAND ISLANDS
Fair Isle to: Lerwick 5hrs. (Seasonal) Sumburgh 2hrs. 30mins
Mull Head
Papa Westray
PAPA WESTRAY
Knap of Howar
Holland
Holm of Papa Westray Chambered Cairn
Backaskaill
WESTRAY
Rackwick
Noup Head
Noltland
Gayfield
Pierowall
Westray Heritage Centre
Broughton
Braehead
Cleat
B9067
WESTRAY
Midbea
Westside Church
Bay of Tuquoy
B9066
Skelwick
Rapness
THE NORTH SOUND
40mins.
North Ronaldsay
Seal Skerry
NORTH RONALDSAY
Linklet Bay
Hollandstoun
Papa Westray to North Ronaldsay 1hr. 10mins. (Seasonal)
NORTH RONALDSAY FIRTH
Kirkwall to North Ronaldsay 2hrs. 40mins.
Scar
Burness
B9068
Otters Wick
Northwall
Lettan
Start Point
Lady
B9069
Newark
Broughtown
B9070
SANDAY
SANDAY
Overbister
Calf of Eday
Carrick Ho
Calfsound
Kettletoft
Tres Ness
Benstonhall
Braeswick
Laminess
Quoyness Chambered Cairn
Millbounds
Stove
EDAY
Sanday Sound
35mins
B9063
EDAY
Backaland
Southside
Veness
1hr.
20mins.
Kirkwall to Westray 1hr. 25mins.
WESTRAY FIRTH
Wasbister
B9064
Midhowe Broch
Midhowe Chambered Cairn
ROUSAY
Sourin
St Magnus Kirk
Westside Cairns
Brinian
Egilsay
Westness
Frotoft
15mins.
Kirkwall to Papa Westray 1hr. 50mins.
STRONSAY FIRTH
Kirkwall to Eday, Sanday & Stronsay
STRONSAY
Whitehall
B9060
Odie
Samsonslane
Everbay
Rothiesholm
B9061
B9062
Grobister
Kirbuster
Dishes
Cott
Holland
STRONSAY
Earl's Palace
Brough of Birsay
Abune-the-Hill
The Barony
Kirbuster Museum
Costa
Church
Broch of Gurness
Georth
Stenso
A967
Twatt
Hillside
Redland
Marwick
A967
B9056
Beaquoy
B9057
Woodwick
Tingwall
Cubbie Row's Castle
St Mary's Chapel
Wyre
Gairsay
Quoyloo
Skelbrae
Dounby
Click Mill
Northdyke
Mirbister
Corrigall Farm
Hackland
Skara Brae Prehistoric Village
Skaill
Sandwick
Corrigall
A966
Gorseness
Skaill House
Hestwall
Ness of Tenston
Brough
Russland
Settiscarth
Isbister
Wide Firth
B9058
Burroughston
Edmonstone
SHAPINSAY
Crossgate
Balfour
B9059
Newlot
Auskerry Sound
Auskerry
Yesnaby
Voy
B9055
Netherbrough
Bimbister
Rennibister Earth House
Grimeston
A986
Finstown
Kirbister
A965
Quholm
Brodgar
Stenness
Cuween Hill
Grimbister
Work
Orkney
Kirkwall
Outertown
Cairn
Tormiston Mill
Heddle
Wideford Hill
Yinstay
Linksness
Stromness
Cairston
Clouston
MAINLAND
Scapa
Holodespark
Tankerness
KIRKWALL
Kirkwall (Hatston) to: Aberdeen 7hrs. 15mins. Lerwick (Holmsgarth) 7hrs. 45mins.
A964
A964
Kirbister
Greenigoe
Borrowstonehill
Toab
Deerness
Skaills
Graemsay
Clestrain
DANGER AREA
Hobbister
A961
A960
B9050
Murra
Moaness
Petertown
Orphir
Swanbister
Smoogro
Highland Park Distillery
Gritley
Orgil
Houton
Earl's Bu
Midland
Foubister
B9052
Upper Sanday
Stromness to Scrabster 1hr. 30mins.
Old Man of Hoy
Quoyness
Scapa Flow
St Mary's
Greenwall
Copinsay
Rora Head
Dwarfie Stane
B9047
Cava
35mins.
No. 1
No. 2
Italian Chapel
Cornquoy
Rackwick
No. 3
Northtown
HOY
Fara
Flotta
Burray
Fossil & Heritage Cen.
Scapa Flow
Lyness
B9045
Burray Village
Southtown
Lowertown
No. 4
Rinnigill
Uppertown
Grimness
Flotta
B9046
Ronaldsvoe
St Margaret's Hope
North Ness
Herston
Quindry
Longhope
B9047
Hackness
Widewall
Aikers
Saltness
Melsetter
Wyng
B9042
Sandwick
Lythes
Hurliness
Osmondwall
Brims
South Walls
SOUTH RONALDSAY
A961
Linklater
Swona
Burwick
Cleat
Tomb of the Eagles
Liddle
Brough
PENTLAND FIRTH
Gills Bay to St Margaret's Hope, Orkney 1hr.
40mins. (Seasonal)
169
Island of Stroma
Nethertown
Uppertown
Pentland Skerries
Stromness 1hr. 30mins.
DUNNET HEAD
Castle of Mey
East Mey
A836
DUNCANSBY HEAD
Brough
Scarfskerry
Ham
Rattar
Kirkstyle
Huna
Last House
Brims Ness
Hunspow
Corsback
Mey
Gills
Caithness Horizons
West Dunnet
Seadrift
Barrock
Upper Gills
Warse
Canisbay
John o' Groats
Duncansby Stacks
Crosskirk
Scrabster
A9
West Murkle
Dunnet
Inkstack
Forss
A836
Thurso
East Murkle
Greenland
Brabster
A99
Skiall
Janetstown
Castletown
Lochend
Tofts
Skirza
Achreamie
Lythmore
Millbank
Olrig
Tain
Greenland
Freswick
Glengolly
Dixonfield
Mains
Slickly
Stemster
Newlands
Weydale
B876
Reaster
Alterwall
Westfield
of Geise
Geise
Durran
Bowermadden
Caithness Broch Centre
Knockglass
Achscrabster
A9
Hillclay
Sortat
Auckengill
Sordale
Bowertower
Lyth
Lyth Arts Centre
Nybster
B870
Braal
Knockdee
Halcro
Howe
Keiss
Keiss Castle
Broubster
Calder
Gerston
Castle
Roadside
Corsback
Hastigrow
Kirk
Mireland
A99
Scale 10 miles to 1 inch 1:633,600
0 5 10 15 Miles
0 5 10 15 20 Kilometres
PAGE NOT CONTINUED

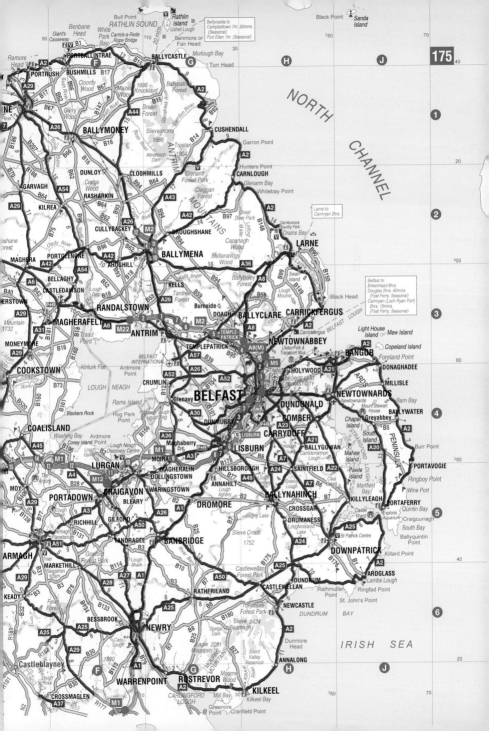

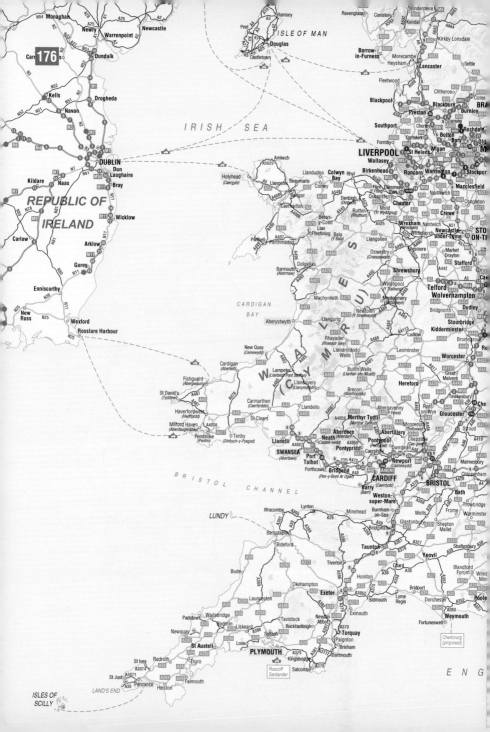

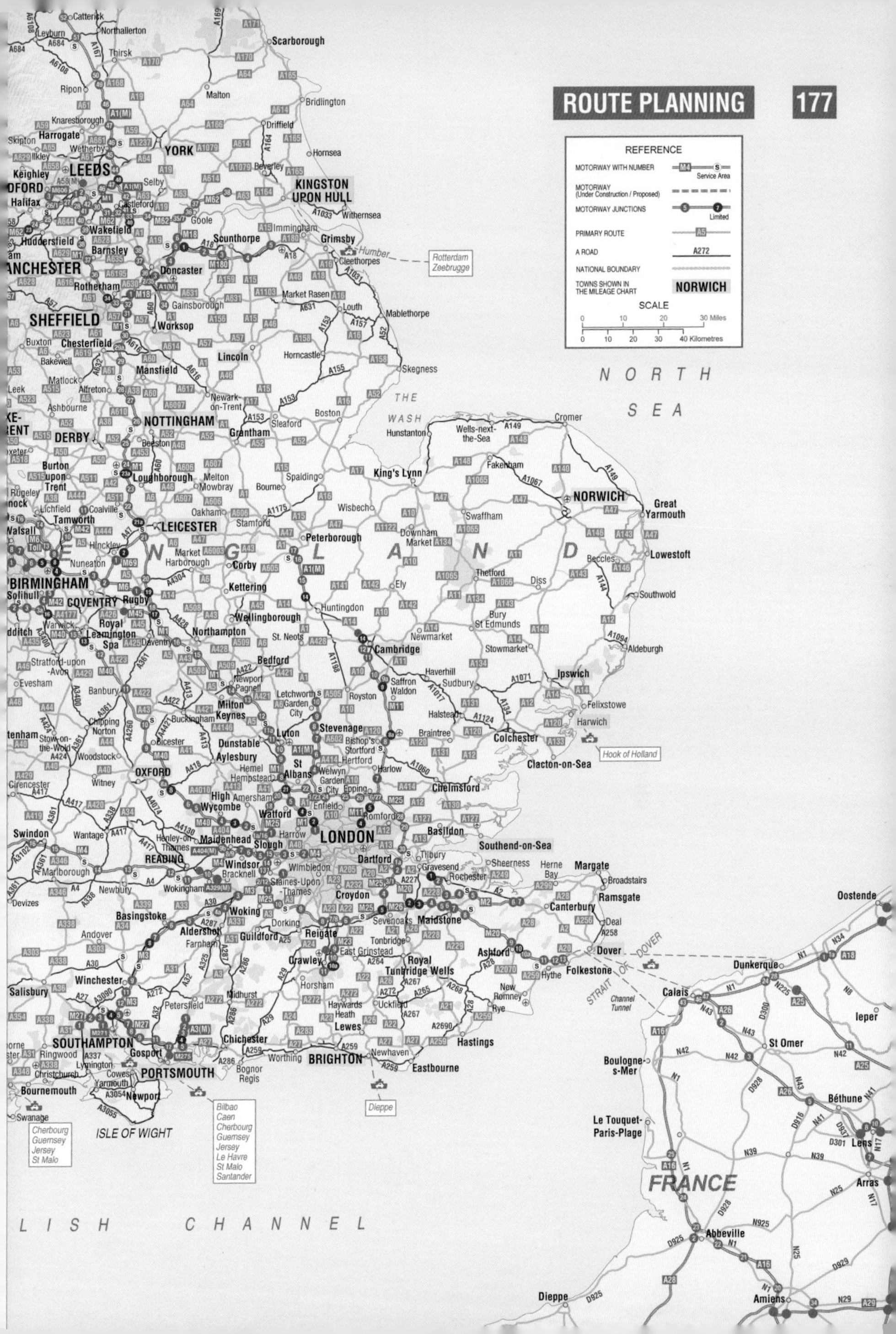

REFERENCE

MOTORWAY WITH NUMBER ......... M4 — S Service Area

MOTORWAY
(Under Construction / Proposed) ........ = = = =

MOTORWAY JUNCTIONS ......... S — 7 Limited

PRIMARY ROUTE ......... A6

A ROAD ......... A272

NATIONAL BOUNDARY

TOWNS SHOWN IN
THE MILEAGE CHART ......... **NORWICH**

SCALE
0        10        20        30 Miles
0    10    20    30    40 Kilometres

NORTH

SEA

THE WASH

E N G L A N D

Rotterdam
Zeebrugge

Hook of Holland

Dieppe

Bilbao
Caen
Cherbourg
Guernsey
Jersey
Le Havre
St Malo
Santander

Cherbourg
Guernsey
Jersey
St Malo

ISLE OF WIGHT

E N G L I S H     C H A N N E L

Oostende

F R A N C E

STRAIT
Channel
Tunnel

Dieppe

Amiens

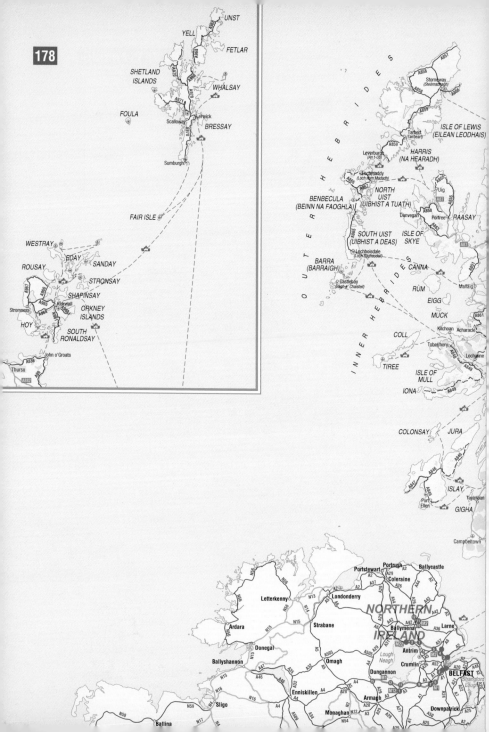

UNST
YELL
FETLAR
SHETLAND
ISLANDS
WHALSAY
FOULA
BRESSAY
Scalloway Lerwick
Sumburgh

FAIR ISLE

WESTRAY
EDAY SANDAY
ROUSAY
STRONSAY
SHAPINSAY
Kirkwall
Stromness ORKNEY
HOY ISLANDS
SOUTH
RONALDSAY
John o'Groats
Thurso

ISLE OF LEWIS
(EILEAN LEODHAIS)
Stornoway
(Steòrnabhagh)
Tarbert
(Tairbeart)
HARRIS
Leverburgh (NA HEARADH)
(An t-Ob)
Lochmaddy
(Loch nam Madadh)
NORTH Uig
BENBECULA UIST
(BEINN NA FAOGHLA) (UIBHIST A TUATH) RAASAY
Dunvegan
Portree
SOUTH UIST ISLE OF
(UIBHIST A DEAS) SKYE
Lochboisdale
(Loch Baghasdail)
BARRA CANNA
(BARRAIGH)
Castlebay RÙM
(Bàgh a' Chaisteil)
EIGG
MUCK
Kilchoan Acharacle

COLL
Tobermory Lochaline
TIREE

ISLE OF
MULL
IONA

COLONSAY JURA

ISLAY
Port
Ellen GIGHA

Campbeltown

Portrush
Portstewart Ballycastle
Coleraine
Letterkenny Londonderry
NORTHERN
Ardara Strabane Ballymena Larne
IRELAND
Antrim
Donegal Lough Crumlin
Ballyshannon Omagh Neagh
Dungannon BELFAST
Enniskillen
Armagh
Sligo Monaghan Downpatrick
Ballina

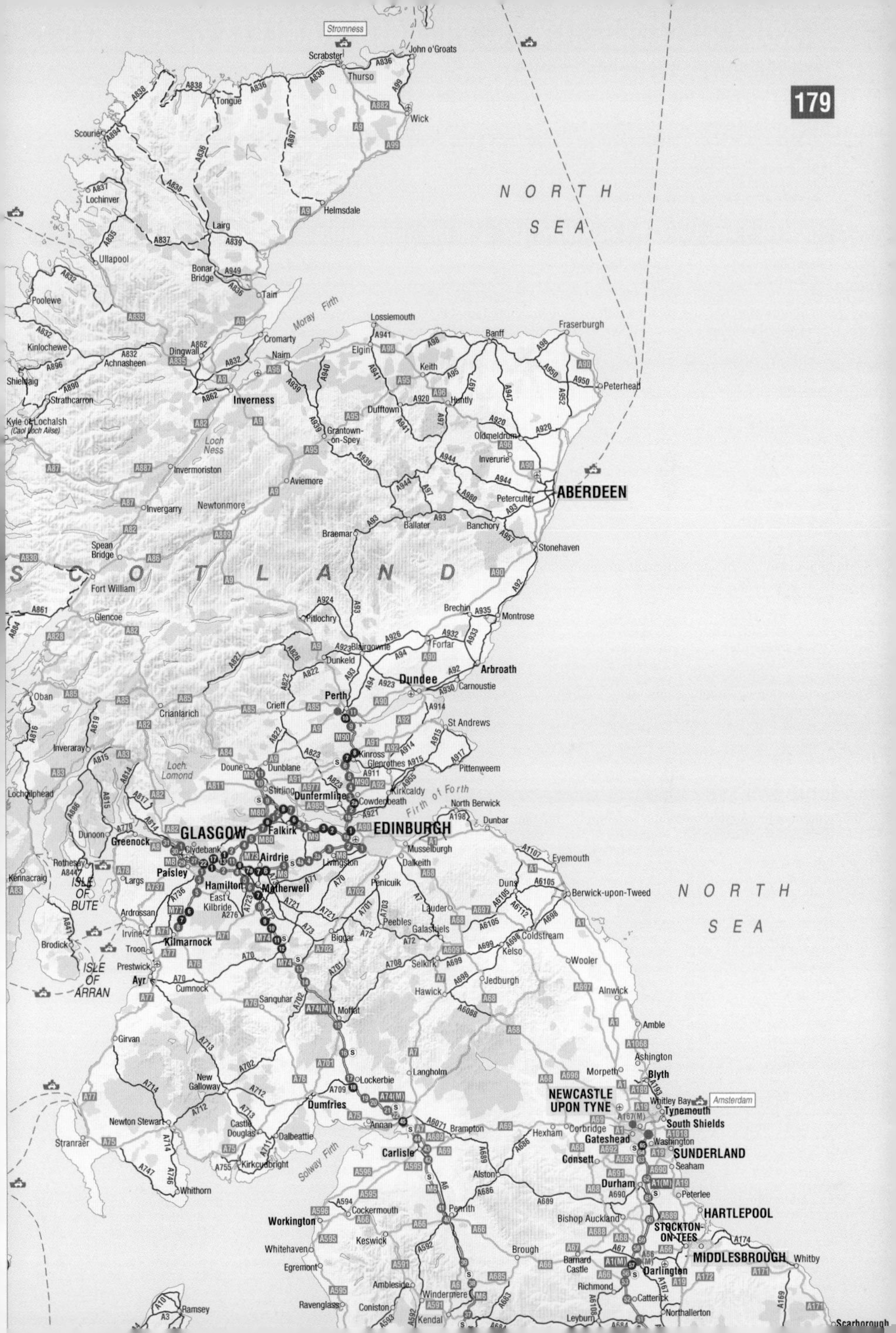

SCOTLAND

NORTH SEA

Stromness
Scrabster
Thurso
John o'Groats
Tongue
Scourie
Wick
Helmsdale
Lochinver
Lairg
Ullapool
Bonar Bridge
Tain
Poolewe
Cromarty
Lossiemouth
Bantf
Fraserburgh
Kinlochewe
Dingwall
Nairn
Elgin
Keith
Peterhead
Achnasheen
Inverness
Dufftown
Huntly
Oldmeldrum
Shieldaig
Kyle of Lochalsh
(Caol Loch Aillse)
Loch Ness
Grantown-on-Spey
Inverurie
Strathcarron
Invermoriston
Aviemore
Peterculter
ABERDEEN
Invergarry
Newtonmore
Spean Bridge
Braemar
Ballater
Banchory
Stonehaven
Fort William
Glencoe
Pitlochry
Brechin
Montrose
Oban
Crianlarich
Dunkeld
Blairgowrie
Forfar
Arbroath
Inveraray
Loch Lomond
Crieff
Dundee
Carnoustie
Lochgilphead
Doune
Dunblane
Perth
St Andrews
Dunoon
Stirling
Kinross
Glenrothes
Pittenweem
Rothesay
GLASGOW
Falkirk
Dunfermline
Kirkcaldy
ISLE OF BUTE
Greenock
Clydebank
Cowdenbeath
North Berwick
Largs
Paisley
Airdrie
EDINBURGH
Dunbar
Ardrossan
Hamilton
Livingston
Musselburgh
Eyemouth
Irvine
East Kilbride
Motherwell
Dalkeith
Duns
Berwick-upon-Tweed
Troon
Kilmarnock
Penicuik
Lauder
Prestwick
Peebles
Galashiels
Kelso
Ayr
Biggar
Selkirk
Coldstream
Cumnock
Wooler
Girvan
Sanquhar
Moffat
Hawick
Jedburgh
Alnwick
New Galloway
Langholm
Amble
Newton Stewart
Lockerbie
Morpeth
Blyth
Stranraer
Dumfries
Annan
Brampton
Ashington
Whitley Bay
Amsterdam
Castle Douglas
NEWCASTLE UPON TYNE
Tynemouth
Dalbeattie
Corbridge
Hexham
South Shields
Kirkcudbright
Carlisle
Gateshead
SUNDERLAND
Whithorn
Consett
Seaham
Alston
Durham
Peterlee
Workington
Cockermouth
Penrith
Bishop Auckland
HARTLEPOOL
Whitehaven
Keswick
STOCKTON-ON-TEES
Egremont
Brough
Barnard Castle
Darlington
MIDDLESBROUGH
Whitby
Ravenglass
Ambleside
Richmond
Catterick
Ramsey
Coniston
Kendal
Leyburn
Northallerton
Scarborough

NORTH SEA

# INDEX TO CITIES, TOWNS, VILLAGES, HAMLETS & AIRPORTS

(1) A strict alphabetical order is used e.g. An Dùnan follows Andreas but precedes Andwell.

(2) The map reference given refers to the actual map square in which the town spot or built-up area is located and not to the place name.

(3) Where two or more places of the same name occur in the same County or Unitary Authority, the nearest large town is also given;
e.g. Achiemore. High nr. Durness . . . .2D **166** indicates that Achiemore is located in square 2D on page **166** and is situated near Durness in the Unitary Authority of Highland.

(4) Only one reference is given although due to page overlaps the place may appear on more than one page.

(5) Major towns and destinations are shown in bold, i.e. **Aberdeen.** Aber . . . .3G **153**

## COUNTIES and UNITARY AUTHORITIES with the abbreviations used in this index

Aberdeen : Aber
Aberdeenshire : Abers
Angus : Ang
Antrim & Newtownabbey : Ant
Ards & North Down : Ards
Argyll & Bute : Arg
Armagh, Banbridge & Craigavon : Arm
Bath & N E Somerset : Bath
Bedford : Bed
Belfast : Bel
Blackburn with Darwen : Bkbn
Blackpool : Bkpl
Blaenau Gwent : Blae
Bournemouth : Bour
Bracknell Forest : Brac
Bridgend : B'end
Brighton & Hove : Brig
Bristol : Bris
Buckinghamshire : Buck
Caerphilly : Cphy
Cambridgeshire : Cambs
Cardiff : Card
Carmarthenshire : Carm
Causeway Coast & Glens : Caus
Central Bedfordshire : C Beds
Ceredigion : Cdgn
Cheshire East : Ches E
Cheshire West & Chester : Ches W
Clackmannanshire : Clac
Conwy : Cnwy
Cornwall : Corn
Cumbria : Cumb

Darlington : Darl
Denbighshire : Den
Derby : Derb
Derbyshire : Derbs
Derry & Strabane : Derr
Devon : Devn
Dorset : Dors
Dundee : D'dee
Durham : Dur
East Ayrshire : E Ayr
East Dunbartonshire : E Dun
East Lothian : E Lot
East Renfrewshire : E Ren
East Riding of Yorkshire : E Yor
East Sussex : E Sus
Edinburgh : Edin
Essex : Essx
Falkirk : Falk
Fermanagh & Omagh : Ferm
Fife : Fife
Flintshire : Flin
Glasgow : Glas
Gloucestershire : Glos
Greater London : G Lon
Greater Manchester : G Man
Gwynedd : Gwyn
Halton : Hal
Hampshire : Hants
Hartlepool : Hart
Herefordshire : Here
Hertfordshire : Herts

Highland : High
Inverclyde : Inv
Isle of Anglesey : IOA
Isle of Man : IOM
Isle of Wight : IOW
Isles of Scilly : IOS
Kent : Kent
Kingston upon Hull : Hull
Lancashire : Lanc
Leicester : Leic
Leicestershire : Leics
Lincolnshire : Linc
Lisburn & Castlereagh : Lis
Luton : Lutn
Medway : Medw
Merseyside : Mers
Merthyr Tydfil : Mer T
Mid & East Antrim : ME Ant
Middlesbrough : Midd
Midlothian : Midl
Mid Ulster : M Ulst
Milton Keynes : Mil
Monmouthshire : Mon
Moray : Mor
Neath Port Talbot : Neat
Newport : Newp
Newry, Mourne & Down : New M
Norfolk : Norf
Northamptonshire : Nptn
North Ayrshire : N Ayr
North East Lincolnshire : NE Lin

North Lanarkshire : N Lan
North Lincolnshire : N Lin
North Somerset : N Som
Northumberland : Nmbd
North Yorkshire : N Yor
Nottingham : Nott
Nottinghamshire : Notts
Orkney : Orkn
Oxfordshire : Oxon
Pembrokeshire : Pemb
Perth & Kinross : Per
Peterborough : Pet
Plymouth : Plym
Poole : Pool
Portsmouth : Port
Powys : Powy
Reading : Read
Redcar & Cleveland : Red C
Renfrewshire : Ren
Rhondda Cynon Taff : Rhon
Rutland : Rut
Scottish Borders : Bord
Shetland : Shet
Shropshire : Shrp
Slough : Slo
Somerset : Som
South Ayrshire : S Ayr
Southend-on-Sea : S'end
South Gloucestershire : S Glo

South Lanarkshire : S Lan
South Yorkshire : S Yor
Staffordshire : Staf
Stirling : Stir
Stockton-on-Tees : Stoc T
Stoke-on-Trent : Stoke
Suffolk : Suff
Surrey : Surr
Swansea : Swan
Swindon : Swin
Telford & Wrekin : Telf
Thurrock : Thur
Torbay : Torb
Torfaen : Torf
Tyne & Wear : Tyne
Vale of Glamorgan, The : V Glam
Warrington : Warr
Warwickshire : Warw
West Berkshire : W Ber
West Dunbartonshire : W Dun
Western Isles : W Isl
West Lothian : W Lot
West Midlands : W Mid
West Sussex : W Sus
West Yorkshire : W Yor
Wiltshire : Wilts
Windsor & Maidenhead : Wind
Wokingham : Wok
Worcestershire : Worc
Wrexham : Wrex
York : York

# INDEX

## A

Abbas Combe. Som . . . . . . . . . .4C 22
Abberley. Worc . . . . . . . . . .4B 60
Abberley Common. Worc . . . .4B 60
Abberton. Essx . . . . . . . . . .4D 54
Abberton. Worc . . . . . . . . . .5D 61
Abberwick. Nmbd . . . . . . . .3F 121
Abbess Roding. Essx . . . . . .4F 53
Abbey. Devn . . . . . . . . . . . .1E 13
Abbey-cwm-hir. Powy . . . . . .3C 58
Abbeydale. S Yor . . . . . . . . .2H 85
Abbeydale Park. S Yor . . . . .2H 85
Abbey Dore. Here . . . . . . . . .2G 47
Abbey Hulton. Stoke . . . . . . .1D 72
Abbey St Bathans. Bord . . . .3D 130
Abbeystead. Lanc . . . . . . . . .4E 97
Abbeytown. Cumb . . . . . . . .4C 112
Abbey Village. Lanc . . . . . . .2E 91
Abbey Wood. G Lon . . . . . . .3F 39
Abbots Bickington. Devn . . . .1D 11
Abbots Bromley. Staf . . . . . .3E 73
Abbotsbury. Dors . . . . . . . . .4A 14
Abbotsham. Devn . . . . . . . . .4E 19
Abbotskerswell. Devn . . . . . .2E 9
Abbots Langley. Herts . . . . .5A 52
Abbots Leigh. N Som . . . . . .4A 34
Abbotsley. Cambs . . . . . . . .5B 64
Abbots Morton. Worc . . . . . .5E 61
Abbots Ripton. Cambs . . . . .3B 64

Abbot's Salford. Warw . . . . .5E 61
Abbotstone. Hants . . . . . . . .3D 24
Abbots Worthy. Hants . . . . . .3C 24
Abbotts Ann. Hants . . . . . . .2B 24
Abcott. Shrp . . . . . . . . . . . .3F 59
Abdon. Shrp . . . . . . . . . . . .2H 59
Abenhall. Glos . . . . . . . . . .4B 48
Aber. Cdgn . . . . . . . . . . . . .1E 45
Aberarder. Cdgn . . . . . . . . .4D 56
Aberafan. Neat . . . . . . . . . .3G 31
Aberaman. Rhon . . . . . . . . .5D 46
Aberangell. Gwyn . . . . . . . .4H 69
Aberarad. Carm . . . . . . . . . .1H 43
Aberarder. High . . . . . . . . .1A 150
Aberargie. Per . . . . . . . . . .2D 136
Aberarth. Cdgn . . . . . . . . . .4D 57
Aberavon. Neat . . . . . . . . . .3G 31
Aber-banc. Cdgn . . . . . . . . .1D 44
Aberbargoed. Cphy . . . . . . .2E 33
Aberbechan. Powy . . . . . . . .1D 58
Aberbeeg. Blae . . . . . . . . . .5F 47
Aberbowlan. Carm . . . . . . . .2G 45
Aberbran. Powy . . . . . . . . . .3C 46
Abercanaid. Mer T . . . . . . . .5D 46
Abercarn. Cphy . . . . . . . . . .2F 33
Abercegir. Powy . . . . . . . . .5H 69
Aberchalder. High . . . . . . . .3F 149
Aberchirder. Abers . . . . . . . .3D 160
Abercorn. W Lot . . . . . . . . .2D 129
Abercraf. Powy . . . . . . . . . .4B 46

Abercregan. Neat . . . . . . . . .2B 32
Abercrombie. Fife . . . . . . . .3H 137
Abercwmboi. Rhon . . . . . . . .2D 32
Abercych. Pemb . . . . . . . . .1C 44
**Abercynon.** Rhon . . . . . . . . .2D 32
Aber-Cywarch. Gwyn . . . . . .4A 70
Aberdalgie. Per . . . . . . . . .1C 136
**Aberdâr.** Rhon . . . . . . . . . .5C 46
**Aberdare.** Rhon . . . . . . . . .5C 46
Aberdaron. Gwyn . . . . . . . . .3A 68
**Aberdaugleddau.** Pemb . . . .4D 42
**Aberdeen.** Aber . . . . . .3G **153**
Aberdeen International
Airport. Aber . . . . . . . . .2F **153**
Aberdesach. Gwyn . . . . . . . .5D 80
Aberdour. Fife . . . . . . . . . .1E 129
Aberdovey. Gwyn . . . . . . . . .1F 57
Aberdulais. Neat . . . . . . . . .5A 46
Aberdyfi. Gwyn . . . . . . . . . .1F 57
Aberedw. Powy . . . . . . . . . .1D 46
Abereiddy. Pemb . . . . . . . . .1B 42
Abererch. Gwyn . . . . . . . . . .2C 68
Aberfan. Mer T . . . . . . . . . .5D 46
Aberfeldy. Per . . . . . . . . . .4F 143
Aberffraw. IOA . . . . . . . . . .4C 80
Aberffrwd. Cdgn . . . . . . . . .3F 57
Aberford. W Yor . . . . . . . . .1E 93
Aberfoyle. Stir . . . . . . . . . .3E 135
Abergarw. B'end . . . . . . . . .3C 32
Abergarwed. Neat . . . . . . . .5B 46
**Abergavenny.** Mon . . . . . . .4G 47
Abergele. Cnwy . . . . . . . . . .3B 82

Aber-Giâr. Carm . . . . . . . . .1F 45
Abergorlech. Carm . . . . . . . .2F 45
Abergwaun. Pemb . . . . . . . .1D 42
Abergwesyn. Powy . . . . . . . .5A 58
Abergwili. Carm . . . . . . . . .3E 45
Abergwynfi. Neat . . . . . . . . .2B 32
Abergwyngregyn. Gwyn . . . . .3F 81
Abergynolwyn. Gwyn . . . . . .5F 69
Aberhafesp. Powy . . . . . . . .1C 58
Aberhonddu. Powy . . . . . . . .3D 46
Aberhosan. Powy . . . . . . . . .1H 57
Aberkenfig. B'end . . . . . . . .3B 32
Aberlady. E Lot . . . . . . . . .1A 130
Aberlemno. Ang . . . . . . . . .3E 145
Aberllefenni. Gwyn . . . . . . .5G 69
Abermaw. Gwyn . . . . . . . . .4F 69
Abermeurig. Cdgn . . . . . . . .5E 57
Aber-miwl. Powy . . . . . . . . .1D 58
Abermule. Powy . . . . . . . . .1D 58
Abernant. Carm . . . . . . . . . .2H 43
Abernant. Rhon . . . . . . . . . .5D 46
Abernethy. Per . . . . . . . . . .2D 136
Abernyte. Per . . . . . . . . . . .5B 144
Aber-oer. Wrex . . . . . . . . . .1E 71
**Aberpennar.** Rhon . . . . . . . .2D 32
Aberporth. Cdgn . . . . . . . . .5B 56
Aberriw. Powy . . . . . . . . . .5D 70
Abersoch. Gwyn . . . . . . . . .3C 68
Abersychan. Torf . . . . . . . . .5F 47
**Abertawe.** Swan . . . . . . . . .3F 31
Aberteifi. Cdgn . . . . . . . . .1B 44
Aberthin. V Glam . . . . . . . . .4D 32

**Abertillery.** Blae . . . . . . . . .5F 47
Abertridwr. Cphy . . . . . . . . .3E 32
**Abertyleri.** Blae . . . . . . . . .5F 47
Abertysswg. Cphy . . . . . . . .5E 47
Aberuthven. Per . . . . . . . . .2B 136
Aber Village. Powy . . . . . . . .3E 46
Aberwheeler. Den . . . . . . . .4C 82
Aberyscir. Powy . . . . . . . . . .3C 46
**Aberystwyth.** Cdgn . . . . . . .2E 57
Abhainn Suidhe. W Isl . . . . .7C 171
**Abingdon-on-Thames.**
Oxon . . . . . . . . . . . . . . .2C 36
Abinger Common. Surr . . . . .1C 26
Abinger Hammer. Surr . . . . .1B 26
Abington. S Lan . . . . . . . . .2B 118
Ab Lench. Worc . . . . . . . . . .5E 61
Ab Kettleby. Leics . . . . . . . .3E 74
Ablington. Glos . . . . . . . . . .5G 49
Ablington. Wilts . . . . . . . . . .2G 23
Abney. Derbs . . . . . . . . . . .3F 85
Aboyne. Abers . . . . . . . . . .4C 152
**Abram.** G Man . . . . . . . . . .4E 90
Abriachan. High . . . . . . . . .5H 157
Abridge. Essx . . . . . . . . . . .1F 39
Abronhill. N Lan . . . . . . . . .2A 128
Abson. S Glo . . . . . . . . . . .4C 34
Abthorpe. Nptn . . . . . . . . . .1E 51
Abune-the-Hill. Orkn . . . . . .5B 172
Aby. Linc . . . . . . . . . . . . . .3D 88
Acairseid. W Isl . . . . . . . . .8C 170
Acaster Malbis. York . . . . . .5H 99

Acaster Selby —Alpraham

Acaster Selby. N Yor 5H 99
Accott. Devn 3G 19
**Accrington**. Lanc 2F 91
Acha. Arg 3C 138
Achachork. High 4D 155
Achadh a' Chuirn. High 1E 147
Achahoish. Arg 2F 125
Achaleven. Arg 5D 140
Achallader. Arg 4H 141
Acha Mor. W Isl 5F 171
Achanalt. High 2E 157
Achandunie. High 1A 158
Ach' an Todhair. High 1E 141
Achany. High 3C 164
Achaphubuil. High 1E 141
Acharacle. High 2A 140
Acharn. Ang 1B 144
Acharn. Per 4E 143
Acharole. High 3E 169
Achateny. High 2G 139
Achavanich. High 4D 169
Achdalieu. High 1E 141
Achduart. High 3E 163
Achentoul. High 5A 168
Achfary. High 5C 166
Achfrish. High 2C 164
Achgarve. High 4C 162
Achiemore. High
nr. Durness 2D 166
nr. Thurso 3A 168
A' Chill. High 3A 146
Achiltibuie. High 3E 163
Achina. High 2H 167
Achinahuagh. High 2F 167
Achindarroch. High 3E 141
Achinduich. High 3C 164
Achinduin. Arg 5C 140
Achininver. High 2F 167
Achintee. High 4B 156
Achintraid. High 5H 155
Achleck. Arg 4F 139
Achlorachan. High 3F 157
Achluachrach. High 5E 149
Achlyness. High 3C 166
Achmelvich. High 1E 163
Achmony. High 5H 157
Achmore. High
nr. Stromeferry 5A 156
nr. Ullapool 4E 163
Achnacarnin. High 1E 163
Achnacarry. High 5D 148
Achnaclerach. High 2G 157
Achnacloich. High 3D 147
Ach na Cloiche. High 3D 147
Achnaconeran. High 2G 149
Achnacroish. Arg 4C 140
Achnafalnich. Arg 1B 134
Achnagarron. High 1A 158
Achnagoul. Arg 3H 133
Achnaha. High 2F 139
Achnahanat. High 4C 164
Achnahannet. High 1D 151
Achnairn. High 2C 164
Achnamara. Arg 1F 125
Achnanellan. High 5C 148
Achnasheen. High 3D 156
Achnashellach. High 4C 156
Achosnich. High 2F 139
Achow. High 5E 169
Achranich. High 4B 140
Achreamie. High 2C 168
Achriabhach. High 2F 141
Achriesgill. High 3C 166
Achrimsdale. High 3G 165
Achscrabster. High 2C 168
Achtoty. High 2G 167
Achurch. Nptn 2H 63
Achuvoldrach. High 3F 167
Achvaich. High 4E 164
Achvoan. High 3E 165
Ackenthwaite. Cumb 1E 97
Ackergill. High 3F 169
Ackergillshore. High 3F 169
Acklam. Midd 3B 106
Acklam. N Yor 3B 100
Ackleton. Shrp 1B 60
Acklington. Nmbd 4G 121
Ackton. W Yor 2E 93
Ackworth Moor Top.
W Yor 3E 93
Acle. Norf 4G 79
Acocks Green. W Mid 2F 61
Acol. Kent 4H 41
Acomb. Nmbd 3C 114
Acomb. York 4H 99
Aconbury. Here 2A 48
Acre. G Man 4H 91
Acre. Lanc 2F 91
Acrefair. Wrex 1E 71
Acrise. Kent 1F 29
Acton. Ches E 5A 84
Acton. Dors 5E 15
**Acton**. G Lon 2C 38
Acton. Shrp 2F 59
Acton. Staf 1C 72
Acton. Suff 1B 54
Acton. Worc 4C 60
Acton. Wrex 5F 83
Acton Beauchamp. Here 5A 60
Acton Bridge. Ches W 3H 83
Acton Burnell. Shrp 5H 71
Acton Green. Here 5A 60
Acton Pigott. Shrp 5H 71
Acton Round. Shrp 1A 60
Acton Scott. Shrp 2G 59
Acton Trussell. Staf 4D 72
Acton Turville. S Glo 3D 34
Adabroc. W Isl 1H 171
Adam's Hill. Worc 3D 60
Adbaston. Staf 3B 72
Adber. Dors 4B 22
Adderbury. Oxon 2C 50
Adderley. Shrp 2A 72
Adderstone. Nmbd 1F 121
Addiewell. W Lot 3C 128
Addingham. W Yor 5C 98
Addington. Buck 3F 51
Addington. G Lon 4E 39
Addington. Kent 5A 40
Addinston. Bord 4B 130
Addiscombe. G Lon 4E 39
**Addlestone**. Surr 4B 38
Addlethorpe. Linc 4E 89
Adeney. Telf 4B 72
Adfa. Powy 5C 70
Adforton. Here 3G 59
Adgestone. IOW 4D 16
Adisham. Kent 5G 41
Adlestrop. Glos 3H 49
Adlingfleet. E Yor 2B 94
Adlington. Ches E 2D 84
Adlington. Lanc 3E 90
Admaston. Staf 3E 73
Admaston. Telf 4A 72
Admington. Warw 1H 49
Adpar. Cdgn 1D 44
Adsborough. Som 4F 21
Adstock. Buck 2F 51
Adstone. Nptn 5C 62
Adversane. W Sus 3B 26
Advie. High 5F 159
Adwalton. W Yor 2C 92
Adwell. Oxon 2E 37
**Adwick le Street**. S Yor 4F 93
Adwick upon Dearne.
S Yor 4E 93
Adziel. Abers 3G 161
Ae. Dum 1A 112
Affleck. Abers 1F 153
Affpuddle. Dors 3D 14
Affric Lodge. High 1D 148
Afon-wen. Flin 3D 82
Agglethorpe. N Yor 1C 98
Aglionby. Cumb 4F 113
Ahoghill. ME Ant 2F 175
Aigburth. Mers 2F 83
Aiginis. W Isl 4G 171
Aike. E Yor 5E 101
Aikers. Orkn 8D 172
Aiketgate. Cumb 5F 113
Aikhead. Cumb 5D 112
Aikton. Cumb 4D 112
Ailey. Here 1G 47
Ailsworth. Pet 1A 64
Ainderby Quernhow. N Yor 1F 99
Ainderby Steeple. N Yor 5A 106
Aingers Green. Essx 3E 54
Ainsdale. Mers 3B 90
Ainsdale-on-Sea. Mers 3B 90
Ainstable. Cumb 5G 113
Ainsworth. G Man 3F 91
Ainthorpe. N Yor 4E 107
Aintree. Mers 1F 83
Aird. Arg 3E 133
Aird. Dum 3F 109
Aird. High
nr. Port Henderson 1G 155
nr. Tarskavaig 3D 147
Aird. W Isl
on Benbecula 3C 170
on Isle of Lewis 4H 171
The Aird. High 3D 154
Aird a Bhasair. High 3E 147
Aird a Mhachair. W Isl 4C 170
Aird a Mhulaidh. W Isl 6D 171
Aird Asaig. W Isl 7D 171
Aird Dhail. W Isl 1G 171
Airdens. High 4D 164
Airdeny. Arg 1G 133
Aird Mhidhinis. W Isl 8C 170
Aird Mhighe. W Isl
nr. Ceann a Bhaigh 8D 171
nr. Fionnsabhagh 9C 171
Aird Mhor. W Isl on Barra 8C 170
on South Uist 4D 170
**Airdrie**. N Lan 3A 128
Aird Shleibhe. W Isl 9D 171
Aird Thunga. W Isl 4G 171
Aird Uig. W Isl 4C 171
Airedale. W Yor 2E 93
Airidh a Bhruaich. W Isl 6E 171
Airies. Dum 3E 109
Airmyn. E Yor 2H 93
Airntully. Per 5H 143
Airor. High 3F 147
Airth. Falk 1C 128
Airton. N Yor 4B 98
Aisby. Linc
nr. Gainsborough 1F 87
nr. Grantham 2H 75
Aisgernis. W Isl 6C 170
Aish. Devn
nr. Buckfastleigh 2C 8
nr. Totnes 3E 9
Aisholt. Som 3E 21
Aiskew. N Yor 1E 99
Aislaby. N Yor
nr. Pickering 1B 100
nr. Whitby 4F 107
Aislaby. Stoc T 3B 106
Aisthorpe. Linc 2G 87
Aith. Shet
on Fetlar 3H 173
on Mainland 6E 173
Aithsetter. Shet 8F 173
Akeld. Nmbd 2D 120
Akeley. Buck 2F 51
Akenham. Suff 1E 55
Albaston. Corn 5E 11
Alberbury. Shrp 4F 71
Albert Town. Pemb 3D 42
Albert Village. Leics 4H 73
Albourne. W Sus 4D 26
Albrighton. Shrp
nr. Shrewsbury 4G 71
nr. Telford 5C 72
Alburgh. Norf 2E 67
Albury. Herts 3E 53
Albury. Surr 1B 26
Albyfield. Cumb 4G 113
Alby Hill. Norf 2D 78
Alcaig. High 3H 157
Alcaston. Shrp 2G 59
Alcester. Warw 5E 61
Alciston. E Sus 5G 27
Alcombe. Som 2C 20
Alconbury. Cambs 3A 64
Alconbury Weston. Cambs 3A 64
Aldborough. Norf 2D 78
Aldborough. N Yor 3G 99
Aldbourne. Wilts 4A 36
Aldbrough. E Yor 1F 95
Aldbrough St John. N Yor 3F 105
Aldbury. Herts 4H 51
Aldcliffe. Lanc 3D 96
Aldclune. Per 2G 143
Aldeburgh. Suff 5G 67
Aldeby. Norf 1G 67
Aldenham. Herts 1C 38
Alderbury. Wilts 4G 23
Aldercar. Derbs 1B 74
Alderford. Norf 4D 78
Alderholt. Dors 1G 15
Alderley. Glos 2C 34
Alderley Edge. Ches E 3C 84
Aldermaston. W Ber 5D 36
Aldermaston Soke. Hants 5E 36
Aldermaston Wharf. W Ber 5E 36
Alderminster. Warw 1H 49
Alder Moor. Staf 3G 73
Aldersey Green. Ches W 5G 83
**Aldershot**. Hants 1G 25
Alderton. Glos 2F 49
Alderton. Nptn 1F 51
Alderton. Shrp 3G 71
Alderton. Suff 1G 55
Alderton. Wilts 3D 34
Alderton Fields. Glos 2F 49
Alderwasley. Derbs 5H 85
Aldfield. N Yor 3E 99
Aldford. Ches W 5G 83
Aldgate. Rut 5G 75
Aldham. Essx 3C 54
Aldham. Suff 1D 54
Aldingbourne. W Sus 5A 26
Aldingham. Cumb 2B 96
Aldington. Kent 2E 29
Aldington. Worc 1F 49
Aldington Frith. Kent 2E 29
Aldochlay. Arg 4C 134
Aldon. Shrp 3G 59
Aldoth. Cumb 5C 112
Aldreth. Cambs 3D 64
**Aldridge**. W Mid 5E 73
Aldringham. Suff 4G 67
Aldsworth. Glos 4G 49
Aldsworth. W Sus 2F 17
Aldwark. Derbs 5G 85
Aldwark. N Yor 3G 99
Aldwick. W Sus 3H 17
Aldwincle. Nptn 2H 63
Aldworth. W Ber 4D 36
Alexandria. W Dun 1E 127
Aley. Som 3E 21
Aley Green. C Beds 4A 52
Alfardisworthy. Devn 1C 10
Alfington. Devn 3E 12
Alfold. Surr 2B 26
Alfold Bars. W Sus 2B 26
Alfold Crossways. Surr 2B 26
Alford. Abers 2C 152
Alford. Linc 3D 88
Alford. Som 3B 22
**Alfreton**. Derbs 5B 86
Alfrick. Worc 5B 60
Alfrick Pound. Worc 5B 60
Alfriston. E Sus 5G 27
Algarkirk. Linc 2B 76
Alhampton. Som 3B 22
Aline Lodge. W Isl 6D 171
Alkborough. N Lin 2B 94
Alkerton. Oxon 1B 50
Alkham. Kent 1G 29
Alkington. Shrp 2H 71
Alkmonton. Derbs 2F 73
Alladale Lodge. High 5B 164
Allaleigh. Devn 3E 9
Allanbank. N Lan 4B 128
Allanton. N Lan 4B 128
Allanton. Bord 4E 131
Allaston. Glos 5B 48
Allbrook. Hants 4C 24
All Cannings. Wilts 5F 35
Allendale Town. Nmbd 4B 114
Allen End. Warw 1F 61
Allenheads. Nmbd 5B 114
Allensford. Dur 5D 115
Allen's Green. Herts 4E 53
Allensmore. Here 2H 47
Allenton. Derb 2A 74
Aller. Som 4H 21
Allerby. Cumb 1B 102
Allercombe. Devn 3D 12
Allerford. Som 2C 20
Allerston. N Yor 1C 100
Allerthorpe. E Yor 5B 100
Allerton. Mers 2G 83
Allerton. W Yor 1B 92
Allerton Bywater. W Yor 2E 93
Allerton Mauleverer. N Yor 4G 99
Allesley. W Mid 2G 61
Allestree. Derb 2H 73
Allet. Corn 4B 6
Allexton. Leics 5F 75
Allgreave. Ches E 4D 84
Allhallows. Medw 3C 40
Allhallows-on-Sea. Medw 3C 40
Alligin Shuas. High 3H 155
Allimore Green. Staf 4C 72
Allington. Kent 5B 40
Allington. Linc 1F 75
Allington. Wilts
nr. Amesbury 3H 23
nr. Devizes 5F 35
Allithwaite. Cumb 2C 96
**Alloa**. Clac 4A 136
Allonby. Cumb 5B 112
Allostock. Ches W 3B 84
Alloway. S Ayr 3C 116
Allowenshay. Som 1G 13
All Saints South Elmham.
Suff 2F 67
Allscott. Shrp 1B 60
Allscott. Telf 4A 72
All Stretton. Shrp 1G 59
Allt. Carm 5F 45
Alltami. Flin 4E 83
Alltgobhlach. N Ayr 5G 125
Alltmawr. Powy 1D 46
Alltnacaillich. High 4E 167
Allt na h' Airbhe. High 4F 163
Alltour. High 5E 148
Alltsigh. High 2G 149
Alltwalis. Carm 2E 45
Alltwen. Neat 5H 45
Alltyblacca. Cdgn 1F 45
Allt-y-goed. Pemb 1B 44
Almeley. Here 5F 59
Almeley Wootton. Here 5F 59
Almer. Dors 3E 15
Almholme. S Yor 4F 93
Almington. Staf 2B 72
Alminstone Cross. Devn 4D 18
Almodington. W Sus 3G 17
Almondbank. Per 1C 136
Almondbury. W Yor 3B 92
Almondsbury. S Glo 3B 34
Alne. N Yor 3G 99
Alness. High 2A 158
Alnessferry. High 2A 158
Alnham. Nmbd 3D 121
Alnmouth. Nmbd 3G 121
Alnwick. Nmbd 3F 121
Alphamstone. Essx 2B 54
Alpheton. Suff 5A 66
Alphington. Devn 3C 12
Alpington. Norf 5E 79
Alport. Derbs 4G 85
Alport. Powy 1E 59
Alpraham. Ches E 5H 83

Alresford—Ashbury


Alresford. *Essx* 3D 54
Alrewas. *Staf* 4F 73
**Alsager**. *Ches E* 5B 84
Alsagers Bank. *Staf* 1C 72
Alsop en le Dale. *Derbs* 5F 85
Alston. *Cumb* 5A 114
Alston. *Devn* 2G 13
Alstone. *Glos* 2E 49
Alstone. *Som* 2G 21
Alstonefield. *Staf* 5F 85
Alston Sutton. *Som* 1H 21
Alswear. *Devn* 4H 19
Altandhu. *High* 2D 163
Altanduin. *High* 1F 165
Altarnun. *Corn* 4C 10
Altass. *High* 3B 164
Alterwall. *High* 2E 169
Altgaltraig. *Arg* 2B 126
Altham. *Lanc* 1F 91
Althorne. *Essx* 1D 40
Althorpe. *N Lin* 4B 94
Altnabreac. *High* 4C 168
Altnacealgach. *High* 2G 163
Altnafeadh. *High* 3G 141
Altnaharra. *High* 5F 167
Altofts. *W Yor* 2D 93
Alton. *Derbs* 4A 86
**Alton**. *Hants* 3F 25
Alton. *Staf* 1E 73
Alton Barnes. *Wilts* 5G 35
Altonhill. *E Ayr* 1D 116
Alton Pancras. *Dors* 2C 14
Alton Priors. *Wilts* 5G 35
**Altrincham**. *G Man* 2B 84
Altrua. *High* 4E 149
Alva. *Clac* 4A 136
Alvanley. *Ches W* 3G 83
Alvaston. *Derb* 2A 74
Alvechurch. *Worc* 3E 61
Alvecote. *Warw* 5G 73
Alvediston. *Wilts* 4E 23
Alveley. *Shrp* 2B 60
Alverdiscott. *Devn* 4F 19
Alverstoke. *Hants* 3D 16
Alverstone. *IOW* 4D 16
Alverthorpe. *W Yor* 2D 92
Alverton. *Notts* 1E 75
Alves. *Mor* 2F 159
Alvescot. *Oxon* 5A 50
Alveston. *S Glo* 3B 34
Alveston. *Warw* 5G 61
Alvie. *High* 3C 150
Alvingham. *Linc* 1C 88
Alvington. *Glos* 5B 48
Alwalton. *Cambs* 1A 64
Alweston. *Dors* 1B 14
Alwington. *Devn* 4E 19
Alwinton. *Nmbd* 4D 120
Alwoodley. *W Yor* 5E 99
Alyth. *Per* 4B 144
Amatnatua. *High* 4B 164
Am Baile. *W Isl* 7C 170
Ambaston. *Derbs* 2B 74
Ambergate. *Derbs* 5H 85
Amber Hill. *Linc* 1B 76
Amberley. *Glos* 5D 48
Amberley. *W Sus* 4B 26
Amble. *Nmbd* 4G 121
Amblecote. *W Mid* 2C 60
Ambler Thorn. *W Yor* 2A 92
Ambleside. *Cumb* 4E 103
Ambleston. *Pemb* 2E 43
Ambrosden. *Oxon* 4E 50
Amcotts. *N Lin* 3B 94
**Amersham**. *Buck* 1A 38
Amerton. *Staf* 3D 73
Amesbury. *Wilts* 2G 23
Amisfield. *Dum* 1B 112
Amlwch. *IOA* 1D 80
Amlwch Port. *IOA* 1D 80
**Ammanford**. *Carm* 4G 45
Amotherby. *N Yor* 2B 100
Ampfield. *Hants* 4B 24
Ampleforth. *N Yor* 2H 99
Ampleforth College. *N Yor* 2H 99
Ampney Crucis. *Glos* 5F 49
Ampney St Mary. *Glos* 5F 49
Ampney St Peter. *Glos* 5F 49
Amport. *Hants* 2A 24
Ampthill. *C Beds* 2A 52
Ampton. *Suff* 3A 66
Amroth. *Pemb* 4F 43
Amulree. *Per* 5G 143
Amwell. *Herts* 4B 52
Anaheilt. *High* 2C 140
An Àird. *High* 3D 147
An Camus Darach. *High* 4E 147
Ancaster. *Linc* 1G 75
Anchor. *Shrp* 2D 58
Anchorsholme. *Lanc* 5C 96
Anchor Street. *Norf* 3F 79
An Cnoc. *W Isl* 4G 171
An Cnoc Ard. *W Isl* 1H 171
An Coroghon. *High* 3A 146
Ancroft. *Nmbd* 5G 131
Ancrum. *Bord* 2A 120
Ancton. *W Sus* 5A 26
Anderby. *Linc* 3E 89
Anderby Creek. *Linc* 3E 89
Anderson. *Dors* 3D 15
Anderton. *Ches W* 3A 84
Andertons Mill. *Lanc* 3D 90
**Andover**. *Hants* 2B 24
Andover Down. *Hants* 2B 24
Andoversford. *Glos* 4F 49
Andreas. *IOM* 2D 108
An Dùnan. *High* 1D 147
Andwell. *Hants* 1E 25
Anelog. *Gwyn* 3A 68
Anfield. *Mers* 1F 83
Angarrack. *Corn* 3C 4
Angelbank. *Shrp* 3H 59
Angersleigh. *Som* 1E 13
Angerton. *Cumb* 4D 112
Angle. *Pemb* 4C 42
An Gleann Ur. *W Isl* 4G 171
Angmering. *W Sus* 5B 26
Angmering-on-Sea. *W Sus* 5B 26
Angram. *N Yor*
nr. Keld 5B 104
nr. York 5H 99
Anick. *Nmbd* 3C 114
Ankerbold. *Derbs* 4A 86
Ankerville. *High* 1C 158
Anlaby. *E Yor* 2D 94
Anlaby Park. *Hull* 2D 94
An Leth Meadhanach. *W Isl* 7C 170
Anmer. *Norf* 3G 77
Anmore. *Hants* 1E 17
Annahilt. *Lis* 5G 175
Annalong. *New M* 6H 175
Annan. *Dum* 3D 112
Annaside. *Cumb* 1A 96
Annat. *Arg* 1H 133
Annat. *High* 3A 156
Annathill. *N Lan* 2A 128
Anna Valley. *Hants* 2B 24
Annbank. *S Ayr* 2D 116
Annesley. *Notts* 5C 86
Annesley Woodhouse. *Notts* 5C 86
**Annfield Plain**. *Dur* 4E 115
Annscroft. *Shrp* 5G 71
An Sailean. *High* 2A 140
Ansdell. *Lanc* 2B 90
Ansford. *Som* 3B 22
Ansley. *Warw* 1G 61
Anslow. *Staf* 3G 73
Anslow Gate. *Staf* 3F 73
Ansteadbrook. *Surr* 2A 26
Anstey. *Herts* 2E 53
Anstey. *Leics* 5C 74
Anston. *S Lan* 5D 128
Anstruther Easter. *Fife* 3H 137
Anstruther Wester. *Fife* 3H 137
Ansty. *Warw* 2A 62
Ansty. *W Sus* 3D 27
Ansty. *Wilts* 4E 23
An Taobh Tuath. *W Isl* 1E 170
An t-Aodann Ban. *High* 3C 154
An t Ath Leathann. *High* 1E 147
An Teanga. *High* 3E 147
Anthill Common. *Hants* 1E 17
Anthorn. *Cumb* 4C 112
Antingham. *Norf* 2E 79
An t-Ob. *W Isl* 9C 171
Anton's Gowt. *Linc* 1B 76
Antony. *Corn* 3A 8
An t-Ord. *High* 2E 147
**Antrim**. *Ant* 3G 175
Antrobus. *Ches W* 3A 84
Anvil Corner. *Devn* 2D 10
Anwick. *Linc* 5A 88
Anwoth. *Dum* 4C 110
Apethorpe. *Nptn* 1H 63
Apeton. *Staf* 4C 72
Apley. *Linc* 3A 88
Apperknowle. *Derbs* 3A 86
Apperley. *Glos* 3D 48
Apperley Dene. *Nmbd* 4D 114
Appersett. *N Yor* 5B 104
Appin. *Arg* 4D 140
Appleby. *N Lin* 3C 94
Appleby-in-Westmorland.
*Cumb* 2H 103
Appleby Magna. *Leics* 5H 73
Appleby Parva. *Leics* 5H 73
Applecross. *High* 4G 155
Appledore. *Devn*
nr. Bideford 3E 19
nr. Tiverton 1D 12
Appledore. *Kent* 3D 28
Appledore Heath. *Kent* 2D 28
Appleford. *Oxon* 2D 36
Applegarthtown. *Dum* 1C 112
Applemore. *Hants* 2B 16
Appleshaw. *Hants* 2B 24
Applethwaite. *Cumb* 2D 102
Appleton. *Hal* 2H 83
Appleton. *Oxon* 5C 50
Appleton-le-Moors. *N Yor* 1B 100
Appleton-le-Street. *N Yor* 2B 100
Appleton Roebuck. *N Yor* 5H 99
Appleton Thorn. *Warr* 2A 84
Appleton Wiske. *N Yor* 4A 106
Appletree. *Nptn* 1C 50
Appletreehall. *Bord* 3H 119
Appletreewick. *N Yor* 3C 98
Appley. *Som* 4D 20
Appley Bridge. *Lanc* 3D 90
Apse Heath. *IOW* 4D 16
Apsley End. *C Beds* 2B 52
Apuldram. *W Sus* 2G 17
Arabella. *High* 1C 158
Arasaig. *High* 5E 147
Arbeadie. *Abers* 4D 152
Arberth. *Pemb* 3F 43
Arbirlot. *Ang* 4F 145
Arborfield. *Wok* 5F 37
Arborfield Cross. *Wok* 5F 37
Arborfield Garrison. *Wok* 5F 37
Arbourthorne. *S Yor* 2A 86
**Arbroath**. *Ang* 4F 145
Arbuthnott. *Abers* 1H 145
Arcan. *High* 3H 157
Archargary. *High* 3H 167
Archdeacon Newton. *Darl* 3F 105
Archiestown. *Mor* 4G 159
Arclid. *Ches E* 4B 84
Arclid Green. *Ches E* 4B 84
Ardachu. *High* 3D 164
Ardalanish. *Arg* 2A 132
Ardaneaskan. *High* 5H 155
Ardarroch. *High* 5H 155
Ardbeg. *Arg*
nr. Dunoon 1C 126
on Islay 5C 124
on Isle of Bute 3B 126
Ardcharnich. *High* 5F 163
Ardchiavaig. *Arg* 2A 132
Ardchonnell. *Arg* 2G 133
Ardchrishnish. *Arg* 1B 132
Ardchronie. *High* 5D 164
Ardchullarie. *Stir* 2E 135
Ardchyle. *Stir* 1E 135
Ard-dhubh. *High* 4G 155
Arddleen. *Powy* 4E 71
Arddlîn. *Powy* 4E 71
Ardechive. *High* 4D 148
Ardeley. *Herts* 3D 52
Ardelve. *High* 1A 148
Arden. *Arg* 1E 127
Ardendrain. *High* 5H 157
Arden Hall. *N Yor* 5C 106
Ardens Grafton. *Warw* 5F 61
Ardentinny. *Arg* 1C 126
Ardeonaig. *Stir* 5D 142
Ardersier. *High* 3B 158
Ardery. *High* 2B 140
Ardessie. *High* 5E 163
Ardfern. *Arg* 3F 133
Ardfernal. *Arg* 2D 124
Ardfin. *Arg* 3C 124
Ardgartan. *Arg* 3B 134
Ardgay. *High* 4D 164
Ardglass. *New M* 6J 175
Ardgour. *High* 2E 141
Ardheslaig. *High* 3G 155
Ardindrean. *High* 5F 163
Ardingly. *W Sus* 3E 27
Ardington. *Oxon* 3C 36
Ardlamont House. *Arg* 3A 126
Ardleigh. *Essx* 3D 54
Ardler. *Per* 4B 144
Ardley. *Oxon* 3D 50
Ardlui. *Arg* 2C 134
Ardlussa. *Arg* 1E 125
Ardmair. *High* 4F 163
Ardmay. *Arg* 3B 134
Ardminish. *Arg* 5E 125
Ardmolich. *High* 1B 140
Ardmore. *High*
nr. Kinlochbervie 3C 166
nr. Tain 5E 164
Ardnacross. *Arg* 4G 139
Ardnadam. *Arg* 1C 126
Ardnagrask. *High* 4H 157
Ardnamurach. *High* 4G 147
Ardnarff. *High* 5A 156
Ardnastang. *High* 2C 140
Ardoch. *Per* 5H 143
Ardochy House. *High* 3E 148
Ardpatrick. *Arg* 3F 125
Ardrishaig. *Arg* 1G 125
Ardroag. *High* 4B 154
Ardross. *High* 1A 158
**Ardrossan**. *N Ayr* 5D 126
Ardshealach. *High* 2A 140
Ardsley. *S Yor* 4D 93
Ardslignish. *High* 2G 139
Ardtalla. *Arg* 4C 124
Ardtalnaig. *Per* 5E 142
Ardtoe. *High* 1A 140
Arduaine. *Arg* 2E 133
Ardullie. *High* 2H 157
Ardvasar. *High* 3E 147
Ardvorlich. *Per* 1F 135
Ardwell. *Dum* 5G 109
Ardwell. *Mor* 5A 160
Arean. *High* 1A 140
Areley Common. *Worc* 3C 60
Areley Kings. *Worc* 3C 60
Arford. *Hants* 3G 25
Argoed. *Cphy* 2E 33
Argoed Mill. *Powy* 4B 58
Aridhglas. *Arg* 2B 132
Arinacrinachd. *High* 3G 155
Arinagour. *Arg* 3D 138
Arisaig. *High* 5E 147
Ariundle. *High* 2C 140
Arivegaig. *High* 2A 140
Arkendale. *N Yor* 3F 99
Arkesden. *Essx* 2E 53
Arkholme. *Lanc* 2E 97
Arkle Town. *N Yor* 4D 104
Arkley. *G Lon* 1D 38
Arksey. *S Yor* 4F 93
Arkwright Town. *Derbs* 3B 86
Arlecdon. *Cumb* 3B 102
Arlescote. *Warw* 1B 50
Arlesey. *C Beds* 2B 52
Arleston. *Telf* 4A 72
Arley. *Ches E* 2A 84
Arlingham. *Glos* 4C 48
Arlington. *Devn* 2G 19
Arlington. *E Sus* 5G 27
Arlington. *Glos* 5G 49
Arlington Beccott. *Devn* 2G 19
Armadail. *High* 3E 147
Armadale. *High*
nr. Isleornsay 3E 147
nr. Strathy 2H 167
Armadale. *W Lot* 3C 128
**Armagh**. *Arm* 5E 175
Armathwaite. *Cumb* 5G 113
Arminghall. *Norf* 5E 79
Armitage. *Staf* 4E 73
Armitage Bridge. *W Yor* 3B 92
Armley. *W Yor* 1C 92
The Arms. *Norf* 1A 66
Armscote. *Warw* 1H 49
Armston. *Nptn* 2H 63
**Armthorpe**. *S Yor* 4G 93
Arncliffe. *N Yor* 2B 98
Arncliffe Cote. *N Yor* 2B 98
Arncroach. *Fife* 3H 137
Arne. *Dors* 4E 15
Arnesby. *Leics* 1D 62
Arnicle. *Arg* 2B 122
Arnisdale. *High* 2G 147
Arnish. *High* 4E 155
Arniston. *Midl* 3G 129
Arnol. *W Isl* 3F 171
Arnold. *E Yor* 5F 101
**Arnold**. *Notts* 1C 74
Arnprior. *Stir* 4F 135
Arnside. *Cumb* 2D 96
Aros Mains. *Arg* 4G 139
Arpafeelie. *High* 3A 158
Arrad Foot. *Cumb* 1C 96
Arram. *E Yor* 5E 101
Arras. *E Yor* 5D 100
Arrathorne. *N Yor* 5E 105
Arreton. *IOW* 4D 16
Arrington. *Cambs* 5C 64
Arrochar. *Arg* 3B 134
Arrow. *Warw* 5E 61
Arscaig. *High* 2C 164
Artafallie. *High* 4A 158
Arthington. *W Yor* 5E 99
Arthingworth. *Nptn* 2E 63
Arthog. *Gwyn* 4F 69
Arthrath. *Abers* 5G 161
Arthurstone. *Per* 4B 144
Artington. *Surr* 1A 26
Arundel. *W Sus* 5B 26
Asby. *Cumb* 2B 102
Ascog. *Arg* 3C 126
**Ascot**. *Wind* 4A 38
Ascott-under-Wychwood.
*Oxon* 4B 50
Asenby. *N Yor* 2F 99
Asfordby. *Leics* 4E 74
Asfordby Hill. *Leics* 4E 74
Asgarby. *Linc*
nr. Horncastle 4C 88
nr. Sleaford 1A 76
Ash. *Devn* 4E 9
Ash. *Dors* 1D 14
Ash. *Kent*
nr. Sandwich 5G 41
nr. Swanley 4H 39
Ash. *Som* 4H 21
Ash. *Surr* 1G 25
Ashampstead. *W Ber* 4D 36
Ashbocking. *Suff* 5D 66
Ashbourne. *Derbs* 1F 73
Ashbrittle. *Som* 4D 20
Ashbrook. *Shrp* 1G 59
Ashburton. *Devn* 2D 8
Ashbury. *Devn* 3F 11

Ashbury. *Oxon* ... 3A 36
Ashby. *N Lin* ... 4B 94
Ashby by Partney. *Linc* ... 4D 88
Ashby cum Fenby. *NE Lin* ... 4F 95
Ashby de la Launde. *Linc* ... 5H 87
**Ashby-de-la-Zouch.** *Leics* ... 4A 74
Ashby Folville. *Leics* ... 4E 74
Ashby Magna. *Leics* ... 1C 62
Ashby Parva. *Leics* ... 2C 62
Ashby Puerorum. *Linc* ... 3C 88
Ashby St Ledgars. *Nptn* ... 4C 62
Ashby St Mary. *Norf* ... 5F 79
Aschurch. *Glos* ... 2E 49
Ashcombe. *Devn* ... 5C 12
Ashcott. *Som* ... 3H 21
Ashdon. *Essx* ... 1F 53
Ashe. *Hants* ... 2D 24
Asheldham. *Essx* ... 5C 54
Ashen. *Essx* ... 1H 53
Ashendon. *Buck* ... 4F 51
Ashey. *IOW* ... 4D 16
Ashfield. *Hants* ... 1B 16
Ashfield. *Here* ... 3A 48
Ashfield. *Shrp* ... 2H 59
Ashfield. *Stir* ... 3G 135
Ashfield. *Suff* ... 4E 66
Ashfield Green. *Suff* ... 3E 67
Ashfold Crossways. *W Sus* ... 3D 26
Ashford. *Devn*
 nr. Barnstaple ... 3F 19
 nr. Kingsbridge ... 4C 8
Ashford. *Hants* ... 1G 15
**Ashford.** *Kent* ... 1E 28
Ashford. *Surr* ... 3B 38
Ashford Bowdler. *Shrp* ... 3H 59
Ashford Carbonel. *Shrp* ... 3H 59
Ashford Hill. *Hants* ... 5D 36
Ashford in the Water.
 *Derbs* ... 4F 85
Ashgill. *S Lan* ... 5A 128
Ash Green. *Warw* ... 2H 61
Ashgrove. *Mor* ... 2G 159
Ashill. *Devn* ... 1D 12
Ashill. *Norf* ... 5A 78
Ashill. *Som* ... 1G 13
Ashingdon. *Essx* ... 1C 40
**Ashington.** *Nmbd* ... 1F 115
Ashington. *W Sus* ... 4C 26
Ashkirk. *Bord* ... 2G 119
Ashleworth. *Glos* ... 3D 48
Ashley. *Cambs* ... 4F 65
Ashley. *Ches E* ... 2B 84
Ashley. *Dors* ... 2G 15
Ashley. *Glos* ... 2E 35
Ashley. *Hants*
 nr. New Milton ... 3A 16
 nr. Winchester ... 3B 24
Ashley. *Kent* ... 1H 29
Ashley. *Nptn* ... 1E 63
Ashley. *Staf* ... 2B 72
Ashley. *Wilts* ... 5D 34
Ashley Green. *Buck* ... 5H 51
Ashley Heath. *Dors* ... 2G 15
Ashley Heath. *Staf* ... 2B 72
Ashley Moor. *Here* ... 4G 59
Ash Magna. *Shrp* ... 2H 71
Ashmanhaugh. *Norf* ... 3F 79
Ashmansworth. *Hants* ... 1C 24
Ashmansworthy. *Devn* ... 1D 10
Ashmead Green. *Glos* ... 2C 34
Ash Mill. *Devn* ... 4A 20
Ashmill. *Devn* ... 3D 11
Ashmore. *Dors* ... 1E 15
Ashmore Green. *W Ber* ... 5D 36
Ashorne. *Warw* ... 5H 61
Ashover. *Derbs* ... 4A 86
Ashow. *Warw* ... 3H 61
Ash Parva. *Shrp* ... 2H 71
Ashperton. *Here* ... 1B 48
Ash Priors. *Som* ... 4E 21
Ashreigney. *Devn* ... 1G 11
Ash Street. *Suff* ... 1D 54
Ashtead. *Surr* ... 5C 38

Ash Thomas. *Devn* ... 1D 12
Ashton. *Corn* ... 4D 4
Ashton. *Here* ... 4H 59
Ashton. *Inv* ... 2D 126
Ashton. *Nptn*
 nr. Oundle ... 2H 63
 nr. Roade ... 1F 51
Ashton. *Pet* ... 5A 76
Ashton Common. *Wilts* ... 1D 23
Ashton Hayes. *Ches W* ... 4H 83
**Ashton-in-Makerfield.**
 *G Man* ... 1H 83
Ashton Keynes. *Wilts* ... 2F 35
Ashton under Hill. *Worc* ... 2E 49
**Ashton-under-Lyne.** *G Man* ... 1D 84
Ashton upon Mersey.
 *G Man* ... 1B 84
Ashurst. *Hants* ... 1B 16
Ashurst. *Kent* ... 2G 27
Ashurst. *Lanc* ... 4C 90
Ashurst. *W Sus* ... 4C 26
Ashurst Wood. *W Sus* ... 2F 27
Ash Vale. *Surr* ... 1G 25
Ashwater. *Devn* ... 3D 11
Ashwell. *Herts* ... 2C 52
Ashwell. *Rut* ... 4F 75
Ashwellthorpe. *Norf* ... 1D 66
Ashwick. *Som* ... 2B 22
Ashwicken. *Norf* ... 4G 77
Ashwood. *Staf* ... 2C 60
Askam in Furness. *Cumb* ... 2B 96
Askern. *S Yor* ... 3F 93
Askerswell. *Dors* ... 3A 14
Askett. *Buck* ... 5G 51
Askham. *Cumb* ... 2G 103
Askham. *Notts* ... 3E 87
Askham Bryan. *York* ... 5H 99
Askham Richard. *York* ... 5H 99
Askrigg. *N Yor* ... 5C 104
Askwith. *N Yor* ... 5D 98
Aslackby. *Linc* ... 2H 75
Aslacton. *Norf* ... 1D 66
Aslockton. *Notts* ... 1E 75
Aspatria. *Cumb* ... 5C 112
Aspenden. *Herts* ... 3D 52
Asperton. *Linc* ... 2B 76
Aspley Guise. *C Beds* ... 2H 51
Aspley Heath. *C Beds* ... 2H 51
Aspull. *G Man* ... 4E 90
Asselby. *E Yor* ... 2H 93
Assington. *Suff* ... 2C 54
Assington Green. *Suff* ... 5G 65
Astbury. *Ches E* ... 4C 84
Astcote. *Nptn* ... 5D 62
Asterby. *Linc* ... 3B 88
Asterley. *Shrp* ... 5F 71
Asterton. *Shrp* ... 1F 59
Asthall. *Oxon* ... 4A 50
Asthall Leigh. *Oxon* ... 4B 50
Astle. *High* ... 4E 165
Astley. *G Man* ... 4F 91
Astley. *Shrp* ... 4H 71
Astley. *Warw* ... 2H 61
Astley. *Worc* ... 4B 60
Astley Abbotts. *Shrp* ... 1B 60
Astley Bridge. *G Man* ... 3F 91
Astley Cross. *Worc* ... 4C 60
Aston. *Ches E* ... 1A 72
Aston. *Ches W* ... 3H 83
Aston. *Derbs*
 nr. Hope ... 2F 85
 nr. Sudbury ... 2F 73
Aston. *Flin* ... 4F 83
Aston. *Here* ... 4G 59
Aston. *Herts* ... 3C 52
Aston. *Oxon* ... 5B 50
Aston. *Shrp*
 nr. Bridgnorth ... 1C 60
 nr. Wem ... 3H 71
Aston. *S Yor* ... 2B 86
Aston. *Staf* ... 1B 72
Aston. *Telf* ... 5A 72
Aston. *W Mid* ... 1E 61
Aston. *Wok* ... 3F 37

Aston Abbotts. *Buck* ... 3G 51
Aston Botterell. *Shrp* ... 2A 60
Aston-by-Stone. *Staf* ... 2D 72
Aston Cantlow. *Warw* ... 5F 61
Aston Clinton. *Buck* ... 4G 51
Aston Crews. *Here* ... 3B 48
Aston Cross. *Glos* ... 2E 49
Aston End. *Herts* ... 3C 52
Aston Eyre. *Shrp* ... 1A 60
Aston Fields. *Worc* ... 4D 60
Aston Flamville. *Leics* ... 1B 62
Aston Ingham. *Here* ... 3B 48
Aston juxta Mondrum.
 *Ches E* ... 5A 84
Astonlane. *Shrp* ... 1A 60
Aston le Walls. *Nptn* ... 5B 62
Aston Magna. *Glos* ... 2G 49
Aston Munslow. *Shrp* ... 2H 59
Aston on Carrant. *Glos* ... 2E 49
Aston on Clun. *Shrp* ... 2F 59
Aston-on-Trent. *Derbs* ... 3B 74
Aston Pigott. *Shrp* ... 5F 71
Aston Rogers. *Shrp* ... 5F 71
Aston Rowant. *Oxon* ... 2F 37
Aston Sandford. *Buck* ... 5F 51
Aston Somerville. *Worc* ... 2F 49
Aston Subedge. *Glos* ... 1G 49
Aston Tirrold. *Oxon* ... 3D 36
Aston Upthorpe. *Oxon* ... 3D 36
Astrop. *Nptn* ... 2D 50
Astwick. *C Beds* ... 2C 52
Astwood. *Mil* ... 1H 51
Astwood Bank. *Worc* ... 4E 61
Aswarby. *Linc* ... 2H 75
Aswardby. *Linc* ... 3C 88
Atcham. *Shrp* ... 5H 71
Atch Lench. *Worc* ... 5E 61
Athelhampton. *Dors* ... 3C 14
Athelington. *Suff* ... 3E 66
Athelney. *Som* ... 4G 21
Athelstaneford. *E Lot* ... 2B 130
Atherfield Green. *IOW* ... 5C 16
Atherington. *Devn* ... 4F 19
Atherington. *W Sus* ... 5B 26
Athersley. *S Yor* ... 4D 92
**Atherstone.** *Warw* ... 1H 61
Atherstone on Stour. *Warw* ... 5G 61
**Atherton.** *G Man* ... 4E 91
Ath-Tharracail. *High* ... 2A 140
Atlow. *Derbs* ... 1G 73
Attadale. *High* ... 5B 156
Attenborough. *Notts* ... 2C 74
Atterby. *Linc* ... 1G 87
Atterley. *Shrp* ... 1A 60
Atterton. *Leics* ... 1A 62
Attleborough. *Norf* ... 1C 66
Attleborough. *Warw* ... 1A 62
Attlebridge. *Norf* ... 4D 78
Atwick. *E Yor* ... 4F 101
Atworth. *Wilts* ... 5D 34
Auberrow. *Here* ... 1H 47
Aubourn. *Linc* ... 4G 87
Aucharnie. *Abers* ... 4D 160
Auchattie. *Abers* ... 4D 152
Auchavan. *Ang* ... 2A 144
Auchbreck. *Mor* ... 1G 151
Auchenback. *E Ren* ... 4G 127
Auchenblae. *Abers* ... 1G 145
Auchenbrack. *Dum* ... 5G 117
Auchenbreck. *Arg* ... 1B 126
Auchencairn. *Dum*
 nr. Dalbeattie ... 4E 111
 nr. Dumfries ... 1A 112
Auchencarroch. *W Dun* ... 1F 127
Auchencrow. *Bord* ... 3E 131
Auchendennan. *Arg* ... 1E 127
Auchendinny. *Midl* ... 3F 129
Auchengray. *S Lan* ... 4C 128
Auchenhalrig. *Mor* ... 2A 160
Auchenheath. *S Lan* ... 5B 128
Auchenlochan. *Arg* ... 2A 126
Auchenmade. *N Ayr* ... 5E 127
Auchenmalg. *Dum* ... 4H 109
Auchentiber. *N Ayr* ... 5E 127

Auchenvennel. *Arg* ... 1D 126
Auchindrain. *Arg* ... 3H 133
Auchininna. *Abers* ... 4D 160
Auchinleck. *Dum* ... 2B 110
Auchinleck. *E Ayr* ... 2E 117
Auchinloch. *N Lan* ... 2H 127
Auchinstarry. *N Lan* ... 2A 128
Auchleven. *Abers* ... 1D 152
Auchlochan. *S Lan* ... 1H 117
Auchlunachan. *High* ... 5F 163
Auchmillan. *E Ayr* ... 2E 117
Auchmithie. *Ang* ... 4F 145
Auchmuirbridge. *Fife* ... 3E 136
Auchmull. *Ang* ... 1E 145
Auchnacree. *Ang* ... 2D 144
Auchnafree. *Per* ... 5F 143
Auchnagallin. *High* ... 5E 159
Auchnagatt. *Abers* ... 4G 161
Aucholzie. *Abers* ... 4H 151
Auchreddie. *Abers* ... 4F 161
Auchterarder. *Per* ... 2B 136
Auchteraw. *High* ... 3F 149
Auchterderran. *Fife* ... 4E 136
Auchterhouse. *Ang* ... 5C 144
Auchtermuchty. *Fife* ... 2E 137
Auchterneed. *High* ... 3G 157
Auchtertool. *Fife* ... 4E 136
Auchtertyre. *High* ... 1G 147
Auchtubh. *Stir* ... 1E 135
Auckengill. *High* ... 2F 169
Auckley. *S Yor* ... 4G 93
**Audenshaw.** *G Man* ... 1D 84
Audlem. *Ches E* ... 1A 72
Audley. *Staf* ... 5B 84
Audley End. *Essx* ... 2F 53
Audmore. *Staf* ... 3C 72
Auds. *Abers* ... 2D 160
Aughertree. *Cumb* ... 1D 102
Aughton. *E Yor* ... 1H 93
Aughton. *Lanc*
 nr. Lancaster ... 3E 97
 nr. Ormskirk ... 4B 90
**Aughton.** *Shrp* ... 1H 23
Aughton. *Wilts* ... 1H 23
Aughton Park. *Lanc* ... 4C 90
Auldearn. *High* ... 3D 158
Aulden. *Here* ... 5G 59
Auldgirth. *Dum* ... 1G 111
Auldhouse. *S Lan* ... 4H 127
Ault a' chruinn. *High* ... 1B 148
Aultbea. *High* ... 5C 162
Aultdearg. *High* ... 2E 157
Aultgrishan. *High* ... 5B 162
Aultguish Inn. *High* ... 1F 157
Ault Hucknall. *Derbs* ... 4B 86
Aultibea. *High* ... 1H 165
Aultiphurst. *High* ... 2A 168
Aultivullin. *High* ... 2A 168
Aultmore. *Mor* ... 3B 160
Aultnamain Inn. *High* ... 5D 164
Aunby. *Linc* ... 4H 75
Aunsby. *Linc* ... 2H 75
Aust. *S Glo* ... 3A 34
Austerfield. *S Yor* ... 1D 86
Austen Fen. *Linc* ... 1C 88
Austrey. *Warw* ... 5G 73
Austwick. *N Yor* ... 3G 97
Authorpe. *Linc* ... 2D 88
Authorpe Row. *Linc* ... 3E 89
Avebury. *Wilts* ... 5G 35
Avebury Trusloe. *Wilts* ... 5F 35
Aveley. *Thur* ... 2G 39
Avening. *Glos* ... 2D 35
Averham. *Notts* ... 5E 87
Aveton Gifford. *Devn* ... 4C 8
Avielochan. *High* ... 2D 150
Aviemore. *High* ... 2C 150
Avington. *Hants* ... 3D 24
Avoch. *High* ... 3B 158
Avon. *Hants* ... 3G 15
Avonbridge. *Falk* ... 2C 128
Avon Dassett. *Warw* ... 5B 62
Avonmouth. *Bris* ... 4A 34
Avonwick. *Devn* ... 3D 8

Awbridge. *Hants* ... 4B 24
Awkmanton. *Devn* ... 2E 13
Awliscombe. *Devn* ... 2E 13
Awre. *Glos* ... 5C 48
Awsworth. *Notts* ... 1B 74
Axbridge. *Som* ... 1H 21
Axford. *Hants* ... 2E 24
Axford. *Wilts* ... 5H 35
Axminster. *Devn* ... 3G 13
Axmouth. *Devn* ... 3F 13
Aycliffe Village. *Dur* ... 2F 105
Aydon. *Nmbd* ... 3D 114
Aykley Heads. *Dur* ... 5F 115
Aylburton. *Glos* ... 5B 48
Aylburton Common. *Glos* ... 5B 48
Ayle. *Nmbd* ... 5A 114
Aylesbeare. *Devn* ... 3D 12
**Aylesbury.** *Buck* ... 4G 51
Aylesby. *NE Lin* ... 4F 95
Aylescott. *Devn* ... 1G 11
**Aylesford.** *Kent* ... 5B 40
Aylesham. *Kent* ... 5G 41
Aylestone. *Leic* ... 5C 74
Aylmerton. *Norf* ... 2D 78
Aylsham. *Norf* ... 3D 78
Aylton. *Here* ... 2B 48
Aylworth. *Glos* ... 3G 49
Aymestrey. *Here* ... 4G 59
Aynho. *Nptn* ... 2D 50
Ayot Green. *Herts* ... 4C 52
Ayot St Lawrence. *Herts* ... 4B 52
Ayot St Peter. *Herts* ... 4C 52
**Ayr.** *S Ayr* ... 2C 116
Ayres of Selivoe. *Shet* ... 7D 173
Ayreville. *Torb* ... 2E 9
Aysgarth. *N Yor* ... 1C 98
Ayshford. *Devn* ... 1D 12
Ayside. *Cumb* ... 1C 96
Ayston. *Rut* ... 5F 75
Ayton. *Bord* ... 3F 131
Aywick. *Shet* ... 3G 173
Azerley. *N Yor* ... 2E 99

# B

Babbacombe. *Torb* ... 2F 9
Babbinswood. *Shrp* ... 2F 71
Babbs Green. *Herts* ... 4D 53
Babcary. *Som* ... 4A 22
Babel. *Carm* ... 2B 46
Babell. *Flin* ... 3D 82
Babingley. *Norf* ... 3F 77
Bablock Hythe. *Oxon* ... 5C 50
Babraham. *Cambs* ... 5E 65
Babworth. *Notts* ... 2D 86
Bac. *W Isl* ... 3G 171
Bachau. *IOA* ... 2D 80
Bacheldre. *Powy* ... 1E 59
Bachymbyd Fawr. *Den* ... 4C 82
Backaland. *Orkn* ... 4E 172
Backaskaill. *Orkn* ... 2D 172
Backbarrow. *Cumb* ... 1C 96
Backe. *Carm* ... 3G 43
Backfolds. *Abers* ... 3H 161
Backford. *Ches W* ... 3G 83
Backhill of Clackriach.
 *Abers* ... 4G 161
Backies. *High* ... 4F 165
Backmuir of New Gilston.
 *Fife* ... 3G 137
Back of Keppoch. *High* ... 5E 147
Back Street. *Suff* ... 5G 65
Backwell. *N Som* ... 5H 33
Backworth. *Tyne* ... 2G 115
Bacon End. *Essx* ... 4G 53
Baconsthorpe. *Norf* ... 2D 78
Bacton. *Here* ... 2G 47
Bacton. *Norf* ... 2F 79
Bacton. *Suff* ... 4C 66
Bacton Green. *Norf* ... 2F 79
**Bacup.** *Lanc* ... 2G 91
Badachonacher. *High* ... 1A 158
Badachro. *High* ... 1G 155

# Badanloch Lodge—Barney



Badanloch Lodge. *High* 5H **167**
Badavanich. *High* 3D **156**
Badbury. *Swin* 3G **35**
Badby. *Nptn* 5C **62**
Badcall. *High* 3C **166**
Badcaul. *High* 4E **163**
Baddeley Green. *Stoke* 5D **84**
Baddesley Clinton. *W Mid* 3G **61**
Baddesley Ensor. *Warw* 1G **61**
Baddidarach. *High* 1E **163**
Baddoch. *Abers* 5F **151**
Badenscallie. *High* 3E **163**
Badenscoth. *Abers* 5E **160**
Badentarbat. *High* 2E **163**
Badgall. *Corn* 4C **10**
Badgers Mount. *Kent* 4F **39**
Badgeworth. *Glos* 4E **49**
Badgworth. *Som* 1G **21**
Badicaul. *High* 1F **147**
Badingham. *Suff* 4F **67**
Badlesmere. *Kent* 5E **40**
Badlipster. *High* 4E **169**
Badluarach. *High* 4D **163**
Badminton. *S Glo* 3D **34**
Badnaban. *High* 1E **163**
Badnabay. *High* 4C **166**
Badnagie. *High* 5D **168**
Badnellan. *High* 3F **165**
Badninish. *High* 4E **165**
Badrallach. *High* 4E **163**
Badsey. *Worc* 1F **49**
Badshot Lea. *Surr* 2G **25**
Badsworth. *W Yor* 3E **93**
Badwell Ash. *Suff* 4B **66**
Bae Cinmel. *Cnwy* 2B **82**
**Bae Colwyn**. *Cnwy* 3A **82**
Bae Penrhyn. *Cnwy* 2H **81**
Bagby. *N Yor* 1G **99**
Bag Enderby. *Linc* 3C **88**
Bagendon. *Glos* 5F **49**
Bagginswood. *Shrp* 2A **60**
Bàgh a Chàise. *W Isl* 1E **170**
Bàgh a' Chaisteil. *W Isl* 9B **170**
Bagham. *Kent* 5E **41**
Baghasdal. *W Isl* 7C **170**
Bagh Mor. *W Isl* 3D **170**
Bagh Shiarabhagh. *W Isl* 8C **170**
Bagillt. *Flin* 3E **82**
Baginton. *Warw* 3H **61**
Baglan. *Neat* 2A **32**
Bagley. *Shrp* 3G **71**
Bagley. *Som* 2H **21**
Bagnall. *Staf* 5D **84**
Bagnor. *W Ber* 5C **36**
Bagshot. *Surr* 4A **38**
Bagshot. *Wilts* 5B **36**
Bagstone. *S Glo* 3B **34**
Bagthorpe. *Norf* 2G **77**
Bagthorpe. *Notts* 5B **86**
Bagworth. *Leics* 5B **74**
Bagwy Llydiart. *Here* 3H **47**
**Baildon**. *W Yor* 1B **92**
Baildon Green. *W Yor* 1B **92**
Baile. *W Isl* 1E **170**
Baile Ailein. *W Isl* 5E **171**
Baile an Truiseil. *W Isl* 2F **171**
Baile Boidheach. *Arg* 2F **125**
Baile Glas. *W Isl* 3D **170**
Bailemeonach. *Arg* 4A **140**
Baile Mhanaich. *W Isl* 3C **170**
Baile Mhartainn. *W Isl* 1C **170**
Baile MhicPhail. *W Isl* 1D **170**
Baile Mor. *W Isl* 2C **170**
Baile Mór. *Arg* 2A **132**
Baile nan Cailleach. *W Isl* 3C **170**
Baile Raghaill. *W Isl* 2C **170**
Bailey Green. *Hants* 4E **25**
Baileyhead. *Cumb* 1G **113**
Bailiesward. *Abers* 5B **160**
Bail' Iochdrach. *W Isl* 3D **170**
Baillieston. *Glas* 3H **127**
Bailrigg. *Lanc* 4D **97**
Bail Uachdraich. *W Isl* 2D **170**
Bail' Ur Tholastaidh. *W Isl* 3H **171**
Bainbridge. *N Yor* 5C **104**
Bainsford. *Falk* 1B **128**
Bainshole. *Abers* 5D **160**
Bainton. *E Yor* 4D **100**
Bainton. *Oxon* 3D **50**
Bainton. *Pet* 5H **75**
Baintown. *Fife* 3F **137**
Baker Street. *Thur* 2H **39**
Bakewell. *Derbs* 4G **85**
Bala. *Gwyn* 2B **70**
Y Bala. *Gwyn* 2B **70**
Balachuirn. *High* 4E **155**
Balbeg. *High*
nr. Cannich 5G **157**
nr. Loch Ness 1G **149**
Balbeggie. *Per* 1D **136**
Balblair. *High*
nr. Bonar Bridge 4C **164**
nr. Invergordon 2B **158**
nr. Inverness 4H **157**
Balby. *S Yor* 4F **93**
Balcathie. *Ang* 5F **145**
Balchladich. *High* 1E **163**
Balchraggan. *High* 4H **157**
Balchrick. *High* 3B **166**
Balcombe. *W Sus* 2E **27**
Balcombe Lane. *W Sus* 2E **27**
Balcurvie. *Fife* 3F **137**
Baldersby. *N Yor* 2F **99**
Baldersby St James. *N Yor* 2F **99**
Balderstone. *Lanc* 1E **91**
Balderton. *Ches W* 4F **83**
Balderton. *Notts* 5F **87**
Baldinnie. *Fife* 2G **137**
Baldock. *Herts* 2C **52**
Baldrine. *IOM* 3D **108**
Baldslow. *E Sus* 4C **28**
Baldwin. *IOM* 3C **108**
Baldwinholme. *Cumb* 4E **113**
Baldwin's Gate. *Staf* 2B **72**
Bale. *Norf* 2C **78**
Balearn. *Abers* 3H **161**
Balemartine. *Arg* 4A **138**
Balephetrish. *Arg* 4B **138**
Balephuil. *Arg* 4A **138**
Balerno. *Edin* 3E **129**
Balevullin. *Arg* 4A **138**
Balfield. *Ang* 2E **145**
Balfour. *Orkn* 6D **172**
Balfron. *Stir* 1G **127**
Balgaveny. *Abers* 4D **160**
Balgonar. *Fife* 4C **136**
Balgowan. *High* 4A **150**
Balgown. *High* 2C **154**
Balgrochan. *E Dun* 2H **127**
Balgy. *High* 3H **155**
Balhalgardy. *Abers* 1E **153**
Baliasta. *Shet* 1H **173**
Baligill. *High* 2A **168**
Balintore. *Ang* 3B **144**
Balintore. *High* 1C **158**
Balintraid. *High* 1B **158**
Balk. *N Yor* 1G **99**
Balkeerie. *Ang* 4C **144**
Balkholme. *E Yor* 2A **94**
Ball. *Shrp* 3F **71**
Ballabeg. *IOM* 4B **108**
Ballacannell. *IOM* 3D **108**
Ballacarnane Beg. *IOM* 3C **108**
Ballachulish. *High* 3E **141**
Ballagyr. *IOM* 3B **108**
Ballajora. *IOM* 2D **108**
Ballaleigh. *IOM* 3C **108**
Ballamodha. *IOM* 4B **108**
Ballantrae. *S Ayr* 1F **109**
Ballards Gore. *Essx* 1D **40**
Ballasalla. *IOM*
nr. Castletown 4B **108**
nr. Kirk Michael 2C **108**
Ballater. *Abers* 4A **152**
Ballaugh. *IOM* 2C **108**
Ballencrieff. *E Lot* 2A **130**
Ballencrieff Toll. *W Lot* 2C **128**
Ballentoul. *Per* 2F **143**
Ball Hill. *Hants* 5C **36**
Ballidon. *Derbs* 5G **85**
Balliemore. *Arg*
nr. Dunoon 1B **126**
nr. Oban 1F **133**
Ballieward. *High* 5E **159**
Ballig. *IOM* 3B **108**
Ballimore. *Stir* 2E **135**
Ballinamallard. *Ferm* 5B **174**
Ballingdon. *Suff* 1B **54**
Ballinger Common. *Buck* 5H **51**
Ballingham. *Here* 2A **48**
Ballingry. *Fife* 4D **136**
Ballinluig. *Per* 3G **143**
Ballintuim. *Per* 3A **144**
Balliveolan. *Arg* 4C **140**
Balloan. *High* 3C **164**
Balloch. *High* 4B **158**
Balloch. *N Lan* 2A **128**
Balloch. *Per* 2H **135**
Balloch. *W Dun* 1E **127**
Ballochan. *Abers* 4C **152**
Ballochgoy. *Arg* 3B **126**
Ballochmyle. *E Ayr* 2E **117**
Ballochroy. *Arg* 4F **125**
Balls Cross. *W Sus* 3A **26**
Ball's Green. *E Sus* 2F **27**
Ballycastle. *Caus* 1G **175**
Ballyclare. *Ant* 3G **175**
Ballygowan. *Ards* 4H **175**
Ballygown. *Arg* 4F **139**
Ballygrant. *Arg* 3B **124**
Ballykelly. *Caus* 1D **174**
**Ballymena**. *ME Ant* 2G **175**
Ballymichael. *N Ayr* 2D **122**
**Ballymoney**. *Caus* 1F **175**
Ballynahinch. *New M* 5H **175**
Ballywater. *Ards* 4J **175**
Balmacara. *High* 1G **147**
Balmaclellan. *Dum* 2D **110**
Balmacqueen. *High* 1D **154**
Balmaha. *Stir* 4D **134**
Balmalcolm. *Fife* 3F **137**
Balmalloch. *N Lan* 2A **128**
Balmeanach. *High* 5E **155**
Balmedie. *Abers* 2G **153**
Balmerino. *Fife* 1F **137**
Balmerlawn. *Hants* 2B **16**
Balmore. *E Dun* 2H **127**
Balmore. *High* 4B **154**
Balmullo. *Fife* 1G **137**
Balmurrie. *Dum* 3H **109**
Balnaboth. *Ang* 2C **144**
Balnabruaich. *High* 1B **158**
Balnabruich. *High* 5D **168**
Balnacoil. *High* 2F **165**
Balnacra. *High* 4B **156**
Balnacroft. *Abers* 4G **151**
Balnageith. *Mor* 3E **159**
Balnaglaic. *High* 5G **157**
Balnagrantach. *High* 5G **157**
Balnaguard. *Per* 3G **143**
Balnahard. *Arg* 4B **132**
Balnain. *High* 5G **157**
Balnakeil. *High* 2D **166**
Balnaknock. *High* 2D **154**
Balnamoon. *Abers* 3G **161**
Balnamoon. *Ang* 2E **145**
Balnapaling. *High* 2B **158**
Balornock. *Glas* 3H **127**
Balquhidder. *Stir* 1E **135**
Balsall. *W Mid* 3G **61**
Balsall Common. *W Mid* 3G **61**
Balscote. *Oxon* 1B **50**
Balsham. *Cambs* 5E **65**
Balstonia. *Thur* 2A **40**
Baltasound. *Shet* 1H **173**
Balterley. *Staf* 5B **84**
Baltersan. *Dum* 3B **110**
Balthangie. *Abers* 3F **161**
Baltonsborough. *Som* 3A **22**
Balvaird. *High* 3H **157**
Balvaird. *Per* 2D **136**
Balvenie. *Mor* 4H **159**
Balvicar. *Arg* 2E **133**
Balvraid. *High* 2G **147**
Balvraid Lodge. *High* 5C **158**
Bamber Bridge. *Lanc* 2D **90**
Bamber's Green. *Essx* 3F **53**
Bamburgh. *Nmbd* 1F **121**
Bamford. *Derbs* 2G **85**
Bamfurlong. *G Man* 4D **90**
Bampton. *Cumb* 3G **103**
Bampton. *Devn* 4C **20**
Bampton. *Oxon* 5B **50**
Bampton Grange. *Cumb* 3G **103**
Banavie. *High* 1F **141**
**Banbridge**. *Arm* 5G **175**
**Banbury**. *Oxon* 1C **50**
Bancffosfelen. *Carm* 4E **45**
Banchory. *Abers* 4D **152**
Banchory-Devenick.
*Abers* 3G **153**
Bancycapel. *Carm* 4E **45**
Bancyfelin. *Carm* 3H **43**
Banc-y-ffordd. *Carm* 2E **45**
Banff. *Abers* 2D **160**
**Bangor**. *Ards* 3J **175**
**Bangor**. *Gwyn* 3E **81**
Bangor-is-y-coed. *Wrex* 1F **71**
Bangors. *Corn* 3C **10**
Bangor's Green. *Lanc* 4B **90**
Banham. *Norf* 2C **66**
Bank. *Hants* 2A **16**
The Bank. *Ches E* 5C **84**
The Bank. *Shrp* 1A **60**
Bankend. *Dum* 3B **112**
Bankfoot. *Per* 5H **143**
Bankglen. *E Ayr* 3F **117**
Bankhead. *Aber* 2F **153**
Bankhead. *Abers* 3D **152**
Bankhead. *S Lan* 5B **128**
Bankland. *Som* 4G **21**
Bank Newton. *N Yor* 4B **98**
Banknock. *Falk* 2A **128**
Banks. *Cumb* 3G **113**
Banks. *Lanc* 2B **90**
Bankshill. *Dum* 1C **112**
Bank Street. *Worc* 4A **60**
Bank Top. *Lanc* 4D **90**
Banners Gate. *W Mid* 1E **61**
Banningham. *Norf* 3E **78**
Banniskirk. *High* 3D **168**
Bannister Green. *Essx* 3G **53**
Bannockburn. *Stir* 4H **135**
**Banstead**. *Surr* 5D **38**
Bantham. *Devn* 4C **8**
Banton. *N Lan* 2A **128**
Banwell. *N Som* 1G **21**
Banyard's Green. *Suff* 3F **67**
Bapchild. *Kent* 4D **40**
Bapton. *Wilts* 3E **23**
Barabhas. *W Isl* 2F **171**
Barabhas Iarach. *W Isl* 3F **171**
Baramore. *High* 1A **140**
Barassie. *S Ayr* 1C **116**
Baravullin. *Arg* 4D **140**
Barbaraville. *High* 1B **158**
Barber Booth. *Derbs* 2F **85**
Barber Green. *Cumb* 1C **96**
Barbhas Uarach. *W Isl* 2F **171**
Barbieston. *S Ayr* 3D **116**
Barbon. *Cumb* 1F **97**
Barbourne. *Worc* 5C **60**
Barbridge. *Ches E* 5A **84**
Barbrook. *Devn* 2H **19**
Barby. *Nptn* 3C **62**
Barby Nortoft. *Nptn* 3C **62**
Barcaldine. *Arg* 4D **140**
Barcheston. *Warw* 2A **50**
Barclose. *Cumb* 3F **113**
Barcombe. *E Sus* 4F **27**
Barcombe Cross. *E Sus* 4F **27**
Barden. *N Yor* 5E **105**
Barden Scale. *N Yor* 4C **98**
Bardfield End Green. *Essx* 2G **53**
Bardfield Saling. *Essx* 3G **53**
Bardister. *Shet* 4E **173**
Bardnabeinne. *High* 4E **164**
Bardney. *Linc* 4A **88**
Bardon. *Leics* 4B **74**
Bardon Mill. *Nmbd* 3A **114**
Bardowie. *E Dun* 2G **127**
Bardrainney. *Inv* 2E **127**
Bardsea. *Cumb* 2C **96**
Bardsey. *W Yor* 5F **99**
Bardsley. *G Man* 4H **91**
Bardwell. *Suff* 3B **66**
Bare. *Lanc* 3D **96**
Barelees. *Nmbd* 1C **120**
Barewood. *Here* 5F **59**
Barford. *Hants* 3G **25**
Barford. *Norf* 5D **78**
Barford. *Warw* 4G **61**
Barford St John. *Oxon* 2C **50**
Barford St Martin. *Wilts* 3F **23**
Barford St Michael. *Oxon* 2C **50**
Barfrestone. *Kent* 5G **41**
Bargeddie. *N Lan* 3H **127**
**Bargod**. *Cphy* 2E **33**
**Bargoed**. *Cphy* 2E **33**
Bargrennan. *Dum* 2A **110**
Barham. *Cambs* 3A **64**
Barham. *Kent* 5G **41**
Barham. *Suff* 5D **66**
Barharrow. *Dum* 4D **110**
Bar Hill. *Cambs* 4C **64**
Barholm. *Linc* 4H **75**
Barkby. *Leics* 5D **74**
Barkestone-le-Vale. *Leics* 2E **75**
Barkham. *Wok* 5F **37**
**Barking**. *G Lon* 2F **39**
Barking. *Suff* 5C **66**
Barkingside. *G Lon* 2F **39**
Barking Tye. *Suff* 5C **66**
Barkisland. *W Yor* 3A **92**
Barkston. *Linc* 1G **75**
Barkston Ash. *N Yor* 1E **93**
Barkway. *Herts* 2D **53**
Barlanark. *Glas* 3H **127**
Barlaston. *Staf* 2C **72**
Barlavington. *W Sus* 4A **26**
Barlborough. *Derbs* 3B **86**
Barlby. *N Yor* 1G **93**
Barlestone. *Leics* 5B **74**
Barley. *Herts* 2D **53**
Barley. *Lanc* 5H **97**
Barley Mow. *Tyne* 4F **115**
Barleythorpe. *Rut* 5F **75**
Barling. *Essx* 2D **40**
Barlings. *Linc* 3H **87**
Barlow. *Derbs* 3H **85**
Barlow. *N Yor* 2G **93**
Barlow. *Tyne* 3E **115**
Barmby Moor. *E Yor* 5B **100**
Barmby on the Marsh.
*E Yor* 2G **93**
Barmer. *Norf* 2H **77**
Barming. *Kent* 5B **40**
Barming Heath. *Kent* 5B **40**
Barmoor. *Nmbd* 1E **121**
Barmouth. *Gwyn* 4F **69**
Barmpton. *Darl* 3A **106**
Barmston. *E Yor* 4F **101**
Barmulloch. *Glas* 3H **127**
Barnack. *Pet* 5H **75**
Barnacle. *Warw* 2A **62**
Barnard Castle. *Dur* 3D **104**
Barnard Gate. *Oxon* 4C **50**
Barnardiston. *Suff* 1H **53**
Barnbarroch. *Dum* 4F **111**
Barnburgh. *S Yor* 4E **93**
Barnby. *Suff* 2G **67**
Barnby Dun. *S Yor* 4G **93**
Barnby in the Willows.
*Notts* 5F **87**
Barnby Moor. *Notts* 2D **86**
**Barnes**. *G Lon* 3D **38**
Barnes Street. *Kent* 1H **27**
**Barnet**. *G Lon* 1D **38**
Barnetby le Wold. *N Lin* 4D **94**
Barney. *Norf* 2B **78**

Barnham—Belmont


Barnham. *Suff* 3A **66**
Barnham. *W Sus* 5A **26**
Barnham Broom. *Norf* 5C **78**
Barnhead. *Ang* 3F **145**
Barnhill. *D'dee* 5D **145**
Barnhill. *Mor* 3F **159**
Barnhill. *Per* 1D **136**
Barnhills. *Dum* 2E **109**
Barningham. *Dur* 3D **105**
Barningham. *Suff* 3B **66**
Barnoldby le Beck. *NE Lin* 4F **95**
**Barnoldswick**. *Lanc* 5A **98**
Barns Green. *W Sus* 3C **26**
Barnsley. *Glos* 5F **49**
Barnsley. *Shrp* 1B **60**
**Barnsley**. *S Yor* 4D **92**
**Barnstaple**. *Devn* 3F **19**
Barnston. *Essx* 4G **53**
Barnston. *Mers* 2E **83**
Barnstone. *Notts* 2E **75**
Barnt Green. *Worc* 3E **61**
Barnton. *Ches W* 3A **84**
Barnwell. *Cambs* 5D **64**
Barnwell. *Nptn* 2H **63**
Barnwood. *Glos* 4D **48**
Barons Cross. *Here* 5G **59**
The Barony. *Orkn* 5B **172**
Barr. *Dum* 4G **117**
Barr. *S Ayr* 5B **116**
Barra Airport. *W Isl* 8B **170**
Barrachan. *Dum* 5A **110**
Barraglom. *W Isl* 4D **171**
Barrahormid. *Arg* 1F **125**
Barrapol. *Arg* 4A **138**
Barrasford. *Nmbd* 2C **114**
Barravullin. *Arg* 3F **133**
Barregarrow. *IOM* 3C **108**
**Barrhead**. *E Ren* 4G **127**
Barrhill. *S Ayr* 1H **109**
**Barri**. *V Glam* 5E **32**
Barrington. *Cambs* 1D **53**
Barrington. *Som* 1G **13**
Barripper. *Corn* 3D **4**
Barrmill. *N Ayr* 4E **127**
Barrock. *High* 1E **169**
Barrow. *Lanc* 1F **91**
Barrow. *Rut* 4F **75**
Barrow. *Shrp* 5A **72**
Barrow. *Som* 3C **22**
Barrow. *Suff* 4G **65**
Barroway Drove. *Norf* 5E **77**
Barrow Bridge. *G Man* 3E **91**
Barrowburn. *Nmbd* 3C **120**
Barrowby. *Linc* 2F **75**
Barrowcliff. *N Yor* 1E **101**
Barrow Common. *N Som* 5A **34**
Barrowden. *Rut* 5G **75**
Barrowford. *Lanc* 1G **91**
Barrow Gurney. *N Som* 5A **34**
Barrow Haven. *N Lin* 2D **94**
Barrow Hill. *Derbs* 3B **86**
**Barrow-in-Furness**. *Cumb* 3B **96**
Barrow Nook. *Lanc* 4C **90**
Barrow's Green. *Hal* 2H **83**
Barrows Green. *Cumb* 1E **97**
Barrow Street. *Wilts* 3D **22**
Barrow upon Humber.
*N Lin* 2D **94**
Barrow upon Soar. *Leics* 4C **74**
Barrow upon Trent. *Derbs* 3A **74**
Barry. *Ang* 5E **145**
**Barry**. *V Glam* 5E **32**
Barry Island. *V Glam* 5E **32**
Barsby. *Leics* 4D **74**
Barsham. *Suff* 2F **67**
Barston. *W Mid* 3G **61**
Bartestree. *Here* 1A **48**
Barthol Chapel. *Abers* 5F **161**
Bartholomew Green. *Essx* 3H **53**
Barthomley. *Ches E* 5B **84**
Bartley. *Hants* 1B **16**
Bartley Green. *W Mid* 2E **61**
Bartlow. *Cambs* 1F **53**
Barton. *Cambs* 5D **64**
Barton. *Ches W* 5G **83**
Barton. *Cumb* 2F **103**
Barton. *Glos* 3G **49**
Barton. *IOW* 4D **16**
Barton. *Lanc*
nr. Ormskirk 4B **90**
nr. Preston 1D **90**
Barton. *N Som* 1G **21**
Barton. *N Yor* 4F **105**
Barton. *Oxon* 5D **50**
Barton. *Torb* 2F **9**
Barton. *Warw* 5F **61**
Barton Bendish. *Norf* 5G **77**
Barton Gate. *Staf* 4F **73**
Barton Green. *Staf* 4F **73**
Barton Hartsthorn. *Buck* 2E **51**
Barton Hill. *N Yor* 3B **100**
Barton in Fabis. *Notts* 2C **74**
Barton in the Beans. *Leics* 5A **74**
Barton-le-Clay. *C Beds* 2A **52**
Barton-le-Street. *N Yor* 2B **100**
Barton-le-Willows. *N Yor* 3B **100**
Barton Mills. *Suff* 3G **65**
**Barton on Sea**. *Hants* 3H **15**
Barton-on-the-Heath.
*Warw* 2A **50**
Barton St David. *Som* 3A **22**
Barton Seagrave. *Nptn* 3F **63**
Barton Stacey. *Hants* 2C **24**
Barton Town. *Devn* 2G **19**
Barton Turf. *Norf* 3F **79**
Barton-Under-Needwood.
*Staf* 4F **73**
Barton-upon-Humber. *N Lin* 2D **94**
Barton Waterside. *N Lin* 2D **94**
Barugh Green. *S Yor* 4D **92**
Barway. *Cambs* 3E **65**
Barwell. *Leics* 1B **62**
Barwick. *Herts* 4D **53**
Barwick. *Som* 1A **14**
Barwick in Elmet. *W Yor* 1D **93**
Baschurch. *Shrp* 3G **71**
Bascote. *Warw* 4B **62**
Basford Green. *Staf* 5D **85**
Bashall Eaves. *Lanc* 5F **97**
Bashall Town. *Lanc* 5G **97**
Bashley. *Hants* 3H **15**
**Basildon**. *Essx* 2B **40**
**Basingstoke**. *Hants* 1E **25**
Baslow. *Derbs* 3G **85**
Bason Bridge. *Som* 2G **21**
Bassaleg. *Newp* 3F **33**
Bassendean. *Bord* 5C **130**
Bassenthwaite. *Cumb* 1D **102**
Bassett. *Sotn* 1C **16**
Bassingbourn. *Cambs* 1D **52**
Bassingfield. *Notts* 2D **74**
Bassingham. *Linc* 4G **87**
Bassingthorpe. *Linc* 3G **75**
Bassus Green. *Herts* 3D **52**
Basta. *Shet* 2G **173**
Baston. *Linc* 4A **76**
Bastonford. *Worc* 5C **60**
Bastwick. *Norf* 4G **79**
Batchley. *Worc* 4E **61**
Batchworth. *Herts* 1B **38**
Batcombe. *Dors* 2B **14**
Batcombe. *Som* 3B **22**
Bate Heath. *Ches E* 3A **84**
**Bath**. *Bath* 5C **34**
Bathampton. *Bath* 5C **34**
Bathealton. *Som* 4D **20**
Batheaston. *Bath* 5C **34**
Bathford. *Bath* 5C **34**
**Bathgate**. *W Lot* 3C **128**
Bathley. *Notts* 5E **87**
Bathpool. *Corn* 5C **10**
Bathpool. *Som* 4F **21**
Bathville. *W Lot* 3C **128**
Bathway. *Som* 1A **22**
**Batley**. *W Yor* 2C **92**
Batsford. *Glos* 2G **49**
Batson. *Devn* 5D **8**
Battersby. *N Yor* 4C **106**
**Battersea**. *G Lon* 3D **39**
Battisborough Cross. *Devn* 4C **8**
Battisford. *Suff* 5C **66**
Battisford Tye. *Suff* 5C **66**
Battle. *E Sus* 4B **28**
Battle. *Powy* 2D **46**
Battleborough. *Som* 1G **21**
Battledown. *Glos* 3E **49**
Battlefield. *Shrp* 4H **71**
Battlesbridge. *Essx* 1B **40**
Battlesden. *C Beds* 3H **51**
Battlesea Green. *Suff* 3E **66**
Battleton. *Som* 4C **20**
Battram. *Leics* 5B **74**
Battramsley. *Hants* 3B **16**
Batt's Corner. *Surr* 2G **25**
Bauds of Cullen. *Mor* 2B **160**
Baugh. *Arg* 4B **138**
Baughton. *Worc* 1D **49**
Baughurst. *Hants* 5D **36**
Baulking. *Oxon* 2B **36**
Baumber. *Linc* 3B **88**
Baunton. *Glos* 5F **49**
Baverstock. *Wilts* 3F **23**
Bawburgh. *Norf* 5D **78**
Bawdeswell. *Norf* 3C **78**
Bawdrip. *Som* 3G **21**
Bawdsey. *Suff* 1G **55**
Bawsey. *Norf* 4F **77**
Bawtry. *S Yor* 1D **86**
Baxenden. *Lanc* 2F **91**
Baxterley. *Warw* 1G **61**
Baxter's Green. *Suff* 5G **65**
Bay. *High* 3B **154**
Baybridge. *Hants* 4D **24**
Baybridge. *Nmbd* 4C **114**
Baycliff. *Cumb* 2B **96**
Baydon. *Wilts* 4A **36**
Bayford. *Herts* 5D **52**
Bayford. *Som* 4C **22**
Bayles. *Cumb* 5A **114**
Baylham. *Suff* 5D **66**
Baynard's Green. *Oxon* 3D **50**
Bayston Hill. *Shrp* 5G **71**
Baythorne End. *Essx* 1H **53**
Baythorpe. *Linc* 1B **76**
Bayton. *Worc* 3A **60**
Bayton Common. *Worc* 3B **60**
Bayworth. *Oxon* 5D **50**
Beach. *S Glo* 4C **34**
Beachampton. *Buck* 2F **51**
Beachamwell. *Norf* 5G **77**
Beachley. *Glos* 2A **34**
Beacon. *Devn* 2E **13**
Beacon End. *Essx* 3C **54**
Beacon Hill. *Surr* 3G **25**
Beacon's Bottom. *Buck* 2F **37**
**Beaconsfield**. *Buck* 1A **38**
Beacrabhaic. *W Isl* 8D **171**
Beadlam. *N Yor* 1A **100**
Beadnell. *Nmbd* 2G **121**
Beaford. *Devn* 1F **11**
Beal. *Nmbd* 5G **131**
Beal. *N Yor* 2F **93**
Bealsmill. *Corn* 5D **10**
Beam Hill. *Staf* 3G **73**
Beamhurst. *Staf* 2E **73**
Beaminster. *Dors* 2H **13**
Beamish. *Dur* 4F **115**
Beamond End. *Buck* 1A **38**
Beamsley. *N Yor* 4C **98**
Bean. *Kent* 3G **39**
Beanacre. *Wilts* 5E **35**
Beanley. *Nmbd* 3E **121**
Beaquoy. *Orkn* 5C **172**
Beardwood. *Bkbn* 2E **91**
Beare Green. *Surr* 1C **26**
Bearley. *Warw* 4F **61**
Bearpark. *Dur* 5F **115**
Bearsbridge. *Nmbd* 4A **114**
**Bearsden**. *E Dun* 2G **127**
Bearsted. *Kent* 5B **40**
Bearstone. *Shrp* 2B **72**
Bearwood. *Pool* 3F **15**
Bearwood. *W Mid* 2E **61**
Beattock. *Dum* 4C **118**
Beauchamp Roding. *Essx* 4F **53**
Beauchief. *S Yor* 2H **85**
Beaufort. *Blae* 4E **47**
Beaulieu. *Hants* 2B **16**
Beauly. *High* 4H **157**
Beaumaris. *IOA* 3F **81**
Beaumont. *Cumb* 4E **113**
Beaumont. *Essx* 3E **55**
Beaumont Hill. *Darl* 3F **105**
Beaumont Leys. *Leic* 5C **74**
Beausale. *Warw* 3G **61**
Beauvale. *Notts* 1B **74**
Beauworth. *Hants* 4D **24**
Beaworthy. *Devn* 3E **11**
Beazley End. *Essx* 3H **53**
**Bebington**. *Mers* 2F **83**
Bebside. *Nmbd* 1F **115**
**Beccles**. *Suff* 2G **67**
Becconsall. *Lanc* 2C **90**
Beckbury. *Shrp* 5B **72**
**Beckenham**. *G Lon* 4E **39**
Beckermet. *Cumb* 4B **102**
Beckett End. *Norf* 1G **65**
Beck Foot. *Cumb* 5H **103**
Beckfoot. *Cumb*
nr. Broughton in Furness
1A **96**
nr. Seascale 4C **102**
nr. Silloth 5B **112**
Beckford. *Worc* 2E **49**
Beckhampton. *Wilts* 5F **35**
Beck Hole. *N Yor* 4F **107**
Beckingham. *Linc* 5F **87**
Beckingham. *Notts* 1E **87**
Beckington. *Som* 1D **22**
Beckley. *E Sus* 3C **28**
Beckley. *Hants* 3H **15**
Beckley. *Oxon* 4D **50**
Beck Row. *Suff* 3F **65**
Beck Side. *Cumb*
nr. Cartmel 1C **96**
nr. Ulverston 1B **96**
Beckside. *Cumb* 1F **97**
Beckton. *G Lon* 2F **39**
Beckwithshaw. *N Yor* 4E **99**
Becontree. *G Lon* 2F **39**
Bedale. *N Yor* 1E **99**
Bedburn. *Dur* 1E **105**
Bedchester. *Dors* 1D **14**
Beddau. *Rhon* 3D **32**
Beddgelert. *Gwyn* 1E **69**
Beddingham. *E Sus* 5F **27**
Beddington. *G Lon* 4E **39**
Bedfield. *Suff* 4E **66**
**Bedford**. *Bed* 1A **52**
Bedford. *G Man* 1A **84**
Bedham. *W Sus* 3B **26**
Bedhampton. *Hants* 2F **17**
Bedingfield. *Suff* 4D **66**
Bedingham Green. *Norf* 1E **67**
Bedlam. *N Yor* 3E **99**
Bedlar's Green. *Essx* 3F **53**
**Bedlington**. *Nmbd* 1F **115**
Bedlinog. *Mer T* 5D **46**
Bedminster. *Bris* 4A **34**
Bedmond. *Herts* 5A **52**
Bednall. *Staf* 4D **72**
Bedrule. *Bord* 3A **120**
Bedstone. *Shrp* 3F **59**
Bedwas. *Cphy* 3E **33**
Bedwellty. *Cphy* 5E **47**
**Bedworth**. *Warw* 2A **62**
Beeby. *Leics* 5D **74**
Beech. *Hants* 3E **25**
Beech. *Staf* 2C **72**
Beechcliffe. *W Yor* 5C **98**
Beech Hill. *W Ber* 5E **37**
Beechingstoke. *Wilts* 1F **23**
Beedon. *W Ber* 4C **36**
Beeford. *E Yor* 4F **101**
Beeley. *Derbs* 4G **85**
Beelsby. *NE Lin* 4F **95**
Beenham. *W Ber* 5D **36**
Beeny. *Corn* 3B **10**
Beer. *Devn* 4F **13**
Beer. *Som* 3H **21**
Beercrocombe. *Som* 4G **21**
Beer Hackett. *Dors* 1B **14**
Beesands. *Devn* 4E **9**
Beesby. *Linc* 2D **88**
Beeson. *Devn* 4E **9**
Beeston. *C Beds* 1B **52**
Beeston. *Ches W* 5H **83**
Beeston. *Norf* 4B **78**
**Beeston**. *Notts* 2C **74**
Beeston. *W Yor* 1C **92**
Beeston Regis. *Norf* 1D **78**
Beeswing. *Dum* 3F **111**
Beetham. *Cumb* 2D **97**
Beetham. *Som* 1F **13**
Beetley. *Norf* 4B **78**
Beffcote. *Staf* 4C **72**
Began. *Card* 3F **33**
Begbroke. *Oxon* 4C **50**
Begdale. *Cambs* 5D **76**
Begelly. *Pemb* 4F **43**
Beggar Hill. *Essx* 5G **53**
Beggar's Bush. *Powy* 4E **59**
Beggearn Huish. *Som* 3D **20**
Beguildy. *Powy* 3D **58**
Beighton. *Norf* 5F **79**
**Beighton**. *S Yor* 2B **86**
Beighton Hill. *Derbs* 5G **85**
Beinn Casgro. *W Isl* 5G **171**
Beith. *N Ayr* 4E **127**
Bekesbourne. *Kent* 5F **41**
Belaugh. *Norf* 4E **79**
Belbroughton. *Worc* 3D **60**
Belchalwell. *Dors* 2C **14**
Belchalwell Street. *Dors* 2C **14**
Belchamp Otten. *Essx* 1B **54**
Belchamp St Paul. *Essx* 1A **54**
Belchamp Walter. *Essx* 1B **54**
Belchford. *Linc* 3B **88**
**Belfast**. *Bel* 4H **175**
Belfast City George Best Airport.
*Bel* 4H **175**
Belfast International Airport.
*Ant* 3G **175**
Belfatton. *Abers* 3H **161**
Belford. *Nmbd* 1F **121**
Belgrano. *Cnwy* 3B **82**
Belhaven. *E Lot* 2C **130**
Belhelvie. *Abers* 2G **153**
Belhinnie. *Abers* 1B **152**
Bellabeg. *Abers* 2A **152**
Belladrum. *High* 4H **157**
Bellaghy. *M Ulst* 3F **175**
Bellamore. *S Ayr* 1H **109**
Bellanoch. *Arg* 4F **133**
Bell Busk. *N Yor* 4B **98**
Belleau. *Linc* 3D **88**
Belleheiglash. *Mor* 5F **159**
Bell End. *Worc* 3D **60**
Bellerby. *N Yor* 5E **105**
Bellerby Camp. *N Yor* 5D **105**
Bellever. *Devn* 5G **11**
Belle Vue. *Cumb* 1C **102**
Belle Vue. *Shrp* 4G **71**
Bellfield. *S Lan* 1H **117**
Belliehill. *Ang* 2E **145**
Bellingdon. *Buck* 5H **51**
Bellingham. *Nmbd* 1B **114**
Bellmount. *Norf* 3E **77**
Bellochantuy. *Arg* 2A **122**
Bellsbank. *E Ayr* 4D **117**
Bell's Cross. *Suff* 5D **66**
**Bellshill**. *N Lan* 4A **128**
Bellshill. *Nmbd* 1F **121**
Bellside. *N Lan* 4B **128**
Bellspool. *Bord* 1D **118**
Bellsquarry. *W Lot* 3D **128**
Bells Yew Green. *E Sus* 2H **27**
Belmaduthy. *High* 3A **158**
Belmesthorpe. *Rut* 4H **75**
Belmont. *Bkbn* 3E **91**

| | | | | |
|---|---|---|---|---|
| Belmont. Shet ...1G 173 | Bere Alston. Devn ...2A 8 | Bettws Ifan. Cdgn ...1D 44 | Biggar. Cumb ...3A 96 | Bintree. Norf ...3C 78 |
| Belmont. S Ayr ...2C 116 | Bere Ferrers. Devn ...2A 8 | Bettws Newydd. Mon ...5G 47 | Biggar. S Lan ...1C 118 | Binweston. Shrp ...5F 71 |
| Belnacraig. Abers ...2A 152 | Berepper. Corn ...4D 4 | Betws. Carm ...4G 45 | Biggin. Derbs | Birch. Essx ...4C 54 |
| Belnie. Linc ...2B 76 | Bere Regis. Dors ...3D 14 | Betws Garmon. Gwyn ...5E 81 | nr. Hartington ...5F 85 | Birch. G Man ...4G 91 |
| Belowda. Corn ...2D 6 | Bergh Apton. Norf ...5F 79 | Betws-y-Coed. Cnwy ...5G 81 | nr. Hulland ...1G 73 | Birchall. Staf ...5D 85 |
| Belper. Derbs ...1A 74 | Berinsfield. Oxon ...2D 36 | Betws-yn-Rhos. Cnwy ...3B 82 | Biggin. N Yor ...1F 93 | Bircham Newton. Norf ...2G 77 |
| Belper Lane End. Derbs ...1H 73 | Berkeley. Glos ...2B 34 | Beulah. Cdgn ...1C 44 | Biggings. Shet ...5C 173 | Bircham Tofts. Norf ...2G 77 |
| Belph. Derbs ...3C 86 | Berkhamsted. Herts ...5H 51 | Beulah. Powy ...5B 58 | Biggin Hill. G Lon ...5F 39 | Birchanger. Essx ...3F 53 |
| Belsay. Nmbd ...2E 115 | Berkley. Som ...2D 22 | Beul an Atha. Arg ...3B 124 | Biggleswade. C Beds ...1B 52 | Birch Cross. Staf ...2F 73 |
| Belsford. Devn ...3D 8 | Berkswell. W Mid ...3G 61 | Bevendean. Brig ...5E 27 | Bighouse. High ...2A 168 | Bircher. Here ...4G 59 |
| Belsize. Herts ...5A 52 | Bermondsey. G Lon ...3E 39 | Bevercotes. Notts ...3E 86 | Bighton. Hants ...3E 24 | Birch Green. Essx ...4C 54 |
| Belston. S Ayr ...2C 116 | Bernera. High ...1G 147 | Beverley. E Yor ...1D 94 | Biglands. Cumb ...4D 112 | Birchgrove. Card ...3E 33 |
| Belstone. Devn ...3G 11 | Bernice. Arg ...4A 134 | Beverston. Glos ...2D 34 | Bignall End. Staf ...5C 84 | Birchgrove. Swan ...3G 31 |
| Belstone Corner. Devn ...3G 11 | Bernisdale. High ...3D 154 | Bevington. Glos ...2B 34 | Bignor. W Sus ...4A 26 | Birch Hill. Ches W ...3H 83 |
| Belthorn. Lanc ...2E 91 | Berrick Salome. Oxon ...2E 36 | Bewaldeth. Cumb ...1D 102 | Bigrigg. Cumb ...3B 102 | Birchill. Devn ...2G 13 |
| Beltinge. Kent ...4F 41 | Berriedale. High ...1H 165 | Bewcastle. Cumb ...2G 113 | Big Sand. High ...1G 155 | Birchington. Kent ...4G 41 |
| Beltoft. N Lin ...4B 94 | Berrier. Cumb ...2E 103 | Bewdley. Worc ...3B 60 | Bigton. Shet ...9E 173 | Birchley Heath. Warw ...1G 61 |
| Belton. Leics ...3B 74 | Berriew. Powy ...5D 70 | Bewerley. N Yor ...3D 98 | Bilberry. Corn ...3E 6 | Birchmoor. Warw ...5G 73 |
| Belton. Linc ...2G 75 | Berrington. Nmbd ...5G 131 | Bewholme. E Yor ...4F 101 | Bilborough. Nott ...1C 74 | Birchmoor Green. C Beds ...2H 51 |
| Belton. Norf ...5G 79 | Berrington. Shrp ...5H 71 | Bexfield. Norf ...3C 78 | Bilbrook. Som ...2D 20 | Birchover. Derbs ...4G 85 |
| Belton. N Lin ...4A 94 | Berrington. Worc ...4H 59 | Bexhill. E Sus ...5B 28 | Bilbrook. Staf ...5C 72 | Birch Vale. Derbs ...2E 85 |
| Belton-in-Rutland. Rut ...5F 75 | Berrington Green. Worc ...4H 59 | Bexley. G Lon ...3F 39 | Bilbrough. N Yor ...5H 99 | Birchview. Mor ...5F 159 |
| Beltring. Kent ...1A 28 | Berrington Law. Nmbd ...5F 131 | Bexleyheath. G Lon ...3F 39 | Bilby. Notts ...2D 86 | Birchwood. Linc ...4G 87 |
| Belts of Collonach. Abers ...4D 152 | Berrow. Som ...1G 21 | Bexleyhill. W Sus ...3A 26 | Bildershaw. Dur ...2F 105 | Birchwood. Som ...1F 13 |
| Belvedere. G Lon ...3F 39 | Berrow Green. Worc ...5B 60 | Bexwell. Norf ...5F 77 | Bildeston. Suff ...1C 54 | Birchwood. Warr ...1A 84 |
| Belvoir. Leics ...2F 75 | Berry Cross. Devn ...1E 11 | Beyton. Suff ...4B 66 | Billericay. Essx ...1A 40 | Bircotes. Notts ...1D 86 |
| Bembridge. IOW ...4E 17 | Berry Down Cross. Devn ...2F 19 | Bhalton. W Isl ...4C 171 | Billesdon. Leics ...5E 74 | Birdbrook. Essx ...1H 53 |
| Bemersyde. Bord ...1H 119 | Berry Hill. Glos ...4A 48 | Bhatarsaigh. W Isl ...9B 170 | Billesley. Warw ...5F 61 | Birdfield. Arg ...4G 133 |
| Bemerton. Wilts ...3G 23 | Berry Hill. Pemb ...1A 44 | Bibbington. Derbs ...3E 85 | Billingborough. Linc ...2A 76 | Birdforth. N Yor ...2G 99 |
| Bempton. E Yor ...2F 101 | Berryhillock. Mor ...2C 160 | Bibury. Glos ...5G 49 | Billinge. Mers ...4D 90 | Birdham. W Sus ...3G 17 |
| Benacre. Suff ...2H 67 | Berrynarbor. Devn ...2F 19 | Bicester. Oxon ...3D 50 | Billingford. Norf | Birdholme. Derbs ...4A 86 |
| Ben Alder Lodge. High ...1C 142 | Berry Pomeroy. Devn ...2E 9 | Bickenhall. Som ...1F 13 | nr. Dereham ...3C 78 | Birdingbury. Warw ...4B 62 |
| Ben Armine Lodge. High ...2E 164 | Berryscaur. Dum ...5D 118 | Bickenhill. W Mid ...2F 61 | nr. Diss ...3D 66 | Birdlip. Glos ...4E 49 |
| Benbecula Airport. W Isl ...3C 170 | Berry's Green. G Lon ...5F 39 | Bicker. Linc ...2B 76 | Billingham. Stoc T ...2B 106 | Birdsall. N Yor ...3C 100 |
| Benbuie. Dum ...5G 117 | Bersham. Wrex ...1F 71 | Bicker Bar. Linc ...2B 76 | Billinghay. Linc ...5A 88 | Birds Edge. W Yor ...4C 92 |
| Benchill. G Man ...2C 84 | Berthengam. Flin ...3D 82 | Bicker Gauntlet. Linc ...2B 76 | Billingley. S Yor ...4E 93 | Birds Green. Essx ...5F 53 |
| Benderloch. Arg ...5D 140 | Berwick. E Sus ...5G 27 | Bickershaw. G Man ...4E 91 | Billingshurst. W Sus ...3B 26 | Birdsgreen. Shrp ...2B 60 |
| Benderloch. Herts ...3B 52 | Berwick Bassett. Wilts ...4G 35 | Bickerstaffe. Lanc ...4C 90 | Billingsley. Shrp ...2B 60 | Birdsmoorgate. Dors ...2G 13 |
| Bendronaig Lodge. High ...5C 156 | Berwick Hill. Nmbd ...2E 115 | Bickerton. Ches E ...5H 83 | Billington. C Beds ...3H 51 | Birdston. E Dun ...2H 127 |
| Benenden. Kent ...2C 28 | Berwick St James. Wilts ...3F 23 | Bickerton. Nmbd ...4D 121 | Billington. Lanc ...1F 91 | Birdwell. S Yor ...4D 92 |
| Benfieldside. Dur ...4D 115 | Berwick St John. Wilts ...4E 23 | Bickerton. N Yor ...4G 99 | Billington. Staf ...3C 72 | Birdwood. Glos ...4C 48 |
| Bengate. Norf ...3F 79 | Berwick St Leonard. Wilts ...3E 23 | Bickford. Staf ...4C 72 | Billockby. Norf ...4G 79 | Birgham. Bord ...1B 120 |
| Bengeworth. Worc ...1F 49 | Berwick-upon-Tweed. | Bickington. Devn | Billy Row. Dur ...1E 105 | Birichen. High ...4E 165 |
| Benhall Green. Suff ...4F 67 | Nmbd ...4F 131 | nr. Barnstaple ...3F 19 | Bilsborrow. Lanc ...5E 97 | Birkby. Cumb ...1B 102 |
| Benholm. Abers ...2H 145 | Berwyn. Den ...1D 70 | nr. Newton Abbot ...5A 12 | Bilsby. Linc ...3D 88 | Birkby. N Yor ...4A 106 |
| Beningbrough. N Yor ...4H 99 | Bescaby. Leics ...3F 75 | Bickleigh. Devn | Bilsham. W Sus ...5A 26 | Birkdale. Mers ...3B 90 |
| Benington. Herts ...3C 52 | Bescar. Lanc ...3B 90 | nr. Plymouth ...2B 8 | Bilsington. Kent ...2E 29 | Birkenhead. Mers ...2F 83 |
| Benington. Linc ...1C 76 | Besford. Worc ...1E 49 | nr. Tiverton ...2C 12 | Bilson Green. Glos ...4B 48 | Birkenhills. Abers ...4E 161 |
| Benington Sea End. Linc ...1D 76 | Bessacarr. S Yor ...4G 93 | Bickleton. Devn ...3F 19 | Bilsthorpe. Notts ...4D 86 | Birkenshaw. N Lan ...3H 127 |
| Benllech. IOA ...2E 81 | Bessbrook. New M ...6F 175 | Bickley. N Yor ...5G 107 | Bilston. Midl ...3F 129 | Birkenshaw. W Yor ...2C 92 |
| Benmore Lodge. High ...2H 163 | Bessels Leigh. Oxon ...5C 50 | Bickley Moss. Ches W ...1H 71 | Bilston. W Mid ...1D 60 | Birkhall. Abers ...4H 151 |
| Benacott. Corn ...3C 10 | Bessingby. E Yor ...3F 101 | Bickmarsh. Worc ...1G 49 | Bilstone. Leics ...5A 74 | Birkhill. Ang ...5C 144 |
| Bennah. Devn ...4B 12 | Bessingham. Norf ...2D 78 | Bickerstone. Essx ...5A 54 | Bilting. Kent ...1E 29 | Birkholme. Linc ...3G 75 |
| Bennacarrigan. N Ayr ...3D 122 | Best Beech Hill. E Sus ...2H 27 | Bicknoller. Som ...3E 20 | Bilton. E Yor ...1E 95 | Birkin. N Yor ...2F 93 |
| Bennethead. Cumb ...2F 103 | Besthorpe. Norf ...1C 66 | Bicknor. Kent ...5C 40 | Bilton. Nmbd ...3G 121 | Birley. Here ...5G 59 |
| Benniworth. Linc ...2B 88 | Besthorpe. Notts ...4F 87 | Bickton. Hants ...1G 15 | Bilton. N Yor ...4F 99 | Birling. Kent ...4A 40 |
| Benover. Kent ...1B 28 | Bestwood Village. Notts ...1C 74 | Bicton. Here ...4G 59 | Bilton. Warw ...3B 62 | Birling. Nmbd ...4G 121 |
| Benson. Oxon ...2E 36 | Beswick. E Yor ...5E 101 | Bicton. Shrp | Bilton in Ainsty. N Yor ...5G 99 | Birling Gap. E Sus ...5G 27 |
| Benston. Shet ...6F 173 | Betchworth. Surr ...5D 38 | nr. Bishop's Castle ...2E 59 | Bimbister. Orkn ...6C 172 | Birlingham. Worc ...1E 49 |
| Benstonhall. Orkn ...4E 172 | Bethania. Cdgn ...4E 57 | nr. Shrewsbury ...4G 71 | Binbrook. Linc ...1B 88 | Birmingham. W Mid ...2E 61 |
| Bent. Abers ...1F 145 | Bethania. Gwyn | Bicton Heath. Shrp ...4G 71 | Binchester. Dur ...1F 105 | Birmingham Airport. |
| Benthall. Shrp ...5A 72 | nr. Blaenau Ffestiniog ...1G 69 | Bidborough. Kent ...1G 27 | Bincombe. Dors ...4B 14 | W Mid ...2F 61 |
| Bentham. Glos ...4E 49 | nr. Caernarfon ...5F 81 | Biddenden. Kent ...2C 28 | Bindal. High ...5G 165 | Birnam. Per ...4H 143 |
| Bentlawnt. Shrp ...5F 71 | Bethel. Gwyn | Biddenden Green. Kent ...1C 28 | Binegar. Som ...2B 22 | Birse. Abers ...4C 152 |
| Bentley. E Yor ...1D 94 | nr. Bala ...2B 70 | Biddenham. Bed ...5H 63 | Bines Green. W Sus ...4C 26 | Birsemore. Abers ...4C 152 |
| Bentley. Hants ...2F 25 | nr. Caernarfon ...4E 81 | Biddestone. Wilts ...4D 34 | Binfield. Brac ...4G 37 | Birstall. Leics ...5C 74 |
| Bentley. S Yor ...4F 93 | Bethel. IOA ...3C 80 | Biddisham. Som ...1G 21 | Binfield Heath. Oxon ...4F 37 | Birstall. W Yor ...2C 92 |
| Bentley. Suff ...2E 54 | Bethersden. Kent ...1D 28 | Biddlesden. Buck ...1E 51 | Bingfield. Nmbd ...2C 114 | Birstall Smithies. W Yor ...2C 92 |
| Bentley. Warw ...1G 61 | Bethesda. Gwyn ...4F 81 | Biddlestone. Nmbd ...4D 120 | Bingham. Notts ...2E 74 | Birstwith. N Yor ...4E 99 |
| Bentley. W Mid ...1D 61 | Bethesda. Pemb ...3E 43 | Biddulph. Staf ...5C 84 | Bingham's Melcombe. | Birthorpe. Linc ...2A 76 |
| Bentley Heath. Herts ...1D 38 | Bethlehem. Carm ...3G 45 | Biddulph Moor. Staf ...5D 84 | Dors ...2C 14 | Birtle. G Man ...3G 91 |
| Bentley Heath. W Mid ...3F 61 | Bethnal Green. G Lon ...2E 39 | Bideford. Devn ...4E 19 | Bingley. W Yor ...1B 92 | Birtley. Here ...4F 59 |
| Bentpath. Dum ...5F 119 | Betley. Staf ...1B 72 | Bidford-on-Avon. Warw ...5E 61 | Bings Heath. Shrp ...4H 71 | Birtley. Nmbd ...2B 114 |
| Bents. W Lot ...3C 128 | Betsham. Kent ...3H 39 | Bidlake. Devn ...4F 11 | Binham. Norf ...2B 78 | Birtley. Tyne ...4F 115 |
| Bentworth. Hants ...2E 25 | Betteshanger. Kent ...5H 41 | Bidston. Mers ...2E 83 | Binley. Hants ...1C 24 | Birtsmorton. Worc ...2D 48 |
| Benvie. D'dee ...5C 144 | Bettiscombe. Dors ...3H 13 | Bielby. E Yor ...5B 100 | Binley. W Mid ...3A 62 | Birts Street. Worc ...2C 48 |
| Benville. Dors ...2A 14 | Bettisfield. Wrex ...2G 71 | Bieldside. Aber ...3F 153 | Binnegar. Dors ...4D 15 | Bisbrooke. Rut ...1F 63 |
| Benwell. Tyne ...3F 115 | Betton. Shrp ...2A 72 | Bierley. IOW ...5D 16 | Binniehill. Falk ...2B 128 | Bisham. Wind ...3G 37 |
| Benwick. Cambs ...1C 64 | Betton Strange. Shrp ...5H 71 | Bierley. W Yor ...1B 92 | Binsoe. N Yor ...2E 99 | Bishampton. Worc ...5D 61 |
| Beoley. Worc ...4E 61 | Bettws. B'end ...3C 32 | Bierton. Buck ...4G 51 | Binstead. IOW ...3D 16 | Bish Mill. Devn ...4H 19 |
| Beoraidbeg. High ...4E 147 | Bettws. Newp ...2F 33 | Bigbury. Devn ...4C 8 | Binsted. Hants ...2F 25 | Bishop Auckland. Dur ...2F 105 |
| Bepton. W Sus ...1G 17 | Bettws Bledrws. Cdgn ...5E 57 | Bigbury-on-Sea. Devn ...4C 8 | Binsted. W Sus ...5A 26 | Bishopbridge. Linc ...1H 87 |
| Berden. Essx ...3E 53 | Bettws Cedewain. Powy ...1D 58 | Bigby. Linc ...4D 94 | Binton. Warw ...5F 61 | Bishopbriggs. E Dun ...2H 127 |
| | Bettws Gwerfil Goch. Den ...1C 70 | | | Bishop Burton. E Yor ...1C 94 |

Bishopdown. Wilts ...3G 23
Bishop Middleham. Dur ...1A 106
Bishopmill. Mor ...2G 159
Bishop Monkton. N Yor ...3F 99
Bishop Norton. Linc ...1G 87
Bishopsbourne. Kent ...5F 41
Bishops Cannings. Wilts ...5F 35
Bishop's Castle. Shrp ...2F 59
Bishop's Caundle. Dors ...1B 14
Bishop's Cleeve. Glos ...3E 49
Bishop's Down. Dors ...1B 14
Bishop's Frome. Here ...1B 48
Bishop's Green. Essx ...4G 53
Bishop's Green. Hants ...5D 36
Bishop's Hull. Som ...4F 21
Bishop's Itchington. Warw ...5A 62
Bishops Lydeard. Som ...4E 21
Bishop's Norton. Glos ...3D 48
Bishop's Nympton. Devn ...4A 20
Bishop's Offley. Staf ...3B 72
Bishop's Stortford. Herts ...3E 53
Bishop's Sutton. Hants ...3E 24
Bishop's Tachbrook. Warw ...4H 61
Bishop's Tawton. Devn ...3F 19
Bishopsteignton. Devn ...5C 12
Bishopstoke. Hants ...1C 16
Bishopstone. Swan ...4E 31
Bishopstone. Buck ...4G 51
Bishopstone. E Sus ...5F 27
Bishopstone. Here ...1H 47
Bishopstone. Swin ...3H 35
Bishopstone. Wilts ...4F 23
Bishopstrow. Wilts ...2D 23
Bishop Sutton. Bath ...1A 22
Bishop's Waltham. Hants ...1D 16
Bishopswood. Som ...1F 13
Bishopsworth. Bris ...5A 34
Bishop Thornton. N Yor ...3E 99
Bishopthorpe. York ...5H 99
Bishopton. Darl ...2A 106
Bishopton. Dum ...5B 110
Bishopton. N Yor ...2E 99
Bishopton. Ren ...2F 127
Bishopton. Warw ...5F 61
Bishop Wilton. E Yor ...4B 100
Bishton. Newp ...3G 33
Bishton. Staf ...3E 73
Bisley. Glos ...5E 49
Bisley. Surr ...5A 38
Bispham. Bkpl ...5C 96
Bispham Green. Lanc ...3C 90
Bissoe. Corn ...4B 6
Bisterne. Hants ...2G 15
Bisterne Close. Hants ...2H 15
Bitchfield. Linc ...3G 75
Bittadon. Devn ...2F 19
Bittaford. Devn ...3C 8
Bittering. Norf ...4B 78
Bitterley. Shrp ...3H 59
Bitterne. Sotn ...1C 16
Bitteswell. Leics ...2C 62
Bitton. S Glo ...5B 34
Bix. Oxon ...3F 37
Bixter. Shet ...6E 173
Blaby. Leics ...1C 62
Blackawton. Devn ...3E 9
Black Bank. Cambs ...2E 65
Black Barn. Linc ...3D 76
Blackborough. Devn ...2D 12
Blackborough. Norf ...4F 77
Blackborough End. Norf ...4F 77
Black Bourton. Oxon ...5A 50
Blackboys. E Sus ...3G 27
Blackbrook. Derbs ...1H 73
Blackbrook. Mers ...1H 83
Blackbrook. Staf ...2B 72
Blackbrook. Surr ...1C 26
Blackburn. Abers ...2F 153
Blackburn. Bkbn ...2E 91
Blackburn. W Lot ...3D 128
Black Callerton. Tyne ...3E 115
Black Carr. Norf ...1C 66
Black Clauchrie. S Ayr ...1H 109

Black Corries. High ...3G 141
Black Crofts. Arg ...5D 140
Black Cross. Corn ...2D 6
Blackden Heath. Ches E ...3B 84
Blackditch. Oxon ...5C 50
Black Dog. Devn ...2B 12
Blackdog. Abers ...2G 153
Blackdown. Dors ...2G 13
Blackdyke. Cumb ...4C 112
Blacker Hill. S Yor ...4D 92
Blackfen. G Lon ...3F 39
Blackfield. Hants ...2C 16
Blackford. Cumb ...3E 113
Blackford. Per ...3A 136
Blackford. Shrp ...2H 59
Blackfordby. Leics ...4H 73
Blackgang. IOW ...5C 16
Blackhall. Edin ...2F 129
Blackhall. Ren ...3F 127
Blackhall Colliery. Dur ...1B 106
Blackhall Mill. Tyne ...4E 115
Blackhall Rocks. Dur ...1B 106
Blackham. E Sus ...2F 27
Blackhaugh. Essx ...3D 54
Blackheath. G Lon ...3E 39
Blackheath. Suff ...3G 67
Blackheath. Surr ...1B 26
Blackheath. W Mid ...2D 61
Black Heddon. Nmbd ...2D 115
Black Hill. Warw ...5G 61
Blackhill. Abers ...4H 161
Blackhill. High ...3C 154
Blackhills. Abers ...2G 161
Blackhills. High ...3D 158
Blackjack. Linc ...2B 76
Blackland. Wilts ...5F 35
Black Lane. G Man ...4F 91
Blackleach. Lanc ...1C 90
Blackley. G Man ...4G 91
Blackley. W Yor ...3B 92
Blacklunans. Per ...2A 144
Blackmill. B'end ...3C 32
Blackmoor. G Man ...4E 91
Blackmoor. Hants ...3F 25
Blackmoor Gate. Devn ...2G 19
Blackmore. Essx ...5G 53
Blackmore End. Essx ...2H 53
Blackmore End. Herts ...4B 52
Black Mount. Arg ...4G 141
Blackness. Falk ...2D 128
Blacknest. Hants ...2F 25
Blackney. Dors ...3H 13
Blacknoll. Dors ...4D 14
Black Notley. Essx ...3A 54
Blacko. Lanc ...5A 98
Black Pill. Swan ...3F 31
Blackpool. Bkpl ...1B 90
Blackpool. Devn ...4E 9
Blackpool Corner. Dors ...3G 13
Blackpool Gate. Cumb ...2G 113
Blackridge. W Lot ...3B 128
Blackrock. Arg ...3B 124
Blackrock. Mon ...4F 47
Blackrod. G Man ...3E 90
Blackshaw. Dum ...3B 112
Blackshaw Head. W Yor ...2H 91
Blackshaw Moor. Staf ...5E 85
Blacksmith's Green. Suff ...4D 66
Blacksnape. Bkbn ...2F 91
Blackstone. W Sus ...4D 26
Black Street. Suff ...2G 67
Black Tar. Pemb ...4D 43
Blackthorn. Oxon ...4E 50
Blackthorpe. Suff ...4B 66
Blacktoft. E Yor ...2B 94
Blacktop. Aber ...3F 153
Black Torrington. Devn ...2E 11
Blacktown. Newp ...3F 33
Blackwall Tunnel. G Lon ...2E 39
Blackwater. Corn ...4B 6
Blackwater. Hants ...1G 25

Blackwater. IOW ...4D 16
Blackwater. Som ...1F 13
Blackwaterfoot. N Ayr ...3C 122
Blackwell. Darl ...3F 105
Blackwell. Derbs
  nr. Alfreton ...5B 86
  nr. Buxton ...3F 85
Blackwell. Som ...4D 20
Blackwell. Warw ...1A 50
Blackwell. Worc ...3D 61
Blackwood. Cphy ...2E 32
Blackwood. Dum ...1G 111
Blackwood. S Lan ...5A 128
Blackwood Hill. Staf ...5D 84
Blacon. Ches W ...4F 83
Bladnoch. Dum ...4B 110
Bladon. Oxon ...4C 50
Blaenannerch. Cdgn ...1C 44
Blaenau Dolwyddelan.
  ...5F 81
Blaenau Ffestiniog. Gwyn ...1G 69
Blaenavon. Torf ...5F 47
Blaenawey. Mon ...4F 47
Blaen Celyn. Cdgn ...5C 56
Blaen Clydach. Rhon ...2C 32
Blaencwm. Rhon ...2C 32
Blaendulais. Neat ...5B 46
Blaenffos. Pemb ...1F 43
Blaengarw. B'end ...2C 32
Blaen-geuffordd. Cdgn ...2F 57
Blaengwrach. Neat ...5B 46
Blaengwynfi. Neat ...2B 32
Blaenllechau. Rhon ...2C 32
Blaenpennal. Cdgn ...4F 57
Blaenplwyf. Cdgn ...3E 57
Blaenporth. Cdgn ...1C 44
Blaenrhondda. Rhon ...2C 32
Blaenwaun. Carm ...2G 43
Blaen-y-coed. Carm ...2H 43
Blagdon. N Som ...1A 22
Blagdon. Torb ...2E 9
Blagdon Hill. Som ...1F 13
Blagill. Cumb ...5A 114
Blaguegate. Lanc ...4C 90
Blaich. High ...1E 141
Blain. High ...2A 140
Blaina. Blae ...5F 47
Blair Atholl. Per ...2F 143
Blairbeg. Arg ...4G 135
Blairgowrie. Per ...4A 144
Blairhall. Fife ...1D 128
Blairingone. Per ...4B 136
Blairlogie. Stir ...4A 136
Blairmore. Abers ...5B 160
Blairmore. Arg ...1C 126
Blairmore. High ...3B 166
Blairquhanan. W Dun ...1F 127
Blaisdon. Glos ...4C 48
Blakebrook. Worc ...3C 60
Blakedown. Worc ...3C 60
Blake End. Essx ...3H 53
Blakemere. Here ...1G 47
Blakeney. Glos ...5B 48
Blakeney. Norf ...1C 78
Blakenhall. Ches E ...1B 72
Blakeshall. Worc ...2C 60
Blakesley. Nptn ...5D 62
Blanchland. Nmbd ...4C 114
Blandford Camp. Dors ...2E 15
Blandford Forum. Dors ...2D 15
Blandford St Mary. Dors ...2D 15
Bland Hill. N Yor ...4E 98
Blandy. High ...2G 167
Blanefield. Stir ...2G 127
Blankney. Linc ...4H 87
Blarmachfoldach. High ...2E 141
Blarnalearoch. High ...4F 163
Blashford. Hants ...2G 15
Blaston. Leics ...1F 63
Blatchbridge. Som ...2C 22
Blathaisbhal. W Isl ...1D 170
Blatherwycke. Nptn ...1G 63
Blawith. Cumb ...1B 96

Blaxhall. Suff ...5F 67
Blaxton. S Yor ...4G 93
Blaydon. Tyne ...3E 115
Bleadney. Som ...2H 21
Bleadon. N Som ...1G 21
Blean. Kent ...4F 41
Bleary. Arm ...5F 175
Bleasby. Linc ...2A 88
Bleasby. Notts ...1E 74
Bleasby Moor. Linc ...2A 88
Bleasdale. Lanc ...5E 97
Blebocraigs. Fife ...2G 137
Bleddfa. Powy ...4E 58
Bledington. Glos ...3H 49
Bledlow. Buck ...5F 51
Bledlow Ridge. Buck ...2F 37
Blencarn. Cumb ...1H 103
Blencogo. Cumb ...5C 112
Blendworth. Hants ...1F 17
Blennerhasset. Cumb ...5C 112
Bletchingdon. Oxon ...4D 50
Bletchingley. Surr ...5E 39
Bletchley. Mil ...2G 51
Bletchley. Shrp ...2A 72
Bletherston. Pemb ...2E 43
Bletsoe. Bed ...5H 63
Blewbury. Oxon ...3D 36
Blickling. Norf ...3D 78
Blidworth. Notts ...5C 86
Blindburn. Nmbd ...3C 120
Blindcrake. Cumb ...1C 102
Blindley Heath. Surr ...1E 27
Blisland. Corn ...5B 10
Blissford. Hants ...1G 15
Bliss Gate. Worc ...3B 60
Blists Hill. Telf ...5A 72
Blisworth. Nptn ...5E 63
Blithbury. Staf ...3E 73
Blitterlees. Cumb ...4C 112
Blockley. Glos ...2G 49
Blofield. Norf ...5F 79
Blofield Heath. Norf ...4F 79
Blo' Norton. Norf ...3C 66
Bloomfield. Bord ...2H 119
Blore. Staf ...1F 73
Blount's Green. Staf ...2E 73
Bloxham. Oxon ...2C 50
Bloxholm. Linc ...5H 87
Bloxwich. W Mid ...5D 73
Bloxworth. Dors ...3D 15
Blubberhouses. N Yor ...4D 98
Blue Anchor. Som ...2D 20
Blue Anchor. Swan ...3E 31
Blue Bell Hill. Kent ...4B 40
Blue Row. Essx ...4D 54
Bluetown. Kent ...5D 40
Blundeston. Suff ...1H 67
Blunham. C Beds ...5A 64
Blunsdon St Andrew.
  Swin ...3G 35
Bluntington. Worc ...3C 60
Bluntisham. Cambs ...3C 64
Blunts. Corn ...2H 7
Blurton. Stoke ...1C 72
Blyborough. Linc ...1G 87
Blyford. Suff ...3G 67
Blymhill. Staf ...4C 72
Blymhill Lawns. Staf ...4C 72
Blyth. Nmbd ...1G 115
Blyth. Notts ...2D 86
Blyth. Bord ...5E 129
Blyth Bank. Bord ...5E 129
Blyth Bridge. Bord ...5E 129
Blythburgh. Suff ...3G 67
The Blythe. Staf ...3E 73
Blythe Bridge. Staf ...1D 72
Blythe Marsh. Staf ...1D 72
Blyton. Linc ...1F 87
Boarhills. Fife ...2H 137
Boarhunt. Hants ...2E 16
Boar's Head. G Man ...4D 90
Boarshead. E Sus ...2G 27
Boars Hill. Oxon ...5C 50
Boarstall. Buck ...4E 51

Boasley Cross. Devn ...3F 11
Boath. High ...1H 157
Boat of Garten. High ...2D 150
Bobbing. Kent ...4C 40
Bobbington. Staf ...1C 60
Bobbingworth. Essx ...5F 53
Bocaddon. Corn ...3F 7
Bocking. Essx ...3A 54
Bocking Churchstreet.
  Essx ...3A 54
Boddam. Abers ...4H 161
Boddam. Shet ...10E 173
Boddington. Glos ...3D 48
Bodedern. IOA ...2C 80
Bodelwyddan. Den ...3C 82
Bodenham. Here ...5H 59
Bodenham. Wilts ...4G 23
Bodewryd. IOA ...1C 80
Bodfari. Den ...3C 82
Bodham. Norf ...1D 78
Bodiam. E Sus ...3B 28
Bodicote. Oxon ...2C 50
Bodieve. Corn ...1D 6
Bodinnick. Corn ...3F 7
Bodle Street Green. E Sus ...4A 28
Bodmin. Corn ...2E 7
Bodnant. Cnwy ...3H 81
Bodney. Norf ...1H 65
Bodorgan. IOA ...4C 80
Bodrane. Corn ...2G 7
Bodsham. Kent ...1F 29
Boduan. Gwyn ...2C 68
Bodymoor Heath. Warw ...1F 61
The Bog. Shrp ...1F 59
Bogallan. High ...3A 158
Bogbrae Croft. Abers ...5H 161
Bogend. S Ayr ...1C 116
Boghall. Midl ...3F 129
Boghall. W Lot ...3C 128
Boghead. S Lan ...5A 128
Bogindollo. Arg ...3D 144
Bogmoor. Mor ...2A 160
Bogniebrae. Abers ...4C 160
Bognor Regis. W Sus ...3H 17
Bograxie. Abers ...2E 152
Bogside. N Lan ...4B 128
Bogton. Abers ...3D 160
Bogue. Dum ...1D 110
Bohenie. High ...5E 149
Bohortha. Corn ...5C 6
Boirseam. W Isl ...9C 171
Bokiddick. Corn ...2E 7
Bolam. Dur ...2E 105
Bolam. Nmbd ...1D 115
Bolberry. Devn ...5C 8
Bold Heath. Mers ...2H 83
Boldon. Tyne ...3G 115
Boldon Colliery. Tyne ...3G 115
Boldre. Hants ...3B 16
Boldron. Dur ...3D 104
Bole. Notts ...2E 87
Bolehall. Staf ...5G 73
Bolehill. Derbs ...5G 85
Bolenowe. Corn ...5A 6
Boleside. Bord ...1G 119
Bolham. Devn ...1C 12
Bolham Water. Devn ...1E 13
Bolingey. Corn ...3B 6
Bollington. Ches E ...3D 84
Bolney. W Sus ...3D 26
Bolnhurst. Bed ...5H 63
Bolshan. Arg ...3F 145
Bolsover. Derbs ...3B 86
Bolsterstone. S Yor ...1G 85
Bolstone. Here ...2A 48
Boltachan. Per ...3F 143
Boltby. N Yor ...1G 99
Bolton. Cumb ...2H 103
Bolton. E Lot ...2B 130
Bolton. E Yor ...4B 100
Bolton. G Man ...4F 91
Bolton. Nmbd ...3F 121
Bolton Abbey. N Yor ...4C 98

Bolton-by-Bowland. Lanc ....5G 97
Boltonfellend. Cumb ........3F 113
Boltongate. Cumb ...........5D 112
Bolton Green. Lanc .........3D 90
Bolton-le-Sands. Lanc ......3D 97
Bolton Low Houses.
  Cumb ...................5D 112
Bolton New Houses.
  Cumb ...................5D 112
Bolton-on-Swale. N Yor .....5F 105
Bolton Percy. N Yor ........5H 99
Bolton Town End. Lanc ......3D 97
Bolton upon Dearne.
  S Yor ...................4E 93
Bolton Wood Lane.
  Cumb ...................5D 112
Bolventor. Corn ............5B 10
Bomarsund. Nmbd ...........1F 115
Bomere Heath. Shrp .........4G 71
Bonar Bridge. High .........4D 164
Bonawe. Arg ................5E 141
Bonby. N Lin ...............3D 94
Boncath. Pemb ..............1G 43
Bonchester Bridge. Bord ....3H 119
Bonchurch. IOW ............5D 16
Bond End. Staf .............4F 73
Bondleigh. Devn ............2G 11
Bonds. Lanc ................5D 97
Bonehill. Devn .............5H 11
Bonehill. Staf .............5F 73
Bo'ness. Falk ..............1C 128
Boney Hay. Staf ............4E 73
Bonham. Wilts ..............3C 22
Bonhill. W Dun .............2E 127
Boningale. Shrp ............5C 72
Bonjedward. Bord ...........2A 120
Bonkle. N Lan ..............4B 128
Bonnington. Ang ............5E 145
Bonnington. Edin ...........3E 129
Bonnington. Kent ...........2E 29
Bonnybank. Fife ............3F 137
Bonnybridge. Falk ..........1B 128
Bonnykelly. Abers ..........3F 161
Bonnyrigg. Midl ............3G 129
Bonnyton. Ang ..............5C 144
Bonnytown. Fife ............2H 137
Bonsall. Derbs .............5G 85
Bont. Mon .................4G 47
Bontddu. Gwyn .............4F 69
Bont Dolgadfan. Powy ......5A 70
Y Bont-Faen. V Glam .......4C 32
Bontgoch. Cdgn ............2F 57
Bonthorpe. Linc ...........3D 89
Bont Newydd. Gwyn .........1G 69
Bont-newydd. Cnwy .........3C 82
Bontnewydd. Cdgn ..........4F 57
Bontnewydd. Gwyn ..........4D 81
Bontuchel. Den ............5C 82
Bonvilston. V Glam ........4D 32
Bon-y-maen. Swan ..........3F 31
Booker. Buck ..............2G 37
Booley. Shrp ..............3H 71
Boorley Green. Hants ......1D 16
Boosbeck. Red C ...........3D 106
Boot. Cumb ...............4C 102
Booth. W Yor .............2A 92
Boothby Graffoe. Linc .....5G 87
Boothby Pagnell. Linc .....2G 75
Booth Green. Ches E .......2D 84
Booth of Toft. Shet .......4F 173
Boothstown. G Man .........4F 91
Boothville. Nptn ..........4E 63
Bootle. Cumb .............1A 96
Bootle. Mers .............1F 83
Booton. Norf .............3D 78
Booze. N Yor .............4D 104
Boquhan. Stir ............1G 127
Boraston. Shrp ...........3A 60
Borden. Kent .............4C 40
Borden. W Sus ...........4G 25
Bordlands. Bord ..........5E 129
Bordley. N Yor ...........3B 98
Bordon. Hants ...........3F 25
Boreham. Essx ...........5A 54

Boreham. Wilts ...........2D 23
Boreham Street. E Sus ....4A 28
Borehamwood. Herts .......1C 38
Boreland. Dum ...........5D 118
Boreston. Devn ..........3D 8
Borestone Brae. Stir .....4G 135
Boreton. Shrp ...........5H 71
Borgh. W Isl
  on Barra ..............8B 170
  on Benbecula ..........3C 170
  on Berneray ...........1E 170
  on Isle of Lewis ......2E 171
Borghasdal. W Isl ........9C 171
Borghastan. W Isl ........3D 171
Borgh na Sgiotaig. High ..1C 154
Borgie. High .............3G 167
Borgue. Dum .............5D 110
Borgue. High ............1H 165
Borley. Essx .............1B 54
Borley Green. Essx .......1B 54
Borley Green. Suff .......4B 66
Borlum. High ............1H 149
Bornais. W Isl ...........6C 170
Bornesketaig. High .......1C 154
Boroughbridge. N Yor .....3F 99
Borough Green. Kent ......5H 39
Borreraig. High ..........3A 154
Borrobol Lodge. High .....1F 165
Borrodale. High ..........4A 154
Borrowash. Derbs .........2B 74
Borrowby. N Yor
  nr. Northallerton .....1G 99
  nr. Whitby ...........3E 107
Borrowston. High .........4F 169
Borrowstonehill. Orkn ....7D 172
Borstal. Medw ...........4B 40
Borth. Cdgn .............2F 57
Borthwick. Midl ..........4G 129
Borth-y-Gest. Gwyn .......2E 69
Borve. High .............4D 154
Borwick. Lanc ...........2E 97
Bosbury. Here ...........1B 48
Boscastle. Corn ..........3A 10
Boscombe. Bour ..........3G 15
Boscombe. Wilts .........3H 23
Boscoppa. Corn ..........3E 7
Bosham. W Sus ..........2G 17
Bosherston. Pemb ........5D 42
Bosley. Ches E ..........4D 84
Bossall. N Yor ..........3B 100
Bossiney. Corn ..........4A 10
Bossingham. Kent ........1F 29
Bossington. Som .........2B 20
Bostadh. W Isl ..........3D 171
Bostock Green. Ches W ...4A 84
Boston. Linc ............1C 76
Boston Spa. W Yor .......5G 99
Boswarthen. Corn ........3B 4
Boswinger. Corn .........4D 6
Botallack. Corn .........3A 4
Botany Bay. G Lon .......1D 39
Botcheston. Leics .......5B 74
Botesdale. Suff .........3C 66
Bothal. Nmbd ...........1F 115
Bothampstead. W Ber .....4D 36
Bothamsall. Notts .......3D 86
Bothel. Cumb ...........1C 102
Bothenhampton. Dors .....3H 13
Bothwell. S Lan .........4A 128
Botley. Buck ...........5H 51
Botley. Hants ..........1D 16
Botley. Oxon ...........5C 50
Botloe's Green. Glos ....3C 48
Botolph Claydon. Buck ...3F 51
Botolphs. W Sus ........5C 26
Bottacks. High .........2G 157
Bottesford. Leics .......2F 75
Bottesford. N Lin .......4B 94
Bottisham. Cambs .......4E 65
Bottlesford. Wilts ......1G 23
Bottomcraig. Fife .......1F 137
Bottom o' th' Moor.
  G Man ...............3E 91

Botton. N Yor ...........4D 107
Botton Head. Lanc .......3F 97
Bottreaux Mill. Devn .....4B 20
Botus Fleming. Corn ......2A 8
Botwnnog. Gwyn .........2B 68
Bough Beech. Kent .......1F 27
Boughrood. Powy .........2E 47
Boughspring. Glos .......2A 34
Boughton. Norf ..........5F 77
Boughton. Nptn ..........4E 63
Boughton. Notts .........4D 86
Boughton Aluph. Kent ....1E 29
Boughton Green. Kent ....5B 40
Boughton Lees. Kent .....1E 28
Boughton Malherbe. Kent .1C 28
Boughton Monchelsea.
  Kent .................5B 40
Boughton under Blean.
  Kent .................5E 41
Bouldby. Red C ..........3E 107
Bouldnor. IOW ..........4B 16
Bouldon. Shrp ..........2H 59
Boulder. Nmbd ..........3G 121
Boulston. Pemb ..........3D 42
Boultham. Linc .........4G 87
Boulton. Derb ..........2A 74
Bournbrook. W Mid ......2E 61
Bourne. Linc ...........3H 75
The Bourne. Surr .......2G 25
Bourne End. Bed ........4H 63
Bourne End. Buck .......3G 37
Bourne End. C Beds .....1H 51
Bourne End. Herts ......5A 52
Bournemouth. Bour .......3F 15
Bournemouth Airport.
  Dors ................3G 15
Bournes Green. Glos ....5E 49
Bournes Green. S'end ....2D 40
Bournheath. Worc .......3D 60
Bournmoor. Dur .........4G 115
Bournville. W Mid ......2E 61
Bourton. Dors ..........3C 22
Bourton. N Som .........5G 33
Bourton. Oxon ..........3H 35
Bourton. Shrp ..........1H 59
Bourton. Wilts .........5F 35
Bourton on Dunsmore.
  Warw ................3B 62
Bourton-on-the-Hill. Glos .2G 49
Bourton-on-the-Water.
  Glos ................3G 49
Bousd. Arg ............2D 138
Bousta. Shet ..........6D 173
Boustead Hill. Cumb ....4D 112
Bouth. Cumb ...........1C 96
Bouthwaite. N Yor ......2D 98
Boveney. Buck .........3A 38
Boveridge. Dors ........1F 15
Boverton. V Glam .......5C 32
Bovey Tracey. Devn .....5B 12
Bovingdon. Herts .......5A 52
Bovingdon Green. Buck ...3G 37
Bovinger. Essx .........5F 53
Bovington Camp. Dors ...4D 14
Bow. Devn .............2H 11
Bowbank. Dur ..........2C 104
Bow Brickhill. Mil ......2H 51
Bowbridge. Glos ........5D 48
Bowburn. Dur ..........1A 106
Bowcombe. IOW ........4C 16
Bowd. Devn ...........4E 12
Bowden. Devn ..........4E 9
Bowden. Bord ..........1H 119
Bowden Hill. Wilts .....5E 35
Bowdens. Som .........4H 21
Bowderdale. Cumb ......4H 103
Bowdon. G Man ........2B 84
Bower. Nmbd ..........1A 114
Bowerchalke. Wilts .....4F 23
Bowerhill. Wilts .......5E 35
Bower Hinton. Som .....1H 13

Bowermadden. High ......2E 169
Bowers. Staf ..........2C 72
Bowers Gifford. Essx ....2B 40
Bowershall. Fife .......4C 136
Bowertower. High .......2E 169
Bowes. Dur ............3C 104
Bowgreave. Lanc .......5D 97
Bowhousebog. N Lan ....4B 128
Bowithick. Corn ........4B 10
Bowland Bridge. Cumb ..1D 96
Bowlees. Dur ..........2C 104
Bowley. Here ..........5H 59
Bowlhead Green. Surr ...2A 26
Bowling. W Dun ........2F 127
Bowling. W Yor ........1B 92
Bowling Bank. Wrex .....1F 71
Bowling Green. Worc ....5C 60
Bowmanstead. Cumb .....5E 102
Bowmore. Arg ..........4B 124
Bowness-on-Solway.
  Cumb ................3D 112
Bowness-on-Windermere.
  Cumb ................5F 103
Bow of Fife. Fife ......2F 137
Bowriefauld. Ang .......4E 145
Bowscale. Cumb ........1E 103
Bowsden. Nmbd .........5F 131
Bowside Lodge. High ....2A 168
Bowston. Cumb .........5F 103
Bow Street. Cdgn .......2F 57
Bowthorpe. Norf ........5D 78
Box. Glos .............5D 48
Box. Wilts ............5D 34
Boxbush. Glos .........3B 48
Box End. Bed ..........1A 52
Boxford. Suff .........1C 54
Boxford. W Ber ........4C 36
Boxgrove. W Sus .......5A 26
Box Hill. Wilts ........5D 34
Boxley. Kent ..........5B 40
Boxmoor. Herts ........5A 52
Box's Shop. Corn ......2C 10
Boxted. Essx ..........2C 54
Boxted. Suff ..........5H 65
Boxted Cross. Essx .....2D 54
Boxworth. Cambs .......4C 64
Boxworth End. Cambs ...4C 64
Boyden Gate. Kent ......4G 41
Boylestone. Derbs ......2F 73
Boynton. E Yor .........3F 101
Boys Hill. Dors ........1B 14
Boythorpe. Derbs .......4A 86
Boyton. Corn ..........3D 10
Boyton. Suff ..........1G 55
Boyton. Wilts .........3E 23
Boyton Cross. Essx .....5G 53
Boyton End. Essx .......2G 53
Boyton End. Suff .......1H 53
Bozeat. Nptn ..........5G 63
Braaid. IOM ...........4C 108
Brabling Green. Suff ....4E 67
Brabourne. Kent .......1F 29
Brabourne Lees. Kent ...1E 29
Brabster. High .........2F 169
Bracadale. High ........5C 154
Braceborough. Linc .....4H 75
Bracebridge. Linc ......4G 87
Bracebridge Heath. Linc .4G 87
Braceby. Linc .........2H 75
Bracewell. Lanc ........5A 98
Brackenber. Cumb .......3A 104
Brackenfield. Derbs .....5A 86
Brackenlands. Cumb .....5D 112
Brackenthwaite. Cumb ...5D 112
Brackenthwaite. N Yor ...4E 99
Brackla. B'end .........4C 32
Brackla. High .........3C 158
Bracklesham. W Sus .....3G 17

Brackletter. High ......5D 148
Brackley. Nptn ........2D 50
Brackley Hatch. Nptn ...1E 51
Brackloch. High ........1F 163
Bracknell. Brac ........5G 37
Braco. Per ............3H 135
Bracobrae. Mor ........3C 160
Bracon. N Lin ........4A 94
Bracon Ash. Norf .......1D 66
Bradbourne. Derbs .....5G 85
Bradbury. Dur .........2A 106
Bradda. IOM ...........4A 108
Bradden. Nptn .........1E 51
Bradenham. Buck .......2G 37
Bradenham. Norf .......5B 78
Bradenstoke. Wilts .....4F 35
Bradfield. Essx ........2E 55
Bradfield. Norf ........2E 79
Bradfield. W Ber .......4E 36
Bradfield Combust. Suff .5A 66
Bradfield Green. Ches E .5A 84
Bradfield Heath. Essx ...3E 55
Bradfield St Clare. Suff .5B 66
Bradfield St George. Suff .4B 66
Bradford. Derbs ........4G 85
Bradford. Devn .........2E 11
Bradford. Nmbd ........1F 121
Bradford. W Yor .......1B 92
Bradford Abbas. Dors ...1A 14
Bradford Barton. Devn ..1B 12
Bradford Leigh. Wilts ...5D 34
Bradford-on-Avon. Wilts .5D 34
Bradford-on-Tone. Som ..4E 21
Bradford Peverell. Dors .3B 14
Bradiford. Devn ........3F 19
Brading. IOW ..........4E 16
Bradley. Ches W .......3H 83
Bradley. Derbs .........1G 73
Bradley. Glos ..........2C 34
Bradley. Hants ........2E 25
Bradley. NE Lin .......4F 95
Bradley. N Yor .........1C 98
Bradley. Staf ..........4C 72
Bradley. W Mid ........1D 60
Bradley. W Yor ........2B 92
Bradley. Wrex .........5F 83
Bradley Cross. Som .....1H 21
Bradley Green. Ches W ..1H 71
Bradley Green. Som .....3F 21
Bradley Green. Warw ....5G 73
Bradley Green. Worc ....4D 61
Bradley in the Moors. Staf .1E 73
Bradley Stoke. S Glo ....3A 34
Bradlow. Here .........2C 48
Bradmore. Notts .......2C 74
Bradmore. W Mid .......1C 60
Bradninch. Devn .......2D 12
Bradnop. Staf .........5E 85
Bradpole. Dors ........3H 13
Bradshaw. G Man .......3F 91
Bradstone. Devn .......4D 11
Bradwall Green. Ches E ..4B 84
Bradway. S Yor ........2H 85
Bradwell. Derbs ........2F 85
Bradwell. Essx ........3B 54
Bradwell. Mil .........2G 51
Bradwell. Norf .........5H 79
Bradwell-on-Sea. Essx ..5D 54
Bradwell Waterside. Essx .5C 54
Bradworthy. Devn .......1D 10
Brae. High ............5C 162
Brae. Shet ............5E 173
Braeantra. High ........1H 157
Braefield. High ........5G 157
Braefindon. High .......3A 158
Braegrum. Per .........1C 136
Braehead. Ang .........3F 145
Braehead. Dum .........4B 110
Braehead. Orkn ........3D 172
Braehead. S Lan
  nr. Coalburn ........1H 117
  nr. Forth ...........4C 128

Braehoulland—Broadfield


Braehoulland. *Shet* 4D **173**
Braemar. *Abers* 4F **151**
Braemore. *High*
nr. Dunbeath 5C **168**
nr. Ullapool 1D **156**
Brae of Achnahaird. *High* 2E **163**
Brae Roy Lodge. *High* 4F **149**
Braeside. *Abers* 5G **161**
Braeside. *Inv* 2D **126**
Braes of Coul. *Ang* 3B **144**
Braeswick. *Orkn* 4F **172**
Braetongue. *High* 3F **167**
Braeval. *Stir* 3E **135**
Braevallich. *Arg* 3G **133**
Braewick. *Shet* 6E **173**
Brafferton. *Darl* 2F **105**
Brafferton. *N Yor* 2G **99**
Brafield-on-the-Green. *Nptn* 5F **63**
Bragar. *W Isl* 3E **171**
Bragbury End. *Herts* 3C **52**
Bragleenbeg. *Arg* 1G **133**
Braichmelyn. *Gwyn* 4F **81**
Braides. *Lanc* 4D **96**
Braidwood. *S Lan* 5B **128**
Braigo. *Arg* 3A **124**
Brailsford. *Derbs* 1G **73**
**Braintree**. *Essx* 3A **54**
Braiseworth. *Suff* 3D **66**
Braishfield. *Hants* 4B **24**
Braithwaite. *Cumb* 2D **102**
Braithwaite. *S Yor* 3G **93**
Braithwaite. *W Yor* 5C **98**
Braithwell. *S Yor* 1C **86**
Brakefield Green. *Norf* 5C **78**
Bramber. *W Sus* 4C **26**
Brambridge. *Hants* 4C **24**
Bramcote. *Notts* 2C **74**
Bramcote. *Warw* 2B **62**
Bramdean. *Hants* 4E **24**
Bramerton. *Norf* 5E **79**
Bramfield. *Herts* 4C **52**
Bramfield. *Suff* 3F **67**
Bramford. *Suff* 1E **54**
**Bramhall**. *G Man* 2C **84**
Bramham. *W Yor* 5G **99**
Bramhope. *W Yor* 5E **99**
Bramley. *Hants* 1E **25**
Bramley. *S Yor* 1B **86**
Bramley. *Surr* 1B **26**
Bramley. *W Yor* 1C **92**
Bramley Green. *Hants* 1E **25**
Bramley Head. *N Yor* 4D **98**
Bramley Vale. *Derbs* 4B **86**
Bramling. *Kent* 5G **41**
Brampford Speke. *Devn* 3C **12**
Brampton. *Cambs* 3B **64**
Brampton. *Cumb*
nr. Appleby-in-Westmorland 2H **103**
nr. Carlisle 3G **113**
Brampton. *Linc* 3F **87**
Brampton. *Norf* 3E **78**
Brampton. *S Yor* 4E **93**
Brampton. *Suff* 2G **67**
Brampton Abbotts. *Here* 3B **48**
Brampton Ash. *Nptn* 2E **63**
Brampton Bryan. *Here* 3F **59**
Brampton en le Morthen. *S Yor* 2B **86**
Bramshall. *Staf* 2E **73**
Bramshaw. *Hants* 1A **16**
Bramshill. *Hants* 5F **37**
Bramshott. *Hants* 3G **25**
Branault. *High* 2G **139**
Brancaster. *Norf* 1G **77**
Brancaster Staithe. *Norf* 1G **77**
Brancepeth. *Dur* 1F **105**
Branch End. *Nmbd* 3D **114**
Branchill. *Mor* 3E **159**
Brand End. *Linc* 1C **76**
Branderburgh. *Mor* 1G **159**
Brandesburton. *E Yor* 5F **101**
Brandeston. *Suff* 4E **67**
Brand Green. *Glos* 3C **48**
Brandhill. *Shrp* 3G **59**
Brandis Corner. *Devn* 2E **11**
Brandish Street. *Som* 2C **20**
Brandiston. *Norf* 3D **78**
Brandon. *Dur* 1F **105**
Brandon. *Linc* 1G **75**
Brandon. *Nmbd* 3E **121**
Brandon. *Suff* 2G **65**
Brandon. *Warw* 3B **62**
Brandon Bank. *Cambs* 2F **65**
Brandon Creek. *Norf* 1F **65**
Brandon Parva. *Norf* 5C **78**
Brandsby. *N Yor* 2H **99**
Brandy Wharf. *Linc* 1H **87**
Brane. *Corn* 4B **4**
Bran End. *Essx* 3G **53**
Branksome. *Pool* 3F **15**
Bransbury. *Hants* 2C **24**
Bransby. *Linc* 3F **87**
Branscombe. *Devn* 4E **13**
Bransford. *Worc* 5B **60**
Bransgore. *Hants* 3G **15**
Bransholme. *Hull* 1E **94**
Bransley. *Shrp* 3A **60**
Branston. *Leics* 3F **75**
Branston. *Linc* 4H **87**
Branston. *Staf* 3G **73**
Branston Booths. *Linc* 4H **87**
Branstone. *IOW* 4D **16**
Bransty. *Cumb* 3A **102**
Brant Broughton. *Linc* 5G **87**
Brantham. *Suff* 2E **54**
Branthwaite. *Cumb*
nr. Caldbeck 1D **102**
nr. Workington 2B **102**
Brantingham. *E Yor* 2C **94**
Branton. *Nmbd* 3E **121**
Branton. *S Yor* 4G **93**
Branton Green. *N Yor* 3G **99**
Branxholme. *Bord* 3G **119**
Branxton. *Nmbd* 1C **120**
Brassington. *Derbs* 5G **85**
Brasted. *Kent* 5F **39**
Brasted Chart. *Kent* 5F **39**
The Bratch. *Staf* 1C **60**
Brathens. *Abers* 4D **152**
Bratoft. *Linc* 4D **88**
Brattleby. *Linc* 2G **87**
Bratton. *Som* 2C **20**
Bratton. *Telf* 4A **72**
Bratton. *Wilts* 1E **23**
Bratton Clovelly. *Devn* 3E **11**
Bratton Fleming. *Devn* 3G **19**
Bratton Seymour. *Som* 4B **22**
Braughing. *Herts* 3D **53**
Braulen Lodge. *High* 5E **157**
Braunston. *Nptn* 4C **62**
Braunstone Town. *Leics* 5C **74**
Braunston-in-Rutland. *Rut* 5F **75**
Braunton. *Devn* 3E **19**
Brawby. *N Yor* 2B **100**
Brawl. *High* 2A **168**
Brawlbin. *High* 3C **168**
Bray. *Wind* 3A **38**
Braybrooke. *Nptn* 2E **63**
Brayford. *Devn* 3G **19**
Bray Shop. *Corn* 5D **10**
Braystones. *Cumb* 4B **102**
Brayton. *N Yor* 1G **93**
Bray Wick. *Wind* 4G **37**
Brazacott. *Corn* 3C **10**
Brea. *Corn* 4A **6**
Breach. *W Sus* 2F **17**
Breachwood Green. *Herts* 3B **52**
Breacleit. *W Isl* 4D **171**
Breaden Heath. *Shrp* 2G **71**
Breadsall. *Derbs* 1A **74**
Breadstone. *Glos* 5C **48**
Breage. *Corn* 4D **4**
Breakachy. *High* 4G **157**
Breakish. *High* 1E **147**
Bream. *Glos* 5B **48**
Breamore. *Hants* 1G **15**
Bream's Meend. *Glos* 5B **48**
Brean. *Som* 1F **21**
Breanais. *W Isl* 5B **171**
Brearton. *N Yor* 3F **99**
Breascleit. *W Isl* 4E **171**
Breaston. *Derbs* 2B **74**
Brecais Ard. *High* 1E **147**
Brecais Iosal. *High* 1E **147**
Brechfa. *Carm* 2F **45**
Brechin. *Ang* 3F **145**
Breckles. *Norf* 1B **66**
Brecon. *Powy* 3D **46**
**Bredbury**. *G Man* 1D **84**
Brede. *E Sus* 4C **28**
Bredenbury. *Here* 5A **60**
Bredfield. *Suff* 5E **67**
Bredgar. *Kent* 4C **40**
Bredhurst. *Kent* 4B **40**
Bredicot. *Worc* 5D **60**
Bredon. *Worc* 2E **49**
Bredon's Norton. *Worc* 2E **49**
Bredwardine. *Here* 1G **47**
Breedon on the Hill. *Leics* 3B **74**
Breibhig. *W Isl*
on Barra 9B **170**
on Isle of Lewis 4G **171**
Breich. *W Lot* 3C **128**
Breightmet. *G Man* 4F **91**
Breighton. *E Yor* 1H **93**
Breinton. *Here* 2H **47**
Breinton Common. *Here* 2H **47**
Breiwick. *Shet* 7F **173**
Brelston Green. *Here* 3A **48**
Bremhill. *Wilts* 4E **35**
Brenachie. *High* 1B **158**
Brenchley. *Kent* 1A **28**
Brendon. *Devn* 2A **20**
**Brent Cross**. *G Lon* 2D **38**
Brent Eleigh. *Suff* 1C **54**
**Brentford**. *G Lon* 3C **38**
Brentingby. *Leics* 4E **75**
Brent Knoll. *Som* 1G **21**
Brent Pelham. *Herts* 2E **53**
**Brentwood**. *Essx* 1G **39**
Brenzett. *Kent* 3E **28**
Brereton. *Staf* 4E **73**
Brereton Cross. *Staf* 4E **73**
Brereton Green. *Ches E* 4B **84**
Brereton Heath. *Ches E* 4C **84**
Bressingham. *Norf* 2C **66**
Bretby. *Derbs* 3G **73**
Bretford. *Warw* 3B **62**
Bretforton. *Worc* 1F **49**
Bretherdale Head. *Cumb* 4G **103**
Bretherton. *Lanc* 2C **90**
Brettabister. *Shet* 6F **173**
Brettenham. *Norf* 2B **66**
Brettenham. *Suff* 5B **66**
Bretton. *Flin* 4F **83**
Bretton. *Pet* 5A **76**
Brewlands Bridge. *Ang* 2A **144**
Brewood. *Staf* 5C **72**
Briantspuddle. *Dors* 3D **14**
Bricket Wood. *Herts* 5B **52**
Bricklehampton. *Worc* 1E **49**
Bride. *IOM* 1D **108**
Bridekirk. *Cumb* 1C **102**
Bridell. *Pemb* 1B **44**
Bridestowe. *Devn* 4F **11**
Brideswell. *Abers* 5C **160**
Bridford. *Devn* 4B **12**
Bridge. *Corn* 4A **6**
Bridge. *Kent* 5F **41**
Bridge. *Som* 2G **13**
Bridge End. *Bed* 5H **63**
Bridge End. *Cumb*
nr. Broughton in Furness 5D **102**
nr. Dalston 5E **113**
Bridge End. *Linc* 2A **76**
Bridge End. *Shet* 8E **173**
Bridgefoot. *Ang* 5C **144**
Bridgefoot. *Cumb* 2B **102**
Bridge Green. *Essx* 2E **53**
Bridgehampton. *Som* 4A **22**
Bridge Hewick. *N Yor* 2F **99**
Bridgehill. *Dur* 4D **115**
Bridgemary. *Hants* 2D **16**
Bridgemere. *Ches E* 1B **72**
Bridgemont. *Derbs* 2E **85**
Bridgend. *Abers*
nr. Huntly 5C **160**
nr. Peterhead 5H **161**
Bridgend. *Ang*
nr. Brechin 2E **145**
nr. Kirriemuir 4C **144**
Bridgend. *Arg*
nr. Lochgilphead 4F **133**
on Islay 3B **124**
**Bridgend**. *B'end* 3C **32**
Bridgend. *Cumb* 3E **103**
Bridgend. *Devn* 4B **8**
Bridgend. *Fife* 2F **137**
Bridgend. *High* 3F **157**
Bridgend. *Mor* 5A **160**
Bridgend. *Per* 1D **136**
Bridgend. *W Lot* 2D **128**
Bridgend of Lintrathen. *Ang* 3B **144**
Bridgeness. *Falk* 1D **128**
Bridge of Alford. *Abers* 2C **152**
Bridge of Allan. *Stir* 4G **135**
Bridge of Avon. *Mor* 5F **159**
Bridge of Awe. *Arg* 1H **133**
Bridge of Balgie. *Per* 4C **142**
Bridge of Brown. *High* 1F **151**
Bridge of Cally. *Per* 3A **144**
Bridge of Canny. *Abers* 4D **152**
Bridge of Dee. *Dum* 3E **111**
Bridge of Don. *Aber* 2G **153**
Bridge of Dun. *Ang* 3F **145**
Bridge of Dye. *Abers* 5D **152**
Bridge of Earn. *Per* 2D **136**
Bridge of Ericht. *Per* 3C **142**
Bridge of Feugh. *Abers* 4E **152**
Bridge of Gairn. *Abers* 4A **152**
Bridge of Gaur. *Per* 3C **142**
Bridge of Muchalls. *Abers* 4F **153**
Bridge of Oich. *High* 3F **149**
Bridge of Orchy. *Arg* 5H **141**
Bridge of Walls. *Shet* 6D **173**
Bridge of Weir. *Ren* 3E **127**
Bridge Reeve. *Devn* 1G **11**
Bridgerule. *Devn* 2C **10**
Bridge Sollers. *Here* 1H **47**
Bridge Street. *Suff* 1B **54**
Bridge Town. *Warw* 5G **61**
Bridgetown. *Devn* 2E **9**
Bridgetown. *Som* 3C **20**
Bridge Trafford. *Ches W* 3G **83**
Bridgeyate. *S Glo* 4B **34**
Bridgham. *Norf* 2B **66**
**Bridgnorth**. *Shrp* 1B **60**
Bridgtown. *Staf* 5D **73**
**Bridgwater**. *Som* 3G **21**
**Bridlington**. *E Yor* 3F **101**
**Bridport**. *Dors* 3H **13**
Bridstow. *Here* 3A **48**
**Brierfield**. *Lanc* 1G **91**
Brierley. *Glos* 4B **48**
Brierley. *Here* 5G **59**
Brierley. *S Yor* 3E **93**
Brierley Hill. *W Mid* 2D **60**
Brierton. *Hart* 1B **106**
Briestfield. *W Yor* 3C **92**
Brigg. *N Lin* 4D **94**
Briggate. *Norf* 3F **79**
Briggswath. *N Yor* 4F **107**
Brigham. *Cumb* 1B **102**
Brigham. *E Yor* 4E **101**
**Brighouse**. *W Yor* 2B **92**
Brighstone. *IOW* 4C **16**
Brightgate. *Derbs* 5G **85**
Brighthampton. *Oxon* 5B **50**
Brightholmlee. *S Yor* 1G **85**
Brightley. *Devn* 3G **11**
Brightling. *E Sus* 3A **28**
Brightlingsea. *Essx* 4D **54**
**Brighton**. *Brig* 5E **27**
Brighton. *Corn* 3D **6**
Brighton Hill. *Hants* 2E **24**
Brightons. *Falk* 2C **128**
Brightwalton. *W Ber* 4C **36**
Brightwalton Green. *W Ber* 4C **36**
Brightwell. *Suff* 1F **55**
Brightwell Baldwin. *Oxon* 2E **37**
Brightwell-cum-Sotwell. *Oxon* 2D **36**
Brigmerston. *Wilts* 2G **23**
Brignall. *Dur* 3D **104**
Brig o' Turk. *Stir* 3E **135**
Brigsley. *NE Lin* 4F **95**
Brigsteer. *Cumb* 1D **97**
Brigstock. *Nptn* 2G **63**
Brill. *Buck* 4E **51**
Brill. *Corn* 4E **5**
Brilley. *Here* 1F **47**
Brimaston. *Pemb* 2D **42**
Brimfield. *Here* 4H **59**
Brimington. *Derbs* 3B **86**
Brimley. *Devn* 5B **12**
Brimpsfield. *Glos* 4E **49**
Brimpton. *W Ber* 5D **36**
Brims. *Orkn* 9B **172**
Brimscombe. *Glos* 5D **48**
Brimstage. *Mers* 2F **83**
Brincliffe. *S Yor* 2H **85**
Brind. *E Yor* 1H **93**
Brindister. *Shet*
nr. West Burrafirth 6D **173**
nr. West Lerwick 8F **173**
Brindle. *Lanc* 2D **90**
Brindley. *Ches E* 5H **83**
Brindley Ford. *Stoke* 5C **84**
Brineton. *Staf* 4C **72**
Bringhurst. *Leics* 1F **63**
Bringsty Common. *Here* 5A **60**
Brington. *Cambs* 3H **63**
Brinian. *Orkn* 5D **172**
Briningham. *Norf* 2C **78**
Brinkhill. *Linc* 3C **88**
Brinkley. *Cambs* 5F **65**
Brinklow. *Warw* 3B **62**
Brinkworth. *Wilts* 3F **35**
Brinscall. *Lanc* 2E **91**
Brinscombe. *Som* 1H **21**
Brinsley. *Notts* 1B **74**
Brinsworth. *S Yor* 2B **86**
Brinton. *Norf* 2C **78**
Brisco. *Cumb* 4F **113**
Brisley. *Norf* 3B **78**
Brislington. *Bris* 4B **34**
Brissenden Green. *Kent* 2D **28**
**Bristol**. *Bris* 4A **34**
Bristol Airport. *N Som* 5A **34**
Briston. *Norf* 2C **78**
Britannia. *Lanc* 2G **91**
Britford. *Wilts* 4G **23**
Brithdir. *Cphy* 5E **47**
Brithdir. *Cdgn* 1D **44**
Brithdir. *Gwyn* 4G **69**
Briton Ferry. *Neat* 3G **31**
Britwell Salome. *Oxon* 2E **37**
**Brixham**. *Torb* 3F **9**
Brixton. *Devn* 3B **8**
**Brixton**. *G Lon* 3E **39**
Brixton Deverill. *Wilts* 3D **22**
Brixworth. *Nptn* 3E **63**
Brize Norton. *Oxon* 5B **50**
The Broad. *Here* 4G **59**
Broad Alley. *Worc* 4C **60**
Broad Blunsdon. *Swin* 2G **35**
Broadbottom. *G Man* 1D **85**
Broadbridge. *W Sus* 2G **17**
Broadbridge Heath. *W Sus* 2C **26**
Broad Campden. *Glos* 2G **49**
Broad Chalke. *Wilts* 4F **23**
Broadclyst. *Devn* 3C **12**
Broadfield. *Inv* 2E **127**

# Broadfield—Buckland



Broadfield. *Pemb* 4F 43
Broadfield. *W Sus* 2D 26
Broadford. *High* 1E 147
Broadford Bridge. *W Sus* 3B 26
Broadgate. *Cumb* 1A 96
Broad Green. *Cambs* 5F 65
Broad Green. *C Beds* 1H 51
Broad Green. *Worc*
nr. Bromsgrove 3D 61
nr. Worcester 5B 60
Broad Haven. *Pemb* 3C 42
Broadhaven. *High* 3F 169
Broad Heath. *Staf* 3C 72
Broadheath. *G Man* 2B 84
Broadheath. *Worc* 4A 60
Broadheath Common. *Worc* 5C 60
Broadhembury. *Devn* 2E 12
Broadhempston. *Devn* 2E 9
Broad Hill. *Cambs* 3E 65
Broad Hinton. *Wilts* 4G 35
Broadholme. *Derbs* 1A 74
Broadholme. *Linc* 3F 87
Broadlay. *Carm* 5D 44
Broad Laying. *Hants* 5C 36
Broadley. *Lanc* 3G 91
Broadley. *Mor* 2A 160
Broadley Common. *Essx* 5E 53
Broad Marston. *Worc* 1G 49
Broadmayne. *Dors* 4C 14
Broadmere. *Hants* 2E 24
Broadmoor. *Pemb* 4E 43
Broad Oak. *Carm* 3F 45
Broad Oak. *Cumb* 5C 102
Broad Oak. *Devn* 3D 12
Broad Oak. *Dors* 1C 14
Broad Oak. *E Sus*
nr. Hastings 4C 28
nr. Heathfield 3H 27
Broad Oak. *Here* 3H 47
Broad Oak. *Kent* 4F 41
Broadoak. *Dors* 3H 13
Broadoak. *Glos* 4B 48
Broadoak. *Hants* 1D 16
Broadrashes. *Mor* 3B 160
Broadsea. *Abers* 2G 161
Broad's Green. *Essx* 4G 53
Broadshard. *Som* 1H 13
**Broadstairs**. *Kent* 4H 41
Broadstone. *Pool* 3F 15
Broadstone. *Shrp* 2H 59
Broad Street. *E Sus* 4C 28
Broad Street. *Kent*
nr. Ashford 1F 29
nr. Maidstone 5C 40
Broad Street Green. *Essx* 5B 54
Broad Town. *Wilts* 4F 35
Broadwas. *Worc* 5B 60
Broadwath. *Cumb* 4F 113
Broadway. *Carm*
nr. Kidwelly 5D 45
nr. Laugharne 4G 43
Broadway. *Pemb* 3C 42
Broadway. *Som* 1G 13
Broadway. *Suff* 3F 67
Broadway. *Worc* 2F 49
Broadwell. *Glos*
nr. Cinderford 4A 48
nr. Stow-on-the-Wold 3H 49
Broadwell. *Oxon* 5A 50
Broadwell. *Warw* 4B 62
Broadwell House. *Nmbd* 4C 114
Broadwey. *Dors* 4B 14
Broadwindsor. *Dors* 2H 13
Broadwoodkelly. *Devn* 2G 11
Broadwoodwidger. *Devn* 4E 11
Broallan. *High* 4G 157
Brobury. *Here* 1G 47
Brochel. *High* 4E 155
Brockamin. *Worc* 5B 60
Brockbridge. *Hants* 1E 16
Brockdish. *Norf* 3E 66
Brockencote. *Worc* 3C 60
Brockenhurst. *Hants* 2A 16
Brocketsbrae. *S Lan* 1H 117
Brockford Street. *Suff* 4D 66
Brockhall. *Nptn* 4D 62
Brockham. *Surr* 1C 26
Brockhampton. *Glos*
nr. Bishop's Cleeve 3E 49
nr. Sevenhampton 3F 49
Brockhampton. *Here* 2A 48
Brockhill. *Bord* 2F 119
Brockholes. *W Yor* 3B 92
Brockhurst. *Hants* 2D 16
Brocklesby. *Linc* 3E 95
Brockley. *N Som* 5H 33
Brockley Corner. *Suff* 3H 65
Brockley Green. *Suff*
nr. Bury St Edmunds 1H 53
nr. Haverhill 5H 65
Brockleymoor. *Cumb* 1F 103
Brockmoor. *W Mid* 2D 60
Brockton. *Shrp*
nr. Bishop's Castle 2F 59
nr. Madeley 5B 72
nr. Much Wenlock 1H 59
nr. Pontesbury 5F 71
Brockton. *Staf* 2C 72
Brockton. *Telf* 4B 72
Brockweir. *Glos* 5A 48
Brockworth. *Glos* 4D 49
Brocton. *Staf* 4D 72
Brodick. *N Ayr* 2E 123
Brodie. *Mor* 3D 159
Brodiesord. *Abers* 3C 160
Brodsworth. *S Yor* 4F 93
Brogaig. *High* 2D 154
Brogborough. *C Beds* 2H 51
Brokenborough. *Wilts* 3E 35
Broken Cross. *Ches E* 3C 84
Bromborough. *Mers* 2F 83
Bromdon. *Shrp* 2A 60
Brome. *Suff* 3D 66
Brome Street. *Suff* 3D 66
Bromeswell. *Suff* 5F 67
Bromfield. *Cumb* 5C 112
Bromfield. *Shrp* 3G 59
Bromford. *W Mid* 1F 61
Bromham. *Bed* 5H 63
Bromham. *Wilts* 5E 35
**Bromley**. *G Lon* 4F 39
Bromley. *Herts* 3E 53
Bromley. *Shrp* 1B 60
Bromley Cross. *G Man* 3F 91
Bromley Green. *Kent* 2D 28
Bromley Wood. *Staf* 3F 73
Brompton. *Medw* 4B 40
Brompton. *N Yor*
nr. Northallerton 5A 106
nr. Scarborough 1D 100
Brompton. *Shrp* 5H 71
Brompton-on-Swale.
*N Yor* 5F 105
Brompton Ralph. *Som* 3D 20
Brompton Regis. *Som* 3C 20
Bromsash. *Here* 3B 48
Bromsberrow. *Glos* 2C 48
Bromsberrow Heath. *Glos* 2C 48
**Bromsgrove**. *Worc* 3D 60
Bromstead Heath. *Staf* 4B 72
Bromyard. *Here* 5A 60
Bromyard Downs. *Here* 5A 60
Bronaber. *Gwyn* 2G 69
Broncroft. *Shrp* 2H 59
Brongest. *Cdgn* 1D 44
Brongwyn. *Cdgn* 1C 44
Bronington. *Wrex* 2G 71
Bronllys. *Powy* 2E 47
Bronnant. *Cdgn* 4F 57
Bronwydd Arms. *Carm* 3E 45
Bronydd. *Powy* 1F 47
Bronygarth. *Shrp* 2E 71
Brook. *Carm* 4G 43
Brook. *Hants*
nr. Cadnam 1A 16
nr. Romsey 4B 24
Brook. *IOW* 4B 16
Brook. *Kent* 1E 29
Brook. *Surr*
nr. Guildford 1B 26
nr. Haslemere 2A 26
Brooke. *Norf* 1E 67
Brooke. *Rut* 5F 75
Brookenby. *Linc* 1B 88
Brook End. *Worc* 1D 48
Brookend. *Glos* 5B 48
Brookfield. *Lanc* 1D 90
Brookfield. *Ren* 3F 127
Brookhouse. *Lanc* 3E 97
Brookhouse. *S Yor* 2C 86
Brookhouse Green.
*Ches E* 4C 84
Brookhouses. *Staf* 1D 73
Brookhurst. *Mers* 2F 83
Brookland. *Kent* 3D 28
Brooklands. *G Man* 1B 84
Brooklands. *Shrp* 1H 71
Brookmans Park. *Herts* 5C 52
Brooks. *Powy* 1D 58
Brooksby. *Leics* 4D 74
Brooks Green. *W Sus* 3C 26
Brook Street. *Essx* 1G 39
Brook Street. *Kent* 2D 28
Brook Street. *W Sus* 3E 27
Brookthorpe. *Glos* 4D 48
Brookville. *Norf* 1G 65
Brookwood. *Surr* 5A 38
Broom. *C Beds* 1B 52
Broom. *Fife* 3F 137
Broom. *Warw* 5E 61
Broome. *Norf* 1F 67
Broome. *Shrp*
nr. Cardington 1H 59
nr. Craven Arms 2G 59
Broome. *Worc* 3D 60
Broomedge. *Warr* 2B 84
Broomend. *Abers* 2E 153
Broomer's Corner. *W Sus* 3C 26
Broomfield. *Abers* 5G 161
Broomfield. *Essx* 4H 53
Broomfield. *Kent*
nr. Herne Bay 4F 41
nr. Maidstone 5C 40
Broomfield. *Som* 3F 21
Broomfleet. *E Yor* 2B 94
Broom Green. *Norf* 3B 78
Broomhall. *Ches E* 1A 72
Broomhall. *Wind* 4A 38
Broomhaugh. *Nmbd* 3D 114
Broom Hill. *Dors* 2F 15
Broom Hill. *Worc* 3D 60
Broomhill. *High*
nr. Grantown-on-Spey
1D 151
nr. Invergordon 1B 158
Broomhill. *Norf* 5F 77
Broomhill. *S Yor* 4E 93
Broomhillbank. *Dum* 5D 118
Broomholm. *Norf* 2F 79
Broomlands. *Dum* 4C 118
Broomley. *Nmbd* 3D 114
Broom of Moy. *Mor* 3E 159
Broompark. *Dur* 5F 115
Broom's Green. *Glos* 2C 48
Brora. *High* 3G 165
Broseley. *Shrp* 5A 72
Brotherhouse Bar. *Linc* 4B 76
Brotheridge Green. *Worc* 1D 48
Brotherlee. *Dur* 1C 104
Brothertoft. *Linc* 1B 76
Brotherton. *N Yor* 2E 93
Brotton. *Red C* 3D 107
Broubster. *High* 2C 168
Brough. *Cumb* 3A 104
Brough. *Derbs* 2F 85
Brough. *E Yor* 2C 94
Brough. *High* 1E 169
Brough. *Notts* 5F 87
Brough. *Orkn*
nr. Finstown 6C 172
nr. St Margaret's Hope
9D 172
Brough. *Shet*
nr. Benston 6F 173
nr. Booth of Toft 4F 173
on Bressay 7G 173
on Whalsay 5G 173
Broughall. *Shrp* 1H 71
Brougham. *Cumb* 2G 103
Brough Lodge. *Shet* 2G 173
Broughshane. *ME Ant* 2G 175
Brough Sowerby. *Cumb* 3A 104
Broughton. *Cambs* 3B 64
Broughton. *Flin* 4F 83
Broughton. *Hants* 3B 24
Broughton. *Lanc* 1D 90
Broughton. *Mil* 2G 51
Broughton. *Nptn* 3F 63
Broughton. *N Lin* 4C 94
Broughton. *N Yor*
nr. Malton 2B 100
nr. Skipton 4B 98
Broughton. *Orkn* 3D 172
Broughton. *Oxon* 2C 50
Broughton. *Bord* 1D 118
Broughton. *Staf* 2B 72
Broughton. *V Glam* 4C 32
Broughton Astley. *Leics* 1C 62
Broughton Beck. *Cumb* 1B 96
Broughton Cross. *Cumb* 1B 102
Broughton Gifford. *Wilts* 5D 35
Broughton Green. *Worc* 4D 60
Broughton Hackett. *Worc* 5D 60
Broughton in Furness. *Cumb* 1B 96
Broughton Mills. *Cumb* 5D 102
Broughton Moor. *Cumb* 1B 102
Broughton Park. *G Man* 4G 91
Broughton Poggs. *Oxon* 5H 49
Broughtown. *Orkn* 3F 172
Broughty Ferry. *D'dee* 5D 144
Browland. *Shet* 6D 173
Brownbread Street. *E Sus* 4A 28
Brown Candover. *Hants* 3D 24
Brown Edge. *Lanc* 3B 90
Brown Edge. *Staf* 5D 84
Brownhill. *Bkbn* 1E 91
Brownhill. *Shrp* 3G 71
Brownhills. *Shrp* 2A 72
**Brownhills**. *W Mid* 5E 73
Brown Knowl. *Ches W* 5G 83
Brownlow. *Ches E* 4C 84
Brownlow Heath. *Ches E* 4C 84
Brown's Green. *W Mid* 1E 61
Brownshill. *Glos* 5D 49
Brownston. *Devn* 3C 8
Brownstone. *Devn* 2A 12
Browston Green. *Norf* 5G 79
Broxa. *N Yor* 5G 107
Broxbourne. *Herts* 5D 52
Broxburn. *E Lot* 2C 130
**Broxburn**. *W Lot* 2D 128
Broxholme. *Linc* 3G 87
Broxted. *Essx* 3F 53
Broxton. *Ches W* 5G 83
Broxwood. *Here* 5F 59
Broyle Side. *E Sus* 4F 27
Brù. *W Isl* 3F 171
Bruach Mairi. *W Isl* 4G 171
Bruairnis. *W Isl* 8C 170
Bruan. *High* 5F 169
Bruar Lodge. *Per* 1F 143
Brucehill. *W Dun* 2E 127
Brucklay. *Abers* 3G 161
Bruera. *Ches W* 4G 83
Bruern Abbey. *Oxon* 3A 50
Bruichladdich. *Arg* 3A 124
Bruisyard. *Suff* 4F 67
Bruisyard Street. *Suff* 4F 67
Brund. *Staf* 4F 85
Brundall. *Norf* 5F 79
Brundish. *Norf* 1F 67
Brundish. *Suff* 4E 67
Brundish Street. *Suff* 3E 67
Brunery. *High* 1B 140
Brunswick Village. *Tyne* 2F 115
Brunthwaite. *W Yor* 5C 98
Bruntingthorpe. *Leics* 1D 62
Brunton. *Fife* 1F 137
Brunton. *Nmbd* 2G 121
Brunton. *Wilts* 1H 23
Brushford. *Devn* 2G 11
Brushford. *Som* 4C 20
Brusta. *W Isl* 1E 170
Bruton. *Som* 3B 22
Bryanston. *Dors* 2D 14
Bryant's Bottom. *Buck* 2G 37
Brydekirk. *Dum* 2C 112
Brymbo. *Cnwy* 3H 81
**Brymbo**. *Wrex* 5E 83
Brympton D'Evercy. *Som* 1A 14
Bryn. *Carm* 5F 45
Bryn. *G Man* 4D 90
Bryn. *Neat* 2B 32
Bryn. *Shrp* 2E 59
Brynamman. *Carm* 4H 45
Brynberian. *Pemb* 1F 43
Brynbryddan. *Neat* 2A 32
Bryncae. *Rhon* 3C 32
Bryncethin. *B'end* 3C 32
Bryncir. *Gwyn* 1D 69
Bryncoch. *Neat* 3G 31
Bryncroes. *Gwyn* 2B 68
Bryncrug. *Gwyn* 5F 69
Bryn Du. *IOA* 3C 80
Bryn Eden. *Gwyn* 3G 69
Bryn Eglwys. *Gwyn* 4F 81
Bryneglwys. *Den* 1D 70
Brynford. *Flin* 3D 82
Bryn Gates. *G Man* 4D 90
Bryn Golau. *Rhon* 3D 32
Bryngwran. *IOA* 3C 80
Bryngwyn. *Mon* 5G 47
Bryngwyn. *Powy* 1E 47
Bryn-henllan. *Pemb* 1E 43
Brynhoffnant. *Cdgn* 5C 56
Bryn-llwyn. *Den* 2C 82
Brynllywarch. *Powy* 2D 58
Bryn-mawr. *Gwyn* 2B 68
**Brynmawr**. *Blae* 4E 47
Brynmenyn. *B'end* 3C 32
Brynmill. *Swan* 3F 31
Brynna. *Rhon* 3C 32
Brynrefail. *Gwyn* 4E 81
Brynrefail. *IOA* 2D 81
Brynsadler. *Rhon* 3D 32
Bryn-Saith Marchog. *Den* 5C 82
Brynsiencyn. *IOA* 4D 81
Brynteg. *IOA* 2D 81
Brynteg. *Wrex* 5F 83
Brynygwenyn. *Mon* 4G 47
Bryn-y-maen. *Cnwy* 3H 81
Buaile nam Bodach.
*W Isl* 8C 170
Bualintur. *High* 1C 146
Bubbenhall. *Warw* 3A 62
Bubwith. *E Yor* 1H 93
Buccleuch. *Bord* 3F 119
Buchanan Smithy. *Stir* 1F 127
Buchanhaven. *Abers* 4H 161
Buchanty. *Per* 1B 136
Buchany. *Stir* 3G 135
Buchley. *E Dun* 2G 127
Buchlyvie. *Stir* 4E 135
Buckabank. *Cumb* 5E 113
Buckden. *Cambs* 4A 64
Buckden. *N Yor* 2B 98
Buckenham. *Norf* 5F 79
Buckerell. *Devn* 2E 12
Buckfast. *Devn* 2D 8
Buckfastleigh. *Devn* 2D 8
**Buckhaven**. *Fife* 4F 137
Buckholm. *Bord* 1G 119
Buckholt. *Here* 4A 48
Buckhorn Weston. *Dors* 4C 22
Buckhurst Hill. *Essx* 1F 39
Buckie. *Mor* 2B 160
**Buckingham**. *Buck* 2E 51
Buckland. *Buck* 4G 51
Buckland. *Glos* 2F 49
Buckland. *Here* 5H 59

Buckland. Herts ....................2D 52
Buckland. Kent .....................1H 29
Buckland. Oxon .....................2B 36
Buckland. Surr .....................5D 38
Buckland. Surr .....................4E 19
Buckland Brewer. Devn ..............4E 19
Buckland Common. Buck .............5H 51
Buckland Dinham. Som ..............1C 22
Buckland Filleigh. Devn ............2E 11
Buckland in the Moor. Devn .....5H 11
Buckland Monachorum.
   Devn ...........................2A 8
Buckland Newton. Dors .............2B 14
Buckland Ripers. Dors .............4B 14
Buckland St Mary. Som .............1F 13
Buckland-tout-Saints. Devn .........4D 8
Bucklebury. W Ber ..................4D 36
Bucklegate. Linc ...................2C 76
Buckleigh. Devn ....................4E 19
Buckler's Hard. Hants ..............3C 16
Bucklesham. Suff ...................1F 55
Buckley. Flin ......................4E 83
Buckley Green. Warw ...............4F 61
Buckley Hill. Mers .................1F 83
Bucklow Hill. Ches E ...............2B 84
Buckminster. Leics .................3F 75
Bucknall. Linc .....................4A 88
Bucknall. Stoke ....................1D 72
Bucknell. Oxon .....................3D 50
Bucknell. Shrp .....................3F 59
Buckpool. Mor .....................2B 160
Bucksburn. Aber ...................3F 153
Buck's Cross. Devn .................4D 18
Bucks Green. W Sus ................2B 26
Buckshaw Village. Lanc ............2D 90
Bucks Hill. Herts .................5A 52
Bucks Horn Oak. Hants .............2G 25
Buck's Mills. Devn .................4D 18
Buckton. E Yor ....................2F 101
Buckton. Here ......................3F 59
Buckton. Nmbd .....................1E 121
Buckton Vale. G Man ...............4H 91
Buckworth. Cambs ...................3A 64
Budby. Notts .......................4D 86
Bude. Corn .........................2C 10
Budge's Shop. Corn ................3H 7
Budlake. Devn ......................2C 12
Budle. Nmbd .......................1F 121
Budleigh Salterton. Devn ...........4D 12
Budock Water. Corn ................5B 6
Buerton. Ches E ...................1A 72
Buffler's Holt. Buck ...............2E 51
Bugbrooke. Nptn ...................5D 62
Buglawton. Ches E ..................4C 84
Bugle. Corn ........................3E 6
Bugthorpe. E Yor ..................4B 100
Buildwas. Shrp .....................5A 72
Builth Road. Powy ..................5C 58
Builth Wells. Powy .................5C 58
Bulbourne. Herts ...................4H 51
Bulby. Linc ........................3H 75
Bulcote. Notts .....................1D 74
Buldoo. High ......................2B 168
Bulford. Wilts .....................2G 23
Bulford Camp. Wilts ................2G 23
Bulkeley. Ches E ...................5H 83
Bulkington. Warw ..................2A 62
Bulkington. Wilts ..................1E 23
Bulkworthy. Devn ...................1D 11
Bullamoor. N Yor ..................5A 106
Bull Bay. IOA ......................1D 80
Bullbridge. Derbs ..................5A 86
Bullgill. Cumb ....................1B 102
Bull Hill. Hants ...................3B 16
Bullinghope. Here ..................2A 48
Bull's Green. Herts ................4C 52
Bullwood. Arg .....................2C 126
Bulmer. Essx .......................1B 54
Bulmer. N Yor .....................3A 100
Bulmer Tye. Essx ...................2B 54
Bulphan. Thur ......................2H 39
Bulverhythe. E Sus .................5B 28
Bulwark. Abers ....................4G 161
Bulwell. Nott ......................1C 74
Bulwick. Nptn ......................1G 63

Bumble's Green. Essx ...............5E 53
Bun Abhainn Eadarra.
   W Isl ..........................7D 171
Bunacaimb. High ...................5E 147
Bun a' Mhuilinn. W Isl ............7C 170
Bunarkaig. High ...................5D 148
Bunbury. Ches E ....................5H 83
Bunchrew. High .....................4A 158
Bundalloch. High ..................1A 148
Buness. Shet ......................1H 173
Bunessan. Arg .....................1A 132
Bungay. Suff .......................2F 67
Bunkegivie. High ..................2H 149
Bunker's Hill. Cambs ...............5D 76
Bunker's Hill. Suff ................5H 79
Bunkers Hill. Linc .................5B 88
Bunloit. High .....................1H 149
Bunny. Notts .......................3C 74
Bunoich. High .....................3F 149
Bunree. High ......................2E 141
Bunroy. High ......................5E 149
Buntait. High .....................5G 157
Buntingford. Herts .................3D 52
Bunting's Green. Essx ..............2B 54
Bunwell. Norf ......................1D 66
Burbage. Derbs .....................3E 85
Burbage. Leics .....................1B 62
Burbage. Wilts .....................5H 35
Burcher. Here ......................4F 59
Burchett's Green. Wind .............3G 37
Burcombe. Wilts ....................3F 23
Burcot. Oxon .......................2D 36
Burcot. Worc .......................3D 61
Burcote. Shrp ......................1B 60
Burcott. Buck ......................3G 51
Burcott. Som .......................2A 22
Burdale. N Yor .....................3C 100
Burdrop. Oxon ......................2B 50
Bures. Suff ........................2C 54
The Burf. Worc .....................4C 60
Burford. Oxon ......................4A 50
Burford. Shrp ......................4H 59
Burg. Arg .........................4E 139
Burgate Great Green. Suff .........3C 66
Burgate Little Green. Suff ........3C 66
Burgess Hill. W Sus ................4E 27
Burgh. Suff ........................5E 67
Burgh by Sands. Cumb ..............4E 113
Burgh Castle. Norf .................5G 79
Burghclere. Hants ..................5C 36
Burghead. Mor .....................2F 159
Burghfield. W Ber ..................5E 37
Burghfield Common. W Ber ..........5E 37
Burghfield Hill. W Ber .............5E 37
Burgh Heath. Surr ..................5D 38
Burghill. Here .....................1H 47
Burgh le Marsh. Linc ...............4E 89
Burgh Muir. Abers .................2E 153
Burgh next Aylsham. Norf ...........3E 78
Burgh on Bain. Linc ................2B 88
Burgh St Margaret. Norf ...........4G 79
Burgh St Peter. Norf ...............1G 67
Burghwallis. S Yor .................3F 93
Burham. Kent .......................4B 40
Buriton. Hants .....................4F 25
Burland. Ches E ....................5A 84
Burland. Shet .....................8E 173
Burlawn. Corn ......................1D 6
Burleigh. Glos .....................5D 48
Burleigh. Wind .....................4G 37
Burlescombe. Devn ..................1D 12
Burleston. Dors ....................3C 14
Burlestone. Devn ...................4E 9
Burley. Hants ......................2H 15
Burley. Rut ........................4F 75
Burley. W Yor ......................1C 92
Burleydam. Ches E ..................1A 72
Burley Gate. Here ..................1A 48
Burley in Wharfedale.
   W Yor ...........................5D 98
Burley Street. Hants ...............2H 15
Burley Woodhead. W Yor ............5D 98
Burlingjobb. Powy ..................5E 59

Burlington. Shrp ...................4B 72
Burlton. Shrp ......................3G 71
Burmantofts. W Yor .................1D 92
Burmarsh. Kent .....................2F 29
Burmington. Warw ...................2A 50
Burn. N Yor ........................2F 93
Burnage. G Man .....................1C 84
Burnaston. Derbs ...................2G 73
Burnbanks. Cumb ...................3G 103
Burnby. E Yor .....................5C 100
Burncross. S Yor ...................1H 85
Burneside. Cumb ...................5G 103
Burness. Orkn .....................3F 172
Burneston. N Yor ...................1F 99
Burnett. Bath ......................5B 34
Burnfoot. E Ayr ...................4D 116
Burnfoot. Per ......................3B 136
Burnfoot. Bord
   nr. Hawick .....................3H 119
   nr. Roberton ...................3G 119
Burngreave. S Yor .................2A 86
Burnham. Buck ......................2A 38
Burnham. N Lin .....................3D 94
Burnham Deepdale. Norf .............1H 77
Burnham Green. Herts ...............4C 52
Burnham Market. Norf ...............1H 77
Burnham Norton. Norf ...............1H 77
Burnham-on-Crouch. Essx ............1D 40
Burnham-on-Sea. Som ...............2G 21
Burnham Overy Staithe.
   Norf ...........................1H 77
Burnham Overy Town.
   ................................1H 77
Burnham Thorpe. Norf ..............1A 78
Burnhaven. Abers ..................4H 161
Burnhead. Dum ....................5A 118
Burnhervie. Abers .................2E 153
Burnhill Green. Staf ...............5B 72
Burnhope. Dur .....................5E 115
Burnhouse. N Ayr ..................4E 127
Burniston. N Yor ..................5H 107
Burnlee. W Yor .....................4B 92
Burnley. Lanc ......................1G 91
Burnmouth. Bord ...................3F 131
Burn Naze. Lanc ....................5C 96
Burn of Cambus. Stir ..............3G 135
Burnopfield. Dur ..................4E 115
Burnsall. N Yor ....................3C 98
Burnside. Ang .....................3E 145
Burnside. Ant .....................3G 175
Burnside. E Yor ....................3E 117
Burnside. Per ......................3D 136
Burnside. Shet .....................4D 173
Burnside. S Lan ...................4H 127
Burnside. W Lot
   nr. Broxburn ...................2D 129
   nr. Winchburgh .................2D 128
Burntcommon. Surr ..................5B 38
Burnt Heath. Essx ..................3D 54
Burnt Hill. W Ber ..................4D 36
Burnt Houses. Dur .................2E 105
Burntisland. Fife .................1F 129
Burnt Oak. G Lon ...................1D 38
Burnton. E Ayr ....................4D 117
Burntstalk. Norf ...................2G 77
Burntwood. Staf ....................5E 73
Burntwood Green. Staf ..............5E 73
Burnt Yates. N Yor .................3E 99
Burnwynd. Edin ....................3E 129
Burpham. Surr ......................5B 38
Burpham. W Sus .....................5B 26
Burradon. Nmbd ....................4D 121
Burradon. Tyne ....................2F 115
Burrafirth. Shet ..................1H 173
Burraton. Corn .....................3A 8
Burravoe. Shet
   nr. North Roe ..................3E 173
   on Mainland ....................5E 173
   on Yell ........................4G 173
Burray Village. Orkn ..............8D 172
Burrells. Cumb ....................3H 103

Burrelton. Per ....................5A 144
Burridge. Hants ....................1D 16
Burridge. Som ......................2G 13
Burrill. High .....................5E 169
Burrill. N Yor .....................1E 99
Burringham. N Lin ..................4B 94
Burrington. Devn ..................2G 11
Burrington. Here ...................3G 59
Burrington. N Som ..................1H 21
Burrough End. Cambs ................5F 65
Burrough Green. Cambs ..............5F 65
Burrough on the Hill.
   Leics ...........................4E 75
Burroughston. Orkn ................5E 172
Burrow. Devn .......................4D 12
Burrow. Som ........................2C 20
Burrowbridge. Som ..................4G 21
Burrowhill. Surr ...................4A 38
Burry. Swan ........................3D 30
Burry Green. Swan ..................3D 30
Burry Port. Carm ...................5E 45
Burscough. Lanc ....................3C 90
Burscough Bridge. Lanc .............3C 90
Bursea. E Yor ......................1B 94
Burshill. E Yor ...................5E 101
Bursledon. Hants ...................2C 16
Burslem. Stoke .....................1C 72
Burstall. Suff .....................1D 54
Burstock. Dors .....................2H 13
Burston. Devn ......................2H 11
Burston. Norf ......................2D 66
Burston. Staf ......................2D 72
Burstow. Surr ......................1E 27
Burstwick. E Yor ...................2F 95
Burtersett. N Yor ..................1A 98
Burtholme. Cumb ...................3G 113
Burthwaite. Cumb ..................5F 113
Burtle. Som ........................2H 21
Burtoft. Linc ......................2B 76
Burton. Ches W
   nr. Kelsall .....................4H 83
   nr. Neston ......................3F 83
Burton. Dors
   nr. Christchurch ................3G 15
   nr. Dorchester ..................3B 14
Burton. Nmbd ......................1F 121
Burton. Pemb .......................4D 43
Burton. Som ........................2E 21
Burton. Wrex .......................5F 83
Burton. Wilts
   nr. Chippenham ..................4D 34
   nr. Warminster ..................3D 22
Burton Agnes. E Yor ...............3F 101
Burton Bradstock. Dors .............4H 13
Burton-by-Lincoln. Linc ...........3G 87
Burton Coggles. Linc ...............3G 75
Burton Constable. E Yor ...........1E 95
Burton Corner. Linc ................1C 76
Burton End. Cambs .................1G 53
Burton End. Essx ...................3F 53
Burton Fleming. E Yor .............2E 101
Burton Green. Warw ................3G 61
Burton Green. Wrex .................5F 83
Burton Hastings. Warw ..............2B 62
Burton-in-Kendal. Cumb .............2E 97
Burton in Lonsdale. N Yor .........2F 97
Burton Joyce. Notts ................1D 74
Burton Latimer. Nptn ...............3G 63
Burton Lazars. Leics ...............4E 75
Burton Leonard. N Yor ..............3F 99
Burton on the Wolds.
   Leics ...........................3C 74
Burton Overy. Leics ................1D 62
Burton Pedwardine. Linc ............1A 76
Burton Pidsea. E Yor ...............1F 95
Burton Salmon. N Yor ...............2E 93
Burton's Green. Essx ..............3B 54
Burton Stather. N Lin ..............3B 94
Burton upon Stather.
   N Lin ...........................3B 94
Burton upon Trent. Staf ............3G 73
Burton Wolds. Leics ................3D 74
Burtonwood. Warr ...................1H 83

Burwardsley. Ches W ................5H 83
Burwarton. Shrp ....................2A 60
Burwash. E Sus .....................3A 28
Burwash Common. E Sus .............3H 27
Burwash Weald. E Sus ...............3A 28
Burwell. Cambs .....................4E 65
Burwell. Linc ......................3C 88
Burwen. IOA ........................1D 80
Burwick. Orkn .....................9D 172
Bury. Cambs ........................2B 64
Bury. G Man ........................3G 91
Bury. Som ..........................4C 20
Bury. W Sus ........................4B 26
Bury End. Worc .....................2F 49
Bury Green. Herts ..................3E 53
Bury St Edmunds. Suff ..............4H 65
Burythorpe. N Yor .................3B 100
Busbridge. Surr ....................1A 26
Busby. E Ren ......................4G 127
Busby. Per ........................1C 136
Buscot. Oxon .......................2H 35
Bush. Corn .........................2C 10
Bush Bank. Here ....................5G 59
Bushbury. W Mid ....................5D 72
Bushby. Leics ......................5D 74
Bushey. Dors .......................4E 15
Bushey. Herts ......................1C 38
Bushey Heath. Herts ................1C 38
Bush Green. Norf
   nr. Attleborough ................1C 66
   nr. Harleston ...................2E 66
Bush Green. Suff ...................5B 66
Bushley. Worc ......................2D 49
Bushley Green. Worc ...............2D 48
Bushmead. Bed .....................4A 64
Bushmills. Caus ...................1F 175
Bushmoor. Shrp ....................2G 59
Bushton. Wilts .....................4F 35
Bushy Common. Norf .................4B 78
Busk. Cumb ........................5H 113
Buslingthorpe. Linc ................2H 87
Bussage. Glos ......................5D 48
Bussex. Som ........................3G 21
Busta. Shet .......................5E 173
Butcher's Cross. E Sus .............3G 27
Butcombe. N Som ....................5A 34
Bute Town. Cphy ....................5E 46
Butleigh. Som ......................3A 22
Butleigh Wootton. Som ..............3A 22
Butlers Marston. Warw ..............1B 50
Butley. Suff .......................5F 67
Butley High Corner. Suff ..........1G 55
Butlocks Heath. Hants ..............2C 16
Butterburn. Cumb ..................2H 113
Buttercrambe. N Yor ...............4B 100
Butterknowle. Dur .................2E 105
Butterleigh. Devn ..................2C 12
Buttermere. Cumb ..................3C 102
Buttermere. Wilts ..................5B 36
Buttershaw. W Yor ..................2B 92
Butterstone. Per ...................4H 143
Butterton. Staf
   nr. Leek ........................5E 85
   nr. Stoke-on-Trent .............1C 72
Butterwick. Dur ...................2A 106
Butterwick. Linc ...................1C 76
Butterwick. N Yor
   nr. Malton ......................2B 100
   nr. Weaverthorpe ...............2D 101
Butteryhaugh. Nmbd ...............5A 120
Butt Green. Ches E .................5A 84
Buttington. Powy ...................5E 71
Buttonbridge. Shrp .................3B 60
Buttonoak. Shrp ....................3B 60
Buttsash. Hants ....................2C 16
Butt's Green. Essx .................5A 54
Butt Yeats. Lanc ...................3E 97
Buxhall. Suff ......................5C 66
Buxted. E Sus ......................3F 27
Buxton. Derbs ......................3E 85
Buxton. Norf .......................3E 78
Buxworth. Derbs ....................2E 85
Bwcle. Flin ........................4E 83

Bwlch. Powy ...3E 47
Bwlchderwin. Gwyn ...1D 68
Bwlchgwyn. Wrex ...5E 83
Bwlch-Llan. Cdgn ...5E 57
Bwlchnewydd. Carm ...3D 44
Bwlchtocyn. Gwyn ...3C 68
Bwlch-y-cibau. Powy ...4D 70
Bwlchyddar. Powy ...3D 70
Bwlch-y-fadfa. Cdgn ...1E 45
Bwlch-y-ffridd. Powy ...1C 58
Bwlch y Garreg. Powy ...1C 58
Bwlch-y-groes. Pemb ...1G 43
Bwlch-y-sarnau. Powy ...3C 58
Bybrook. Kent ...1E 28
Byermoor. Tyne ...4E 115
Byers Garth. Dur ...5G 115
Byers Green. Dur ...1F 105
Byfield. Nptn ...5C 62
**Byfleet.** Surr ...4B 38
Byford. Here ...1G 47
Bygrave. Herts ...2C 52
Byker. Tyne ...3F 115
Byland Abbey. N Yor ...2H 99
Bylchau. Cnwy ...4B 82
Byley. Ches W ...4B 84
Bynea. Carm ...3E 31
Byram. N Yor ...2E 93
Byrness. Nmbd ...4B 120
Bystock. Devn ...4D 12
Bythorn. Cambs ...3H 63
Byton. Here ...4F 59
Bywell. Nmbd ...3D 114
Byworth. W Sus ...3A 26

# C

Cabharstadh. W Isl ...6F 171
Cabourne. Linc ...4E 95
Cabrach. Arg ...3C 124
Cabrach. Mor ...1A 152
Cabus. Lanc ...5D 97
Cadbury. Devn ...2C 12
Cadder. E Dun ...2H 127
Caddington. C Beds ...4A 52
Caddonfoot. Bord ...1G 119
Cadeby. Leics ...5B 74
Cadeby. S Yor ...4F 93
Cadeleigh. Devn ...2C 12
Cade Street. E Sus ...3H 27
Cadgwith. Corn ...5E 5
Cadham. Fife ...3E 137
Cadishead. G Man ...1B 84
Cadle. Swan ...3F 31
Cadley. Lanc ...1D 90
Cadley. Wilts
   nr. Ludgershall ...1H 23
   nr. Marlborough ...5H 35
Cadmore End. Buck ...2F 37
Cadnam. Hants ...1A 16
Cadney. N Lin ...4D 94
Cadole. Flin ...4E 82
Cadoxton-juxta-Neath.
   Neat ...3A 32
Cadwell. Herts ...2B 52
Cadwst. Den ...2C 70
Caeathro. Gwyn ...4E 81
Caehopkin. Powy ...4B 46
Caenby. Linc ...2G 87
Caerau. B'end ...2B 32
Caerau. Card ...4E 33
Cae'r-bont. Powy ...4B 46
Cae'r-bryn. Carm ...4F 45
Caerdeon. Gwyn ...4F 69
**Caerdydd.** Card ...4E 33
Caerfarchell. Pemb ...2B 42
**Caerffili.** Cphy ...3E 33
**Caerfyrddin.** Carm ...4E 45
Caergeiliog. IOA ...3C 80
Caergwrle. Flin ...5F 83
**Caergybi.** IOA ...2B 80
Caerlaverock. Per ...2A 136
Caerleon. Newp ...2G 33
Caerllion. Carm ...2G 43

Caerllion. Newp ...2G 33
**Caernarfon.** Gwyn ...4D 81
**Caerphilly.** Cphy ...3E 33
Caersws. Powy ...1C 58
Caerwedros. Cdgn ...5C 56
Caerwent. Mon ...2H 33
Caerwys. Flin ...3D 82
Caim. IOA ...2F 81
Caio. Carm ...2G 45
Cairinis. W Isl ...2D 170
Cairisiadar. W Isl ...4C 171
Cairminis. W Isl ...9C 171
Cairnbaan. Arg ...4F 133
Cairnbulg. Abers ...2H 161
Cairncross. Ang ...1D 145
Cairndow. Arg ...2A 134
Cairness. Abers ...2H 161
Cairneyhill. Fife ...1D 128
Cairngarroch. Dum ...5F 109
Cairnhill. Abers ...5D 160
Cairnie. Abers ...4B 160
Cairnorrie. Abers ...4F 161
Cairnryan. Dum ...3F 109
Cairston. Orkn ...6B 172
Caister-on-Sea. Norf ...4H 79
Caistor. Linc ...4E 94
Caistor St Edmund. Norf ...5E 79
Caistron. Nmbd ...4D 121
Cakebole. Worc ...3C 60
Calais Street. Suff ...1C 54
Calanais. W Isl ...4E 171
Calbost. W Isl ...6G 171
Calbourne. IOW ...4C 16
Calceby. Linc ...3C 88
Calcot. Glos ...4F 49
Calcot Row. W Ber ...4E 37
Calcott. Kent ...4F 41
Calcott. Shrp ...4G 71
Caldback. Shet ...1H 173
Caldbeck. Cumb ...1E 102
Caldbergh. N Yor ...1C 98
Caldecote. Cambs
   nr. Cambridge ...5C 64
   nr. Peterborough ...2A 64
Caldecote. Herts ...2C 52
Caldecote. Nptn ...5D 62
Caldecote. Warw ...1A 62
Caldecott. Nptn ...4G 63
Caldecott. Oxon ...2C 36
Caldecott. Rut ...1F 63
Calder Bridge. Cumb ...4B 102
Calderbank. N Lan ...3A 128
Calderbrook. G Man ...3H 91
Caldercruix. N Lan ...3B 128
Calder Grove. W Yor ...3D 92
Calder Mains. High ...3C 168
Caldermill. S Lan ...5H 127
Calder Vale. Lanc ...5E 97
Calderwood. S Lan ...4H 127
**Caldicot.** Mon ...3H 33
Caldwell. Derbs ...4G 73
Caldwell. N Yor ...3E 105
Caldy. Mers ...2E 83
Calebrack. Cumb ...1E 103
Calford Green. Suff ...1G 53
Calfsound. Orkn ...4E 172
Calgary. Arg ...3E 139
California. Cambs ...2E 65
California. Falk ...2C 128
California. Norf ...4H 79
California. Suff ...1E 55
Calke. Derbs ...3A 74
Callakille. High ...3F 155
Callaly. Nmbd ...4E 121
Callander. Stir ...3F 135
Callaughton. Shrp ...1A 60
Callendoun. Arg ...1E 127
Callestick. Corn ...3B 6
Calligarry. High ...3E 147
Callington. Corn ...2H 7
Callingwood. Staf ...3F 73
Callow. Here ...2H 47

Callowell. Glos ...5D 48
Callow End. Worc ...1D 48
Callow Hill. Wilts ...3F 35
Callow Hill. Worc
   nr. Bewdley ...3B 60
   nr. Redditch ...4E 61
Calmore. Hants ...1B 16
Calmsden. Glos ...5F 49
**Calne.** Wilts ...4E 35
Calow. Derbs ...3B 86
Calshot. Hants ...2C 16
Calstock. Corn ...2A 8
Calstone Wellington.
   Wilts ...5F 35
Calthorpe. Norf ...2D 78
Calthorpe Street. Norf ...3G 79
Calthwaite. Cumb ...5F 113
Calton. N Yor ...4B 98
Calton. Staf ...5F 85
Calveley. Ches E ...5H 83
Calver. Derbs ...3G 85
Calverhall. Shrp ...2A 72
Calverleigh. Devn ...1C 12
Calverley. W Yor ...1C 92
Calvert. Buck ...3E 51
Calverton. Mil ...2F 51
Calverton. Notts ...1D 74
Calvine. Per ...2F 143
Calvo. Cumb ...4C 112
Cam. Glos ...2C 34
Camaghael. High ...1F 141
Camas-luinie. High ...1B 148
Camasnacroise. High ...3C 140
Camastianavaig. High ...5E 155
Camasunary. High ...2D 146
Camault Muir. High ...4H 157
Camb. Shet ...2G 173
Camber. E Sus ...4D 28
**Camberley.** Surr ...5G 37
**Camberwell.** G Lon ...3E 39
Camblesforth. N Yor ...2G 93
Cambo. Nmbd ...1D 114
Cambois. Nmbd ...1G 115
**Camborne.** Corn ...5A 6
Cambourne. Cambs ...5C 64
**Cambridge.** Cambs ...5D 64
Cambridge. Glos ...5C 48
Cambrose. Corn ...4A 6
Cambus. Clac ...4A 136
Cambusbarron. Stir ...4G 135
Cambuskenneth. Stir ...4H 135
**Cambuslang.** S Lan ...3H 127
Cambusnethan. N Lan ...4B 128
Cambus o' May. Abers ...4B 152
**Camden Town.** G Lon ...2D 39
Cameley. Bath ...1B 22
Camelford. Corn ...4B 10
Camelon. Falk ...1B 128
Camelsdale. W Sus ...3G 25
Camer's Green. Worc ...2C 48
Camerton. Bath ...1B 22
Camerton. Cumb ...1B 102
Camerton. E Yor ...2F 95
Camghouran. Per ...3C 142
Camlough. New M ...6F 175
Cammachmore. Abers ...4G 153
Cammeringham. Linc ...2G 87
Camore. High ...4E 165
Camp, The. Glos ...5E 49
Campbelton. N Ayr ...4C 126
Campbeltown. Arg ...3B 122
Campbeltown Airport.
   Arg ...3A 122
Campmuir. Per ...5B 144
Campsall. S Yor ...3F 93
Campsea Ashe. Suff ...5F 67
Camps End. Cambs ...1G 53
Campton. C Beds ...2B 52
Camptoun. E Lot ...2B 130
Camptown. Bord ...3A 120
Camrose. Pemb ...2D 42
Camserney. Per ...4F 143
Camster. High ...4E 169

Camus Croise. High ...2E 147
Camuscross. High ...2E 147
Camusdarach. High ...4E 147
Camusnagaul. High
   nr. Fort William ...1E 141
   nr. Little Loch Broom ...5E 163
Camusteel. High ...4G 155
Camusterrach. High ...4G 155
Camusvrachan. Per ...4D 142
Canada. Hants ...1A 16
Canadia. E Sus ...4B 28
Canaston Bridge. Pemb ...3E 43
Candlesby. Linc ...4D 88
Candle Street. Suff ...3C 66
Candy Mill. S Lan ...5D 128
Cane End. Oxon ...4E 37
Canewdon. Essx ...1D 40
Canford Cliffs. Pool ...4F 15
Canford Heath. Pool ...3F 15
Canford Magna. Pool ...3F 15
Cangate. Norf ...4F 79
Canham's Green. Suff ...4C 66
Canholes. Derbs ...3E 85
Canisbay. High ...1F 169
Canley. W Mid ...3H 61
Cann. Dors ...4D 22
Cann Common. Dors ...4D 23
Cannich. High ...5F 157
Cannington. Som ...3F 21
**Cannock.** Staf ...4D 73
Cannock Wood. Staf ...4E 73
Canonbie. Dum ...2E 113
Canon Bridge. Here ...1H 47
Canon Frome. Here ...1B 48
Canon Pyon. Here ...1H 47
Canons Ashby. Nptn ...5C 62
Canonstown. Corn ...3C 4
**Canterbury.** Kent ...5F 41
Cantley. Norf ...5F 79
Cantley. S Yor ...4G 93
Cantlop. Shrp ...5H 71
Canton. Card ...4E 33
Cantray. High ...4B 158
Cantraybruich. High ...4B 158
Cantraywood. High ...4B 158
Cantsdam. Fife ...4D 136
Cantsfield. Lanc ...2F 97
**Canvey Island.** Essx ...2B 40
Canwick. Linc ...4G 87
Canworthy Water. Corn ...3C 10
Caol. High ...1F 141
Caolas. Arg ...4B 138
Caolas. W Isl ...9B 170
Caolas Liubharsaigh.
   W Isl ...4D 170
Caolas Scalpaigh. W Isl ...8E 171
Caolas Stocinis. W Isl ...8D 171
Caol Ila. Arg ...2C 124
Caol Loch Ailse. High ...1F 147
Caol Reatha. High ...1F 147
Capel. Kent ...1H 27
Capel. Surr ...1C 26
Capel Bangor. Cdgn ...2F 57
Capel Betws Lleucu. Cdgn ...5F 57
Capel Coch. IOA ...2D 80
Capel Curig. Cnwy ...5G 81
Capel Cynon. Cdgn ...1D 45
Capel Dewi. Carm ...3E 45
Capel Dewi. Cdgn
   nr. Aberystwyth ...2F 57
   nr. Llandysul ...1E 45
Capel Garmon. Cnwy ...5H 81
Capel Green. Suff ...1G 55
Capel Gwyn. IOA ...3C 80
Capel Gwynfe. Carm ...3H 45
Capel Hendre. Carm ...4F 45
Capel Isaac. Carm ...3F 45
Capel Iwan. Carm ...1G 43
Capel-le-Ferne. Kent ...2G 29
Capel Llanilltern. Card ...4D 32
Capel Mawr. IOA ...3D 80
Capel Newydd. Pemb ...1G 43
Capel St Andrew. Suff ...1G 55

Capel St Mary. Suff ...2D 54
Capel Seion. Carm ...4F 45
Capel Seion. Cdgn ...3F 57
Capel Uchaf. Gwyn ...1D 68
Capel-y-ffin. Powy ...2F 47
Capenhurst. Ches W ...3F 83
Capernwray. Lanc ...2E 97
Capheaton. Nmbd ...1D 114
Cappercleuch. Bord ...2E 119
Capplegill. Dum ...4D 118
Capton. Devn ...3E 9
Capton. Som ...3D 20
Caputh. Per ...5H 143
Caradon Town. Corn ...5C 10
Carbis Bay. Corn ...3C 4
Carbost. High
   nr. Loch Harport ...5C 154
   nr. Portree ...4D 154
Carbrook. S Yor ...2A 86
Carbrooke. Norf ...5B 78
Carburton. Notts ...3D 86
Carcluie. S Ayr ...3C 116
Car Colston. Notts ...1E 74
Carcroft. S Yor ...4F 93
Cardenden. Fife ...4E 136
Cardeston. Shrp ...4F 71
Cardewlees. Cumb ...4E 113
**Cardiff.** Card ...4E 33
Cardiff Airport. V Glam ...5D 32
**Cardigan.** Cdgn ...1B 44
Cardinal's Green. Cambs ...1G 53
Cardington. Bed ...1A 52
Cardington. Shrp ...1H 59
Cardinham. Corn ...2F 7
Cardno. Abers ...2G 161
Cardow. Mor ...4F 159
Cardross. Arg ...2E 127
Cardurnock. Cumb ...4C 112
Careby. Linc ...4H 75
Careston. Ang ...2E 145
Carew. Pemb ...4E 43
Carew Cheriton. Pemb ...4E 43
Carew Newton. Pemb ...4E 43
Carey. Here ...2A 48
Carfin. N Lan ...4A 128
Carfrae. Bord ...4B 130
Cargate Green. Norf ...4F 79
Cargenbridge. Dum ...2G 111
Cargill. Per ...5A 144
Cargo. Cumb ...4E 113
Cargreen. Corn ...2A 8
Carham. Nmbd ...1C 120
Carhampton. Som ...2D 20
Carharrack. Corn ...4B 6
Carie. Per
   nr. Loch Rannah ...3D 142
   nr. Loch Tay ...5D 142
Carisbrooke. IOW ...4C 16
Cark. Cumb ...2C 96
Carkeel. Corn ...2A 8
Carlabhagh. W Isl ...3E 171
Carland Cross. Corn ...3C 6
Carlby. Linc ...4H 75
Carlbury. Darl ...3F 105
Carlby. Linc ...4H 75
Carlecotes. S Yor ...4B 92
Carleen. Corn ...4D 4
Carlesmoor. N Yor ...2D 98
Carleton. Cumb
   nr. Carlisle ...4F 113
   nr. Egremont ...4B 102
   nr. Penrith ...2G 103
Carleton. Lanc ...5C 96
Carleton. N Yor ...5B 98
Carleton. W Yor ...2E 93
Carleton Forehoe. Norf ...5C 78
Carleton Rode. Norf ...1D 66
Carleton St Peter. Norf ...5F 79
Carlidnack. Corn ...4E 5
Carlingcott. Bath ...1B 22
Carlin How. Red C ...3E 107
**Carlisle.** Cumb ...4F 113
Carloonan. Arg ...2H 133
Carlops. Bord ...4E 129
Carlton. Bed ...5G 63

Carlton—Chapel

Carlton. *Cambs* 5F **65**
Carlton. *Leics* 5A **74**
Carlton. *N Yor*
nr. Helmsley 1A **100**
nr. Middleham 1C **98**
nr. Selby 2G **93**
**Carlton**. *Notts* 1D **74**
Carlton. *S Yor* 3D **92**
Carlton. *Stoc T* 2A **106**
Carlton. *Suff* 4F **67**
Carlton. *W Yor* 2D **92**
Carlton Colville. *Suff* 1H **67**
Carlton Curlieu. *Leics* 1D **62**
Carlton Husthwaite. *N Yor* 2G **99**
Carlton in Cleveland.
*N Yor* 4C **106**
Carlton in Lindrick. *Notts* 2C **86**
Carlton-le-Moorland. *Linc* 5G **87**
Carlton Miniott. *N Yor* 1F **99**
Carlton-on-Trent. *Notts* 4F **87**
Carlton Scroop. *Linc* 1G **75**
**Carluke**. *S Lan* 4B **128**
Carlyon Bay. *Corn* 3E **7**
**Carmarthen**. *Carm* 4E **45**
Carmel. *Carm* 4F **45**
Carmel. *Flin* 3D **82**
Carmel. *Gwyn* 5D **81**
Carmel. *IOA* 2C **80**
Carmichael. *S Lan* 1B **118**
Carmunnock. *Glas* 4H **127**
Carmyle. *Glas* 3H **127**
Carmyllie. *Ang* 4E **145**
Carnaby. *E Yor* 3F **101**
Carnach. *High*
nr. Lochcarron 1C **148**
nr. Ullapool 4E **163**
Carnach. *Mor* 4E **159**
Carnach. *W Isl* 8E **171**
Carnachy. *High* 3H **167**
Carnain. *Arg* 3B **124**
Carnais. *W Isl* 4C **171**
Carnan. *Arg* 4B **138**
Carnan. *W Isl* 4C **170**
Carnbee. *Fife* 3H **137**
Carnbo. *Per* 3C **136**
Carn Brea Village. *Corn* 4A **6**
Carndu. *High* 1A **148**
Carne. *Corn* 5D **6**
Carnell. *S Ayr* 1D **116**
Carnforth. *Lanc* 2E **97**
Carn-gorm. *High* 1B **148**
Carnhedryn. *Pemb* 2C **42**
Carnhell Green. *Corn* 3D **4**
Carnie. *Abers* 3F **153**
Carnkie. *Corn*
nr. Falmouth 5B **6**
nr. Redruth 5A **6**
Carnkief. *Corn* 3B **6**
Carno. *Powy* 1B **58**
Carnock. *Fife* 1D **128**
Carnon Downs. *Corn* 4B **6**
**Carnoustie**. *Ang* 5E **145**
Carntyne. *Glas* 3H **127**
Carnwath. *S Lan* 5C **128**
Carnyorth. *Corn* 3A **4**
Carol Green. *W Mid* 3G **61**
Carpalla. *Corn* 3D **6**
Carperby. *N Yor* 1C **98**
Carradale. *Arg* 2C **122**
Carragraich. *W Isl* 8D **171**
Carrbridge. *High* 1D **150**
Carr Cross. *Lanc* 3B **90**
Carreglefn. *IOA* 2C **80**
Carrhouse. *N Lin* 4A **94**
Carrick Castle. *Arg* 4A **134**
**Carrickfergus**. *ME Ant* 3H **175**
Carrick Ho. *Orkn* 4E **172**
Carriden. *Falk* 1D **128**
Carrington. *G Man* 1B **84**
Carrington. *Linc* 5C **88**
Carrington. *Midl* 3G **129**
Carrog. *Cnwy* 1G **69**
Carrog. *Den* 1D **70**
Carron. *Falk* 1B **128**
Carron. *Mor* 4G **159**
Carronbridge. *Dum* 5A **118**
Carronshore. *Falk* 1B **128**
Carrow Hill. *Mon* 2H **33**
Carr Shield. *Nmbd* 5B **114**
Carrutherstown. *Dum* 2C **112**
Carr Vale. *Derbs* 4B **86**
Carrville. *Dur* 5G **115**
Carryduff. *Lis* 4H **175**
Carsaig. *Arg* 1C **132**
Carscreugh. *Dum* 3H **109**
Carsegowan. *Dum* 4B **110**
Carse House. *Arg* 3F **125**
Carseriggan. *Dum* 3A **110**
Carsethorn. *Dum* 4A **112**
**Carshalton**. *G Lon* 4D **39**
Carsington. *Derbs* 5G **85**
Carskiey. *Arg* 5A **122**
Carsluith. *Dum* 4B **110**
Carsphairn. *Dum* 5E **117**
Carstairs. *S Lan* 5C **128**
Carstairs Junction. *S Lan* 5C **128**
Cartbridge. *Surr* 5B **38**
Carterhaugh. *Ang* 4D **144**
Carter's Clay. *Hants* 4B **24**
**Carterton**. *Oxon* 5A **50**
Carterway Heads. *Nmbd* 4D **114**
Carthew. *Corn* 3E **6**
Carthorpe. *N Yor* 1F **99**
Cartington. *Nmbd* 4E **121**
Cartland. *S Lan* 5B **128**
Cartmel. *Cumb* 2C **96**
Cartmel Fell. *Cumb* 1D **96**
Cartworth. *W Yor* 4B **92**
Carwath. *Cumb* 5E **112**
Carway. *Carm* 5E **45**
Carwinley. *Cumb* 2F **113**
Cascob. *Powy* 4E **59**
**Cas-gwent**. *Mon* 2A **34**
Cash Feus. *Fife* 3E **136**
Cashlie. *Per* 4B **142**
Cashmoor. *Dors* 1E **15**
Cas-Mael. *Pemb* 2E **43**
**Casnewydd**. *Newp* 3G **33**
Cassington. *Oxon* 4C **50**
Cassop. *Dur* 1A **106**
Castell. *Cnwy* 4G **81**
Castell. *Den* 4D **82**
Castell Hendre. *Pemb* 2E **43**
**Castell-Nedd**. *Neat* 2A **32**
Castell Newydd Emlyn.
*Carm* 1D **44**
Castell-y-bwch. *Torf* 2F **33**
Casterton. *Cumb* 2F **97**
Castle. *Som* 2A **22**
Castle Acre. *Norf* 4H **77**
Castle Ashby. *Nptn* 5F **63**
Castlebay. *W Isl* 9B **170**
Castle Bolton. *N Yor* 5D **104**
Castle Bromwich. *W Mid* 2F **61**
Castle Bytham. *Linc* 4G **75**
Castlebythe. *Pemb* 2E **43**
Castle Caereinion. *Powy* 5D **70**
Castle Camps. *Cambs* 1G **53**
Castle Carrock. *Cumb* 4G **113**
Castle Cary. *Som* 3B **22**
Castlecary. *N Lan* 2A **128**
Castle Combe. *Wilts* 4D **34**
Castlecraig. *High* 2C **158**
Castledawson. *M Ulst* 3F **175**
Castlederg. *Derr* 3B **174**
Castle Donington. *Leics* 3B **74**
Castle Douglas. *Dum* 3E **111**
Castle Eaton. *Swin* 2G **35**
Castle Eden. *Dur* 1B **106**
**Castleford**. *W Yor* 2E **93**
Castle Frome. *Here* 1B **48**
Castle Green. *Surr* 4A **38**
Castle Green. *Warw* 3G **61**
Castle Gresley. *Derbs* 4G **73**
Castle Heaton. *Nmbd* 5F **131**
Castle Hedingham. *Essx* 2A **54**
Castle Hill. *Kent* 1A **28**
Castle Hill. *Suff* 1E **55**
Castlehill. *Per* 5B **144**
Castlehill. *S Lan* 4B **128**
Castlehill. *W Dun* 2E **127**
Castle Kennedy. *Dum* 4G **109**
Castle Lachlan. *Arg* 4H **133**
Castlemartin. *Pemb* 5D **42**
Castlemilk. *Glas* 4H **127**
Castlemorris. *Pemb* 1D **42**
Castlemorton. *Worc* 2C **48**
Castle O'er. *Dum* 5E **119**
Castle Park. *N Yor* 3F **107**
Castlerigg. *Cumb* 2D **102**
Castle Rising. *Norf* 3F **77**
Castlerock. *Caus* 1E **174**
Castleside. *Dur* 5D **115**
Castlethorpe. *Mil* 1F **51**
Castleton. *Abers* 4F **151**
Castleton. *Arg* 1G **125**
Castleton. *Derbs* 2F **85**
Castleton. *G Man* 3G **91**
Castleton. *Mor* 1F **151**
Castleton. *Newp* 3F **33**
Castleton. *N Yor* 4D **107**
Castleton. *Per* 2B **136**
Castletown. *Cumb* 1G **103**
Castletown. *Dors* 5B **14**
Castletown. *High* 2D **169**
Castletown. *IOM* 5B **108**
Castletown. *Tyne* 4G **115**
Castlewellan. *New M* 6H **175**
Castley. *N Yor* 5E **99**
Caston. *Norf* 1B **66**
Castor. *Pet* 1A **64**
Caswell. *Swan* 4E **31**
Catacol. *N Ayr* 5H **125**
Catbrook. *Mon* 5A **48**
Catchems End. *Worc* 3B **60**
Catchgate. *Dur* 4E **115**
Catcleugh. *Nmbd* 4B **120**
Catcliffe. *S Yor* 2B **86**
Catcott. *Som* 3G **21**
**Caterham**. *Surr* 5E **39**
Catfield. *Norf* 3F **79**
Catfield Common. *Norf* 3F **79**
Catfirth. *Shet* 6F **173**
**Catford**. *G Lon* 3E **39**
Catforth. *Lanc* 1C **90**
Cathcart. *Glas* 3G **127**
Cathedine. *Powy* 3E **47**
Catherine-de-Barnes.
*W Mid* 2F **61**
Catherington. *Hants* 1E **17**
Catherston Leweston.
*Dors* 3G **13**
Catherton. *Shrp* 3A **60**
Catisfield. *Hants* 2D **16**
Catlodge. *High* 4A **150**
Catlowdy. *Cumb* 2F **113**
Catmore. *W Ber* 3C **36**
Caton. *Devn* 5A **12**
Caton. *Lanc* 3E **97**
Catrine. *E Ayr* 2E **117**
Cat's Ash. *Newp* 2G **33**
Catsfield. *E Sus* 4B **28**
Catsgore. *Som* 4A **22**
Catshill. *Worc* 3D **60**
Cattal. *N Yor* 4G **99**
Cattawade. *Suff* 2E **54**
Catterall. *Lanc* 5E **97**
Catterick. *N Yor* 5F **105**
Catterick Bridge. *N Yor* 5F **105**
Catterick Garrison.
*N Yor* 5E **105**
Catterlen. *Cumb* 1F **103**
Catterline. *Abers* 1H **145**
Catterton. *N Yor* 5H **99**
Catteshall. *Surr* 1A **26**
Catthorpe. *Leics* 3C **62**
Cattistock. *Dors* 3A **14**
Catton. *Nmbd* 4B **114**
Catton. *N Yor* 2F **99**
Catwick. *E Yor* 5F **101**
Catworth. *Cambs* 3H **63**
Caudle Green. *Glos* 4E **49**
Caulcott. *Oxon* 3D **50**
Cauldhame. *Stir* 4F **135**
Cauldmill. *Bord* 3H **119**
Cauldon. *Staf* 1E **73**
Cauldon Lowe. *Staf* 1E **73**
Cauldwells. *Abers* 3E **161**
Caulkerbush. *Dum* 4G **111**
Caulside. *Dum* 1F **113**
Caunsall. *Worc* 2C **60**
Caunton. *Notts* 4E **87**
Causewayend. *S Lan* 1C **118**
Causewayhead. *Stir* 4H **135**
Causey Park. *Nmbd* 5F **121**
Caute. *Devn* 1E **11**
Cautley. *Cumb* 5H **103**
Cavendish. *Suff* 1B **54**
Cavendish Bridge. *Leics* 3B **74**
Cavenham. *Suff* 3G **65**
Caversfield. *Oxon* 3D **50**
Caversham. *Read* 4F **37**
Caversham Heights.
*Read* 4F **37**
Caverswall. *Staf* 1D **72**
Cawdor. *High* 3C **158**
Cawkwell. *Linc* 2B **88**
Cawood. *N Yor* 1F **93**
Cawsand. *Corn* 3A **8**
Cawston. *Norf* 3D **78**
Cawston. *Warw* 3B **62**
Cawthorne. *N Yor* 1B **100**
Cawthorne. *S Yor* 4C **92**
Cawthorpe. *Linc* 3H **75**
Cawton. *N Yor* 2A **100**
Caxton. *Cambs* 5C **64**
Caynham. *Shrp* 3H **59**
Caythorpe. *Linc* 1G **75**
Caythorpe. *Notts* 1D **74**
Cayton. *N Yor* 1E **101**
Ceallan. *W Isl* 3D **170**
Ceann a Bhaigh. *W Isl*
on North Uist 2C **170**
on Scalpay 8E **171**
on South Harris 8D **171**
Ceann a Bhàigh. *W Isl* 9C **171**
Ceannacroc Lodge. *High* 2E **149**
Ceann a Deas Loch Baghasdail.
*W Isl* 7C **170**
Ceann an Leothaid. *High* 5E **147**
Ceann a Tuath Loch
Baghasdail. *W Isl* 6C **170**
Ceann Loch Ailleart. *High* 5F **147**
Ceann Loch Muideirt.
*High* 1B **140**
Ceann-na-Cleithe. *W Isl* 8D **171**
Ceann Shìphoirt. *W Isl* 6E **171**
Ceann Tarabhaigh. *W Isl* 6E **171**
Cearsiadar. *W Isl* 5F **171**
Ceathramh Meadhanach.
*W Isl* 1D **170**
Cefn Berain. *Cnwy* 4B **82**
Cefn-brith. *Cnwy* 5B **82**
Cefn-bryn-brain. *Carm* 4H **45**
Cefn Bychan. *Cphy* 2F **33**
Cefn-bychan. *Flin* 4D **82**
Cefncaeau. *Carm* 3E **31**
Cefn Canol. *Powy* 2E **71**
Cefn Coch. *Powy* 5C **70**
Cefn-coch. *Powy* 3D **70**
Cefn-coed-y-cymmer.
*Mer T* 5D **46**
Cefn Cribwr. *B'end* 3B **32**
Cefn-ddwysarn. *Gwyn* 2B **70**
Cefn Einion. *Shrp* 2E **59**
Cefneithin. *Carm* 4F **45**
Cefn Glas. *B'end* 3B **32**
Cefngorwydd. *Powy* 1C **46**
Cefn Llwyd. *Cdgn* 2F **57**
Cefn-mawr. *Wrex* 1E **71**
Cefn-y-bedd. *Flin* 5F **83**
Cefn-y-coed. *Powy* 1D **58**
Cefn-y-pant. *Carm* 2F **43**
Cegidfa. *Powy* 4E **70**
Ceinewydd. *Cdgn* 5C **56**
Cellan. *Cdgn* 1G **45**
Cellardyke. *Fife* 3H **137**
Cellarhead. *Staf* 1D **72**
Cemaes. *IOA* 1C **80**
Cemmaes. *Powy* 5H **69**
Cemmaes Road. *Powy* 5H **69**
Cenarth. *Cdgn* 1C **44**
Cenin. *Gwyn* 1D **68**
Ceos. *W Isl* 5F **171**
Ceres. *Fife* 2G **137**
Ceri. *Powy* 2D **58**
Cerist. *Powy* 2B **58**
Cerne Abbas. *Dors* 2B **14**
Cerney Wick. *Glos* 2F **35**
Cerrigceinwen. *IOA* 3D **80**
Cerrigydrudion. *Cnwy* 1B **70**
Cess. *Norf* 4G **79**
Cessford. *Bord* 2B **120**
Ceunant. *Gwyn* 4E **81**
Chaceley. *Glos* 2D **48**
Chacewater. *Corn* 4B **6**
Chackmore. *Buck* 2E **51**
Chacombe. *Nptn* 1C **50**
**Chadderton**. *G Man* 4H **91**
Chaddesden. *Derb* 2A **74**
Chaddesden Common.
*Derb* 2A **74**
Chaddesley Corbett. *Worc* 3C **60**
Chaddlehanger. *Devn* 5E **11**
Chaddleworth. *W Ber* 4C **36**
Chadlington. *Oxon* 3B **50**
Chadshunt. *Warw* 5H **61**
Chadstone. *Nptn* 5F **63**
Chad Valley. *W Mid* 2E **61**
Chadwell. *Leics* 3E **75**
Chadwell. *Shrp* 4B **72**
Chadwell Heath. *G Lon* 2F **39**
Chadwell St Mary. *Thur* 3H **39**
Chadwick End. *W Mid* 3G **61**
Chadwick Green. *Mers* 1H **83**
Chaffcombe. *Som* 1G **13**
Chafford Hundred. *Thur* 3H **39**
Chagford. *Devn* 4H **11**
Chailey. *E Sus* 4E **27**
Chain Bridge. *Linc* 1C **76**
Chainbridge. *Cambs* 5D **76**
Chainhurst. *Kent* 1B **28**
Chalbury. *Dors* 2F **15**
Chalbury Common. *Dors* 2F **15**
Chaldon. *Surr* 5E **39**
Chaldon Herring. *Dors* 4C **14**
Chale. *IOW* 5C **16**
Chale Green. *IOW* 5C **16**
Chalfont Common. *Buck* 1B **38**
Chalfont St Giles. *Buck* 1A **38**
**Chalfont St Peter**. *Buck* 2B **38**
Chalford. *Glos* 5D **49**
Chalgrove. *Oxon* 2E **37**
Chalk. *Kent* 3A **40**
Chalk End. *Essx* 4G **53**
Chalk Hill. *Glos* 3G **49**
Challaborough. *Devn* 4C **8**
Challacombe. *Devn* 2G **19**
Challister. *Shet* 5G **173**
Challoch. *Dum* 3A **110**
Challock. *Kent* 5E **40**
Chalton. *C Beds*
nr. Bedford 5A **64**
nr. Luton 3A **52**
Chalton. *Hants* 1F **17**
Chalvington. *E Sus* 5G **27**
Champany. *Falk* 2D **128**
Chance Inn. *Fife* 2F **137**
Chancery. *Cdgn* 3E **57**
Chandler's Cross. *Herts* 1B **38**
Chandler's Cross. *Worc* 2C **48**
Chandler's Ford. *Hants* 4C **24**
Chanlockfoot. *Dum* 4G **117**
Channel's End. *Bed* 5A **64**
**Channel Tunnel**. *Kent* 2F **29**
Channerwick. *Shet* 9F **173**
Chantry. *Som* 2C **22**
Chantry. *Suff* 1E **55**
Chapel. *Cumb* 1D **102**
Chapel. *Fife* 4E **137**

Chapel Allerton. Som . . . . . . . .1H 21
Chapel Allerton. W Yor . . . . . . .1C 92
Chapel Amble. Corn . . . . . . . . .1D 6
Chapel Brampton. Nptn . . . . . . .4E 63
Chapelbridge. Cambs . . . . . . . .1B 64
Chapel Chorlton. Staf . . . . . . .2C 72
Chapel Cleeve. Som . . . . . . . . .2D 20
Chapel End. C Beds . . . . . . . . .1A 52
Chapel-en-le-Frith. Derbs . . . . .2E 85
Chapelfield. Abers . . . . . . . . .2G 145
Chapelgate. Linc . . . . . . . . . .3D 76
Chapel Green. Warw
  nr. Coventry . . . . . . . . . . .2G 61
  nr. Southam . . . . . . . . . . . .4B 62
Chapel Haddlesey. N Yor . . . . . .2F 93
Chapel Hill. Abers . . . . . . . . .5H 161
Chapel Hill. Linc . . . . . . . . .5B 88
Chapel Hill. Mon . . . . . . . . . .5A 48
Chapelhill. Per
  nr. Glencarse . . . . . . . . . . .1E 136
  nr. Harrietfield . . . . . . . . .5H 143
Chapelknowe. Dum . . . . . . . . . .2E 112
Chapel Lawn. Shrp . . . . . . . . .3F 59
Chapel le Dale. N Yor . . . . . . .2G 97
Chapel Milton. Derbs . . . . . . . .2E 85
Chapel of Garioch. Abers . . . . .1E 152
Chapel Row. W Ber . . . . . . . . .5D 36
Chapels. Cumb . . . . . . . . . . .1B 96
Chapel St Leonards. Linc . . . . .3E 89
Chapel Stile. Cumb . . . . . . . . .4E 102
Chapelthorpe. W Yor . . . . . . . .3D 92
Chapelton. Ang . . . . . . . . . . .4F 145
Chapelton. Devn . . . . . . . . . .4F 19
Chapelton. High
  nr. Grantown-on-Spey . . . . . . .2D 150
  nr. Inverness . . . . . . . . . .3H 157
Chapelton. S Lan . . . . . . . . . .5H 127
Chapel Town. Corn . . . . . . . . .3C 6
Chapeltown. Bkbn . . . . . . . . . .3F 91
Chapeltown. Mor . . . . . . . . . .1G 151
Chapeltown. S Yor . . . . . . . . .1A 86
Chapmanslade. Wilts . . . . . . . .2D 22
Chapmans Well. Devn . . . . . . . .3D 10
Chapmore End. Herts . . . . . . . .4D 52
Chappel. Essx . . . . . . . . . . .3B 54
Chard. Som . . . . . . . . . . . . .2G 13
Chard Junction. Dors . . . . . . . .2G 13
Chardstock. Devn . . . . . . . . . .2G 13
Charfield. S Glo . . . . . . . . . .2C 34
Charing. Kent . . . . . . . . . . .1D 28
Charing Heath. Kent . . . . . . . .1D 28
Charing Hill. Kent . . . . . . . . .5D 40
Charingworth. Glos . . . . . . . . .2H 49
Charlbury. Oxon . . . . . . . . . .4B 50
Charlcombe. Bath . . . . . . . . . .5C 34
Charlcutt. Wilts . . . . . . . . . .4E 35
Charlecote. Warw . . . . . . . . . .5G 61
Charles. Devn . . . . . . . . . . .3G 19
Charlesfield. Dum . . . . . . . . .3C 112
Charleshill. Surr . . . . . . . . .2G 25
Charleston. Ang . . . . . . . . . .4C 144
Charleston. Ren . . . . . . . . . .3F 127
Charlestown. Aber . . . . . . . . .3G 153
Charlestown. Abers . . . . . . . . .2H 161
Charlestown. Corn . . . . . . . . .3E 7
Charlestown. Dors . . . . . . . . .5B 14
Charlestown. Fife . . . . . . . . .1D 128
Charlestown. G Man . . . . . . . . .4G 91
Charlestown. High
  nr. Gairloch . . . . . . . . . . .1H 155
  nr. Inverness . . . . . . . . . .4A 158
Charlestown. W Yor . . . . . . . . .2H 91
Charlestown of Aberlour.
  Mor . . . . . . . . . . . . . . . .4G 159
Charles Tye. Suff . . . . . . . . .5C 66
Charlesworth. Derbs . . . . . . . .1E 85
Charlton. G Lon . . . . . . . . . .3F 39
Charlton. Hants . . . . . . . . . .2B 24
Charlton. Herts . . . . . . . . . .3B 52
Charlton. Nptn . . . . . . . . . . .2D 50
Charlton. Nmbd . . . . . . . . . . .1B 114
Charlton. Oxon . . . . . . . . . . .3C 36

Charlton. Som
  nr. Radstock . . . . . . . . . . .1B 22
  nr. Shepton Mallet . . . . . . . .2B 22
  nr. Taunton . . . . . . . . . . . .4F 21
Charlton. Telf . . . . . . . . . . .4H 71
Charlton. W Sus . . . . . . . . . .1G 17
Charlton. Wilts
  nr. Malmesbury . . . . . . . . . .3E 35
  nr. Pewsey . . . . . . . . . . . .1G 23
  nr. Shaftesbury . . . . . . . . .4E 23
Charlton. Worc
  nr. Evesham . . . . . . . . . . . .1F 49
  nr. Stourport-on-Severn
  . . . . . . . . . . . . . . . . . .3C 60
Charlton Abbots. Glos . . . . . . .3F 49
Charlton Adam. Som . . . . . . . . .4A 22
Charlton All Saints. Wilts . . . .4G 23
Charlton Down. Dors . . . . . . . .3B 14
Charlton Horethorne. Som . . . . .4B 22
Charlton Kings. Glos . . . . . . . .3E 49
Charlton Mackrell. Som . . . . . . .4A 22
Charlton Marshall. Dors . . . . . .2E 15
Charlton Musgrove. Som . . . . . . .4C 22
Charlton-on-Otmoor. Oxon . . . . .4D 50
Charlton on the Hill. Dors . . . .2D 15
Charlwood. Hants . . . . . . . . . .3E 25
Charlwood. Surr . . . . . . . . . .1D 26
Charlynch. Som . . . . . . . . . . .3F 21
Charminster. Dors . . . . . . . . .3B 14
Charmouth. Dors . . . . . . . . . .3G 13
Charndon. Buck . . . . . . . . . . .3E 51
Charney Bassett. Oxon . . . . . . .2B 36
Charnock Green. Lanc . . . . . . . .3D 90
Charnock Richard. Lanc . . . . . . .3D 90
Charsfield. Suff . . . . . . . . . .5E 67
The Chart. Kent . . . . . . . . . .5F 39
Chart Corner. Kent . . . . . . . . .5B 40
Charter Alley. Hants . . . . . . . .1D 24
Charterhouse. Som . . . . . . . . .1H 21
Charterville Allotments.
  Oxon . . . . . . . . . . . . . . .4B 50
Chartham. Kent . . . . . . . . . . .5F 41
Chartham Hatch. Kent . . . . . . . .5F 41
Chartridge. Buck . . . . . . . . . .5H 51
Chart Sutton. Kent . . . . . . . . .5B 40
Charvil. Wok . . . . . . . . . . . .4F 37
Charwelton. Nptn . . . . . . . . . .5C 62
Chase Terrace. Staf . . . . . . . .5E 73
Chasetown. Staf . . . . . . . . . .5E 73
Chastleton. Oxon . . . . . . . . . .3H 49
Chasty. Devn . . . . . . . . . . . .2D 10
Chatburn. Lanc . . . . . . . . . . .5G 97
Chatcull. Staf . . . . . . . . . . .2B 72
Chatham. Medw . . . . . . . . . . .4B 40
Chatham Green. Essx . . . . . . . .4H 53
Chathill. Nmbd . . . . . . . . . . .2F 121
Chatley. Worc . . . . . . . . . . .4C 60
Chattenden. Medw . . . . . . . . . .3B 40
Chatteris. Cambs . . . . . . . . . .2C 64
Chattisham. Suff . . . . . . . . . .1D 54
Chatton. Nmbd . . . . . . . . . . .2E 121
Chatwall. Shrp . . . . . . . . . . .1H 59
Chaulden. Herts . . . . . . . . . .5A 52
Chaul End. C Beds . . . . . . . . .3A 52
Chawleigh. Devn . . . . . . . . . .1H 11
Chawley. Oxon . . . . . . . . . . .5C 50
Chawston. Bed . . . . . . . . . . .5A 64
Chawton. Hants . . . . . . . . . . .3F 25
Chaxhill. Glos . . . . . . . . . . .4C 48
Cheadle. G Man . . . . . . . . . . .2C 84
Cheadle. Staf . . . . . . . . . . .1E 73
Cheadle Hulme. G Man . . . . . . . .2C 84
Cheapside. Wind . . . . . . . . . .4A 38
Chearsley. Buck . . . . . . . . . .4F 51
Chebsey. Staf . . . . . . . . . . .3C 72
Checkendon. Oxon . . . . . . . . . .3E 37
Checkley. Ches E . . . . . . . . . .1B 72
Checkley. Here . . . . . . . . . . .2A 48
Checkley. Staf . . . . . . . . . . .2E 73
Chedburgh. Suff . . . . . . . . . .5G 65
Cheddar. Som . . . . . . . . . . . .1H 21
Cheddington. Buck . . . . . . . . .4H 51
Cheddleton. Staf . . . . . . . . . .5D 84

Cheddon Fitzpaine. Som . . . . . . .4F 21
Chedglow. Wilts . . . . . . . . . .2E 35
Chedgrave. Norf . . . . . . . . . .1F 67
Chedington. Dors . . . . . . . . . .2H 13
Chediston. Suff . . . . . . . . . .3F 67
Chediston Green. Suff . . . . . . .3F 67
Chedworth. Glos . . . . . . . . . .4F 49
Chedzoy. Som . . . . . . . . . . . .3G 21
Cheeseman's Green. Kent . . . . . .2E 29
Cheetham Hill. G Man . . . . . . . .4G 91
Cheglinch. Devn . . . . . . . . . .2F 19
Cheldon. Devn . . . . . . . . . . .1H 11
Chelford. Ches E . . . . . . . . . .3C 84
Chellaston. Derb . . . . . . . . . .2A 74
Chellington. Bed . . . . . . . . . .5G 63
Chelmarsh. Shrp . . . . . . . . . .2B 60
Chelmick. Shrp . . . . . . . . . . .1G 59
Chelmondiston. Suff . . . . . . . .2F 55
Chelmorton. Derbs . . . . . . . . .4F 85
Chelmsford. Essx . . . . . . . . . .5H 53
Chelsea. G Lon . . . . . . . . . . .3D 38
Chelsfield. G Lon . . . . . . . . .4F 39
Chelsham. Surr . . . . . . . . . . .5E 39
Chelston. Som . . . . . . . . . . .4E 21
Chelsworth. Suff . . . . . . . . . .1C 54
Cheltenham. Glos . . . . . . . . . .3E 49
Chelveston. Nptn . . . . . . . . . .4G 63
Chelvey. N Som . . . . . . . . . . .5H 33
Chelwood. Bath . . . . . . . . . . .5B 34
Chelwood Common. E Sus . . . . . .3F 27
Chelwood Gate. E Sus . . . . . . .3F 27
Chelworth. Wilts . . . . . . . . . .2E 35
Chelworth Lower Green.
  Wilts . . . . . . . . . . . . . . .2F 35
Chelworth Upper Green.
  Wilts . . . . . . . . . . . . . . .2F 35
Chelynch. Som . . . . . . . . . . .2B 22
Cheney Longville. Shrp . . . . . .2G 59
Chenies. Buck . . . . . . . . . . .1B 38
Chepstow. Mon . . . . . . . . . . .2A 34
Chequerfield. W Yor . . . . . . . .2E 93
Chequers Corner. Norf . . . . . . .5D 77
Cherhill. Wilts . . . . . . . . . .4F 35
Cherington. Glos . . . . . . . . . .2E 35
Cherington. Warw . . . . . . . . . .2A 50
Cheriton. Devn . . . . . . . . . . .2H 19
Cheriton. Hants . . . . . . . . . .4D 24
Cheriton. Kent . . . . . . . . . . .2G 29
Cheriton. Pemb . . . . . . . . . . .5D 43
Cheriton. Swan . . . . . . . . . . .3D 30
Cheriton Bishop. Devn . . . . . . .3A 12
Cheriton Cross. Devn . . . . . . . .3A 12
Cheriton Fitzpaine. Devn . . . . .2B 12
Cherrington. Telf . . . . . . . . .3A 72
Cherrybank. Per . . . . . . . . . .1D 136
Cherry Burton. E Yor . . . . . . . .5D 101
Cherry Green. Herts . . . . . . . .3D 52
Cherry Hinton. Cambs . . . . . . . .5D 65
Cherry Willingham. Linc . . . . . .3H 87
Chertsey. Surr . . . . . . . . . . .4B 38
Cheselbourne. Dors . . . . . . . . .3C 14
Chesham. Buck . . . . . . . . . . .5H 51
Chesham. G Man . . . . . . . . . . .3G 91
Chesham Bois. Buck . . . . . . . . .1A 38
Cheshunt. Herts . . . . . . . . . .5D 52
Cheslyn Hay. Staf . . . . . . . . .5D 73
Chessetts Wood. Warw . . . . . . . .3F 61
Chessington. G Lon . . . . . . . . .4C 38
Chester. Ches W . . . . . . . . . .4G 83
Chesterblade. Som . . . . . . . . .2B 22
Chesterfield. Derbs . . . . . . . .3A 86
Chesterfield. Staf . . . . . . . . .5F 73
Chesterhope. Nmbd . . . . . . . . .1B 114
Chester Moor. Dur . . . . . . . . .5F 115
Chesters. Bord . . . . . . . . . . .3A 120
Chesterton. Cambs
  nr. Cambridge . . . . . . . . . . .4D 64
  nr. Peterborough . . . . . . . . .1A 64
Chesterton. Glos . . . . . . . . . .5F 49
Chesterton. Oxon . . . . . . . . . .3D 50
Chesterton. Shrp . . . . . . . . . .1B 60
Chesterton. Staf . . . . . . . . . .1C 72
Chesterton Green. Warw . . . . . . .5H 61

Chesterwood. Nmbd . . . . . . . . .3B 114
Chestfield. Kent . . . . . . . . . .4F 41
Cheston. Devn . . . . . . . . . . .3C 8
Cheswardine. Shrp . . . . . . . . .2B 72
Cheswell. Telf . . . . . . . . . . .4B 72
Cheswick. Nmbd . . . . . . . . . . .5G 131
Cheswick Green. W Mid . . . . . . .3F 61
Chetnole. Dors . . . . . . . . . . .2B 14
Chettiscombe. Devn . . . . . . . . .1C 12
Chettisham. Cambs . . . . . . . . .2E 65
Chettle. Dors . . . . . . . . . . .1E 15
Chetton. Shrp . . . . . . . . . . .1A 60
Chetwode. Buck . . . . . . . . . . .3E 51
Chetwynd Aston. Telf . . . . . . . .4B 72
Cheveley. Cambs . . . . . . . . . .4F 65
Chevening. Kent . . . . . . . . . .5F 39
Chevington. Suff . . . . . . . . . .5G 65
Chevithorne. Devn . . . . . . . . .1C 12
Chew Magna. Bath . . . . . . . . . .5A 34
Chew Moor. G Man . . . . . . . . . .4E 91
Chew Stoke. Bath . . . . . . . . . .5A 34
Chewton Keynsham. Bath . . . . . .5B 34
Chewton Mendip. Som . . . . . . . .1A 22
Chicacott. Devn . . . . . . . . . .3G 11
Chickerley. Mil . . . . . . . . . .1H 51
Chichester. W Sus . . . . . . . . .2G 17
Chickerell. Dors . . . . . . . . . .4B 14
Chickering. Suff . . . . . . . . . .3E 66
Chicklade. Wilts . . . . . . . . . .3E 23
Chicksands. C Beds . . . . . . . . .2B 52
Chickward. Here . . . . . . . . . .5E 59
Chidden. Hants . . . . . . . . . . .1E 17
Chiddingfold. Surr . . . . . . . . .2A 26
Chiddingly. E Sus . . . . . . . . .4G 27
Chiddingstone. Kent . . . . . . . .1G 27
Chiddingstone Causeway.
  Kent . . . . . . . . . . . . . . .1G 27
Chiddingstone Hoath. Kent . . . . .1F 27
Chideock. Dors . . . . . . . . . . .3H 13
Chidgley. Som . . . . . . . . . . .3D 20
Chidham. W Sus . . . . . . . . . . .2F 17
Chieveley. W Ber . . . . . . . . . .4C 36
Chignal St James. Essx . . . . . .5G 53
Chignal Smealy. Essx . . . . . . . .4G 53
Chigwell. Essx . . . . . . . . . . .1F 39
Chigwell Row. Essx . . . . . . . . .1F 39
Chilbolton. Hants . . . . . . . . .2B 24
Chilcomb. Hants . . . . . . . . . .4D 24
Chilcombe. Dors . . . . . . . . . .3A 14
Chilcompton. Som . . . . . . . . . .1B 22
Chilcote. Leics . . . . . . . . . .4G 73
Childer Thornton. Ches W . . . . .3F 83
Child Okeford. Dors . . . . . . . .1D 14
Childrey. Oxon . . . . . . . . . . .3B 36
Child's Ercall. Shrp . . . . . . . .3A 72
Childswickham. Worc . . . . . . . .2F 49
Childwall. Mers . . . . . . . . . .2G 83
Childwick Green. Herts . . . . . . .4B 52
Chilfrome. Dors . . . . . . . . . .3A 14
Chilgrove. W Sus . . . . . . . . . .1G 17
Chilham. Kent . . . . . . . . . . .5E 41
Chilhampton. Wilts . . . . . . . . .3F 23
Chilla. Devn . . . . . . . . . . . .2E 11
Chilland. Hants . . . . . . . . . .3D 24
Chillaton. Devn . . . . . . . . . .4E 11
Chillenden. Kent . . . . . . . . . .5G 41
Chillerton. IOW . . . . . . . . . .4C 16
Chillesford. Suff . . . . . . . . .5F 67
Chillingham. Nmbd . . . . . . . . .2E 121
Chillington. Devn . . . . . . . . .4D 9
Chillington. Som . . . . . . . . . .1G 13
Chilmark. Wilts . . . . . . . . . .3E 23
Chilmington Green. Kent . . . . . .1D 28
Chilson. Oxon . . . . . . . . . . .4B 50
Chilsworthy. Corn . . . . . . . . .5E 11
Chilsworthy. Devn . . . . . . . . .2D 10
Chiltern Green. C Beds . . . . . .4B 52
Chilthorne Domer. Som . . . . . . .1A 14
Chilton. Buck . . . . . . . . . . .4E 51
Chilton. Devn . . . . . . . . . . .2B 12
Chilton. Dur . . . . . . . . . . . .2F 105
Chilton. Oxon . . . . . . . . . . .3C 36
Chilton Candover. Hants . . . . . .2D 24
Chilton Cantelo. Som . . . . . . . .4A 22

Chilton Foliat. Wilts . . . . . . .4B 36
Chilton Lane. Dur . . . . . . . . .1A 106
Chilton Polden. Som . . . . . . . .3G 21
Chilton Street. Suff . . . . . . . .1A 54
Chilton Trinity. Som . . . . . . . .3F 21
Chilwell. Notts . . . . . . . . . .2C 74
Chilworth. Hants . . . . . . . . . .1C 16
Chilworth. Surr . . . . . . . . . .1B 26
Chimney. Oxon . . . . . . . . . . .5B 50
Chimney Street. Suff . . . . . . . .1H 53
Chineham. Hants . . . . . . . . . .1E 25
Chingford. G Lon . . . . . . . . . .1E 39
Chinley. Derbs . . . . . . . . . . .2E 85
Chinnor. Oxon . . . . . . . . . . .5F 51
Chipley. Som . . . . . . . . . . . .4E 20
Chipnall. Shrp . . . . . . . . . . .2B 72
Chippenham. Cambs . . . . . . . . .4F 65
Chippenham. Wilts . . . . . . . . .4E 35
Chipperfield. Herts . . . . . . . .5A 52
Chipping. Herts . . . . . . . . . .2D 52
Chipping. Lanc . . . . . . . . . . .5F 97
Chipping Campden. Glos . . . . . .2G 49
Chipping Hill. Essx . . . . . . . .4B 54
Chipping Norton. Oxon . . . . . . .3B 50
Chipping Ongar. Essx . . . . . . . .5F 53
Chipping Sodbury. S Glo . . . . . .3C 34
Chipping Warden. Nptn . . . . . . .1C 50
Chipstable. Som . . . . . . . . . .4D 20
Chipstead. Kent . . . . . . . . . .5G 39
Chipstead. Surr . . . . . . . . . .5D 38
Chirbury. Shrp . . . . . . . . . . .1E 59
Chirk. Wrex . . . . . . . . . . . .2E 71
Chirmorie. S Ayr . . . . . . . . . .2H 109
Chirnside. Bord . . . . . . . . . .4E 131
Chirnsidebridge. Bord . . . . . . .4E 131
Chirton. Wilts . . . . . . . . . . .1F 23
Chisbridge Cross. Buck . . . . . .3G 37
Chisbury. Wilts . . . . . . . . . .5A 36
Chiselborough. Som . . . . . . . . .1H 13
Chiseldon. Swin . . . . . . . . . .4G 35
Chiselhampton. Oxon . . . . . . . .2D 36
Chiserley. W Yor . . . . . . . . . .2A 92
Chislehurst. G Lon . . . . . . . . .3F 39
Chislet. Kent . . . . . . . . . . .4G 41
Chiswell. Dors . . . . . . . . . . .5B 14
Chiswell Green. Herts . . . . . . .5B 52
Chiswick. G Lon . . . . . . . . . .3D 38
Chisworth. Derbs . . . . . . . . . .1D 85
Chitcombe. E Sus . . . . . . . . . .3C 28
Chithurst. W Sus . . . . . . . . . .4G 25
Chittering. Cambs . . . . . . . . .4D 65
Chitterne. Wilts . . . . . . . . . .2E 23
Chittlehamholt. Devn . . . . . . . .4G 19
Chittlehampton. Devn . . . . . . . .4G 19
Chittoe. Wilts . . . . . . . . . . .5E 35
Chivelstone. Devn . . . . . . . . .5D 9
Chivenor. Devn . . . . . . . . . . .3F 19
Chobham. Surr . . . . . . . . . . .4A 38
Cholderton. Wilts . . . . . . . . .2H 23
Cholesbury. Buck . . . . . . . . . .5H 51
Chollerford. Nmbd . . . . . . . . .2C 114
Chollerton. Nmbd . . . . . . . . . .2C 114
Cholsey. Oxon . . . . . . . . . . .3D 36
Cholstrey. Here . . . . . . . . . .5G 59
Chop Gate. N Yor . . . . . . . . . .5C 106
Choppington. Nmbd . . . . . . . . .1F 115
Chopwell. Tyne . . . . . . . . . . .4E 115
Chorley. Ches E . . . . . . . . . .5H 83
Chorley. Lanc . . . . . . . . . . .3D 90
Chorley. Shrp . . . . . . . . . . .2A 60
Chorley. Staf . . . . . . . . . . .4E 73
Chorleywood. Herts . . . . . . . . .1B 38
Chorlton. Ches E . . . . . . . . . .5B 84
Chorlton-cum-Hardy.
  G Man . . . . . . . . . . . . . . .1C 84
Chorlton Lane. Ches W . . . . . . .1G 71
Choulton. Shrp . . . . . . . . . . .2F 59
Chrishall. Essx . . . . . . . . . .2E 53
Christchurch. Cambs . . . . . . . .1D 65
Christchurch. Devn . . . . . . . . .3G 15
Christchurch. Glos . . . . . . . . .4A 48
Christian Malford. Wilts . . . . .4E 35
Christleton. Ches W . . . . . . . .4G 83

Christmas Common—Cloughton


Christmas Common. *Oxon* 2F **37**
Christon. *N Som* 1G **21**
Christon Bank. *Nmbd* 2G **121**
Christow. *Devn* 4B **12**
Chryston. *N Lan* 2H **127**
Chuck Hatch. *E Sus* 2F **27**
Chudleigh. *Devn* 5B **12**
Chudleigh Knighton. *Devn* 5B **12**
Chulmleigh. *Devn* 1G **11**
Chunal. *Derbs* 1E **85**
Church. *Lanc* 2F **91**
Churcham. *Glos* 4C **48**
Church Aston. *Telf* 4B **72**
Church Brampton. *Nptn* 4E **62**
Church Brough. *Cumb* 3A **104**
Church Broughton. *Derbs* 2G **73**
Church Corner. *Suff* 2G **67**
Church Crookham. *Hants* 1G **25**
Churchdown. *Glos* 3D **49**
Church Eaton. *Staf* 4C **72**
Church End. *Cambs*
nr. Cambridge 5D **65**
nr. Over 3C **64**
nr. Sawtry 2B **64**
nr. Wisbech 5C **76**
Church End. *C Beds*
nr. Stotfold 2B **52**
nr. Totternhoe 3H **51**
Church End. *E Yor* 4E **101**
Church End. *Essx*
nr. Braintree 3H **53**
nr. Great Dunmow 3G **53**
nr. Saffron Walden 1F **53**
Church End. *Glos* 5C **48**
Church End. *Hants* 1E **25**
Church End. *Linc*
nr. Donington 2B **76**
nr. North Somercotes 1D **88**
Church End. *Norf* 4E **77**
Church End. *Warw*
nr. Coleshill 1G **61**
nr. Nuneaton 1G **61**
Church End. *Wilts* 4F **35**
Churchend. *Essx* 1E **40**
Church Enstone. *Oxon* 3B **50**
Church Fenton. *N Yor* 1F **93**
Church Green. *Devn* 3E **13**
Church Gresley. *Derbs* 4G **73**
Church Hanborough. *Oxon* 4C **50**
Church Hill. *Ches W* 4A **84**
Church Hill. *Worc* 4E **61**
Church Hougham. *Kent* 1G **29**
Church Houses. *N Yor* 5D **106**
Churchill. *Devn*
nr. Axminster 2G **13**
nr. Barnstaple 2F **19**
Churchill. *N Som* 1H **21**
Churchill. *Oxon* 3A **50**
Churchill. *Worc*
nr. Kidderminster 3C **60**
nr. Worcester 5D **60**
Churchinford. *Som* 1F **13**
Church Knowle. *Dors* 4E **15**
Church Laneham. *Notts* 3F **87**
Church Langley. *Essx* 5E **53**
Church Langton. *Leics* 1E **62**
Church Lawford. *Warw* 3B **62**
Church Lawton. *Ches E* 5C **84**
Church Leigh. *Staf* 2E **73**
Church Lench. *Worc* 5E **61**
Church Mayfield. *Staf* 1F **73**
Church Minshull. *Ches E* 4A **84**
Church Norton. *W Sus* 3G **17**
Churchover. *Warw* 2C **62**
Church Preen. *Shrp* 1H **59**
Church Pulverbatch. *Shrp* 5G **71**
Churchstanton. *Som* 1E **13**
Church Stoke. *Powy* 1E **59**
Churchstow. *Devn* 4D **8**
Church Stowe. *Nptn* 5D **62**
Church Street. *Kent* 3B **40**
Church Stretton. *Shrp* 1G **59**
Church Town. *Leics* 4A **74**
Church Town. *N Lin* 4A **94**
Churchtown. *Cumb* 5E **113**
Churchtown. *Derbs* 4G **85**
Churchtown. *Devn* 2G **19**
Churchtown. *IOM* 2D **108**
Churchtown. *Lanc* 5D **97**
Churchtown. *Mers* 3B **90**
Churchtown. *Shrp* 2E **59**
Church Village. *Rhon* 3D **32**
Church Warsop. *Notts* 4C **86**
Church Westcote. *Glos* 3H **49**
Church Wilne. *Derbs* 2B **74**
Churnsike Lodge. *Nmbd* 2H **113**
Churston Ferrers. *Torb* 3F **9**
Churt. *Surr* 3G **25**
Churton. *Ches W* 5G **83**
Churwell. *W Yor* 2C **92**
Chute Standen. *Wilts* 1B **24**
Chwilog. *Gwyn* 2D **68**
Chwittfordd. *Flin* 3D **82**
Chyandour. *Corn* 3B **4**
Cilan Uchaf. *Gwyn* 3B **68**
Cilcain. *Flin* 4D **82**
Cilcennin. *Cdgn* 4E **57**
Cilfrew. *Neat* 5A **46**
Cilfynydd. *Rhon* 2D **32**
Cilgerran. *Pemb* 1B **44**
Cilgeti. *Pemb* 4F **43**
Cilgwyn. *Carm* 3H **45**
Cilgwyn. *Pemb* 1E **43**
Ciliau Aeron. *Cdgn* 5D **57**
Cill Amhlaidh. *W Isl* 4C **170**
Cill Donnain. *W Isl* 6C **170**
Cille a' Bhacstair. *High* 2C **154**
Cille Bhrighde. *W Isl* 7C **170**
Cille Pheadair. *W Isl* 7C **170**
Cilmaengwyn. *Neat* 5H **45**
Cilmeri. *Powy* 5C **58**
Cilmery. *Powy* 5C **58**
Cilrhedyn. *Pemb* 1G **43**
Cilsan. *Carm* 3F **45**
Ciltalgarth. *Gwyn* 1A **70**
Ciltwrch. *Powy* 1E **47**
Cilybebyll. *Neat* 5H **45**
Cilycwm. *Carm* 1A **46**
Cimla. *Neat* 2A **32**
**Cinderford**. *Glos* 4B **48**
Cinderhill. *Derbs* 1A **74**
Cippenham. *Slo* 2A **38**
Cippyn. *Pemb* 1B **44**
Cirbhig. *W Isl* 3D **171**
Circebost. *W Isl* 4D **171**
**Cirencester**. *Glos* 5F **49**
City. *Powy* 1E **58**
City. *V Glam* 4C **32**
The City. *Buck* 2F **37**
City Airport. *G Lon* 2F **39**
City Centre. *Stoke* 1C **72**
City Dulas. *IOA* 2D **80**
City of Derry Airport. *Derr* 1D **174**
**City of London**. *G Lon* 2E **39**
Clabhach. *Arg* 3C **138**
Clachaig. *Arg* 1C **126**
Clachaig. *High*
nr. Kinlochleven 3F **141**
nr. Nethy Bridge 2E **151**
Clachamish. *High* 3C **154**
Clachan. *Arg*
on Kintyre 4F **125**
on Lismore 4C **140**
Clachan. *High*
nr. Bettyhill 2H **167**
nr. Staffin 2D **155**
nr. Uig 1D **154**
on Raasay 5E **155**
Clachan Farm. *Arg* 2A **134**
Clachan na Luib. *W Isl* 2D **170**
Clachan of Campsie. *E Dun* 2H **127**
Clachan of Glendaruel. *Arg* 1A **126**
Clachan-Seil. *Arg* 2E **133**
Clachan Shannda. *W Isl* 1D **170**
Clachan Strachur. *Arg* 3H **133**
Clachbreck. *Arg* 2F **125**
Clachnaharry. *High* 4A **158**
Clachtoll. *High* 1E **163**
Clackmannan. *Clac* 4B **136**
**Clackmannanshire Bridge**. *Clac* 1C **128**
Clackmarras. *Mor* 3G **159**
**Clacton-on-Sea**. *Essx* 4E **55**
Cladach a Chaolais. *W Isl* 2C **170**
Cladach Chairinis. *W Isl* 3D **170**
Cladach Chirceboist. *W Isl* 2C **170**
Cladach Iolaraigh. *W Isl* 2C **170**
Cladich. *Arg* 1H **133**
Cladswell. *Worc* 5E **61**
Claggan. *High*
nr. Fort William 1F **141**
nr. Lochaline 3B **140**
Claigan. *High* 3B **154**
Clandown. *Bath* 1B **22**
Clanfield. *Hants* 1E **17**
Clanfield. *Oxon* 5A **50**
Clanville. *Hants* 2B **24**
Clanville. *Som* 3B **22**
Claonaig. *Arg* 4G **125**
Clapgate. *Dors* 2F **15**
Clapgate. *Herts* 3E **53**
Clapham. *Bed* 5H **63**
Clapham. *Devn* 4B **12**
**Clapham**. *G Lon* 3D **39**
Clapham. *N Yor* 3G **97**
Clapham. *W Sus* 5B **26**
Clap Hill. *Kent* 2E **29**
Clappers. *Bord* 4F **131**
Clappersgate. *Cumb* 4E **103**
Clapphoull. *Shet* 9F **173**
Clapton. *Som*
nr. Crewkerne 2H **13**
nr. Radstock 1B **22**
Clapton in Gordano. *N Som* 4H **33**
Clapton-on-the-Hill. *Glos* 4G **49**
Clapworthy. *Devn* 4G **19**
Clara Vale. *Tyne* 3E **115**
Clarbeston. *Pemb* 2E **43**
Clarbeston Road. *Pemb* 2E **43**
Clarborough. *Notts* 2E **87**
Clare. *Suff* 1A **54**
Clarebrand. *Dum* 3E **111**
Clarencefield. *Dum* 3B **112**
Clarilaw. *Bord* 3H **119**
Clark's Green. *Surr* 2C **26**
Clark's Hill. *Linc* 3C **76**
**Clarkston**. *E Ren* 4G **127**
Clasheddy. *High* 2G **167**
Clashindarroch. *Abers* 5B **160**
Clashmore. *High*
nr. Dornoch 5E **165**
nr. Stoer 1E **163**
Clashnessie. *High* 5A **166**
Clashnoir. *Mor* 1G **151**
Clate. *Shet* 5G **173**
Clathick. *Per* 1H **135**
Clathy. *Per* 2B **136**
Clatt. *Abers* 1C **152**
Clatter. *Powy* 1B **58**
Clatterford. *IOW* 4C **16**
Clatworthy. *Som* 3D **20**
Claudy. *Derr* 2D **174**
Claughton. *Lanc*
nr. Caton 3E **97**
nr. Garstang 5E **97**
Claughton. *Mers* 2E **83**
Claverdon. *Warw* 4F **61**
Claverham. *N Som* 5H **33**
Clavering. *Essx* 2E **53**
Claverley. *Shrp* 1B **60**
Claverton. *Bath* 5C **34**
Clawdd-côch. *V Glam* 4D **32**
Clawdd-newydd. *Den* 5C **82**
Clawson Hill. *Leics* 3E **75**
Clawton. *Devn* 3D **10**
Claxby. *Linc*
nr. Alford 3D **88**
nr. Market Rasen 1A **88**
Claxton. *Norf* 5F **79**
Claxton. *N Yor* 3A **100**
Claybrooke Magna. *Leics* 2B **62**
Claybrooke Parva. *Leics* 2B **62**
Clay Common. *Suff* 2G **67**
Clay Coton. *Nptn* 3C **62**
**Clay Cross**. *Derbs* 4A **86**
Claydon. *Oxon* 5B **62**
Claydon. *Suff* 5D **66**
Clay End. *Herts* 3D **52**
Claygate. *Dum* 2E **113**
Claygate. *Kent* 1B **28**
Claygate. *Surr* 4C **38**
Claygate Cross. *Kent* 5H **39**
Clayhall. *Hants* 3E **16**
Clayhanger. *Devn* 4D **20**
Clayhanger. *W Mid* 5E **73**
Clayhidon. *Devn* 1E **13**
Clay Hill. *Bris* 4B **34**
Clayhill. *E Sus* 3C **28**
Clayhill. *Hants* 2B **16**
Clayhithe. *Cambs* 4E **65**
Clayholes. *Ang* 5E **145**
Clay Lake. *Linc* 3B **76**
Clayock. *High* 3D **168**
Claypits. *Glos* 5C **48**
Claypole. *Linc* 1F **75**
Claythorpe. *Linc* 3D **88**
Clayton. *G Man* 1C **84**
Clayton. *S Yor* 4E **93**
Clayton. *Staf* 1C **72**
Clayton. *W Sus* 4E **27**
Clayton. *W Yor* 1B **92**
Clayton Green. *Lanc* 2D **90**
Clayton-le-Moors. *Lanc* 1F **91**
Clayton-le-Woods. *Lanc* 2D **90**
Clayton West. *W Yor* 3C **92**
Clayworth. *Notts* 2E **87**
Cleadale. *High* 5C **146**
Cleadon. *Tyne* 3G **115**
Clearbrook. *Devn* 2B **8**
Clearwell. *Glos* 5A **48**
Cleasby. *N Yor* 3F **105**
Cleat. *Orkn*
nr. Braehead 3D **172**
nr. St Margaret's Hope 9D **172**
Cleatlam. *Dur* 3E **105**
Cleator. *Cumb* 3B **102**
Cleator Moor. *Cumb* 3B **102**
**Cleckheaton**. *W Yor* 2B **92**
Cleedownton. *Shrp* 2H **59**
Cleehill. *Shrp* 3H **59**
Cleekhimin. *N Lan* 4A **128**
Clee St Margaret. *Shrp* 2H **59**
Cleestanton. *Shrp* 3H **59**
**Cleethorpes**. *NE Lin* 4G **95**
Cleeton St Mary. *Shrp* 3A **60**
Cleeve. *N Som* 5H **33**
Cleeve. *Oxon* 3E **36**
Cleeve Hill. *Glos* 3E **49**
Cleeve Prior. *Worc* 1F **49**
Clehonger. *Here* 2H **47**
Cleigh. *Arg* 1F **133**
Cleish. *Per* 4C **136**
Cleland. *N Lan* 4B **128**
Clench Common. *Wilts* 5G **35**
Clenchwarton. *Norf* 3E **77**
Clennell. *Nmbd* 4D **120**
Clent. *Worc* 3D **60**
Cleobury Mortimer. *Shrp* 3A **60**
Cleobury North. *Shrp* 2A **60**
Clephanton. *High* 3C **158**
Clerkhill. *High* 2H **167**
Clestrain. *Orkn* 7C **172**
Clevancy. *Wilts* 4F **35**
**Clevedon**. *N Som* 4H **33**
Cleveley. *Oxon* 3B **50**
**Cleveleys**. *Lanc* 5C **96**
Clevelode. *Worc* 1D **48**
Cleverton. *Wilts* 3E **35**
Clewer. *Som* 1H **21**
Cley next the Sea. *Norf* 1C **78**
Cliaid. *W Isl* 8B **170**
Cliasmol. *W Isl* 7C **171**
Clibberswick. *Shet* 1H **173**
Cliburn. *Cumb* 2G **103**
Cliddesden. *Hants* 2E **25**
Clieves Hills. *Lanc* 4B **90**
Cliff. *Warw* 1G **61**
Cliffburn. *Ang* 4F **145**
Cliffe. *Medw* 3B **40**
Cliffe. *N Yor*
nr. Darlington 3F **105**
nr. Selby 1G **93**
Cliff End. *E Sus* 4C **28**
Cliffe Woods. *Medw* 3B **40**
Clifford. *Here* 1F **47**
Clifford. *W Yor* 5G **99**
Clifford Chambers. *Warw* 5F **61**
Clifford's Mesne. *Glos* 3C **48**
Cliffsend. *Kent* 4H **41**
Clifton. *Bris* 4A **34**
Clifton. *C Beds* 2B **52**
Clifton. *Cumb* 2G **103**
Clifton. *Derbs* 1F **73**
Clifton. *Devn* 2G **19**
Clifton. *G Man* 4F **91**
Clifton. *Lanc* 1C **90**
Clifton. *Nmbd* 1F **115**
Clifton. *N Yor* 5D **98**
Clifton. *Nott* 2C **74**
Clifton. *Oxon* 2C **50**
Clifton. *S Yor* 1C **86**
Clifton. *Stir* 5H **141**
Clifton. *W Yor* 2B **92**
Clifton. *Worc* 1D **48**
Clifton. *York* 4H **99**
Clifton Campville. *Staf* 4G **73**
Clifton Hampden. *Oxon* 2D **36**
Clifton Hill. *Worc* 4B **60**
Clifton Reynes. *Mil* 5G **63**
Clifton upon Dunsmore. *Warw* 3C **62**
Clifton upon Teme. *Worc* 4B **60**
Cliftonville. *Kent* 3H **41**
Cliftonville. *Norf* 2F **79**
Climping. *W Sus* 5A **26**
Climpy. *S Lan* 4C **128**
Clink. *Som* 2C **22**
Clint. *N Yor* 4E **99**
Clint Green. *Norf* 4C **78**
Clintmains. *Bord* 1A **120**
Cliobh. *W Isl* 4C **171**
Clipiau. *Gwyn* 4H **69**
Clippesby. *Norf* 4G **79**
Clippings Green. *Norf* 4C **78**
Clipsham. *Rut* 4G **75**
Clipston. *Nptn* 2E **62**
Clipston. *Notts* 2D **74**
Clipstone. *Notts* 4C **86**
**Clitheroe**. *Lanc* 5G **97**
Cliuthar. *W Isl* 8D **171**
Clive. *Shrp* 3H **71**
Clivocast. *Shet* 1G **173**
Clixby. *Linc* 4D **94**
Clocaenog. *Den* 5C **82**
Clochan. *Mor* 2B **160**
Clochforbie. *Abers* 3F **161**
Clock Face. *Mers* 1H **83**
Cloddiau. *Powy* 5E **70**
Cloddymoss. *Mor* 2D **159**
Clodock. *Here* 3G **47**
Cloford. *Som* 2C **22**
Cloghmills. *Caus* 2F **175**
Clola. *Abers* 4H **161**
Clophill. *C Beds* 2A **52**
Clopton. *Nptn* 2H **63**
Clopton Corner. *Suff* 5E **66**
Clopton Green. *Suff* 5G **65**
Closeburn. *Dum* 5A **118**
Close Clark. *IOM* 4B **108**
Closworth. *Som* 1A **14**
Clothall. *Herts* 2C **52**
Clotton. *Ches W* 4H **83**
Clough. *G Man* 3H **91**
Clough. *W Yor* 3A **92**
Clough Foot. *W Yor* 2H **91**
Cloughton. *N Yor* 5H **107**

# Cloughton Newlands—Coniston Cold



Cloughton Newlands. *N Yor* 5H **107**
Clousta. *Shet* 6E **173**
Clouston. *Orkn* 6B **172**
Clova. *Abers* 1B **152**
Clova. *Ang* 1C **144**
Clovelly. *Devn* 4D **18**
Clovenfords. *Bord* 1G **119**
Clovenstone. *Abers* 2E **153**
Clovullin. *High* 2E **141**
Clowne. *Derbs* 3B **86**
Clows Top. *Worc* 3B **60**
Cloy. *Wrex* 1F **71**
Cluanie Inn. *High* 2C **148**
Cluanie Lodge. *High* 2C **148**
Cluddley. *Telf* 4A **72**
Clun. *Shrp* 2F **59**
Y Clun. *Neat* 5B **46**
Clunas. *High* 4C **158**
Clunbury. *Shrp* 2F **59**
Clunderwen. *Pemb* 3F **43**
Clune. *High* 1B **150**
Clunes. *High* 5E **148**
Clungunford. *Shrp* 3F **59**
Clunie. *Per* 4A **144**
Clunton. *Shrp* 2F **59**
Cluny. *Fife* 4E **137**
Clutton. *Bath* 1B **22**
Clutton. *Ches W* 5G **83**
Clwt-y-bont. *Gwyn* 4E **81**
Clwydfagwyr. *Mer T* 5D **46**
Clydach. *Mon* 4F **47**
**Clydach**. *Swan* 5G **45**
Clydach Vale. *Rhon* 2C **32**
**Clydebank**. *W Dun* 3G **127**
Clydey. *Pemb* 1G **43**
Clyffe Pypard. *Wilts* 4F **35**
Clynder. *Arg* 1D **126**
Clyne. *Neat* 5B **46**
Clynelish. *High* 3F **165**
Clynnog-fawr. *Gwyn* 1D **68**
Clyro. *Powy* 1F **47**
Clyst Honiton. *Devn* 3C **12**
Clyst Hydon. *Devn* 2D **12**
Clyst St George. *Devn* 4C **12**
Clyst St Lawrence. *Devn* 2D **12**
Clyst St Mary. *Devn* 3C **12**
Clyth. *High* 5E **169**
Cnip. *W Isl* 4C **171**
Cnoc Amhlaigh. *W Isl* 4H **171**
Cnwcau. *Pemb* 1C **44**
Cnwch Coch. *Cdgn* 3F **57**
Coad's Green. *Corn* 5C **10**
Coal Aston. *Derbs* 3A **86**
Coalbrookdale. *Telf* 5A **72**
Coalbrookvale. *Blae* 5E **47**
Coalburn. *S Lan* 1H **117**
Coalburns. *Tyne* 3E **115**
Coalcleugh. *Nmbd* 5B **114**
Coaley. *Glos* 5C **48**
Coalford. *Abers* 4F **153**
Coalhall. *E Ayr* 3D **116**
Coalhill. *Essx* 1B **40**
Coalisland. *M Ulst* 4E **175**
Coalpit Heath. *S Glo* 3B **34**
Coal Pool. *W Mid* 5E **73**
Coalport. *Telf* 5B **72**
Coalsnaughton. *Clac* 4B **136**
Coaltown of Balgonie. *Fife* 4F **137**
Coaltown of Wemyss. *Fife* 4F **137**
**Coalville**. *Leics* 4B **74**
Coalway. *Glos* 4A **48**
Coanwood. *Nmbd* 4H **113**
Coat. *Som* 4H **21**
**Coatbridge**. *N Lan* 3A **128**
Coatdyke. *N Lan* 3A **128**
Coate. *Swin* 3G **35**
Coate. *Wilts* 5F **35**
Coates. *Cambs* 1C **64**
Coates. *Glos* 5E **49**
Coates. *Linc* 2G **87**
Coates. *W Sus* 4A **26**
Coatham. *Red C* 2C **106**
Coatham Mundeville. *Darl* 2F **105**
Cobbaton. *Devn* 4G **19**
Coberley. *Glos* 4E **49**
Cobhall Common. *Here* 2H **47**
Cobham. *Kent* 4A **40**
**Cobham**. *Surr* 5C **38**
Cobnash. *Here* 4G **59**
Coburg. *Devn* 5B **12**
Cockayne. *N Yor* 5D **106**
Cockayne Hatley. *C Beds* 1C **52**
Cock Bank. *Wrex* 1F **71**
Cock Bridge. *Abers* 3G **151**
Cockburnspath. *Bord* 2D **130**
Cock Clarks. *Essx* 5B **54**
Cockenzie and Port Seton. *E Lot* 2H **129**
Cockerham. *Lanc* 4D **96**
Cockermouth. *Cumb* 1C **102**
Cockernhoe. *Herts* 3B **52**
Cockfield. *Dur* 2E **105**
Cockfield. *Suff* 5B **66**
Cockfosters. *G Lon* 1D **39**
Cock Gate. *Here* 4G **59**
Cock Green. *Essx* 4G **53**
Cocking. *W Sus* 1G **17**
Cocking Causeway. *W Sus* 1G **17**
Cockington. *Torb* 2E **9**
Cocklake. *Som* 2H **21**
Cocklaw. *Abers* 4H **161**
Cocklaw. *Nmbd* 2C **114**
Cockley Beck. *Cumb* 4D **102**
Cockley Cley. *Norf* 5G **77**
Cockmuir. *Abers* 3G **161**
Cockpole Green. *Wok* 3F **37**
Cockshutford. *Shrp* 2H **59**
Cockshutt. *Shrp* 3G **71**
Cockthorpe. *Norf* 1B **78**
Cockwood. *Devn* 4C **12**
Cockyard. *Derbs* 3E **85**
Cockyard. *Here* 2H **47**
Codda. *Corn* 5B **10**
Coddenham. *Suff* 5D **66**
Coddenham Green. *Suff* 5D **66**
Coddington. *Ches W* 5G **83**
Coddington. *Here* 1C **48**
Coddington. *Notts* 5F **87**
Codford. *Wilts* 3E **23**
Codicote. *Herts* 4C **52**
Codmore Hill. *W Sus* 3B **26**
Codnor. *Derbs* 1B **74**
Codrington. *S Glo* 4C **34**
**Codsall**. *Staf* 5C **72**
Codsall Wood. *Staf* 5C **72**
**Coed Duon**. *Cphy* 2E **33**
Coedely. *Rhon* 3D **32**
Coedglasson. *Powy* 4C **58**
Coedkernew. *Newp* 3F **33**
Coed Morgan. *Mon* 4G **47**
Coedpoeth. *Wrex* 5E **83**
Coedway. *Powy* 4F **71**
Coed-y-bryn. *Cdgn* 1D **44**
Coed-y-paen. *Mon* 2G **33**
Coed Ystumgwern. *Gwyn* 3E **69**
Coelbren. *Powy* 4B **46**
Coffinswell. *Devn* 2E **9**
Cofton Hackett. *Worc* 3E **61**
Cogan. *V Glam* 4E **33**
Cogenhoe. *Nptn* 4F **63**
Cogges. *Oxon* 5B **50**
Coggeshall. *Essx* 3B **54**
Coggeshall Hamlet. *Essx* 3B **54**
Coggins Mill. *E Sus* 3G **27**
Coignafearn Lodge. *High* 2A **150**
Coig Peighinnean. *W Isl* 1H **171**
Coig Peighinnean Bhuirgh. *W Isl* 2G **171**
Coilleag. *W Isl* 7C **170**
Coillemore. *High* 1A **158**
Coillore. *High* 5C **154**
Coire an Fhuarain. *W Isl* 4E **171**
Coity. *B'end* 3C **32**
Cokhay Green. *Derbs* 3G **73**
Col. *W Isl* 3G **171**
Colaboll. *High* 2C **164**
Colan. *Corn* 2C **6**
Colaton Raleigh. *Devn* 4D **12**
Colbost. *High* 4B **154**
Colburn. *N Yor* 5E **105**
Colby. *Cumb* 2H **103**
Colby. *IOM* 4B **108**
Colby. *Norf* 2E **78**
**Colchester**. *Essx* 3D **54**
Cold Ash. *W Ber* 5D **36**
Cold Ashby. *Nptn* 3D **62**
Cold Ashton. *S Glo* 4C **34**
Cold Aston. *Glos* 4G **49**
Coldbackie. *High* 3G **167**
Cold Blow. *Pemb* 3F **43**
Cold Brayfield. *Mil* 5G **63**
Cold Cotes. *N Yor* 2G **97**
Coldean. *Brig* 5E **27**
Coldeast. *Devn* 5B **12**
Colden. *W Yor* 2H **91**
Colden Common. *Hants* 4C **24**
Coldfair Green. *Suff* 4G **67**
Coldham. *Cambs* 5D **76**
Coldham. *Staf* 5C **72**
Cold Hanworth. *Linc* 2H **87**
Cold Harbour. *Dors* 3E **15**
Coldharbour. *Corn* 4B **6**
Coldharbour. *Glos* 5A **48**
Coldharbour. *Kent* 5G **39**
Coldharbour. *Surr* 1C **26**
Cold Hatton. *Telf* 3A **72**
Cold Hatton Heath. *Telf* 3A **72**
Cold Hesledon. *Dur* 5H **115**
Cold Hiendley. *W Yor* 3D **92**
Cold Higham. *Nptn* 5D **62**
Coldingham. *Bord* 3F **131**
Cold Kirby. *N Yor* 1H **99**
Coldmeece. *Staf* 2C **72**
Cold Northcott. *Corn* 4C **10**
Cold Norton. *Essx* 5B **54**
Cold Overton. *Leics* 4F **75**
Coldrain. *Per* 3C **136**
Coldred. *Kent* 1G **29**
Coldridge. *Devn* 2G **11**
Cold Row. *Lanc* 5C **96**
Coldstream. *Bord* 5E **131**
Coldwaltham. *W Sus* 4B **26**
Coldwell. *Here* 2H **47**
Coldwells. *Abers* 5H **161**
Coldwells Croft. *Abers* 1C **152**
Cole. *Shet* 5E **173**
Cole. *Som* 3B **22**
Colebatch. *Shrp* 2F **59**
Colebrook. *Devn* 2D **12**
Colebrooke. *Devn* 3A **12**
Coleburn. *Mor* 3G **159**
Coleby. *Linc* 4G **87**
Coleby. *N Lin* 3B **94**
Cole End. *Warw* 2G **61**
Coleford. *Devn* 2A **12**
**Coleford**. *Glos* 4A **48**
Coleford. *Som* 2B **22**
Colegate End. *Norf* 2D **66**
Cole Green. *Herts* 4C **52**
Cole Henley. *Hants* 1C **24**
Colehill. *Dors* 2F **15**
Coleman Green. *Herts* 4B **52**
Coleman's Hatch. *E Sus* 2F **27**
Colemere. *Shrp* 2G **71**
Colemore. *Hants* 3F **25**
Colemore Green. *Shrp* 1B **60**
Coleorton. *Leics* 4B **74**
**Coleraine**. *Caus* 1E **175**
Colerne. *Wilts* 4D **34**
Colesbourne. *Glos* 4F **49**
Colesden. *Bed* 5A **64**
Coles Green. *Worc* 5B **60**
Coleshill. *Buck* 1A **38**
Coleshill. *Oxon* 2H **35**
Coleshill. *Warw* 2G **61**
Colestocks. *Devn* 2D **12**
Colethrop. *Glos* 4D **48**
Coley. *Bath* 1A **22**
Colgate. *W Sus* 2D **26**
Colinsburgh. *Fife* 3G **137**
Colinton. *Edin* 3F **129**
Colintraive. *Arg* 2B **126**
Colkirk. *Norf* 3B **78**
Collace. *Per* 5B **144**
Collam. *W Isl* 8D **171**
Collaton. *Devn* 5D **8**
Collaton St Mary. *Torb* 2E **9**
College of Roseisle. *Mor* 2F **159**
Collessie. *Fife* 2E **137**
Collier Row. *G Lon* 1F **39**
Colliers End. *Herts* 3D **52**
Collier Street. *Kent* 1B **28**
Colliery Row. *Tyne* 5G **115**
Collieston. *Abers* 1H **153**
Collin. *Dum* 2B **112**
Collingbourne Ducis. *Wilts* 1H **23**
Collingbourne Kingston. *Wilts* 1H **23**
Collingham. *Notts* 4F **87**
Collingham. *W Yor* 5F **99**
Collingtree. *Nptn* 5E **63**
Collins Green. *Warr* 1H **83**
Collins Green. *Worc* 5B **60**
Colliston. *Ang* 4F **145**
Colliton. *Devn* 2D **12**
Collydean. *Fife* 3E **137**
Collyweston. *Nptn* 5G **75**
Colmonell. *S Ayr* 1G **109**
Colmworth. *Bed* 5A **64**
Colnbrook. *Slo* 3B **38**
Colne. *Cambs* 3C **64**
**Colne**. *Lanc* 5A **98**
Colne Engaine. *Essx* 2B **54**
Colney. *Norf* 5D **78**
Colney Heath. *Herts* 5C **52**
Colney Street. *Herts* 5B **52**
Coln Rogers. *Glos* 5F **49**
Coln St Aldwyns. *Glos* 5G **49**
Coln St Dennis. *Glos* 4F **49**
Colpitts Grange. *Nmbd* 4C **114**
Colpy. *Abers* 5D **160**
Colscott. *Devn* 1D **10**
Colsterdale. *N Yor* 1D **98**
Colsterworth. *Linc* 3G **75**
Colston Bassett. *Notts* 2E **74**
Colstoun House. *E Lot* 2B **130**
Coltfield. *Mor* 2F **159**
Colthouse. *Cumb* 5E **103**
Coltishall. *Norf* 4E **79**
Coltness. *N Lan* 4B **128**
Colton. *Cumb* 1C **96**
Colton. *Norf* 5D **78**
Colton. *N Yor* 5H **99**
Colton. *Staf* 3E **73**
Colton. *W Yor* 1D **92**
Colt's Hill. *Kent* 1H **27**
Col Uarach. *W Isl* 4G **171**
Colvend. *Dum* 4F **111**
Colvister. *Shet* 2G **173**
Colwall. *Here* 1C **48**
Colwall Green. *Here* 1C **48**
Colwell. *Nmbd* 2C **114**
Colwich. *Staf* 3E **73**
Colwick. *Notts* 1D **74**
Colwinston. *V Glam* 4C **32**
Colworth. *W Sus* 5A **26**
**Colwyn Bay**. *Cnwy* 3A **82**
Colyford. *Devn* 3F **13**
Colyton. *Devn* 3F **13**
Combe. *Devn* 2D **8**
Combe. *Here* 4F **59**
Combe. *Oxon* 4C **50**
Combe. *W Ber* 5B **36**
Combe Almer. *Dors* 3E **15**
Combebow. *Devn* 4E **11**
Combe Down. *Bath* 5C **34**
Combe Fishacre. *Devn* 2E **9**
Combe Florey. *Som* 3E **21**
Combe Hay. *Bath* 5C **34**
Combeinteignhead. *Devn* 5C **12**
Combe Martin. *Devn* 2F **19**
Combe Moor. *Here* 4F **59**
Comber. *Ards* 4H **175**
Combe Raleigh. *Devn* 2E **13**
Comberbach. *Ches W* 3A **84**
Comberford. *Staf* 5F **73**
Comberton. *Cambs* 5C **64**
Comberton. *Here* 4G **59**
Combe St Nicholas. *Som* 1G **13**
Combpyne. *Devn* 3F **13**
Combridge. *Staf* 2E **73**
Combrook. *Warw* 5H **61**
Combs. *Derbs* 3E **85**
Combs. *Suff* 5C **66**
Combs Ford. *Suff* 5C **66**
Combwich. *Som* 2F **21**
Comers. *Abers* 3D **152**
Comhampton. *Worc* 4C **60**
Comins Coch. *Cdgn* 2F **57**
Comley. *Shrp* 1G **59**
Commercial End. *Cambs* 4E **65**
Commins. *Powy* 3D **70**
Commins Coch. *Powy* 5H **69**
The Common. *Wilts*
nr. Salisbury 3H **23**
nr. Swindon 3F **35**
Commondale. *N Yor* 3D **106**
Common End. *Cumb* 2B **102**
Common Hill. *Here* 2A **48**
Common Moor. *Corn* 2G **7**
Common Side. *Derbs* 3H **85**
Commonside. *Ches W* 3H **83**
Commonside. *Derbs* 1G **73**
Compstall. *G Man* 1D **84**
Compton. *Devn* 2E **9**
Compton. *Hants* 4C **24**
Compton. *Staf* 2C **60**
Compton. *Surr* 1A **26**
Compton. *W Ber* 4D **36**
Compton. *W Sus* 1F **17**
Compton. *Wilts* 1G **23**
Compton Abbas. *Dors* 1D **15**
Compton Abdale. *Glos* 4F **49**
Compton Bassett. *Wilts* 4F **35**
Compton Beauchamp. *Oxon* 3A **36**
Compton Bishop. *Som* 1G **21**
Compton Chamberlayne. *Wilts* 4F **23**
Compton Dando. *Bath* 5B **34**
Compton Dundon. *Som* 3H **21**
Compton Greenfield. *S Glo* 3A **34**
Compton Martin. *Bath* 1A **22**
Compton Pauncefoot. *Som* 4B **22**
Compton Valence. *Dors* 3A **14**
Comrie. *Fife* 1D **128**
Comrie. *Per* 1G **135**
Conaglen. *High* 2E **141**
Conchra. *Arg* 1B **126**
Conchra. *High* 1A **148**
Conder Green. *Lanc* 4D **96**
Conderton. *Worc* 2E **49**
Condicote. *Glos* 3G **49**
Condorrat. *N Lan* 2A **128**
Condover. *Shrp* 5G **71**
Coneyhurst. *W Sus* 3C **26**
Coneysthorpe. *N Yor* 2B **100**
Coneythorpe. *N Yor* 4F **99**
Coney Weston. *Suff* 3B **66**
Conford. *Hants* 3G **25**
Congdon's Shop. *Corn* 5C **10**
Congerstone. *Leics* 5A **74**
Congham. *Norf* 3G **77**
**Congleton**. *Ches E* 4C **84**
Congl-y-wal. *Gwyn* 1G **69**
Congresbury. *N Som* 5H **33**
Congreve. *Staf* 4D **72**
Conham. *S Glo* 4B **34**
Conicaval. *Mor* 3D **159**
Coningsby. *Linc* 5B **88**
Conington. *Cambs*
nr. Fenstanton 4C **64**
nr. Sawtry 2A **64**
**Conisbrough**. *S Yor* 1C **86**
Conisby. *Arg* 3A **124**
Conisholme. *Linc* 1D **88**
Coniston. *Cumb* 5E **102**
Coniston. *E Yor* 1E **95**
Coniston Cold. *N Yor* 4B **98**

Conistone. N Yor . . . . . . . . . . . .3B 98
**Connah's Quay.** Flin . . . . . . . . .3E 83
Connel. Arg . . . . . . . . . . . . . . . .5D 140
Connel Park. E Ayr . . . . . . . . .3F 117
Connista. High . . . . . . . . . . . . .1D 154
Connor Downs. Corn . . . . . . . .3C 4
Conock. Wilts . . . . . . . . . . . . . .1F 23
Conon Bridge. High . . . . . . . . .3H 157
Cononley. N Yor . . . . . . . . . . . .5B 98
Cononsyth. Ang . . . . . . . . . . . .4E 145
Conordan. High . . . . . . . . . . . .5E 155
Consall. Staf . . . . . . . . . . . . . . .1D 73
**Consett.** Dur . . . . . . . . . . . . . .4E 115
Constable Burton. N Yor . . . . .5E 105
Constantine. Corn . . . . . . . . . . .4E 5
Constantine Bay. Corn . . . . . . .1C 6
Contin. High . . . . . . . . . . . . . . .3G 157
Contullich. High . . . . . . . . . . . .1A 158
Conwy. Cnwy . . . . . . . . . . . . . .3G 81
Conyer. Kent . . . . . . . . . . . . . . .4D 40
Conyer's Green. Suff . . . . . . . . .4A 66
Cooden. E Sus . . . . . . . . . . . . .5B 28
Cooil. IOM . . . . . . . . . . . . . . . .4C 108
Cookbury. Devn . . . . . . . . . . . .2E 11
Cookbury Wick. Devn . . . . . . . .2D 11
Cookham. Wind . . . . . . . . . . . .3G 37
Cookham Dean. Wind . . . . . . .3G 37
Cookham Rise. Wind . . . . . . . .3G 37
Cookhill. Worc . . . . . . . . . . . . . .5E 61
Cookley. Suff . . . . . . . . . . . . . . .3F 67
Cookley. Worc . . . . . . . . . . . . . .2C 60
Cookley Green. Oxon . . . . . . . .2E 37
Cookney. Abers . . . . . . . . . . . .4F 153
Cooksbridge. E Sus . . . . . . . . .4F 27
Cooksey Green. Worc . . . . . . . .4D 60
Cookshill. Staf . . . . . . . . . . . . . .1D 72
Cooksmill Green. Essx . . . . . . .5G 53
**Cookstown.** M Ulst . . . . . . . . .4E 175
Coolham. W Sus . . . . . . . . . . . .3C 26
Cooling. Medw . . . . . . . . . . . . .3B 40
Cooling Street. Medw . . . . . . . .3B 40
Coombe. Corn
    nr. Bude . . . . . . . . . . . . . .1C 10
    nr. St Austell . . . . . . . . . . .3D 6
    nr. Truro . . . . . . . . . . . . . .4C 6
Coombe. Devn
    nr. Sidmouth . . . . . . . . . . .3E 12
    nr. Teignmouth . . . . . . . . .5C 12
Coombe. Glos . . . . . . . . . . . . . .2C 34
Coombe. Hants . . . . . . . . . . . .4E 25
Coombe. Wilts . . . . . . . . . . . . .1G 23
Coombe Bissett. Wilts . . . . . . .4G 23
Coombe Hill. Glos . . . . . . . . . .3D 49
Coombe Keynes. Dors . . . . . . .4D 14
Coombes. W Sus . . . . . . . . . . .5C 26
Coopersale. Essx . . . . . . . . . . .5E 53
Coopersale Street. Essx . . . . . .5E 53
Cooper's Corner. Kent . . . . . . .1F 27
Cooper Street. Kent . . . . . . . . .5H 41
Cootham. W Sus . . . . . . . . . . .4B 26
Copalder Corner. Cambs . . . . . .1C 64
Copdock. Suff . . . . . . . . . . . . . .1E 54
Copford. Essx . . . . . . . . . . . . . .3C 54
Copford Green. Essx . . . . . . . . .3C 54
Copgrove. N Yor . . . . . . . . . . . .3F 99
Copister. Shet . . . . . . . . . . . . . .4F 173
Cople. Bed . . . . . . . . . . . . . . . .1B 52
Copley. Dur . . . . . . . . . . . . . . . .2D 105
Coplow Dale. Derbs . . . . . . . . .3F 85
Copmanthorpe. York . . . . . . . . .5H 99
Copp. Lanc . . . . . . . . . . . . . . . .1C 90
Coppathorne. Corn . . . . . . . . . .2C 10
Coppenhall. Ches E . . . . . . . . . .5B 84
Coppenhall. Staf . . . . . . . . . . . .4D 72
Coppenhall Moss. Ches E . . . . .5B 84
Copperhouse. Corn . . . . . . . . . .3C 4
Coppicegate. Shrp . . . . . . . . . . .2B 60
Coppingford. Cambs . . . . . . . . .2A 64
Copplestone. Devn . . . . . . . . . .2A 12
Coppull. Lanc . . . . . . . . . . . . . .3D 90
Coppull Moor. Lanc . . . . . . . . .3D 90
Copsale. W Sus . . . . . . . . . . . .3C 26
Copshaw Holm. Bord . . . . . . . .1F 113
Copster Green. Lanc . . . . . . . . .1E 91

Copston Magna. Warw . . . . . . .2B 62
Copt Green. Warw . . . . . . . . . .4F 61
Copthall Green. Essx . . . . . . . .5E 53
Copt Heath. W Mid . . . . . . . . .3F 61
Copt Hewick. N Yor . . . . . . . . .2F 99
Copthill. Dur . . . . . . . . . . . . . . .5B 114
Copthorne. W Sus . . . . . . . . . .2E 27
Coptiviney. Shrp . . . . . . . . . . . .2G 71
Copy's Green. Norf . . . . . . . . . .2B 78
Copythorne. Hants . . . . . . . . . .1B 16
Corbridge. Nmbd . . . . . . . . . . .3C 114
**Corby.** Nptn . . . . . . . . . . . . . .2F 63
Corby Glen. Linc . . . . . . . . . . . .3G 75
Cordon. N Ayr . . . . . . . . . . . . . .2E 123
Coreley. Shrp . . . . . . . . . . . . . . .3A 60
Corfe. Som . . . . . . . . . . . . . . . . .1F 13
Corfe Castle. Dors . . . . . . . . . .4E 15
Corfe Mullen. Dors . . . . . . . . . .3E 15
Corfton. Shrp . . . . . . . . . . . . . . .2G 59
Corgarff. Abers . . . . . . . . . . . . .3G 151
Corhampton. Hants . . . . . . . . . .4E 24
Corlae. Dum . . . . . . . . . . . . . . .5F 117
Corlannau. Neat . . . . . . . . . . . .2A 32
Corley. Warw . . . . . . . . . . . . . .2H 61
Corley Ash. Warw . . . . . . . . . . .2G 61
Corley Moor. Warw . . . . . . . . . .2G 61
Cormiston. S Lan . . . . . . . . . . . .1C 118
Cornaa. IOM . . . . . . . . . . . . . . .3D 108
Cornaigbeg. Arg . . . . . . . . . . . .4A 138
Cornaigmore. Arg
    on Coll . . . . . . . . . . . . . . .2D 138
    on Tiree . . . . . . . . . . . . . .4A 138
Corner Row. Lanc . . . . . . . . . . .1C 90
Corney. Cumb . . . . . . . . . . . . . .5C 102
Cornforth. Dur . . . . . . . . . . . . .1A 106
Cornhill. Abers . . . . . . . . . . . . . .3C 160
Cornhill. High . . . . . . . . . . . . . .4C 164
Cornhill-on-Tweed. Nmbd . . . . .1C 120
Cornholme. W Yor . . . . . . . . . .2H 91
Cornish Hall End. Essx . . . . . . .2G 53
Cornquoy. Orkn . . . . . . . . . . . . .7E 172
Cornriggs. Dur . . . . . . . . . . . . . .5B 114
Cornsay. Dur . . . . . . . . . . . . . . .5E 115
Cornsay Colliery. Dur . . . . . . . .5E 115
Corntown. High . . . . . . . . . . . . .3H 157
Corntown. V Glam . . . . . . . . . .4C 32
Cornwall Airport Newquay.
    Corn . . . . . . . . . . . . . . . .2C 6
Cornwell. Oxon . . . . . . . . . . . . .3A 50
Cornwood. Devn . . . . . . . . . . . .3C 8
Cornworthy. Devn . . . . . . . . . . .3E 9
Corpach. High . . . . . . . . . . . . . .1E 141
Corpusty. Norf . . . . . . . . . . . . . .3D 78
Corra. High . . . . . . . . . . . . . . . .3F 111
Corran. High
    nr. Arnisdale . . . . . . . . . . .2E 141
    nr. Fort William . . . . . . . . .3A 148
Corrany. IOM . . . . . . . . . . . . . .3D 108
Corribeg. High . . . . . . . . . . . . .1D 141
Corrie. N Ayr . . . . . . . . . . . . . . .5B 126
Corrie Common. Dum . . . . . . . .1D 112
Corriecravie. N Ayr . . . . . . . . . .3D 122
Corriekinloch. High . . . . . . . . .1A 164
Corriemoillie. High . . . . . . . . . .2F 157
Corrievarkie Lodge. Per . . . . . .1C 142
Corrievorrie. High . . . . . . . . . . .1B 150
Corrigall. Orkn . . . . . . . . . . . . . .6C 172
Corrimony. High . . . . . . . . . . . .5F 157
Corringham. Linc . . . . . . . . . . . .1F 87
**Corringham.** Thur . . . . . . . . . .2B 40
Corris. Gwyn . . . . . . . . . . . . . . .5G 69
Corris Uchaf. Gwyn . . . . . . . . . .5G 69
Corrour Shooting Lodge.
    High . . . . . . . . . . . . . . . . .2B 142
Corry. High . . . . . . . . . . . . . . . .1E 147
Corrybrough. High . . . . . . . . . .1C 150
Corrygills. N Ayr . . . . . . . . . . . .2E 123
Corry of Ardnagrask. High . . . .4H 157
Corsback. High
    nr. Dunnet . . . . . . . . . . . .1E 169
    nr. Halkirk . . . . . . . . . . . .3E 169
Corscombe. Dors . . . . . . . . . . .2A 14
Corse. Abers . . . . . . . . . . . . . . .4D 160
Corse. Glos . . . . . . . . . . . . . . . .3C 48

Corsehill. Abers . . . . . . . . . . . .3G 161
Corse Lawn. Worc . . . . . . . . . . .2D 48
Corse of Kinnoir. Abers . . . . . .4C 160
**Corsham.** Wilts . . . . . . . . . . . .4D 34
Corsley. Wilts . . . . . . . . . . . . . .2D 22
Corsley Heath. Wilts . . . . . . . . .2D 22
Corsock. Dum . . . . . . . . . . . . . .2E 111
Corston. Bath . . . . . . . . . . . . . .5B 34
Corston. Wilts . . . . . . . . . . . . . .3E 35
Corstorphine. Edin . . . . . . . . . .2F 129
Cortachy. Ang . . . . . . . . . . . . . .3C 144
Corton. Suff . . . . . . . . . . . . . . . .1H 67
Corton. Wilts . . . . . . . . . . . . . . .2E 23
Corton Denham. Som . . . . . . . .4B 22
Corwar House. S Ayr . . . . . . . . .1H 109
Corwen. Den . . . . . . . . . . . . . . .1C 70
Coryates. Dors . . . . . . . . . . . . .4B 14
Coryton. Devn . . . . . . . . . . . . . .4E 11
Coryton. Thur . . . . . . . . . . . . . . .2B 40
Cosby. Leics . . . . . . . . . . . . . . .1C 62
Coscote. Oxon . . . . . . . . . . . . .3D 36
Coseley. W Mid . . . . . . . . . . . . .1D 60
Cosgrove. Nptn . . . . . . . . . . . . .1F 51
Cosham. Port . . . . . . . . . . . . . . .2E 17
Cosheston. Pemb . . . . . . . . . . .4E 43
Coskills. N Lin . . . . . . . . . . . . . .3D 94
Cosmeston. V Glam . . . . . . . . . .5E 33
Cossall. Notts . . . . . . . . . . . . . .1B 74
Cossington. Leics . . . . . . . . . . .4D 74
Cossington. Som . . . . . . . . . . .2G 21
Costa. Orkn . . . . . . . . . . . . . . . .5C 172
Costessey. Norf . . . . . . . . . . . . .4D 78
Costock. Notts . . . . . . . . . . . . .3C 74
Coston. Leics . . . . . . . . . . . . . . .3F 75
Coston. Norf . . . . . . . . . . . . . . .5C 78
Cote. Oxon . . . . . . . . . . . . . . . .5B 50
Cotebrook. Ches W . . . . . . . . . .4H 83
Cotehill. Cumb . . . . . . . . . . . . .4F 113
Cotes. Cumb . . . . . . . . . . . . . . .1D 97
Cotes. Leics . . . . . . . . . . . . . . . .3C 74
Cotes. Staf . . . . . . . . . . . . . . . .2C 72
Cotesbach. Leics . . . . . . . . . . .2C 62
Cotes Heath. Staf . . . . . . . . . . .2C 72
Cotford St Luke. Som . . . . . . . .4E 21
Cotgrave. Notts . . . . . . . . . . . . .2D 74
Cotham. Notts . . . . . . . . . . . . . .1E 75
Cothelstone. Som . . . . . . . . . . .3E 21
Cotheridge. Worc . . . . . . . . . . . .5B 60
Cotherstone. Dur . . . . . . . . . . . .3D 104
Cothill. Oxon . . . . . . . . . . . . . . .2C 36
Cotland. Mon . . . . . . . . . . . . . .5A 48
Cotleigh. Devn . . . . . . . . . . . . . .2F 13
Cotmanhay. Derbs . . . . . . . . . . .1B 74
Coton. Cambs . . . . . . . . . . . . . .5D 64
Coton. Nptn . . . . . . . . . . . . . . . .3D 62
Coton. Staf
    nr. Gnosall . . . . . . . . . . . .3C 72
    nr. Stone . . . . . . . . . . . . . .2D 73
    nr. Tamworth . . . . . . . . . .5F 73
Coton Clanford. Staf . . . . . . . . .3C 72
Coton Hayes. Staf . . . . . . . . . . .2D 73
Coton Hill. Shrp . . . . . . . . . . . . .4G 71
Coton in the Clay. Staf . . . . . . .3F 73
Coton in the Elms. Derbs . . . . .4G 73
Cotonwood. Shrp . . . . . . . . . . .2H 71
Cotonwood. Staf . . . . . . . . . . . .3C 72
Cott. Devn . . . . . . . . . . . . . . . . .2D 9
Cott. Orkn . . . . . . . . . . . . . . . . .5F 172
Cottam. E Yor . . . . . . . . . . . . . .3D 101
Cottam. Lanc . . . . . . . . . . . . . . .1D 90
Cottam. Notts . . . . . . . . . . . . . .3F 87
Cottartown. High . . . . . . . . . . . .5E 159
Cottatown. Nptn . . . . . . . . . . . .4E 63
Cottenham. Cambs . . . . . . . . . .4D 64
Cotterdale. N Yor . . . . . . . . . . .5B 104
Cottered. Herts . . . . . . . . . . . . .3D 52
Cotterstock. Nptn . . . . . . . . . . .1H 63
Cottesbrooke. Nptn . . . . . . . . . .3E 62
Cottesmore. Rut . . . . . . . . . . . .4G 75
Cottingham. E Yor . . . . . . . . . . .1D 94
Cottingham. Nptn . . . . . . . . . . .1F 63
Cottingley. W Yor . . . . . . . . . . .1B 92

Cottisford. Oxon . . . . . . . . . . . .2D 50
Cotton. Staf . . . . . . . . . . . . . . . .1E 73
Cotton. Suff . . . . . . . . . . . . . . . .4C 66
Cotton End. Bed . . . . . . . . . . . .1A 52
Cottown. Abers . . . . . . . . . . . . .4F 161
Cotts. Devn . . . . . . . . . . . . . . . .2A 8
Cotwalton. Staf . . . . . . . . . . . . .2D 72
Couch's Mill. Corn . . . . . . . . . . .3F 7
Coughton. Here . . . . . . . . . . . . .3A 48
Coughton. Warw . . . . . . . . . . . .4E 61
Coulags. High . . . . . . . . . . . . . .4B 156
Coulby Newham. Midd . . . . . . .3C 106
Coulderton. Cumb . . . . . . . . . . .4A 102
Coulin Lodge. High . . . . . . . . . .3C 156
Coull. Abers . . . . . . . . . . . . . . . .3C 152
Coulport. Arg . . . . . . . . . . . . . . .1D 126
**Coulsdon.** G Lon . . . . . . . . . . .5D 39
Coulston. Wilts . . . . . . . . . . . . . .1E 23
Coulter. S Lan . . . . . . . . . . . . . .1C 118
Coultings. Som . . . . . . . . . . . . .2F 21
Coulton. N Yor . . . . . . . . . . . . .2A 100
Cound. Shrp . . . . . . . . . . . . . . . .5H 71
Coundon. Dur . . . . . . . . . . . . . .2F 105
Coundon Grange. Dur . . . . . . . .2F 105
Countersett. N Yor . . . . . . . . . .1B 98
Countess. Wilts . . . . . . . . . . . . .2G 23
Countess Cross. Essx . . . . . . . .2B 54
Countesthorpe. Leics . . . . . . . . .1C 62
Countisbury. Devn . . . . . . . . . . .2H 19
Coupar Angus. Per . . . . . . . . . .4B 144
Coupe Green. Lanc . . . . . . . . . .2D 90
Coupland. Cumb . . . . . . . . . . . .3A 104
Coupland. Nmbd . . . . . . . . . . .1D 120
Cour. Arg . . . . . . . . . . . . . . . . . .5G 125
Courance. Dum . . . . . . . . . . . . .5C 118
Court-at-Street. Kent . . . . . . . . .2E 29
Courteachan. High . . . . . . . . . .4E 147
Courteenhall. Nptn . . . . . . . . . .5E 63
Court Henry. Carm . . . . . . . . . .3F 45
Courtsend. Essx . . . . . . . . . . . . .1E 41
Courtway. Som . . . . . . . . . . . . .3F 21
Cousland. Midl . . . . . . . . . . . . . .3G 129
Cousley Wood. E Sus . . . . . . . . .2A 28
Coustonn. Arg . . . . . . . . . . . . . .2B 126
Cove. Arg . . . . . . . . . . . . . . . . . .1D 126
Cove. Devn . . . . . . . . . . . . . . . . .1C 12
Cove. Hants . . . . . . . . . . . . . . . .1G 25
Cove. High . . . . . . . . . . . . . . . . .4C 162
Cove. Bord . . . . . . . . . . . . . . . . .2D 130
Cove Bay. Aber . . . . . . . . . . . . .3G 153
Covehithe. Suff . . . . . . . . . . . . .2H 67
Coven. Staf . . . . . . . . . . . . . . . .5D 72
Coveney. Cambs . . . . . . . . . . . .2D 65
Covenham St Bartholomew.
    Linc . . . . . . . . . . . . . . . . .1C 88
Covenham St Mary. Linc . . . . . .1C 88
Coven Heath. Staf . . . . . . . . . . .5D 72
**Coventry.** W Mid . . . . . . . . . . .3H 61
Coverack. Corn . . . . . . . . . . . . . .5E 5
Coverham. N Yor . . . . . . . . . . . .1D 98
Covesea. Mor . . . . . . . . . . . . . .1F 159
Covingham. Swin . . . . . . . . . . . .3G 35
Covington. Cambs . . . . . . . . . . .3H 63
Covington. S Lan . . . . . . . . . . . .1B 118
Cowan Bridge. Lanc . . . . . . . . .2F 97
Cowan Head. Cumb . . . . . . . . .5F 103
Cowbar. Red C . . . . . . . . . . . . .3E 107
Cowbeech. E Sus . . . . . . . . . . . .4H 27
Cowbit. Linc . . . . . . . . . . . . . . . .4B 76
Cowbridge. V Glam . . . . . . . . . .4C 32
Cowden. Kent . . . . . . . . . . . . . .1F 27
**Cowdenbeath.** Fife . . . . . . . . .4D 136
Cowdenburn. Bord . . . . . . . . . .4F 129
Cowdened. Fife . . . . . . . . . . . . .4D 136
Cowers Lane. Derbs . . . . . . . . .1H 73
**Cowes.** IOW . . . . . . . . . . . . . .3C 16
Cowesby. N Yor . . . . . . . . . . . . .1G 99
Cowfold. W Sus . . . . . . . . . . . . .3D 26
Cowfords. Mor . . . . . . . . . . . . . .2H 159
Cowgill. Cumb . . . . . . . . . . . . . .1G 97
Cowie. Abers . . . . . . . . . . . . . . .5F 153
Cowie. Stir . . . . . . . . . . . . . . . . .1B 128
Cowlam. E Yor . . . . . . . . . . . . . .3D 100
Cowley. Devn . . . . . . . . . . . . . . .3C 12

Cowley. Glos . . . . . . . . . . . . . . .4E 49
Cowley. G Lon . . . . . . . . . . . . . .2B 38
Cowley. Oxon . . . . . . . . . . . . . . .5D 50
Cowley. Staf . . . . . . . . . . . . . . . .4C 72
Cowleymoor. Devn . . . . . . . . . .1C 12
Cowling. Lanc . . . . . . . . . . . . . . .3D 90
Cowling. N Yor
    nr. Bedale . . . . . . . . . . . .1E 99
    nr. Glusburn . . . . . . . . . . .5B 98
Cowlinge. Suff . . . . . . . . . . . . . .5G 65
Cowmes. W Yor . . . . . . . . . . . . .3B 92
Cowpe. Lanc . . . . . . . . . . . . . . .2G 91
Cowpen. Nmbd . . . . . . . . . . . . .1F 115
Cowpen Bewley. Stoc T . . . . . .2B 106
Cowplain. Hants . . . . . . . . . . . . .1E 17
Cowshill. Dur . . . . . . . . . . . . . . .5B 114
Cowslip Green. N Som . . . . . . .5H 33
Cowstrandburn. Fife . . . . . . . . .4C 136
Cowthorpe. N Yor . . . . . . . . . . .4G 99
Coxall. Here . . . . . . . . . . . . . . . .3F 59
Coxbank. Ches E . . . . . . . . . . . .1A 72
Coxbench. Derbs . . . . . . . . . . . .1A 74
Cox Common. Suff . . . . . . . . . .2G 67
Coxford. Norf . . . . . . . . . . . . . . .3H 77
Cox Green. Surr . . . . . . . . . . . . .2B 26
Cox Green. Tyne . . . . . . . . . . . .4G 115
Coxgreen. Staf . . . . . . . . . . . . . .2C 60
Coxheath. Kent . . . . . . . . . . . . .5B 40
Coxhoe. Dur . . . . . . . . . . . . . . .1A 106
Coxley. Som . . . . . . . . . . . . . . . .2A 22
Coxwold. N Yor . . . . . . . . . . . . .2H 99
Coychurch. B'end . . . . . . . . . . .3C 32
Coylton. S Ayr . . . . . . . . . . . . . .3D 116
Coylumbridge. High . . . . . . . . .2D 150
Coynach. Abers . . . . . . . . . . . . .3B 152
Coynachie. Abers . . . . . . . . . . .5B 160
Coytrahen. B'end . . . . . . . . . . . .3B 32
Crabbs Cross. Worc . . . . . . . . . .4E 61
Crabgate. Norf . . . . . . . . . . . . . .3C 78
Crab Orchard. Dors . . . . . . . . . .2F 15
Crabtree. W Sus . . . . . . . . . . . .3D 26
Crabtree Green. Wrex . . . . . . . .1F 71
Crackaig. High . . . . . . . . . . . . . .2G 165
Crackenthorpe. Cumb . . . . . . .2H 103
Crackington Haven. Corn . . . . .3B 10
Crackley. Staf . . . . . . . . . . . . . . .5C 84
Crackley. Warw . . . . . . . . . . . . .3G 61
Crackleybank. Shrp . . . . . . . . . .4B 72
Crackpot. N Yor . . . . . . . . . . . .5C 104
Cracoe. N Yor . . . . . . . . . . . . . .3B 98
Craddock. Devn . . . . . . . . . . . . .1D 12
Cradhlastadh. W Isl . . . . . . . . .4C 171
Cradley. Here . . . . . . . . . . . . . . .1C 48
Cradley. W Mid . . . . . . . . . . . . .2D 60
Cradoc. Powy . . . . . . . . . . . . . . .2D 46
Crafthole. Corn . . . . . . . . . . . . .3H 7
Crafton. Buck . . . . . . . . . . . . . . .4G 51
Cragabus. Arg . . . . . . . . . . . . . .5B 124
Crag Foot. Lanc . . . . . . . . . . . .2D 97
Craggan. High . . . . . . . . . . . . .1E 151
Cragganmore. Mor . . . . . . . . . .5F 159
Cragganvallie. High . . . . . . . . .5H 157
Craggie. High . . . . . . . . . . . . . .2F 165
Craggiemore. High . . . . . . . . . .5B 158
Cragg Vale. W Yor . . . . . . . . . . .2A 92
Craghead. Dur . . . . . . . . . . . . .4F 115
Crai. Powy . . . . . . . . . . . . . . . . .3B 46
Craichie. Ang . . . . . . . . . . . . . .4E 145
Craig. Arg . . . . . . . . . . . . . . . . .5E 141
Craig. Dum . . . . . . . . . . . . . . . .2D 111
Craig. High
    nr. Achnashellach . . . . . .4C 156
    nr. Lower Diabaig . . . . . .2G 155
    nr. Stromeferry . . . . . . . .5H 155
Craiganour Lodge. Per . . . . . . .3D 142
**Craigavon.** Arm . . . . . . . . . . . .5F 175
Craigbrack. High . . . . . . . . . . .4A 134
Craig-Cefn-Parc. Swan . . . . . . .5G 45
Craigdallie. Per . . . . . . . . . . . . .1E 137
Craigdam. Abers . . . . . . . . . . .5F 161
Craigdarroch. E Ayr . . . . . . . . .4F 117
Craigdarroch. High . . . . . . . . . .3G 157
Craigdhu. High . . . . . . . . . . . . .4G 157
Craigearn. Abers . . . . . . . . . . .2E 152

Craigellachie. Mor . . . . . . . . . .4G 159
Craigend. Per . . . . . . . . . . . . . .1D 136
Craigendoran. Arg . . . . . . . . . .1E 126
Craigends. Ren . . . . . . . . . . . .3F 127
Craigenputtock. Dum . . . . . . . .1E 111
Craigens. E Ayr . . . . . . . . . . . .3E 117
Craighall. Edin . . . . . . . . . . . . .2E 129
Craighead. Fife . . . . . . . . . . . .2H 137
Craighouse. Arg . . . . . . . . . . .3D 124
Craigie. Abers . . . . . . . . . . . . .2G 153
Craigie. D'dee . . . . . . . . . . . . .5D 144
Craigie. Per
  nr. Blairgowrie . . . . . . . .4A 144
  nr. Perth . . . . . . . . . . . .1D 136
Craigie. S Ayr . . . . . . . . . . . . .1D 116
Craigielaw. E Lot . . . . . . . . . . .2A 130
Craiglemine. Dum . . . . . . . . . .5B 110
Craig-llwyn. Shrp . . . . . . . . . . .3E 71
Craiglockhart. Edin . . . . . . . . .2F 129
Craig Lodge. Arg . . . . . . . . . . .2B 126
Craigmalloch. E Ayr . . . . . . . .5D 117
Craigmaud. Abers . . . . . . . . . .3F 161
Craigmill. Stir . . . . . . . . . . . . .4H 135
Craigmillar. Edin . . . . . . . . . . .2F 129
Craigmore. Arg . . . . . . . . . . . .3C 126
Craigmuie. Dum . . . . . . . . . . .1E 111
Craignair. Dum . . . . . . . . . . . .3F 111
Craignant. Shrp . . . . . . . . . . . .2E 71
Craigneuk. N Lan
  nr. Airdrie . . . . . . . . . . . .3A 128
  nr. Motherwell . . . . . . . .4A 128
Craignure. Arg . . . . . . . . . . . .5B 140
Craigo. Ang . . . . . . . . . . . . . .2F 145
Craigrory. High . . . . . . . . . . . .4A 158
Craigrothie. Fife . . . . . . . . . . .2F 137
Craigs. Dum . . . . . . . . . . . . . .2D 112
The Craigs. High . . . . . . . . . . .4B 164
Craigshill. W Lot . . . . . . . . . . .3D 128
Craigton. Aber . . . . . . . . . . . . .3F 153
Craigton. Abers . . . . . . . . . . . .3E 152
Craigton. Ang
  nr. Carnoustie . . . . . . . . .5E 145
  nr. Kirriemuir . . . . . . . . .3C 144
Craigton. High . . . . . . . . . . . . .4A 158
Craigtown. High . . . . . . . . . . . .3A 168
Craig-y-Duke. Neat . . . . . . . . . .5H 45
Craig-y-nos. Powy . . . . . . . . . . .4B 46
Craik. Bord . . . . . . . . . . . . . . .4F 119
Crail. Fife . . . . . . . . . . . . . . . .3H 137
Crailing. Bord . . . . . . . . . . . . .2A 120
Crailinghall. Bord . . . . . . . . . .2A 120
Crakehill. N Yor . . . . . . . . . . . .2G 99
Crakemarsh. Staf . . . . . . . . . . .2E 73
Crambe. N Yor . . . . . . . . . . . .3B 100
Crambeck. N Yor . . . . . . . . . .3B 100
Cramlington. Nmbd . . . . . . . . .2F 115
Cramond. Edin . . . . . . . . . . . .2E 129
Cramond Bridge. Edin . . . . . . .2E 129
Cranage. Ches E . . . . . . . . . . . .4B 84
Cranberry. Staf . . . . . . . . . . . . .2C 72
Cranborne. Dors . . . . . . . . . . . .1F 15
Cranbourne. Brac . . . . . . . . . . .3A 38
Cranbrook. Devon . . . . . . . . . . .3D 12
Cranbrook. Kent . . . . . . . . . . . .2B 28
Cranbrook Common. Kent . . . . .2B 28
Crane Moor. S Yor . . . . . . . . . .4D 92
Crane's Corner. Norf . . . . . . . . .4B 78
Cranfield. C Beds . . . . . . . . . . .1H 51
Cranford. G Lon . . . . . . . . . . . .3C 38
Cranford St Andrew. Nptn . . . . .3G 63
Cranford St John. Nptn . . . . . . .3G 63
Cranham. Glos . . . . . . . . . . . . .4D 49
Cranham. G Lon . . . . . . . . . . . .2G 39
Crank. Mers . . . . . . . . . . . . . . .1H 83
Cranleigh. Surr . . . . . . . . . . . . .2B 26
Cranley. Suff . . . . . . . . . . . . . .3D 66
Cranloch. Mor . . . . . . . . . . . . .3G 159
Cranmer Green. Suff . . . . . . . . .3C 66
Cranmore. IOW . . . . . . . . . . . .3C 16
Cranmore. Som . . . . . . . . . . . .5A 76
Crannich. Arg . . . . . . . . . . . . .4G 139
Crannoch. Mor . . . . . . . . . . . .3B 160
Cranoe. Leics . . . . . . . . . . . . . .1E 63
Cransford. Suff . . . . . . . . . . . . .4F 67

Cranshaws. Bord . . . . . . . . . . .3C 130
Cranstal. IOM . . . . . . . . . . . . .1D 108
Crantock. Corn . . . . . . . . . . . . . .2B 6
Cranwell. Linc . . . . . . . . . . . . .1H 75
Cranwich. Norf . . . . . . . . . . . . .1G 65
Cranworth. Norf . . . . . . . . . . . .5B 78
Craobh Haven. Arg . . . . . . . . .3E 133
Craobhnaclag. High . . . . . . . .4G 157
Crapstone. Devn . . . . . . . . . . . . .2B 8
Crarae. Arg . . . . . . . . . . . . . . .4G 133
Crask. High
  nr. Bettyhill . . . . . . . . . .2H 167
  nr. Lairg . . . . . . . . . . . .1C 164
Crask of Aigas. High . . . . . . . .4G 157
Craster. Nmbd . . . . . . . . . . . .2G 121
Craswall. Here . . . . . . . . . . . . . .2F 47
Cratfield. Suff . . . . . . . . . . . . . .3F 67
Crathes. Abers . . . . . . . . . . . .4E 153
Crathie. Abers . . . . . . . . . . . . .4G 151
Crathie. High . . . . . . . . . . . . .4H 149
Crathorne. N Yor . . . . . . . . . . .4B 106
Craven Arms. Shrp . . . . . . . . . .2G 59
Crawcrook. Tyne . . . . . . . . . . .3E 115
Crawford. Lanc . . . . . . . . . . . . .4C 90
Crawford. S Lan . . . . . . . . . . .2B 118
Crawfordsdyke. S Lan . . . . . . . .4B 128
Crawfordjohn. S Lan . . . . . . . .2A 118
Crawick. Dum . . . . . . . . . . . . .3G 117
Crawley. Devn . . . . . . . . . . . . . .2F 13
Crawley. Hants . . . . . . . . . . . . . .3C 24
Crawley. Oxon . . . . . . . . . . . . .4B 50
Crawley. W Sus . . . . . . . . . . . .2D 26
Crawley Down. W Sus . . . . . . . .2E 27
Crawley End. Essx . . . . . . . . . . .1E 53
Crawley Side. Dur . . . . . . . . . .5C 114
Crawshawbooth. Lanc . . . . . . . .2G 91
Crawton. Abers . . . . . . . . . . . .5F 153
Cray. N Yor . . . . . . . . . . . . . . .2B 98
Cray. Per . . . . . . . . . . . . . . . .2A 144
Crayford. G Lon . . . . . . . . . . . .3G 39
Crayke. N Yor . . . . . . . . . . . . . .2H 99
Craymere Beck. Norf . . . . . . . . .2C 78
Crays Hill. Essx . . . . . . . . . . . . .1B 40
Cray's Pond. Oxon . . . . . . . . . . .3E 37
Crazies Hill. Wok . . . . . . . . . . . .3F 37
Creacombe. Devn . . . . . . . . . . .1B 12
Creagan. Arg . . . . . . . . . . . . .4D 140
Creag Aoil. High . . . . . . . . . . .1F 141
Creag Ghoraidh. W Isl . . . . . . .4C 170
Creaguaineach Lodge.
  High . . . . . . . . . . . . . . .2H 141
Creamore Bank. Shrp . . . . . . . . .2H 71
Creaton. Nptn . . . . . . . . . . . . . .3E 62
Creca. Dum . . . . . . . . . . . . . .2D 112
Credenhill. Here . . . . . . . . . . . . .1H 47
Crediton. Devn . . . . . . . . . . . . .2B 12
Creebridge. Dum . . . . . . . . . . .3B 110
Creech. Dors . . . . . . . . . . . . . .4E 15
Creech Heathfield. Som . . . . . . . .4F 21
Creech St Michael. Som . . . . . . .4F 21
Creed. Corn . . . . . . . . . . . . . . . .4D 6
Creekmoor. Pool . . . . . . . . . . . .3E 15
Creekmouth. G Lon . . . . . . . . . .2F 39
Creeting St Mary. Suff . . . . . . . .5C 66
Creeting St Peter. Suff . . . . . . . .5C 66
Creeton. Linc . . . . . . . . . . . . . .3H 75
Creetown. Dum . . . . . . . . . . . .4B 110
Creggans. Arg . . . . . . . . . . . . .3H 133
Cregneash. IOM . . . . . . . . . . .5A 108
Cregrina. Powy . . . . . . . . . . . . .5D 58
Creich. Arg . . . . . . . . . . . . . . .2B 132
Creich. Fife . . . . . . . . . . . . . . .1F 137
Creighton. Staf . . . . . . . . . . . . . .2E 73
Creigiau. Card . . . . . . . . . . . . . .3D 32
Cremyll. Corn . . . . . . . . . . . . . . .3A 8
Crendell. Dors . . . . . . . . . . . . . .1F 15
Crepkill. High . . . . . . . . . . . . .4D 154
Cressage. Shrp . . . . . . . . . . . . .5H 71
Cressbrook. Derbs . . . . . . . . . . .3F 85
Cresselly. Pemb . . . . . . . . . . . . .4E 43
Cressing. Essx . . . . . . . . . . . . . .3A 54
Cresswell. Nmbd . . . . . . . . . . .5G 121
Cresswell. Staf . . . . . . . . . . . . .2D 73
Cresswell Quay. Pemb . . . . . . . .4E 43

Creswell. Derbs . . . . . . . . . . . . .3C 86
Creswell Green. Staf . . . . . . . . . .4E 73
Cretingham. Suff . . . . . . . . . . . .4E 67
Crewe. Ches E . . . . . . . . . . . . .5B 84
Crewe-by-Farndon. Ches W . . .5G 83
Crewgreen. Powy . . . . . . . . . . . .4F 71
Crewkerne. Som . . . . . . . . . . . .2H 13
Crews Hill. G Lon . . . . . . . . . . . .5D 52
Crewton. Derb . . . . . . . . . . . . . .2A 74
Crianlarich. Stir . . . . . . . . . . . .1C 134
Cribbs Causeway. S Glo . . . . . .3A 34
Cribyn. Cdgn . . . . . . . . . . . . . . .5E 57
Criccieth. Gwyn . . . . . . . . . . . . .2D 69
Crich. Derbs . . . . . . . . . . . . . . .5A 86
Crichton. Midl . . . . . . . . . . . . .3G 129
Crick. Mon . . . . . . . . . . . . . . . .3H 33
Crick. Nptn . . . . . . . . . . . . . . . .3C 62
Cricket Hill. Hants . . . . . . . . . . .5G 37
Cricket Malherbie. Som . . . . . . .1G 13
Cricket St Thomas. Som . . . . . . .2G 13
Crickham. Som . . . . . . . . . . . . .2H 21
Crickheath. Shrp . . . . . . . . . . . . .3E 71
Crickhowell. Powy . . . . . . . . . . . .4F 47
Cricklade. Wilts . . . . . . . . . . . . .2G 35
Cricklewood. G Lon . . . . . . . . . .2D 38
Cridling Stubbs. N Yor . . . . . . . .2F 93
Crieff. Per . . . . . . . . . . . . . . . .1A 136
Criftins. Shrp . . . . . . . . . . . . . . .2F 71
Criggion. Powy . . . . . . . . . . . . . .4E 71
Crigglestone. W Yor . . . . . . . . . .3D 92
Crimchard. Som . . . . . . . . . . . .2G 13
Crimdon Park. Dur . . . . . . . . . .1B 106
Crimond. Abers . . . . . . . . . . . .3H 161
Crimonmogate. Abers . . . . . . . .3H 161
Crimplesham. Norf . . . . . . . . . . .5F 77
Crimscote. Warw . . . . . . . . . . . .1H 49
Crinan. Arg . . . . . . . . . . . . . . .4E 133
Cringleford. Norf . . . . . . . . . . . .5D 78
Crinow. Pemb . . . . . . . . . . . . . .3F 43
Cripplesease. Corn . . . . . . . . . . . .3C 4
Cripplestyle. Dors . . . . . . . . . . . .1F 15
Cripp's Corner. E Sus . . . . . . . . .3B 28
Croanford. Corn . . . . . . . . . . . . .5A 10
Crockenhill. Kent . . . . . . . . . . . .4G 39
Crocker End. Oxon . . . . . . . . . . .3F 37
Crockerhill. Hants . . . . . . . . . . . .2D 16
Crockernwell. Devn . . . . . . . . . . .3A 12
Crocker's Ash. Here . . . . . . . . . .4A 48
Crockerton. Wilts . . . . . . . . . . . .2D 22
Crocketford. Dum . . . . . . . . . . .2F 111
Crockey Hill. York . . . . . . . . . . .5A 100
Crockham Hill. Kent . . . . . . . . . . .5F 39
Crockhurst Street. Kent . . . . . . . .1H 27
Crockleford Heath. Essx . . . . . . .3D 54
Croeserw. Neat . . . . . . . . . . . . .2B 32
Croes-Goch. Pemb . . . . . . . . . . .1C 42
Croes Hywel. Mon . . . . . . . . . . .4G 47
Croes-lan. Cdgn . . . . . . . . . . . . .1D 45
Croesor. Gwyn . . . . . . . . . . . . . .1F 69
Croesoswallt. Shrp . . . . . . . . . . .3E 71
Croesyceiliog. Carm . . . . . . . . . .4E 45
Croesyceiliog. Torf . . . . . . . . . . .2G 33
Croes-y-mwyalch. Torf . . . . . . . .2G 33
Croesywaun. Gwyn . . . . . . . . . . .5E 81
Croford. Som . . . . . . . . . . . . . . .4E 20
Croft. Leics . . . . . . . . . . . . . . . .1C 62
Croft. Linc . . . . . . . . . . . . . . . . .4E 89
Croft. Warr . . . . . . . . . . . . . . . . .1A 84
Croftamie. Stir . . . . . . . . . . . . .1F 127
Croftfoot. Glas . . . . . . . . . . . . .3G 127
Croftmill. Per . . . . . . . . . . . . . .5F 143
Crofton. Cumb . . . . . . . . . . . . .4E 112
Crofton. W Yor . . . . . . . . . . . . . .3D 93
Crofton. Wilts . . . . . . . . . . . . . . .5A 36
Croft-on-Tees. N Yor . . . . . . . . .4F 105
Crofts. Dum . . . . . . . . . . . . . . .2E 111
Crofts of Benachielt. High . . . . .5D 169
Crofts of Dipple. Mor . . . . . . . .3H 159
Crofty. Swan . . . . . . . . . . . . . . .3E 31
Croggan. Arg . . . . . . . . . . . . .1E 132
Croglin. Cumb . . . . . . . . . . . . .5G 113
Croich. High . . . . . . . . . . . . . . .4B 164
Croick. High . . . . . . . . . . . . . . .3A 168

Croig. Arg . . . . . . . . . . . . . . . .3E 139
Cromarty. High . . . . . . . . . . . . .2B 158
Crombie. Fife . . . . . . . . . . . . . .1D 128
Cromdale. High . . . . . . . . . . . .1E 151
Cromer. Herts . . . . . . . . . . . . . . .3C 52
Cromer. Norf . . . . . . . . . . . . . . . .1E 78
Cromford. Derbs . . . . . . . . . . . . .5G 85
Cromhall. S Glo . . . . . . . . . . . . .2B 34
Cromor. W Isl . . . . . . . . . . . . . .5G 171
Cromra. High . . . . . . . . . . . . . .5H 149
Cromwell. Notts . . . . . . . . . . . . . .4E 87
Cronberry. E Ayr . . . . . . . . . . . .2F 117
Crondall. Hants . . . . . . . . . . . . . .2F 25
The Cronk. IOM . . . . . . . . . . . .2C 108
Cronk-y-Voddy. IOM . . . . . . . . .3C 108
Cronton. Mers . . . . . . . . . . . . . .2G 83
Crook. Cumb . . . . . . . . . . . . . . .5F 103
Crook. Dur . . . . . . . . . . . . . . . .1E 105
Crookdake. Cumb . . . . . . . . . . .5C 112
Crooke. G Man . . . . . . . . . . . . . .4D 90
Crookedholm. E Ayr . . . . . . . . .1D 116
Crooked Soley. Wilts . . . . . . . . . .4B 36
Crookes. S Yor . . . . . . . . . . . . . .2H 85
Crookgate Bank. Dur . . . . . . . .4E 115
Crookhall. Dur . . . . . . . . . . . . .4E 115
Crookham. Nmbd . . . . . . . . . . .1D 120
Crookham. W Ber . . . . . . . . . . . .5D 36
Crookham Village. Hants . . . . . . .1F 25
Crooklands. Cumb . . . . . . . . . . .1E 97
Crook of Devon. Per . . . . . . . . .3C 136
Crookston. Glas . . . . . . . . . . . .3G 127
Cropredy. Oxon . . . . . . . . . . . . .1C 50
Cropston. Leics . . . . . . . . . . . . . .4C 74
Cropthorne. Worc . . . . . . . . . . . .1E 49
Cropton. N Yor . . . . . . . . . . . . .1B 100
Cropwell Bishop. Notts . . . . . . . .2D 74
Cropwell Butler. Notts . . . . . . . . .2D 74
Cros. W Isl . . . . . . . . . . . . . . . .1H 171
Crosbie. N Ayr . . . . . . . . . . . . . .4D 126
Crosbost. W Isl . . . . . . . . . . . . .5F 171
Crosby. Cumb . . . . . . . . . . . . .1B 102
Crosby. IOM . . . . . . . . . . . . . .4C 108
Crosby. N Lin . . . . . . . . . . . . . .3B 94
Crosby Court. N Yor . . . . . . . . .5A 106
Crosby Garrett. Cumb . . . . . . . .4A 104
Crosby Ravensworth.
  Cumb . . . . . . . . . . . . .3H 103
Crosby Villa. Cumb . . . . . . . . . .1B 102
Croscombe. Som . . . . . . . . . . . .2A 22
Crosland Moor. W Yor . . . . . . . .3B 92
Cross. Som . . . . . . . . . . . . . . . .1H 21
Crossaig. Arg . . . . . . . . . . . . . .4G 125
Crossapol. Arg . . . . . . . . . . . . .4A 138
Cross Ash. Mon . . . . . . . . . . . . .4H 47
Cross-at-Hand. Kent . . . . . . . . . .1B 28
Crossbush. W Sus . . . . . . . . . . .5B 26
Crosscanonby. Cumb . . . . . . . .1B 102
Crossdale Street. Norf . . . . . . . . .2E 79
Cross End. Essx . . . . . . . . . . . . .2B 54
Crossens. Mers . . . . . . . . . . . . .2B 90
Crossford. Fife . . . . . . . . . . . . .1D 128
Crossford. S Lan . . . . . . . . . . . .5B 128
Cross Foxes. Gwyn . . . . . . . . . . .4G 69
Crossgar. New M . . . . . . . . . . . .5H 175
Crossgate. Orkn . . . . . . . . . . . .6D 172
Crossgate. Staf . . . . . . . . . . . . . .2D 72
Crossgatehall. E Lot . . . . . . . . .3G 129
Crossgates. Fife . . . . . . . . . . . .1E 129
Crossgates. N Yor . . . . . . . . . . .1E 101
Crossgates. Powy . . . . . . . . . . . .4C 58
Crossgill. Lanc . . . . . . . . . . . . . . .3E 97
Cross Green. Devn . . . . . . . . . . .4D 11
Cross Green. Staf . . . . . . . . . . . .5D 72
Cross Green. Suff
  nr. Cockfield . . . . . . . . . .5A 66
  nr. Hitcham . . . . . . . . . . .5B 66
Cross Hands. Carm . . . . . . . . . . .4F 45
Crosshands. Carm . . . . . . . . . . . .2F 43
Crosshands. E Ayr . . . . . . . . . .1D 117
Cross Green. Devn . . . . . . . . . . .4D 11
Cross Hill. Derbs . . . . . . . . . . . .1B 74
Cross Hill. Glos . . . . . . . . . . . . .2A 34
Crosshill. E Ayr . . . . . . . . . . . .2D 117

Crosshill. Fife . . . . . . . . . . . . . .4D 136
Crosshill. S Ayr . . . . . . . . . . . . .4C 116
Crosshills. High . . . . . . . . . . . .1A 158
Cross Holme. N Yor . . . . . . . . . .5C 106
Crosshouse. E Ayr . . . . . . . . . .1C 116
Cross Houses. Shrp . . . . . . . . . .5H 71
Crossings. Cumb . . . . . . . . . . .2G 113
Cross Inn. Cdgn
  nr. Aberaeron . . . . . . . . . .4E 57
  nr. New Quay . . . . . . . . .5C 56
Cross Inn. Rhon . . . . . . . . . . . . .3D 32
Crosskeys. Cphy . . . . . . . . . . . . .2F 33
Crosskirk. High . . . . . . . . . . . .2C 168
Crosslands. Cumb . . . . . . . . . . . .1C 96
Cross Lane Head. Shrp . . . . . . . .1B 60
Cross Lanes. Corn . . . . . . . . . . . .4D 5
Cross Lanes. Dur . . . . . . . . . . .3D 104
Cross Lanes. N Yor . . . . . . . . . . .3H 99
Cross Lanes. Wrex . . . . . . . . . . . .1F 71
Crosslanes. Shrp . . . . . . . . . . . . .4F 71
Crosslee. Ren . . . . . . . . . . . . . .3F 127
Crossmaglen. New M . . . . . . . .6F 175
Crossmichael. Dum . . . . . . . . .3E 111
Crossmoor. Lanc . . . . . . . . . . . .1C 90
Cross Oak. Powy . . . . . . . . . . . . .3E 46
Cross of Jackston. Abers . . . . . .5E 161
Cross o' th' Hands. Derbs . . . . . .1G 73
Crossroads. Abers
  nr. Aberdeen . . . . . . . . .3G 153
  nr. Banchory . . . . . . . . .4E 153
Crossroads. E Ayr . . . . . . . . . . .1D 116
Cross Side. Devn . . . . . . . . . . . .4B 20
Cross Street. Suff . . . . . . . . . . . .3D 66
Crosston. Ang . . . . . . . . . . . . .3E 145
Cross Town. Ches E . . . . . . . . . .3B 84
Crossway. Mon . . . . . . . . . . . . . .4H 47
Crossway. Powy . . . . . . . . . . . . .5C 58
Crossway Green. Mon . . . . . . . .2A 34
Crossway Green. Worc . . . . . . . . .4C 60
Crossways. Dors . . . . . . . . . . . . .4C 14
Crosswell. Pemb . . . . . . . . . . . . .1F 43
Crosswood. Cdgn . . . . . . . . . . . .3F 57
Crosthwaite. Cumb . . . . . . . . . .5F 103
Croston. Lanc . . . . . . . . . . . . . . .3C 90
Crostwick. Norf . . . . . . . . . . . . . .4E 79
Crostwight. Norf . . . . . . . . . . . . .3F 79
Crothair. W Isl . . . . . . . . . . . . . .4D 171
Crouch. Kent . . . . . . . . . . . . . . .5H 39
Croucheston. Wilts . . . . . . . . . . .4F 23
Crouch Hill. Dors . . . . . . . . . . . .1C 14
Croughton. Nptn . . . . . . . . . . . .2D 50
Crovie. Abers . . . . . . . . . . . . . .2F 161
Crow. Hants . . . . . . . . . . . . . . . .2G 15
Crowan. Corn . . . . . . . . . . . . . . . .3D 4
Crowborough. E Sus . . . . . . . . .2G 27
Crowcombe. Som . . . . . . . . . . . .3E 21
Crowcroft. Worc . . . . . . . . . . . . .5B 60
Crowdecote. Derbs . . . . . . . . . . .4F 85
Crowden. Derbs . . . . . . . . . . . . .1E 85
Crowden. Devn . . . . . . . . . . . . . .3E 11
Crowdhill. Hants . . . . . . . . . . . . .1C 16
Crowdon. N Yor . . . . . . . . . . . .5G 107
Crow Edge. S Yor . . . . . . . . . . . .4B 92
Crow End. Cambs . . . . . . . . . . . .5C 64
Crowfield. Nptn . . . . . . . . . . . . . .1E 50
Crowfield. Suff . . . . . . . . . . . . . .5D 66
Crow Green. Essx . . . . . . . . . . . .1G 39
Crow Hill. Here . . . . . . . . . . . . . .3B 48
Crowhurst. E Sus . . . . . . . . . . . .4B 28
Crowhurst. Surr . . . . . . . . . . . . . .1E 27
Crowhurst Lane End. Surr . . . . . .1E 27
Crowland. Linc . . . . . . . . . . . . . .4B 76
Crowland. Suff . . . . . . . . . . . . . .3C 66
Crowlas. Corn . . . . . . . . . . . . . . . .3C 4
Crowle. N Lin . . . . . . . . . . . . . . .3A 94
Crowle. Worc . . . . . . . . . . . . . . .5D 60
Crowle Green. Worc . . . . . . . . . .5D 60
Crowmarsh Gifford. Oxon . . . . . .3E 36
Crown Corner. Suff . . . . . . . . . . .3E 67
Crownthorpe. Norf . . . . . . . . . . . .5C 78
Crowntown. Corn . . . . . . . . . . . . .3D 4
Crows-an-wra. Corn . . . . . . . . . . .4A 4

Crowshill. *Norf* . . . . . . . . . . . .5B 78
**Crowthorne.** *Brac* . . . . . . . . . .5G 37
Crowton. *Ches W* . . . . . . . . . . .3H 83
Croxall. *Staf* . . . . . . . . . . . . . . .4F 73
Croxby. *Linc* . . . . . . . . . . . . . . .1A 88
Croxdale. *Dur* . . . . . . . . . . . . .1F 105
Croxden. *Staf* . . . . . . . . . . . . . .2E 73
Croxley Green. *Herts* . . . . . . . .1B 38
Croxton. *Cambs* . . . . . . . . . . . .4B 64
Croxton. *Norf*
    nr. Fakenham . . . . . . . . . . .2B 78
    nr. Thetford . . . . . . . . . . . . .2A 66
Croxton. *N Lin* . . . . . . . . . . . . .3D 94
Croxton. *Staf* . . . . . . . . . . . . . .2B 72
Croxtonbank. *Staf* . . . . . . . . . .2B 72
Croxton Green. *Ches E* . . . . . . .5H 83
Croxton Kerrial. *Leics* . . . . . . . .3F 75
Croy. *High* . . . . . . . . . . . . . . . .4B 158
Croy. *N Lan* . . . . . . . . . . . . . . .2A 128
Croyde. *Devn* . . . . . . . . . . . . . .3E 19
Croydon. *Cambs* . . . . . . . . . . . .1D 52
**Croydon.** *G Lon* . . . . . . . . . . . .4E 39
Crubenbeg. *High* . . . . . . . . . . .4A 150
Crubenmore Lodge. *High* . . . .4A 150
Cruckmeole. *Shrp* . . . . . . . . . .5G 71
Cruckton. *Shrp* . . . . . . . . . . . . .4G 71
Cruden Bay. *Abers* . . . . . . . . .5H 161
Crudgington. *Telf* . . . . . . . . . . .4A 72
Crudie. *Abers* . . . . . . . . . . . . .3E 161
Crudwell. *Wilts* . . . . . . . . . . . . .2E 35
Cruft. *Devn* . . . . . . . . . . . . . . . .3F 11
Crug. *Powy* . . . . . . . . . . . . . . .3D 58
Crughywel. *Powy* . . . . . . . . . . .4F 47
Crugmeer. *Corn* . . . . . . . . . . . . .1D 6
Crugybar. *Carm* . . . . . . . . . . . .2G 45
Crug-y-byddar. *Powy* . . . . . . . .2D 58
Crulabhig. *W Isl* . . . . . . . . . . . .4D 171
Crumlin. *Ant* . . . . . . . . . . . . . .4G 175
Crumlin. *Cphy* . . . . . . . . . . . . . .2F 33
Crumpsall. *G Man* . . . . . . . . . .4G 91
Crumpsbrook. *Shrp* . . . . . . . . . .3A 60
Crundale. *Kent* . . . . . . . . . . . . .1E 29
Crundale. *Pemb* . . . . . . . . . . . .3D 42
Cruwys Morchard. *Devn* . . . . . .1B 12
Crux Easton. *Hants* . . . . . . . . .1C 24
Cruxton. *Dors* . . . . . . . . . . . . . .3B 14
Crwbin. *Carm* . . . . . . . . . . . . . .4E 45
Cryers Hill. *Buck* . . . . . . . . . . .2G 37
Crynant. *Neat* . . . . . . . . . . . . . .5A 46
Crystal Palace. *G Lon* . . . . . . . .3E 39
Cuaich. *High* . . . . . . . . . . . . . .5A 150
Cuaig. *High* . . . . . . . . . . . . . . .3G 155
Cuan. *Arg* . . . . . . . . . . . . . . . .2E 133
Cubbington. *Warw* . . . . . . . . . .4H 61
Cubert. *Corn* . . . . . . . . . . . . . . . .3B 6
Cubley. *S Yor* . . . . . . . . . . . . . .4C 92
Cubley Common. *Derbs* . . . . . .2F 73
Cublington. *Buck* . . . . . . . . . . .3G 51
Cublington. *Here* . . . . . . . . . . . .2G 47
Cuckfield. *W Sus* . . . . . . . . . . .3E 27
Cucklington. *Som* . . . . . . . . . . .4C 22
Cuckney. *Notts* . . . . . . . . . . . . .3C 86
Cuckron. *Shet* . . . . . . . . . . . . .6F 173
Cuddesdon. *Oxon* . . . . . . . . . . .5E 50
Cuddington. *Buck* . . . . . . . . . . .4F 51
Cuddington. *Ches W* . . . . . . . . .3A 84
Cuddington Heath. *Ches W* . . .1G 71
Cuddy Hill. *Lanc* . . . . . . . . . . . .1C 90
Cudham. *G Lon* . . . . . . . . . . . . .5F 39
Cudliptown. *Devn* . . . . . . . . . . .5F 11
Cudworth. *Som* . . . . . . . . . . . . .1G 13
**Cudworth.** *S Yor* . . . . . . . . . . .4D 93
Cudworth. *Surr* . . . . . . . . . . . . .1D 26
Cuerdley Cross. *Warr* . . . . . . . .2H 83
Cuffley. *Herts* . . . . . . . . . . . . . .5D 52
Cuidhir. *W Isl* . . . . . . . . . . . . . .8B 170
Cuidhsiadar. *W Isl* . . . . . . . . . .2H 171
Cuidhtinis. *W Isl* . . . . . . . . . . . .9C 171
Culbo. *High* . . . . . . . . . . . . . . .2A 158
Culbokie. *High* . . . . . . . . . . . . .3A 158
Culburnie. *High* . . . . . . . . . . . .4G 157
Culcabock. *High* . . . . . . . . . . .4A 158
Culcharry. *High* . . . . . . . . . . . .3C 158

Culcheth. *Warr* . . . . . . . . . . . . . .1A 84
Culduie. *High* . . . . . . . . . . . . . .4G 155
Culeave. *High* . . . . . . . . . . . . . .4C 164
Culford. *Staf* . . . . . . . . . . . . . . .3H 65
Culgaith. *Cumb* . . . . . . . . . . . .2H 103
Culham. *Oxon* . . . . . . . . . . . . . .2D 36
Culkein. *High* . . . . . . . . . . . . . .1E 163
Culkein Drumbeg. *High* . . . . . .5B 166
Culkerton. *Glos* . . . . . . . . . . . . .2E 35
Cullen. *Mor* . . . . . . . . . . . . . . .2C 160
Cullercoats. *Tyne* . . . . . . . . . . .2G 115
Cullicudden. *High* . . . . . . . . . .2A 158
Cullingworth. *W Yor* . . . . . . . . .1A 92
Cullipool. *Arg* . . . . . . . . . . . . . .2E 133
Cullivoe. *Shet* . . . . . . . . . . . . . .1G 173
Culloch. *Per* . . . . . . . . . . . . . . .2G 135
Culloden. *High* . . . . . . . . . . . . .4B 158
Cullompton. *Devn* . . . . . . . . . . .2D 12
Culm Davy. *Devn* . . . . . . . . . . . .1E 13
Culmington. *Shrp* . . . . . . . . . . .2G 59
Culmstock. *Devn* . . . . . . . . . . . .1E 12
Culnacraig. *High* . . . . . . . . . . .3E 163
Culnacnoc. *High* . . . . . . . . . . . .2E 155
Culnady. *M Ulst* . . . . . . . . . . . .6E 174
Culrain. *High* . . . . . . . . . . . . . .4C 164
Culross. *Fife* . . . . . . . . . . . . . . .1C 128
Culroy. *S Ayr* . . . . . . . . . . . . . . .3C 116
Culswick. *Shet* . . . . . . . . . . . . .7D 173
Cults. *Aber* . . . . . . . . . . . . . . . .3F 153
Cults. *Aber* . . . . . . . . . . . . . . .5C 160
Cults. *Fife* . . . . . . . . . . . . . . . . .3F 137
Cultybraggan Camp. *Per* . . . . .1G 135
Culver. *Devn* . . . . . . . . . . . . . . .3B 12
Culverlane. *Devn* . . . . . . . . . . . . .2D 8
Culverstone Green. *Kent* . . . . .4H 39
Culverthorpe. *Linc* . . . . . . . . . .1H 75
Culworth. *Nptn* . . . . . . . . . . . . .1D 50
Culzie Lodge. *High* . . . . . . . . .1H 157
Cumberlow Green. *Herts* . . . . .2D 52
**Cumbernauld.** *N Lan* . . . . . . . .2A 128
Cumbernauld Village.
    *N Lan* . . . . . . . . . . . . . . . .2A 128
Cumberworth. *Linc* . . . . . . . . . .3E 89
Cumdivock. *Cumb* . . . . . . . . . .5E 113
Cuminestown. *Abers* . . . . . . . .3F 161
Cumledge Mill. *Bord* . . . . . . . .4D 130
Cumlewick. *Shet* . . . . . . . . . . . .9F 173
Cummersdale. *Cumb* . . . . . . . .4E 113
Cummertrees. *Dum* . . . . . . . . .3C 112
Cummingstown. *Mor* . . . . . . . .2F 159
Cumnock. *E Ayr* . . . . . . . . . . . .2E 117
Cumnor. *Oxon* . . . . . . . . . . . . . .5C 50
Cumrew. *Cumb* . . . . . . . . . . . .4G 113
Cumwhinton. *Cumb* . . . . . . . . .4F 113
Cumwhitton. *Cumb* . . . . . . . . .4G 113
Cundall. *N Yor* . . . . . . . . . . . . . .2G 99
Cunninghamhead. *N Ayr* . . . . .5E 127
Cunning Park. *S Ayr* . . . . . . . .3C 116
Cunningsburgh. *Shet* . . . . . . . .9F 173
Cunnister. *Shet* . . . . . . . . . . . .2G 173
Cupar. *Fife* . . . . . . . . . . . . . . . .2F 137
Cupar Muir. *Fife* . . . . . . . . . . .2F 137
Curbar. *Derbs* . . . . . . . . . . . . . .3G 85
Curborough. *Staf* . . . . . . . . . . . .4F 73
Curbridge. *Hants* . . . . . . . . . . .1D 16
Curbridge. *Oxon* . . . . . . . . . . . .5B 50
Curdridge. *Hants* . . . . . . . . . . .1D 16
Curdworth. *Warw* . . . . . . . . . . .1F 61
Curland. *Som* . . . . . . . . . . . . . .1F 13
Curland Common. *Som* . . . . . . .1F 13
Curridge. *W Ber* . . . . . . . . . . . .4C 36
Currie. *Edin* . . . . . . . . . . . . . . .3E 129
Curry Mallet. *Som* . . . . . . . . . .4G 21
Curry Rivel. *Som* . . . . . . . . . . .4G 21
Curtisden Green. *Kent* . . . . . . . .1B 28
Curtisknowle. *Devn* . . . . . . . . . . .3D 8
Cury. *Corn* . . . . . . . . . . . . . . . . .4D 5
Cusgarne. *Corn* . . . . . . . . . . . . .4B 6
Cushendall. *Caus* . . . . . . . . . . .1G 175
Cusop. *Here* . . . . . . . . . . . . . . .1F 47
Cusworth. *S Yor* . . . . . . . . . . . .4F 93
Cutcombe. *Som* . . . . . . . . . . . .3C 20

Cuthill. *E Lot* . . . . . . . . . . . . . .2G 129
Cutiau. *Gwyn* . . . . . . . . . . . . . .4F 69
Cutlers Green. *Essx* . . . . . . . . .2F 53
Cutmadoc. *Corn* . . . . . . . . . . . . .2E 7
Cutnall Green. *Worc* . . . . . . . . .4C 60
Cutsdean. *Glos* . . . . . . . . . . . . .2F 49
Cutthorpe. *Derbs* . . . . . . . . . . .3H 85
Cuttiford's Door. *Som* . . . . . . . .1G 13
Cuttivett. *Corn* . . . . . . . . . . . . . .2H 7
Cutts. *Shet* . . . . . . . . . . . . . . .8E 173
Cuttybridge. *Pemb* . . . . . . . . . .3D 42
Cuttyhill. *Abers* . . . . . . . . . . . .3H 161
Cuxham. *Oxon* . . . . . . . . . . . . .2E 37
Cuxton. *Medw* . . . . . . . . . . . . . .4B 40
Cuxwold. *Linc* . . . . . . . . . . . . . .4E 95
Cwm. *Blae* . . . . . . . . . . . . . . . .5E 47
Cwm. *Den* . . . . . . . . . . . . . . . .3C 82
Cwm. *Powy* . . . . . . . . . . . . . . . .1E 59
Cwmafan. *Neat* . . . . . . . . . . . . .2A 32
Cwmaman. *Rhon* . . . . . . . . . . . .2C 32
Cwmann. *Carm* . . . . . . . . . . . . .1F 45
Cwmbach. *Carm* . . . . . . . . . . . .2G 43
Cwmbach. *Powy* . . . . . . . . . . . .2E 47
Cwmbach. *Rhon* . . . . . . . . . . . .5D 46
Cwmbach Llechrhyd.
    *Powy* . . . . . . . . . . . . . . . . .5C 58
Cwmbelan. *Powy* . . . . . . . . . . .2B 58
**Cwmbran.** *Torf* . . . . . . . . . . . . .2F 33
Cwmbrwyno. *Cdgn* . . . . . . . . . .2G 57
Cwm Capel. *Carm* . . . . . . . . . .5E 45
Cwmcarn. *Cphy* . . . . . . . . . . . . .2F 33
Cwmcarvan. *Mon* . . . . . . . . . . .5H 47
Cwm-celyn. *Blae* . . . . . . . . . . . .5F 47
Cwmcerdinen. *Swan* . . . . . . . . .5G 45
Cwm-Cewydd. *Gwyn* . . . . . . . . .4A 70
Cwm-cou. *Cdgn* . . . . . . . . . . . . .1C 44
Cwmcych. *Pemb* . . . . . . . . . . . .1G 43
Cwmdare. *Rhon* . . . . . . . . . . . . .5C 46
Cwmdu. *Carm* . . . . . . . . . . . . . .2G 45
Cwmdu. *Powy* . . . . . . . . . . . . . .3E 47
Cwmduad. *Carm* . . . . . . . . . . . .2D 45
Cwmerfyn. *Cdgn* . . . . . . . . . . . .2F 57
Cwmfelin. *B'end* . . . . . . . . . . . .3B 32
Cwmfelin Boeth. *Carm* . . . . . . .3F 43
Cwmfelinfach. *Cphy* . . . . . . . . .2E 33
Cwmfelin Mynach. *Carm* . . . . .2G 43
Cwmffrwd. *Carm* . . . . . . . . . . . .4E 45
Cwmgiedd. *Powy* . . . . . . . . . . . .4A 46
Cwmgors. *Neat* . . . . . . . . . . . . .4H 45
Cwmgwili. *Carm* . . . . . . . . . . . .4F 45
Cwmgwrach. *Neat* . . . . . . . . . . .5B 46
Cwmhiraeth. *Carm* . . . . . . . . . .1H 43
Cwmifor. *Carm* . . . . . . . . . . . . .3G 45
Cwmisfael. *Carm* . . . . . . . . . . . .4E 45
Cwm-Llinau. *Powy* . . . . . . . . . .5H 69
Cwmllynfell. *Neat* . . . . . . . . . . .4H 45
Cwm-mawr. *Carm* . . . . . . . . . . .4F 45
Cwm-miles. *Carm* . . . . . . . . . . .2F 43
Cwmorgan. *Carm* . . . . . . . . . . .1G 43
Cwmparc. *Rhon* . . . . . . . . . . . . .2C 32
Cwm Penmachno. *Cnwy* . . . . .1G 69
Cwmpennar. *Rhon* . . . . . . . . . . .5D 46
Cwm Plysgog. *Pemb* . . . . . . . . .1B 44
Cwmrhos. *Powy* . . . . . . . . . . . . .3E 47
Cwmsychpant. *Cdgn* . . . . . . . . .1E 45
Cwmsyfiog. *Cphy* . . . . . . . . . . .5E 47
Cwmsymlog. *Cdgn* . . . . . . . . . .2F 57
Cwmtillery. *Blae* . . . . . . . . . . . .5F 47
Cwm-twrch Isaf. *Powy* . . . . . . .5A 46
Cwm-twrch Uchaf. *Powy* . . . . .4A 46
Cwmwysg. *Powy* . . . . . . . . . . . .3B 46
Cwm-y-glo. *Gwyn* . . . . . . . . . . .4E 81
Cwmyoy. *Mon* . . . . . . . . . . . . . .3G 47
Cwmystwyth. *Cdgn* . . . . . . . . . .3G 57
Cwrt. *Gwyn* . . . . . . . . . . . . . . . .5F 69
Cwrtnewydd. *Cdgn* . . . . . . . . . .1E 45
Cwrt-y-Cadno. *Carm* . . . . . . . . .1G 45
Cydweli. *Carm* . . . . . . . . . . . . . .5E 45
Cyffylliog. *Den* . . . . . . . . . . . . . .5C 82
Cymau. *Flin* . . . . . . . . . . . . . . . .5E 83
Cymer. *Neat* . . . . . . . . . . . . . . .2B 32
Cymmer. *Neat* . . . . . . . . . . . . . .2B 32
Cymmer. *Rhon* . . . . . . . . . . . . .2D 32

Cyncoed. *Card* . . . . . . . . . . . . . .3E 33
Cynghordy. *Carm* . . . . . . . . . . .2B 46
Cynheidre. *Carm* . . . . . . . . . . . .5E 45
Cynonville. *Neat* . . . . . . . . . . . .2B 32
Cynwyd. *Den* . . . . . . . . . . . . . . .1C 70
Cynwyl Elfed. *Carm* . . . . . . . . .3D 44
Cywarch. *Gwyn* . . . . . . . . . . . . .4A 70

## D

Dacre. *Cumb* . . . . . . . . . . . . . .2F 103
Dacre. *N Yor* . . . . . . . . . . . . . . .3D 98
Dacre Banks. *N Yor* . . . . . . . . . .3D 98
Daddry Shield. *Dur* . . . . . . . . .1B 104
Dadford. *Buck* . . . . . . . . . . . . . .2E 51
Dadlington. *Leics* . . . . . . . . . . . .1B 62
Dafen. *Carm* . . . . . . . . . . . . . . .5F 45
Daffy Green. *Norf* . . . . . . . . . . .5B 78
Dagdale. *Staf* . . . . . . . . . . . . . .2E 73
**Dagenham.** *G Lon* . . . . . . . . . .2F 39
Daggons. *Dors* . . . . . . . . . . . . .1G 15
Daglingworth. *Glos* . . . . . . . . . .5E 49
Dagnall. *Buck* . . . . . . . . . . . . . .4H 51
Dagtail End. *Worc* . . . . . . . . . . .4E 61
Dail. *Arg* . . . . . . . . . . . . . . . . . .5E 141
Dail Beag. *W Isl* . . . . . . . . . . . .3E 171
Dail bho Dheas. *W Isl* . . . . . . .1G 171
Dailly. *S Ayr* . . . . . . . . . . . . . . .4B 116
Dail Mor. *W Isl* . . . . . . . . . . . . .3E 171
Dairsie. *Fife* . . . . . . . . . . . . . . .2G 137
Daisy Bank. *W Mid* . . . . . . . . . .1E 61
Daisy Hill. *G Man* . . . . . . . . . . .4E 91
Daisy Hill. *W Yor* . . . . . . . . . . . .1B 92
Dalabrog. *W Isl* . . . . . . . . . . . .6C 170
Dalavich. *Arg* . . . . . . . . . . . . . .2G 133
Dalbeattie. *Dum* . . . . . . . . . . . .3F 111
Dalblair. *E Ayr* . . . . . . . . . . . . . .3F 117
Dalbury. *Derbs* . . . . . . . . . . . . . .2G 73
Dalby. *IOM* . . . . . . . . . . . . . . . .4B 108
Dalby Wolds. *Leics* . . . . . . . . . .3D 74
Dalchalm. *High* . . . . . . . . . . . . .3G 165
Dalcharn. *High* . . . . . . . . . . . .3G 167
Dalchork. *High* . . . . . . . . . . . . .2C 164
Dalchreichart. *High* . . . . . . . . .2E 149
Dalchruin. *Per* . . . . . . . . . . . . .2G 135
Dalcross. *High* . . . . . . . . . . . . .4B 158
Dalderby. *Linc* . . . . . . . . . . . . . .4B 88
Dale. *Cumb* . . . . . . . . . . . . . . .5G 113
Dale. *Pemb* . . . . . . . . . . . . . . . .4C 42
Dale Abbey. *Derbs* . . . . . . . . . .2B 74
Dalebank. *Derbs* . . . . . . . . . . . .4A 86
Dale Bottom. *Cumb* . . . . . . . . .2D 102
Dale Head. *Cumb* . . . . . . . . . .3F 103
Dalehouse. *N Yor* . . . . . . . . . . .3E 107
Dalelia. *High* . . . . . . . . . . . . . . .2B 140
Dale of Walls. *Shet* . . . . . . . . .6C 173
Dalgarven. *N Ayr* . . . . . . . . . . .5D 126
Dalgety Bay. *Fife* . . . . . . . . . . .1E 129
Dalginross. *Per* . . . . . . . . . . . .1G 135
Dalguise. *Per* . . . . . . . . . . . . . .4G 143
Dalhalvaig. *High* . . . . . . . . . . .3A 168
Dalham. *Suff* . . . . . . . . . . . . . . .4G 65
Dalintart. *Arg* . . . . . . . . . . . . . .1F 133
Dalkeith. *Midl* . . . . . . . . . . . . .3G 129
Dallas. *Mor* . . . . . . . . . . . . . . .3F 159
Dalleagles. *E Ayr* . . . . . . . . . . . .3E 117
Dall House. *Per* . . . . . . . . . . . .3C 142
Dallinghoo. *Suff* . . . . . . . . . . . . .5E 67
Dallington. *E Sus* . . . . . . . . . . . .4A 28
Dallow. *N Yor* . . . . . . . . . . . . . .2D 98
Dalmally. *Arg* . . . . . . . . . . . . . .1A 134
Dalmarnock. *Glas* . . . . . . . . . .3H 127
Dalmellington. *E Ayr* . . . . . . . .4D 117
Dalmeny. *Edin* . . . . . . . . . . . . .2E 129
Dalmigavie. *High* . . . . . . . . . . .2B 150
Dalmilling. *S Ayr* . . . . . . . . . . .2C 116
**Darlington.** *Darl* . . . . . . . . . . .3F 105
    nr. Alness . . . . . . . . . . . . . .2A 158
    nr. Rogart . . . . . . . . . . . . . .3E 164
Dalmuir. *W Dun* . . . . . . . . . . . .2F 127
Dalmunach. *Mor* . . . . . . . . . . .4G 159
Dalnabreck. *High* . . . . . . . . . . .2B 140
Dalnacardoch Lodge. *Per* . . . .1E 142

Dalnamein Lodge. *Per* . . . . . . .2E 143
Dalnaspidal Lodge. *Per* . . . . . .1D 142
Dalnatrat. *High* . . . . . . . . . . . .3D 140
Dalnavie. *High* . . . . . . . . . . . . .1A 158
Dalnawillan Lodge. *High* . . . . .4C 168
Dalness. *High* . . . . . . . . . . . . .3F 141
Dalnessie. *High* . . . . . . . . . . . .2D 164
Dalqueich. *Per* . . . . . . . . . . . . .3C 136
Dalquharn. *S Ayr* . . . . . . . . . . .5C 116
Dalreavoch. *High* . . . . . . . . . . .3E 165
Dalreoch. *Per* . . . . . . . . . . . . . .2C 136
Dalry. *Edin* . . . . . . . . . . . . . . . .2F 129
Dalry. *N Ayr* . . . . . . . . . . . . . . .5D 126
Dalrymple. *E Ayr* . . . . . . . . . . .3C 116
Dalscote. *Nptn* . . . . . . . . . . . . . .5D 62
Dalserf. *S Lan* . . . . . . . . . . . . . .4B 128
Dalsmirren. *Arg* . . . . . . . . . . . .4A 122
Dalston. *Cumb* . . . . . . . . . . . . .4E 113
Dalswinton. *Dum* . . . . . . . . . . .1G 111
Dalton. *Dum* . . . . . . . . . . . . . .2C 112
Dalton. *Lanc* . . . . . . . . . . . . . . .4C 90
Dalton. *Nmbd*
    nr. Hexham . . . . . . . . . . . .4C 114
    nr. Ponteland . . . . . . . . . .2E 115
Dalton. *N Yor*
    nr. Richmond . . . . . . . . . . .4E 105
    nr. Thirsk . . . . . . . . . . . . . . .2G 99
Dalton. *S Lan* . . . . . . . . . . . . . .4H 127
Dalton. *S Yor* . . . . . . . . . . . . . . .1B 86
Dalton-in-Furness. *Cumb* . . . . .2B 96
Dalton-le-Dale. *Dur* . . . . . . . . .5H 115
Dalton Magna. *S Yor* . . . . . . . . .1B 86
Dalton-on-Tees. *N Yor* . . . . . . .4F 105
Dalton Piercy. *Hart* . . . . . . . . .1B 106
Daltot. *Arg* . . . . . . . . . . . . . . . .1F 125
Dalvey. *High* . . . . . . . . . . . . . . .5F 159
Dalwhinnie. *High* . . . . . . . . . .5A 150
Dalwood. *Devn* . . . . . . . . . . . . . .2F 13
Damerham. *Hants* . . . . . . . . . .1G 15
Damgate. *Norf*
    nr. Acle . . . . . . . . . . . . . . . .4G 79
    nr. Martham . . . . . . . . . . . .4G 79
Dam Green. *Norf* . . . . . . . . . . . .2C 66
Damhead. *Mor* . . . . . . . . . . . . .3E 159
Danaway. *Kent* . . . . . . . . . . . . .4C 40
Danbury. *Essx* . . . . . . . . . . . . . .5A 54
Danby. *N Yor* . . . . . . . . . . . . . .4E 107
Danby Botton. *N Yor* . . . . . . . .4D 107
Danby Wiske. *N Yor* . . . . . . . . .5A 106
Danderhall. *Midl* . . . . . . . . . . .3G 129
Danebank. *Ches E* . . . . . . . . . . .2D 85
Danebridge. *Ches E* . . . . . . . . .4D 84
Dane End. *Herts* . . . . . . . . . . . .3D 52
Danehill. *E Sus* . . . . . . . . . . . . .3F 27
Danesford. *Shrp* . . . . . . . . . . . .1B 60
Daneshill. *Hants* . . . . . . . . . . . .1E 25
Danesmoor. *Derbs* . . . . . . . . . .4B 86
Dangerous Corner. *Lanc* . . . . . .3D 90
Daniel's Water. *Kent* . . . . . . . . .1D 28
Dan's Castle. *Dur* . . . . . . . . . .1E 105
Danzey Green. *Warw* . . . . . . . . .4F 61
Dapple Heath. *Staf* . . . . . . . . . .3E 73
Darenth. *Kent* . . . . . . . . . . . . . .3G 39
Daresbury. *Hal* . . . . . . . . . . . . . .2H 83
Darfield. *S Yor* . . . . . . . . . . . . . .4E 93
Dargate. *Kent* . . . . . . . . . . . . . .4E 41
Dargill. *Per* . . . . . . . . . . . . . . .2A 136
Darite. *Corn* . . . . . . . . . . . . . . . .2G 7
Darlaston. *W Mid* . . . . . . . . . . .1D 61
Darley. *N Yor* . . . . . . . . . . . . . . .4E 98
Darley Abbey. *Derb* . . . . . . . . . .2H 73
Darley Bridge. *Derbs* . . . . . . . .4G 85
Darley Dale. *Derbs* . . . . . . . . . .4G 85
Darley Head. *N Yor* . . . . . . . . . .4D 98
Darlingscott. *Warw* . . . . . . . . . .1H 49
Darliston. *Shrp* . . . . . . . . . . . . .2H 71
Darlton. *Notts* . . . . . . . . . . . . . .3E 87
Darmsden. *Suff* . . . . . . . . . . . . .5C 66
Darnall. *S Yor* . . . . . . . . . . . . . .2A 86
Darnford. *Abers* . . . . . . . . . . . .4E 153
Darnford. *Staf* . . . . . . . . . . . . . .5F 73

Darnhall. Ches W .........4A 84
Darnick. Bord ...........1H 119
Darowen. Powy ..........5H 69
Darra. Abers ...........4E 161
Darracott. Devn .........3E 19
Darras Hall. Nmbd ......2E 115
Darrington. W Yor ........2E 93
Darrow Green. Norf ......2E 67
Darsham. Suff ..........4G 67
Dartfield. Abers ........3H 161
**Dartford. Kent** ..........3G 39
**Dartford-Thurrock**
    **River Crossing.** Kent ...3G 39
Dartington. Devn ........2D 9
Dartmeet. Devn .........5G 11
Dartmouth. Devn .........3E 9
**Darton.** S Yor ..........3D 92
Darvel. E Ayr ..........1E 117
**Darwen.** Bkbn ..........2E 91
Dassels. Herts .........3D 53
Datchet. Wind ..........3A 38
Datchworth. Herts .......4C 52
Datchworth Green. Herts ..4C 52
Daubhill. G Man ........4F 91
Dauntsey. Wilts .........3E 35
Dauntsey Green. Wilts ....3E 35
Dauntsey Lock. Wilts .....3E 35
Dava. Mor .............5E 159
Davenham. Ches W .......3A 84
**Daventry.** Nptn .........4C 62
Davidson's Mains. Edin ...2F 129
Davidston. High ........2B 158
Davidstow. Corn .........4B 10
David's Well. Powy .......3C 58
Davington. Dum .........4E 119
Daviot. Abers ..........1E 153
Daviot. High ..........5B 158
Davyhulme. G Man ......1B 84
Daw Cross. N Yor .......4E 99
Dawdon. Dur ..........5H 115
Dawesgreen. Surr .......1D 26
Dawley. Telf ..........5A 72
**Dawlish.** Devn .........5C 12
Dawlish Warren. Devn ....5C 12
Dawn. Cnwy ..........3A 82
Daws Heath. Essx .......2C 40
Dawshill. Worc .........5C 60
Daw's House. Corn .......4D 10
Dawsmere. Linc ........2D 76
Dayhills. Staf .........2D 72
Dayhouse Bank. Worc ....3D 60
Daylesford. Glos .......3H 49
Daywall. Shrp .........2E 71
Ddol. Flin ............1D 82
Ddol Cownwy. Powy .....4C 70
Deadman's Cross. C Beds .1B 52
Deadwater. Nmbd ......5A 120
Deaf Hill. Dur .........1A 106
**Deal.** Kent ...........5H 41
Dean. Cumb ..........2B 102
Dean. Devn
    nr. Combe Martin ....2G 19
    nr. Lynton .........2H 19
Dean. Dors ...........1E 15
Dean. Hants
    nr. Bishop's Waltham ..1D 16
    nr. Winchester ......3C 24
Dean. Oxon ..........3B 50
Dean. Som ...........2B 22
Dean Bank. Dur ........1F 105
Deanburnhaugh. Bord ....3F 119
Dean Cross. Devn .......2F 19
Deane. Hants ..........1D 24
Deanich Lodge. High ....5A 164
Deanland. Dors ........1E 15
Deanlane End. W Sus ....1F 17
Dean Park. Shrp ........4A 60
Dean Prior. Devn .......2D 8
Dean Row. Ches E .......2C 84
Deans. W Lot ..........3D 128
Deanscales. Cumb ......2B 102
Deanshanger. Nptn .....1F 51
Deanston. Stir .........3G 135
Dearham. Cumb ........1B 102

Dearne Valley. S Yor ......4D 93
Debach. Suff ...........5E 67
Debden. Essx ..........2F 53
Debden Green.
    nr. Loughton .......1F 39
    nr. Saffron Walden ...2F 53
Debenham. Suff ........4D 66
Dechmont. W Lot .......2D 128
Deddington. Oxon ......2C 50
Dedham. Essx ..........2D 54
Dedham Heath. Essx ....2D 54
Deebank. Abers ........4D 152
Deene. Nptn ..........1G 63
Deenethorpe. Nptn .....1G 63
Deepcar. S Yor .........1G 85
Deepcut. Surr .........5A 38
Deepdale. Cumb ........1G 97
Deepdale. N Lin ........3D 94
Deepdale. N Yor .......2A 98
Deeping Gate. Pet ......5A 76
Deeping St James. Linc ..4A 76
Deeping St Nicholas. Linc ..4B 76
Deerhill. Mor .........3B 160
Deerhurst. Glos ........3D 48
Deerhurst Walton. Glos ..3D 49
Deerness. Orkn ........7E 172
Defford. Worc .........1E 49
Defynnog. Powy ........3C 46
Deganwy. Cnwy ........3G 81
Deighton. N Yor .......4A 106
Deighton. W Yor .......3B 92
Deighton. York ........5A 100
Deiniolen. Gwyn .......4E 81
Delabole. Corn ........4A 10
Delamere. Ches W ......4H 83
Delfour. High .........3C 150
The Dell. Suff .........1G 67
Delliefure. High ........5E 159
Delly End. Oxon .......4B 50
Delny. High ..........1B 158
Delph. G Man .........4H 91
Delves. Dur ..........5E 115
The Delves. W Mid .....1E 61
Delvin End. Essx .......2A 54
Dembleby. Linc ........2H 75
Demelza. Corn .........2D 6
The Den. N Ayr ........4E 127
Denaby Main. S Yor .....1B 86
Denbeath. Fife .........4F 137
Denbigh. Den .........4C 82
Denbury. Devn .........2E 9
Denby. Derbs ..........1A 74
Denby Common. Derbs ..1B 74
Denby Dale. W Yor .....4C 92
Denchworth. Oxon .....2B 36
Dendron. Cumb ........2B 96
Deneside. Dur .........5H 115
Denford. Nptn .........3G 63
Dengie. Essx ..........5C 54
Denham. Buck .........2B 38
Denham. Suff
    nr. Bury St Edmunds ..4G 65
    nr. Eye ...........3D 66
Denham Green. Buck ...2B 38
Denham Street. Suff ....3D 66
Denhead. Abers
    nr. Ellon .........5G 161
    nr. Strichen ......3G 161
Denhead. Fife .........2G 137
Denholm. Bord ........3H 119
Denholme. W Yor ......1A 92
Denholme Clough. W Yor ..1A 92
Denholme Gate. W Yor ..1A 92
Denio. Gwyn ..........2C 68
Denmead. Hants .......1E 17
Dennington. Suff ......4E 67
**Denny.** Falk ..........1B 128
Denny End. Cambs .....4D 65
Dennyloanhead. Falk ...1B 128
Den of Lindores. Fife ...2E 137
Denshaw. G Man .......3H 91
Denside. Abers ........4F 153
Densole. Kent .........1G 29
Denston. Suff .........5G 65

Denstone. Staf .........1F 73
Denstroude. Kent .......4F 41
Dent. Cumb ...........1G 97
Denton. Cambs ........2A 64
Denton. Darl .........3F 105
Denton. E Sus .........5F 27
**Denton.** G Man .........1D 84
Denton. Kent ..........1G 29
Denton. Linc ..........2F 75
Denton. Norf ..........2E 67
Denton. Nptn ..........5F 63
Denton. N Yor .........5D 98
Denton. Oxon ..........5D 50
Denver. Norf ..........5F 77
Denwick. Nmbd ........3G 121
Deopham. Norf ........5C 78
Deopham Green. Norf ..1C 66
Depden. Suff ..........5G 65
Depden Green. Suff ....5G 65
**Deptford.** G Lon .......3E 39
Deptford. Wilts ........3F 23
**Derby.** Derb ..........2A 74
Derbyhaven. IOM .......5B 108
Derculich. Per .........3F 143
**Dereham.** Norf .........4B 78
Deri. Cphy ...........5E 47
Derril. Devn ..........2D 10
Derringstone. Kent .....1G 29
Derrington. Shrp .......1A 60
Derrington. Staf .......3C 72
Derriton. Devn .........2D 10
**Derry.** Derr ...........2C 174
Derryguaig. Arg ........5F 139
Derry Hill. Wilts .......4E 35
Derrythorpe. N Lin .....4B 94
Dersingham. Norf ......2F 77
Dervaig. Arg ..........3F 139
Derwen. Den ..........5C 82
Derwen Gam. Cdgn .....5D 56
Derwenlas. Powy .......1G 57
Desborough. Nptn ......2F 63
Desford. Leics .........5B 74
Detchant. Nmbd ........1E 121
Dethick. Derbs ........5H 85
Detling. Kent .........5B 40
Deuchar. Ang .........2D 144
Deuddwr. Powy ........4E 71
Devauden. Mon ........2H 33
**Devizes.** Wilts .........5F 35
Devonport. Plym .......3A 8
Devonside. Clac .......4B 136
Devoran. Corn .........5B 6
Dewartown. Midl .......3G 129
Dewlish. Dors .........3C 14
Dewsall Court. Here ....2H 47
**Dewsbury.** W Yor ......2C 92
Dexbeer. Devon ........2C 10
Dhoon. IOM ..........3D 108
Dhoor. IOM ...........2D 108
Dhowin. IOM ..........1D 108
Dial Green. W Sus ......3A 26
Dial Post. W Sus .......4C 26
Dibberford. Dors .......2H 13
Dibden. Hants .........2C 16
Dibden Purlieu. Hants ..2C 16
Dickleburgh. Norf ......2D 66
Didbrook. Glos .........2F 49
**Didcot.** Oxon ..........2D 36
Diddington. Cambs .....4A 64
Diddlebury. Shrp .......2H 59
Didley. Here ..........2H 47
Didling. W Sus .........1G 17
Didmarton. Glos .......3D 34
Didsbury. G Man .......1C 84
Didworthy. Devn .......2C 8
Digby. Linc ...........5H 87
Digg. High ...........2D 154
Diggle. G Man .........4A 92
Digmoor. Lanc .........4C 90
Digswell. Herts ........4C 52
Dihewyd. Cdgn ........5D 57
Dilham. Norf ..........3F 79

Dilhorne. Staf .........1D 72
Dillarburn. S Lan .......5B 128
Dillington. Cambs ......4A 64
Dilston. Nmbd .........3C 114
Dilton Marsh. Wilts .....2D 22
Dilwyn. Here ..........5G 59
Dimmer. Som .........3B 22
Dimple. G Man .........3F 91
Dinas. Carm ..........1G 43
Dinas. Gwyn
    nr. Caernarfon ......5D 81
    nr. Tudweiliog ......2B 68
Dinas Cross. Pemb .....1E 43
Dinas Dinlle. Gwyn .....5D 80
Dinas Mawddwy. Gwyn ..4A 70
Dinas Powys. V Glam ...4E 33
Dinbych. Den ..........4C 82
Dinbych-y-Pysgod. Pemb ..4F 43
Dinckley. Lanc .........1E 91
Dinder. Som ..........2A 22
Dinedor. Here .........2A 48
Dinedor Cross. Here ....2A 48
Dingestow. Mon ........4H 47
Dingle. Mers ..........2F 83
Dingleden. Kent ........2C 28
Dingleton. Bord ........1H 119
Dingley. Nptn .........2E 63
Dingwall. High ........3H 157
Dinmael. Cnwy ........1C 70
Dinnet. Abers .........4B 152
Dinnington. S Yor ......2C 86
Dinnington. Som .......1H 13
Dinnington. Tyne ......2F 115
Dinorwig. Gwyn .......4E 81
Dinton. Buck ..........4F 51
Dinton. Wilts .........3F 23
Dinworthy. Devn .......1D 10
Dipley. Hants .........1F 25
Dippen. Arg ..........2B 122
Dippenhall. Surr .......2G 25
Dippertown. Devn ......4E 11
Dippin. N Ayr .........3E 123
Dipple. S Ayr .........4B 116
Diptford. Devn .........3D 8
Dipton. Dur ...........4E 115
Dirleton. E Lot ........1B 130
Dirt Pot. Nmbd ........5B 114
Discoed. Powy .........4E 59
Diseworth. Leics .......3B 74
Dishes. Orkn ..........5F 172
Dishforth. N Yor .......2F 99
Disley. Ches E .........2D 85
Diss. Norf ...........3D 66
Disserth. Powy ........5C 58
Distington. Cumb ......2B 102
Ditcheat. Som .........3B 22
Ditchingham. Norf .....1F 67
Ditchling. E Sus .......4E 27
Ditteridge. Wilts .......5D 34
Dittisham. Devn ........3E 9
Ditton. Hal ...........2G 83
Ditton. Kent ..........5B 40
Ditton Green. Cambs ...5F 65
Ditton Priors. Shrp .....2A 60
Divach. High ..........1G 149
Dixonfield. High .......2D 168
Dixton. Glos ..........2E 49
Dixton. Mon ..........4A 48
Dizzard. Corn .........3B 10
Doagh. Ant ...........3G 175
Dobcross. G Man .......4H 91
Dobs Hill. Flin ........4F 83
Dobson's Bridge. Shrp ..2G 71
Dobwalls. Corn ........2G 7
Doccombe. Devn .......4A 12
Dochgarroch. High .....4A 158
Docking. Norf .........2G 77
Docklow. Here ........5H 59
Dockray. Cumb ........2E 103
Doc Penfro. Pemb ......4D 42
Dodbrooke. Devn .......4D 8
Doddenham. Worc .....5B 60
Doddinghurst. Essx ....1G 39

Doddington. Cambs .....1C 64
Doddington. Kent ......5D 40
Doddington. Linc ......3G 87
Doddington. Nmbd .....1D 121
Doddington. Shrp ......3A 60
Doddiscombsleigh. Devn ..4B 12
Doddshill. Norf ........2G 77
Dodford. Nptn .........4D 62
Dodford. Worc ........3D 60
Dodington. Som ........2E 21
Dodington. S Glo ......3C 34
Dodleston. Ches W .....4F 83
Dods Leigh. Staf .......2E 73
Dodworth. S Yor .......4D 92
Doe Lea. Derbs ........4B 86
Dogdyke. Linc .........5B 88
Dogmersfield. Hants ...1F 25
Dogsthorpe. Pet .......5B 76
Dog Village. Devn ......3C 12
Dolanog. Powy .........4C 70
Dolau. Powy ..........4D 58
Dolau. Rhon ..........3D 32
Dolbenmaen. Gwyn ....1E 69
Doley. Staf ...........3B 72
Dol-fâch. Powy ........5B 70
Dolfach. Powy .........3B 58
Dolfor. Powy ..........2D 58
Dolgarrog. Cnwy .......4G 81
Dolgellau. Gwyn .......4G 69
Dolgoch. Gwyn ........5F 69
Dol-gran. Carm ........2E 45
Dolhelfa. Powy ........3B 58
Doll. High ...........3F 165
Dollar. Clac ..........4B 136
Dolley Green. Powy .....4E 59
Dollingstown. Arm .....5G 175
Dollwen. Cdgn ........2F 57
Dolphin. Flin .........3D 82
Dolphinholme. Lanc ....4E 97
Dolphinton. S Lan ......5E 129
Dolton. Devn .........1F 11
Dolwen. Cnwy .........3A 82
Dolwyddelan. Cnwy .....5G 81
Dol-y-Bont. Cdgn ......2F 57
Dolyhir. Powy .........5E 59
Domgay. Powy .........4E 71
Donaghadee. Ards .....4J 175
**Doncaster.** S Yor .......4F 93
Doncaster Sheffield Airport.
    S Yor ...........1D 86
Donhead St Andrew. Wilts ..4E 23
Donhead St Mary. Wilts ..4E 23
Doniford. Som .........2D 20
Donington. Linc .......2B 76
Donington. S Yor .......5C 72
Donington. W Ber ......5C 36
Donington. W Sus ......2G 17
Donington Eaudike. Linc ..2B 76
Donington le Heath. Leics ..4B 74
Donington on Bain. Linc ..2B 88
Donington South Ing. Linc ..2B 76
Donisthorpe. Leics .....4H 73
Donkey Street. Kent ....2F 29
Donkey Town. Surr .....4A 38
Donna Nook. Linc ......1D 88
Donnington. Glos ......3G 49
Donnington. Here ......2C 48
Donnington. Shrp ......5H 71
Donnington. Telf ......4B 72
Donnington. W Ber .....5C 36
Donnington. W Sus .....2G 17
Donyatt. Som .........1G 13
Doomsday Green. W Sus ..3C 26
Doonfoot. S Ayr .......3C 116
Doonholm. S Ayr ......3C 116
Dorback Lodge. High ...2E 151
**Dorchester.** Dors .......3B 14
Dorchester on Thames.
    Oxon ............2D 36
Dordon. Warw .........5G 73
Dore. S Yor ..........2H 85
Dores. High ..........5H 157
**Dorking.** Surr .........1C 26
Dorking Tye. Suff ......2C 54
Dormansland. Surr .....1F 27
Dormans Park. Surr ....1E 27

**Dormanstown—Dunstan**


Dormanstown. *Red C* 2C **106**
Dormington. *Here* 1A **48**
Dormston. *Worc* 5D **61**
Dorn. *Glos* 2H **49**
Dorney. *Buck* 3A **38**
Dornie. *High* 1A **148**
Dornoch. *High* 5E **165**
Dornock. *Dum* 3D **112**
Dorrery. *High* 3C **168**
Dorridge. *W Mid* 3F **61**
Dorrington. *Linc* 5H **87**
Dorrington. *Shrp* 5G **71**
Dorsington. *Warw* 1G **49**
Dorstone. *Here* 1G **47**
Dorton. *Buck* 4E **51**
Dosthill. *Staf* 5G **73**
Dotham. *IOA* 3C **80**
Dottery. *Dors* 3H **13**
Doublebois. *Corn* 2F **7**
Dougarie. *N Ayr* 2C **122**
Doughton. *Glos* 2D **35**
Douglas. *IOM* 4C **108**
Douglas. *S Lan* 1H **117**
Douglastown. *Ang* 4D **144**
Douglas Water. *S Lan* 1A **118**
Doulting. *Som* 2B **22**
Dounby. *Orkn* 5B **172**
Doune. *High*
nr. Kingussie 2C **150**
nr. Lairg 3B **164**
Doune. *Stir* 3G **135**
Dounie. *High*
nr. Bonar Bridge 4C **164**
nr. Tain 5D **164**
Dounreay, Upper & Lower.
*High* 2B **168**
Doura. *N Ayr* 5E **127**
Dousland. *Devn* 2B **8**
Dovaston. *Shrp* 3F **71**
Dove Holes. *Derbs* 3E **85**
Dovenby. *Cumb* 1B **102**
**Dover**. *Kent* 1H **29**
Dovercourt. *Essx* 2F **55**
Doverdale. *Worc* 4C **60**
Doveridge. *Derbs* 2F **73**
Doversgreen. *Surr* 1D **26**
Dowally. *Per* 4H **143**
Dowbridge. *Lanc* 1C **90**
Dowdeswell. *Glos* 4F **49**
Dowlais. *Mer T* 5D **46**
Dowland. *Devn* 1F **11**
Dowlands. *Devn* 3F **13**
Dowles. *Worc* 3B **60**
Dowlesgreen. *Wok* 5G **37**
Dowlish Wake. *Som* 1G **13**
The Down. *Shrp* 1A **60**
Downall Green. *Mers* 4D **90**
Down Ampney. *Glos* 2G **35**
Downderry. *Corn*
nr. Looe 3H **7**
nr. St Austell 3D **6**
Downe. *G Lon* 4F **39**
Downend. *IOW* 4D **16**
Downend. *S Glo* 4B **34**
Downend. *W Ber* 4C **36**
Down Field. *Cambs* 3F **65**
Downfield. *D'dee* 5C **144**
Downgate. *Corn*
nr. Kelly Bray 5D **10**
nr. Upton Cross 5C **10**
Downham. *Essx* 1B **40**
Downham. *Lanc* 5G **97**
Downham. *Nmbd* 1C **120**
Downham Market. *Norf* 5F **77**
Down Hatherley. *Glos* 3D **48**
Downhead. *Som*
nr. Frome 2B **22**
nr. Yeovil 4A **22**
Downholland Cross. *Lanc* 4B **90**
Downholme. *N Yor* 5E **105**
Downies. *Abers* 4G **153**
Downley. *Buck* 2G **37**
**Downpatrick**. *New M* 5H **175**
Down St Mary. *Devn* 2H **11**
Downside. *Som*
nr. Chilcompton 1B **22**
nr. Shepton Mallet 2B **22**
Downside. *Surr* 5C **38**
Down Thomas. *Devn* 3B **8**
Downton. *Hants* 3A **16**
Downton. *Wilts* 4G **23**
Downton on the Rock.
*Here* 3G **59**
Dowsby. *Linc* 3A **76**
Dowsdale. *Linc* 4B **76**
Dowthwaitehead. *Cumb* 2E **103**
Doxey. *Staf* 3D **72**
Doxford. *Nmbd* 2F **121**
Doynton. *S Glo* 4C **34**
Drabblegate. *Norf* 3E **78**
Draethen. *Cphy* 3F **33**
Draffan. *S Lan* 5A **128**
Dragonby. *N Lin* 3C **94**
Dragon's Green. *W Sus* 3C **26**
Drakelow. *Worc* 2C **60**
Drakemyre. *N Ayr* 4D **126**
Drakes Broughton. *Worc* 1E **49**
Drakes Cross. *Worc* 3E **61**
Drakewalls. *Corn* 5E **11**
Draperstown. *M Ulst* 3E **174**
Draughton. *Nptn* 3E **63**
Draughton. *N Yor* 4C **98**
Drax. *N Yor* 2G **93**
Draycot. *Oxon* 5E **51**
Draycote. *Warw* 3B **62**
Draycot Foliat. *Swin* 4G **35**
Draycott. *Derbs* 2B **74**
Draycott. *Glos* 2G **49**
Draycott. *Shrp* 1C **60**
Draycott. *Som*
nr. Cheddar 1H **21**
nr. Yeovil 4A **22**
Draycott. *Worc* 1D **48**
Draycott in the Clay. *Staf* 3F **73**
Draycott in the Moors.
*Staf* 1D **73**
Drayford. *Devn* 1A **12**
Drayton. *Leics* 1F **63**
Drayton. *Linc* 2B **76**
Drayton. *Norf* 4D **78**
Drayton. *Nptn* 4C **62**
Drayton. *Oxon*
nr. Abingdon 2C **36**
nr. Banbury 1C **50**
Drayton. *Port* 2E **17**
Drayton. *Som* 4H **21**
Drayton. *Warw* 5F **61**
Drayton. *Worc* 3D **60**
Drayton Bassett. *Staf* 5F **73**
Drayton Beauchamp. *Buck* 4H **51**
Drayton Parslow. *Buck* 3G **51**
Drayton St Leonard. *Oxon* 2D **36**
Drebley. *N Yor* 4C **98**
Dreenhill. *Pemb* 3D **42**
Y Dref. *Gwyn* 2D **69**
Drefach. *Carm*
nr. Meidrim 4F **45**
nr. Newcastle Emlyn 2D **44**
nr. Tumble 2G **43**
Drefach. *Cdgn* 1E **45**
Dreghorn. *N Ayr* 1C **116**
Drellingore. *Kent* 1G **29**
Drem. *E Lot* 2B **130**
**Y Drenewydd**. *Powy* 1D **58**
Dreumasdal. *W Isl* 5C **170**
Drewsteignton. *Devn* 3H **11**
Driby. *Linc* 3C **88**
Driffield. *E Yor* 4E **101**
Driffield. *Glos* 2F **35**
Drift. *Corn* 4B **4**
Drigg. *Cumb* 5B **102**
Drighlington. *W Yor* 2C **92**
Drimnin. *High* 3G **139**
Drimpton. *Dors* 2H **13**
Dringhoe. *E Yor* 4F **101**
Drinisiadar. *W Isl* 8D **171**
Drinkstone. *Suff* 4B **66**
Drinkstone Green. *Suff* 4B **66**
Drointon. *Staf* 3E **73**
**Droitwich Spa**. *Worc* 4C **60**
Droman. *High* 3B **166**
Dromore. *Arm* 5G **175**
Dromore. *Ferm* 4C **174**
Dron. *Per* 2D **136**
**Dronfield**. *Derbs* 3A **86**
Dronfield Woodhouse.
*Derbs* 3H **85**
Drongan. *E Ayr* 3D **116**
Dronley. *Ang* 5C **144**
Droop. *Dors* 2C **14**
Drope. *V Glam* 4E **32**
Droxford. *Hants* 1E **16**
**Droylsden**. *G Man* 1C **84**
Druggers End. *Worc* 2C **48**
Druid. *Den* 1C **70**
Druid's Heath. *W Mid* 5E **73**
Druidston. *Pemb* 3C **42**
Druim. *High* 3D **158**
Druimarbin. *High* 1E **141**
Druim Fhearna. *High* 2E **147**
Druimindarroch. *High* 5E **147**
Druim Saighdinis. *W Isl* 2D **170**
Drum. *Per* 3C **136**
Drumaness. *New M* 5H **175**
Drumbeg. *High* 5B **166**
Drumblade. *Abers* 4C **160**
Drumbuie. *Dum* 1C **110**
Drumbuie. *High* 5G **155**
Drumburgh. *Cumb* 4D **112**
Drumburn. *Dum* 3A **112**
Drumchapel. *Glas* 2G **127**
Drumchardine. *High* 4H **157**
Drumchork. *High* 5C **162**
Drumclog. *S Lan* 1F **117**
Drumeldrie. *Fife* 3G **137**
Drumelzier. *Bord* 1D **118**
Drumfearn. *High* 2E **147**
Drumgask. *High* 4A **150**
Drumgelloch. *N Lan* 3A **128**
Drumgley. *Ang* 3D **144**
Drumguish. *High* 4B **150**
Drumin. *Mor* 5F **159**
Drumindorsair. *High* 4G **157**
Drumlamford House.
*S Ayr* 2H **109**
Drumlasie. *Abers* 3D **152**
Drumlemble. *Arg* 4A **122**
Drumlithie. *Abers* 5E **153**
Drummoddie. *Dum* 5A **110**
Drummond. *High* 2A **158**
Drummore. *Dum* 5E **109**
Drummuir. *Mor* 4A **160**
Drumnadrochit. *High* 5H **157**
Drumnagorrach. *Mor* 3C **160**
Drumnakilly. *Ferm* 4D **174**
Drumoak. *Abers* 4E **153**
Drumrunie. *High* 3F **163**
Drumry. *W Dun* 2G **127**
Drums. *Abers* 1G **153**
Drumsleet. *Dum* 2G **111**
Drumsmittal. *High* 4A **158**
Drums of Park. *Abers* 3C **160**
Drumsturdy. *Ang* 5D **145**
Drumtochty Castle. *Abers* 5D **152**
Drumuie. *High* 4D **154**
Drumuillie. *High* 1D **150**
Drumvaich. *Stir* 3F **135**
Drumwhindle. *Abers* 5G **161**
Drunkendub. *Ang* 4F **145**
Drury. *Flin* 4E **83**
Drury Square. *Norf* 4B **78**
Drybeck. *Cumb* 3H **103**
Drybridge. *Mor* 2B **160**
Drybridge. *N Ayr* 1C **116**
Drybrook. *Glos* 4B **48**
Drybrook. *Here* 4A **48**
Dryburgh. *Bord* 1H **119**
Dry Doddington. *Linc* 1F **75**
Dry Drayton. *Cambs* 4C **64**
Drym. *Corn* 3D **4**
Drymen. *Stir* 1F **127**
Drymuir. *Abers* 4G **161**
Drynachan Lodge. *High* 5C **158**
Drynie Park. *High* 3H **157**
Drynoch. *High* 5D **154**
Dry Sandford. *Oxon* 5C **50**
Dryslwyn. *Carm* 3F **45**
Dry Street. *Essx* 2A **40**
Dryton. *Shrp* 5H **71**
Dubford. *Abers* 2E **161**
Dubiton. *Abers* 3D **160**
Dubton. *Ang* 3E **145**
Duchally. *High* 2A **164**
Duck End. *Essx* 3G **53**
Duckington. *Ches W* 5G **83**
Ducklington. *Oxon* 5B **50**
Duckmanton. *Derbs* 3B **86**
Duck Street. *Hants* 2B **24**
Dudbridge. *Glos* 5D **48**
Duddenhoe End. *Essx* 2E **53**
Duddingston. *Edin* 2F **129**
Duddington. *Nptn* 5G **75**
Duddleswell. *E Sus* 3F **27**
Duddo. *Nmbd* 5F **131**
Duddon. *Ches W* 4H **83**
Duddon Bridge. *Cumb* 1A **96**
Dudleston. *Shrp* 2F **71**
Dudleston Heath. *Shrp* 2F **71**
Dudley. *Tyne* 2F **115**
**Dudley**. *W Mid* 2D **60**
Dudston. *Shrp* 1E **59**
Dudwells. *Pemb* 2D **42**
Duffield. *Derbs* 1H **73**
Duffryn. *Neat* 2B **32**
Dufftown. *Mor* 4H **159**
Duffus. *Mor* 2F **159**
Dufton. *Cumb* 2H **103**
Duggleby. *N Yor* 3C **100**
Duirinish. *High* 5G **155**
Duisdalemore. *High* 2E **147**
Duisdeil Mòr. *High* 2E **147**
Duisky. *High* 1E **141**
Dukesfield. *Nmbd* 4C **114**
Dukestown. *Blae* 5E **47**
**Dukinfield**. *G Man* 1D **84**
Dulas. *IOA* 2D **81**
Dulcote. *Som* 2A **22**
Dulford. *Devn* 2D **12**
Dull. *Per* 4F **143**
Dullatur. *N Lan* 2A **128**
Dullingham. *Cambs* 5F **65**
Dullingham Ley. *Cambs* 5F **65**
Dulnain Bridge. *High* 1D **151**
Duloe. *Bed* 4A **64**
Duloe. *Corn* 3G **7**
Dulverton. *Som* 4C **20**
Dulwich. *G Lon* 3E **39**
**Dumbarton**. *W Dun* 2F **127**
Dumbleton. *Glos* 2F **49**
Dumfin. *Arg* 1E **127**
**Dumfries**. *Dum* 2A **112**
Dumgoyne. *Stir* 1G **127**
Dummer. *Hants* 2D **24**
Dumpford. *W Sus* 4G **25**
Dun. *Ang* 2F **145**
Dunagoil. *Arg* 4B **126**
Dunalastair. *Per* 3E **142**
Dunan. *High* 1D **147**
Dunball. *Som* 2G **21**
Dunbar. *E Lot* 2C **130**
Dunbeath. *High* 5D **168**
Dunbeg. *Arg* 5C **140**
Dunblane. *Stir* 3G **135**
Dunbog. *Fife* 2E **137**
Dunbridge. *Hants* 4B **24**
Duncanston. *Abers* 1C **152**
Duncanston. *High* 3H **157**
Dun Charlabhaigh. *W Isl* 3D **171**
Dunchideock. *Devn* 4B **12**
Dunchurch. *Warw* 3B **62**
Duncote. *Nptn* 5D **62**
Duncow. *Dum* 1A **112**
Duncrievie. *Per* 3D **136**
Duncton. *W Sus* 4A **26**
**Dundee**. *D'dee* 5D **144**
Dundee Airport. *D'dee* 1F **137**
Dundon. *Som* 3H **21**
**Dundonald**. *Lis* 4H **175**
Dundonald. *S Ayr* 1C **116**
Dundonnell. *High* 5E **163**
Dundraw. *Cumb* 5D **112**
Dundreggan. *High* 2F **149**
Dundrennan. *Dum* 5E **111**
Dundridge. *Hants* 1D **16**
Dundrum. *New M* 6H **175**
Dundry. *N Som* 5A **34**
Dunecht. *Abers* 3E **153**
**Dunfermline**. *Fife* 1D **129**
Dunford Bridge. *S Yor* 4B **92**
**Dungannon**. *M Ulst* 4E **174**
Dungate. *Kent* 5D **40**
Dunge. *Wilts* 1D **23**
Dungeness. *Kent* 4E **29**
Dungiven. *Caus* 2D **174**
Dungworth. *S Yor* 2G **85**
Dunham-on-the-Hill.
*Ches W* 3G **83**
Dunham-on-Trent. *Notts* 3F **87**
Dunhampton. *Worc* 4C **60**
Dunham Town. *G Man* 2B **84**
Dunham Woodhouses.
*G Man* 2B **84**
Dunholme. *Linc* 3H **87**
Dunino. *Fife* 2H **137**
Dunipace. *Falk* 1B **128**
Dunira. *Per* 1G **135**
Dunkeld. *Per* 4H **143**
Dunkerton. *Bath* 1C **22**
Dunkeswell. *Devn* 2E **13**
Dunkeswick. *N Yor* 5F **99**
Dunkirk. *Kent* 5E **41**
Dunkirk. *S Glo* 3C **34**
Dunkirk. *Staf* 5C **84**
Dunkirk. *Wilts* 5E **35**
Dunk's Green. *Kent* 5H **39**
Dunlappie. *Ang* 2E **145**
Dunley. *Hants* 1C **24**
Dunley. *Worc* 4B **60**
Dunlichity Lodge. *High* 5A **158**
Dunlop. *E Ayr* 5F **127**
Dunloy. *Caus* 2F **175**
Dunmaglass Lodge.
*High* 1H **149**
Dunmore. *Arg* 3F **125**
Dunmore. *Falk* 1B **128**
Dunmore. *High* 4H **157**
Dunmurry. *Bel* 4G **175**
Dunnet. *High* 1E **169**
Dunnichen. *Ang* 4E **145**
Dunning. *Per* 2C **136**
Dunnington. *E Yor* 4F **101**
Dunnington. *Warw* 5E **61**
Dunnington. *York* 4A **100**
Dunningwell. *Cumb* 1A **96**
Dunnockshaw. *Lanc* 2G **91**
**Dunoon**. *Arg* 2C **126**
Dunphail. *Mor* 4E **159**
Dunragit. *Dum* 4G **109**
Dunrostan. *Arg* 1F **125**
Duns. *Bord* 4D **130**
Dunsby. *Linc* 3A **76**
Dunscar. *G Man* 3F **91**
Dunscore. *Dum* 1F **111**
Dunscroft. *S Yor* 4G **93**
Dunsdale. *Red C* 3D **106**
Dunsden Green. *Oxon* 4F **37**
Dunsfold. *Surr* 2B **26**
Dunsford. *Devn* 4B **12**
Dunshalt. *Fife* 2E **137**
Dunshillock. *Abers* 4G **161**
Dunsley. *N Yor* 3F **107**
Dunsley. *Staf* 2C **60**
Dunsmore. *Buck* 5G **51**
Dunsop Bridge. *Lanc* 4F **97**
**Dunstable**. *C Beds* 3A **52**
Dunstal. *Staf* 3E **73**
Dunstall. *Staf* 3F **73**
Dunstall Green. *Suff* 4G **65**
Dunstall Hill. *W Mid* 5D **72**
Dunstan. *Nmbd* 3G **121**

Dunster—East Markham


Dunster. *Som* 2C **20**
Duns Tew. *Oxon* 3C **50**
Dunston. *Linc* 4H **87**
Dunston. *Norf* 5E **79**
Dunston. *Staf* 4D **72**
Dunston. *Tyne* 3F **115**
Dunstone. *Devn* 3B **8**
Dunston Heath. *Staf* 4D **72**
Dunsville. *S Yor* 4G **93**
Dunswell. *E Yor* 1D **94**
Dunsyre. *S Lan* 5D **128**
Dunterton. *Devn* 5D **11**
Duntisbourne Abbots.
*Glos* 5E **49**
Duntisbourne Leer. *Glos* 5E **49**
Duntisbourne Rouse. *Glos* 5E **49**
Duntish. *Dors* 2B **14**
Duntocher. *W Dun* 2F **127**
Dunton. *Buck* 3G **51**
Dunton. *C Beds* 1C **52**
Dunton. *Norf* 2A **78**
Dunton Bassett. *Leics* 1C **62**
Dunton Green. *Kent* 5G **39**
Dunton Patch. *Norf* 2A **78**
Duntulm. *High* 1D **154**
Dunure. *S Ayr* 3B **116**
Dunvant. *Swan* 3E **31**
Dunvegan. *High* 4B **154**
Dunwich. *Suff* 3G **67**
Dunwood. *Staf* 5D **84**
Durdar. *Cumb* 4F **113**
Durgates. *E Sus* 2H **27**
**Durham**. *Dur* 5F **115**
Durham Tees Valley Airport.
*Darl* 3A **106**
Durisdeer. *Dum* 4A **118**
Durisdeermill. *Dum* 4A **118**
Durkar. *W Yor* 3D **92**
Durleigh. *Som* 3F **21**
Durley. *Hants* 1D **16**
Durley. *Wilts* 5H **35**
Durley Street. *Hants* 1D **16**
Durlow Common. *Here* 2B **48**
Durnamuck. *High* 4E **163**
Durness. *High* 2E **166**
Durno. *Abers* 1E **152**
Durns Town. *Hants* 3A **16**
Duror. *High* 3D **141**
Durran. *Arg* 3G **133**
Durran. *High* 2D **169**
Durrant Green. *Kent* 2C **28**
Durrants. *Hants* 1F **17**
Durrington. *W Sus* 5C **26**
Durrington. *Wilts* 2G **23**
**Dursley**. *Glos* 2C **34**
Dursley Cross. *Glos* 4B **48**
Durston. *Som* 4F **21**
Durweston. *Dors* 2D **14**
Dury. *Shet* 6F **173**
Duston. *Nptn* 4E **63**
Duthil. *High* 1D **150**
Dutlas. *Powy* 3E **58**
Duton Hill. *Essx* 3G **53**
Dutson. *Corn* 4D **10**
Dutton. *Ches W* 3H **83**
Duxford. *Cambs* 1E **53**
Duxford. *Oxon* 2B **36**
Dwygyfylchi. *Cnwy* 3G **81**
Dwyran. *IOA* 4D **80**
Dyce. *Aber* 2F **153**
Dyffryn. *B'end* 2B **32**
Dyffryn. *Carm* 2H **43**
Dyffryn. *Pemb* 1D **42**
Dyffryn. *V Glam* 4D **32**
Dyffryn Ardudwy. *Gwyn* 3E **69**
Dyffryn Castell. *Cdgn* 2G **57**
Dyffryn Ceidrych. *Carm* 3H **45**
Dyffryn Cellwen. *Neat* 5B **46**
Dyke. *Linc* 3A **76**
Dyke. *Mor* 3D **159**
Dykehead. *Ang* 2C **144**
Dykehead. *N Lan* 3B **128**
Dykehead. *Stir* 4E **135**
Dykend. *Ang* 3B **144**
Dykesfield. *Cumb* 4E **112**
Dylife. *Powy* 1A **58**
Dymchurch. *Kent* 3F **29**
Dymock. *Glos* 2C **48**
Dyrham. *S Glo* 4C **34**
Dysart. *Fife* 4F **137**
Dyserth. *Den* 3C **82**


## E


Eachwick. *Nmbd* 2E **115**
Eadar Dha Fhadhail. *W Isl* 4C **171**
Eagland Hill. *Lanc* 5D **96**
Eagle. *Linc* 4F **87**
Eagle Barnsdale. *Linc* 4F **87**
Eagle Moor. *Linc* 4F **87**
**Eaglescliffe**. *Stoc T* 3B **106**
Eaglesfield. *Cumb* 2B **102**
Eaglesfield. *Dum* 2D **112**
Eaglesham. *E Ren* 4G **127**
Eaglethorpe. *Nptn* 1H **63**
Eagley. *G Man* 3F **91**
Eairy. *IOM* 4B **108**
Eakley Lanes. *Mil* 5F **63**
Eakring. *Notts* 4D **86**
Ealand. *N Lin* 3A **94**
**Ealing**. *G Lon* 2C **38**
Eallabus. *Arg* 3B **124**
Eals. *Nmbd* 4H **113**
Eamont Bridge. *Cumb* 2G **103**
Earby. *Lanc* 5B **98**
Earcroft. *Bkbn* 2E **91**
Eardington. *Shrp* 1B **60**
Eardisland. *Here* 5G **59**
Eardisley. *Here* 1G **47**
Eardiston. *Shrp* 3F **71**
Eardiston. *Worc* 4A **60**
Earith. *Cambs* 3C **64**
Earlais. *High* 2C **154**
Earle. *Nmbd* 2D **121**
Earlesfield. *Linc* 2G **75**
Earlestown. *Mers* 1H **83**
Earley. *Wok* 4F **37**
Earlham. *Norf* 5D **78**
Earlish. *High* 2C **154**
Earls Barton. *Nptn* 4F **63**
Earls Colne. *Essx* 3B **54**
Earls Common. *Worc* 5D **60**
Earl's Croome. *Worc* 1D **48**
Earlsdon. *W Mid* 3H **61**
Earlsferry. *Fife* 3G **137**
Earlsford. *Abers* 5F **161**
Earl's Green. *Suff* 4C **66**
Earlsheaton. *W Yor* 2C **92**
**Earl Shilton**. *Leics* 1B **62**
Earl Soham. *Suff* 4E **67**
Earl Sterndale. *Derbs* 4E **85**
Earlston. *E Ayr* 1D **116**
Earlston. *Bord* 1H **119**
Earl Stonham. *Suff* 5D **66**
Earlstoun. *Dum* 1D **110**
Earlswood. *Mon* 2H **33**
Earlswood. *Warw* 3F **61**
Earlyvale. *Bord* 4F **129**
Earnley. *W Sus* 3G **17**
Earsairidh. *W Isl* 9C **170**
Earsdon. *Tyne* 2G **115**
Earsham. *Norf* 2F **67**
Earsham Street. *Suff* 3E **67**
Earswick. *York* 4A **100**
Eartham. *W Sus* 5A **26**
Earthcott Green. *S Glo* 3B **34**
Easby. *N Yor*
nr. Great Ayton 4C **106**
nr. Richmond 4E **105**
Easdale. *Arg* 2E **133**
Easebourne. *W Sus* 4G **25**
Easenhall. *Warw* 3B **62**
Eashing. *Surr* 1A **26**
Easington. *Buck* 4E **51**
Easington. *Dur* 5H **115**
Easington. *E Yor* 3G **95**
Easington. *Nmbd* 1F **121**
Easington. *Oxon*
nr. Banbury 2C **50**
nr. Watlington 2E **37**
Easington. *Red C* 3E **107**
Easington Colliery. *Dur* 5H **115**
Easington Lane. *Tyne* 5G **115**
Easingwold. *N Yor* 2H **99**
Eassie. *Ang* 4C **144**
Eassie and Nevay. *Ang* 4C **144**
East Aberthaw. *V Glam* 5D **32**
Eastacombe. *Devn* 4F **19**
Eastacott. *Devn* 4G **19**
East Allington. *Devn* 4D **8**
East Anstey. *Devn* 4B **20**
East Anton. *Hants* 2B **24**
East Appleton. *N Yor* 5F **105**
East Ardsley. *W Yor* 2D **92**
East Ashley. *Devn* 1G **11**
East Ashling. *W Sus* 2G **17**
East Aston. *Hants* 2C **24**
East Ayton. *N Yor* 1D **101**
East Barkwith. *Linc* 2A **88**
East Barnby. *N Yor* 3F **107**
East Barnet. *G Lon* 1D **39**
East Barns. *E Lot* 2D **130**
East Barsham. *Norf* 2B **78**
East Beach. *W Sus* 3G **17**
East Beckham. *Norf* 2D **78**
East Bedfont. *G Lon* 3B **38**
East Bennan. *N Ayr* 3D **123**
East Bergholt. *Suff* 2D **54**
East Bierley. *W Yor* 2C **92**
East Bilney. *Norf* 4B **78**
East Blatchington. *E Sus* 5F **27**
East Bloxworth. *Dors* 3D **15**
East Boldre. *Hants* 2B **16**
East Bolton. *Nmbd* 3F **121**
Eastbourne. *Darl* 3F **105**
**Eastbourne**. *E Sus* 5H **27**
East Brent. *Som* 1G **21**
East Bridge. *Suff* 4G **67**
East Bridgford. *Notts* 1D **74**
East Briscoe. *Dur* 3C **104**
East Buckland. *Devn*
nr. Barnstaple 3G **19**
nr. Thurlestone 4C **8**
East Budleigh. *Devn* 4D **12**
Eastburn. *W Yor* 5C **98**
East Burnham. *Buck* 2A **38**
East Burrafirth. *Shet* 6E **173**
East Burton. *Dors* 4D **14**
Eastbury. *Herts* 1B **38**
Eastbury. *W Ber* 4B **36**
East Butsfield. *Dur* 5E **115**
East Butterleigh. *Devn* 2C **12**
East Butterwick. *N Lin* 4B **94**
Eastby. *N Yor* 4C **98**
East Calder. *W Lot* 3D **129**
East Carleton. *Norf* 5D **78**
East Carlton. *Nptn* 2F **63**
East Carlton. *W Yor* 5E **98**
East Chaldon. *Dors* 4C **14**
East Challow. *Oxon* 3B **36**
East Charleton. *Devn* 4D **8**
East Chelborough. *Dors* 2A **14**
East Chiltington. *E Sus* 4E **27**
East Chinnock. *Som* 1H **13**
East Chisenbury. *Wilts* 1G **23**
Eastchurch. *Kent* 3D **40**
East Clandon. *Surr* 5B **38**
East Claydon. *Buck* 3F **51**
East Clevedon. *N Som* 4H **33**
East Clyne. *High* 3F **165**
East Clyth. *High* 5E **169**
East Coker. *Som* 1A **14**
East Combe. *Som* 3E **21**
Eastcombe. *Glos* 5D **49**
East Common. *N Yor* 1G **93**
East Compton. *Som* 2B **22**
East Cornworthy. *Devn* 3E **9**
Eastcote. *G Lon* 2C **38**
Eastcote. *Nptn* 5D **62**
Eastcote. *W Mid* 3F **61**
Eastcott. *Corn* 1C **10**
Eastcott. *Wilts* 1F **23**
East Cottingwith. *E Yor* 5B **100**
Eastcourt. *Wilts*
nr. Pewsey 5H **35**
nr. Tetbury 2E **35**
East Cowes. *IOW* 3D **16**
East Cowick. *E Yor* 2G **93**
East Cowton. *N Yor* 4A **106**
East Cramlington. *Nmbd* 2F **115**
East Cranmore. *Som* 2B **22**
East Creech. *Dors* 4E **15**
East Croachy. *High* 1A **150**
East Dean. *E Sus* 5G **27**
East Dean. *Glos* 3B **48**
East Dean. *Hants* 4A **24**
East Dean. *W Sus* 4A **26**
East Down. *Devn* 2G **19**
East Drayton. *Notts* 3E **87**
East Dundry. *N Som* 5A **34**
East Ella. *Hull* 2D **94**
East End. *Cambs* 3C **64**
East End. *Dors* 3E **15**
East End. *E Yor*
nr. Ulrome 4F **101**
nr. Withernsea 2F **95**
East End. *Hants*
nr. Lymington 3B **16**
nr. Newbury 5C **36**
East End. *Herts* 3E **53**
East End. *Kent*
nr. Minster 3D **40**
nr. Tenterden 2C **28**
East End. *N Som* 4H **33**
East End. *Oxon* 4B **50**
East End. *Som* 1A **22**
East End. *Suff* 2E **54**
Easter Ardross. *High* 1A **158**
Easter Balgedie. *Per* 3D **136**
Easter Balmoral. *Abers* 4G **151**
Easter Brae. *High* 2A **158**
Easter Buckieburn. *Stir* 1A **128**
Easter Compton. *S Glo* 3A **34**
Easter Fearn. *High* 5D **164**
Easter Galcantray. *High* 4C **158**
Eastergate. *W Sus* 5A **26**
Easterhouse. *Glas* 3H **127**
Easter Howgate. *Midl* 3F **129**
Easter Kinkell. *High* 3H **157**
Easter Lednathie. *Ang* 2C **144**
Easter Ogil. *Ang* 2D **144**
Easter Ord. *Abers* 3F **153**
Easter Quarff. *Shet* 8F **173**
Easter Rhynd. *Per* 2D **136**
Easter Skeld. *Shet* 7E **173**
Easter Suddie. *High* 3A **158**
Easterton. *Wilts* 1F **23**
Eastertown. *Som* 1G **21**
Easter Tulloch. *Abers* 1G **145**
East Everleigh. *Wilts* 1H **23**
East Farleigh. *Kent* 5B **40**
East Farndon. *Nptn* 2E **62**
East Ferry. *Linc* 1F **87**
Eastfield. *N Lan*
nr. Caldercruix 3B **128**
nr. Harthill 3B **128**
**Eastfield**. *N Yor* 1E **101**
Eastfield. *S Lan* 3H **127**
Eastfield Hall. *Nmbd* 4G **121**
East Fortune. *E Lot* 2B **130**
East Garforth. *W Yor* 1E **93**
East Garston. *W Ber* 4B **36**
Eastgate. *Dur* 1C **104**
Eastgate. *Norf* 3D **78**
East Ginge. *Oxon* 3C **36**
East Gores. *Essx* 3B **54**
East Goscote. *Leics* 4D **74**
East Grafton. *Wilts* 5A **36**
East Green. *Suff* 5F **65**
East Grimstead. *Wilts* 4H **23**
**East Grinstead**. *W Sus* 2E **27**
East Guldeford. *E Sus* 3D **28**
East Haddon. *Nptn* 4D **62**
East Hagbourne. *Oxon* 3D **36**
East Halton. *N Lin* 2E **95**
**East Ham**. *G Lon* 2F **39**
Eastham. *Mers* 2F **83**
Eastham. *Worc* 4A **60**
Eastham Ferry. *Mers* 2F **83**
Easthampstead. *Brac* 5G **37**
Easthampton. *Here* 4G **59**
East Hanney. *Oxon* 2C **36**
East Hanningfield. *Essx* 5A **54**
East Hardwick. *W Yor* 3E **93**
East Harling. *Norf* 2B **66**
East Harlsey. *N Yor* 5B **106**
East Harptree. *Bath* 1A **22**
East Hartford. *Nmbd* 2F **115**
East Harting. *W Sus* 1G **17**
East Hatch. *Wilts* 4E **23**
East Hatley. *Cambs* 5B **64**
Easthaugh. *Norf* 4C **78**
East Hauxwell. *N Yor* 5E **105**
East Haven. *Ang* 5E **145**
Eastheath. *Wok* 5G **37**
East Heckington. *Linc* 1A **76**
East Hedleyhope. *Dur* 5E **115**
East Helmsdale. *High* 2H **165**
East Hendred. *Oxon* 3C **36**
East Heslerton. *N Yor* 2D **100**
East Hoathly. *E Sus* 4G **27**
East Holme. *Dors* 4D **15**
Easthope. *Shrp* 1H **59**
Easthorpe. *Essx* 3C **54**
Easthorpe. *Leics* 2F **75**
East Horrington. *Som* 2A **22**
East Horsley. *Surr* 5B **38**
East Horton. *Nmbd* 1E **121**
Easthouses. *Midl* 3G **129**
East Howe. *Bour* 3F **15**
East Huntspill. *Som* 2G **21**
East Hyde. *C Beds* 4B **52**
East Ilsley. *W Ber* 3C **36**
Eastington. *Devn* 2H **11**
Eastington. *Glos*
nr. Northleach 4G **49**
nr. Stonehouse 5C **48**
East Keal. *Linc* 4C **88**
East Kennett. *Wilts* 5G **35**
East Keswick. *W Yor* 5F **99**
**East Kilbride**. *S Lan* 4H **127**
East Kirkby. *Linc* 4C **88**
East Knapton. *N Yor* 2C **100**
East Knighton. *Dors* 4D **14**
East Knowstone. *Devn* 4B **20**
East Knoyle. *Wilts* 3D **23**
East Kyloe. *Nmbd* 1E **121**
East Lambrook. *Som* 1H **13**
East Langdon. *Kent* 1H **29**
East Langton. *Leics* 1E **63**
East Langwell. *High* 3E **164**
East Lavant. *W Sus* 2G **17**
East Lavington. *W Sus* 4A **26**
East Layton. *N Yor* 4E **105**
Eastleach Martin. *Glos* 5H **49**
Eastleach Turville. *Glos* 5G **49**
East Leake. *Notts* 3C **74**
East Learmouth. *Nmbd* 1C **120**
East Leigh. *Devn*
nr. Crediton 2G **11**
nr. Modbury 3C **8**
Eastleigh. *Devn* 4E **19**
**Eastleigh**. *Hants* 1C **16**
East Lexham. *Norf* 4A **78**
East Lilburn. *Nmbd* 2E **121**
Eastling. *Kent* 5D **40**
East Linton. *E Lot* 2B **130**
East Liss. *Hants* 4F **25**
East Lockinge. *Oxon* 3C **36**
East Looe. *Corn* 3G **7**
East Lound. *N Lin* 1E **87**
East Lulworth. *Dors* 4D **14**
East Lutton. *N Yor* 3D **100**
East Lydford. *Som* 3A **22**
East Lyng. *Som* 4G **21**
East Mains. *Abers* 4D **152**
East Malling. *Kent* 5B **40**
East Marden. *W Sus* 1G **17**
East Markham. *Notts* 3E **87**

East Marton. N Yor ....4B 98
East Meon. Hants ....4E 25
East Mersea. Essx ....4D 54
East Mey. High ....1F 169
East Midlands Airport. Leics ..3B 74
East Molesey. Surr ....4C 38
Eastmoor. Norf ....5G 77
East Morden. Dors ....3E 15
East Morton. W Yor ....5D 98
East Ness. N Yor ....2A 100
East Newton. E Yor ....1F 95
East Newton. N Yor ....2A 100
Eastney. Port ....3E 17
Eastnor. Here ....2C 48
East Norton. Leics ....5E 75
East Nynehead. Som ....4E 21
East Oakley. Hants ....1D 24
Eastoft. N Lin ....3B 94
East Ogwell. Devn ....5B 12
Easton. Cambs ....3A 64
Easton. Cumb
  nr. Burgh by Sands ..4D 112
  nr. Longtown ....2F 113
Easton. Devn ....4H 11
Easton. Dors ....5B 14
Easton. Hants ....3D 24
Easton. Linc ....3G 75
Easton. Norf ....4D 78
Easton. Som ....2A 22
Easton. Suff ....5E 67
Easton. Wilts ....4D 35
Easton Grey. Wilts ....3D 35
Easton-in-Gordano. N Som ..4A 34
Easton Maudit. Nptn ....5F 63
Easton on the Hill. Nptn ..5H 75
Easton Royal. Wilts ....5H 35
East Orchard. Dors ....1D 14
East Ord. Nmbd ....4F 131
East Panson. Devn ....3D 10
East Peckham. Kent ....1A 28
East Pennard. Som ....3A 22
East Perry. Cambs ....4A 64
East Pitcorthie. Fife ....3H 137
East Portlemouth. Devn ....5D 8
East Prawle. Devn ....5D 9
East Preston. W Sus ....5B 26
East Putford. Devn ....1D 10
East Quantoxhead. Som ..2E 21
East Rainton. Tyne ....5G 115
East Ravendale. NE Lin ..1B 88
East Raynham. Norf ....3A 78
Eastrea. Cambs ....1B 64
East Rhidorroch Lodge.
  High ....4G 163
Eastriggs. Dum ....3D 112
East Rigton. W Yor ....5F 99
Eastrington. E Yor ....2A 94
East Rounton. N Yor ....4B 106
East Row. N Yor ....3F 107
East Rudham. Norf ....3H 77
East Runton. Norf ....1D 78
East Ruston. Norf ....3F 79
Eastry. Kent ....5H 41
East Saltoun. E Lot ....3A 130
East Shaws. Dur ....3D 105
East Shefford. W Ber ..4B 36
Eastshore. Shet ....10E 173
East Sleekburn. Nmbd ..1F 115
East Somerton. Norf ....4G 79
East Stockwith. Linc ....1E 87
East Stoke. Dors ....4D 14
East Stoke. Notts ....1E 75
East Stoke. Som ....1H 13
East Stour. Dors ....4D 22
East Stourmouth. Kent ..4G 41
East Stowford. Devn ....4G 19
East Stratton. Hants ....2D 24
East Studdal. Kent ....1H 29
East Taphouse. Corn ....2F 7
East-the-Water. Devn ....4E 19
East Thirston. Nmbd ....5F 121
East Tilbury. Thur ....3A 40
East Tisted. Hants ....3F 25
East Torrington. Linc ....2A 88

East Tuddenham. Norf ....4C 78
East Tytherley. Hants ....4A 24
East Tytherton. Wilts ....4E 35
East Village. Devn ....2B 12
Eastville. Linc ....5D 88
East Wall. Shrp ....1H 59
East Walton. Norf ....4G 77
East Week. Devn ....3G 11
Eastwell. Leics ....3E 75
East Wellow. Hants ....4B 24
East Wemyss. Fife ....4F 137
East Whitburn. W Lot ..3C 128
Eastwick. Herts ....4E 53
Eastwick. Shet ....4E 173
East Williamston. Pemb ..4E 43
East Winch. Norf ....4F 77
East Winterslow. Wilts ..3H 23
East Wittering. W Sus ..3F 17
East Witton. N Yor ....1D 98
Eastwood. Notts ....1B 74
Eastwood. S'end ....2C 40
East Woodburn. Nmbd ..1C 114
Eastwood End. Cambs ..1D 64
East Woodhay. Hants ....5C 36
East Woodlands. Som ..2C 22
East Worldham. Hants ..3F 25
East Worlington. Devn ..1A 12
East Wretham. Norf ....1B 66
East Youlstone. Devn ....1C 10
Eathorpe. Warw ....4A 62
Eaton. Ches E ....4C 84
Eaton. Ches W ....4H 83
Eaton. Leics ....3E 75
Eaton. Norf
  nr. Heacham ....2F 77
  nr. Norwich ....5E 78
Eaton. Notts ....3E 86
Eaton. Oxon ....5C 50
Eaton. Shrp
  nr. Bishop's Castle ..2F 59
  nr. Church Stretton ..2H 59
Eaton Bishop. Here ....2H 47
Eaton Bray. C Beds ....3H 51
Eaton Constantine. Shrp ..5H 71
Eaton Hastings. Oxon ..2A 36
Eaton Socon. Cambs ....5A 64
Eaton upon Tern. Shrp ..3A 72
Eau Brink. Norf ....4E 77
Eaves Green. W Mid ....2G 61
Ebberley Hill. Devn ....1F 11
Ebberston. N Yor ....1C 100
Ebbesbourne Wake. Wilts ..4E 23
Ebblake. Dors ....2G 15
Ebbsfleet. Kent ....3H 39
Ebbw Vale. Blae ....5E 47
Ebchester. Dur ....4E 115
Ebernoe. W Sus ....3A 26
Ebford. Devn ....4C 12
Ebley. Glos ....5D 48
Ebnal. Ches W ....1G 71
Ebrington. Glos ....1G 49
Ecchinswell. Hants ....1D 24
Ecclefechan. Dum ....2C 112
Eccles. G Man ....1B 84
Eccles. Kent ....4B 40
Eccles. Bord ....5D 130
Ecclesall. S Yor ....2H 85
Ecclesfield. S Yor ....1A 86
Eccles Green. Here ....1G 47
Eccleshall. Staf ....3C 72
Eccleshill. W Yor ....1B 92
Ecclesmachan. W Lot ..2D 128
Eccles on Sea. Norf ....3G 79
Eccles Road. Norf ....1C 66
Eccleston. Ches W ....4G 83
Eccleston. Lanc ....3D 90
Eccleston. Mers ....1G 83
Eccup. W Yor ....5E 99
Echt. Abers ....3E 153
Eckford. Bord ....2B 120
Eckington. Derbs ....3B 86
Eckington. Worc ....1E 49
Ecton. Nptn ....4F 63
Edale. Derbs ....2F 85

Eday Airport. Orkn ....4E 172
Edburton. W Sus ....4D 26
Edderside. Cumb ....5C 112
Edderton. High ....5E 164
Eddington. Kent ....4F 41
Eddington. W Ber ....5B 36
Eddleston. Bord ....5F 129
Eddlewood. S Lan ....4A 128
Edenbridge. Kent ....1F 27
Edendonich. Arg ....1A 134
Edenfield. Lanc ....3F 91
Edenhall. Cumb ....1G 103
Edenham. Linc ....3H 75
Edensor. Derbs ....3G 85
Edentaggart. Arg ....4C 134
Edenthorpe. S Yor ....4G 93
Eden Vale. Dur ....1B 106
Edern. Gwyn ....2B 68
Edgarley. Som ....3A 22
Edgbaston. W Mid ....2E 61
Edgcott. Buck ....3E 51
Edgcott. Som ....3B 20
Edge. Glos ....5D 48
Edge. Shrp ....5F 71
Edgebolton. Shrp ....3H 71
Edge End. Glos ....4A 48
Edgefield. Norf ....2C 78
Edgefield Street. Norf ..2C 78
Edge Green. Ches W ....5G 83
Edgehead. Midl ....3G 129
Edgeley. Shrp ....1H 71
Edgeside. Lanc ....2G 91
Edgeworth. Glos ....5E 49
Edgiock. Worc ....4E 61
Edgmond. Telf ....4B 72
Edgmond Marsh. Telf ..3B 72
Edgton. Shrp ....2F 59
Edgware. G Lon ....1C 38
Edgworth. Bkbn ....3F 91
Edinbane. High ....3C 154
Edinburgh. Edin ....2F 129
Edinburgh Airport. Edin ..2E 129
Edingale. Staf ....4G 73
Edingley. Notts ....5D 86
Edingthorpe. Norf ....2F 79
Edington. Som ....3G 21
Edington. Wilts ....1E 23
Edingworth. Som ....1G 21
Edistone. Devn ....4C 18
Edithmead. Som ....2G 21
Edith Weston. Rut ....5G 75
Edlaston. Derbs ....1F 73
Edlesborough. Buck ....4H 51
Edlingham. Nmbd ....4F 121
Edlington. Linc ....3B 88
Edmondsham. Dors ....1F 15
Edmondsley. Dur ....5F 115
Edmondthorpe. Leics ..4F 75
Edmonstone. Orkn ....5E 172
Edmonton. Corn ....1D 6
Edmonton. G Lon ....1E 39
Edmundbyers. Dur ....4D 114
Ednam. Bord ....1B 120
Ednaston. Derbs ....1G 73
Edney Common. Essx ....5G 53
Edrom. Bord ....4E 131
Edstaston. Shrp ....2H 71
Edstone. Warw ....4F 61
Edvin Loach. Here ....5A 60
Edwalton. Notts ....2C 74
Edwardstone. Suff ....1C 54
Edwardsville. Mer T ....2D 32
Edwinsford. Carm ....2G 45
Edwinstowe. Notts ....4D 86
Edworth. C Beds ....1C 52
Edwyn Ralph. Here ....5A 60
Edzell. Ang ....2F 145
Efail-fach. Neat ....2A 32
Efail Isaf. Rhon ....3D 32
Efailnewydd. Gwyn ....2C 68
Efail-rhyd. Powy ....3D 70
Efailwen. Carm ....2F 43
Efenechtyd. Den ....5D 82
Effingham. Surr ....5C 38
Effingham Common. Surr ..5C 38

Effirth. Shet ....6E 173
Effinch. Staf ....4F 73
Efford. Devn ....2B 12
Efstigarth. Shet ....2F 173
Egbury. Hants ....1C 24
Egdon. Worc ....5D 60
Egerton. G Man ....3F 91
Egerton. Kent ....1D 28
Egerton Forstal. Kent ..1C 28
Eggborough. N Yor ....2F 93
Eggbuckland. Plym ....3A 8
Eggesford. Devn ....1G 11
Eggington. C Beds ....3H 51
Egginton. Derbs ....3G 73
Egglescliffe. Stoc T ....3B 106
Eggleston. Dur ....2C 104
Egham. Surr ....3B 38
Egham Hythe. Surr ....3B 38
Egleton. Rut ....5F 75
Eglingham. Nmbd ....3F 121
Eglinton. Derr ....1D 174
Egloshayle. Corn ....5A 10
Egloskerry. Corn ....4C 10
Eglwysbach. Cnwy ....3H 81
Eglwys-Brewis. V Glam ..5D 32
Eglwys Fach. Cdgn ....1F 57
Eglwyswrw. Pemb ....1F 43
Egmanton. Notts ....4E 87
Egmere. Norf ....2B 78
Egremont. Cumb ....3B 102
Egremont. Mers ....1F 83
Egton. N Yor ....4F 107
Egton Bridge. N Yor ....4F 107
Egypt. Buck ....2A 38
Egypt. Hants ....2C 24
Eight Ash Green. Essx ..3C 54
Eight Mile Burn. Midl ..4E 129
Eignaig. High ....4B 140
Eilanreach. High ....2G 147
Eildon. Bord ....1H 119
Eileanach Lodge. High ..2H 157
Eilean Fhlodaigh. W Isl ..3D 170
Eilean Iarmain. High ....2F 147
Einacleit. W Isl ....5D 171
Eisgein. W Isl ....6F 171
Eisingrug. Gwyn ....2F 69
Elan Village. Powy ....4B 58
Elberton. S Glo ....3B 34
Elbridge. W Sus ....5A 26
Elburton. Plym ....3B 8
Elcho. Per ....1D 136
Elcombe. Swin ....3G 35
Elcot. W Ber ....5B 36
Eldernell. Cambs ....1C 64
Eldersfield. Worc ....2D 48
Elderslie. Ren ....3F 127
Elder Street. Essx ....2F 53
Eldon. Dur ....2F 105
Eldroth. N Yor ....3G 97
Eldwick. W Yor ....5D 98
Elfhowe. Cumb ....5F 103
Elford. Nmbd ....1F 121
Elford. Staf ....4F 73
Elford Closes. Cambs ..3D 65
Elgin. Mor ....2G 159
Elgol. High ....2D 146
Elham. Kent ....1F 29
Elie. Fife ....3G 137
Eling. Hants ....1B 16
Eling. W Ber ....4D 36
Elishaw. Nmbd ....5C 120
Elizafield. Dum ....2B 112
Elkesley. Notts ....3D 86
Elkington. Nptn ....3D 62
Elkins Green. Essx ....5G 53
Elkstone. Glos ....4E 49
Ellan. High ....1C 150
Elland. W Yor ....2B 92
Ellary. Arg ....2F 125
Ellastone. Staf ....1F 73
Ellbridge. Corn ....2A 8
Ellel. Lanc ....4D 97
Ellemford. Bord ....3D 130
Ellenabeich. Arg ....2E 133

Ellenborough. Cumb ....1B 102
Ellenbrook. Herts ....5C 52
Ellenhall. Staf ....3C 72
Ellen's Green. Surr ....2B 26
Ellerbeck. N Yor ....5B 106
Ellerburn. N Yor ....1C 100
Ellerby. N Yor ....3E 107
Ellerdine. Telf ....3A 72
Ellerdine Heath. Telf ..3A 72
Ellerhayes. Devn ....2C 12
Elleric. Arg ....4E 141
Ellerker. E Yor ....2C 94
Ellerton. E Yor ....1H 93
Ellerton. Shrp ....3B 72
Ellerton-on-Swale. N Yor ..5F 105
Ellesborough. Buck ....5G 51
Ellesmere. Shrp ....2G 71
Ellesmere Port. Ches W ..3G 83
Ellingham. Hants ....2G 15
Ellingham. Nmbd ....2F 121
Ellingham. Norf ....1F 67
Ellingstring. N Yor ....1D 98
Ellington. Cambs ....3A 64
Ellington. Nmbd ....5G 121
Ellington Thorpe. Cambs ..3A 64
Elliot. Ang ....5F 145
Ellisfield. Hants ....2E 25
Ellishadder. High ....2E 155
Ellistown. Leics ....4B 74
Ellon. Abers ....5G 161
Ellonby. Cumb ....1F 103
Ellough. Suff ....2G 67
Elloughton. E Yor ....2C 94
Ellwood. Glos ....5A 48
Elm. Cambs ....5D 76
Elmbridge. Glos ....4D 48
Elmbridge. Worc ....4D 60
Elmdon. Essx ....2E 53
Elmdon. W Mid ....2F 61
Elmdon Heath. W Mid ..2F 61
Elmesthorpe. Leics ....1B 62
Elmfield. IOW ....3E 16
Elm Hill. Dors ....4D 22
Elmhurst. Staf ....4F 73
Elmley Castle. Worc ....1E 49
Elmley Lovett. Worc ....4C 60
Elmore. Glos ....4C 48
Elmore Back. Glos ....4C 48
Elm Park. G Lon ....2G 39
Elmscott. Devn ....4C 18
Elmsett. Suff ....1D 54
Elmstead. Essx ....3D 54
Elmstead Heath. Essx ..3D 54
Elmstead Market. Essx ..3D 54
Elmstone. Kent ....4G 41
Elmstone Hardwicke.
  Glos ....3E 49
Elmswell. E Yor ....4D 101
Elmswell. Suff ....4B 66
Elmton. Derbs ....3C 86
Elphin. High ....2G 163
Elphinstone. E Lot ....2G 129
Elrick. Abers ....3F 153
Elrick. Mor ....1B 152
Elrig. Dum ....5A 110
Elsdon. Nmbd ....5D 120
Elsecar. S Yor ....1A 86
Elsenham. Essx ....3F 53
Elsfield. Oxon ....4D 50
Elsham. N Lin ....3D 94
Elsing. Norf ....4C 78
Elslack. N Yor ....5B 98
Elsrickle. S Lan ....5D 128
Elstead. Surr ....1A 26
Elsted. W Sus ....1G 17
Elsted Marsh. W Sus ....4G 25
Elsthorpe. Linc ....3H 75
Elstob. Dur ....2A 106
Elston. Devn ....2A 12
Elston. Lanc ....1E 90
Elston. Notts ....1E 75
Elston. Wilts ....2F 23
Elstone. Devn ....1G 11

| | | | | | | | |
|---|---|---|---|---|---|---|---|
| Elstow. Bed | .1A 52 | Eorabus. Arg | .1A 132 | Ettington. Warw | .1A 50 | Eye. Suff | .3D 66 |
| Elstree. Herts | .1C 38 | Eoropaidh. W Isl | .1H 171 | Etton. E Yor | .5D 101 | Eye Green. Pet | .5B 76 |
| Elstronwick. E Yor | .1F 95 | Epney. Glos | .4C 48 | Etton. Pet | .5A 76 | Eyemouth. Bord | .3F 131 |
| Elswick. Lanc | .1C 90 | Epperstone. Notts | .1D 74 | Ettrick. Bord | .3E 119 | Eyeworth. C Beds | .1C 52 |
| Elswick. Tyne | .3F 115 | Epping. Essx | .5E 53 | Ettrickbridge. Bord | .2F 119 | Eyhorne Street. Kent | .5C 40 |
| Elsworth. Cambs | .4C 64 | Epping Green. Essx | .5E 53 | Etwall. Derbs | .2G 73 | Eyke. Suff | .5F 67 |
| Elterwater. Cumb | .4E 103 | Epping Green. Herts | .5C 52 | Eudon Burnell. Shrp | .2B 60 | Eynesbury. Cambs | .5A 64 |
| Eltham. G Lon | .3F 39 | Epping Upland. Essx | .5E 53 | Eudon George. Shrp | .2A 60 | Eynort. High | .1B 146 |
| Eltisley. Cambs | .5B 64 | Eppleby. N Yor | .3E 105 | Euston. Suff | .3A 66 | Eynsford. Kent | .4G 39 |
| Elton. Cambs | .1H 63 | Eppleworth. E Yor | .1D 94 | Euxton. Lanc | .3D 90 | Eynsham. Oxon | .5C 50 |
| Elton. Ches W | .3G 83 | Epsom. Surr | .4D 38 | Evanstown. B'end | .3C 32 | Eyre. High | |
| Elton. Derbs | .4G 85 | Epwell. Oxon | .1B 50 | Evanton. High | .2A 158 | on Isle of Skye | .3D 154 |
| Elton. Glos | .4C 48 | Epworth. N Lin | .4A 94 | Evedon. Linc | .1H 75 | on Raasay | .5E 155 |
| Elton. G Man | .3F 91 | Epworth Turbary. N Lin | .4A 94 | Evelix. High | .4E 165 | Eythorne. Kent | .1G 29 |
| Elton. Here | .3G 59 | Erbistock. Wrex | .1F 71 | Evendine. Here | .1C 48 | Eyton. Here | .4G 59 |
| Elton. Notts | .2E 75 | Erbusaig. High | .1F 147 | Evenjobb. Powy | .4E 59 | Eyton. Shrp | |
| Elton. Stoc T | .3B 106 | Erchless Castle. High | .4G 157 | Evenley. Nptn | .2D 50 | nr. Bishop's Castle | .2F 59 |
| Elton Green. Ches W | .3G 83 | Erdington. W Mid | .1F 61 | Evenlode. Glos | .3H 49 | nr. Shrewsbury | .4F 71 |
| Eltringham. Nmbd | .3D 115 | Eredine. Arg | .3G 133 | Even Swindon. Swin | .3G 35 | Eyton. Wrex | .1F 71 |
| Elvanfoot. S Lan | .3B 118 | Eriboll. High | .3E 167 | Evenwood. Dur | .2E 105 | Eyton on Severn. Shrp | .5H 71 |
| Elvaston. Derbs | .2B 74 | Ericstane. Dum | .3C 118 | Evenwood Gate. Dur | .2E 105 | Eyton upon the Weald |
| Elveden. Suff | .3H 65 | Eridge Green. E Sus | .2G 27 | Everbay. Orkn | .5F 172 | Moors. Telf | .4A 72 |
| Elvetham Heath. Hants | .1F 25 | Erines. Arg | .2G 125 | Evercreech. Som | .3B 22 | | |
| Elvingston. E Lot | .2A 130 | Eriswell. Suff | .3G 65 | Everdon. Nptn | .5C 62 | | |
| Elvington. Kent | .5G 41 | Erith. G Lon | .3F 39 | Everingham. E Yor | .5C 100 | **F** | |
| Elvington. York | .5B 100 | Erlestoke. Wilts | .1E 23 | Everleigh. Wilts | .1H 23 | | |
| Elwick. Hart | .1B 106 | Ermine. Linc | .3G 87 | Everley. N Yor | .1D 100 | Faccombe. Hants | .1B 24 |
| Elwick. Nmbd | .1F 121 | Ermington. Devn | .3C 8 | Eversholt. C Beds | .2H 51 | Faceby. N Yor | .4B 106 |
| Elworth. Ches E | .4B 84 | Ernesettle. Plym | .3A 8 | Evershot. Dors | .2A 14 | Faddiley. Ches E | .5H 83 |
| Elworth. Dors | .4A 14 | Erpingham. Norf | .2D 78 | Eversley. Hants | .5F 37 | Fadmoor. N Yor | .1A 100 |
| Elworthy. Som | .3D 20 | Erriott Wood. Kent | .5D 40 | Eversley Centre. Hants | .5F 37 | Fagwyr. Swan | .5G 45 |
| Ely. Cambs | .2E 65 | Errogie. High | .1H 149 | Eversley Cross. Hants | .5F 37 | Faichem. High | .3E 149 |
| Ely. Card | .4E 33 | Errol. Per | .1E 137 | Everthorpe. E Yor | .1C 94 | Faifley. W Dun | .2G 127 |
| Emberton. Mil | .1G 51 | Errol Station. Per | .1E 137 | Everton. C Beds | .5B 64 | Fail. S Ayr | .2D 116 |
| Embleton. Cumb | .1C 102 | Erskine. Ren | .2F 127 | Everton. Hants | .3A 16 | Failand. N Som | .4A 34 |
| Embleton. Hart | .2B 106 | Erskine Bridge. Ren | .2F 127 | Everton. Mers | .1F 83 | Failford. S Ayr | .2D 116 |
| Embleton. Nmbd | .2G 121 | Ervie. Dum | .3F 109 | Everton. Notts | .1D 86 | Failsworth. G Man | .4H 91 |
| Embo. High | .4F 165 | Erwarton. Suff | .2F 55 | Evertown. Dum | .2E 113 | Fairbourne. Gwyn | .4F 69 |
| Emborough. Som | .1B 22 | Erwood. Powy | .1D 46 | Evesbatch. Here | .1B 48 | Fairbourne Heath. Kent | .5C 40 |
| Embo Street. High | .4F 165 | Eryholme. N Yor | .4A 106 | Evesham. Worc | .1F 49 | Fairburn. N Yor | .2E 93 |
| Embsay. N Yor | .4C 98 | Eryrys. Den | .5E 82 | Evington. Leic | .5D 74 | Fairfield. Derbs | .3E 85 |
| Emery Down. Hants | .2A 16 | Escalls. Corn | .4A 4 | Ewden Village. S Yor | .1G 85 | Fairfield. Kent | .3D 28 |
| Emley. W Yor | .3C 92 | Escomb. Dur | .1E 105 | Ewdness. Shrp | .1B 60 | Fairfield. Worc | |
| Emmbrook. Wok | .5F 37 | Escrick. N Yor | .5A 100 | Ewell. Surr | .4D 38 | nr. Bromsgrove | .3D 60 |
| Emmer Green. Read | .4F 37 | Esgair. Carm | | Ewell Minnis. Kent | .1G 29 | nr. Evesham | .1F 49 |
| Emmington. Oxon | .5F 51 | nr. Carmarthen | .3D 45 | Ewelme. Oxon | .2E 37 | Fairford. Glos | .5G 49 |
| Emneth. Norf | .5D 77 | nr. St Clears | .3G 43 | Ewen. Glos | .2F 35 | Fair Green. Norf | .4F 77 |
| Emneth Hungate. Norf | .5E 77 | Esgairgeiliog. Powy | .5G 69 | Ewenny. V Glam | .4C 32 | Fair Hill. Cumb | .1G 103 |
| Empingham. Rut | .5G 75 | Esh. Dur | .5E 115 | Ewerby. Linc | .1A 76 | Fairhill. S Lan | .4A 128 |
| Empshott. Hants | .3F 25 | Esher. Surr | .4C 38 | Ewes. Dum | .5F 119 | Fair Isle Airport. Shet | .1B 172 |
| Emsworth. Hants | .2F 17 | Esholt. W Yor | .5D 98 | Ewesley. Nmbd | .5E 121 | Fairlands. Surr | .5A 38 |
| Enborne. W Ber | .5C 36 | Eshott. Nmbd | .5G 121 | Ewhurst. Surr | .1B 26 | Fairlie. N Ayr | .4D 126 |
| Enborne Row. W Ber | .5C 36 | Eshton. N Yor | .4B 98 | Ewhurst Green. E Sus | .3B 28 | Fairlight. E Sus | .4C 28 |
| Enchmarsh. Shrp | .1H 59 | Esh Winning. Dur | .5E 115 | Ewhurst Green. Surr | .2B 26 | Fairlight Cove. E Sus | .4C 28 |
| Enderby. Leics | .1C 62 | Eskadale. High | .5G 157 | Ewloe. Flin | .4E 83 | Fairmile. Devn | .3D 12 |
| Endmoor. Cumb | .1E 97 | Eskbank. Midl | .3G 129 | Ewloe. Flin | .4E 83 | Fairmile. Surr | .4C 38 |
| Endon. Staf | .5D 84 | Eskdale Green. Cumb | .4C 102 | Ewood Bridge. Lanc | .2F 91 | Fairmilehead. Edin | .3F 129 |
| Endon Bank. Staf | .5D 84 | Eskdalemuir. Dum | .5E 119 | Eworthy. Devn | .3E 11 | Fair Oak. Devn | .1D 12 |
| Enfield. G Lon | .1E 39 | Eskham. Linc | .1C 88 | Ewshot. Hants | .1G 25 | Fair Oak. Hants | |
| Enfield Wash. G Lon | .1E 39 | Esknish. Arg | .3B 124 | Ewyas Harold. Here | .3G 47 | nr. Eastleigh | .1C 16 |
| Enford. Wilts | .1G 23 | Esk Valley. N Yor | .4F 107 | Exbourne. Devn | .2G 11 | nr. Kingsclere | .5D 36 |
| Engine Common. S Glo | .3B 34 | Eslington Hall. Nmbd | .3E 121 | Exbury. Hants | .2C 16 | Fairoak. Staf | .2B 72 |
| Englefield. W Ber | .4E 37 | Esprick. Lanc | .1C 90 | Exceat. E Sus | .5G 27 | Fair Oak Green. Hants | .5E 37 |
| Englefield Green. Surr | .3A 38 | Essendine. Rut | .4H 75 | Exebridge. Som | .4C 20 | Fairseat. Kent | .4H 39 |
| Englesea-brook. Ches E | .5B 84 | Essendon. Herts | .5C 52 | Exelby. N Yor | .1E 99 | Fairstead. Essx | .4A 54 |
| English Bicknor. Glos | .4A 48 | Essich. High | .5A 158 | Exeter. Devn | .3C 12 | Fairstead. Norf | .4F 77 |
| Englishcombe. Bath | .5C 34 | Essington. Staf | .5D 72 | Exeter Airport. Devn | .3D 12 | Fairwarp. E Sus | .3F 27 |
| English Frankton. Shrp | .3G 71 | Eston. Red C | .3C 106 | Exford. Som | .3B 20 | Fairwater. Card | .4E 33 |
| Enham Alamein. Hants | .2B 24 | Estover. Plym | .3B 8 | Exfords Green. Shrp | .5G 71 | Fairy Cross. Devn | .4E 19 |
| Enmore. Som | .3F 21 | Eswick. Shet | .6F 173 | Exhall. Warw | .5F 61 | Fakenham. Norf | .2B 78 |
| Ennerdale Bridge. Cumb | .3B 102 | Etal. Nmbd | .1D 120 | Exlade Street. Oxon | .3E 37 | Fakenham Magna. Suff | .3B 66 |
| Enniscaven. Corn | .3D 6 | Etchilhampton. Wilts | .5F 35 | Exminster. Devn | .4C 12 | Fala. Midl | .3H 129 |
| Enniskillen. Ferm | .5B 174 | Etchingham. E Sus | .3B 28 | Exmouth. Devn | .4D 12 | Fala Dam. Midl | .3H 129 |
| Enoch. Dum | .4A 118 | Etchinghill. Kent | .2F 29 | Exnaboe. Shet | .10E 173 | Falcon. Here | .2B 48 |
| Enochdhu. Per | .2H 143 | Etchinghill. Staf | .4E 73 | Exning. Suff | .4F 65 | Faldingworth. Linc | .2H 87 |
| Ensay. Arg | .4E 139 | Etherley Dene. Dur | .2E 105 | Exton. Devn | .4C 12 | Falfield. S Glo | .2B 34 |
| Ensbury. Bour | .3F 15 | Ethie Haven. Ang | .4F 145 | Exton. Hants | .4E 24 | Y Fali. IOA | .3B 80 |
| Ensdon. Shrp | .4G 71 | Etling Green. Norf | .4C 78 | Exton. Rut | .4G 75 | Falkenham. Suff | .2F 55 |
| Ensis. Devn | .4F 19 | Etloe. Glos | .5B 48 | Exton. Som | .3C 20 | Falkirk. Falk | .1B 128 |
| Enson. Staf | .3D 72 | Eton. Wind | .3A 38 | Exwick. Devn | .3C 12 | Falkland. Fife | .3E 137 |
| Enstone. Oxon | .3B 50 | Eton Wick. Wind | .3A 38 | Eyam. Derbs | .3G 85 | Fallin. Stir | .4H 135 |
| Enterkinfoot. Dum | .4A 118 | Etteridge. High | .4A 150 | Eydon. Nptn | .5C 62 | Fallowfield. G Man | .1C 84 |
| Enville. Staf | .2C 60 | Ettersgill. Dur | .2B 104 | Eye. Here | .4G 59 | Falmer. E Sus | .5E 27 |
| Eolaigearraidh. W Isl | .8C 170 | Ettiley Heath. Ches E | .4B 84 | Eye. Pet | .5B 76 | Falmouth. Corn | .5C 6 |

| | | |
|---|---|---|
| Falsgrave. N Yor | .1E 101 |
| Falstone. Nmbd | .1A 114 |
| Fanagmore. High | .4B 166 |
| Fancott. C Beds | .3A 52 |
| Fanellan. High | .4G 157 |
| Fangdale Beck. N Yor | .5C 106 |
| Fangfoss. E Yor | .4B 100 |
| Fankerton. Falk | .1A 128 |
| Fanmore. Arg | .4F 139 |
| Fanner's Green. Essx | .4G 53 |
| Fannich Lodge. High | .2E 156 |
| Fans. Bord | .5C 130 |
| Farcet. Cambs | .1B 64 |
| Far Cotton. Nptn | .5E 63 |
| Fareham. Hants | .2D 16 |
| Farewell. Staf | .4E 73 |
| Far Forest. Worc | .3B 60 |
| Farforth. Linc | .3C 88 |
| Far Green. Glos | .5C 48 |
| Far Hoarcross. Staf | .3F 73 |
| Faringdon. Oxon | .2A 36 |
| Farington. Lanc | .2D 90 |
| Farlam. Cumb | .4G 113 |
| Farleigh. N Som | .5H 33 |
| Farleigh. Surr | .4E 39 |
| Farleigh Hungerford. Som | .1D 22 |
| Farleigh Wallop. Hants | .2E 24 |
| Farleigh Wick. Wilts | .5D 34 |
| Farlesthorpe. Linc | .3D 88 |
| Farleton. Cumb | .1E 97 |
| Farleton. Lanc | .3E 97 |
| Farley. High | .4G 157 |
| Farley. Shrp | |
| nr. Shrewsbury | .5F 71 |
| nr. Telford | .5A 72 |
| Farley. Staf | .1E 73 |
| Farley. Wilts | .4H 23 |
| Farley Green. Suff | .5G 65 |
| Farley Green. Surr | .1B 26 |
| Farley Hill. Wok | .5F 37 |
| Farley's End. Glos | .4C 48 |
| Farlington. N Yor | .3A 100 |
| Farlington. Port | .2E 17 |
| Farlow. Shrp | .2A 60 |
| Farmborough. Bath | .5B 34 |
| Farmcote. Glos | .3F 49 |
| Farmcote. Shrp | .1B 60 |
| Farmington. Glos | .4G 49 |
| Far Moor. G Man | .4D 90 |
| Farmoor. Oxon | .5C 50 |
| Farmtown. Mor | .3C 160 |
| Farnah Green. Derbs | .1H 73 |
| Farnborough. G Lon | .4F 39 |
| Farnborough. Hants | .1G 25 |
| Farnborough. Warw | .1C 50 |
| Farnborough. W Ber | .3C 36 |
| Farncombe. Surr | .1A 26 |
| Farndish. Bed | .4G 63 |
| Farndon. Ches W | .5G 83 |
| Farndon. Notts | .5E 87 |
| Farnell. Ang | .3F 145 |
| Farnham. Dors | .1E 15 |
| Farnham. Essx | .3E 53 |
| Farnham. N Yor | .3F 99 |
| Farnham. Suff | .4F 67 |
| Farnham. Surr | .2G 25 |
| Farnham Common. | |
| Buck | .2A 38 |
| Farnham Green. Essx | .3E 53 |
| Farnham Royal. Buck | .2A 38 |
| Farnhill. N Yor | .5C 98 |
| Farningham. Kent | .4G 39 |
| Farnley. N Yor | .5E 98 |
| Farnley Tyas. W Yor | .3B 92 |
| Farnsfield. Notts | .5D 86 |
| Farnworth. G Man | .4F 91 |
| Farnworth. Hal | .2H 83 |
| Far Oakridge. Glos | .5E 49 |
| Farr. High | |
| nr. Bettyhill | .2H 167 |
| nr. Inverness | .5A 158 |
| nr. Kingussie | .3C 150 |
| Farraline. High | .1H 149 |
| Farrington. Devn | .3D 12 |

Farrington—Folda

Farrington. *Dors* 1D **14**
Farrington Gurney. *Bath* 1B **22**
Far Sawrey. *Cumb* 5E **103**
Farsley. *W Yor* 1C **92**
Farthinghoe. *Nptn* 2D **50**
Farthingstone. *Nptn* 5D **62**
Farthorpe. *Linc* 3B **88**
Fartown. *W Yor* 3B **92**
Farway. *Devn* 3E **13**
Fasag. *High* 3A **156**
Fascadale. *High* 1G **139**
Fasnacloich. *Arg* 4E **141**
Fassfern. *High* 1E **141**
Fatfield. *Tyne* 4G **115**
Faugh. *Cumb* 4G **113**
Fauld. *Staf* 3F **73**
Fauldhouse. *W Lot* 3C **128**
Faulkbourne. *Essx* 4A **54**
Faulkland. *Som* 1C **22**
Fauls. *Shrp* 2H **71**
Faverdale. *Darl* 3F **105**
**Faversham**. *Kent* 4E **40**
Fawdington. *N Yor* 2G **99**
Fawfieldhead. *Staf* 4E **85**
Fawkham Green. *Kent* 4G **39**
Fawler. *Oxon* 4B **50**
Fawley. *Buck* 3F **37**
**Fawley**. *Hants* 2C **16**
Fawley. *W Ber* 3B **36**
Fawley Chapel. *Here* 3A **48**
Fawton. *Corn* 2F **7**
Faxfleet. *E Yor* 2B **94**
Faygate. *W Sus* 2D **26**
Fazakerley. *Mers* 1F **83**
Fazeley. *Staf* 5F **73**
Feagour. *High* 4H **149**
Fearann Dhomhnaill. *High* 3E **147**
Fearby. *N Yor* 1D **98**
Fearn. *High* 1C **158**
Fearnan. *Per* 4E **142**
Fearnbeg. *High* 3G **155**
Fearnhead. *Warr* 1A **84**
Fearnmore. *High* 2G **155**
Featherstone. *Staf* 5D **72**
**Featherstone**. *W Yor* 2E **93**
Featherstone Castle. *Nmbd* 3H **113**
Feckenham. *Worc* 4E **61**
Feering. *Essx* 3B **54**
Feetham. *N Yor* 5C **104**
Feizor. *N Yor* 3G **97**
Felbridge. *Surr* 2E **27**
Felbrigg. *Norf* 2E **78**
Felcourt. *Surr* 1E **27**
Felden. *Herts* 5A **52**
Felhampton. *Shrp* 2G **59**
Felindre. *Carm*
nr. Llandeilo 3F **45**
nr. Llandovery 2G **45**
nr. Newcastle Emlyn 2D **44**
Felindre. *Powy* 2D **58**
Felindre. *Swan* 5G **45**
Felindre Farchog. *Pemb* 1F **43**
Felinfach. *Cdgn* 5E **57**
Felinfach. *Powy* 2D **46**
Felinfoel. *Carm* 5F **45**
Felingwmisaf. *Carm* 3F **45**
Felingwmuchaf. *Carm* 3F **45**
Y Felinheli. *Gwyn* 4E **81**
Felin Newydd. *Powy*
nr. Newtown 5C **70**
nr. Oswestry 3E **70**
Felin Wnda. *Cdgn* 1D **44**
Felinwynt. *Cdgn* 5B **56**
Felixkirk. *N Yor* 1G **99**
**Felixstowe**. *Suff* 2F **55**
Felixstowe Ferry. *Suff* 2G **55**
Felkington. *Nmbd* 5F **131**
Fell End. *Cumb* 5A **104**
**Felling**. *Tyne* 3F **115**
Fell Side. *Cumb* 1E **102**
Felmersham. *Bed* 5G **63**
Felmingham. *Norf* 3E **79**
Felpham. *W Sus* 3H **17**
Felsham. *Suff* 5B **66**
Felsted. *Essx* 3G **53**
**Feltham**. *G Lon* 3C **38**
Felthamhill. *Surr* 3B **38**
Felthorpe. *Norf* 4D **78**
Felton. *Here* 1A **48**
Felton. *N Som* 5A **34**
Felton. *Nmbd* 4F **121**
Felton Butler. *Shrp* 4F **71**
Feltwell. *Norf* 1G **65**
Fenay Bridge. *W Yor* 3B **92**
Fence. *Lanc* 1G **91**
Fence Houses. *Tyne* 4G **115**
Fencott. *Oxon* 4D **50**
Fen Ditton. *Cambs* 4D **65**
Fen Drayton. *Cambs* 4C **64**
Fen End. *Linc* 3B **76**
Fen End. *W Mid* 3G **61**
Fenham. *Nmbd* 5G **131**
Fenham. *Tyne* 3F **115**
Fenhouses. *Linc* 1B **76**
Feniscowles. *Bkbn* 2E **91**
Feniton. *Devn* 3D **12**
Fenn Green. *Shrp* 2B **60**
**Y Fenni**. *Mon* 4G **47**
Fenn's Bank. *Wrex* 2H **71**
Fenn Street. *Medw* 3B **40**
Fenny Bentley. *Derbs* 5F **85**
Fenny Bridges. *Devn* 3E **12**
Fenny Compton. *Warw* 5B **62**
Fenny Drayton. *Leics* 1H **61**
Fenny Stratford. *Mil* 2G **51**
Fenrother. *Nmbd* 5F **121**
Fenstanton. *Cambs* 4C **64**
Fen Street. *Norf* 1C **66**
Fenton. *Cambs* 3C **64**
Fenton. *Cumb* 4G **113**
Fenton. *Linc*
nr. Caythorpe 5F **87**
nr. Saxilby 3F **87**
Fenton. *Nmbd* 1D **120**
Fenton. *Notts* 2E **87**
Fenton. *Stoke* 1C **72**
Fentonadle. *Corn* 5A **10**
Fenton Barns. *E Lot* 1B **130**
Fenwick. *E Ayr* 5F **127**
Fenwick. *Nmbd*
nr. Berwick-upon-Tweed 5G **131**
nr. Hexham 2D **114**
Fenwick. *S Yor* 3F **93**
Feochaig. *Arg* 4B **122**
Feock. *Corn* 5C **6**
Feolin Ferry. *Arg* 3C **124**
Feorlan. *Arg* 5A **122**
Ferindonald. *High* 3E **147**
Feriniquarrie. *High* 3A **154**
Fern. *Ang* 2D **145**
**Ferndale**. *Rhon* 2C **32**
**Ferndown**. *Dors* 2F **15**
Ferness. *High* 4D **158**
Fernham. *Oxon* 2A **36**
Fernhill. *W Sus* 1E **27**
Fernhill Heath. *Worc* 5C **60**
Fernhurst. *W Sus* 4G **25**
Fernieflatt. *Abers* 1H **145**
Ferniegair. *S Lan* 4A **128**
Fernilea. *High* 5C **154**
Fernilee. *Derbs* 3E **85**
Ferrensby. *N Yor* 3F **99**
Ferriby Sluice. *N Lin* 2C **94**
Ferring. *W Sus* 5B **26**
Ferrybridge. *W Yor* 2E **93**
Ferryden. *Ang* 3G **145**
Ferry Hill. *Cambs* 2C **64**
Ferryhill. *Aber* 3G **153**
**Ferryhill**. *Dur* 1F **105**
Ferryhill Station. *Dur* 1A **106**
Ferryside. *Carm* 4D **44**
Ferryton. *High* 2A **158**
Fersfield. *Norf* 2C **66**
Fersit. *High* 1A **142**
Y Ferwig. *Cdgn* 1B **44**
Feshiebridge. *High* 3C **150**
Fetcham. *Surr* 5C **38**
Fetterangus. *Abers* 3G **161**
Fettercairn. *Abers* 1F **145**
Fewcott. *Oxon* 3D **50**
Fewston. *N Yor* 4D **98**
Ffairfach. *Carm* 3G **45**
Ffair Rhos. *Cdgn* 4G **57**
Ffaldybrenin. *Carm* 1G **45**
Ffarmers. *Carm* 1G **45**
Ffawyddog. *Powy* 4F **47**
**Y Fflint**. *Flin* 3E **83**
Ffodun. *Powy* 5E **71**
Ffont-y-gari. *V Glam* 5D **32**
Y Ffor. *Gwyn* 2C **68**
Fforest. *Carm* 5F **45**
Fforest-fach. *Swan* 3F **31**
Fforest Goch. *Neat* 5H **45**
Ffostrasol. *Cdgn* 1D **44**
Ffos-y-ffin. *Cdgn* 4D **56**
Ffrith. *Flin* 5E **83**
Ffwl-y-mwn. *V Glam* 5D **32**
Ffynnon-ddrain. *Carm* 3E **45**
Ffynnongroyw. *Flin* 2D **82**
Ffynnon Gynydd. *Powy* 1E **47**
Ffynnon-oer. *Cdgn* 5E **57**
Fiag Lodge. *High* 1B **164**
Fidden. *Arg* 2B **132**
Fiddington. *Glos* 2E **49**
Fiddington. *Som* 2F **21**
Fiddleford. *Dors* 1D **14**
Fiddlers Hamlet. *Essx* 5E **53**
Field. *Staf* 2E **73**
Field Assarts. *Oxon* 4B **50**
Field Broughton. *Cumb* 1C **96**
Field Dalling. *Norf* 2C **78**
Field Head. *Leics* 5B **74**
Fieldhead. *Cumb* 1F **103**
Fifehead Magdalen. *Dors* 4C **22**
Fifehead Neville. *Dors* 1C **14**
Fifehead St Quintin. *Dors* 1C **14**
Fife Keith. *Mor* 3B **160**
Fifield. *Oxon* 4H **49**
Fifield. *Wilts* 1G **23**
Fifield. *Wind* 3A **38**
Fifield Bavant. *Wilts* 4F **23**
Figheldean. *Wilts* 2G **23**
Filby. *Norf* 4G **79**
Filey. *N Yor* 1F **101**
Filford. *Dors* 3H **13**
Filgrave. *Mil* 1G **51**
Filkins. *Oxon* 5H **49**
Filleigh. *Devn*
nr. Crediton 1H **11**
nr. South Molton 4G **19**
Fillingham. *Linc* 2G **87**
Fillongley. *Warw* 2G **61**
Filton. *S Glo* 4B **34**
Fimber. *E Yor* 3C **100**
Finavon. *Ang* 3D **145**
Fincham. *Norf* 5F **77**
Finchampstead. *Wok* 5F **37**
Fincharn. *Arg* 3G **133**
Finchdean. *Hants* 1F **17**
Finchingfield. *Essx* 2G **53**
**Finchley**. *G Lon* 1D **38**
Findern. *Derbs* 2H **73**
Findhorn. *Mor* 2E **159**
Findhorn Bridge. *High* 1C **150**
Findochty. *Mor* 2B **160**
Findo Gask. *Per* 1C **136**
Findon. *Abers* 4G **153**
Findon. *W Sus* 5C **26**
Findon Mains. *High* 2A **158**
Findon Valley. *W Sus* 5C **26**
Finedon. *Nptn* 3G **63**
Fingal Street. *Suff* 3E **66**
Fingest. *Buck* 2F **37**
Finghall. *N Yor* 1D **98**
Fingland. *Cumb* 4D **112**
Fingland. *Dum* 3G **117**
Finglesham. *Kent* 5H **41**
Fingringhoe. *Essx* 3D **54**
Finiskaig. *High* 4A **148**
Finmere. *Oxon* 2E **51**
Finnart. *Per* 3C **142**
Finningham. *Suff* 4C **66**
Finningley. *S Yor* 1D **86**
Finnygaud. *Abers* 3D **160**
**Finsbury**. *G Lon* 2E **39**
Finstall. *Worc* 4D **61**
Finsthwaite. *Cumb* 1C **96**
Finstock. *Oxon* 4B **50**
Finstown. *Orkn* 6C **172**
Fintona. *Ferm* 4C **174**
Fintry. *Abers* 3E **161**
Fintry. *D'dee* 5D **144**
Fintry. *Stir* 1H **127**
Finwood. *Warw* 4F **61**
Finzean. *Abers* 4D **152**
Fionnphort. *Arg* 2B **132**
Fionnsabhagh. *W Isl* 9C **171**
Firbeck. *S Yor* 2C **86**
Firby. *N Yor*
nr. Bedale 1E **99**
nr. Malton 3B **100**
Firgrove. *G Man* 3H **91**
Firle. *E Sus* 5F **27**
Firsby. *Linc* 4D **88**
Firsdown. *Wilts* 3H **23**
First Coast. *High* 4D **162**
Firth. *Shet* 4F **173**
Fir Tree. *Dur* 1E **105**
Fishbourne. *IOW* 3D **16**
Fishbourne. *W Sus* 2G **17**
Fishburn. *Dur* 1A **106**
Fishcross. *Clac* 4A **136**
Fisherford. *Abers* 5D **160**
Fisherrow. *E Lot* 2G **129**
Fisher's Pond. *Hants* 4C **24**
Fisher's Row. *Lanc* 5D **96**
Fisherstreet. *W Sus* 2A **26**
Fisherton. *High* 3B **158**
Fisherton. *S Ayr* 3B **116**
Fisherton de la Mere. *Wilts* 3E **23**
Fishguard. *Pemb* 1D **42**
Fishlake. *S Yor* 3G **93**
Fishley. *Norf* 4G **79**
Fishnish. *Arg* 4A **140**
Fishpond Bottom. *Dors* 3G **13**
Fishponds. *Bris* 4B **34**
Fishpool. *Glos* 3B **48**
Fishpool. *G Man* 3G **91**
Fishpools. *Powy* 4D **58**
Fishtoft. *Linc* 1C **76**
Fishtoft Drove. *Linc* 1C **76**
Fishwick. *Bord* 4F **131**
Fiskavaig. *High* 5C **154**
Fiskerton. *Linc* 3H **87**
Fiskerton. *Notts* 5E **87**
Fitch. *Shet* 7E **173**
Fitling. *E Yor* 1F **95**
Fittleton. *Wilts* 2G **23**
Fittleworth. *W Sus* 4B **26**
Fitton End. *Cambs* 4D **76**
Fitz. *Shrp* 4G **71**
Fitzhead. *Som* 4E **20**
Fitzwilliam. *W Yor* 3E **93**
Fiunary. *High* 4A **140**
Five Ash Down. *E Sus* 3F **27**
Five Ashes. *E Sus* 3G **27**
Five Bells. *Som* 2D **20**
Five Bridges. *Here* 1B **48**
Fivehead. *Som* 4G **21**
Fivelanes. *Corn* 4C **10**
Fivemiletown. *M Ulst* 5C **174**
Five Oak Green. *Kent* 1H **27**
Five Oaks. *W Sus* 3B **26**
Five Roads. *Carm* 5E **45**
Five Ways. *Warw* 3G **61**
Flack's Green. *Essx* 4A **54**
Flackwell Heath. *Buck* 3G **37**
Fladbury. *Worc* 1E **49**
Fladda. *Shet* 3E **173**
Fladdabister. *Shet* 8F **173**
Flagg. *Derbs* 4F **85**
Flamborough. *E Yor* 2G **101**
Flamstead. *Herts* 4A **52**
Flansham. *W Sus* 5A **26**
Flasby. *N Yor* 4B **98**
Flash. *Staf* 4E **85**
Flashader. *High* 3C **154**
The Flatt. *Cumb* 2G **113**
Flaunden. *Herts* 5A **52**
Flawborough. *Notts* 1E **75**
Flawith. *N Yor* 3G **99**
Flax Bourton. *N Som* 5A **34**
Flaxby. *N Yor* 4F **99**
Flaxholme. *Derbs* 1H **73**
Flaxley. *Glos* 4B **48**
Flaxley Green. *Staf* 4E **73**
Flaxpool. *Som* 3E **21**
Flaxton. *N Yor* 3A **100**
Fleck. *Shet* 10E **173**
Fleckney. *Leics* 1D **62**
Flecknoe. *Warw* 4C **62**
Fledborough. *Notts* 3F **87**
Fleet. *Dors* 4B **14**
**Fleet**. *Hants*
nr. Farnborough 1G **25**
Fleet. *Hants*
nr. South Hayling 2F **17**
Fleet. *Linc* 3C **76**
Fleet Hargate. *Linc* 3C **76**
Fleetville. *Herts* 5B **52**
**Fleetwood**. *Lanc* 5C **96**
Fleggburgh. *Norf* 4G **79**
Fleisirin. *W Isl* 4H **171**
Flemingston. *V Glam* 5D **32**
Flemington. *S Lan*
nr. Glasgow 3H **127**
nr. Strathaven 5A **128**
Flempton. *Suff* 4H **65**
Fleoideabhagh. *W Isl* 9C **171**
Fletcher's Green. *Kent* 1G **27**
Fletchertown. *Cumb* 5D **112**
Fletching. *E Sus* 3F **27**
Fleuchary. *High* 4E **165**
Flexbury. *Corn* 2C **10**
Flexford. *Surr* 1A **26**
Flimby. *Cumb* 1B **102**
Flimwell. *E Sus* 2B **28**
**Flint**. *Flin* 3E **83**
Flintham. *Notts* 1E **75**
Flint Mountain. *Flin* 3E **83**
Flinton. *E Yor* 1F **95**
Flintsham. *Here* 5F **59**
Flishinghurst. *Kent* 2B **28**
Flitcham. *Norf* 3G **77**
Flitton. *C Beds* 2A **52**
**Flitwick**. *C Beds* 2A **52**
Flixborough. *N Lin* 3B **94**
Flixton. *G Man* 1B **84**
Flixton. *N Yor* 2E **101**
Flixton. *Suff* 2F **67**
Flockton. *W Yor* 3C **92**
Flodden. *Nmbd* 1D **120**
Flodigarry. *High* 1D **154**
Flood's Ferry. *Cambs* 1C **64**
Flookburgh. *Cumb* 2C **96**
Flordon. *Norf* 1D **66**
Flore. *Nptn* 4D **62**
Flotterton. *Nmbd* 4D **121**
Flowton. *Suff* 1D **54**
Flushing. *Abers* 4H **161**
Flushing. *Corn* 5C **6**
Fluxton. *Devn* 3D **12**
Flyford Flavell. *Worc* 5D **61**
Fobbing. *Thur* 2B **40**
Fochabers. *Mor* 3H **159**
Fochriw. *Cphy* 5E **46**
Fockerby. *N Lin* 3B **94**
Fodderty. *High* 3H **157**
Foddington. *Som* 4A **22**
Foel. *Powy* 4B **70**
Foffarty. *Ang* 4D **144**
Foggathorpe. *E Yor* 1A **94**
Fogo. *Bord* 5D **130**
Fogorig. *Bord* 5D **130**
Foindle. *High* 4B **166**
Folda. *Ang* 2A **144**

Fole. Staf ...2E 73
Foleshill. W Mid ...2A 62
Foley Park. Worc ...3C 60
Folke. Dors ...1B 14
Folkestone. Kent ...2G 29
Folkingham. Linc ...2H 75
Folkington. E Sus ...5G 27
Folksworth. Cambs ...2A 64
Folkton. N Yor ...2E 101
Folla Rule. Abers ...5E 161
Follifoot. N Yor ...4F 99
The Folly. Herts ...4B 52
Folly Cross. Devn ...2E 11
Folly Gate. Devn ...3F 11
Fonmon. V Glam ...5D 32
Fonthill Bishop. Wilts ...3E 23
Fonthill Gifford. Wilts ...3E 23
Fontmell Magna. Dors ...1D 14
Fontwell. W Sus ...5A 26
Font-y-gary. V Glam ...5D 32
Foodieash. Fife ...2F 137
Foolow. Derbs ...3F 85
Footdee. Aber ...3G 153
Footherley. Staf ...5F 73
Foots Cray. G Lon ...3F 39
Forbestown. Abers ...2A 152
Force Forge. Cumb ...5E 103
Force Mills. Cumb ...5E 103
Forcett. N Yor ...3E 105
Ford. Arg ...3F 133
Ford. Buck ...5F 51
Ford. Derbs ...2B 86
Ford. Devn
  nr. Bideford ...4E 19
  nr. Holbeton ...3C 8
  nr. Salcombe ...4D 9
Ford. Glos ...3F 49
Ford. Nmbd ...1D 120
Ford. Plym ...3A 8
Ford. Shrp ...4G 71
Ford. Som
  nr. Wells ...1A 22
  nr. Wiveliscombe ...4D 20
Ford. Staf ...5E 85
Ford. W Sus ...5B 26
Ford. Wilts
  nr. Chippenham ...4D 34
  nr. Salisbury ...3G 23
Forda. Devn ...3E 19
Ford Barton. Devn ...1C 12
Fordcombe. Kent ...1G 27
Fordell. Fife ...1E 129
Forden. Powy ...5E 71
Ford End. Essx ...4G 53
Forder Green. Devn ...2D 9
Ford Green. Lanc ...5D 97
Fordham. Cambs ...3F 65
Fordham. Essx ...3C 54
Fordham. Norf ...1F 65
Fordham Heath. Essx ...3C 54
Fordhouses. W Mid ...5D 72
Fordie. Per ...1G 135
Fordingbridge. Hants ...1G 15
Fordington. Linc ...3D 88
Fordon. E Yor ...2E 101
Fordoun. Abers ...1G 145
Ford Street. Essx ...3C 54
Ford Street. Som ...1E 13
Fordton. Devn ...3B 12
Fordwells. Oxon ...4B 50
Fordwich. Kent ...5F 41
Fordyce. Abers ...2C 160
Forebridge. Staf ...3D 72
Foremark. Derbs ...3H 73
Forest. N Yor ...4F 105
Forestburn Gate. Nmbd ...5E 121
Foresterseat. Mor ...3F 159
Forest Green. Glos ...2D 34
Forest Green. Surr ...1C 26
Forest Hall. Cumb ...4G 103
Forest Head. Cumb ...4G 113
Forest Hill. Oxon ...5D 50
Forest-in-Teesdale. Dur ...2B 104

Forest Lodge. Per ...1G 143
Forest Mill. Clac ...4B 136
Forest Row. E Sus ...2F 27
Forestside. W Sus ...1F 17
Forest Town. Notts ...4C 86
Forfar. Ang ...3D 144
Forgandenny. Per ...2C 136
Forge. Powy ...1G 57
Forge. Here ...5F 59
Forge Side. Torf ...5F 47
Forgewood. N Lan ...4A 128
Forgie. Mor ...3A 160
Forgue. Abers ...4D 160
Formby. Mers ...4B 90
Forncett End. Norf ...1D 66
Forncett St Mary. Norf ...1D 66
Forncett St Peter. Norf ...1D 66
Forneth. Per ...4H 143
Fornham All Saints. Suff ...4H 65
Fornham St Martin. Suff ...4A 66
Forres. Mor ...3E 159
Forrestfield. N Lan ...3B 128
Forrest Lodge. Dum ...1C 110
Forsbrook. Staf ...1D 72
Forse. High ...5E 169
Forsinard. High ...4A 168
Forss. High ...2C 168
The Forstal. Kent ...2E 29
Forston. Dors ...3B 14
Fort Augustus. High ...3F 149
Fortevoit. Per ...2C 136
Fort George. High ...3B 158
Forth. S Lan ...4C 128
Forthampton. Glos ...2D 48
Forthay. Glos ...2C 34
Fortingall. Per ...4E 143
Forton. Hants ...2C 24
Forton. Lanc ...4D 97
Forton. Shrp ...4G 71
Forton. Som ...2G 13
Forton. Staf ...3B 72
Forton Heath. Shrp ...4G 71
Fortrie. Abers ...4D 160
Fortrose. High ...3B 158
Fortuneswell. Dors ...5B 14
Forty Green. Buck ...1A 38
Forty Hill. G Lon ...1E 39
Forward Green. Suff ...5C 66
Fosbury. Wilts ...1B 24
Foscot. Oxon ...3H 49
Fosdyke. Linc ...2C 76
Foss. Per ...3E 143
Fossebridge. Glos ...4F 49
Foster Street. Essx ...5E 53
Foston. Derbs ...2F 73
Foston. Leics ...1D 62
Foston. Linc ...1F 75
Foston on the Wolds.
  E Yor ...4F 101
Fotherby. Linc ...1C 88
Fothergill. Cumb ...1B 102
Fotheringhay. Nptn ...1H 63
Foubister. Orkn ...7E 172
Foula Airport. Shet ...8A 173
Foulbridge. Cumb ...5F 113
Foulden. Norf ...1G 65
Foulden. Bord ...4F 131
Foul Mile. E Sus ...4H 27
Foulridge. Lanc ...5A 98
Foulsham. Norf ...3C 78
Fountainhall. Bord ...5H 129
The Four Alls. Shrp ...2A 72
Four Ashes. Staf
  nr. Cannock ...5D 72
  nr. Kinver ...2C 60
Four Ashes. Suff ...3C 66
Four Crosses. Powy
  nr. Llanerfyl ...5C 70
  nr. Llanymynech ...4E 71
Four Crosses. Staf ...5D 72

Four Elms. Kent ...1F 27
Four Forks. Som ...3F 21
Four Gotes. Cambs ...4D 76
Four Lane End. S Yor ...4C 92
Four Lane Ends. Lanc ...4E 97
Four Lanes. Corn ...5A 6
Four Marks. Hants ...3E 25
Four Mile Bridge. IOA ...3B 80
Four Oaks. E Sus ...3C 28
Four Oaks. Glos ...3B 48
Four Oaks. W Mid ...2G 61
Four Roads. Carm ...5E 45
Four Roads. IOM ...5B 108
Fourstones. Nmbd ...3B 114
Four Throws. Kent ...3B 28
Fovant. Wilts ...4F 23
Foveran. Abers ...1G 153
Fowey. Corn ...3F 7
Fowlershill. Aber ...2G 153
Fowley Common. Warr ...1A 84
Fowlis. Ang ...5C 144
Fowlis Wester. Per ...1B 136
Fowlmere. Cambs ...1E 53
Fownhope. Here ...2A 48
Fox Corner. Surr ...5A 38
Foxcote. Glos ...4F 49
Foxcote. Som ...1C 22
Foxdale. IOM ...4B 108
Foxearth. Essx ...1B 54
Foxfield. Cumb ...1B 96
Foxham. Wilts ...4E 35
Fox Hatch. Essx ...1G 39
Foxhole. Corn ...3D 6
Foxholes. N Yor ...2E 101
Foxhunt Green. E Sus ...4G 27
Fox Lane. Hants ...1G 25
Foxley. Norf ...3C 78
Foxley. Nptn ...5D 62
Foxley. Wilts ...3D 35
Foxlydiate. Worc ...4E 61
Fox Street. Essx ...3D 54
Foxt. Staf ...1E 73
Foxton. Cambs ...1E 53
Foxton. Dur ...2A 106
Foxton. Leics ...2D 62
Foxton. N Yor ...5B 106
Foxup. N Yor ...2A 98
Foxwist Green. Ches W ...4A 84
Foxwood. Shrp ...3A 60
Foy. Here ...3A 48
Foyers. High ...1G 149
Foynesfield. High ...3C 158
Fraddam. Corn ...3C 4
Fraddon. Corn ...3D 6
Fradley. Staf ...4F 73
Fradley South. Staf ...4F 73
Fradswell. Staf ...2D 73
Fraisthorpe. E Yor ...3F 101
Framfield. E Sus ...3F 27
Framingham Earl. Norf ...5E 79
Framingham Pigot. Norf ...5E 79
Framlingham. Suff ...4E 67
Frampton. Dors ...3B 14
Frampton. Linc ...2C 76
Frampton Cotterell. S Glo ...3B 34
Frampton Mansell. Glos ...5E 49
Frampton on Severn. Glos ...5C 48
Frampton West End. Linc ...1B 76
Framsden. Suff ...5D 66
Framwellgate Moor. Dur ...5F 115
Franche. Worc ...3C 60
Frandley. Ches W ...3A 84
Frankby. Mers ...2E 83
Frankfort. Norf ...3F 79
Frankley. Worc ...2D 61
Frank's Bridge. Powy ...5D 58
Frankton. Warw ...3B 62
Frankwell. Shrp ...4G 71
Frant. E Sus ...2G 27
Fraserburgh. Abers ...2G 161
Frating Green. Essx ...3D 54
Fratton. Port ...2E 17
Freathy. Corn ...3A 8

Freckenham. Suff ...3F 65
Freckleton. Lanc ...2C 90
Freeby. Leics ...3F 75
Freefolk Priors. Hants ...2C 24
Freehay. Staf ...1E 73
Freeland. Oxon ...4C 50
Freester. Shet ...6F 173
Freethorpe. Norf ...5G 79
Freiston. Linc ...1C 76
Freiston Shore. Linc ...1C 76
Fremington. Devn ...3F 19
Fremington. N Yor ...5D 104
Frenchay. S Glo ...4B 34
Frenchbeer. Devn ...4G 11
Frenich. Stir ...3D 134
Frensham. Surr ...2G 25
Frenze. Norf ...2D 66
Fresgoe. High ...2B 168
Freshfield. Mers ...4A 90
Freshford. Bath ...5C 34
Freshwater. IOW ...4B 16
Freshwater Bay. IOW ...4B 16
Freshwater East. Pemb ...5E 43
Fressingfield. Suff ...3E 67
Freston. Suff ...2E 55
Freswick. High ...2F 169
Fretherne. Glos ...5C 48
Frettenham. Norf ...4E 79
Freuchie. Fife ...3E 137
Freystrop. Pemb ...3D 42
Friar's Gate. E Sus ...2F 27
Friar Waddon. Dors ...4B 14
Friday Bridge. Cambs ...5D 76
Friday Street. E Sus ...5H 27
Friday Street. Surr ...1C 26
Fridaythorpe. E Yor ...4C 100
Friden. Derbs ...4F 85
Friern Barnet. G Lon ...1D 39
Friesthorpe. Linc ...2H 87
Frieston. Linc ...1G 75
Frieth. Buck ...2F 37
Friezeland. Notts ...5B 86
Frilford. Oxon ...2C 36
Frilsham. W Ber ...4D 36
Frimley. Surr ...1G 25
Frimley Green. Surr ...1G 25
Frindsbury. Medw ...4B 40
Fring. Norf ...2G 77
Fringford. Oxon ...3E 50
Frinsted. Kent ...5C 40
Frinton-on-Sea. Essx ...4F 55
Friockheim. Ang ...4E 145
Friog. Gwyn ...4F 69
Frisby. Leics ...5E 74
Frisby on the Wreake.
  Leics ...4D 74
Friskney. Linc ...5D 88
Friskney Eaudyke. Linc ...5D 88
Friston. E Sus ...5G 27
Friston. Suff ...4G 67
Fritchley. Derbs ...5A 86
Fritham. Hants ...1H 15
Frith Bank. Linc ...1C 76
Frith Common. Worc ...4A 60
Frithelstock. Devn ...1E 11
Frithelstock Stone. Devn ...1E 11
Frithsden. Herts ...5A 52
Frithville. Linc ...5C 88
Frittenden. Kent ...1C 28
Frittiscombe. Devn ...4E 9
Fritton. Norf
  nr. Great Yarmouth ...5G 79
  nr. Long Stratton ...1E 67
Fritwell. Oxon ...3D 50
Frizinghall. W Yor ...1B 92
Frizington. Cumb ...3B 102
Frobost. W Isl ...6C 170
Frocester. Glos ...5C 48
Frochas. Powy ...5D 70
Frodesley. Shrp ...5H 71
Frodingham. N Lin ...3C 94
Frodsham. Ches W ...3H 83
Froggatt. Derbs ...3G 85
Froghall. Staf ...1E 73

Frogham. Hants ...1G 15
Frogham. Kent ...5G 41
Frogmore. Devn ...4D 8
Frogmore. Hants ...5G 37
Frogmore. Herts ...5B 52
Frognall. Linc ...4A 76
Frogshall. Norf ...2E 79
Frogwell. Corn ...2H 7
Frolesworth. Leics ...1C 62
Frome. Som ...2C 22
Fromefield. Som ...2C 22
Frome St Quintin. Dors ...2A 14
Fromes Hill. Here ...1B 48
Fron. Gwyn ...2C 68
Fron. Powy
  nr. Llandrindod Wells ...4C 58
  nr. Newtown ...1D 58
  nr. Welshpool ...5E 71
Y Fron. Gwyn ...5E 81
Froncysyllte. Wrex ...1E 71
Frongoch. Gwyn ...2B 70
Fron Isaf. Wrex ...1E 71
Fronoleu. Gwyn ...2G 69
Frosterley. Dur ...1D 104
Frotoft. Orkn ...5D 172
Froxfield. C Beds ...2H 51
Froxfield. Wilts ...5A 36
Froxfield Green. Hants ...4F 25
Fryern Hill. Hants ...4C 24
Fryerning. Essx ...5G 53
Fryton. N Yor ...2A 100
Fugglestone St Peter.
  Wilts ...3G 23
Fulbeck. Linc ...5G 87
Fulbourn. Cambs ...5E 65
Fulbrook. Oxon ...4A 50
Fulflood. Hants ...3C 24
Fulford. Som ...4F 21
Fulford. Staf ...2D 72
Fulford. York ...5A 100
Fulham. G Lon ...3D 38
Fulking. W Sus ...4D 26
Fuller's Moor. Ches W ...5G 83
Fuller Street. Essx ...4H 53
Fullerton. Hants ...3B 24
Fulletby. Linc ...3B 88
Full Sutton. E Yor ...4B 100
Fullwood. E Ayr ...4F 127
Fulmer. Buck ...2A 38
Fulmodeston. Norf ...2B 78
Fulnetby. Linc ...3H 87
Fulney. Linc ...3B 76
Fulstow. Linc ...1C 88
Fulthorpe. Stoc T ...2B 106
Fulwell. Tyne ...4G 115
Fulwood. Lanc ...1D 90
Fulwood. Notts ...5B 86
Fulwood. Som ...1F 13
Fulwood. S Yor ...2G 85
Fundenhall. Norf ...1D 66
Funtington. W Sus ...2G 17
Funtley. Hants ...2D 16
Funzie. Shet ...2H 173
Furley. Devn ...2F 13
Furnace. Arg ...3H 133
Furnace. Carm ...5F 45
Furnace. Cdgn ...1F 57
Furnace. E Sus ...3F 27
Furnace Vale. Derbs ...2E 85
Furneux Pelham. Herts ...3E 53
Furzebrook. Dors ...4E 15
Furzehill. Devn ...2H 19
Furzehill. Dors ...2F 15
Furzeley Corner. Hants ...1E 17
Furzey Lodge. Hants ...2B 16
Furzley. Hants ...1A 16
Fyfield. Essx ...5F 53
Fyfield. Glos ...5H 49
Fyfield. Hants ...2A 24
Fyfield. Oxon ...2C 36
Fyfield. Wilts ...5G 35
The Fylde. Lanc ...1B 90
Fylingthorpe. N Yor ...4G 107

Fyning. W Sus ...4G 25
Fyvie. Abers ...5E 161

## G

Gabhsann bho Dheas. W Isl ...2G 171
Gabhsann bho Thuath. W Isl ...2G 171
Gabroc Hill. E Ayr ...4F 127
Gadbrook. Surr ...1D 26
Gaddesby. Leics ...4D 74
Gadfa. IOA ...2D 80
Gadgirth. S Ayr ...2D 116
Gaer. Powy ...3E 47
Gaerwen. IOA ...3D 81
Gagingwell. Oxon ...3C 50
Gaick Lodge. High ...5B 150
Gailey. Staf ...4D 72
Gainford. Dur ...3E 105
Gainsborough. Linc ...1F 87
Gainsborough. Suff ...1E 55
Gainsford End. Essx ...2H 53
Gairletter. Arg ...1C 126
Gairloch. Abers ...3E 153
Gairloch. High ...1H 155
Gairlochy. High ...5D 148
Gairney Bank. Per ...4D 136
Gairnshiel Lodge. Abers ...3G 151
Gaisgill. Cumb ...4H 103
Gaitsgill. Cumb ...5E 113
Galashiels. Bord ...1G 119
Galgate. Lanc ...4D 97
Galhampton. Som ...4B 22
Gallatown. Fife ...4E 137
Galley Common. Warw ...1H 61
Galleyend. Essx ...5H 53
Galleywood. Essx ...5H 53
Gallin. Per ...4C 142
Gallowfauld. Ang ...4D 144
Gallowhill. Per ...5A 144
Gallowhill. Ren ...3F 127
Gallowhills. Abers ...3H 161
Gallows Green. Staf ...1E 73
Gallows Green. Worc ...4D 60
Gallowstree Common. Oxon ...3E 37
Galltair. High ...1G 147
Gallt Melyd. Den ...2C 82
Galmington. Som ...4F 21
Galmisdale. High ...5C 146
Galmpton. Devn ...4C 8
Galmpton. Torb ...3E 9
Galmpton Warborough. Torb ...3E 9
Galphay. N Yor ...2E 99
Galston. E Ayr ...1D 117
Galton. Dors ...4C 14
Galtrigill. High ...3A 154
Gamblesby. Cumb ...1H 103
Gamelsby. Cumb ...4D 112
Gamesley. Derbs ...1E 85
Gamlingay. Cambs ...5B 64
Gamlingay Cinques. Cambs ...5B 64
Gamlingay Great Heath. Cambs ...5B 64
Gammaton. Devn ...4E 19
Gammersgill. N Yor ...1C 98
Gamston. Notts
  nr. Nottingham ...2D 74
  nr. Retford ...3E 86
Ganarew. Here ...4A 48
Ganavan. Arg ...5C 140
Ganborough. Glos ...3G 49
Gang. Corn ...2H 7
Ganllwyd. Gwyn ...3G 69
Gannochy. Ang ...1E 145
Gannochy. Per ...1D 136
Gansclet. High ...4F 169
Ganstead. E Yor ...1E 95
Ganthorpe. N Yor ...2A 100
Ganton. N Yor ...2D 101
Gants Hill. G Lon ...2F 39

Gappah. Devn ...5B 12
Garafad. High ...2D 155
Garboldisham. Norf ...2C 66
Garden City. Flin ...4F 83
Gardeners Green. Wok ...5G 37
Gardenstown. Abers ...2F 161
Garden Village. S Yor ...1G 85
Garden Village. Swan ...3E 31
Garderhouse. Shet ...7E 173
Gardham. E Yor ...5D 100
Gardie. Shet
  on Papa Stour ...5C 173
  on Unst ...1H 173
Gardie Ho. Shet ...7F 173
Gare Hill. Wilts ...2C 22
Garelochhead. Arg ...4B 134
Garford. Oxon ...2C 36
Garforth. W Yor ...1E 93
Gargrave. N Yor ...4B 98
Gargunnock. Stir ...4G 135
Garleffin. S Ayr ...1F 109
Garlieston. Dum ...5B 110
Garlinge Green. Kent ...5F 41
Garlogie. Abers ...3E 153
Garmelow. Staf ...3B 72
Garmond. Abers ...3F 161
Garmondsway. Dur ...1A 106
Garmony. Arg ...4A 140
Garmouth. Mor ...2H 159
Garmston. Shrp ...5A 72
Garnant. Carm ...4G 45
Garndiffaith. Torf ...5F 47
Garndolbenmaen. Gwyn ...1D 69
Garnett Bridge. Cumb ...5G 103
Garnfadryn. Gwyn ...2B 68
Garnkirk. N Lan ...3H 127
Garnlydan. Blae ...4E 47
Garnsgate. Linc ...3D 76
Garnswllt. Swan ...5G 45
Garn yr Erw. Torf ...4F 47
Garrabost. W Isl ...4H 171
Garrallan. E Ayr ...3E 117
Garras. Corn ...4E 5
Garreg. Gwyn ...1F 69
Garrigill. Cumb ...5A 114
Garriston. N Yor ...5E 105
Garrogie Lodge. High ...2H 149
Garros. High ...2D 155
Garrow. Per ...4F 143
Garsdale. Cumb ...1G 97
Garsdale Head. Cumb ...5A 104
Garsdon. Wilts ...3E 35
Garshall Green. Staf ...2D 72
Garsington. Oxon ...5D 50
Garstang. Lanc ...5D 97
Garston. Mers ...2G 83
Garswood. Mers ...1H 83
Gartcosh. N Lan ...3H 127
Garth. B'end ...2B 32
Garth. Cdgn ...2F 57
Garth. Gwyn ...2E 69
Garth. IOM ...4C 108
Garth. Powy
  nr. Builth Wells ...1C 46
  nr. Knighton ...3E 59
Garth. Shet
  nr. Sandness ...6D 173
  nr. Skellister ...6F 173
Garth. Wrex ...1E 71
Garthamlock. Glas ...3H 127
Garthbrengy. Powy ...2D 46
Gartheli. Cdgn ...5E 57
Garthmyl. Powy ...1D 58
Garthorpe. Leics ...3F 75
Garthorpe. N Lin ...3B 94
Garth Owen. Powy ...1D 58
Garth Place. Cphy ...3E 33
Garth Row. Cumb ...5G 103
Gartly. Abers ...5C 160
Gartmore. Stir ...4E 135
Gartness. N Lan ...3A 128
Gartness. Stir ...1G 127
Gartocharn. W Dun ...1F 127
Garton. E Yor ...1F 95

Garton-on-the-Wolds. E Yor ...4D 101
Gartsherrie. N Lan ...3A 128
Gartymore. High ...2H 165
Garvagh. Caus ...2E 175
Garvald. E Lot ...2B 130
Garvamore. High ...4H 149
Garvard. Arg ...4A 132
Garvault. High ...5H 167
Garve. High ...2F 157
Garvestone. Norf ...5C 78
Garvie. Arg ...4H 133
Garvock. Abers ...1G 145
Garvock. Inv ...2D 126
Garway. Here ...3H 47
Garway Common. Here ...3H 47
Garway Hill. Here ...3H 47
Garwick. Linc ...1A 76
Gaskan. High ...1C 140
Gasper. Wilts ...3C 22
Gastard. Wilts ...5D 35
Gasthorpe. Norf ...2B 66
Gatcombe. IOW ...4C 16
Gateacre. Mers ...2G 83
Gatebeck. Cumb ...1E 97
Gate Burton. Linc ...2F 87
Gateforth. N Yor ...2F 93
Gatehead. E Ayr ...1C 116
Gate Helmsley. N Yor ...4A 100
Gatehouse. Nmbd ...1A 114
Gatehouse of Fleet. Dum ...4D 110
Gatelawbridge. Dum ...5B 118
Gateley. Norf ...3B 78
Gatenby. N Yor ...1F 99
Gatesgarth. Cumb ...3C 102
Gateshead. Tyne ...3F 115
Gatesheath. Ches W ...4G 83
Gateside. Ang
  nr. Forfar ...4D 144
  nr. Kirriemuir ...4C 144
Gateside. Fife ...3D 136
Gateside. N Ayr ...4E 127
Gathurst. G Man ...4D 90
Gatley. G Man ...2C 84
Gatton. Surr ...5D 39
Gattonside. Bord ...1H 119
Gatwick Airport. W Sus ...1D 26
Gaufron. Powy ...4B 58
Gaulby. Leics ...5D 74
Gauldry. Fife ...1F 137
Gaultree. Norf ...5D 77
Gaunt's Common. Dors ...2F 15
Gaunt's Earthcott. S Glo ...3B 34
Gautby. Linc ...3A 88
Gavinton. Bord ...4D 130
Gawber. S Yor ...4D 92
Gawcott. Buck ...2E 51
Gawsworth. Ches E ...4C 84
Gawthorpe. W Yor ...2C 92
Gawthrop. Cumb ...1F 97
Gawthwaite. Cumb ...1B 96
Gay Bowers. Essx ...5A 54
Gaydon. Warw ...5A 62
Gayfield. Orkn ...2D 172
Gayhurst. Mil ...1G 51
Gayle. N Yor ...1A 98
Gayles. N Yor ...4E 105
Gay Street. W Sus ...3B 26
Gayton. Mers ...2E 83
Gayton. Norf ...4G 77
Gayton. Nptn ...5E 62
Gayton. Staf ...3D 73
Gayton le Marsh. Linc ...2D 88
Gayton le Wold. Linc ...2B 88
Gayton Thorpe. Norf ...4G 77
Gaywood. Norf ...3F 77
Gazeley. Suff ...4G 65
Gearraidh Bhailteas. W Isl ...6C 170
Gearraidh Bhaird. W Isl ...6F 171
Gearraidh ma Monadh. W Isl ...7C 170
Gearraidh na h-Aibhne. W Isl ...4E 171

Geary. High ...2B 154
Geddes. High ...3C 158
Gedding. Suff ...5B 66
Geddington. Nptn ...2F 63
Gedintailor. High ...5E 155
Gedling. Notts ...1D 74
Gedney. Linc ...3D 76
Gedney Broadgate. Linc ...3D 76
Gedney Drove End. Linc ...3D 76
Gedney Dyke. Linc ...3D 76
Gedney Hill. Linc ...4C 76
Geeston. Rut ...5G 75
Geilston. Arg ...2E 127
Geirinis. W Isl ...4C 170
Geise. High ...2D 168
Geisiadar. W Isl ...4D 171
Gelder Shiel. Abers ...5G 151
Geldeston. Norf ...1F 67
Gell. Cnwy ...4A 82
Gelli. Pemb ...3E 43
Gelli. Rhon ...2C 32
Gellifor. Den ...4D 82
Gelligaer. Cphy ...2E 33
Y Gelli Gandryll. Powy ...1F 47
Gellilydan. Gwyn ...2F 69
Gellinudd. Neat ...5H 45
Gellyburn. Per ...5H 143
Gellywen. Carm ...2G 43
Gelston. Dum ...4E 111
Gelston. Linc ...1G 75
Gembling. E Yor ...4F 101
Geneva. Cdgn ...5D 56
Gentleshaw. Staf ...4E 73
Geocrab. W Isl ...8D 171
George Best Belfast City Airport. Bel ...4H 175
Georgefield. Dum ...5E 118
Georgeham. Devn ...3E 19
George Nympton. Devn ...4H 19
Georgetown. Blae ...5E 47
Georgetown. Ren ...3F 127
Georth. Orkn ...5C 172
Gerlan. Gwyn ...4F 81
Germansweek. Devn ...3E 11
Germoe. Corn ...4C 4
Gerrans. Corn ...5C 6
Gerrard's Bromley. Staf ...2B 72
Gerrards Cross. Buck ...2A 38
Gerston. High ...3D 168
Gestingthorpe. Essx ...2B 54
Gethsemane. Pemb ...1A 44
Geuffordd. Powy ...4E 70
Gibraltar. Buck ...4F 51
Gibraltar. Linc ...5E 89
Gibraltar. Suff ...5D 66
Gibsmere. Notts ...1E 74
Giddeahall. Wilts ...4D 34
Gidea Park. G Lon ...2G 39
Gidleigh. Devn ...4G 11
Giffnock. E Ren ...4G 127
Gifford. E Lot ...3B 130
Giffordtown. Fife ...2E 137
Giggetty. Staf ...1C 60
Giggleswick. N Yor ...3H 97
Gignog. Pemb ...2C 42
Gilberdyke. E Yor ...2B 94
Gilbert's End. Worc ...1D 48
Gilbert's Green. Warw ...3F 61
Gilchriston. E Lot ...3A 130
Gilcrux. Cumb ...1C 102
Gildersome. W Yor ...2C 92
Gildingwells. S Yor ...2C 86
Gilesgate Moor. Dur ...5F 115
Gileston. V Glam ...5D 32
Gilfach. Cphy ...2E 33
Gilfach Goch. Rhon ...3C 32
Gilfachreda. Cdgn ...5D 56
Gilford. Arm ...5F 175
Gilgarran. Cumb ...2B 102
Gillamoor. N Yor ...5D 107
Gillan. Corn ...4E 5
Gillar's Green. Mers ...1G 83
Gillen. High ...3B 154

Gilling East. N Yor ...2A 100
Gillingham. Dors ...4D 22
Gillingham. Medw ...4B 40
Gillingham. Norf ...1G 67
Gilling West. N Yor ...4E 105
Gillock. High ...3E 169
Gillow Heath. Staf ...5C 84
Gills. High ...1F 169
Gill's Green. Kent ...2B 28
Gilmanscleuch. Bord ...2F 119
Gilmerton. Edin ...3F 129
Gilmerton. Per ...1A 136
Gilmonby. Dur ...3C 104
Gilmorton. Leics ...2C 62
Gilsland. Nmbd ...3H 113
Gilsland Spa. Cumb ...3H 113
Gilston. Bord ...4H 129
Giltbrook. Notts ...1B 74
Gilwern. Mon ...4F 47
Gimingham. Norf ...2E 79
Giosla. W Isl ...5D 171
Gipping. Suff ...4C 66
Gipsey Bridge. Linc ...1B 76
Gipton. W Yor ...1D 92
Girdle Toll. N Ayr ...5E 127
Girlsta. Shet ...6F 173
Girsby. N Yor ...4A 106
Girthon. Dum ...4D 110
Girton. Cambs ...4D 64
Girton. Notts ...4F 87
Girvan. S Ayr ...5A 116
Gisburn. Lanc ...5H 97
Gisleham. Suff ...2H 67
Gislingham. Suff ...3C 66
Gissing. Norf ...2D 66
Gittisham. Devn ...3E 13
Gladestry. Powy ...5E 59
Gladsmuir. E Lot ...2A 130
Glaichbea. High ...5H 157
Glais. Swan ...5H 45
Glaisdale. N Yor ...4E 107
Glame. High ...4E 155
Glamis. Ang ...4C 144
Glanaman. Carm ...4G 45
Glan-Conwy. Cnwy ...5H 81
Glandford. Norf ...1C 78
Glan Duar. Carm ...1F 45
Glandwr. Blae ...5F 47
Glandwr. Pemb ...2F 43
Glan-Dwyfach. Gwyn ...1D 69
Glandy Cross. Carm ...2F 43
Glandyfi. Cdgn ...1F 57
Glangrwyney. Powy ...4F 47
Glanmule. Powy ...1D 58
Glan-rhyd. Pemb ...1F 43
Glan-rhyd. Powy ...5A 46
Glanrhyd. Gwyn ...2B 68
Glanrhyd. Pemb ...1B 44
Glanton. Nmbd ...3E 121
Glanton Pyke. Nmbd ...3E 121
Glanvilles Wootton. Dors ...2B 14
Glan-y-don. Flin ...3D 82
Glan-y-nant. Powy ...2B 58
Glan-yr-afon. Gwyn ...1C 70
Glan-yr-afon. IOA ...2F 81
Glan-yr-afon. Powy ...5C 70
Glan-y-wern. Gwyn ...2F 69
Glapthorn. Nptn ...1H 63
Glapwell. Derbs ...4B 86
Glas Aird. Arg ...4A 132
Glas-allt Shiel. Abers ...5G 151
Glasbury. Powy ...2E 47
Glaschoil. High ...5E 159
Glascoed. Den ...3B 82
Glascoed. Mon ...5G 47
Glascote. Staf ...5G 73
Glascwm. Powy ...5D 58
Glasfryn. Cnwy ...5B 82
Glasgow. Glas ...3G 127
Glasgow Airport. Ren ...3F 127
Glasgow Prestwick Airport. S Ayr ...2C 116
Glashvin. High ...2D 154
Glasinfryn. Gwyn ...4E 81

Glas na Cardaich. *High* . . . . . .4E 147
Glasnacardoch. *High* . . . . . . . .4E 147
Glasnakille. *High* . . . . . . . . . . .2D 146
Glaspwll. *Cdgn* . . . . . . . . . . . . . .1G 57
Glassburn. *High* . . . . . . . . . . . .5F 157
Glassenbury. *Kent* . . . . . . . . . . .2B 28
Glasserton. *Dum* . . . . . . . . . . . .5B 110
Glassford. *S Lan* . . . . . . . . . . . .5A 128
Glassgreen. *Mor* . . . . . . . . . . . .2G 159
Glasshouse. *Glos* . . . . . . . . . . . . .3C 48
Glasshouses. *N Yor* . . . . . . . . .3D 98
Glasson. *Cumb* . . . . . . . . . . . .3D 112
Glasson. *Lanc* . . . . . . . . . . . . . .4D 96
Glassonby. *Cumb* . . . . . . . . . .1G 103
Glasterlaw. *Ang* . . . . . . . . . . . .3E 145
Glaston. *Rut* . . . . . . . . . . . . . . . . .5F 75
Glastonbury. *Som* . . . . . . . . . . . .3H 21
Glatton. *Cambs* . . . . . . . . . . . . .2A 64
Glazebrook. *Warr* . . . . . . . . . . . .1A 84
Glazebury. *Warr* . . . . . . . . . . . . .1A 84
Glazeley. *Shrp* . . . . . . . . . . . . . . .2B 60
Gleadless. *S Yor* . . . . . . . . . . . . .2A 86
Gleadsmoss. *Ches E* . . . . . . . .4C 84
Gleann Dail bho Dheas.
  *W Isl* . . . . . . . . . . . . .7C 170
Gleann Tholastaidh. *W Isl* . . . .3H 171
Gleann Uige. *High* . . . . . . . . . .1A 140
Gleaston. *Cumb* . . . . . . . . . . . . .2B 96
Glecknabae. *Arg* . . . . . . . . . . . . .3B 126
Gledrid. *Shrp* . . . . . . . . . . . . . . . .2E 71
Gleiniant. *Powy* . . . . . . . . . . . . . .1B 58
Glemsford. *Suff* . . . . . . . . . . . . . .1B 54
Glen. *Dum* . . . . . . . . . . . . . . . .4C 110
Glenancross. *High* . . . . . . . . . .4E 147
Glenbarr. *Arg* . . . . . . . . . . . . . . .2A 122
Glenbeg. *High* . . . . . . . . . . . . . .2G 139
Glen Bernisdale. *High* . . . . . .4D 154
Glenbervie. *Abers* . . . . . . . . . . .5E 153
Glenboig. *N Lan* . . . . . . . . . . . .3A 128
Glenborrodale. *High* . . . . . . . . .2A 140
Glenbranter. *Arg* . . . . . . . . . . . .4A 134
Glenbreck. *Bord* . . . . . . . . . . . . .2C 118
Glenbrein Lodge. *High* . . . . . . .2G 149
Glenbrittle. *High* . . . . . . . . . . . . .1C 146
Glenbuchat Lodge. *Abers* . . . . .2H 151
Glenbuck. *E Ayr* . . . . . . . . . . . .2G 117
Glenburn. *Ren* . . . . . . . . . . . . . .3F 127
Glencalvie Lodge. *High* . . . . . .5B 164
Glencaple. *Dum* . . . . . . . . . . . .3A 112
Glencarron Lodge. *High* . . . . . .3C 156
Glencarse. *Per* . . . . . . . . . . . . .1D 136
Glencassley Castle. *High* . . . . .3B 164
Glencat. *Abers* . . . . . . . . . . . . .4C 152
Glencoe. *High* . . . . . . . . . . . . . .3F 141
Glen Cottage. *High* . . . . . . . . . .5E 147
Glencraig. *Fife* . . . . . . . . . . . . .4D 136
Glendale. *High* . . . . . . . . . . . . .4A 154
Glendevon. *Per* . . . . . . . . . . . . . .3B 136
Glendoebeg. *High* . . . . . . . . . . .3G 149
Glendoick. *Per* . . . . . . . . . . . . . .1E 136
Glendoune. *S Ayr* . . . . . . . . . . .5A 116
Glenduckie. *Fife* . . . . . . . . . . . . .2E 137
Gleneagles. *Per* . . . . . . . . . . . . .3B 136
Glenegedale. *Arg* . . . . . . . . . . . .4B 124
Glenegedale Lots. *Arg* . . . . . . .4B 124
Glenelg. *High* . . . . . . . . . . . . . .2G 147
Glenernie. *Mor* . . . . . . . . . . . . . .4E 159
Glenesslin. *Dum* . . . . . . . . . . . . .1F 111
Glenfarg. *Per* . . . . . . . . . . . . . . .2D 136
Glenfarquhar Lodge.
  *Abers* . . . . . . . . . . . . .5E 152
Glenferness Mains. *High* . . . . . .4D 158
Glenfeshie Lodge. *High* . . . . . .4C 150
Glenfiddich Lodge. *Mor* . . . . . .5H 159
Glenfield. *Leics* . . . . . . . . . . . . . .5C 74
Glenfinnan. *High* . . . . . . . . . . . .5B 148
Glenfintaig Lodge. *High* . . . . . .5E 148
Glenfoot. *Per* . . . . . . . . . . . . . . .2D 136
Glenfyne Lodge. *Arg* . . . . . . . . .2B 134
Glengap. *Dum* . . . . . . . . . . . . .4D 110
Glengarnock. *N Ayr* . . . . . . . . . .4E 126
Glengolly. *High* . . . . . . . . . . . . .2D 168

Glengorm Castle. *Arg* . . . . . . . . .3F 139
Glengrasco. *High* . . . . . . . . . . .4D 154
Glenhead Farm. *Ang* . . . . . . . .2B 144
Glen House. *Bord* . . . . . . . . . . .1E 119
Glenhurich. *High* . . . . . . . . . . . .2C 140
Glenkerry. *Bord* . . . . . . . . . . . . .3E 119
Glenkiln. *Dum* . . . . . . . . . . . . . . .2F 111
Glenkindie. *Abers* . . . . . . . . . . .2B 152
Glen Maye. *IOM* . . . . . . . . . . . .4B 108
Glenmavis. *N Lan* . . . . . . . . . . .3A 128
Glenmazeran Lodge. *High* . . . . .1B 150
Glenmidge. *Dum* . . . . . . . . . . . .1F 111
Glen Mona. *IOM* . . . . . . . . . . .3D 108
Glenmore. *High* . . . . . . . . . . . . . . .
  nr. Glenborrodale . . . . . .2G 139
  nr. Kingussie . . . . . . . . . . .3D 151
  on Isle of Skye . . . . . . . . . .4D 154
Glenmoy. *Ang* . . . . . . . . . . . . . .2D 144
Glennoe. *Arg* . . . . . . . . . . . . . . .5E 141
Glen of Coachford. *Abers* . . . . .4B 160
Glenogil. *Ang* . . . . . . . . . . . . . . .2D 144
Glen Parva. *Leics* . . . . . . . . . . . .1C 62
Glenprosen Village. *Ang* . . . . . .2C 144
Glenree. *N Ayr* . . . . . . . . . . . . . .3D 122
Glenridding. *Cumb* . . . . . . . . . . .3E 103
Glenrosa. *N Ayr* . . . . . . . . . . . . .2E 123
Glenrothes. *Fife* . . . . . . . . . . . . .3E 137
Glensanda. *High* . . . . . . . . . . . . .4C 140
Glensaugh. *Abers* . . . . . . . . . . .1F 145
Glenshero Lodge. *High* . . . . . . .4H 149
Glensluain. *Arg* . . . . . . . . . . . . .4H 133
Glenstockadale. *Dum* . . . . . . . . .3F 109
Glenstriven. *Arg* . . . . . . . . . . . . .2B 126
Glen Tanar House. *Abers* . . . . .4B 152
Glentham. *Linc* . . . . . . . . . . . . . .1H 87
Glenton. *Abers* . . . . . . . . . . . . .1D 152
Glentress. *Bord* . . . . . . . . . . . . .1E 119
Glentromie Lodge. *High* . . . . . .4B 150
Glentrool Lodge. *Dum* . . . . . . . .1B 110
Glentrool Village. *Dum* . . . . . . .2A 110
Glentruim House. *High* . . . . . . .4A 150
Glentworth. *Linc* . . . . . . . . . . . . .2G 87
Glenuig. *High* . . . . . . . . . . . . . .1A 140
Glen Village. *Falk* . . . . . . . . . . .2B 128
Glen Vine. *IOM* . . . . . . . . . . . .4C 108
Glenwhilly. *Dum* . . . . . . . . . . . . .2G 109
Glenzierfoot. *Dum* . . . . . . . . . . .2E 113
Glespin. *S Lan* . . . . . . . . . . . . . .2H 117
Gletness. *Shet* . . . . . . . . . . . . . .6F 173
Glewstone. *Here* . . . . . . . . . . . . . .3A 48
Glib Cheois. *W Isl* . . . . . . . . . . .5F 171
Glinton. *Pet* . . . . . . . . . . . . . . . . .5A 76
Glooston. *Leics* . . . . . . . . . . . . . .1E 63
**Glossop.** *Derbs* . . . . . . . . . . . . .1E 85
Gloster Hill. *Nmbd* . . . . . . . . . . .4G 121
**Gloucester.** *Glos* . . . . . . . . . . . .4D 48
Gloucestershire Airport.
  *Glos* . . . . . . . . . . . . . . . .3D 49
Glusburn. *N Yor* . . . . . . . . . . . . .5C 98
Glutt Lodge. *High* . . . . . . . . . . . .5B 168
Glutton Bridge. *Derbs* . . . . . . . .4E 85
Gluvian. *Corn* . . . . . . . . . . . . . . . .2D 6
Glympton. *Oxon* . . . . . . . . . . . . .3C 50
Glyn. *Cnwy* . . . . . . . . . . . . . . . . .3A 82
Glynarthen. *Cdgn* . . . . . . . . . . . .1D 44
Glynbrochan. *Powy* . . . . . . . . . . .2B 58
Glyn Ceiriog. *Wrex* . . . . . . . . . . .2E 70
Glyncoch. *Rhon* . . . . . . . . . . . . . .2D 32
Glyncorrwg. *Neat* . . . . . . . . . . . . .2B 32
Glynde. *E Sus* . . . . . . . . . . . . . . .5F 27

Glyndebourne. *E Sus* . . . . . . . . .4F 27
Glyndyfrdwy. *Den* . . . . . . . . . . .1D 70
**Glyn Ebwy.** *Blae* . . . . . . . . . . . .5E 47
Glynllan. *B'end* . . . . . . . . . . . . . .3C 32
Glyn-neath. *Neat* . . . . . . . . . . . . .5B 46
Glynogwr. *B'end* . . . . . . . . . . . . .3C 32
Glyntaff. *Rhon* . . . . . . . . . . . . . . .3D 32
Glyntawe. *Powy* . . . . . . . . . . . . . .4B 46
Glynteg. *Carm* . . . . . . . . . . . . . . .2D 44
Gnosall. *Staf* . . . . . . . . . . . . . . . .3C 72
Gnosall Heath. *Staf* . . . . . . . . . .3C 72
Goadby. *Leics* . . . . . . . . . . . . . . .1E 63
Goadby Marwood. *Leics* . . . . . .3E 75
Goatacre. *Wilts* . . . . . . . . . . . . . . .4F 35
Goathill. *Dors* . . . . . . . . . . . . . . . .1B 14
Goathland. *N Yor* . . . . . . . . . . .4F 107
Goathurst. *Som* . . . . . . . . . . . . . .3F 21
Goathurst Common. *Kent* . . . . . .5F 39
Goat Lees. *Kent* . . . . . . . . . . . . . .1E 28
Gobernuisgach Lodge.
  *High* . . . . . . . . . . . . .4E 167
Gobernuisgeach. *High* . . . . . . . .5B 168
Gobhaig. *W Isl* . . . . . . . . . . . . .7C 171
Gobowen. *Shrp* . . . . . . . . . . . . . .2F 71
**Godalming.** *Surr* . . . . . . . . . . . . .1A 26
Goddard's Corner. *Suff* . . . . . . . .4E 67
Goddard's Green. *Kent* . . . . . . . . .
  nr. Benenden . . . . . . . . . . .2C 28
  nr. Cranbrook . . . . . . . . . . .2B 28
Goddards' Green. *W Sus* . . . . . .3D 27
Godford Cross. *Devn* . . . . . . . . .2E 13
Godleybrook. *Staf* . . . . . . . . . . . .1D 73
Godmanchester. *Cambs* . . . . . . .3B 64
Godmanstone. *Dors* . . . . . . . . . .3B 14
Godmersham. *Kent* . . . . . . . . . . .5E 41
Godolphin Cross. *Corn* . . . . . . . . .3D 4
Godre'r-graig. *Neat* . . . . . . . . . . .5A 46
Godshill. *Hants* . . . . . . . . . . . . . .1G 15
Godshill. *IOW* . . . . . . . . . . . . . . .4D 16
Godstone. *Staf* . . . . . . . . . . . . . . .2E 73
Godstone. *Surr* . . . . . . . . . . . . . .5E 39
Goetre. *Mon* . . . . . . . . . . . . . . . . .5G 47
Goff's Oak. *Herts* . . . . . . . . . . . . .5D 52
Gogar. *Edin* . . . . . . . . . . . . . . . .2E 129
Goginan. *Cdgn* . . . . . . . . . . . . . . .2F 57
Golan. *Gwyn* . . . . . . . . . . . . . . . .1E 69
Golant. *Corn* . . . . . . . . . . . . . . . . . .3F 7
Golberdon. *Corn* . . . . . . . . . . . . .5D 10
**Golborne.** *G Man* . . . . . . . . . . .1A 84
Golcar. *W Yor* . . . . . . . . . . . . . . .3A 92
Goldcliff. *Newp* . . . . . . . . . . . . . . .3G 33
Golden Cross. *E Sus* . . . . . . . . .4G 27
Golden Green. *Kent* . . . . . . . . . .1H 27
Golden Grove. *Carm* . . . . . . . . . .4F 45
Golden Grove. *N Yor* . . . . . . . .4F 107
Golden Hill. *Pemb* . . . . . . . . . . . .2D 43
Goldenhill. *Stoke* . . . . . . . . . . . . .5C 84
Golden Pot. *Hants* . . . . . . . . . . . .2F 25
Golden Valley. *Glos* . . . . . . . . . .3E 49
Golders Green. *G Lon* . . . . . . . .2D 38
Goldfinger. *Essx* . . . . . . . . . . . . . .5C 54
Gold Hill. *Norf* . . . . . . . . . . . . . . .1E 65
Golding. *Shrp* . . . . . . . . . . . . . . .5H 71
Goldington. *Bed* . . . . . . . . . . . . .5H 63
Goldsborough. *N Yor* . . . . . . . . . . . .
  nr. Harrogate . . . . . . . . . .4F 99
  nr. Whitby . . . . . . . . . . . . .3F 107
Goldsithney. *Corn* . . . . . . . . . . . . . .3C 4
Goldstone. *Kent* . . . . . . . . . . . . .4G 41
Goldstone. *Shrp* . . . . . . . . . . . . . .3B 72
Goldthorpe. *S Yor* . . . . . . . . . . . .4E 93
Goldworthy. *Devn* . . . . . . . . . . . .4D 19
Golfa. *Powy* . . . . . . . . . . . . . . . . .3D 70
Gollanfield. *High* . . . . . . . . . . . .3C 158
Gollinglith Foot. *N Yor* . . . . . . . .1D 98
Golsoncott. *Som* . . . . . . . . . . . . .3D 20
Golspie. *High* . . . . . . . . . . . . . .4F 165
Gomeldon. *Wilts* . . . . . . . . . . . . .3G 23
Gomersal. *W Yor* . . . . . . . . . . . . .2C 92
Gometra House. *Arg* . . . . . . . . .4E 139
Gomshall. *Surr* . . . . . . . . . . . . . .1B 26
Gonalston. *Notts* . . . . . . . . . . . . .1D 74
Gonerby Hill Foot. *Linc* . . . . . . .2G 75
Gonfirth. *Shet* . . . . . . . . . . . . . . .5E 173

Good Easter. *Essx* . . . . . . . . . . . .4G 53
Gooderstone. *Norf* . . . . . . . . . . . .5G 77
Goodleigh. *Devn* . . . . . . . . . . . . . .3G 19
Goodmanham. *E Yor* . . . . . . . . .5C 100
Goodmayes. *G Lon* . . . . . . . . . . .2F 39
Goodnestone. *Kent* . . . . . . . . . . . . .
  nr. Aylesham . . . . . . . . . . .5G 41
  nr. Faversham . . . . . . . . . .4E 41
Goodrich. *Here* . . . . . . . . . . . . . .4A 48
Goodrington. *Torb* . . . . . . . . . . . . .3E 9
Goodshaw. *Lanc* . . . . . . . . . . . . .2G 91
Goodshaw Fold. *Lanc* . . . . . . . . .2G 91
Goodstone. *Devn* . . . . . . . . . . . . .5A 12
Goodwick. *Pemb* . . . . . . . . . . . . .1D 42
Goodworth Clatford. *Hants* . . . . .2B 24
**Goole.** *E Yor* . . . . . . . . . . . . . . .2H 93
Goom's Hill. *Worc* . . . . . . . . . . . .5E 61
Goonabarn. *Corn* . . . . . . . . . . . . . .3D 6
Goonbell. *Corn* . . . . . . . . . . . . . . .4B 6
Goonhavern. *Corn* . . . . . . . . . . . . .3B 6
Goonlaze. *Corn* . . . . . . . . . . . . . . .5B 6
Goonvrea. *Corn* . . . . . . . . . . . . . . .4B 6
Goose Green. *Cumb* . . . . . . . . . .1E 97
Goose Green. *S Glo* . . . . . . . . . .3C 34
Gooseham. *Corn* . . . . . . . . . . . .1C 10
Goosewell. *Plym* . . . . . . . . . . . . . .3B 8
Goosey. *Oxon* . . . . . . . . . . . . . . .2B 36
Goosnargh. *Lanc* . . . . . . . . . . . .1D 90
Goostrey. *Ches E* . . . . . . . . . . . .3B 84
Gorcott Hill. *Warw* . . . . . . . . . . . .4E 61
  nr. Evesham . . . . . . . . . . .2E 49
Gord. *Shet* . . . . . . . . . . . . . . . . .9F 173
Gordon. *Bord* . . . . . . . . . . . . . . .5C 130
Gordonbush. *High* . . . . . . . . . . .3F 165
Gordonstown. *Abers* . . . . . . . . . . . . .
  nr. Cornhill . . . . . . . . . . . . .3C 160
  nr. Fyvie . . . . . . . . . . . . . .5E 160
Gorebridge. *Midl* . . . . . . . . . . . .3G 129
Gorefield. *Cambs* . . . . . . . . . . . . .4D 76
Gores. *Wilts* . . . . . . . . . . . . . . . .1G 23
Gorgie. *Edin* . . . . . . . . . . . . . . .2F 129
Goring. *Oxon* . . . . . . . . . . . . . . . .3E 36
Goring-by-Sea. *W Sus* . . . . . . . .5C 26
Goring Heath. *Oxon* . . . . . . . . . .4E 37
Gorleston-on-Sea. *Norf* . . . . . . . .5H 79
Gornalwood. *W Mid* . . . . . . . . . .1D 60
Gorran Churchtown. *Corn* . . . . . . .4D 6
Gorran Haven. *Corn* . . . . . . . . . . .4E 6
Gorran High Lanes. *Corn* . . . . . . .4D 6
Gors. *Cdgn* . . . . . . . . . . . . . . . . .3F 57
Gorsedd. *Flin* . . . . . . . . . . . . . . . .3D 82
**Gorseinon.** *Swan* . . . . . . . . . . . .3E 31
Gorseness. *Orkn* . . . . . . . . . . . .6D 172
Gorseybank. *Derbs* . . . . . . . . . . .5G 85
Gorsgoch. *Cdgn* . . . . . . . . . . . . .5D 57
Gorslas. *Carm* . . . . . . . . . . . . . . .4F 45
Gorsley. *Glos* . . . . . . . . . . . . . . . .3B 48
Gorsley Common. *Here* . . . . . . . .3B 48
Gorstan. *High* . . . . . . . . . . . . . .2F 157
Gorstella. *Ches W* . . . . . . . . . . . .4F 83
Gorsty Common. *Here* . . . . . . . . .2H 47
Gorsty Hill. *Staf* . . . . . . . . . . . . . .3F 73
Gortantaoid. *Arg* . . . . . . . . . . . .2B 124
Gorteneorn. *High* . . . . . . . . . . . .2A 140
Gortenfern. *High* . . . . . . . . . . . .2A 140
Gorton. *G Man* . . . . . . . . . . . . . . .1C 84
Gosbeck. *Suff* . . . . . . . . . . . . . . .5D 66
Gosberton. *Linc* . . . . . . . . . . . . . .2B 76
Gosberton Cheal. *Linc* . . . . . . . . .3B 76
Gosberton Clough. *Linc* . . . . . . . .3A 76
Goseley Dale. *Derbs* . . . . . . . . . .3H 73
Gosfield. *Essx* . . . . . . . . . . . . . . .3A 54
Gosford. *Oxon* . . . . . . . . . . . . . . .4D 50
Gosforth. *Cumb* . . . . . . . . . . . . .4B 102
Gosforth. *Tyne* . . . . . . . . . . . . . .3F 115
Gosmore. *Herts* . . . . . . . . . . . . . .3B 52
Gospel End. *Staf* . . . . . . . . . . . . .1C 60
**Gosport.** *Hants* . . . . . . . . . . . . . .3E 16
Gossabrough. *Shet* . . . . . . . . . .3G 173
Gossington. *Glos* . . . . . . . . . . . . .5C 48
Gossops Green. *W Sus* . . . . . . . .2D 26
Goswick. *Nmbd* . . . . . . . . . . . . .5G 131
Gotham. *Notts* . . . . . . . . . . . . . . .2C 74
Gotherington. *Glos* . . . . . . . . . . . .3E 49
Gott. *Arg* . . . . . . . . . . . . . . . . . . .4B 138

Gott. *Shet* . . . . . . . . . . . . . . . . .7F 173
Goudhurst. *Kent* . . . . . . . . . . . . . .2B 28
Goulceby. *Linc* . . . . . . . . . . . . . . .3B 88
Goundon. *Abers* . . . . . . . . . . . . .1H 145
Gourock. *Inv* . . . . . . . . . . . . . . . .2D 126
Govan. *Glas* . . . . . . . . . . . . . . . .3G 127
Govanhill. *Glas* . . . . . . . . . . . . . .3G 127
Goverton. *Notts* . . . . . . . . . . . . . . .1E 74
Goveton. *Devn* . . . . . . . . . . . . . . . .4D 8
Govilon. *Mon* . . . . . . . . . . . . . . . .4F 47
Gowanhill. *Abers* . . . . . . . . . . . .2H 161
Gowdall. *E Yor* . . . . . . . . . . . . . . .2G 93
Gowerton. *Swan* . . . . . . . . . . . . . .3E 31
Gowkhall. *Fife* . . . . . . . . . . . . . . .1D 128
Gowthorpe. *E Yor* . . . . . . . . . . .4B 100
Goxhill. *E Yor* . . . . . . . . . . . . . . . .5F 101
Goxhill. *N Lin* . . . . . . . . . . . . . . . .2E 94
Goxhill Haven. *N Lin* . . . . . . . . . .2E 94
Goytre. *Neat* . . . . . . . . . . . . . . . . .3A 32
Grabhair. *W Isl* . . . . . . . . . . . . . .6F 171
Graby. *Linc* . . . . . . . . . . . . . . . . . .3H 75
Graffham. *W Sus* . . . . . . . . . . . . . .4A 26
Grafham. *Cambs* . . . . . . . . . . . . .4A 64
Grafham. *Surr* . . . . . . . . . . . . . . . .1B 26
Grafton. *Here* . . . . . . . . . . . . . . . .2H 47
Grafton. *N Yor* . . . . . . . . . . . . . . .3G 99
Grafton. *Oxon* . . . . . . . . . . . . . . .5A 50
Grafton. *Shrp* . . . . . . . . . . . . . . . .4G 71
Grafton. *Worc* . . . . . . . . . . . . . . . . . .
  nr. Evesham . . . . . . . . . . .2E 49
  nr. Leominster . . . . . . . . . .4H 59
Grafton Flyford. *Worc* . . . . . . . . .5D 60
Grafton Regis. *Nptn* . . . . . . . . . . .1F 51
Grafton Underwood. *Nptn* . . . . . .2G 63
Grafty Green. *Kent* . . . . . . . . . . . .1C 28
Graianrhyd. *Den* . . . . . . . . . . . . . .5E 82
Graig. *Carm* . . . . . . . . . . . . . . . . .5E 45
Graig. *Cnwy* . . . . . . . . . . . . . . . . .3H 81
Graig. *Den* . . . . . . . . . . . . . . . . . .3C 82
Graig-fechan. *Den* . . . . . . . . . . . .5D 82
Graig Penllyn. *V Glam* . . . . . . . . .4C 32
Grain. *Medw* . . . . . . . . . . . . . . . . .3C 40
Grainsby. *Linc* . . . . . . . . . . . . . . . .1B 88
Grainthorpe. *Linc* . . . . . . . . . . . . .1C 88
Grainthorpe Fen. *Linc* . . . . . . . . .1C 88
Graiselound. *N Lin* . . . . . . . . . . . .1E 87
Gramasdail. *W Isl* . . . . . . . . . . .3D 170
Grampound. *Corn* . . . . . . . . . . . . . .4D 6
Grampound Road. *Corn* . . . . . . . .3D 6
Granborough. *Buck* . . . . . . . . . . . .3F 51
Granby. *Notts* . . . . . . . . . . . . . . . .2E 75
Grandborough. *Warw* . . . . . . . . . .4B 62
Grandpont. *Oxon* . . . . . . . . . . . . .5D 50
Grandtully. *Per* . . . . . . . . . . . . . .3G 143
Grange. *Cumb* . . . . . . . . . . . . . .3D 102
Grange. *E Yor* . . . . . . . . . . . . . .1D 116
Grange. *Here* . . . . . . . . . . . . . . . .3G 59
Grange. *Mers* . . . . . . . . . . . . . . . .2E 82
The Grange. *N Yor* . . . . . . . . . . .1E 137
Grange. *Per* . . . . . . . . . . . . . . . .1E 136
**Grangemouth.** *Falk* . . . . . . . . . .1C 128
Grange of Lindores. *Fife* . . . . . .2E 137
Grange-over-Sands. *Cumb* . . . . .2D 96
Grangepans. *Falk* . . . . . . . . . . .1D 128
Grangetown. *Card* . . . . . . . . . . . . .4E 33
Grangetown. *Red C* . . . . . . . . . .2C 106
Grange Villa. *Dur* . . . . . . . . . . . .4F 115
Granish. *High* . . . . . . . . . . . . . . .2C 150
Gransmoor. *E Yor* . . . . . . . . . . . .4F 101
Granston. *Pemb* . . . . . . . . . . . . .1C 42
Grantchester. *Cambs* . . . . . . . . . .5D 64
**Grantham.** *Linc* . . . . . . . . . . . . .2G 75
Grantley. *N Yor* . . . . . . . . . . . . . .3E 99
Grantlodge. *Abers* . . . . . . . . . . .2E 152
Granton. *Edin* . . . . . . . . . . . . . .2F 129
Grantown-on-Spey. *High* . . . . . .1E 151
Grantshouse. *Bord* . . . . . . . . . .3E 130
Grappenhall. *Warr* . . . . . . . . . . . .2A 84
Grasby. *Linc* . . . . . . . . . . . . . . . . .4D 94
Grasmere. *Cumb* . . . . . . . . . . . .4E 103

Grasscroft. G Man . . . . . .4H 91
Grassendale. Mers . . . . . .2F 83
Grassgarth. Cumb . . . . . .5E 113
Grassholme. Dur . . . . . .2C 104
Grassington. N Yor . . . . . .3C 98
Grassmoor. Derbs . . . . . .4B 86
Grassthorpe. Notts . . . . . .4E 87
Grateley. Hants . . . . . .2A 24
Gratton. Devn . . . . . .1D 11
Gratton. Staf . . . . . .5D 84
Gratwich. Staf . . . . . .2E 73
Graveley. Cambs . . . . . .4B 64
Graveley. Herts . . . . . .3C 52
Gravelhill. Shrp . . . . . .4G 71
Gravel Hole. G Man . . . . . .4H 91
Gravelly Hill. W Mid . . . . . .1F 61
Graven. Shet . . . . . .4F 173
Graveney. Kent . . . . . .4E 41
Gravesend. Kent . . . . . .3H 39
Grayingham. Linc . . . . . .1G 87
Grayrigg. Cumb . . . . . .5G 103
Grays. Thur . . . . . .3H 39
Grayshott. Hants . . . . . .3G 25
Grayson Green. Cumb . . . . . .2A 102
Grayswood. Surr . . . . . .2A 26
Graythorp. Hart . . . . . .2C 106
Grazeley. Wok . . . . . .5E 37
Grealin. High . . . . . .2E 155
Greasbrough. S Yor . . . . . .1B 86
Greasby. Mers . . . . . .2E 83
Great Abington. Cambs . . . . . .1F 53
Great Addington. Nptn . . . . . .3G 63
Great Alne. Warw . . . . . .5F 61
Great Altcar. Lanc . . . . . .4B 90
Great Amwell. Herts . . . . . .4D 52
Great Asby. Cumb . . . . . .3H 103
Great Ashfield. Suff . . . . . .4B 66
Great Ayton. N Yor . . . . . .3C 106
Great Baddow. Essx . . . . . .5H 53
Great Bardfield. Essx . . . . . .2G 53
Great Barford. Bed . . . . . .5A 64
Great Barr. W Mid . . . . . .1E 61
Great Barrington. Glos . . . . . .4H 49
Great Barrow. Ches W . . . . . .4G 83
Great Barton. Suff . . . . . .4A 66
Great Barugh. N Yor . . . . . .2B 100
Great Bavington. Nmbd . . . . . .1C 114
Great Bealings. Suff . . . . . .1F 55
Great Bedwyn. Wilts . . . . . .5A 36
Great Bentley. Essx . . . . . .3E 54
Great Billing. Nptn . . . . . .4F 63
Great Bircham. Norf . . . . . .2G 77
Great Blakenham. Suff . . . . . .5D 66
Great Blencow. Cumb . . . . . .1F 103
Great Bolas. Telf . . . . . .3A 72
Great Bookham. Surr . . . . . .5C 38
Great Bosullow. Corn . . . . . .3B 4
Great Bourton. Oxon . . . . . .1C 50
Great Bowden. Leics . . . . . .2E 63
Great Bradley. Suff . . . . . .5F 65
Great Braxted. Essx . . . . . .4B 54
Great Bricett. Suff . . . . . .5C 66
Great Brickhill. Buck . . . . . .2H 51
Great Bridgeford. Staf . . . . . .3C 72
Great Brington. Nptn . . . . . .4D 62
Great Bromley. Essx . . . . . .3D 54
Great Broughton. Cumb . . . . . .1B 102
Great Broughton. N Yor . . . . . .4C 106
Great Budworth. Ches W . . . . . .3A 84
Great Burdon. Darl . . . . . .3A 106
Great Burstead. Essx . . . . . .1A 40
Great Busby. N Yor . . . . . .4C 106
Great Canfield. Essx . . . . . .4F 53
Great Carlton. Linc . . . . . .2D 88
Great Casterton. Rut . . . . . .5G 75
Great Chalfield. Wilts . . . . . .5D 34
Great Chart. Kent . . . . . .1D 28
Great Chatwell. Staf . . . . . .4B 72
Great Chesterford. Essx . . . . . .1F 53
Great Cheverell. Wilts . . . . . .1E 23
Great Chilton. Dur . . . . . .1F 105
Great Chishill. Cambs . . . . . .2E 53
Great Clacton. Essx . . . . . .4E 55
Great Cliff. W Yor . . . . . .3D 92

Great Clifton. Cumb . . . . . .2B 102
Great Coates. NE Lin . . . . . .3F 95
Great Comberton. Worc . . . . . .1E 49
Great Corby. Cumb . . . . . .4F 113
Great Cornard. Suff . . . . . .1B 54
Great Cowden. E Yor . . . . . .5G 101
Great Coxwell. Oxon . . . . . .2A 36
Great Crakehall. N Yor . . . . . .5F 105
Great Cransley. Nptn . . . . . .3F 63
Great Cressingham. Norf . . . . . .5A 78
Great Crosby. Mers . . . . . .4B 90
Great Cubley. Derbs . . . . . .2F 73
Great Dalby. Leics . . . . . .4E 75
Great Doddington. Nptn . . . . . .4F 63
Great Doward. Here . . . . . .4A 48
Great Dunham. Norf . . . . . .4A 78
Great Dunmow. Essx . . . . . .3G 53
Great Durnford. Wilts . . . . . .3G 23
Great Easton. Essx . . . . . .3G 53
Great Easton. Leics . . . . . .1F 63
Great Eccleston. Lanc . . . . . .5D 96
Great Edstone. N Yor . . . . . .1B 100
Great Ellingham. Norf . . . . . .1C 66
Great Elm. Som . . . . . .2C 22
Great Eppleton. Tyne . . . . . .5G 115
Great Eversden. Cambs . . . . . .5C 64
Great Fencote. N Yor . . . . . .5F 105
Great Finborough. Suff . . . . . .5C 66
Greatford. Linc . . . . . .4H 75
Great Fransham. Norf . . . . . .4A 78
Great Gaddesden. Herts . . . . . .4A 52
Great Gate. Staf . . . . . .1E 73
Great Gidding. Cambs . . . . . .2A 64
Great Givendale. E Yor . . . . . .4C 100
Great Glemham. Suff . . . . . .4F 67
Great Glen. Leics . . . . . .1D 62
Great Gonerby. Linc . . . . . .2F 75
Great Gransden. Cambs . . . . . .5B 64
Great Green. Norf . . . . . .2E 67
Great Green. Suff
    nr. Lavenham . . . . . .5B 66
    nr. Palgrave . . . . . .3D 66
Great Habton. N Yor . . . . . .2B 100
Great Hale. Linc . . . . . .1A 76
Great Hallingbury. Essx . . . . . .4F 53
Greatham. Hants . . . . . .3F 25
Greatham. Hart . . . . . .2B 106
Greatham. W Sus . . . . . .4B 26
Great Hampden. Buck . . . . . .5G 51
Great Harrowden. Nptn . . . . . .3F 63
Great Harwood. Lanc . . . . . .1F 91
Great Haseley. Oxon . . . . . .5E 51
Great Hatfield. E Yor . . . . . .5F 101
Great Haywood. Staf . . . . . .3D 73
Great Heath. W Mid . . . . . .2H 61
Great Heck. N Yor . . . . . .2F 93
Great Henny. Essx . . . . . .2B 54
Great Hinton. Wilts . . . . . .1E 23
Great Hockham. Norf . . . . . .1B 66
Great Holland. Essx . . . . . .4F 55
Great Horkesley. Essx . . . . . .2C 54
Great Hormead. Herts . . . . . .3E 53
Great Horton. W Yor . . . . . .1B 92
Great Horwood. Buck . . . . . .2F 51
Great Houghton. Nptn . . . . . .5E 63
Great Houghton. S Yor . . . . . .4E 93
Great Hucklow. Derbs . . . . . .3F 85
Great Kelk. E Yor . . . . . .4F 101
Great Kendale. E Yor . . . . . .3E 101
Great Kimble. Buck . . . . . .5G 51
Great Kingshill. Buck . . . . . .2G 37
Great Langdale. Cumb . . . . . .4D 102
Great Langton. N Yor . . . . . .5F 105
Great Leighs. Essx . . . . . .4H 53
Great Limber. Linc . . . . . .4E 95
Great Linford. Mil . . . . . .1G 51
Great Livermere. Suff . . . . . .3A 66
Great Longstone. Derbs . . . . . .3G 85
Great Lumley. Dur . . . . . .5F 115
Great Lyth. Shrp . . . . . .5G 71
Great Malvern. Worc . . . . . .1C 48
Great Maplestead. Essx . . . . . .2B 54
Great Marton. Bkpl . . . . . .1B 90
Great Massingham. Norf . . . . . .3G 77

Great Melton. Norf . . . . . .5D 78
Great Milton. Oxon . . . . . .5E 51
Great Missenden. Buck . . . . . .5G 51
Great Mitton. Lanc . . . . . .1F 91
Great Mongeham. Kent . . . . . .5H 41
Great Moulton. Norf . . . . . .1D 66
Great Munden. Herts . . . . . .3D 52
Great Musgrave. Cumb . . . . . .3A 104
Great Ness. Shrp . . . . . .4F 71
Great Notley. Essx . . . . . .3H 53
Great Oak. Mon . . . . . .5G 47
Great Oakley. Essx . . . . . .3E 55
Great Oakley. Nptn . . . . . .2F 63
Great Offley. Herts . . . . . .3B 52
Great Ormside. Cumb . . . . . .3A 104
Great Orton. Cumb . . . . . .4E 113
Great Ouseburn. N Yor . . . . . .3G 99
Great Oxendon. Nptn . . . . . .2E 63
Great Oxney Green. Essx . . . . . .5G 53
Great Parndon. Essx . . . . . .5E 53
Great Paxton. Cambs . . . . . .4B 64
Great Plumpton. Lanc . . . . . .1B 90
Great Plumstead. Norf . . . . . .4F 79
Great Ponton. Linc . . . . . .2G 75
Great Potheridge. Devn . . . . . .1F 11
Great Preston. W Yor . . . . . .2E 93
Great Raveley. Cambs . . . . . .2B 64
Great Rissington. Glos . . . . . .4G 49
Great Rollright. Oxon . . . . . .2B 50
Great Ryburgh. Norf . . . . . .3B 78
Great Ryle. Nmbd . . . . . .3E 121
Great Ryton. Shrp . . . . . .5G 71
Great Saling. Essx . . . . . .3H 53
Great Salkeld. Cumb . . . . . .1G 103
Great Sampford. Essx . . . . . .2G 53
Great Sankey. Warr . . . . . .2H 83
Great Saredon. Staf . . . . . .5D 72
Great Saxham. Suff . . . . . .4G 65
Great Shefford. W Ber . . . . . .4B 36
Great Shelford. Cambs . . . . . .5D 64
Great Shoddesden. Hants . . . . . .2A 24
Great Smeaton. N Yor . . . . . .4A 106
Great Snoring. Norf . . . . . .2B 78
Great Somerford. Wilts . . . . . .3E 35
Great Stainton. Darl . . . . . .2A 106
Great Stambridge. Essx . . . . . .1C 40
Great Staughton. Cambs . . . . . .4A 64
Great Steeping. Linc . . . . . .4D 88
Great Stonar. Kent . . . . . .5H 41
Greatstone-on-Sea. Kent . . . . . .3E 29
Great Strickland. Cumb . . . . . .2G 103
Great Stukeley. Cambs . . . . . .3B 64
Great Sturton. Linc . . . . . .3B 88
Great Sutton. Ches W . . . . . .3F 83
Great Sutton. Shrp . . . . . .2H 59
Great Swinburne. Nmbd . . . . . .2C 114
Great Tew. Oxon . . . . . .3B 50
Great Tey. Essx . . . . . .3B 54
Great Thirkleby. N Yor . . . . . .2G 99
Great Thorness. IOW . . . . . .3C 16
Great Thurlow. Suff . . . . . .5F 65
Great Torr. Devn . . . . . .4C 8
Great Torrington. Devn . . . . . .1E 11
Great Tosson. Nmbd . . . . . .4E 121
Great Totham North. Essx . . . . . .4B 54
Great Totham South. Essx . . . . . .4B 54
Great Tows. Linc . . . . . .1B 88
Great Urswick. Cumb . . . . . .2B 96
Great Wakering. Essx . . . . . .2D 40
Great Waldingfield. Suff . . . . . .1C 54
Great Walsingham. Norf . . . . . .2B 78
Great Waltham. Essx . . . . . .4G 53
Great Warley. Essx . . . . . .1G 39
Great Washbourne. Glos . . . . . .2E 49
Great Wenham. Suff . . . . . .2D 54
Great Whelnetham. Suff . . . . . .5A 66
Great Whittington. Nmbd . . . . . .2D 114
Great Wigborough. Essx . . . . . .4C 54
Great Wilbraham. Cambs . . . . . .5E 65
Great Wilne. Derbs . . . . . .2B 74
Great Wishford. Wilts . . . . . .3F 23
Great Witchingham. Norf . . . . . .3D 78
Great Witcombe. Glos . . . . . .4E 49
Great Witley. Worc . . . . . .4B 60

Great Wolford. Warw . . . . . .2H 49
Greatworth. Nptn . . . . . .1D 50
Great Wratting. Suff . . . . . .1G 53
Great Wymondley. Herts . . . . . .3C 52
Great Wyrley. Staf . . . . . .5D 73
Great Wytheford. Shrp . . . . . .4H 71
Great Yarmouth. Norf . . . . . .5H 79
Great Yeldham. Essx . . . . . .2A 54
Grebby. Linc . . . . . .4D 88
Greeba Castle. IOM . . . . . .3C 108
The Green. Cumb . . . . . .1A 96
The Green. Wilts . . . . . .3D 22
Greenbank. Shet . . . . . .1G 173
Greenbottom. Corn . . . . . .4B 6
Greenburn. W Lot . . . . . .3C 128
Greencroft. Dur . . . . . .4E 115
Greendown. Som . . . . . .1A 22
Greendykes. Nmbd . . . . . .2E 121
Green End. Bed
    nr. Bedford . . . . . .1A 52
    nr. Little Staughton . . . . . .4A 64
Green End. Herts
    nr. Buntingford . . . . . .2D 52
    nr. Stevenage . . . . . .3D 52
Green End. N Yor . . . . . .4F 107
Green End. Warw . . . . . .2G 61
Greenfield. Arg . . . . . .4B 134
Greenfield. C Beds . . . . . .2A 52
Greenfield. Flin . . . . . .3D 82
Greenfield. G Man . . . . . .4H 91
Greenfield. Oxon . . . . . .2F 37
Greenfoot. N Lan . . . . . .3A 128
Greenford. G Lon . . . . . .2C 38
Greengairs. N Lan . . . . . .2A 128
Greengate. Norf . . . . . .4C 78
Greengill. Cumb . . . . . .1C 102
Greenhalgh. Lanc . . . . . .1C 90
Greenham. Dors . . . . . .2H 13
Greenham. Som . . . . . .4D 20
Greenham. W Ber . . . . . .5C 36
Green Hammerton. N Yor . . . . . .4G 99
Greenhaugh. Nmbd . . . . . .1A 114
Greenhead. Nmbd . . . . . .3H 113
Green Heath. Staf . . . . . .4D 73
Greenhill. Dum . . . . . .2C 112
Greenhill. Falk . . . . . .2B 128
Greenhill. Kent . . . . . .4F 41
Greenhill. S Yor . . . . . .2H 85
Greenhill. Worc . . . . . .3C 60
Greenhithe. Kent . . . . . .3G 39
Greenholm. E Ayr . . . . . .1E 117
Greenhow Hill. N Yor . . . . . .3D 98
Greenigoe. Orkn . . . . . .7D 172
Greenland. High . . . . . .2E 169
Greenland Mains. High . . . . . .2E 169
Greenlands. Worc . . . . . .4E 61
Green Lane. Shrp . . . . . .3A 72
Green Lane. Worc . . . . . .4E 61
Greenlaw. Bord . . . . . .5D 130
Greenlea. Dum . . . . . .2B 112
Greenloaning. Per . . . . . .3H 135
Greenmount. G Man . . . . . .3F 91
Greenmow. Shet . . . . . .9F 173
Greenock. Inv . . . . . .2D 126
Greenock Mains. E Ayr . . . . . .2F 117
Greenodd. Cumb . . . . . .1C 96
Green Ore. Som . . . . . .1A 22
Greenrow. Cumb . . . . . .4C 112
Greens. Abers . . . . . .4F 161
Greensgate. Norf . . . . . .4D 78
Greenside. Tyne . . . . . .3E 115
Greensidehill. Nmbd . . . . . .3D 121
Greens Norton. Nptn . . . . . .1E 51
Greenstead Green. Essx . . . . . .3B 54
Greensted Green. Essx . . . . . .5F 53
Green Street. Herts . . . . . .1C 38
Green Street. Suff . . . . . .3D 66
Green Street Green. G Lon . . . . . .4F 39
Green Street Green. Kent . . . . . .3G 39
Greenstreet Green. Suff . . . . . .1D 54
Green Tye. Herts . . . . . .4E 53
Greenwall. Orkn . . . . . .7E 172
Greenway. Pemb . . . . . .1E 43

Greenway. V Glam . . . . . .4D 32
Greenwell. Cumb . . . . . .4G 113
Greenwich. G Lon . . . . . .3E 39
Greet. Glos . . . . . .2F 49
Greete. Shrp . . . . . .3H 59
Greetham. Linc . . . . . .3C 88
Greetham. Rut . . . . . .4G 75
Greetland. W Yor . . . . . .2A 92
Gregson Lane. Lanc . . . . . .2D 90
Grein. W Isl . . . . . .8B 170
Greinetobht. W Isl . . . . . .1D 170
Greinton. Som . . . . . .3H 21
Gremista. Shet . . . . . .7F 173
Grenaby. IOM . . . . . .4B 108
Grendon. Nptn . . . . . .4F 63
Grendon. Warw . . . . . .1G 61
Grendon Common. Warw . . . . . .1G 61
Grendon Green. Here . . . . . .5H 59
Grendon Underwood. Buck . . . . . .3E 51
Grenofen. Devn . . . . . .5E 11
Grenoside. S Yor . . . . . .1H 85
Greosabhagh. W Isl . . . . . .8D 171
Gresford. Wrex . . . . . .5F 83
Gresham. Norf . . . . . .2D 78
Greshornish. High . . . . . .3C 154
Gressenhall. Norf . . . . . .4B 78
Gressingham. Lanc . . . . . .3E 97
Greta Bridge. Dur . . . . . .3D 105
Gretna. Dum . . . . . .3E 112
Gretna Green. Dum . . . . . .3E 112
Gretton. Glos . . . . . .2F 49
Gretton. Nptn . . . . . .1G 63
Gretton. Shrp . . . . . .1H 59
Grewelthorpe. N Yor . . . . . .2E 99
Greyabbey. Ards . . . . . .4J 175
Greygarth. N Yor . . . . . .2D 98
Grey Green. N Lin . . . . . .4A 94
Greylake. Som . . . . . .3G 21
Greysouthen. Cumb . . . . . .2B 102
Greysteel. Caus . . . . . .1D 174
Greystoke. Cumb . . . . . .1F 103
Greystoke Gill. Cumb . . . . . .2F 103
Greystone. Ang . . . . . .4E 145
Greystones. S Yor . . . . . .2H 85
Greywell. Hants . . . . . .1F 25
Griais. W Isl . . . . . .3G 171
Grianan. W Isl . . . . . .4G 171
Gribthorpe. E Yor . . . . . .1A 94
Gribun. Arg . . . . . .5F 139
Griff. Warw . . . . . .2A 62
Griffithstown. Torf . . . . . .2F 33
Griffydam. Leics . . . . . .4B 74
Griggs Green. Hants . . . . . .3G 25
Grimbister. Orkn . . . . . .6C 172
Grimeford Village. Lanc . . . . . .3E 90
Grimeston. Orkn . . . . . .6C 172
Grimethorpe. S Yor . . . . . .4E 93
Griminis. W Isl
    on Benbecula . . . . . .3C 170
    on North Uist . . . . . .1C 170
Grimister. Shet . . . . . .2F 173
Grimley. Worc . . . . . .4C 60
Grimness. Orkn . . . . . .8D 172
Grimoldby. Linc . . . . . .2C 88
Grimpo. Shrp . . . . . .3F 71
Grimsargh. Lanc . . . . . .1D 90
Grimsbury. Oxon . . . . . .1C 50
Grimsby. NE Lin . . . . . .4F 95
Grimscote. Nptn . . . . . .5D 62
Grimscott. Corn . . . . . .2C 10
Grimshaw. Bkbn . . . . . .2F 91
Grimshaw Green. Lanc . . . . . .3C 90
Grimsthorpe. Linc . . . . . .3H 75
Grimston. E Yor . . . . . .1F 95
Grimston. Leics . . . . . .3D 74
Grimston. Norf . . . . . .3B 114
Grimston. York . . . . . .4A 100
Grimstone. Dors . . . . . .3B 14
Grimstone End. Suff . . . . . .4B 66
Grinacombe Moor. Devn . . . . . .3E 11
Grindale. E Yor . . . . . .2F 101
Grindhill. Devn . . . . . .3E 11
Grindiscol. Shet . . . . . .8F 173
Grindle. Shrp . . . . . .5B 72

Grindleford—Hamstall Ridware


Grindleford. *Derbs* 3G **85**
Grindleton. *Lanc* 5G **97**
Grindley. *Staf* 3E **73**
Grindley Brook. *Shrp* 1H **71**
Grindlow. *Derbs* 3F **85**
Grindon. *Nmbd* 5F **131**
Grindon. *Staf* 5E **85**
Gringley on the Hill. *Notts* 1E **87**
Grinsdale. *Cumb* 4E **113**
Grinshill. *Shrp* 3H **71**
Grinton. *N Yor* 5D **104**
Griomsidar. *W Isl* 5G **171**
Grishipoll. *Arg* 3C **138**
Grisling Common. *E Sus* 3F **27**
Gristhorpe. *N Yor* 1E **101**
Griston. *Norf* 1B **66**
Gritley. *Orkn* 7E **172**
Grittenham. *Wilts* 3F **35**
Grittleton. *Wilts* 3D **34**
Grizebeck. *Cumb* 1B **96**
Grizedale. *Cumb* 5E **103**
Grobister. *Orkn* 5F **172**
Grobsness. *Shet* 5E **173**
Groby. *Leics* 5C **74**
Groes. *Cnwy* 4C **82**
Groes. *Neat* 3A **32**
Groes-faen. *Rhon* 3D **32**
Groesffordd. *Gwyn* 2B **68**
Groesffordd. *Powy* 3D **46**
Groeslon. *Gwyn* 5D **81**
Groes-lwyd. *Powy* 4E **70**
Groes-wen. *Cphy* 3E **33**
Grogport. *Arg* 5G **125**
Groigearraidh. *W Isl* 4C **170**
Gromford. *Suff* 5F **67**
Gronant. *Flin* 2C **82**
Groombridge. *E Sus* 2G **27**
Grosmont. *Mon* 3H **47**
Grosmont. *N Yor* 4F **107**
Groton. *Suff* 1C **54**
Grove. *Dors* 5B **14**
Grove. *Kent* 4G **41**
Grove. *Notts* 3E **87**
Grove. *Oxon* 2B **36**
The Grove. *Dum* 2A **112**
The Grove. *Worc* 1D **48**
Grovehill. *E Yor* 1D **94**
Grove Park. *G Lon* 3F **39**
Grovesend. *Swan* 5F **45**
Grub Street. *Staf* 3B **72**
Grudie. *High* 2F **157**
Gruids. *High* 3C **164**
Gruinard House. *High* 4D **162**
Gruinart. *Arg* 3A **124**
Grulinbeg. *Arg* 3A **124**
Gruline. *Arg* 4G **139**
Grummore. *High* 5G **167**
Grundisburgh. *Suff* 5E **66**
Gruting. *Shet* 7D **173**
Grutness. *Shet* 10F **173**
Gualachulain. *High* 4F **141**
Gualin House. *High* 3D **166**
Guardbridge. *Fife* 2G **137**
Guarlford. *Worc* 1D **48**
Guay. *Per* 4H **143**
Gubblecote. *Herts* 4H **51**
Guestling Green. *E Sus* 4C **28**
Guestling Thorn. *E Sus* 4C **28**
Guestwick. *Norf* 3C **78**
Guestwick Green. *Norf* 3C **78**
Guide. *Bkbn* 2F **91**
Guide Post. *Nmbd* 1F **115**
Guilden Down. *Shrp* 2F **59**
Guilden Morden. *Cambs* 1C **52**
Guilden Sutton. *Ches W* 4G **83**
**Guildford**. *Surr* 1A **26**
Guildtown. *Per* 5A **144**
Guilsborough. *Nptn* 3D **62**
Guilsfield. *Powy* 4E **70**
Guineaford. *Devn* 3F **19**
**Guisborough**. *Red C* 3D **106**
Guiseley. *W Yor* 5D **98**
Guist. *Norf* 3B **78**
Guiting Power. *Glos* 3F **49**
Gulberwick. *Shet* 8F **173**
Gullane. *E Lot* 1A **130**
Gulling Green. *Suff* 5H **65**
Gulval. *Corn* 3B **4**
Gulworthy. *Devn* 5E **11**
Gumfreston. *Pemb* 4F **43**
Gumley. *Leics* 1D **62**
Gunby. *E Yor* 1H **93**
Gunby. *Linc* 3G **75**
Gundleton. *Hants* 3E **24**
Gun Green. *Kent* 2B **28**
Gun Hill. *E Sus* 4G **27**
Gunn. *Devn* 3G **19**
Gunnerside. *N Yor* 5C **104**
Gunnerton. *Nmbd* 2C **114**
Gunness. *N Lin* 3B **94**
Gunnislake. *Corn* 5E **11**
Gunnista. *Shet* 7F **173**
Gunsgreenhill. *Bord* 3F **131**
Gunstone. *Staf* 5C **72**
Gunthorpe. *Norf* 2C **78**
Gunthorpe. *N Lin* 1F **87**
Gunthorpe. *Notts* 1D **74**
Gunthorpe. *Pet* 5A **76**
Gunville. *IOW* 4C **16**
Gupworthy. *Som* 3C **20**
Gurnard. *IOW* 3C **16**
Gurney Slade. *Som* 2B **22**
Gurnos. *Powy* 5A **46**
Gussage All Saints. *Dors* 1F **15**
Gussage St Andrew. *Dors* 1E **15**
Gussage St Michael. *Dors* 1E **15**
Guston. *Kent* 1H **29**
Gutcher. *Shet* 2G **173**
Guthram Gowt. *Linc* 3A **76**
Guthrie. *Ang* 3E **145**
Guyhirn. *Cambs* 5D **76**
Guyhirn Gull. *Cambs* 5C **76**
Guy's Head. *Linc* 3D **77**
Guy's Marsh. *Dors* 4D **22**
Guyzance. *Nmbd* 4G **121**
Gwaelod-y-garth. *Card* 3E **32**
Gwaenynog Bach. *Den* 4C **82**
Gwaenysgor. *Flin* 2C **82**
Gwalchmai. *IOA* 3C **80**
Gwastad. *Pemb* 2E **43**
Gwaun-Cae-Gurwen. *Neat* 4H **45**
Gwbert. *Cdgn* 1B **44**
Gweek. *Corn* 4E **5**
Gwehelog. *Mon* 5G **47**
Gwenddwr. *Powy* 1D **46**
Gwennap. *Corn* 4B **6**
Gwenter. *Corn* 5E **5**
Gwernaffield. *Flin* 4E **82**
Gwernesney. *Mon* 5H **47**
Gwernogle. *Carm* 2F **45**
Gwern-y-go. *Powy* 1E **58**
Gwernymynydd. *Flin* 4E **82**
Gwersyllt. *Wrex* 5F **83**
Gwespyr. *Flin* 2D **82**
Gwinear. *Corn* 3C **4**
Gwithian. *Corn* 2C **4**
Gwredog. *IOA* 2D **80**
Gwyddelwern. *Den* 1C **70**
Gwyddgrug. *Carm* 2E **45**
Gwynfryn. *Wrex* 5E **83**
Gwystre. *Powy* 4C **58**
Gwytherin. *Cnwy* 4A **82**
Gyfelia. *Wrex* 1F **71**
Gyffin. *Cnwy* 3G **81**


## H


Haa of Houlland. *Shet* 1G **173**
Habberley. *Shrp* 5G **71**
Habblesthorpe. *Notts* 2E **87**
Habergham. *Lanc* 1G **91**
Habin. *W Sus* 4G **25**
Habrough. *NE Lin* 3E **95**
Haceby. *Linc* 2H **75**
Hacheston. *Suff* 5F **67**
Hackenthorpe. *S Yor* 2B **86**
Hackford. *Norf* 5C **78**
Hackforth. *N Yor* 5F **105**
Hackland. *Orkn* 5C **172**
Hackleton. *Nptn* 5F **63**
Hackman's Gate. *Worc* 3C **60**
Hackness. *N Yor* 5G **107**
Hackness. *Orkn* 8C **172**
**Hackney**. *G Lon* 2E **39**
Hackthorn. *Linc* 2G **87**
Hackthorpe. *Cumb* 2G **103**
Haclait. *W Isl* 4D **170**
Haconby. *Linc* 3A **76**
Hadden. *Bord* 1B **120**
Haddenham. *Buck* 5F **51**
Haddenham. *Cambs* 3D **64**
Haddenham End Field. *Cambs* 3D **64**
Haddington. *E Lot* 2B **130**
Haddington. *Linc* 4G **87**
Haddiscoe. *Norf* 1G **67**
Haddo. *Abers* 5F **161**
Haddon. *Cambs* 1A **64**
Hademore. *Staf* 5F **73**
Hadfield. *Derbs* 1E **85**
Hadham Cross. *Herts* 4E **53**
Hadham Ford. *Herts* 3E **53**
Hadleigh. *Essx* 2C **40**
Hadleigh. *Suff* 1D **54**
Hadleigh Heath. *Suff* 1C **54**
Hadley. *Telf* 4A **72**
Hadley. *Worc* 4C **60**
Hadley End. *Staf* 3F **73**
Hadley Wood. *G Lon* 1D **38**
Hadlow. *Kent* 1H **27**
Hadlow Down. *E Sus* 3G **27**
Hadnall. *Shrp* 3H **71**
Hadstock. *Essx* 1F **53**
Hadston. *Nmbd* 4G **121**
Hady. *Derbs* 3A **86**
Hadzor. *Worc* 4D **60**
Haffenden Quarter. *Kent* 1C **28**
Haggate. *Lanc* 1G **91**
Haggbeck. *Cumb* 2F **113**
Haggersta. *Shet* 7E **173**
Haggerston. *Nmbd* 5G **131**
Haggrister. *Shet* 4E **173**
Hagley. *Here* 1A **48**
Hagley. *Worc* 2D **60**
Hagnaby. *Linc* 4C **88**
Hagworthingham. *Linc* 4C **88**
Haigh. *G Man* 4E **90**
Haigh Moor. *W Yor* 2C **92**
Haighton Green. *Lanc* 1D **90**
Haile. *Cumb* 4B **102**
Hailes. *Glos* 2F **49**
Hailey. *Herts* 4D **52**
Hailey. *Oxon* 4B **50**
**Hailsham**. *E Sus* 5G **27**
Hail Weston. *Cambs* 4A **64**
Hainault. *G Lon* 1F **39**
Hainford. *Norf* 4E **78**
Hainton. *Linc* 2A **88**
Hainworth. *W Yor* 1A **92**
Haisthorpe. *E Yor* 3F **101**
Hakin. *Pemb* 4C **42**
Halam. *Notts* 5D **86**
Halbeath. *Fife* 1E **129**
Halberton. *Devn* 1D **12**
Halcro. *High* 2E **169**
Hale. *Cumb* 2E **97**
**Hale**. *G Man* 2B **84**
Hale. *Hal* 2G **83**
Hale. *Hants* 1G **15**
Hale. *Surr* 2G **25**
Hale Bank. *Hal* 2G **83**
Halebarns. *G Man* 2B **84**
Hales. *Norf* 1F **67**
Hales. *Staf* 2B **72**
Halesgate. *Linc* 3C **76**
Hales Green. *Derbs* 1F **73**
**Halesowen**. *W Mid* 2D **60**
Hale Street. *Kent* 1A **28**
Halesworth. *Suff* 3F **67**
Halewood. *Mers* 2G **83**
Halford. *Shrp* 2G **59**
Halford. *Warw* 1A **50**
Halfpenny. *Cumb* 1E **97**
Halfpenny Furze. *Carm* 3G **43**
Halfpenny Green. *Staf* 1C **60**
Halfway. *Carm*
  nr. Llandeilo 2G **45**
  nr. Llandovery 2B **46**
Halfway. *S Yor* 2B **86**
Halfway. *W Ber* 5C **36**
Halfway House. *Shrp* 4F **71**
Halfway Houses. *Kent* 3D **40**
Halgabron. *Corn* 4A **10**
**Halifax**. *W Yor* 2A **92**
Halistra. *High* 3B **154**
Halket. *E Ayr* 4F **127**
Halkirk. *High* 3D **168**
Halkyn. *Flin* 3E **82**
Hall. *E Ren* 4F **127**
Hallam Fields. *Derbs* 1B **74**
Halland. *E Sus* 4G **27**
The Hallands. *N Lin* 2D **94**
Hallaton. *Leics* 1E **63**
Hallatrow. *Bath* 1B **22**
Hallbank. *Cumb* 5H **103**
Hallbankgate. *Cumb* 4G **113**
Hall Dunnerdale. *Cumb* 5D **102**
Hallen. *S Glo* 3A **34**
Hall End. *Bed* 1A **52**
Hallgarth. *Dur* 5G **115**
Hall Green. *Ches E* 5C **84**
Hall Green. *Norf* 2D **66**
Hall Green. *W Mid* 2F **61**
Hall Green. *W Yor* 3D **92**
Hall Green. *Wrex* 1G **71**
Halliburton. *Bord* 5C **130**
Hallin. *High* 3B **154**
Halling. *Medw* 4B **40**
Hallington. *Linc* 2C **88**
Hallington. *Nmbd* 2C **114**
Halloughton. *Notts* 5D **86**
Hallow. *Worc* 5C **60**
Hallow Heath. *Worc* 5C **60**
Hallowsgate. *Ches W* 4H **83**
Hallsands. *Devn* 5E **9**
Hall's Green. *Herts* 3C **52**
Hallspill. *Devn* 4E **19**
Hallthwaites. *Cumb* 1A **96**
Hall Waberthwaite. *Cumb* 5C **102**
Hallwood Green. *Glos* 2B **48**
Hallworthy. *Corn* 4B **10**
Hallyne. *Bord* 5E **129**
Halmer End. *Staf* 1C **72**
Halmond's Frome. *Here* 1B **48**
Halmore. *Glos* 5B **48**
Halnaker. *W Sus* 5A **26**
Halsall. *Lanc* 3B **90**
Halse. *Nptn* 1D **50**
Halse. *Som* 4E **21**
Halsetown. *Corn* 3C **4**
Halsham. *E Yor* 2F **95**
Halsinger. *Devn* 3F **19**
**Halstead**. *Essx* 2B **54**
Halstead. *Kent* 4F **39**
Halstead. *Leics* 5E **75**
Halstock. *Dors* 2A **14**
Halsway. *Som* 3E **21**
Haltcliff Bridge. *Cumb* 1E **103**
Haltham. *Linc* 4B **88**
Haltoft End. *Linc* 1C **76**
Halton. *Buck* 5G **51**
Halton. *Hal* 2H **83**
Halton. *Lanc* 3E **97**
Halton. *Nmbd* 3C **114**
Halton. *W Yor* 1D **92**
Halton. *Wrex* 2F **71**
Halton East. *N Yor* 4C **98**
Halton Fenside. *Linc* 4D **88**
Halton Gill. *N Yor* 2A **98**
Halton Holegate. *Linc* 4D **88**
Halton Lea Gate. *Nmbd* 4H **113**
Halton Moor. *W Yor* 1D **92**
Halton Shields. *Nmbd* 3D **114**
Halton West. *N Yor* 4H **97**
Haltwhistle. *Nmbd* 3A **114**
Halvergate. *Norf* 5G **79**
Halwell. *Devn* 3D **9**
Halwill. *Devn* 3E **11**
Halwill Junction. *Devn* 3E **11**
Ham. *Devn* 2F **13**
Ham. *Glos* 2B **34**
Ham. *G Lon* 3C **38**
Ham. *High* 1E **169**
Ham. *Kent* 5H **41**
Ham. *Plym* 3A **8**
Ham. *Shet* 8A **173**
Ham. *Som*
  nr. Ilminster 1F **13**
  nr. Taunton 4F **21**
  nr. Wellington 4E **21**
Ham. *Wilts* 5B **36**
Hambleden. *Buck* 3F **37**
Hambledon. *Hants* 1E **17**
Hambledon. *Surr* 2A **26**
Hamble-le-Rice. *Hants* 2C **16**
Hambleton. *Lanc* 5C **96**
Hambleton. *N Yor* 1F **93**
Hambridge. *Som* 4G **21**
Hambrook. *S Glo* 4B **34**
Hambrook. *W Sus* 2F **17**
Ham Common. *Dors* 4D **22**
Hameringham. *Linc* 4C **88**
Hamerton. *Cambs* 3A **64**
Ham Green. *Here* 1C **48**
Ham Green. *Kent* 4C **40**
Ham Green. *N Som* 4A **34**
Ham Green. *Worc* 4E **61**
Ham Hill. *Kent* 4A **40**
Hamilton. *Leic* 5D **74**
**Hamilton**. *S Lan* 4A **128**
Hamister. *Shet* 5G **173**
Hammer. *W Sus* 3G **25**
**Hammersmith**. *G Lon* 3D **38**
Hammerwich. *Staf* 5E **73**
Hammerwood. *E Sus* 2F **27**
Hammill. *Kent* 5G **41**
Hammond Street. *Herts* 5D **52**
Hammoon. *Dors* 1D **14**
Hamnavoe. *Shet*
  nr. Braehoulland 3D **173**
  nr. Burland 8E **173**
  nr. Lunna 4F **173**
  on Yell 3F **173**
Hamp. *Som* 3G **21**
Hampden Park. *E Sus* 5G **27**
Hampen. *Glos* 4F **49**
Hamperden End. *Essx* 2F **53**
Hamperley. *Shrp* 2G **59**
Hampnett. *Glos* 4F **49**
Hampole. *S Yor* 3F **93**
Hampreston. *Dors* 3F **15**
**Hampstead**. *G Lon* 2D **38**
Hampstead Norreys. *W Ber* 4D **36**
Hampsthwaite. *N Yor* 4E **99**
Hampton. *Devn* 3F **13**
Hampton. *G Lon* 3C **38**
Hampton. *Kent* 4F **41**
Hampton. *Shrp* 2B **60**
Hampton. *Swin* 2G **35**
Hampton. *Worc* 1F **49**
Hampton Bishop. *Here* 2A **48**
Hampton Fields. *Glos* 2D **35**
Hampton Hargate. *Pet* 1A **64**
Hampton Heath. *Ches W* 1H **71**
Hampton in Arden. *W Mid* 2G **61**
Hampton Loade. *Shrp* 2B **60**
Hampton Lovett. *Worc* 4C **60**
Hampton Lucy. *Warw* 5G **61**
Hampton Magna. *Warw* 4G **61**
Hampton on the Hill. *Warw* 4G **61**
Hampton Poyle. *Oxon* 4D **50**
Hampton Wick. *G Lon* 4C **38**
Hamptworth. *Wilts* 1H **15**
Hamrow. *Norf* 3B **78**
Hamsey. *E Sus* 4F **27**
Hamsey Green. *Surr* 5E **39**
Hamstall Ridware. *Staf* 4F **73**

Hamstead—Hawkshead

Hamstead. IOW 3C 16
Hamstead. W Mid 1E 61
Hamstead Marshall. W Ber 5C 36
Hamsterley. Dur
nr. Consett 4E 115
nr. Wolsingham 1E 105
Hamsterley Mill. Dur 4E 115
Ham Street. Som 3A 22
Hamstreet. Kent 2E 28
Hamworthy. Pool 3E 15
Hanbury. Staf 3F 73
Hanbury. Worc 4D 60
Hanbury Woodend. Staf 3F 73
Hanby. Linc 2H 75
Hanchurch. Staf 1C 72
Hand and Pen. Devn 3D 12
Handbridge. Ches W 4G 83
Handcross. W Sus 2D 26
Handforth. Ches E 2C 84
Handley. Ches W 5G 83
Handley. Derbs 4A 86
Handsacre. Staf 4E 73
Handsworth. S Yor 2B 86
Handsworth. W Mid 1E 61
Handy Cross. Buck 2G 37
Hanford. Dors 1D 14
Hanford. Stoke 1C 72
Hangersley. Hants 2G 15
Hanging Houghton. Nptn 3E 63
Hanging Langford. Wilts 3F 23
Hangleton. Brig 5D 26
Hangleton. W Sus 5B 26
Hanham. S Glo 4B 34
Hanham Green. S Glo 4B 34
Hankelow. Ches E 1A 72
Hankerton. Wilts 2E 35
Hankham. E Sus 5H 27
**Hanley**. Stoke 1C 72
Hanley Castle. Worc 1D 48
Hanley Childe. Worc 4A 60
Hanley Swan. Worc 1D 48
Hanley William. Worc 4A 60
Hanlith. N Yor 3B 98
Hanmer. Wrex 2G 71
Hannaborough. Devn 2F 11
Hannaford. Devn 4G 19
Hannah. Linc 3E 89
Hannington. Hants 1D 24
Hannington. Nptn 3F 63
Hannington. Swin 2G 35
Hannington Wick. Swin 2G 35
Hanscombe End. C Beds 2B 52
Hanslope. Mil 1G 51
Hanthorpe. Linc 3H 75
Hanwell. G Lon 2C 38
Hanwell. Oxon 1C 50
Hanwood. Shrp 5G 71
Hanworth. G Lon 3C 38
Hanworth. Norf 2D 78
Happas. Ang 4D 144
Happendon. S Lan 1A 118
Happisburgh. Norf 2F 79
Happisburgh Common. Norf 3F 79
Hapsford. Ches W 3G 83
Hapton. Lanc 1F 91
Hapton. Norf 1D 66
Harberton. Devn 3D 9
Harbertonford. Devn 3D 9
Harbledown. Kent 5F 41
Harborne. W Mid 2E 61
Harborough Magna. Warw 3B 62
Harbottle. Nmbd 4D 120
Harbourneford. Devn 2D 8
Harbours Hill. Worc 4D 60
Harbridge. Hants 1G 15
Harbury. Warw 4A 62
Harby. Leics 2E 75
Harby. Notts 3F 87
Harcombe. Devn 3E 13
Harcombe Bottom. Devn 3G 13
Harcourt. Corn 5C 6
Harden. W Yor 1A 92
Hardenhuish. Wilts 4E 35
Hardgate. Abers 3E 153
Hardgate. Dum 3F 111
Hardham. W Sus 4B 26
Hardingham. Norf 5C 78
Hardingstone. Nptn 5E 63
Hardings Wood. Staf 5C 84
Hardington. Som 1C 22
Hardington Mandeville. Som 1A 14
Hardington Marsh. Som 2A 14
Hardington Moor. Som 1A 14
Hardley. Hants 2C 16
Hardley Street. Norf 5F 79
Hardmead. Mil 1H 51
Hardraw. N Yor 5B 104
Hardstoft. Derbs 4B 86
Hardway. Hants 2E 16
Hardway. Som 3C 22
Hardwick. Buck 4G 51
Hardwick. Cambs 5C 64
Hardwick. Norf 2E 66
Hardwick. Nptn 4F 63
Hardwick. Oxon
nr. Bicester 3D 50
nr. Witney 5B 50
Hardwick. Shrp 1F 59
Hardwick. S Yor 2B 86
Hardwick. Stoc T 2B 106
Hardwick. W Mid 1E 61
Hardwicke. Glos
nr. Cheltenham 3E 49
nr. Gloucester 4C 48
Hardwicke. Here 1F 47
Hardwick Village. Notts 3D 86
Hardy's Green. Essx 3C 54
Hare. Som 1F 13
Hareby. Linc 4C 88
Hareden. Lanc 4F 97
Harefield. G Lon 1B 38
Hare Green. Essx 3D 54
Hare Hatch. Wok 4G 37
Harehill. Derbs 2F 73
Harehills. W Yor 1D 92
Harehope. Nmbd 2E 121
Harelaw. Dum 2F 113
Harelaw. Dur 4E 115
Hareplain. Kent 2C 28
Haresceugh. Cumb 5H 113
Harescombe. Glos 4D 48
Haresfield. Glos 4D 48
Haresfinch. Mers 1H 83
Hareshaw. N Lan 3B 128
Hare Street. Essx 5E 53
Hare Street. Herts 3D 53
Harewood. W Yor 5F 99
Harewood End. Here 3A 48
Harford. Devn 3C 8
Hargate. Norf 1D 66
Hargatewall. Derbs 3F 85
Hargrave. Ches W 4G 83
Hargrave. Nptn 3H 63
Hargrave. Suff 5G 65
Harker. Cumb 3E 113
Harkland. Shet 3F 173
Harkstead. Suff 2E 55
Harlaston. Staf 4G 73
Harlaxton. Linc 2F 75
Harlech. Gwyn 2E 69
Harlequin. Notts 2D 74
Harlescott. Shrp 4H 71
Harleston. Devn 4D 9
Harleston. Norf 2E 67
Harleston. Suff 4C 66
Harlestone. Nptn 4E 62
Harley. Shrp 5H 71
Harley. S Yor 1A 86
Harling Road. Norf 2B 66
Harlington. C Beds 2A 52
Harlington. G Lon 3B 38
Harlington. S Yor 4E 93
Harlosh. High 4B 154
**Harlow**. Essx 4E 53
Harlow Hill. Nmbd 3D 115
Harlsey Castle. N Yor 5B 106
Harlthorpe. E Yor 1H 93
Harlton. Cambs 5C 64
Harlyn Bay. Corn 1C 6
Harman's Cross. Dors 4E 15
Harmby. N Yor 1D 98
Harmer Green. Herts 4C 52
Harmer Hill. Shrp 3G 71
Harmondsworth. G Lon 3B 38
Harmston. Linc 4G 87
Harnage. Shrp 5H 71
Harnham. Nmbd 1D 115
Harnham. Wilts 4G 23
Harnhill. Glos 5F 49
Harold Hill. G Lon 1G 39
Haroldston West. Pemb 3C 42
Haroldswick. Shet 1H 173
Harold Wood. G Lon 1G 39
Harome. N Yor 1A 100
**Harpenden**. Herts 4B 52
Harpford. Devn 3D 12
Harpham. E Yor 3E 101
Harpley. Norf 3G 77
Harpley. Worc 4A 60
Harpole. Nptn 4D 62
Harpsdale. High 3D 168
Harpsden. Oxon 3F 37
Harpswell. Linc 2G 87
Harpurhey. G Man 4G 91
Harpur Hill. Derbs 3E 85
Harraby. Cumb 4F 113
Harracott. Devn 4F 19
Harrapool. High 1E 147
Harrapul. High 1E 147
Harrietfield. Per 1B 136
Harrietsham. Kent 5C 40
Harrington. Cumb 2A 102
Harrington. Linc 3C 88
Harrington. Nptn 2E 63
Harringworth. Nptn 1G 63
Harriseahead. Staf 5C 84
Harriston. Cumb 5C 112
**Harrogate**. N Yor 4F 99
Harrold. Bed 5G 63
Harrop Dale. G Man 4A 92
**Harrow**. G Lon 2C 38
Harrowbarrow. Corn 2H 7
Harrowden. Bed 1A 52
Harrowgate Hill. Darl 3F 105
Harrow on the Hill. G Lon 2C 38
Harrow Weald. G Lon 1C 38
Harry Stoke. S Glo 4B 34
Harston. Cambs 5D 64
Harston. Leics 2F 75
Harswell. E Yor 5C 100
Hart. Hart 1B 106
Hartburn. Nmbd 1D 115
Hartburn. Stoc T 3B 106
Hartest. Suff 5H 65
Hartfield. E Sus 2F 27
Hartford. Cambs 3B 64
Hartford. Ches W 3A 84
Hartford. Som 4C 20
Hartford Bridge. Hants 1F 25
Hartford End. Essx 4G 53
Harthill. Ches W 5H 83
Harthill. N Lan 3C 128
Harthill. S Yor 2B 86
Hartington. Derbs 4F 85
Hartland. Devn 4C 18
Hartland Quay. Devn 4C 18
Hartle. Worc 3D 60
Hartlebury. Worc 3C 60
**Hartlepool**. Hart 1C 106
Hartley. Cumb 4A 104
Hartley. Kent
nr. Cranbrook 2B 28
nr. Dartford 4H 39
Hartley. Nmbd 2G 115
Hartley Green. Staf 3D 73
Hartley Mauditt. Hants 3F 25
Hartley Wespall. Hants 1E 25
Hartley Wintney. Hants 1F 25
Hartlip. Kent 4C 40
Hartmount Holdings. High 1B 158
Hartoft End. N Yor 5E 107
Harton. N Yor 3B 100
Harton. Shrp 2G 59
Harton. Tyne 3G 115
Hartpury. Glos 3D 48
Hartshead. W Yor 2B 92
**Hartshill**. Warw 1H 61
Hartshorne. Derbs 3H 73
Hartsop. Cumb 3F 103
Hart Station. Hart 1B 106
Hartswell. Som 4D 20
Hartwell. Nptn 5E 63
Hartwood. Lanc 3D 90
Hartwood. N Lan 4B 128
Harvel. Kent 4A 40
Harvington. Worc
nr. Evesham 1F 49
nr. Kidderminster 3C 60
Harwell. Oxon 3C 36
**Harwich**. Essx 2F 55
Harwood. Dur 1B 104
Harwood. G Man 3F 91
Harwood Dale. N Yor 5G 107
Harworth. Notts 1D 86
Hascombe. Surr 2A 26
Haselbech. Nptn 3E 62
Haselbury Plucknett. Som 1H 13
Haseley. Warw 4G 61
Hasfield. Glos 3D 48
Hasguard. Pemb 4C 42
Haskayne. Lanc 4B 90
Hasketon. Suff 5E 67
Hasland. Derbs 4A 86
**Haslemere**. Surr 2A 26
**Haslingden**. Lanc 2F 91
Haslingfield. Cambs 5D 64
Haslington. Ches E 5B 84
Hassall. Ches E 5B 84
Hassall Green. Ches E 5B 84
Hassell Street. Kent 1E 29
Hassendean. Bord 2H 119
Hassingham. Norf 5F 79
Hassness. Cumb 3C 102
Hassocks. W Sus 4E 27
Hassop. Derbs 3G 85
Haster. High 3F 169
Hasthorpe. Linc 4D 89
Hastigrow. High 2E 169
Hastingleigh. Kent 1E 29
**Hastings**. E Sus 5C 28
Hastingwood. Essx 5E 53
Hastoe. Herts 5H 51
Haston. Shrp 3H 71
Haswell. Dur 5G 115
Haswell Plough. Dur 5G 115
Hatch. C Beds 1B 52
Hatch Beauchamp. Som 4G 21
Hatch End. G Lon 1C 38
Hatch Green. Som 1G 13
Hatching Green. Herts 4B 52
Hatchmere. Ches W 3H 83
Hatch Warren. Hants 2E 24
Hatcliffe. NE Lin 4F 95
Hatfield. Here 5H 59
**Hatfield**. Herts 5C 52
**Hatfield**. S Yor 4G 93
Hatfield. Worc 5C 60
Hatfield Broad Oak. Essx 4F 53
Hatfield Garden Village. Herts 5C 52
Hatfield Heath. Essx 4F 53
Hatfield Hyde. Herts 4C 52
Hatfield Peverel. Essx 4A 54
Hatfield Woodhouse. S Yor 4G 93
Hatford. Oxon 2B 36
Hatherden. Hants 1B 24
Hatherleigh. Devn 2F 11
Hathern. Leics 3B 74
Hatherop. Glos 5G 49
Hathersage. Derbs 2G 85
Hathersage Booths. Derbs 2G 85
Hatherton. Ches E 1A 72
Hatherton. Staf 4D 72
Hatley St George. Cambs 5B 64
Hatt. Corn 2H 7
Hattersley. G Man 1D 85
Hattingley. Hants 3E 25
Hatton. Abers 5H 161
Hatton. Derbs 2G 73
Hatton. G Lon 3B 38
Hatton. Linc 3A 88
Hatton. Shrp 1G 59
Hatton. Warr 2A 84
Hatton. Warw 4G 61
Hattoncrook. Abers 1F 153
Hatton Heath. Ches W 4G 83
Hatton of Fintray. Abers 2F 153
Haugh. E Ayr 2D 117
Haugh. Linc 3D 88
Haugham. Linc 2C 88
Haugh Head. Nmbd 2E 121
Haughley. Suff 4C 66
Haughley Green. Suff 4C 66
Haugh of Ballechin. Per 3G 143
Haugh of Glass. Mor 5B 160
Haugh of Urr. Dum 3F 111
Haughton. Ches E 5H 83
Haughton. Notts 3D 86
Haughton. Shrp
nr. Bridgnorth 1A 60
nr. Oswestry 3F 71
nr. Shifnal 5B 72
nr. Shrewsbury 4H 71
Haughton. Staf 3C 72
Haughton Green. G Man 1D 84
Haughton le Skerne. Darl 3A 106
Haultwick. Herts 3D 52
Haunn. Arg 4E 139
Haunn. W Isl 7C 170
Haunton. Staf 4G 73
Hauxton. Cambs 5D 64
Havannah. Ches E 4C 84
**Havant**. Hants 2F 17
Haven. Here 5G 59
The Haven. W Sus 2B 26
Haven Bank. Linc 5B 88
Havenstreet. IOW 3D 16
Havercroft. W Yor 3D 93
**Haverfordwest**. Pemb 3D 42
**Haverhill**. Suff 1G 53
Haverigg. Cumb 2A 96
Havering-Atte-Bower. G Lon 1G 39
Havering's Grove. Essx 1A 40
Haversham. Mil 1G 51
Haverthwaite. Cumb 1C 96
Haverton Hill. Stoc T 2B 106
Havyatt. Som 3A 22
**Hawarden**. Flin 4F 83
Hawbridge. Worc 1E 49
Hawcoat. Cumb 2B 96
Hawcross. Glos 2C 48
Hawen. Cdgn 1D 44
Hawes. N Yor 1A 98
Hawes Green. Norf 1E 67
**Hawick**. Bord 3H 119
Hawkchurch. Devn 2G 13
Hawkedon. Suff 5G 65
Hawkenbury. Kent 1C 28
Hawkeridge. Wilts 1D 22
Hawkerland. Devn 4D 12
Hawkesbury. S Glo 3C 34
Hawkesbury. Warw 2A 62
Hawkesbury Upton. S Glo 3C 34
Hawkes End. W Mid 2G 61
Hawk Green. G Man 2D 84
Hawkhurst. Kent 2B 28
Hawkhurst Common. E Sus 4G 27
Hawkinge. Kent 1G 29
Hawkley. Hants 4F 25
Hawkridge. Som 3B 20
Hawksdale. Cumb 5E 113
Hawkshaw. G Man 3F 91
Hawkshead. Cumb 5E 103

# Hawkshead Hill—Heydon



Hawkshead Hill. *Cumb* 5E **103**
Hawkswick. *N Yor* 2B **98**
Hawksworth. *Notts* 1E **75**
Hawksworth. *W Yor* 5D **98**
Hawkwell. *Essx* 1C **40**
Hawley. *Hants* 1G **25**
Hawley. *Kent* 3G **39**
Hawling. *Glos* 3F **49**
Hawnby. *N Yor* 1H **99**
Haworth. *W Yor* 1A **92**
Hawstead. *Suff* 5A **66**
Hawthorn. *Dur* 5H **115**
Hawthorn Hill. *Brac* 4G **37**
Hawthorn Hill. *Linc* 5B **88**
Hawthorpe. *Linc* 3H **75**
Hawton. *Notts* 5E **87**
**Haxby**. *York* 4A **100**
Haxey. *N Lin* 1E **87**
Haybridge. *Shrp* 3A **60**
Haybridge. *Som* 2A **22**
**Haydock**. *Mers* 1H **83**
Haydon. *Bath* 1B **22**
Haydon. *Dors* 1B **14**
Haydon. *Som* 4F **21**
Haydon Bridge. *Nmbd* 3B **114**
Haydon Wick. *Swin* 3G **35**
Haye. *Corn* 2H **7**
Hayes. *G Lon*
nr. Bromley 4F **39**
**Hayes**. *G Lon*
nr. Uxbridge 2B **38**
Hayfield. *Derbs* 2E **85**
Hay Green. *Norf* 4E **77**
Hayhill. *E Ayr* 3D **116**
Haylands. *IOW* 3D **16**
Hayle. *Corn* 3C **4**
Hayley Green. *W Mid* 2D **60**
**Hayling Island**. *Hants* 3F **17**
Hayne. *Devn* 2B **12**
Haynes. *C Beds* 1A **52**
Haynes West End. *C Beds* 1A **52**
Hay-on-Wye. *Powy* 1F **47**
Hayscastle. *Pemb* 2C **42**
Hayscastle Cross. *Pemb* 2D **42**
Hayshead. *Ang* 4F **145**
Hay Street. *Herts* 3D **53**
Hayton. *Aber* 3G **153**
Hayton. *Cumb*
nr. Aspatria 5C **112**
nr. Brampton 4G **113**
Hayton. *E Yor* 5C **100**
Hayton. *Notts* 2E **87**
Hayton's Bent. *Shrp* 2H **59**
Haytor Vale. *Devn* 5A **12**
Haytown. *Devn* 1D **11**
**Haywards Heath**. *W Sus* 3E **27**
Haywood. *S Lan* 4C **128**
Hazelbank. *S Lan* 5B **128**
Hazelbury Bryan. *Dors* 2C **14**
Hazeleigh. *Essx* 5B **54**
Hazeley. *Hants* 1F **25**
**Hazel Grove**. *G Man* 2D **84**
Hazelhead. *S Yor* 4B **92**
Hazelslade. *Staf* 4E **73**
Hazel Street. *Kent* 2A **28**
Hazelton Walls. *Fife* 1F **137**
Hazelwood. *Derbs* 1H **73**
Hazlemere. *Buck* 2G **37**
Hazler. *Shrp* 1G **59**
Hazlerigg. *Tyne* 2F **115**
Hazles. *Staf* 1E **73**
Hazleton. *Glos* 4F **49**
Hazon. *Nmbd* 4F **121**
Heacham. *Norf* 2F **77**
Headbourne Worthy. *Hants* 3C **24**
Headcorn. *Kent* 1C **28**
Headingley. *W Yor* 1C **92**
Headington. *Oxon* 5D **50**
Headlam. *Dur* 3E **105**
Headless Cross. *Worc* 4E **61**
Headley. *Hants*
nr. Haslemere 3G **25**
nr. Kingsclere 5D **36**
Headley. *Surr* 5D **38**
Headley Down. *Hants* 3G **25**
Headley Heath. *Worc* 3E **61**
Headley Park. *Bris* 5A **34**
Head of Muir. *Falk* 1B **128**
Headon. *Notts* 3E **87**
Heads Nook. *Cumb* 4F **113**
Heage. *Derbs* 5A **86**
Healaugh. *N Yor*
nr. Grinton 5D **104**
nr. York 5H **99**
Heald Green. *G Man* 2C **84**
Heale. *Devn* 2G **19**
Healey. *G Man* 3G **91**
Healey. *Nmbd* 4D **114**
Healey. *N Yor* 1D **98**
Healeyfield. *Dur* 5D **114**
Healing. *NE Lin* 3F **95**
Heamoor. *Corn* 3B **4**
Heanish. *Arg* 4B **138**
**Heanor**. *Derbs* 1B **74**
Heanton Punchardon. *Devn* 3F **19**
Heapham. *Linc* 2F **87**
Heartsease. *Powy* 4D **58**
Heasley Mill. *Devn* 3H **19**
Heaste. *High* 2E **147**
Heath. *Derbs* 4B **86**
The Heath. *Norf*
nr. Buxton 3E **79**
nr. Fakenham 3B **78**
nr. Hevingham 3D **78**
The Heath. *Staf* 2E **73**
The Heath. *Suff* 2E **55**
Heath and Reach. *C Beds* 3H **51**
Heath Common. *W Sus* 4C **26**
Heathcote. *Derbs* 4F **85**
Heath Cross. *Devn* 3H **11**
Heathencote. *Nptn* 1F **51**
Heath End. *Hants* 5D **36**
Heath End. *Leics* 3A **74**
Heath End. *W Mid* 5E **73**
Heather. *Leics* 4A **74**
Heatherfield. *High* 4D **155**
Heatherton. *Derb* 2H **73**
Heathfield. *Cambs* 1E **53**
Heathfield. *Cumb* 5C **112**
Heathfield. *Devn* 5B **12**
Heathfield. *E Sus* 3G **27**
Heathfield. *Ren* 3E **126**
Heathfield. *Som*
nr. Lydeard St Lawrence 3E **21**
nr. Norton Fitzwarren 4E **21**
Heath Green. *Worc* 3E **61**
Heathhall. *Dum* 2A **112**
Heath Hayes. *Staf* 4E **73**
Heath Hill. *Shrp* 4B **72**
Heath House. *Som* 2H **21**
Heathrow Airport. *G Lon* 3B **38**
Heathstock. *Devn* 2F **13**
Heathton. *Shrp* 1C **60**
Heathtop. *Derbs* 2G **73**
Heath Town. *W Mid* 1D **60**
Heatley. *Staf* 3E **73**
Heatley. *Warr* 2B **84**
Heaton. *Lanc* 3D **96**
Heaton. *Staf* 4D **84**
Heaton. *Tyne* 3F **115**
Heaton. *W Yor* 1B **92**
Heaton Moor. *G Man* 1C **84**
Heaton's Bridge. *Lanc* 3C **90**
Heaverham. *Kent* 5G **39**
Heavitree. *Devn* 3C **12**
**Hebburn**. *Tyne* 3G **115**
Hebden. *N Yor* 3C **98**
Hebden Bridge. *W Yor* 2H **91**
Hebden Green. *Ches W* 4A **84**
Hebing End. *Herts* 3D **52**
Hebron. *Carm* 2F **43**
Hebron. *Nmbd* 1E **115**
Heck. *Dum* 1B **112**
Heckdyke. *Notts* 1E **87**
Heckfield. *Hants* 5F **37**
Heckfield Green. *Suff* 3D **66**
Heckfordbridge. *Essx* 3C **54**
Heckington. *Linc* 1A **76**
**Heckmondwike**. *W Yor* 2C **92**
Heddington. *Wilts* 5E **35**
Heddle. *Orkn* 6C **172**
Heddon. *Devn* 4G **19**
Heddon-on-the-Wall. *Nmbd* 3E **115**
Hedenham. *Norf* 1F **67**
**Hedge End**. *Hants* 1C **16**
Hedgerley. *Buck* 2A **38**
Hedging. *Som* 4G **21**
Hedley on the Hill. *Nmbd* 4D **115**
Hednesford. *Staf* 4E **73**
Hedon. *E Yor* 2E **95**
Hegdon Hill. *Here* 5H **59**
Heglibister. *Shet* 6E **173**
Heighington. *Darl* 2F **105**
Heighington. *Linc* 4H **87**
Heightington. *Worc* 3B **60**
Heights of Brae. *High* 2H **157**
Heights of Fodderty. *High* 2H **157**
Heights of Kinlochewe. *High* 2C **156**
Heiton. *Bord* 1B **120**
Hele. *Devn*
nr. Exeter 2C **12**
nr. Holsworthy 3D **10**
nr. Ilfracombe 2F **19**
Hele. *Torb* 2F **9**
**Helensburgh**. *Arg* 1D **126**
Helford. *Corn* 4E **5**
Helhoughton. *Norf* 3A **78**
Helions Bumpstead. *Essx* 1G **53**
Helland. *Corn* 5A **10**
Helland. *Som* 4G **21**
Hellandbridge. *Corn* 5A **10**
Hellesdon. *Norf* 4E **78**
Hellesveor. *Corn* 2C **4**
Hellidon. *Nptn* 5C **62**
Hellifield. *N Yor* 4A **98**
Hellingly. *E Sus* 4G **27**
Hellington. *Norf* 5F **79**
Hellister. *Shet* 7E **173**
Helmdon. *Nptn* 1D **50**
Helmingham. *Suff* 5D **66**
Helmington Row. *Dur* 1E **105**
Helmsdale. *High* 2H **165**
Helmshore. *Lanc* 2F **91**
Helmsley. *N Yor* 1A **100**
Helperby. *N Yor* 3G **99**
Helperthorpe. *N Yor* 2D **100**
Helpringham. *Linc* 1A **76**
Helpston. *Pet* 5A **76**
Helsby. *Ches W* 3G **83**
Helsey. *Linc* 3E **89**
Helston. *Corn* 4D **4**
Helstone. *Corn* 4A **10**
Helton. *Cumb* 2G **103**
Helwith. *N Yor* 4D **105**
Helwith Bridge. *N Yor* 3H **97**
Helygain. *Flin* 3E **82**
The Hem. *Shrp* 5B **72**
Hemblington. *Norf* 4F **79**
**Hemel Hempstead**. *Herts* 5A **52**
Hemerdon. *Devn* 3B **8**
Hemingbrough. *N Yor* 1G **93**
Hemingby. *Linc* 3B **88**
Hemingfield. *S Yor* 4D **93**
Hemingford Abbots. *Cambs* 3B **64**
Hemingford Grey. *Cambs* 3B **64**
Hemingstone. *Suff* 5D **66**
Hemington. *Leics* 3B **74**
Hemington. *Nptn* 2H **63**
Hemington. *Som* 1C **22**
Hemley. *Suff* 1F **55**
Hemlington. *Midd* 3B **106**
Hempholme. *E Yor* 4E **101**
Hempnall. *Norf* 1E **67**
Hempnall Green. *Norf* 1E **67**
Hempriggs. *High* 4F **169**
Hemp's Green. *Essx* 3C **54**
Hempstead. *Essx* 2G **53**
Hempstead. *Medw* 4B **40**
Hempstead. *Norf*
nr. Holt 2D **78**
nr. Stalham 3G **79**
Hempsted. *Glos* 4D **48**
Hempton. *Norf* 3B **78**
Hempton. *Oxon* 2C **50**
Hemsby. *Norf* 4G **79**
Hemswell. *Linc* 1G **87**
Hemswell Cliff. *Linc* 2G **87**
Hemsworth. *Dors* 2E **15**
**Hemsworth**. *W Yor* 3E **93**
Hemyock. *Devn* 1E **13**
Henallt. *Carm* 3E **45**
Henbury. *Bris* 4A **34**
Henbury. *Ches E* 3C **84**
Hendomen. *Powy* 1E **58**
**Hendon**. *G Lon* 2D **38**
Hendon. *Tyne* 4H **115**
Hendra. *Corn* 3D **6**
Hendre. *B'end* 3C **32**
Hendreforgan. *Rhon* 3C **32**
Hendy. *Carm* 5F **45**
Heneglwys. *IOA* 3D **80**
Henfeddau Fawr. *Pemb* 1G **43**
Henfield. *S Glo* 4B **34**
Henfield. *W Sus* 4D **26**
Henford. *Devn* 3D **10**
Hengoed. *Cphy* 2E **33**
Hengoed. *Shrp* 2E **71**
Hengrave. *Suff* 4H **65**
Henham. *Essx* 3F **53**
Heniarth. *Powy* 5D **70**
Henlade. *Som* 4F **21**
Henley. *Dors* 2B **14**
Henley. *Shrp*
nr. Church Stretton 2G **59**
nr. Ludlow 3H **59**
Henley. *Som* 3H **21**
Henley. *Suff* 5D **66**
Henley. *W Sus* 4G **25**
Henley Down. *E Sus* 4B **28**
Henley-in-Arden. *Warw* 4F **61**
**Henley-on-Thames**. *Oxon* 3F **37**
Henley Street. *Kent* 4A **40**
Henllan. *Cdgn* 1D **44**
Henllan. *Den* 4C **82**
Henllan. *Mon* 3F **47**
Henllan Amgoed. *Carm* 3F **43**
Henllys. *Torf* 2F **33**
Henlow. *C Beds* 2B **52**
Hennock. *Devn* 4B **12**
Henny Street. *Essx* 2B **54**
Henryd. *Cnwy* 3G **81**
Henry's Moat. *Pemb* 2E **43**
Hensall. *N Yor* 2F **93**
Henshaw. *Nmbd* 3A **114**
Hensingham. *Cumb* 3A **102**
Henstead. *Suff* 2G **67**
Hensting. *Hants* 4C **24**
Henstridge. *Som* 1C **14**
Henstridge Ash. *Som* 4C **22**
Henstridge Bowden. *Som* 4B **22**
Henstridge Marsh. *Som* 4C **22**
Henton. *Oxon* 5F **51**
Henton. *Som* 2H **21**
Henwood. *Corn* 5C **10**
Heogan. *Shet* 7F **173**
Heolgerrig. *Mer T* 5D **46**
Heol Senni. *Powy* 3C **46**
Heol-y-Cyw. *B'end* 3C **32**
Hepburn. *Nmbd* 2E **121**
Hepple. *Nmbd* 4D **121**
Hepscott. *Nmbd* 1F **115**
Heptonstall. *W Yor* 2H **91**
Hepworth. *Suff* 3B **66**
Hepworth. *W Yor* 4B **92**
Herbrandston. *Pemb* 4C **42**
**Hereford**. *Here* 2A **48**
Heribusta. *High* 1D **154**
Heriot. *Bord* 4H **129**
Hermiston. *Edin* 2E **129**
Hermitage. *Dors* 2B **14**
Hermitage. *Bord* 5H **119**
Hermitage. *W Ber* 4D **36**
Hermitage. *W Sus* 2F **17**
Hermon. *Carm*
nr. Llandeilo 3G **45**
nr. Newcastle Emlyn 2D **44**
Hermon. *IOA* 4C **80**
Hermon. *Pemb* 1G **43**
Herne. *Kent* 4F **41**
**Herne Bay**. *Kent* 4F **41**
Herne Common. *Kent* 4F **41**
Herne Pound. *Kent* 5A **40**
Herner. *Devn* 4F **19**
Hernhill. *Kent* 4E **41**
Herodsfoot. *Corn* 2G **7**
Heronden. *Kent* 5G **41**
Herongate. *Essx* 1H **39**
Heronsford. *S Ayr* 1G **109**
Heronsgate. *Herts* 1B **38**
Heron's Ghyll. *E Sus* 3F **27**
Herra. *Shet* 2H **173**
Herriard. *Hants* 2E **25**
Herringfleet. *Suff* 1G **67**
Herringswell. *Suff* 4G **65**
Herrington. *Tyne* 4G **115**
Hersden. *Kent* 4G **41**
Hersham. *Corn* 2C **10**
Hersham. *Surr* 4C **38**
Herstmonceux. *E Sus* 4H **27**
Herston. *Dors* 5F **15**
Herston. *Orkn* 8D **172**
**Hertford**. *Herts* 4D **52**
Hertford Heath. *Herts* 4D **52**
Hertingfordbury. *Herts* 4D **52**
Hesketh. *Lanc* 2C **90**
Hesketh Bank. *Lanc* 2C **90**
Hesketh Lane. *Lanc* 5F **97**
Hesket Newmarket. *Cumb* 1E **103**
Heskin Green. *Lanc* 3D **90**
Hesleden. *Dur* 1B **106**
Hesleyside. *Nmbd* 1B **114**
Heslington. *York* 4A **100**
Hessay. *York* 4H **99**
Hessenford. *Corn* 3H **7**
Hessett. *Suff* 4B **66**
Hessilhead. *N Ayr* 4E **127**
Hessle. *E Yor* 2D **94**
Hestaford. *Shet* 6D **173**
Hest Bank. *Lanc* 3D **96**
Hester's Way. *Glos* 3E **49**
Hestinsetter. *Shet* 7D **173**
Heston. *G Lon* 3C **38**
Hestwall. *Orkn* 6B **172**
**Heswall**. *Mers* 2E **83**
Hethe. *Oxon* 3D **50**
Hethelpit Cross. *Glos* 3C **48**
Hethersett. *Norf* 5D **78**
Hethersgill. *Cumb* 3F **113**
Hetherside. *Cumb* 3F **113**
Hethpool. *Nmbd* 2C **120**
Hett. *Dur* 1F **105**
Hetton. *N Yor* 4B **98**
**Hetton-le-Hole**. *Tyne* 5G **115**
Hetton Steads. *Nmbd* 1E **121**
Heugh. *Nmbd* 2D **115**
Heugh-head. *Abers* 2A **152**
Heveningham. *Suff* 3F **67**
Hever. *Kent* 1F **27**
Heversham. *Cumb* 1D **97**
Hevingham. *Norf* 3D **78**
Hewas Water. *Corn* 4D **6**
Hewelsfield. *Glos* 5A **48**
Hewish. *N Som* 5H **33**
Hewish. *Som* 2H **13**
Hewood. *Dors* 2G **13**
Heworth. *York* 4A **100**
**Hexham**. *Nmbd* 3C **114**
Hextable. *Kent* 3G **39**
Hexton. *Herts* 2B **52**
Hexworthy. *Devn* 5G **11**
Heybridge. *Essx*
nr. Brentwood 1H **39**
nr. Maldon 5B **54**
Heybridge Basin. *Essx* 5B **54**
Heybrook Bay. *Devn* 4A **8**
Heydon. *Cambs* 1E **53**

Heydon. Norf . . . . . . . . . . . . .3D 78
Heydour. Linc . . . . . . . . . . . .2H 75
Heylipol. Arg . . . . . . . . . . .4A 138
Heyop. Powy . . . . . . . . . . . .3E 59
Heysham. Lanc . . . . . . . . . . .3D 96
Heyshott. W Sus . . . . . . . . . .1G 17
Heytesbury. Wilts . . . . . . . . .2E 23
Heythrop. Oxon . . . . . . . . . . .3B 50
**Heywood.** G Man . . . . . . . . .3G 91
Heywood. Wilts . . . . . . . . . . .1D 22
Hibaldstow. N Lin . . . . . . . . .4C 94
Hickleton. S Yor . . . . . . . . . .4E 93
Hickling. Norf . . . . . . . . . . .3G 79
Hickling. Notts . . . . . . . . . . .3D 74
Hickling Green. Norf . . . . . . .3G 79
Hickling Heath. Norf . . . . . . .3G 79
Hickstead. W Sus . . . . . . . . . .3D 26
Hidcote Bartrim. Glos . . . . . . .1G 49
Hidcote Boyce. Glos . . . . . . . .1G 49
Higford. Shrp . . . . . . . . . . . .5B 72
High Ackworth. W Yor . . . . . . .3E 93
Higham. Derbs . . . . . . . . . . .5A 86
Higham. Kent . . . . . . . . . . . .3B 40
Higham. Lanc . . . . . . . . . . . .1G 91
Higham. S Yor . . . . . . . . . . .4D 92
Higham. Suff
    nr. Ipswich . . . . . . . . . . .2D 54
    nr. Newmarket . . . . . . . . .4G 65
Higham Dykes. Nmbd . . . . . . .2E 115
Higham Ferrers. Nptn . . . . . . .4G 63
Higham Gobion. C Beds . . . . . .2B 52
Higham on the Hill. Leics . . . . .1A 62
Highampton. Devn . . . . . . . . .2E 11
Higham Wood. Kent . . . . . . . .1H 27
High Angerton. Nmbd . . . . . . .1D 115
High Auldgirth. Dum . . . . . . . .1G 111
High Bankhill. Cumb . . . . . . . .5G 113
High Banton. N Lan . . . . . . . .1A 128
High Barnet. G Lon . . . . . . . . .1D 38
High Beech. Essx . . . . . . . . . .1F 39
High Bentham. N Yor . . . . . . . .3F 97
High Bickington. Devn . . . . . . .4G 19
High Biggins. Cumb . . . . . . . . .2E 97
High Birkwith. N Yor . . . . . . . .2G 97
High Blantyre. S Lan . . . . . . . .4H 127
High Bonnybridge. Falk . . . . . .2B 128
High Borrans. Cumb . . . . . . . .4F 103
High Bradfield. S Yor . . . . . . . .1G 85
High Bray. Devn . . . . . . . . . . .3G 19
Highbridge. Cumb . . . . . . . . . .5E 113
Highbridge. High . . . . . . . . . .5E 148
Highbridge. Som . . . . . . . . . . .2G 21
Highbrook. W Sus . . . . . . . . . .2E 27
High Brooms. Kent . . . . . . . . .1G 27
High Bullen. Devn . . . . . . . . . .4F 19
Highburton. W Yor . . . . . . . . .3B 92
Highbury. Som . . . . . . . . . . . .2B 22
High Buston. Nmbd . . . . . . . .4G 121
High Callerton. Nmbd . . . . . . .2E 115
High Carlingill. Cumb . . . . . . .4H 103
High Catton. E Yor . . . . . . . . .4B 100
High Church. Nmbd . . . . . . . . .1E 115
Highclere. Hants . . . . . . . . . . .5C 36
Highcliffe. Dors . . . . . . . . . . .3H 15
High Cogges. Oxon . . . . . . . . .5B 50
High Common. Norf . . . . . . . . .5B 78
High Coniscliffe. Darl . . . . . . .3F 105
High Crosby. Cumb . . . . . . . . .4F 113
High Cross. Hants . . . . . . . . . .4F 25
High Cross. Herts . . . . . . . . . .4D 52
High Easter. Essx . . . . . . . . . .4G 53
High Eggborough. N Yor . . . . . .2F 93
High Ellington. N Yor . . . . . . . .1D 98
Higher Alham. Som . . . . . . . . .2B 22
Higher Ansty. Dors . . . . . . . . .2C 14
Higher Ashton. Devn . . . . . . . .4B 12
Higher Ballam. Lanc . . . . . . . .1B 90
Higher Bartle. Lanc . . . . . . . . .1D 90
Higher Bockhampton. Dors . . . .3C 14
Higher Bojewyan. Corn . . . . . .3A 4
High Ercall. Telf . . . . . . . . . . .4H 71
Higher Cheriton. Devn . . . . . . .2E 12
Higher Clovelly. Devn . . . . . . .4D 18
Higher Compton. Plym . . . . . . .3A 8

Higher Dean. Devn . . . . . . . . .2D 8
Higher Dinting. Derbs . . . . . . .1E 85
Higher Dunstone. Devn . . . . . .5H 11
Higher End. G Man . . . . . . . . .4D 90
Higherford. Lanc . . . . . . . . . .5A 98
Higher Gabwell. Devn . . . . . . .2F 9
Higher Halstock Leigh. Dors . . .2A 14
Higher Heysham. Lanc . . . . . . .3D 96
Higher Hurdsfield. Ches E . . . . .3D 84
Higher Kingcombe. Dors . . . . . .3A 14
Higher Kinnerton. Flin . . . . . . .4F 83
Higher Melcombe. Dors . . . . . .2C 14
Higher Penwortham. Lanc . . . . .2D 90
Higher Porthpean. Corn . . . . . .3E 7
Higher Poynton. Ches E . . . . . .2D 84
Higher Shotton. Flin . . . . . . . .4F 83
Higher Shurlach. Ches W . . . . .3A 84
Higher Slade. Devn . . . . . . . . .2F 19
Higher Tale. Devn . . . . . . . . . .2D 12
Higher Town. IOS . . . . . . . . . .1B 4
Higher Town. Som . . . . . . . . . .2C 20
Hightown. Corn . . . . . . . . . . .4C 6
Higher Vexford. Som . . . . . . . .3E 20
Higher Walton. Lanc . . . . . . . .2D 90
Higher Walton. Warr . . . . . . . .2H 83
Higher Whatcombe. Dors . . . . .2D 14
Higher Wheelton. Lanc . . . . . . .2E 90
Higher Whiteleigh. Corn . . . . . .3C 10
Higher Whitley. Ches W . . . . . .2A 84
Higher Wincham. Ches W . . . . .3A 84
Higher Wraxall. Dors . . . . . . . .2A 14
Higher Wych. Ches W . . . . . . .1G 71
Higher Yalberton. Torb . . . . . . .3E 9
Higher Etherley. Dur . . . . . . . .2E 105
High Ferry. Linc . . . . . . . . . . .1C 76
Highfield. E Yor . . . . . . . . . . .1H 93
Highfield. N Ayr . . . . . . . . . . .4E 126
Highfield. Tyne . . . . . . . . . . .4E 115
Highfields Caldecote.
    Cambs . . . . . . . . . . . . . . .5C 64
High Gallowhill. E Dun . . . . . . .2H 127
High Garrett. Essx . . . . . . . . . .3A 54
Highgate. G Lon . . . . . . . . . . .2D 39
Highgate. N Ayr . . . . . . . . . . .4E 127
Highgate. Powy . . . . . . . . . . .1D 58
High Grange. Dur . . . . . . . . . .1E 105
High Green. Cumb . . . . . . . . .4F 103
High Green. Norf . . . . . . . . . . .5D 78
High Green. Shrp . . . . . . . . . .2B 60
High Green. S Yor . . . . . . . . . .1H 85
High Green. W Yor . . . . . . . . .3B 92
High Green. Worc . . . . . . . . . .1D 49
Highgreen Manor. Nmbd . . . . .5C 120
High Halden. Kent . . . . . . . . . .2C 28
High Halstow. Medw . . . . . . . .3B 40
High Ham. Som . . . . . . . . . . .3H 21
High Harrington. Cumb . . . . . . .2B 102
High Haswell. Dur . . . . . . . . . .5G 115
High Hatton. Shrp . . . . . . . . . .3A 72
High Hawsker. N Yor . . . . . . . .4G 107
High Hesket. Cumb . . . . . . . . .5F 113
High Hesleden. Dur . . . . . . . . .1B 106
High Hoyland. S Yor . . . . . . . .3C 92
High Hunsley. E Yor . . . . . . . . .1C 94
High Hurstwood. E Sus . . . . . .3F 27
High Hutton. N Yor . . . . . . . . .3B 100
High Ireby. Cumb . . . . . . . . . .1D 102
High Keil. Arg . . . . . . . . . . . .5A 122
High Kelling. Norf . . . . . . . . . .2D 78
High Kilburn. N Yor . . . . . . . . .2H 99
High Knipe. Cumb . . . . . . . . . .3G 103
High Lands. Dur . . . . . . . . . . .2E 105
The Highlands. Shrp . . . . . . . .2A 60
High Lane. G Man . . . . . . . . . .2D 84
High Lane. Worc . . . . . . . . . . .4A 60
Highlane. Ches E . . . . . . . . . .4C 84
Highlane. Derbs . . . . . . . . . . .2B 86
High Laver. Essx . . . . . . . . . . .5F 53
Highleadon. Glos . . . . . . . . . .3C 48
High Legh. Ches E . . . . . . . . . .2B 84
Highleigh. W Sus . . . . . . . . . .3G 17
High Leven. Stoc T . . . . . . . . .3B 106
Highley. Shrp . . . . . . . . . . . . .2B 60

High Littleton. Bath . . . . . . . . .1B 22
High Longthwaite. Cumb . . . . .5D 112
High Lorton. Cumb . . . . . . . . .2C 102
High Marishes. N Yor . . . . . . . .2C 100
High Marnham. Notts . . . . . . . .3F 87
High Melton. S Yor . . . . . . . . .4F 93
High Mickley. Nmbd . . . . . . . .3D 115
High Moor. Lanc . . . . . . . . . . .3D 90
Highmoor. Cumb . . . . . . . . . .5D 112
Highmoor. Oxon . . . . . . . . . . .3F 37
Highmoor Cross. Oxon . . . . . . .3F 37
Highmoor Hill. Mon . . . . . . . . .3H 33
Highnam. Glos . . . . . . . . . . . .4C 48
High Newport. Tyne . . . . . . . . .4G 115
High Newton. Cumb . . . . . . . . .1D 96
High Newton-by-the-Sea.
    Nmbd . . . . . . . . . . . . . . . .2G 121
High Nibthwaite. Cumb . . . . . .1B 96
High Offley. Staf . . . . . . . . . . .3B 72
High Ongar. Essx . . . . . . . . . . .5F 53
High Onn. Staf . . . . . . . . . . . .4C 72
High Orchard. Glos . . . . . . . . .4D 48
High Park. Mers . . . . . . . . . . .3B 90
High Roding. Essx . . . . . . . . . .4G 53
High Row. Cumb . . . . . . . . . . .1E 103
High Salvington. W Sus . . . . . .5C 26
High Scales. Cumb . . . . . . . . .5C 112
High Shaw. N Yor . . . . . . . . . .5B 104
High Shincliffe. Dur . . . . . . . . .5F 115
High Side. Cumb . . . . . . . . . . .1D 102
High Spen. Tyne . . . . . . . . . . .3E 115
Highsted. Kent . . . . . . . . . . . .4D 40
High Stoop. Dur . . . . . . . . . . .5E 115
High Street. Corn . . . . . . . . . . .3D 6
High Street. Suff
    nr. Aldeburgh . . . . . . . . . . .5G 67
    nr. Bungay . . . . . . . . . . . .2F 67
    nr. Yoxford . . . . . . . . . . . .3G 67
High Street Green. Essx . . . . . .2A 54
Highstreet Green. Surr . . . . . . .2A 26
Hightae. Dum . . . . . . . . . . . .2B 112
High Throston. Hart . . . . . . . . .1B 106
High Town. Staf . . . . . . . . . . .4D 73
Hightown. Ches E . . . . . . . . . .4C 84
Hightown. Mers . . . . . . . . . . .4A 90
Hightown Green. Suff . . . . . . . .5B 66
High Toynton. Linc . . . . . . . . .4B 88
High Trewhitt. Nmbd . . . . . . . .4E 121
High Valleyfield. Fife . . . . . . . .1D 128
Highway. Here . . . . . . . . . . . .1H 47
Highweek. Devn . . . . . . . . . . .5B 12
High Westwood. Dur . . . . . . . .4E 115
Highwood. Staf . . . . . . . . . . .2E 73
Highwood. Worc . . . . . . . . . . .4A 60
High Worsall. N Yor . . . . . . . . .4A 106
Highworth. Swin . . . . . . . . . . .2H 35
High Wray. Cumb . . . . . . . . . .5E 103
High Wych. Herts . . . . . . . . . .4E 53
**High Wycombe.** Buck . . . . . .2G 37
Hilborough. Norf . . . . . . . . . . .5H 77
Hilcott. Wilts . . . . . . . . . . . . .1G 23
Hildenborough. Kent . . . . . . . .1G 27
Hildersham. Cambs . . . . . . . . .1F 53
Hilderstone. Staf . . . . . . . . . . .2D 72
Hilderthorpe. E Yor . . . . . . . . .3F 101
Hilfield. Dors . . . . . . . . . . . . .2B 14
Hilgay. Norf . . . . . . . . . . . . . .1F 65
Hill. S Glo . . . . . . . . . . . . . . .2B 34
Hill. Warw . . . . . . . . . . . . . . .4B 62
Hill. Worc . . . . . . . . . . . . . . .1E 49
The Hill. Cumb . . . . . . . . . . . .1A 96
Hillam. N Yor . . . . . . . . . . . .2F 93
Hillbeck. Cumb . . . . . . . . . . .3A 104
Hillberry. IOM . . . . . . . . . . . .4C 108
Hillborough. Kent . . . . . . . . . .4G 41
Hillbourne. Pool . . . . . . . . . . .3F 15
Hillbrae. Abers
    nr. Aberchirder . . . . . . . . . .4D 160
    nr. Inverurie . . . . . . . . . . .1E 153
    nr. Methlick . . . . . . . . . . . .5F 161
Hill Brow. Hants . . . . . . . . . . .4F 25
Hillbutts. Dors . . . . . . . . . . . .2E 15
Hillclifflane. Derbs . . . . . . . . .1G 73

Hillcommon. Som . . . . . . . . . .4E 21
Hill Deverill. Wilts . . . . . . . . . .2D 22
Hilldyke. Linc . . . . . . . . . . . .1C 76
Hill End. Dur . . . . . . . . . . . . .1D 104
Hill End. Fife . . . . . . . . . . . . .4C 136
Hill End. N Yor . . . . . . . . . . . .4C 98
Hilland. Fife . . . . . . . . . . . . . .1E 129
Hilland. N Lan . . . . . . . . . . . .3B 128
Hilland. Shrp . . . . . . . . . . . . .1C 60
Hilland. Swan . . . . . . . . . . . . .3D 30
Hillersland. Glos . . . . . . . . . . .4A 48
Hillerton. Devn . . . . . . . . . . . .3H 11
Hillesden. Buck . . . . . . . . . . .3E 51
Hillesley. Glos . . . . . . . . . . . .3C 34
Hillfarrance. Som . . . . . . . . . .4E 21
Hill Gate. Here . . . . . . . . . . . .3H 47
Hill Green. Essx . . . . . . . . . . .2E 53
Hill Green. W Ber . . . . . . . . . .4C 36
Hill Head. Hants . . . . . . . . . . .2D 16
Hillhead. Abers . . . . . . . . . . .5C 160
Hillhead. Devn . . . . . . . . . . . .3F 9
Hillhead. S Ayr . . . . . . . . . . .3D 116
Hillhead of Auchentumb.
    Abers . . . . . . . . . . . . . . . .3G 161
Hilliard's Cross. Staf . . . . . . . .4F 73
Hilliclay. High . . . . . . . . . . . .2D 168
Hillingdon. G Lon . . . . . . . . . .2B 38
Hillington. Glas . . . . . . . . . . .3G 127
Hillington. Norf . . . . . . . . . . .3G 77
Hillmorton. Warw . . . . . . . . . .3C 62
Hill of Beath. Fife . . . . . . . . . .4D 136
Hill of Fearn. High . . . . . . . . .1C 158
Hill of Fiddes. Abers . . . . . . . .1G 153
Hill of Keillor. Ang . . . . . . . . .4B 144
Hill of Overbrae. Abers . . . . . .2F 161
Hill Ridware. Staf . . . . . . . . . .4E 73
Hillsborough. Lis . . . . . . . . . . .5G 175
Hillsborough. S Yor . . . . . . . . .1H 85
Hill Side. W Yor . . . . . . . . . . .3B 92
Hillside. Abers . . . . . . . . . . . .4G 153
Hillside. Ang . . . . . . . . . . . . .2G 145
Hillside. Devn . . . . . . . . . . . .2D 8
Hillside. Mers . . . . . . . . . . . .3B 90
Hillside. Orkn . . . . . . . . . . . .5C 172
Hillside. Shet . . . . . . . . . . . . .5F 173
Hillside. Shrp . . . . . . . . . . . . .2A 60
Hillside. Worc . . . . . . . . . . . .4B 60
Hillside of Prieston. Ang . . . . . .5C 144
Hill Somersal. Derbs . . . . . . . .2F 73
Hillstown. Derbs . . . . . . . . . . .4B 86
Hillstreet. Hants . . . . . . . . . . .1B 16
Hillswick. Shet . . . . . . . . . . . .4D 173
Hill Top. Dur
    nr. Barnard Castle . . . . . . .2C 104
    nr. Durham . . . . . . . . . . . .5F 115
    nr. Stanley . . . . . . . . . . . .4E 115
Hill View. Dors . . . . . . . . . . . .3E 15
Hillwell. Shet . . . . . . . . . . . .10E 173
Hill Wootton. Warw . . . . . . . . .4H 61
Hillyland. Per . . . . . . . . . . . . .1C 136
Hilmarton. Wilts . . . . . . . . . . .4F 35
Hilperton. Wilts . . . . . . . . . . .1D 22
Hilperton Marsh. Wilts . . . . . . .1D 22
Hilsea. Port . . . . . . . . . . . . . .2E 17
Hilston. E Yor . . . . . . . . . . . .1F 95
Hiltingbury. Hants . . . . . . . . . .4C 24
Hilton. Cambs . . . . . . . . . . . .4B 64
Hilton. Cumb . . . . . . . . . . . .2A 104
Hilton. Derbs . . . . . . . . . . . . .2G 73
Hilton. Dors . . . . . . . . . . . . .2C 14
Hilton. Dur . . . . . . . . . . . . . .2E 105
Hilton. High . . . . . . . . . . . . . .5E 165
Hilton. Shrp . . . . . . . . . . . . . .1B 60
Hilton. Staf . . . . . . . . . . . . . .5E 73
Hilton. Stoc T . . . . . . . . . . . .3B 106
Hilton of Cadboll. High . . . . . .1C 158
Himbleton. Worc . . . . . . . . . .5D 60
Himley. Staf . . . . . . . . . . . . .1C 60
Hincaster. Cumb . . . . . . . . . .1E 97
Hinchwick. Glos . . . . . . . . . . .3G 49
**Hinckley.** Leics . . . . . . . . . .1B 62
Hinderclay. Suff . . . . . . . . . . .3C 66
Hinderwell. N Yor . . . . . . . . . .3E 107
Hindford. Shrp . . . . . . . . . . . .2F 71

Hindhead. Surr . . . . . . . . . . . .3G 25
**Hindley.** G Man . . . . . . . . . .4E 90
Hindley. Nmbd . . . . . . . . . . .4D 114
Hindley Green. G Man . . . . . . .4E 91
Hindlip. Worc . . . . . . . . . . . . .5C 60
Hindolveston. Norf . . . . . . . . .3C 78
Hindon. Wilts . . . . . . . . . . . . .3E 23
Hindringham. Norf . . . . . . . . . .2B 78
Hingham. Norf . . . . . . . . . . . .5C 78
Hinksford. Staf . . . . . . . . . . . .2C 60
Hinstock. Shrp . . . . . . . . . . . .3A 72
Hintlesham. Suff . . . . . . . . . . .1D 54
Hinton. Hants . . . . . . . . . . . .3H 15
Hinton. Here . . . . . . . . . . . . .2G 47
Hinton. Nptn . . . . . . . . . . . . .5C 62
Hinton. S Glo . . . . . . . . . . . . .4C 34
Hinton Ampner. Hants . . . . . . .4D 24
Hinton Blewett. Bath . . . . . . . .1A 22
Hinton Charterhouse. Bath . . . .1C 22
Hinton-in-the-Hedges. Nptn . . .2D 50
Hinton Martell. Dors . . . . . . . .2F 15
Hinton on the Green. Worc . . . .1F 49
Hinton Parva. Swin . . . . . . . . .3H 35
Hinton St George. Som . . . . . .1H 13
Hinton St Mary. Dors . . . . . . . .1C 14
Hinton Waldrist. Oxon . . . . . . .2B 36
Hints. Shrp . . . . . . . . . . . . . .3A 60
Hints. Staf . . . . . . . . . . . . . . .5F 73
Hinwick. Bed . . . . . . . . . . . . .4G 63
Hinxhill. Kent . . . . . . . . . . . . .1E 29
Hinxton. Cambs . . . . . . . . . . .1E 53
Hinxworth. Herts . . . . . . . . . .1C 52
Hipley. Hants . . . . . . . . . . . . .1E 16
Hipperholme. W Yor . . . . . . . .2B 92
Hipsburn. Nmbd . . . . . . . . . .3G 121
Hipswell. N Yor . . . . . . . . . . .5E 105
Hiraeth. Carm . . . . . . . . . . . .2F 43
Hirn. Abers . . . . . . . . . . . . . .3E 153
Hirnant. Powy . . . . . . . . . . . .3C 70
Hirst. N Lan . . . . . . . . . . . . .3B 128
Hirst. Nmbd . . . . . . . . . . . . .1F 115
First Courtney. N Yor . . . . . . . .2G 93
Hirwaen. Den . . . . . . . . . . . . .4D 82
Hirwaun. Rhon . . . . . . . . . . . .5C 46
Hiscott. Devn . . . . . . . . . . . . .4F 19
Histon. Cambs . . . . . . . . . . . .4D 64
Hitcham. Suff . . . . . . . . . . . . .5B 66
**Hitchin.** Herts . . . . . . . . . . .3B 52
Hittisleigh. Devn . . . . . . . . . . .3H 11
Hittisleigh Barton. Devn . . . . . .3H 11
Hive. E Yor . . . . . . . . . . . . . . .1B 94
Hixon. Staf . . . . . . . . . . . . . .3E 73
Hoaden. Kent . . . . . . . . . . . . .5G 41
Hoar Cross. Staf . . . . . . . . . . .3F 73
Hoarwithy. Here . . . . . . . . . . .3A 48
Hoath. Kent . . . . . . . . . . . . . .4G 41
Yr Hôb. Flin . . . . . . . . . . . . . .5F 83
Hobarris. Shrp . . . . . . . . . . . .3F 59
Hobbister. Orkn . . . . . . . . . . .7C 172
Hobbles Green. Suff . . . . . . . .5G 65
Hobbs Cross. Essx . . . . . . . . .1F 39
Hobkirk. Bord . . . . . . . . . . . .3H 119
Hobson. Dur . . . . . . . . . . . . .4E 115
Hoby. Leics . . . . . . . . . . . . . .4D 74
Hockering. Norf . . . . . . . . . . .4C 78
Hockering Heath. Norf . . . . . . .4C 78
Hockerton. Notts . . . . . . . . . .5E 86
**Hockley.** Essx . . . . . . . . . . .1C 40
Hockley. Staf . . . . . . . . . . . . .5G 73
Hockley. W Mid . . . . . . . . . . .3G 61
Hockley Heath. W Mid . . . . . . .3F 61
Hockliffe. C Beds . . . . . . . . . .3H 51
Hockwold cum Wilton.
    Norf . . . . . . . . . . . . . . . . .2G 65
Hockworthy. Devn . . . . . . . . .1D 12
**Hoddesdon.** Herts . . . . . . . .5D 52
Hoddlesden. Bkbn . . . . . . . . .2F 91
Hoddomcross. Dum . . . . . . . .2C 112
Hodgeston. Pemb . . . . . . . . . .5E 43
Hodley. Powy . . . . . . . . . . . .1D 58
Hodnet. Shrp . . . . . . . . . . . . .3A 72
Hodsoll Street. Kent . . . . . . . .4H 39
Hodson. Swin . . . . . . . . . . . .3G 35

Hodthorpe. *Derbs* . . . . . . . . . . .3C **86**
Hoe. *Norf* . . . . . . . . . . . . . . . . .4B **78**
The Hoe. *Plym* . . . . . . . . . . . . . .3A **8**
Hoe Gate. *Hants* . . . . . . . . . . . .1E **17**
Hoff. *Cumb* . . . . . . . . . . . . . . .3H **103**
Hoffleet Stow. *Linc* . . . . . . . . . .2B **76**
Hogaland. *Shet* . . . . . . . . . . . .4E **173**
Hogben's Hill. *Kent* . . . . . . . . . .5E **41**
Hoggard's Green. *Suff* . . . . . . . .5A **66**
Hoggeston. *Buck* . . . . . . . . . . . .3G **51**
Hoggrill's End. *Warw* . . . . . . . . .1G **61**
Hogha Gearraidh. *W Isl* . . . . . .1C **170**
Hoghton. *Lanc* . . . . . . . . . . . . . .2E **90**
Hoghton Bottoms. *Lanc* . . . . . . .2E **91**
Hognaston. *Derbs* . . . . . . . . . . .5G **85**
Hogsthorpe. *Linc* . . . . . . . . . . . .3E **89**
Hogstock. *Dors* . . . . . . . . . . . . .2E **15**
Holbeach. *Linc* . . . . . . . . . . . . .3C **76**
Holbeach Bank. *Linc* . . . . . . . . .3C **76**
Holbeach Clough. *Linc* . . . . . . . .3C **76**
Holbeach Drove. *Linc* . . . . . . . . .4C **76**
Holbeach Hurn. *Linc* . . . . . . . . .3C **76**
Holbeach St Johns. *Linc* . . . . . . .4C **76**
Holbeach St Marks. *Linc* . . . . . . .2C **76**
Holbeach St Matthew. *Linc* . . . . .2D **76**
Holbeck. *Notts* . . . . . . . . . . . . .3C **86**
Holbeck. *W Yor* . . . . . . . . . . . . .1C **92**
Holbeck Woodhouse. *Notts* . . . . .3C **86**
Holberrow Green. *Worc* . . . . . . . .5E **61**
Holbeton. *Devn* . . . . . . . . . . . . . .3C **8**
Holborn. *G Lon* . . . . . . . . . . . . .2E **39**
Holbrook. *Derbs* . . . . . . . . . . . .1A **74**
Holbrook. *S Yor* . . . . . . . . . . . . .2B **86**
Holbrook. *Suff* . . . . . . . . . . . . .2E **55**
Holburn. *Nmbd* . . . . . . . . . . . .1E **121**
Holbury. *Hants* . . . . . . . . . . . . .2C **16**
Holcombe. *Devn* . . . . . . . . . . . .5C **12**
Holcombe. *G Man* . . . . . . . . . . . .3F **91**
Holcombe. *Som* . . . . . . . . . . . .2B **22**
Holcombe Brook. *G Man* . . . . . . .3F **91**
Holcombe Rogus. *Devn* . . . . . . .1D **12**
Holcot. *Nptn* . . . . . . . . . . . . . . .4E **63**
Holden. *Lanc* . . . . . . . . . . . . . . .5G **97**
Holdenby. *Nptn* . . . . . . . . . . . . .4D **62**
Holder's Green. *Essx* . . . . . . . . .3G **53**
Holdgate. *Shrp* . . . . . . . . . . . . .2H **59**
Holdingham. *Linc* . . . . . . . . . . . .1H **75**
Holditch. *Dors* . . . . . . . . . . . . .2G **13**
Holemoor. *Devn* . . . . . . . . . . . . .2E **11**
Hole Street. *W Sus* . . . . . . . . . . .4C **26**
Holford. *Som* . . . . . . . . . . . . . . .2E **21**
Holker. *Cumb* . . . . . . . . . . . . . .2C **96**
Holkham. *Norf* . . . . . . . . . . . . . .1A **78**
Hollacombe. *Devn* . . . . . . . . . . .2D **11**
Holland. *Orkn*
   on Papa Westray . . . .2D **172**
   on Stronsay . . . . . . .5F **172**
Holland Fen. *Linc* . . . . . . . . . . . .1B **76**
Holland Lees. *Lanc* . . . . . . . . . . .4D **90**
Holland-on-Sea. *Essx* . . . . . . . . .4F **55**
Holland Park. *W Mid* . . . . . . . . . .5E **73**
Hollandstoun. *Orkn* . . . . . . . .2G **172**
Hollesley. *Suff* . . . . . . . . . . . . . .1G **55**
Hollinfare. *Warr* . . . . . . . . . . . . .1A **84**
Hollingbourne. *Kent* . . . . . . . . . .5C **40**
Hollingbury. *Brig* . . . . . . . . . . . .5E **27**
Hollingdon. *Buck* . . . . . . . . . . . .3G **51**
Hollingrove. *E Sus* . . . . . . . . . . .3A **28**
Hollington. *Derbs* . . . . . . . . . . .2G **73**
Hollington. *E Sus* . . . . . . . . . . . .4B **28**
Hollington. *Staf* . . . . . . . . . . . . .2E **73**
Hollington Grove. *Derbs* . . . . . . .2G **73**
Hollingworth. *G Man* . . . . . . . . . .1E **85**
Hollins. *Derbs* . . . . . . . . . . . . .3H **85**
Hollins. *G Man*
   nr. Bury . . . . . . . . . .4G **91**
   nr. Middleton . . . . . . .4G **91**
Hollinsclough. *Staf* . . . . . . . . . .4E **85**
Hollinswood. *Telf* . . . . . . . . . . . .5B **72**
Hollinthorpe. *W Yor* . . . . . . . . . .1D **93**
Hollinwood. *G Man* . . . . . . . . . . .4H **91**
Hollinwood. *Shrp* . . . . . . . . . . . .2H **71**
Hollocombe. *Devn* . . . . . . . . . . .1G **11**
Holloway. *Derbs* . . . . . . . . . . . .5H **85**

Hollowell. *Nptn* . . . . . . . . . . . . .3D **62**
Hollow Meadows. *S Yor* . . . . . . .2G **85**
Hollows. *Dum* . . . . . . . . . . . . .2E **113**
Hollybush. *Cphy* . . . . . . . . . . . . .5E **47**
Hollybush. *E Ayr* . . . . . . . . . . . .3C **116**
Hollybush. *Worc* . . . . . . . . . . . . .2C **48**
Holly End. *Norf* . . . . . . . . . . . . .5D **77**
Holly Hill. *N Yor* . . . . . . . . . . . . .4E **105**
Hollyhurst. *Shrp* . . . . . . . . . . . . .1H **71**
Hollym. *E Yor* . . . . . . . . . . . . . . .2G **95**
Hollywood. *Worc* . . . . . . . . . . . .3E **61**
Holmacott. *Devn* . . . . . . . . . . . . .4F **19**
Holmbridge. *W Yor* . . . . . . . . . . .4B **92**
Holmbury St Mary. *Surr* . . . . . . .1C **26**
Holmbush. *Corn* . . . . . . . . . . . . .3E **7**
Holmcroft. *Staf* . . . . . . . . . . . . .3D **72**
Holme. *Cambs* . . . . . . . . . . . . . .2A **64**
Holme. *Cumb* . . . . . . . . . . . . . .2E **97**
Holme. *N Lin* . . . . . . . . . . . . . . .4C **94**
Holme. *N Yor* . . . . . . . . . . . . . . .1F **99**
Holme. *Notts* . . . . . . . . . . . . . . .5F **87**
Holme. *W Yor* . . . . . . . . . . . . . . .4B **92**
Holmebridge. *Dors* . . . . . . . . . . .4D **15**
Holme Chapel. *Lanc* . . . . . . . . . .2G **91**
Holme Hale. *Norf* . . . . . . . . . . . .5A **78**
Holme Lacy. *Here* . . . . . . . . . . . .2A **48**
Holme Marsh. *Here* . . . . . . . . . . .5F **59**
Holmend. *Dum* . . . . . . . . . . . .4C **118**
Holme next the Sea. *Norf* . . . . . .1G **77**
Holme-on-Spalding-Moor.
   *E Yor* . . . . . . . . . . . . . .1B **94**
Holme on the Wolds. *E Yor* . . . . .5D **100**
Holme Pierrepont. *Notts* . . . . . .2D **74**
Holmer. *Here* . . . . . . . . . . . . . . .1A **48**
Holmer Green. *Buck* . . . . . . . . . .1A **38**
Holmes. *Lanc* . . . . . . . . . . . . . . .3C **90**
Holme St Cuthbert. *Cumb* . . . . .5C **112**
Holmes Chapel. *Ches E* . . . . . . .4B **84**
Holmesfield. *Derbs* . . . . . . . . . . .3H **85**
Holmeswood. *Lanc* . . . . . . . . . . .3C **90**
Holmewood. *Derbs* . . . . . . . . . . .4B **86**
Holmfirth. *W Yor* . . . . . . . . . . . . .4B **92**
Holmhead. *E Ayr* . . . . . . . . . . . .2E **117**
Holmisdale. *High* . . . . . . . . . . .4A **154**
Holm of Drumlanrig. *Dum* . . . . .5H **117**
Holmpton. *E Yor* . . . . . . . . . . . .2G **95**
Holmrook. *Cumb* . . . . . . . . . . . .5B **102**
Holmsgarth. *Shet* . . . . . . . . . . .7F **173**
Holmside. *Dur* . . . . . . . . . . . . . .5F **115**
Holmwrangle. *Cumb* . . . . . . . . . .5G **113**
Holne. *Devn* . . . . . . . . . . . . . . . . .2D **8**
Holsworthy. *Devn* . . . . . . . . . . . .2D **10**
Holsworthy Beacon. *Devn* . . . . . .2D **10**
Holt. *Dors* . . . . . . . . . . . . . . . . .2F **15**
Holt. *Norf* . . . . . . . . . . . . . . . . . .2C **78**
Holt. *Wilts* . . . . . . . . . . . . . . . . .5D **34**
Holt. *Worc* . . . . . . . . . . . . . . . . .4C **60**
Holt. *Wrex* . . . . . . . . . . . . . . . . .5G **83**
Holtby. *York* . . . . . . . . . . . . . . .4A **100**
Holt End. *Hants* . . . . . . . . . . . . .3E **25**
Holt End. *Worc* . . . . . . . . . . . . . .4E **61**
Holt Fleet. *Worc* . . . . . . . . . . . . .4C **60**
Holt Green. *Lanc* . . . . . . . . . . . .4B **90**
Holt Heath. *Dors* . . . . . . . . . . . .2F **15**
Holt Heath. *Worc* . . . . . . . . . . . .4C **60**
Holton. *Oxon* . . . . . . . . . . . . . . .5D **50**
Holton. *Som* . . . . . . . . . . . . . . .4B **22**
Holton. *Suff* . . . . . . . . . . . . . . . .3F **67**
Holton cum Beckering. *Linc* . . . . .2A **88**
Holton Heath. *Dors* . . . . . . . . . . .3E **15**
Holton le Clay. *Linc* . . . . . . . . . .4F **95**
Holton le Moor. *Linc* . . . . . . . . .1H **87**
Holton St Mary. *Suff* . . . . . . . . . .2D **54**
Holt Pound. *Hants* . . . . . . . . . . .2G **25**
Holtsmoers End. *Herts* . . . . . . . .4A **52**
Holtye. *E Sus* . . . . . . . . . . . . . . .2F **27**
Holwell. *Dors* . . . . . . . . . . . . . . .1C **14**
Holwell. *Herts* . . . . . . . . . . . . . . .2B **52**
Holwell. *Leics* . . . . . . . . . . . . . .3E **75**
Holwell. *Oxon* . . . . . . . . . . . . . .5H **49**
Holwell. *Som* . . . . . . . . . . . . . . .2C **22**
Holwick. *Dur* . . . . . . . . . . . . . . .2C **104**
Holworth. *Dors* . . . . . . . . . . . . .4C **14**
Holybourne. *Hants* . . . . . . . . . . .2F **25**

Holy City. *Devn* . . . . . . . . . . . . . .2G **13**
Holy Cross. *Worc* . . . . . . . . . . . .3D **60**
Holyfield. *Essx* . . . . . . . . . . . . . .5D **53**
**Holyhead.** *IOA* . . . . . . . . . . . . . .2B **80**
Holy Island. *Nmbd* . . . . . . . . . .5H **131**
Holymoorside. *Derbs* . . . . . . . . . .4H **85**
Holyport. *Wind* . . . . . . . . . . . . . .4G **37**
Holystone. *Nmbd* . . . . . . . . . . .4D **120**
Holywell. *N Lan* . . . . . . . . . . . .3A **128**
Holywell. *Cambs* . . . . . . . . . . . .3C **64**
Holywell. *Corn* . . . . . . . . . . . . . . .3B **6**
Holywell. *Dors* . . . . . . . . . . . . . .2A **14**
Holywell. *Flin* . . . . . . . . . . . . . . .3D **82**
Holywell. *Glos* . . . . . . . . . . . . . . .2D **35**
Holywell. *Nmbd* . . . . . . . . . . . .2G **115**
Holywell. *Warw* . . . . . . . . . . . . . .4F **61**
Holywell Green. *W Yor* . . . . . . . . .3A **92**
Holywell Lake. *Som* . . . . . . . . . . .4E **20**
Holywell Row. *Suff* . . . . . . . . . . .3G **65**
**Holywood.** *Ards* . . . . . . . . . . . .4H **175**
Holywood. *Dum* . . . . . . . . . . . .1G **111**
Homer. *Shrp* . . . . . . . . . . . . . . . .5A **72**
Homer Green. *Mers* . . . . . . . . . . .4B **90**
Homersfield. *Suff* . . . . . . . . . . . .2E **67**
Hom Green. *Here* . . . . . . . . . . . .3A **48**
Homington. *Wilts* . . . . . . . . . . . .4G **23**
Honeyborough. *Pemb* . . . . . . . . .4D **42**
Honeybourne. *Worc* . . . . . . . . . . .1G **49**
Honeychurch. *Devn* . . . . . . . . . . .2G **11**
Honeydon. *Bed* . . . . . . . . . . . . .5A **64**
Honey Hill. *Kent* . . . . . . . . . . . . .4F **41**
Honey Street. *Wilts* . . . . . . . . . .5G **35**
Honey Tye. *Suff* . . . . . . . . . . . . .2C **54**
Honeywick. *C Beds* . . . . . . . . . . .3H **51**
Honiley. *Warw* . . . . . . . . . . . . . . .3G **61**
Honing. *Norf* . . . . . . . . . . . . . . .3F **79**
Honingham. *Norf* . . . . . . . . . . . .4D **78**
Honington. *Linc* . . . . . . . . . . . . .1G **75**
Honington. *Suff* . . . . . . . . . . . . .3B **66**
Honington. *Warw* . . . . . . . . . . . .1A **50**
Honiton. *Devn* . . . . . . . . . . . . . . .2E **13**
Honley. *W Yor* . . . . . . . . . . . . . . .3B **92**
Honnington. *Telf* . . . . . . . . . . . . .4B **72**
Hoo. *Suff* . . . . . . . . . . . . . . . . . .5E **67**
Hoobrook. *Worc* . . . . . . . . . . . . .3C **60**
Hood Green. *S Yor* . . . . . . . . . . .4D **92**
Hooe. *E Sus* . . . . . . . . . . . . . . .5A **28**
Hooe. *Plym* . . . . . . . . . . . . . . . . .3B **8**
Hooe Common. *E Sus* . . . . . . . . .4A **28**
Hoo Green. *Ches E* . . . . . . . . . . .2B **84**
Hoohill. *Bkpl* . . . . . . . . . . . . . . .1B **90**
Hook. *Cambs* . . . . . . . . . . . . . . .1D **64**
Hook. *E Yor* . . . . . . . . . . . . . . . .2A **94**
Hook. *G Lon* . . . . . . . . . . . . . . . .4C **38**
Hook. *Hants*
   nr. Basingstoke . . . . . .1F **25**
   nr. Fareham . . . . . . . .2D **16**
Hook. *Pemb* . . . . . . . . . . . . . . . .3D **43**
Hook. *Wilts* . . . . . . . . . . . . . . . . .3F **35**
Hook-a-Gate. *Shrp* . . . . . . . . . . .5G **71**
Hook Bank. *Worc* . . . . . . . . . . . .1D **48**
Hooke. *Dors* . . . . . . . . . . . . . . . .2A **14**
Hooker Gate. *Tyne* . . . . . . . . . . .4E **115**
Hookgate. *Staf* . . . . . . . . . . . . . .2B **72**
Hook Green. *Kent*
   nr. Lamberhurst . . . . . .2A **28**
   nr. Meopham . . . . . . . .4H **39**
   nr. Southfleet . . . . . . . .3H **39**
Hook Norton. *Oxon* . . . . . . . . . . .2B **50**
Hook's Cross. *Herts* . . . . . . . . . .3C **52**
Hook Street. *Glos* . . . . . . . . . . . .2B **34**
Hookway. *Devn* . . . . . . . . . . . . . .3B **12**
Hookwood. *Surr* . . . . . . . . . . . . .1D **26**
Hoole. *Ches W* . . . . . . . . . . . . . .4G **83**
Hooley. *Surr* . . . . . . . . . . . . . . . .5D **39**
Hooley Bridge. *G Man* . . . . . . . . .3G **91**
Hooley Brow. *G Man* . . . . . . . . . .3G **91**
Hoo St Werburgh. *Medw* . . . . . . .3B **40**
Hooton. *Ches W* . . . . . . . . . . . . .3F **83**
Hooton Levitt. *S Yor* . . . . . . . . . .1C **86**
Hooton Pagnell. *S Yor* . . . . . . . . .4E **93**
Hooton Roberts. *S Yor* . . . . . . . .1B **86**
Hoove. *Shet* . . . . . . . . . . . . . . .7E **173**
Hope. *Derbs* . . . . . . . . . . . . . . . .2F **85**

Hope. *Flin* . . . . . . . . . . . . . . . . . .5F **83**
Hope. *High* . . . . . . . . . . . . . . . .2E **167**
Hope. *Powy* . . . . . . . . . . . . . . . . .5E **71**
Hope. *Shrp* . . . . . . . . . . . . . . . . .5F **71**
Hope. *Staf* . . . . . . . . . . . . . . . . .5F **85**
Hope Bagot. *Shrp* . . . . . . . . . . . .3H **59**
Hope Bowdler. *Shrp* . . . . . . . . . .1G **59**
Hopedale. *Staf* . . . . . . . . . . . . . .5F **85**
Hope Green. *Ches E* . . . . . . . . . .2D **84**
Hopeman. *Mor* . . . . . . . . . . . . .2F **159**
Hope Mansell. *Here* . . . . . . . . . . .4B **48**
Hopesay. *Shrp* . . . . . . . . . . . . . .2F **59**
Hope's Green. *Essx* . . . . . . . . . . .2B **40**
Hopetown. *W Yor* . . . . . . . . . . . .2D **93**
Hope under Dinmore. *Here* . . . . . .5H **59**
Hopley's Green. *Here* . . . . . . . . . .5F **59**
Hopperton. *N Yor* . . . . . . . . . . . .4G **99**
Hop Pole. *Linc* . . . . . . . . . . . . . .4A **76**
Hopstone. *Shrp* . . . . . . . . . . . . .1B **60**
Hopton. *Derbs* . . . . . . . . . . . . . .5G **85**
Hopton. *Powy* . . . . . . . . . . . . . .1E **59**
Hopton. *Shrp*
   nr. Oswestry . . . . . . . .3F **71**
   nr. Wem . . . . . . . . . . .3H **71**
Hopton. *Staf* . . . . . . . . . . . . . . . .3D **72**
Hopton. *Suff* . . . . . . . . . . . . . . . .3B **66**
Hopton Cangeford. *Shrp* . . . . . . .2H **59**
Hopton Castle. *Shrp* . . . . . . . . . .3F **59**
Hopton Heath. *Staf* . . . . . . . . . . .3D **72**
Hoptonheath. *Shrp* . . . . . . . . . . .3F **59**
Hopton on Sea. *Norf* . . . . . . . . . .5H **79**
Hopton Wafers. *Shrp* . . . . . . . . . .3A **60**
Hopwas. *Staf* . . . . . . . . . . . . . . .5F **73**
Hopwood. *Worc* . . . . . . . . . . . . .3E **61**
Horam. *E Sus* . . . . . . . . . . . . . . .4G **27**
Horbling. *Linc* . . . . . . . . . . . . . . .2A **76**
Horbury. *W Yor* . . . . . . . . . . . . . .3C **92**
Horcott. *Glos* . . . . . . . . . . . . . . .5G **49**
Horden. *Dur* . . . . . . . . . . . . . . .5H **115**
Horderley. *Shrp* . . . . . . . . . . . . .2G **59**
Hordle. *Hants* . . . . . . . . . . . . . . .3A **16**
Hordley. *Shrp* . . . . . . . . . . . . . . .2F **71**
Horeb. *Carm*
   nr. Brechfa . . . . . . . . .3F **45**
   nr. Llanelli . . . . . . . . . .5E **45**
Horeb. *Cdgn* . . . . . . . . . . . . . . . .1D **45**
Horfield. *Bris* . . . . . . . . . . . . . . . .4A **34**
Horgabost. *W Isl* . . . . . . . . . . . .8C **171**
Horham. *Suff* . . . . . . . . . . . . . . .3E **66**
Horkstow. *N Lin* . . . . . . . . . . . . .3C **94**
Horley. *Oxon* . . . . . . . . . . . . . . .1C **50**
**Horley.** *Surr* . . . . . . . . . . . . . . .1D **27**
Horn Ash. *Dors* . . . . . . . . . . . . . .2G **13**
Hornblotton Green. *Som* . . . . . . .3A **22**
Hornby. *Lanc* . . . . . . . . . . . . . . .3E **97**
Hornby. *N Yor*
   nr. Appleton Wiske . . . .4A **106**
   nr. Catterick Garrison
   . . . . . . . . . . . . . . . . .5F **105**
Horncastle. *Linc* . . . . . . . . . . . . .4B **88**
**Hornchurch.** *G Lon* . . . . . . . . . .2G **39**
Horncliffe. *Nmbd* . . . . . . . . . . .5F **131**
Horndean. *Hants* . . . . . . . . . . . .1F **17**
Horndean. *Bord* . . . . . . . . . . . .5E **131**
Horndon. *Devn* . . . . . . . . . . . . . .4F **11**
Horndon on the Hill. *Thur* . . . . . .2A **40**
Horne. *Surr* . . . . . . . . . . . . . . . .1E **27**
Horner. *Som* . . . . . . . . . . . . . . . .2C **20**
Horning. *Norf* . . . . . . . . . . . . . . .4F **79**
Horninghold. *Leics* . . . . . . . . . . .1F **63**
Horninglow. *Staf* . . . . . . . . . . . . .3G **73**
Horningsea. *Cambs* . . . . . . . . . .4D **65**
Horningsham. *Wilts* . . . . . . . . . .2D **22**
Horningtoft. *Norf* . . . . . . . . . . . . .3B **78**
Hornsbury. *Som* . . . . . . . . . . . . .1G **13**
Hornsby. *Cumb* . . . . . . . . . . . .4G **113**
Hornsbygate. *Cumb* . . . . . . . . .4G **113**
Horns Corner. *Kent* . . . . . . . . . . .3B **28**
Horns Cross. *Devn* . . . . . . . . . . .4D **19**
Hornsea. *E Yor* . . . . . . . . . . . . .5G **101**
Hornsea Burton. *E Yor* . . . . . . . .5G **101**
**Hornsey.** *G Lon* . . . . . . . . . . . .2E **39**
Hornton. *Oxon* . . . . . . . . . . . . . .1B **50**
Horpit. *Swin* . . . . . . . . . . . . . . . .3H **35**

Horrabridge. *Devn* . . . . . . . . . . . .2B **8**
Horringer. *Suff* . . . . . . . . . . . . . .4H **65**
Horringford. *IOW* . . . . . . . . . . . .4D **16**
Horrocks Fold. *G Man* . . . . . . . . .3F **91**
Horrocksford. *Lanc* . . . . . . . . . . .5G **97**
Horsbrugh Ford. *Bord* . . . . . . . .1E **119**
Horsebridge. *Devn* . . . . . . . . . . .5E **11**
Horsebridge. *Hants* . . . . . . . . . .3B **24**
Horsebrook. *Staf* . . . . . . . . . . . .4C **72**
Horsecastle. *N Som* . . . . . . . . . .5H **33**
Horsehay. *Telf* . . . . . . . . . . . . . . .5A **72**
Horseheath. *Cambs* . . . . . . . . . .1G **53**
Horsehouse. *N Yor* . . . . . . . . . . .1C **98**
Horsell. *Surr* . . . . . . . . . . . . . . . .5A **38**
Horseman's Green. *Wrex* . . . . . . .1G **71**
Horsenden. *Buck* . . . . . . . . . . . .5F **51**
Horseway. *Cambs* . . . . . . . . . . .2D **64**
Horsey. *Norf* . . . . . . . . . . . . . . . .3G **79**
Horsey. *Som* . . . . . . . . . . . . . . . .3G **21**
Horsford. *Norf* . . . . . . . . . . . . . .4D **78**
**Horsforth.** *W Yor* . . . . . . . . . . . .1C **92**
**Horsham.** *W Sus* . . . . . . . . . . . .2C **26**
Horsham. *Worc* . . . . . . . . . . . . . .5B **60**
Horsham St Faith. *Norf* . . . . . . . .4E **78**
Horsington. *Linc* . . . . . . . . . . . . .4A **88**
Horsington. *Som* . . . . . . . . . . . .4C **22**
Horsley. *Derbs* . . . . . . . . . . . . . .1A **74**
Horsley. *Glos* . . . . . . . . . . . . . . .2D **34**
Horsley. *Nmbd*
   nr. Prudhoe . . . . . . . .3D **115**
   nr. Rochester . . . . . . .5C **120**
Horsley Cross. *Essx* . . . . . . . . . .3E **54**
Horsleycross Street. *Essx* . . . . . .3E **54**
Horsleyhill. *Bord* . . . . . . . . . . . .3H **119**
Horsleyhope. *Dur* . . . . . . . . . . .5D **114**
Horsley Woodhouse.
   *Derbs* . . . . . . . . . . . . .1A **74**
Horsmonden. *Kent* . . . . . . . . . . .1A **28**
Horspath. *Oxon* . . . . . . . . . . . . .5D **50**
Horstead. *Norf* . . . . . . . . . . . . . .4E **79**
Horsted Keynes. *W Sus* . . . . . . . .3E **27**
Horton. *Buck* . . . . . . . . . . . . . . .3H **51**
Horton. *Dors* . . . . . . . . . . . . . . . .2F **15**
Horton. *Lanc* . . . . . . . . . . . . . . .4A **98**
Horton. *Nptn* . . . . . . . . . . . . . . . .5F **63**
Horton. *Shrp* . . . . . . . . . . . . . . . .2G **71**
Horton. *Som* . . . . . . . . . . . . . . . .1G **13**
Horton. *S Glo* . . . . . . . . . . . . . . .3C **34**
Horton. *Staf* . . . . . . . . . . . . . . . .5D **84**
Horton. *Swan* . . . . . . . . . . . . . . .4D **30**
Horton. *Wilts* . . . . . . . . . . . . . . . .5F **35**
Horton. *Wind* . . . . . . . . . . . . . . .3B **38**
Horton Cross. *Som* . . . . . . . . . . .1G **13**
Horton-cum-Studley. *Oxon* . . . . .4D **50**
Horton Grange. *Nmbd* . . . . . . . .2F **115**
Horton Green. *Ches W* . . . . . . . . .1G **71**
Horton Heath. *Hants* . . . . . . . . . .1C **16**
Horton in Ribblesdale.
   *N Yor* . . . . . . . . . . . . . .2H **97**
Horton Kirby. *Kent* . . . . . . . . . . . .4G **39**
Hortonwood. *Telf* . . . . . . . . . . . .4A **72**
**Horwich.** *G Man* . . . . . . . . . . . .3E **91**
Horwich End. *Derbs* . . . . . . . . . .2E **85**
Horwood. *Devn* . . . . . . . . . . . . . .4F **19**
Hoscar. *Lanc* . . . . . . . . . . . . . . .3C **90**
Hose. *Leics* . . . . . . . . . . . . . . . .3E **75**
Hosh. *Per* . . . . . . . . . . . . . . . . .1A **136**
Hosta. *W Isl* . . . . . . . . . . . . . . . .1C **170**
Hoswick. *Shet* . . . . . . . . . . . . . .9F **173**
Hotham. *E Yor* . . . . . . . . . . . . . .1B **94**
Hothfield. *Kent* . . . . . . . . . . . . . .1D **28**
Hoton. *Leics* . . . . . . . . . . . . . . . .3C **74**
Houbie. *Shet* . . . . . . . . . . . . . . .2H **173**
Hough. *Arg* . . . . . . . . . . . . . . . .4A **138**
Hough. *Ches E*
   nr. Crewe . . . . . . . . . .5B **84**
   nr. Wilmslow . . . . . . . .3C **84**
Hougham. *Linc* . . . . . . . . . . . . . .1F **75**
Hough Green. *Hal* . . . . . . . . . . . .2G **83**
Hough-on-the-Hill. *Linc* . . . . . . .1G **75**
Houghton. *Cambs* . . . . . . . . . . . .3B **64**
Houghton. *Cumb* . . . . . . . . . . .4F **113**
Houghton. *Hants* . . . . . . . . . . . .3B **24**
Houghton. *Nmbd* . . . . . . . . . . .3E **115**

Houghton. Pemb .........4D 43
Houghton. W Sus .......4B 26
Houghton Bank. Darl ...2F 105
Houghton Conquest. C Beds ...1A 52
Houghton Green. E Sus ...3D 28
Houghton Green. Warr ...1B 84
Houghton-le-Side. Darl ...2F 105
Houghton-le-Spring. Tyne ...4G 115
Houghton on the Hill. Leics ...5D 74
Houghton Regis. C Beds ...3A 52
Houghton St Giles. Norf ...2B 78
Houlland. Shet
  on Mainland ...6E 173
  on Yell ...4G 173
Houlsyke. N Yor ...4E 107
Houlton. Warw ...3C 62
Hound. Hants ...2C 16
Hound Green. Hants ...1F 25
Houndslow. Bord ...5C 130
Houndsmoor. Som ...4E 21
Houndwood. Bord ...3E 131
Hounsdown. Hants ...1B 16
Hounslow. G Lon ...3C 38
Housabister. Shet ...6F 173
Housay. Shet ...4H 173
Househill. High ...3C 158
Housetter. Shet ...3E 173
Houss. Shet ...8E 173
Houston. Ren ...3F 127
Housty. High ...5D 168
Houton. Orkn ...7C 172
Hove. Brig ...5D 27
Hoveringham. Notts ...1D 74
Hoveton. Norf ...4F 79
Hovingham. N Yor ...2A 100
How. Cumb ...4G 113
How Caple. Here ...2B 48
Howden. E Yor ...2H 93
Howden-le-Wear. Dur ...1E 105
Howe. High ...2F 169
Howe. Norf ...5E 79
Howe. N Yor ...1F 99
The Howe. Cumb ...1D 96
The Howe. IOM ...5A 108
Howe Green. Essx ...5H 53
Howe Green. Warw ...2H 61
Howegreen. Essx ...5B 54
Howell. Linc ...1A 76
Howe End. C Beds ...1A 52
Howe of Teuchar. Abers ...4E 161
Howes. Dum ...3C 112
Howe Street. Essx
  nr. Chelmsford ...4G 53
  nr. Finchingfield ...2G 53
Howey. Powy ...5C 58
Howgate. Midl ...4F 129
Howgill. Lanc ...5H 97
Howgill. N Yor ...4C 98
How Green. Kent ...1F 27
How Hill. Norf ...4F 79
Howick. Nmbd ...3G 121
Howle. Telf ...3A 72
Howle Hill. Here ...3B 48
Howleigh. Som ...1F 13
Howlett End. Essx ...2F 53
Howley. Som ...2F 13
Howley. Warr ...2A 84
Howsham. Bord ...3B 120
Howsham. N Lin ...4D 94
Howsham. N Yor ...3B 100
Howtel. Nmbd ...1C 120
Howt Green. Kent ...4C 40
Howton. Here ...3H 47
Howwood. Ren ...3E 127
Hoxne. Suff ...3D 66
Hoylake. Mers ...2E 82
Hoyland. S Yor ...4D 92
Hoylandswaine. S Yor ...4C 92
Hoyle. W Sus ...4A 26
Hubberholme. N Yor ...2B 98
Hubberston. Pemb ...4C 42
Hubbert's Bridge. Linc ...1B 76
Huby. N Yor
  nr. Harrogate ...5E 99
  nr. York ...3H 99

Hucclecote. Glos ...4D 48
Hucking. Kent ...5C 40
Hucknall. Notts ...1C 74
Huddersfield. W Yor ...3B 92
Huddington. Worc ...5D 60
Huddlesford. Staf ...5F 73
Hudswell. N Yor ...4E 105
Huggate. E Yor ...4C 100
Hugglescote. Leics ...4B 74
Hughenden Valley. Buck ...2G 37
Hughley. Shrp ...1H 59
Hughton. High ...4G 157
Hugh Town. IOS ...1B 4
Hugus. Corn ...4B 6
Huish. Devn ...1F 11
Huish. Wilts ...5G 35
Huish Champflower. Som ...4D 20
Huish Episcopi. Som ...4H 21
Huisinis. W Isl ...6B 171
Hulcote. Nptn ...1F 51
Hulcott. Buck ...4G 51
Hulham. Devn ...4D 12
Hulland. Derbs ...1G 73
Hulland Moss. Derbs ...1G 73
Hulland Ward. Derbs ...1G 73
Hullavington. Wilts ...3D 35
Hullbridge. Essx ...1C 40
Hulme. G Man ...1C 84
Hulme. Staf ...1D 72
Hulme End. Staf ...5F 85
Hulme Walfield. Ches E ...4C 84
Hulverstone. IOW ...4B 16
Hulver Street. Suff ...2G 67
Humber. Devn ...5C 12
Humber. Here ...5H 59
Humber Bridge. N Lin ...2D 94
Humberside Airport. N Lin ...3D 94
Humberston. NE Lin ...4G 95
Humberstone. Leic ...5D 74
Humble. E Lot ...3A 130
Humbleton. E Yor ...1F 95
Humbleton. Nmbd ...2D 121
Humby. Linc ...2H 75
Hume. Bord ...5D 130
Humshaugh. Nmbd ...2C 114
Huna. High ...1F 169
Huncoat. Lanc ...1F 91
Huncote. Leics ...1C 62
Hundall. Derbs ...3A 86
Hunderthwaite. Dur ...2C 104
Hundleby. Linc ...4C 88
Hundle Houses. Linc ...5B 88
Hundleton. Pemb ...4D 42
Hundon. Suff ...1H 53
The Hundred. Here ...4H 59
Hundred Acres. Hants ...1D 16
Hundred House. Powy ...5D 58
Hungarton. Leics ...5D 74
Hungerford. Hants ...1G 15
Hungerford. Shrp ...2H 59
Hungerford. Som ...2D 20
Hungerford. W Ber ...5B 36
Hungerford Newtown.
  W Ber ...4B 36
Hunger Hill. G Man ...4E 91
Hungerton. Linc ...2F 75
Hungladder. High ...1C 154
Hungryhatton. Shrp ...3A 72
Hunmanby. N Yor ...2E 101
Hunmanby Sands. N Yor ...2F 101
Hunningham. Warw ...4A 62
Hunnington. Worc ...2D 60
Hunny Hill. IOW ...4C 16
Hunsdon. Herts ...4E 53
Hunsdonbury. Herts ...4E 53
Hunsingore. N Yor ...4G 99
Hunslet. W Yor ...1D 92
Hunslet Carr. W Yor ...1D 92
Hunsonby. Cumb ...1G 103
Hunspow. High ...1E 169
Hunstanton. Norf ...1F 77
Hunstanworth. Dur ...5C 114
Hunston. Suff ...4B 66

Hunston. W Sus ...2G 17
Hunstrete. Bath ...5B 34
Hunt End. Worc ...4E 61
Hunterfield. Midl ...3G 129
Hunters Forstal. Kent ...4F 41
Hunter's Quay. Arg ...2C 126
Hunthill Lodge. Ang ...1D 144
Huntingdon. Cambs ...3B 64
Huntingfield. Suff ...3F 67
Huntingtower. Per ...1C 136
Huntington. Ches W ...4G 83
Huntington. E Lot ...2A 130
Huntington. Here ...5E 59
Huntington. Staf ...4D 72
Huntington. Telf ...5A 72
Huntington. York ...4A 100
Huntington. Per ...1C 136
Huntley. Glos ...4C 48
Huntly. Staf ...1E 73
Huntly. Abers ...5C 160
Huntlywood. Bord ...5C 130
Hunton. Hants ...3C 24
Hunton. Kent ...1B 28
Hunton. N Yor ...5E 105
Hunton Bridge. Herts ...1B 38
Hunt's Corner. Norf ...2C 66
Huntscott. Som ...2C 20
Huntsham. Devn ...4D 20
Huntshaw. Devn ...4F 19
Huntspill. Som ...2G 21
Huntstile. Som ...3F 21
Huntworth. Som ...3G 21
Hunwick. Dur ...1E 105
Hunworth. Norf ...2C 78
Hurcott. Som
  nr. Ilminster ...1G 13
  nr. Somerton ...4A 22
Hurdcott. Wilts ...3G 23
Hurdley. Powy ...1E 59
Hurdsfield. Ches E ...3D 84
Hurlet. Glas ...3G 127
Hurley. Warw ...1G 61
Hurley. Wind ...3G 37
Hurlford. E Ayr ...1D 116
Hurliness. Orkn ...9B 172
Hurlston Green. Lanc ...3C 90
Hurn. Dors ...3G 15
Hurworth. Dors ...2H 13
Hursley. Hants ...4C 24
Hurst. G Man ...4H 91
Hurst. N Yor ...4D 104
Hurst. Som ...1H 13
Hurst. Wok ...4F 37
Hurstbourne Priors. Hants ...2C 24
Hurstbourne Tarrant. Hants ...1B 24
Hurst Green. Ches E ...1H 71
Hurst Green. E Sus ...3B 28
Hurst Green. Essx ...4D 54
Hurst Green. Lanc ...1E 91
Hurst Green. Surr ...5E 39
Hurstley. Here ...1G 47
Hurstpierpoint. W Sus ...4D 27
Hurstway Common. Here ...1G 47
Hurst Wickham. W Sus ...4D 27
Hurstwood. Lanc ...1G 91
Hurtmore. Surr ...1A 26
Hurworth-on-Tees. Darl ...3A 106
Hurworth Place. Darl ...4F 105
Hury. Dur ...3C 104
Husbands Bosworth. Leics ...2D 62
Husborne Crawley. C Beds ...2H 51
Husthwaite. N Yor ...2H 99
Hutcherleigh. Devn ...3D 9
Hut Green. N Yor ...2F 93
Huthwaite. Notts ...5B 86
Huttoft. Linc ...3E 89
Hutton. Cumb ...2F 103
Hutton. E Yor ...4E 101
Hutton. Essx ...1H 39
Hutton. Lanc ...2C 90
Hutton. N Som ...1G 21

Hutton. Bord ...4F 131
Hutton Bonville. N Yor ...4A 106
Hutton Buscel. N Yor ...1D 100
Hutton Conyers. N Yor ...2F 99
Hutton Cranswick. E Yor ...4E 101
Hutton End. Cumb ...1F 103
Hutton Gate. Red C ...3C 106
Hutton Henry. Dur ...1B 106
Hutton-le-Hole. N Yor ...1B 100
Hutton Magna. Dur ...3E 105
Hutton Mulgrave. N Yor ...4F 107
Hutton Roof. Cumb
  nr. Kirkby Lonsdale ...2E 97
  nr. Penrith ...1E 103
Hutton Rudby. N Yor ...4B 106
Huttons Ambo. N Yor ...3B 100
Hutton Sessay. N Yor ...2G 99
Hutton Village. Red C ...3D 106
Hutton Wandesley. N Yor ...4H 99
Huxham. Devn ...3C 12
Huxham Green. Som ...3A 22
Huxley. Ches W ...4H 83
Huxter. Shet
  on Mainland ...6C 173
  on Whalsay ...5G 173
Huyton. Mers ...1G 83
Hwlffordd. Pemb ...3D 42
Hycemoor. Cumb ...1A 96
Hyde. Glos
  nr. Stroud ...5D 49
  nr. Winchcombe ...3F 49
Hyde. G Man ...1D 84
Hyde Heath. Buck ...5H 51
Hyde Lea. Staf ...4D 72
Hyde Park. S Yor ...4F 93
Hydestile. Surr ...1A 26
Hykeham Bridge. S Lan ...5C 128
Hyndford Bridge. S Lan ...5A 138
Hynish. Arg ...5A 138
Hyssington. Powy ...1F 59
Hythe. Hants ...2C 16
Hythe. Kent ...2F 29
Hythe End. Wind ...3B 38
Hythie. Abers ...3H 161
Hyton. Cumb ...1A 96

# I

Ianstown. Mor ...2B 160
Iarsiadar. W Isl ...4D 171
Ibberton. Dors ...2C 14
Ible. Derbs ...5G 85
Ibrox. Glas ...3G 127
Ibsley. Hants ...2G 15
Ibstock. Leics ...4B 74
Ibstone. Buck ...2F 37
Ibthorpe. Hants ...1B 24
Iburndale. N Yor ...4F 107
Ibworth. Hants ...1D 24
Icelton. N Som ...5G 33
Ichrachan. Arg ...5E 141
Ickburgh. Norf ...1H 65
Ickenham. G Lon ...2B 38
Ickenthwaite. Cumb ...1C 96
Ickford. Buck ...5E 51
Ickham. Kent ...5G 41
Ickleford. Herts ...2B 52
Icklesham. E Sus ...4C 28
Ickleton. Cambs ...1E 53
Icklingham. Suff ...3G 65
Ickwell. C Beds ...1B 52
Icomb. Glos ...3H 49
Idbury. Oxon ...4H 49
Iddesleigh. Devn ...2F 11
Ide. Devn ...3B 12
Ideford. Devn ...5B 12
Ide Hill. Kent ...5F 39
Iden. E Sus ...3D 28
Iden Green. Kent
  nr. Benenden ...2C 28
  nr. Goudhurst ...2B 28
Idle. W Yor ...1B 92
Idless. Corn ...4C 6
Idlicote. Warw ...1A 50

Idmiston. Wilts ...3G 23
Idole. Carm ...4E 45
Idridgehay. Derbs ...1G 73
Idrigill. High ...2C 154
Idstone. Oxon ...3A 36
Iffley. Oxon ...5D 50
Ifield. W Sus ...2D 26
Ifieldwood. W Sus ...2D 26
Ifold. W Sus ...2B 26
Iford. E Sus ...5F 27
Ifton Heath. Shrp ...2F 71
Ightfield. Shrp ...2H 71
Ightham. Kent ...5G 39
Iken. Suff ...5G 67
Ilam. Staf ...5F 85
Ilchester. Som ...4A 22
Ilderton. Nmbd ...2E 121
Ilford. G Lon ...2F 39
Ilford. Som ...1G 13
Ilfracombe. Devn ...2F 19
Ilkeston. Derbs ...1B 74
Ilketshall St Andrew. Suff ...2F 67
Ilketshall St Lawrence. Suff ...2F 67
Ilketshall St Margaret. Suff ...2F 67
Ilkley. W Yor ...5D 98
Illand. Corn ...5C 10
Illey. W Mid ...2D 61
Illidge Green. Ches E ...4B 84
Illington. Norf ...2B 66
Illingworth. W Yor ...2A 92
Illogan. Corn ...4A 6
Illogan Highway. Corn ...4A 6
Illston on the Hill. Leics ...1E 62
Ilmer. Buck ...5F 51
Ilmington. Warw ...1H 49
Ilminster. Som ...1G 13
Ilsington. Devn ...5A 12
Ilsington. Dors ...3C 14
Ilston. Swan ...3E 31
Ilton. N Yor ...2D 98
Ilton. Som ...1G 13
Imachar. N Ayr ...5G 125
Imber. Wilts ...2E 23
Immingham. NE Lin ...3E 95
Immingham Dock. NE Lin ...3F 95
Impington. Cambs ...4D 64
Ince. Ches W ...3G 83
Ince Blundell. Mers ...4B 90
Ince-in-Makerfield. G Man ...4D 90
Inchbae Lodge. High ...2G 157
Inchbare. Ang ...2F 145
Inchberry. Mor ...3H 159
Inchbraoch. Ang ...3G 145
Inchbrook. Glos ...5D 48
Incheril. High ...2C 156
Inchinnan. Ren ...3F 127
Inchlaggan. High ...3D 148
Inchmichael. Per ...1E 137
Inchnadamph. High ...1G 163
Inchree. High ...2E 141
Inchture. Per ...1E 137
Inchyra. Per ...1D 136
Indian Queens. Corn ...3D 6
Ingatestone. Essx ...1H 39
Ingbirchworth. S Yor ...4C 92
Ingestre. Staf ...3D 73
Ingham. Linc ...2G 87
Ingham. Norf ...3F 79
Ingham. Suff ...3A 66
Ingham Corner. Norf ...3F 79
Ingleborough. Norf ...4D 76
Ingleby. Derbs ...3H 73
Ingleby Arncliffe. N Yor ...4B 106
Ingleby Barwick. Stoc T ...3B 106
Ingleby Greenhow. N Yor ...4C 106
Inglegill Green. Dem ...2G 11
Inglemire. Hull ...1D 94
Inglesbatch. Bath ...5C 34
Ingleton. Dur ...2E 105
Ingleton. N Yor ...2F 97
Inglewhite. Lanc ...5E 97
Ingoe. Nmbd ...2D 114
Ingol. Lanc ...1D 90
Ingoldisthorpe. Norf ...2F 77

Ingoldmells. *Linc* . . . . . . . . . .4E 89
Ingoldsby. *Linc* . . . . . . . . . .2H 75
Ingon. *Warw* . . . . . . . . . . . .5G 61
Ingram. *Nmbd* . . . . . . . . . .3E 121
Ingrave. *Essx* . . . . . . . . . . .1H 39
Ingrow. *W Yor* . . . . . . . . . . .1A 92
Ings. *Cumb* . . . . . . . . . . . .5F 103
Ingst. *S Glo* . . . . . . . . . . . .3A 34
Ingthorpe. *Rut* . . . . . . . . . . .5G 75
Ingworth. *Norf* . . . . . . . . . . .3D 78
Inkberrow. *Worc* . . . . . . . . . .5E 61
Inkford. *Worc* . . . . . . . . . . .3E 61
Inkpen. *W Ber* . . . . . . . . . . .5B 36
Inkstack. *High* . . . . . . . . . .1E 169
Innellan. *Arg* . . . . . . . . . . .3C 126
Inner Hope. *Devn* . . . . . . . . . .5C 8
Innerleith. *Fife* . . . . . . . . . .2E 137
Innerleithen. *Bord* . . . . . . . . .1F 119
Innerleven. *Fife* . . . . . . . . . .3F 137
Innermessan. *Dum* . . . . . . . . .3F 109
Innerwick. *E Lot* . . . . . . . . . .2D 130
Innerwick. *Per* . . . . . . . . . .4C 142
Innsworth. *Glos* . . . . . . . . . . .3D 48
Insch. *Abers* . . . . . . . . . . .1D 152
Insh. *High* . . . . . . . . . . . .3C 150
Inshegra. *High* . . . . . . . . . .3C 166
Inshore. *High* . . . . . . . . . .1D 166
Inskip. *Lanc* . . . . . . . . . . . .1C 90
Instow. *Devn* . . . . . . . . . . . .3E 19
Intwood. *Norf* . . . . . . . . . . . .5D 78
Inver. *Abers* . . . . . . . . . . .4G 151
Inver. *High* . . . . . . . . . . . .5F 165
Inver. *Per* . . . . . . . . . . . .4H 143
Inverailort. *High* . . . . . . . . . .5F 147
Inverallligin. *High* . . . . . . . . .3H 155
Inverallochy. *Abers* . . . . . . . .2H 161
Inveramsay. *Abers* . . . . . . . .1E 153
Inveran. *High* . . . . . . . . . . .4C 164
Inveraray. *Arg* . . . . . . . . . . .3H 133
Inverarish. *High* . . . . . . . . . .5E 155
Inverarity. *Ang* . . . . . . . . . .4D 144
Inverarnan. *Stir* . . . . . . . . . .2C 134
Inverarnie. *High* . . . . . . . . . .5A 158
Inverbeg. *Arg* . . . . . . . . . . .4C 134
Inverbervie. *Abers* . . . . . . . .1H 145
Inverboyndie. *Abers* . . . . . . . .2D 160
Invercassley. *High* . . . . . . . .3B 164
Invercharnan. *High* . . . . . . . .4F 141
Inverchoran. *High* . . . . . . . . .3E 157
Invercreran. *Arg* . . . . . . . . . .4E 141
Inverdruie. *High* . . . . . . . . . .2D 150
Inverebrie. *Abers* . . . . . . . . .5G 161
Invereck. *Arg* . . . . . . . . . . .1C 126
Inveresk. *E Lot* . . . . . . . . . .2G 129
Inveresragan. *Arg* . . . . . . . . .5D 141
Inverey. *Abers* . . . . . . . . . .5E 151
Inverfarigaig. *High* . . . . . . . .1H 149
Invergarry. *High* . . . . . . . . . .3F 149
Invergeldie. *Per* . . . . . . . . .1G 135
Invergordon. *High* . . . . . . . . .2B 158
Invergowrie. *Per* . . . . . . . . . .5C 144
Inverguseran. *High* . . . . . . . .3F 147
Inverharroch. *Mor* . . . . . . . . .5A 160
Inverie. *High* . . . . . . . . . . .3F 147
Inverinan. *Arg* . . . . . . . . . .2G 133
Inverinate. *High* . . . . . . . . . .1B 148
Inverkeilor. *Ang* . . . . . . . . . .4F 145
Inverkeithing. *Fife* . . . . . . . .1E 129
Inverkeithny. *Abers* . . . . . . . .4D 160
Inverkip. *Inv* . . . . . . . . . . .2D 126
Inverkirkaig. *High* . . . . . . . . .2E 163
Inverlael. *High* . . . . . . . . . .5F 163
Inverliever Lodge. *Arg* . . . . . .3F 133
Inverliver. *Arg* . . . . . . . . . .5E 141
Inverlochlarig. *Stir* . . . . . . . .2D 134
Inverlochy. *High* . . . . . . . . . .1F 141
Inverlussa. *Arg* . . . . . . . . . .1E 125
Inver Mallie. *High* . . . . . . . . .5D 148
Invermarkie. *Abers* . . . . . . . .5B 160
Invermoriston. *High* . . . . . . . .2G 149
Invernaver. *High* . . . . . . . . . .2H 167
Inverneil House. *Arg* . . . . . . .1G 125
**Inverness.** *High* . . . . . . . . .4A 158
Inverness Airport. *High* . . . . . .3B 158

Invernettie. *Abers* . . . . . . . . .4H 161
Inverpolly Lodge. *High* . . . . . .2E 163
Inverquhomery. *Abers* . . . . . . .4H 161
Inverroy. *High* . . . . . . . . . . .5E 149
Inversanda. *High* . . . . . . . . .3D 140
Invershiel. *High* . . . . . . . . . .2B 148
Invershin. *High* . . . . . . . . . .4C 164
Invershore. *High* . . . . . . . . .5E 169
Inversnaid. *Stir* . . . . . . . . . .3C 134
Inveruglas. *Arg* . . . . . . . . . .4H 161
Inveruglas. *Arg* . . . . . . . . . .3C 134
**Inverurie.** *Abers* . . . . . . . . .1E 153
Invervar. *Per* . . . . . . . . . . .4D 142
Inwardleigh. *Devn* . . . . . . . . . .3F 11
Inworth. *Essx* . . . . . . . . . . .4B 54
Iochdar. *W Isl* . . . . . . . . . .4C 170
Iping. *W Sus* . . . . . . . . . . . .4G 25
Ipplepen. *Devn* . . . . . . . . . . .2E 9
**Ipsden.** *Oxon* . . . . . . . . . . .3E 37
Ipstones. *Staf* . . . . . . . . . .1E 73
**Ipswich.** *Suff* . . . . . . . . . .1E 55
Irby. *Mers* . . . . . . . . . . . . .2E 83
Irby in the Marsh. *Linc* . . . . . .4D 88
Irby upon Humber. *NE Lin* . . . . .4E 95
Irchester. *Nptn* . . . . . . . . . .4G 63
Ireby. *Cumb* . . . . . . . . . . .1D 102
Ireby. *Lanc* . . . . . . . . . . . .2F 97
Ireland. *Shet* . . . . . . . . . . .9E 173
Ireleth. *Cumb* . . . . . . . . . . .2B 96
Ireshopeburn. *Dur* . . . . . . . .1B 104
Ireton Wood. *Derbs* . . . . . . . .1G 73
**Irlam.** *G Man* . . . . . . . . . .1B 84
Irnham. *Linc* . . . . . . . . . . . .3H 75
Iron Acton. *S Glo* . . . . . . . . .3B 34
Iron Bridge. *Cambs* . . . . . . . .1D 65
Ironbridge. *Telf* . . . . . . . . . .5A 72
Iron Cross. *Warw* . . . . . . . . . .5E 61
Ironville. *Derbs* . . . . . . . . . .5B 86
Irstead. *Norf* . . . . . . . . . . . .3F 79
Irthington. *Cumb* . . . . . . . . .3F 113
Irthlingborough. *Nptn* . . . . . . . .3G 63
Irton. *N Yor* . . . . . . . . . . .1E 101
**Irvine.** *N Ayr* . . . . . . . . . .1C 116
Irvine Mains. *N Ayr* . . . . . . . .1C 116
Isabella Pit. *Nmbd* . . . . . . . .1G 115
Isauld. *High* . . . . . . . . . . .2B 168
Isbister. *Orkn* . . . . . . . . . . .6C 172
Isbister. *Shet*
  nr. on Mainland . . . . . . . .2E 173
  nr. on Whalsay . . . . . . . . .5G 173
Isfield. *E Sus* . . . . . . . . . . .4F 27
Isham. *Nptn* . . . . . . . . . . . .3F 63
Island Carr. *N Lin* . . . . . . . . .4C 94
Islay Airport. *Arg* . . . . . . . . .4B 124
Isle Abbotts. *Som* . . . . . . . . .4G 21
Isle Brewers. *Som* . . . . . . . . .4G 21
Isleham. *Cambs* . . . . . . . . . .3F 65
Isle of Man Airport. *IOM* . . . . .5B 108
**Isle of Thanet.** *Kent* . . . . . .4H 41
Isle of Whithorn. *Dum* . . . . . .5B 110
**Isle of Wight.** *IOW* . . . . . . .4C 16
Isleornsay. *High* . . . . . . . . . .2F 147
Islesburgh. *Shet* . . . . . . . . .5E 173
Isles of Scilly Airport. *IOS* . . . .1B 4
Islesteps. *Dum* . . . . . . . . . .2A 112
**Isleworth.** *G Lon* . . . . . . . .3C 38
Isley Walton. *Leics* . . . . . . . .3B 74
Islibhig. *W Isl* . . . . . . . . . .5B 171
**Islington.** *G Lon* . . . . . . . . .2E 39
Islington. *Telf* . . . . . . . . . . .3B 72
Islip. *Nptn* . . . . . . . . . . . .3G 63
Islip. *Oxon* . . . . . . . . . . . .4D 50
Isombridge. *Telf* . . . . . . . . . .4A 72
Istead Rise. *Kent* . . . . . . . . .4A 39
Itchen. *Sotn* . . . . . . . . . . . .1C 16
Itchen Abbas. *Hants* . . . . . . . .3D 24
Itchen Stoke. *Hants* . . . . . . . .3D 24
Itchenor. *W Sus* . . . . . . . . . .2F 17
Itchingfield. *W Sus* . . . . . . . .3C 26
Itchington. *S Glo* . . . . . . . . .3B 34
Itlaw. *Abers* . . . . . . . . . . .3D 160
Itteringham. *Norf* . . . . . . . . .2D 78

Itteringham Common. *Norf* . . . . .3D 78
Itton. *Devn* . . . . . . . . . . . .3G 11
Itton Common. *Mon* . . . . . . . .2H 33
Ivegill. *Cumb* . . . . . . . . . . .5F 113
Ivelet. *N Yor* . . . . . . . . . . .5C 104
Iverchaolain. *Arg* . . . . . . . . .2B 126
Iver Heath. *Buck* . . . . . . . . . .2B 38
Iveston. *Dur* . . . . . . . . . . . .4E 115
Ivetsey Bank. *Staf* . . . . . . . . .4C 72
Ivinghoe. *Buck* . . . . . . . . . .4H 51
Ivinghoe Aston. *Buck* . . . . . . . .4H 51
Ivington. *Here* . . . . . . . . . . .5G 59
Ivington Green. *Here* . . . . . . . .5G 59
Ivybridge. *Devn* . . . . . . . . . . .3C 8
Ivychurch. *Kent* . . . . . . . . . . .3E 29
Ivy Hatch. *Kent* . . . . . . . . . .5G 39
Ivy Todd. *Norf* . . . . . . . . . . .5A 78
Iwade. *Kent* . . . . . . . . . . . .4D 40
Iwerne Courtney. *Dors* . . . . . .1D 14
Iwerne Minster. *Dors* . . . . . . .1D 14
Ixworth. *Suff* . . . . . . . . . . .3B 66
Ixworth Thorpe. *Suff* . . . . . . . .3B 66

## J

Jackfield. *Shrp* . . . . . . . . . . .5A 72
Jack Hill. *N Yor* . . . . . . . . . .4D 98
Jacksdale. *Notts* . . . . . . . . . .5B 86
Jackson. *S Lan* . . . . . . . . . .4G 127
Jacobstow. *Corn* . . . . . . . . . .3B 10
Jacobstowe. *Devn* . . . . . . . . . .2F 11
Jacobs Well. *Surr* . . . . . . . . .5A 38
Jameston. *Pemb* . . . . . . . . . .5E 43
Jamestown. *Dum* . . . . . . . . . .5F 119
Jamestown. *Fife* . . . . . . . . .1E 129
Jamestown. *High* . . . . . . . . .3G 157
Jamestown. *W Dun* . . . . . . . .1E 127
Janetstown. *High*
  nr. Thurso . . . . . . . . . .2C 168
  nr. Wick . . . . . . . . . . . .3F 169
**Jarrow.** *Tyne* . . . . . . . . . .3G 115
Jarvis Brook. *E Sus* . . . . . . . . .3G 27
Jasper's Green. *Essx* . . . . . . . .3H 53
Jaywick. *Essx* . . . . . . . . . . .4E 55
Jedburgh. *Bord* . . . . . . . . . .2A 120
Jeffreyston. *Pemb* . . . . . . . . .4E 43
Jemimaville. *High* . . . . . . . . .2B 158
Jenkins Park. *High* . . . . . . . . .3F 149
Jersey Marine. *Neat* . . . . . . . .3G 31
Jesmond. *Tyne* . . . . . . . . . .3F 115
Jevington. *E Sus* . . . . . . . . . .5G 27
Jingle Street. *Mon* . . . . . . . . .4H 47
Jockey End. *Herts* . . . . . . . . .4A 52
Jodrell Bank. *Ches E* . . . . . . . .3B 84
Johnby. *Cumb* . . . . . . . . . .1F 103
John O'Gaunts. *W Yor* . . . . . . . .2D 92
John o' Groats. *High* . . . . . . .1F 169
John's Cross. *E Sus* . . . . . . . .3B 28
Johnshaven. *Abers* . . . . . . . .2G 145
Johnson Street. *Norf* . . . . . . . .4F 79
Johnston. *Pemb* . . . . . . . . . .3D 42
**Johnstone.** *Ren* . . . . . . . . .3F 127
Johnstonebridge. *Dum* . . . . . .5C 118
Johnstown. *Carm* . . . . . . . . . .4E 45
Johnstown. *Wrex* . . . . . . . . . .1F 71
Joppa. *Edin* . . . . . . . . . . . .2G 129
Joppa. *S Ayr* . . . . . . . . . . .3D 116
Jordan Green. *Norf* . . . . . . . . .3C 78
Jordans. *Buck* . . . . . . . . . . .1A 38
Jordanston. *Pemb* . . . . . . . . .1D 42
Jump. *S Yor* . . . . . . . . . . . .4D 93
Jumpers Common. *Dors* . . . . . . .3G 15
Juniper. *Nmbd* . . . . . . . . . .4C 114
Juniper Green. *Edin* . . . . . . . .3E 129
Jurby East. *IOM* . . . . . . . . .2C 108
Jurby West. *IOM* . . . . . . . . .2C 108
Jury's Gap. *E Sus* . . . . . . . . .4D 28

## K

Kaber. *Cumb* . . . . . . . . . . .3A 104
Kaimend. *S Lan* . . . . . . . . . .5C 128

Kaimes. *Edin* . . . . . . . . . . .3F 129
Kaimrig End. *Bord* . . . . . . . . .5D 129
Kames. *Arg* . . . . . . . . . . . .2A 126
Kames. *E Ayr* . . . . . . . . . . .2F 117
Kea. *Corn* . . . . . . . . . . . . . .4C 6
Keadby. *N Lin* . . . . . . . . . . .3B 94
Keady. *Arm* . . . . . . . . . . . .6E 175
Keal Cotes. *Linc* . . . . . . . . . .4C 88
Kearsley. *G Man* . . . . . . . . . .4F 91
Kearsney. *Kent* . . . . . . . . . . .1G 29
Kearstwick. *Cumb* . . . . . . . . .1F 97
Kearton. *N Yor* . . . . . . . . . .5C 104
Kearvaig. *High* . . . . . . . . . .1C 166
Keasden. *N Yor* . . . . . . . . . .3G 97
Keason. *Corn* . . . . . . . . . . . .2H 7
Keckwick. *Hal* . . . . . . . . . . .2H 83
Keddington. *Linc* . . . . . . . . . .2C 88
Keddington Corner. *Linc* . . . . . .2C 88
Kedington. *Suff* . . . . . . . . . .1H 53
Kedleston. *Derbs* . . . . . . . . .1H 73
Kedlock Feus. *Fife* . . . . . . . .2F 137
Keekle. *Cumb* . . . . . . . . . .3B 102
Keelby. *Linc* . . . . . . . . . . . .3E 95
Keele. *Staf* . . . . . . . . . . . .1C 72
Keeley Green. *Bed* . . . . . . . . .1A 52
Keeston. *Pemb* . . . . . . . . . . .3D 42
Keevil. *Wilts* . . . . . . . . . . . .1E 23
Kegworth. *Leics* . . . . . . . . . .3B 74
Kehelland. *Corn* . . . . . . . . . . .2D 4
**Keig.** *Abers* . . . . . . . . . . .2D 152
**Keighley.** *W Yor* . . . . . . . . .5C 98
Keilarsbrae. *Clac* . . . . . . . . .4A 136
Keillmore. *Arg* . . . . . . . . . .1E 125
Keillor. *Per* . . . . . . . . . . . .4B 144
Keillour. *Per* . . . . . . . . . . .1B 136
Keills. *Arg* . . . . . . . . . . . .3C 124
Keiloch. *Abers* . . . . . . . . . . .4F 151
Keils. *Arg* . . . . . . . . . . . .3D 124
Keinton Mandeville. *Som* . . . . .3A 22
Keir Mill. *Dum* . . . . . . . . . .5A 118
Keirsleywell Row. *Nmbd* . . . . .4A 114
Keisby. *Linc* . . . . . . . . . . . .3H 75
Keisley. *Cumb* . . . . . . . . . .2A 104
Keiss. *High* . . . . . . . . . . . .2F 169
Keith. *Mor* . . . . . . . . . . . .3B 160
Keith Inch. *Abers* . . . . . . . . .4H 161
Kelbrook. *Lanc* . . . . . . . . . . .5B 98
Kelby. *Linc* . . . . . . . . . . . .1H 75
Keld. *Cumb* . . . . . . . . . . . .3G 103
Keld. *N Yor* . . . . . . . . . . . .4B 104
Keldholme. *N Yor* . . . . . . . . .1B 100
Kelfield. *N Lin* . . . . . . . . . . .4B 94
Kelfield. *N Yor* . . . . . . . . . . .1F 93
Kelham. *Notts* . . . . . . . . . . .5E 87
Kellacott. *Devn* . . . . . . . . . . .4E 11
Kellan. *Arg* . . . . . . . . . . . .4G 139
Kellas. *Ang* . . . . . . . . . . . .5D 144
Kellas. *Mor* . . . . . . . . . . . .3F 159
Kellaton. *Devn* . . . . . . . . . . .5E 9
Kelleth. *Cumb* . . . . . . . . . .4H 103
Kelling. *Norf* . . . . . . . . . . .1C 78
Kellingley. *N Yor* . . . . . . . . . .2F 93
Kellington. *N Yor* . . . . . . . . . .2F 93
Kelloe. *Dur* . . . . . . . . . . . .1A 106
Kelloholm. *Dum* . . . . . . . . .3G 117
Kells. *Cumb* . . . . . . . . . . .3A 102
Kells. *ME Ant* . . . . . . . . . .3G 175
Kelly. *Devn* . . . . . . . . . . . .4D 11
Kelly Bray. *Corn* . . . . . . . . . .5D 10
Kelmarsh. *Nptn* . . . . . . . . . .3E 63
Kelmscott. *Oxon* . . . . . . . . . .2H 35
Kelsale. *Suff* . . . . . . . . . . . .4F 67
Kelsall. *Ches W* . . . . . . . . . .4H 83
Kelshall. *Herts* . . . . . . . . . .2D 52
Kelsick. *Cumb* . . . . . . . . . .4C 112
Kelso. *Bord* . . . . . . . . . . .1B 120
Kelstedge. *Derbs* . . . . . . . . . .4H 85
Kelstern. *Linc* . . . . . . . . . . .1B 88
Kelsterton. *Flin* . . . . . . . . . . .3E 83
Kelston. *Bath* . . . . . . . . . . .5C 34
Keltneyburn. *Per* . . . . . . . . . .4E 143
Kelton. *Dum* . . . . . . . . . . .2A 112
Kelton Hill. *Dum* . . . . . . . . .4E 111
Kelty. *Fife* . . . . . . . . . . . .4D 136

Kelvedon. *Essx* . . . . . . . . . . .4B 54
Kelvedon Hatch. *Essx* . . . . . . .1G 39
Kelvinside. *Glas* . . . . . . . . . .3G 127
Kelynack. *Corn* . . . . . . . . . . . .3A 4
Kemback. *Fife* . . . . . . . . . . .2G 137
Kemberton. *Shrp* . . . . . . . . . .5B 72
Kemble. *Glos* . . . . . . . . . . . .2E 35
Kemerton. *Worc* . . . . . . . . . .2E 49
Kemeys Commander.
  *Mon* . . . . . . . . . . . . . . . .5G 47
Kemnay. *Abers* . . . . . . . . . .2E 153
Kempe's Corner. *Kent* . . . . . . .1E 29
Kempley. *Glos* . . . . . . . . . . .3B 48
Kempley Green. *Glos* . . . . . . . .3B 48
Kempsey. *Worc* . . . . . . . . . .1D 48
**Kempston.** *Bed* . . . . . . . . .1A 52
Kempston Hardwick. *Bed* . . . . .1A 52
Kempton. *Shrp* . . . . . . . . . . .2F 59
Kemp Town. *Brig* . . . . . . . . . .5E 27
**Kemsing.** *Kent* . . . . . . . . . .5G 39
Kemsley. *Kent* . . . . . . . . . . .4D 40
Kenardington. *Kent* . . . . . . . . .2D 28
Kenchester. *Here* . . . . . . . . . .1H 47
Kencot. *Oxon* . . . . . . . . . . . .5A 50
**Kendal.** *Cumb* . . . . . . . . . .5G 103
Kendleshire. *S Glo* . . . . . . . . .4B 34
Kenfig. *B'end* . . . . . . . . . . . .3B 32
Kenfig Hill. *B'end* . . . . . . . . . .3B 32
Kengharair. *Arg* . . . . . . . . . . .4F 139
**Kenilworth.** *Warw* . . . . . . . . .3G 61
Kenknock. *Stir* . . . . . . . . . . .5B 142
Kenley. *G Lon* . . . . . . . . . . . .5E 39
Kenley. *Shrp* . . . . . . . . . . . .5H 71
Kenmore. *High* . . . . . . . . . .3G 155
Kenmore. *Per* . . . . . . . . . . .4E 143
Kenn. *Devn* . . . . . . . . . . . . .4C 12
Kenn. *N Som* . . . . . . . . . . . .5H 33
Kennacraig. *Arg* . . . . . . . . . .3G 125
Kenneggy Downs. *Corn* . . . . . . . .4C 4
Kennerleigh. *Devn* . . . . . . . . .2B 12
Kennet. *Clac* . . . . . . . . . . . .4B 136
Kennethmont. *Abers* . . . . . . .1C 152
Kennett. *Cambs* . . . . . . . . . .4G 65
Kennford. *Devn* . . . . . . . . . . .4C 12
Kenninghall. *Norf* . . . . . . . . . .2C 66
Kennington. *Kent* . . . . . . . . . .1E 28
**Kennington.** *Oxon* . . . . . . . . .5D 50
Kennoway. *Fife* . . . . . . . . . .3F 137
Kennyhill. *Suff* . . . . . . . . . . .3F 65
Kennythorpe. *N Yor* . . . . . . . .3B 100
Kenovay. *Arg* . . . . . . . . . . . .4A 138
Kensaleyre. *High* . . . . . . . . . .3D 154
**Kensington.** *G Lon* . . . . . . . .3D 38
Kenstone. *Shrp* . . . . . . . . . . .3H 71
Kensworth. *C Beds* . . . . . . . . .4A 52
Kensworth Common.
  *C Beds* . . . . . . . . . . . . . .4A 52
Kentallen. *High* . . . . . . . . . .3E 141
Kentchurch. *Here* . . . . . . . . . .3H 47
Kentford. *Suff* . . . . . . . . . . .4G 65
Kentisbeare. *Devn* . . . . . . . . .2D 12
Kentisbury. *Devn* . . . . . . . . . .2G 19
Kentisbury Ford. *Devn* . . . . . . .2G 19
Kentmere. *Cumb* . . . . . . . . .4F 103
Kenton. *Devn* . . . . . . . . . . . .4C 12
Kenton. *G Lon* . . . . . . . . . . .2C 38
Kenton. *Suff* . . . . . . . . . . . .4D 66
Kenton Bankfoot. *Tyne* . . . . . .3F 115
Kentra. *High* . . . . . . . . . . .2A 140
Kentrigg. *Cumb* . . . . . . . . . .5G 103
Kents Bank. *Cumb* . . . . . . . . .2C 96
Kent's Green. *Glos* . . . . . . . . .3C 48
Kent's Oak. *Hants* . . . . . . . . . .4B 24
Kent Street. *E Sus* . . . . . . . . . .4B 28
Kent Street. *Kent* . . . . . . . . . .5A 40
Kent Street. *W Sus* . . . . . . . . .3D 26
Kenwick. *Shrp* . . . . . . . . . . . .2G 71
Kenwyn. *Corn* . . . . . . . . . . . .4C 6
Kenyon. *Warr* . . . . . . . . . . . .1A 84
Keoldale. *High* . . . . . . . . . . .2D 166

Keppoch. High .....1B 148
Kepwick. N Yor .....5B 106
Keresley. W Mid .....2H 61
Keresley Newland. Warw .....2H 61
Keristal. IOM .....4C 108
Kerne Bridge. Here .....4A 48
Kerridge. Ches E .....3D 84
Kerris. Corn .....4B 4
Kerrow. High .....5F 157
Kerry. Powy .....2D 58
Kerrycroy. Arg .....3C 126
Kerry's Gate. Here .....2G 47
Kersall. Notts .....4E 86
Kersbrook. Devn .....4D 12
Kerse. Ren .....4E 127
Kersey. Suff .....1D 54
Kershopefoot. Cumb .....1F 113
Kersoe. Worc .....1E 49
Kerswell. Devn .....2D 12
Kerswell Green. Worc .....1D 48
Kesgrave. Suff .....1F 55
Kessingland. Suff .....2H 67
Kessingland Beach. Suff .....2H 67
Kestle. Corn .....4D 6
Kestle Mill. Corn .....3C 6
Keston. G Lon .....4F 39
Keswick. Cumb .....2D 102
Keswick. Norf
  nr. North Walsham .....2F 79
  nr. Norwich .....5E 78
Ketsby. Linc .....3C 88
**Kettering. Nptn** .....3F 63
Ketteringham. Norf .....5D 78
Kettins. Per .....5B 144
Kettlebaston. Suff .....5B 66
Kettlebridge. Fife .....3F 137
Kettlebrook. Staf .....5G 73
Kettleburgh. Suff .....4E 67
Kettleholm. Dum .....2C 112
Kettleness. N Yor .....3F 107
Kettleshulme. Ches E .....3D 85
Kettlesing. N Yor .....4E 98
Kettlesing Bottom. N Yor .....4E 99
Kettlestone. Norf .....2B 78
Kettlethorpe. Linc .....3F 87
Kettletoft. Orkn .....4F 172
Kettlewell. N Yor .....2B 98
Ketton. Rut .....5G 75
Kew. G Lon .....3C 38
Kewaigue. IOM .....4C 108
Kewstoke. N Som .....5G 33
Kexbrough. S Yor .....4C 92
Kexby. Linc .....2F 87
Kexby. York .....4B 100
Keyford. Som .....2C 22
Key Green. Ches E .....4C 84
Key Green. N Yor .....4F 107
Keyham. Leics .....5D 74
Keyhaven. Hants .....3B 16
Keyhead. Abers .....3H 161
Keyingham. E Yor .....2F 95
Keymer. W Sus .....4E 27
Keynsham. Bath .....5B 34
Keysoe. Bed .....4H 63
Keysoe Row. Bed .....4H 63
Key's Toft. Linc .....5D 89
Keyston. Cambs .....3H 63
Key Street. Kent .....4C 40
Keyworth. Notts .....2D 74
Kibblesworth. Tyne .....4F 115
Kibworth Beauchamp. Leics .....1D 62
Kibworth Harcourt. Leics .....1D 62
Kidbrooke. G Lon .....3F 39
Kidburngill. Cumb .....2B 102
Kiddemore Green. Staf .....5C 72
**Kidderminster. Worc** .....3C 60
Kiddington. Oxon .....3C 50
Kidd's Moor. Norf .....5D 78
**Kidlington. Oxon** .....4C 50
Kidmore End. Oxon .....4E 37
Kidnal. Ches W .....1G 71
**Kidsgrove. Staf** .....5C 84
Kidstones. N Yor .....1B 98
Kidwelly. Carm .....5E 45

Kiel Crofts. Arg .....5D 140
Kielder. Nmbd .....5A 120
Kilbagie. Fife .....4B 136
Kilbarchan. Ren .....3F 127
Kilbeg. High .....3E 147
Kilberry. Arg .....3F 125
Kilbirnie. N Ayr .....4E 126
Kilbride. Arg .....1F 133
Kilbride. High .....1D 147
Kilbucho Place. Bord .....1C 118
Kilburn. Derbs .....1A 74
Kilburn. G Lon .....2D 38
Kilburn. N Yor .....2H 99
Kilby. Leics .....1D 62
Kilchattan. Arg .....4A 132
Kilchattan Bay. Arg .....4C 126
Kilchenzie. Arg .....3A 122
Kilcheran. Arg .....5C 140
Kilchiaran. Arg .....3A 124
Kilchoan. High
  nr. Inverie .....4F 147
  nr. Tobermory .....2F 139
Kilchoman. Arg .....3A 124
Kilchrenan. Arg .....1H 133
Kilconquhar. Fife .....3G 137
Kilcot. Glos .....3B 48
Kilcoy. High .....3H 157
Kilcreggan. Arg .....1D 126
Kildale. N Yor .....4D 106
Kildary. High .....1B 158
Kildermorie Lodge. High .....1H 157
Kildonan. High
  nr. Helmsdale .....1G 165
  on Isle of Skye .....3C 154
Kildonan. N Ayr .....3E 123
Kildonnan. High .....5C 146
Kildrummy. Abers .....2B 152
Kildwick. N Yor .....5C 98
Kilfillan. Dum .....4H 109
Kilfinan. Arg .....2H 125
Kilfinnan. High .....4E 149
Kilgetty. Pemb .....4F 43
Kilgour. Fife .....3E 136
Kilgrammie. S Ayr .....4B 116
Kilham. E Yor .....3E 101
Kilham. Nmbd .....1C 120
Kilkeel. New M .....6H 175
Kilkenneth. Arg .....4A 138
Kilkhampton. Corn .....1C 10
Killamarsh. Derbs .....2B 86
Killandrist. Arg .....4C 140
Killay. Swan .....3F 31
Killean. Arg .....5E 125
Killearn. Stir .....1G 127
Killellan. Arg .....4A 122
Killen. High .....3A 158
Killerby. Darl .....3E 105
Killichonan. Per .....3C 142
Killiechronan. Arg .....4G 139
Killiecrankie. Per .....2G 143
Killimster. High .....3E 169
Killin. Stir .....5C 142
Killinghall. N Yor .....4E 99
Killington. Cumb .....1F 97
**Killingworth. Tyne** .....2F 115
Killin Lodge. High .....3H 149
Killinochroch. Arg .....4E 133
Killochyett. Bord .....5A 130
Killundine. High .....4G 139
Killyleagh. New M .....5J 175
Kilmacolm. Inv .....3E 127
Kilmahog. Stir .....3F 135
Kilmahumaig. Arg .....4E 133
Kilmalieu. High .....3C 140
Kilmaluag. High .....1D 154
Kilmany. Fife .....1F 137
Kilmarie. High .....2D 146
**Kilmarnock. E Ayr** .....1D 116
Kilmaron. Fife .....2F 137
Kilmartin. Arg .....4F 133
Kilmaurs. E Ayr .....5F 127
Kilmelford. Arg .....2F 133

Kilmeny. Arg .....3B 124
Kilmersdon. Som .....1B 22
Kilmeston. Hants .....4D 24
Kilmichael Glassary. Arg .....4F 133
Kilmichael of Inverlussa.
  Arg .....1F 125
Kilmington. Devn .....3F 13
Kilmington. Wilts .....3C 22
Kilmoluaig. Arg .....4A 138
Kilmorack. High .....4G 157
Kilmore. Arg .....1F 133
Kilmore. High .....3E 147
Kilmory. Arg .....2F 125
Kilmory. High
  nr. Kilchoan .....1G 139
  on Rùm .....3B 146
Kilmory. N Ayr .....3D 122
Kilmory Lodge. Arg .....3E 132
Kilmote. High .....2G 165
Kilmuir. High
  nr. Dunvegan .....4B 154
  nr. Invergordon .....1B 158
  nr. Inverness .....4A 158
  nr. Uig .....1C 154
Kilmun. Arg .....1C 126
Kilnave. Arg .....2A 124
Kilncadzow. S Lan .....5B 128
Kilndown. Kent .....2B 28
Kiln Green. Here .....4B 48
Kiln Green. Wok .....4G 37
Kilnhill. Cumb .....1D 102
Kilnhurst. S Yor .....1B 86
Kilninian. Arg .....4E 139
Kilninver. Arg .....1F 133
Kiln Pit Hill. Nmbd .....4D 114
Kilnsea. E Yor .....3H 95
Kilnsey. N Yor .....3B 98
Kilnwick. E Yor .....5D 101
Kiloran. Arg .....4A 132
Kilpatrick. N Ayr .....3D 122
Kilpeck. Here .....2H 47
Kilpin. E Yor .....2A 94
Kilpin Pike. E Yor .....2A 94
Kilrea. Caus .....2F 175
Kilrenny. Fife .....3H 137
Kilsby. Nptn .....3C 62
Kilspindie. Per .....1E 136
Kilsyth. N Lan .....2A 128
Kiltarlity. High .....4H 157
Kilton. Som .....2E 21
Kilton Thorpe. Red C .....3D 107
Kilvaxter. High .....2C 154
Kilve. Som .....2E 21
Kilvington. Notts .....1F 75
Kilwinning. N Ayr .....5D 126
Kimberley. Norf .....5C 78
**Kimberley. Notts** .....1B 74
Kimblesworth. Dur .....5F 115
Kimble Wick. Buck .....5G 51
Kimbolton. Cambs .....4H 63
Kimbolton. Here .....4H 59
Kimcote. Leics .....2C 62
Kimmeridge. Dors .....5E 15
Kimmerston. Nmbd .....1D 120
Kimpton. Hants .....2A 24
Kimpton. Herts .....4B 52
Kinbeachie. High .....2A 158
Kinbrace. High .....5A 168
Kinbuck. Stir .....3G 135
Kincaple. Fife .....2G 137
Kincardine. Fife .....1C 128
Kincardine. High .....5D 164
**Kincardine Bridge. Falk** .....1C 128
Kincardine O'Neil. Abers .....4C 152
Kinchrackine. Arg .....1A 134
Kincorth. Aber .....3G 153
Kincraig. High .....3C 150
Kincraigie. Per .....4G 143
Kindallachan. Per .....3G 143
Kineton. Glos .....3F 49
Kineton. Warw .....5H 61
Kinfauns. Per .....1D 136
Kingairloch. High .....3C 140
Kingarth. Arg .....4B 126

Kingcoed. Mon .....5H 47
King Edward. Abers .....3E 160
Kingerby. Linc .....1H 87
Kingham. Oxon .....3A 50
Kingholm Quay. Dum .....2A 112
Kinghorn. Fife .....1F 129
Kingie. High .....3D 148
Kinglassie. Fife .....4E 137
Kingledores. Bord .....2D 118
King o' Muirs. Clac .....4A 136
Kingoodie. Per .....1F 137
King's Acre. Here .....1H 47
Kingsand. Corn .....3A 8
Kingsash. Buck .....5G 51
Kingsbarns. Fife .....2H 137
Kingsbridge. Devn .....4D 8
Kingsbridge. Som .....3C 20
King's Bromley. Staf .....4F 73
Kingsburgh. High .....3C 154
Kingsbury. G Lon .....2C 38
Kingsbury. Warw .....1G 61
Kingsbury Episcopi. Som .....4H 21
Kings Caple. Here .....3A 48
Kingscavil. W Lot .....2D 128
Kingsclere. Hants .....1D 24
King's Cliffe. Nptn .....1H 63
Kings Clipstone. Notts .....4D 86
Kingscote. Glos .....2D 34
Kingscott. Devn .....1F 11
Kings Coughton. Warw .....5E 61
Kingscross. N Ayr .....3E 123
Kingsdon. Som .....4A 22
Kingsdown. Kent .....1H 29
Kingsdown. Swin .....3G 35
Kingsdown. Wilts .....5D 34
Kingseat. Fife .....4D 136
Kingsey. Buck .....5F 51
Kingsfold. Lanc .....2D 90
Kingsfold. W Sus .....2C 26
Kingsford. E Ayr .....5F 127
Kingsford. Worc .....2C 60
Kingsforth. N Lin .....3D 94
Kingsgate. Kent .....3H 41
Kings Green. Glos .....2C 48
Kingshall Street. Suff .....4B 66
Kingsheanton. Devn .....3F 19
King's Heath. W Mid .....2E 61
Kings Hill. Kent .....5A 40
Kingsholm. Glos .....4D 48
Kingshouse. High .....3G 141
Kingshouse. Stir .....1E 135
Kingshurst. W Mid .....2F 61
Kingskerswell. Devn .....2E 9
Kingskettle. Fife .....3F 137
Kingsland. Here .....4G 59
Kingsland. IOA .....2B 80
Kings Langley. Herts .....5A 52
Kingsley. Ches W .....3H 83
Kingsley. Hants .....3F 25
Kingsley. Staf .....1E 73
Kingsley Green. W Sus .....3G 25
Kingsley Holt. Staf .....1E 73
**King's Lynn. Norf** .....3F 77
Kings Meaburn. Cumb .....2H 103
Kings Moss. Mers .....4D 90
Kings Muir. Bord .....1E 119
Kingsmuir. Ang .....4D 145
Kingsmuir. Fife .....3H 137
King's Newnham. Warw .....3B 62
King's Newton. Derbs .....3A 74
Kingsnorth. Kent .....2E 28
Kingsnorth. Medw .....3C 40
King's Norton. Leics .....5D 74
King's Norton. W Mid .....3E 61
Kings Nympton. Devn .....1G 11
Kings Pyon. Here .....5G 59
Kings Ripton. Cambs .....3B 64
Kings Somborne. Hants .....3B 24
King's Stag. Dors .....1C 14
Kings Stanley. Glos .....5D 48
King's Sutton. Nptn .....2C 50
Kingstanding. W Mid .....1E 61
Kingsteignton. Devn .....5B 12
Kingsteps. High .....3D 158

King Sterndale. Derbs .....3E 85
King's Thorn. Here .....2A 48
Kingsthorpe. Nptn .....4E 63
Kingston. Cambs .....5C 64
Kingston. Devn .....4C 8
Kingston. Dors
  nr. Sturminster Newton
  .....2C 14
  nr. Swanage .....5E 15
Kingston. E Lot .....1B 130
Kingston. Hants .....2G 15
Kingston. IOW .....4C 16
Kingston. Kent .....5F 41
Kingston. Mor .....2H 159
Kingston. W Sus .....5B 26
Kingston Bagpuize. Oxon .....2C 36
Kingston Blount. Oxon .....2F 37
Kingston by Sea. W Sus .....5D 26
Kingston Deverill. Wilts .....3D 22
Kingstone. Here .....2H 47
Kingstone. Som .....1G 13
Kingstone. Staf .....3E 73
Kingston Lisle. Oxon .....3B 36
Kingston Maurward. Dors .....3C 14
Kingston near Lewes. E Sus .....5E 27
Kingston on Soar. Notts .....3C 74
Kingston Russell. Dors .....3A 14
Kingston St Mary. Som .....4F 21
Kingston Seymour. N Som .....5H 33
Kingston Stert. Oxon .....5F 51
**Kingston upon Hull. Hull** .....2E 94
**Kingston upon Thames.**
  G Lon .....4C 38
King's Walden. Herts .....3B 52
Kingswear. Devn .....3E 9
Kingswells. Aber .....3F 153
Kingswinford. W Mid .....2C 60
Kingswood. Buck .....4E 51
Kingswood. Glos .....2C 34
Kingswood. Here .....5E 59
Kingswood. Kent .....5C 40
Kingswood. Powy .....5E 71
**Kingswood. S Glo** .....4B 34
Kingswood. Som .....3E 20
Kingswood. Surr .....5D 38
Kingswood. Warw .....3F 61
Kingswood Common. Staf .....5C 72
Kings Worthy. Hants .....3C 24
Kingthorpe. Linc .....3A 88
Kington. Here .....5E 59
Kington. S Glo .....2B 34
Kington. Worc .....5D 61
Kington Langley. Wilts .....4E 35
Kington Magna. Dors .....4C 22
Kington St Michael. Wilts .....4E 35
Kingussie. High .....3B 150
Kingweston. Som .....3A 22
Kinharrachie. Abers .....5G 161
Kinharvie. Dum .....1A 158
Kinkell Bridge. Per .....2B 136
Kinknockie. Abers .....4H 161
Kinkry Hill. Cumb .....2G 113
Kinlet. Shrp .....2B 60
Kinloch. High
  nr. Lochaline .....3A 140
  nr. Loch More .....5D 166
  on Rùm .....4B 146
Kinloch. Per .....4A 144
Kinlochard. Stir .....3D 134
Kinlochbervie. High .....3C 166
Kinlocheil. High .....1D 140
Kinlochewe. High .....2C 156
Kinloch Hourn. High .....3B 148
Kinloch Laggan. High .....5H 149
Kinlochleven. High .....2F 141
Kinloch Lodge. High .....3F 167
Kinlochmoidart. High .....1B 140
Kinlochmore. High .....2F 141
Kinloch Rannoch. Per .....3D 142
Kinlochspelve. Arg .....1D 132
Kinloid. High .....5E 147
Kinloss. Mor .....2E 159
Kinmel Bay. Cnwy .....2B 82

Kinmuck. *Abers* . . . . . . . . . . .2F **153**
Kinnadie. *Abers* . . . . . . . . . . .4G **161**
Kinnaird. *Per* . . . . . . . . . . .1E **137**
Kinneff. *Abers* . . . . . . . . . .1H **145**
Kinnelhead. *Dum* . . . . . . . . .4C **118**
Kinnell. *Ang* . . . . . . . . . . .3F **145**
Kinnerley. *Shrp* . . . . . . . . . .3F **71**
Kinnernie. *Abers* . . . . . . . . .3E **152**
Kinnersley. *Here* . . . . . . . . . .1G **47**
Kinnersley. *Worc* . . . . . . . . .1D **48**
Kinnerton. *Powy* . . . . . . . . . .4E **59**
Kinnerton. *Shrp* . . . . . . . . . .1F **59**
Kinnesswood. *Per* . . . . . . . . .3D **136**
Kinninvie. *Dur* . . . . . . . . . .2D **104**
Kinnordy. *Ang* . . . . . . . . . .3C **144**
Kinoulton. *Notts* . . . . . . . . . .2D **74**
Kinross. *Per* . . . . . . . . . . .3D **136**
Kinrossie. *Per* . . . . . . . . . .5A **144**
Kinsbourne Green. *Herts* . . . . . .4B **52**
Kinsey Heath. *Ches E* . . . . . . . .1A **72**
Kinsham. *Here* . . . . . . . . . . .4F **59**
Kinsham. *Worc* . . . . . . . . . .2E **49**
Kinsley. *W Yor* . . . . . . . . . . .3E **93**
Kinson. *Bour* . . . . . . . . . . .3F **15**
Kintbury. *W Ber* . . . . . . . . . .5B **36**
Kintessack. *Mor* . . . . . . . . . .2E **159**
Kintillo. *Per* . . . . . . . . . . .2D **136**
Kinton. *Here* . . . . . . . . . . .3G **59**
Kinton. *Shrp* . . . . . . . . . . .4F **71**
Kintore. *Abers* . . . . . . . . . .2E **153**
Kintour. *Arg* . . . . . . . . . . .4C **124**
Kintra. *Arg* . . . . . . . . . . .2B **132**
Kintraw. *Arg* . . . . . . . . . . .3F **133**
Kinveachy. *High* . . . . . . . . . .2D **150**
Kinver. *Staf* . . . . . . . . . . . .2C **60**
Kinwarton. *Warw* . . . . . . . . . .5F **61**
Kiplingcotes. *E Yor* . . . . . . . . .5D **100**
Kippax. *W Yor* . . . . . . . . . . .1E **93**
Kippen. *Stir* . . . . . . . . . . .4F **135**
Kippford. *Dum* . . . . . . . . . .4F **111**
Kipping's Cross. *Kent* . . . . . . .1H **27**
Kirbister. *Orkn*
    nr. Hobbister . . . . . . . . .7C **172**
    nr. Quholm . . . . . . . . . .6B **172**
Kirbuster. *Orkn* . . . . . . . . . .5F **172**
Kirby Bedon. *Norf* . . . . . . . . . .5E **79**
Kirby Bellars. *Leics* . . . . . . . . .4E **74**
Kirby Cane. *Norf* . . . . . . . . . .1F **67**
Kirby Cross. *Essx* . . . . . . . . . .3F **55**
Kirby Fields. *Leics* . . . . . . . . . .5C **74**
Kirby Green. *Norf* . . . . . . . . . .1F **67**
Kirby Grindalythe. *N Yor* . . . .3D **100**
Kirby Hill. *N Yor*
    nr. Richmond . . . . . . . . .4E **105**
    nr. Ripon . . . . . . . . . . .3F **99**
Kirby Knowle. *N Yor* . . . . . . . .1G **99**
Kirby-le-Soken. *Essx* . . . . . . . .3F **55**
Kirby Misperton. *N Yor* . . . .2B **100**
Kirby Muxloe. *Leics* . . . . . . . . .5C **74**
Kirby Sigston. *N Yor* . . . . . . . .5B **106**
Kirby Underdale. *E Yor* . . . . . .4C **100**
Kirby Wiske. *N Yor* . . . . . . . . .1F **99**
Kirdford. *W Sus* . . . . . . . . . .3B **26**
Kirk. *High* . . . . . . . . . . . .3E **169**
Kirkabister. *Shet*
    on Bressay . . . . . . . . . . .8F **173**
    on Mainland . . . . . . . . . .6F **173**
Kirkandrews. *Dum* . . . . . . . . .5D **110**
Kirkandrews-on-Eden.
    *Cumb* . . . . . . . . . . . .4E **113**
Kirkapol. *Arg* . . . . . . . . . .4B **138**
Kirkbampton. *Cumb* . . . . . . . .4E **112**
Kirkbean. *Dum* . . . . . . . . . .4A **112**
Kirk Bramwith. *S Yor* . . . . . . . .3G **93**
Kirkbride. *Cumb* . . . . . . . . .4D **112**
Kirkbridge. *N Yor* . . . . . . . . . .5F **105**
Kirkbuddo. *Ang* . . . . . . . . . .4E **145**
Kirkburn. *E Yor* . . . . . . . . . .4D **101**
Kirkburton. *W Yor* . . . . . . . . .3B **92**
Kirkby. *Linc* . . . . . . . . . . .1H **87**
**Kirkby.** *Mers* . . . . . . . . . . .1G **83**
Kirkby. *N Yor* . . . . . . . . . .4C **106**
Kirkby Fenside. *Linc* . . . . . . . .4C **88**
Kirkby Fleetham. *N Yor* . . . . .5F **105**

Kirkby Green. *Linc* . . . . . . . . . .5H **87**
**Kirkby-in-Ashfield.** *Notts* . . . . .5C **86**
Kirkby-in-Furness. *Cumb* . . . . .1B **96**
Kirkby la Thorpe. *Linc* . . . . . . .1A **76**
Kirkby Lonsdale. *Cumb* . . . . . . .2F **97**
Kirkby Malham. *N Yor* . . . . . . . .3A **98**
Kirkby Mallory. *Leics* . . . . . . . .5B **74**
Kirkby Malzeard. *N Yor* . . . . . . .2E **99**
Kirkby Mills. *N Yor* . . . . . . . .1B **100**
Kirkbymoorside. *N Yor* . . . . . .1A **100**
Kirkby on Bain. *Linc* . . . . . . . .4B **88**
Kirkby Overblow. *N Yor* . . . . . . .5F **99**
Kirkby Stephen. *Cumb* . . . . . .4A **104**
Kirkby Thore. *Cumb* . . . . . . . .2H **103**
Kirkby Underwood. *Linc* . . . . .3H **75**
Kirkby Wharfe. *N Yor* . . . . . . . .5H **99**
**Kirkcaldy.** *Fife* . . . . . . . . . .4E **137**
Kirkcambeck. *Cumb* . . . . . . .3G **113**
Kirkcolm. *Dum* . . . . . . . . . .3F **109**
Kirkconnel. *Dum* . . . . . . . . .3G **117**
Kirkconnell. *Dum* . . . . . . . . .3A **112**
Kirkcowan. *Dum* . . . . . . . . . .3A **110**
Kirkcudbright. *Dum* . . . . . . . .4D **111**
Kirkdale. *Mers* . . . . . . . . . . .1F **83**
Kirk Deighton. *N Yor* . . . . . . . .4F **99**
Kirk Ella. *E Yor* . . . . . . . . . . .2D **94**
Kirkfieldbank. *S Lan* . . . . . . . .5B **128**
Kirkforthar Feus. *Fife* . . . . . . .3E **137**
Kirkgunzeon. *Dum* . . . . . . . . .3F **111**
Kirk Hallam. *Derbs* . . . . . . . . .1B **74**
Kirkham. *Lanc* . . . . . . . . . . .1C **90**
Kirkham. *N Yor* . . . . . . . . . .3B **100**
Kirkhamgate. *W Yor* . . . . . . . . .2C **92**
Kirk Hammerton. *N Yor* . . . . . .4G **99**
Kirkharle. *Nmbd* . . . . . . . . . .1D **114**
Kirkheaton. *Nmbd* . . . . . . . . .2D **114**
Kirkheaton. *W Yor* . . . . . . . . . .3B **92**
Kirkhill. *Ang* . . . . . . . . . . .2F **145**
Kirkhill. *High* . . . . . . . . . .4H **157**
Kirkhope. *S Lan* . . . . . . . . . .4B **118**
Kirkhouse. *Bord* . . . . . . . . . .1F **119**
Kirkibost. *High* . . . . . . . . . .2D **146**
Kirkinch. *Ang* . . . . . . . . . . .4C **144**
Kirkinner. *Dum* . . . . . . . . . .3B **110**
**Kirkintilloch.** *E Dun* . . . . . . .2H **127**
Kirk Ireton. *Derbs* . . . . . . . . . .5G **85**
Kirkland. *Cumb*
    nr. Cleator Moor . . . . . . . .3B **102**
    nr. Penrith . . . . . . . . . .1H **103**
    nr. Wigton . . . . . . . . . .5D **112**
Kirkland. *Dum*
    nr. Kirkconnel . . . . . . . . .3G **117**
    nr. Moniaive . . . . . . . . .5H **117**
Kirkland Guards. *Cumb* . . . . . . .5C **112**
Kirk Langley. *Derbs* . . . . . . . . .2G **73**
Kirklauchline. *Dum* . . . . . . . . .4F **109**
Kirkleatham. *Red C* . . . . . . . . .2C **106**
Kirklevington. *Stoc T* . . . . . . . .4B **106**
Kirkley. *Suff* . . . . . . . . . . . .1H **67**
Kirklington. *N Yor* . . . . . . . . . .1F **99**
Kirklington. *Notts* . . . . . . . . . .5D **86**
Kirklinton. *Cumb* . . . . . . . . .3F **113**
Kirkliston. *Edin* . . . . . . . . . .2E **129**
Kirkmabreck. *Dum* . . . . . . . . .4B **110**
Kirkmaiden. *Dum* . . . . . . . . .5E **109**
Kirk Merrington. *Dur* . . . . . . .1F **105**
Kirk Michael. *IOM* . . . . . . . . .2C **108**
Kirkmichael. *Per* . . . . . . . . . .2H **143**
Kirkmichael. *S Ayr* . . . . . . . . .4C **116**
Kirkmuirhill. *S Lan* . . . . . . . . .5A **128**
Kirknewton. *Nmbd* . . . . . . . .1D **120**
Kirknewton. *W Lot* . . . . . . . . .3E **129**
Kirkney. *Abers* . . . . . . . . . . .5C **160**
Kirk of Shotts. *N Lan* . . . . . . .3B **128**
Kirkoswald. *Cumb* . . . . . . . . .5G **113**
Kirkoswald. *S Ayr* . . . . . . . . . .4B **116**
Kirkpatrick. *Dum* . . . . . . . . .5B **118**
Kirkpatrick Durham. *Dum* . . . . .2F **111**
Kirkpatrick-Fleming. *Dum* . . . .2D **112**
**Kirk Sandall.** *S Yor* . . . . . . . .4G **93**
Kirksanton. *Cumb* . . . . . . . . .1A **96**
Kirk Smeaton. *N Yor* . . . . . . . .3F **93**
Kirkstall. *W Yor* . . . . . . . . . . .1C **92**
Kirkstile. *Dum* . . . . . . . . . .5F **119**

Kirkstyle. *High* . . . . . . . . . . .1F **169**
Kirkthorpe. *W Yor* . . . . . . . . . .2D **92**
Kirkton. *Abers*
    nr. Alford . . . . . . . . . . .2D **152**
    nr. Insch . . . . . . . . . . .1D **152**
    nr. Turriff . . . . . . . . . .4F **161**
Kirkton. *Ang*
    nr. Dundee . . . . . . . . . .5D **144**
    nr. Forfar . . . . . . . . . . .4D **144**
    nr. Tarfside . . . . . . . . . .5B **152**
Kirkton. *Dum* . . . . . . . . . .1A **112**
Kirkton. *Fife* . . . . . . . . . . .1F **137**
Kirkton. *High*
    nr. Golspie . . . . . . . . . .4E **165**
    nr. Kyle of Lochalsh . . . .1G **147**
    nr. Lochcarron . . . . . . . .4B **156**
Kirkton. *Bord* . . . . . . . . . . .3H **119**
Kirkton. *S Lan* . . . . . . . . . .2B **118**
Kirktonhill. *W Dun* . . . . . . . . .2E **127**
Kirkton Manor. *Bord* . . . . . . . .1E **118**
Kirkton of Airlie. *Ang* . . . . . . .3C **144**
Kirkton of Auchterhouse.
    *Ang* . . . . . . . . . . . . .5C **144**
Kirkton of Bourtie. *Abers* . . . . .1F **153**
Kirkton of Collace. *Per* . . . . . . .5A **144**
Kirkton of Craig. *Ang* . . . . . . .3G **145**
Kirkton of Culsalmond.
    *Abers* . . . . . . . . . . . .5D **160**
Kirkton of Durris. *Abers* . . . . . .4E **153**
Kirkton of Glenbuchat.
    *Abers* . . . . . . . . . . . .2A **152**
Kirkton of Glenisla. *Ang* . . . . . .2B **144**
Kirkton of Kingoldrum. *Ang* . . .3C **144**
Kirkton of Largo. *Fife* . . . . . . .3G **137**
Kirkton of Lethendy. *Per* . . . . .4A **144**
Kirkton of Logie Buchan.
    *Abers* . . . . . . . . . . . .1G **153**
Kirkton of Maryculter.
    *Abers* . . . . . . . . . . . .4F **153**
Kirkton of Menmuir. *Ang* . . . . .2E **145**
Kirkton of Monikie. *Ang* . . . . . .5E **145**
Kirkton of Oyne. *Abers* . . . . . .1D **152**
Kirkton of Rayne. *Abers* . . . . . .5D **160**
Kirkton of Skene. *Abers* . . . . . .3F **153**
Kirktown. *Abers*
    nr. Fraserburgh . . . . . . .2G **161**
    nr. Peterhead . . . . . . . .3H **161**
Kirktown of Alvah. *Abers* . . . . .2D **160**
Kirktown of Auchterless.
    *Abers* . . . . . . . . . . . .4E **160**
Kirktown of Deskford. *Mor* . . . .2C **160**
Kirktown of Fetteresso.
    *Abers* . . . . . . . . . . . .5F **153**
Kirktown of Mortlach. *Mor* . . . .5H **159**
Kirktown of Slains. *Abers* . . . .1H **153**
Kirkurd. *Bord* . . . . . . . . . . .5E **129**
Kirkwall. *Orkn* . . . . . . . . . . .6D **172**
Kirkwall Airport. *Orkn* . . . . . . .7D **172**
Kirkwhelpington. *Nmbd* . . . . . .1C **114**
Kirk Yetholm. *Bord* . . . . . . . . .2C **120**
Kirmington. *N Lin* . . . . . . . . . .3E **94**
Kirmond le Mire. *Linc* . . . . . . .1A **88**
Kirn. *Arg* . . . . . . . . . . . . .2C **126**
Kirriemuir. *Ang* . . . . . . . . . .3C **144**
Kirstead Green. *Norf* . . . . . . . .1E **67**
Kirtlebridge. *Dum* . . . . . . . . .2D **112**
Kirtleton. *Dum* . . . . . . . . . .1D **112**
Kirtling. *Cambs* . . . . . . . . . . .5F **65**
Kirtling Green. *Cambs* . . . . . . . .5F **65**
Kirtlington. *Oxon* . . . . . . . . . .4D **50**
Kirtomy. *High* . . . . . . . . . . .2H **167**
Kirton. *Linc* . . . . . . . . . . .2C **76**
Kirton. *Notts* . . . . . . . . . . .4D **86**
Kirton. *Suff* . . . . . . . . . . . .2F **55**
Kirton End. *Linc* . . . . . . . . . .1B **76**
Kirton Holme. *Linc* . . . . . . . . .1B **76**
Kirton in Lindsey. *N Lin* . . . . . .1G **87**
Kislingbury. *Nptn* . . . . . . . . .4H **155**
Kites Hardwick. *Warw* . . . . . . . .4B **62**
Kittisford. *Som* . . . . . . . . . . .4D **20**
Kittle. *Swan* . . . . . . . . . . . .4E **31**
Kittybrewster. *Aber* . . . . . . . .3G **153**
Kitwood. *Hants* . . . . . . . . . . .3E **25**

Kivernoll. *Here* . . . . . . . . . . .2H **47**
Kiveton Park. *S Yor* . . . . . . . . .2B **86**
Knaith. *Linc* . . . . . . . . . . . .2F **87**
Knaith Park. *Linc* . . . . . . . . . .2F **87**
Knaphill. *Surr* . . . . . . . . . . .5A **38**
Knapp. *Hants* . . . . . . . . . . . .4C **24**
Knapp. *Per* . . . . . . . . . . . .5B **144**
Knapp. *Som* . . . . . . . . . . . .4G **21**
Knapperfield. *High* . . . . . . . . .3E **169**
Knapton. *Norf* . . . . . . . . . . .2F **79**
Knapton. *York* . . . . . . . . . . .4H **99**
Knapton Green. *Here* . . . . . . . .5G **59**
Knapwell. *Cambs* . . . . . . . . . .4C **64**
**Knaresborough.** *N Yor* . . . . . .4F **99**
Knarsdale. *Nmbd* . . . . . . . . .4H **113**
Knatts Valley. *Kent* . . . . . . . . .4G **39**
Knaven. *Abers* . . . . . . . . . . .4F **161**
Knayton. *N Yor* . . . . . . . . . . .1G **99**
Knebworth. *Herts* . . . . . . . . . .3C **52**
Knedlington. *E Yor* . . . . . . . . .2H **93**
Kneesall. *Notts* . . . . . . . . . . .4E **86**
Kneesworth. *Cambs* . . . . . . . .1D **52**
Kneeton. *Notts* . . . . . . . . . . .1E **74**
Knelston. *Swan* . . . . . . . . . . .4D **30**
Knenhall. *Staf* . . . . . . . . . . .2D **72**
Knightacott. *Devn* . . . . . . . . . .3G **19**
Knightcott. *N Som* . . . . . . . . . .1G **21**
Knightley. *Staf* . . . . . . . . . . .3C **72**
Knightley Dale. *Staf* . . . . . . . . .3C **72**
Knightlow Hill. *Warw* . . . . . . . .3B **62**
Knighton. *Devn* . . . . . . . . . . . .4B **8**
Knighton. *Dors* . . . . . . . . . . .1B **14**
Knighton. *Leic* . . . . . . . . . . .5C **74**
Knighton. *Powy* . . . . . . . . . . .3E **59**
Knighton. *Som* . . . . . . . . . . .2E **21**
Knighton. *Staf*
    nr. Eccleshall . . . . . . . . .3B **72**
    nr. Woore . . . . . . . . . . .1B **72**
Knighton. *Wilts* . . . . . . . . . . .4A **36**
Knighton. *Worc* . . . . . . . . . . .5E **61**
Knighton Common. *Worc* . . . . .3A **60**
Knight's End. *Cambs* . . . . . . . .1D **64**
Knightswood. *Glas* . . . . . . . . .3G **127**
Knightwick. *Worc* . . . . . . . . . .5B **60**
Knill. *Here* . . . . . . . . . . . . .4E **59**
Knipton. *Leics* . . . . . . . . . . . .2F **75**
Knitsley. *Dur* . . . . . . . . . . .5E **115**
Kniveton. *Derbs* . . . . . . . . . . .5G **85**
Knock. *Arg* . . . . . . . . . . . .5G **139**
Knock. *Cumb* . . . . . . . . . . .2H **103**
Knock. *Mor* . . . . . . . . . . . .3C **160**
Knockally. *High* . . . . . . . . . . .5D **168**
Knockan. *Arg* . . . . . . . . . . .1B **132**
Knockan. *High* . . . . . . . . . . .2G **163**
Knockandhu. *Mor* . . . . . . . . .1G **151**
Knockando. *Mor* . . . . . . . . . .4F **159**
Knockarthur. *High* . . . . . . . . .3E **165**
Knockbain. *High* . . . . . . . . . .3A **158**
Knockbreck. *High* . . . . . . . . . .2B **154**
Knockdee. *High* . . . . . . . . . .2D **168**
Knockdolian. *S Ayr* . . . . . . . .1G **109**
Knockdown. *Glos* . . . . . . . . . .3D **34**
Knockenbaird. *Abers* . . . . . . .1D **152**
Knockenkelly. *N Ayr* . . . . . . . .3E **123**
Knockentiber. *E Ayr* . . . . . . . .1C **116**
Knockfarrel. *High* . . . . . . . . . .3H **157**
Knockglass. *High* . . . . . . . . . .2C **168**
Knockholt. *Kent* . . . . . . . . . . .5F **39**
Knockholt Pound. *Kent* . . . . . . .5F **39**
Knockie Lodge. *High* . . . . . . . .2G **149**
Knockin. *Shrp* . . . . . . . . . . . .3F **71**
Knockinlaw. *E Ayr* . . . . . . . . .1D **116**
Knockandhu. . . . . . . . . . . . .5D **169**
Knockrome. *Arg* . . . . . . . . . .2D **124**
Knocksharry. *IOM* . . . . . . . . .3B **108**
Knockshinnoch. *E Ayr* . . . . . . .3D **116**
Knockvennie. *Dum* . . . . . . . . .2E **111**
Knockvologan. *Arg* . . . . . . . . .3B **132**
Knodishall. *Suff* . . . . . . . . . .4G **67**
Knole. *Som* . . . . . . . . . . . .4H **21**
Knollbury. *Mon* . . . . . . . . . .3H **33**
Knolls Green. *Ches E* . . . . . . .3C **84**

Knolton. *Wrex* . . . . . . . . . . .2F **71**
Knook. *Wilts* . . . . . . . . . . . .2E **23**
Knossington. *Leics* . . . . . . . . .5F **75**
Knott. *High* . . . . . . . . . . . .3C **154**
Knott End-on-Sea. *Lanc* . . . . . .5C **96**
Knotting. *Bed* . . . . . . . . . . .4H **63**
Knotting Green. *Bed* . . . . . . . .4H **63**
**Knottingley.** *W Yor* . . . . . . . .2E **93**
Knotts. *Cumb* . . . . . . . . . . .2F **103**
Knotty Ash. *Mers* . . . . . . . . . .1G **83**
Knotty Green. *Buck* . . . . . . . . .1A **38**
Knowbury. *Shrp* . . . . . . . . . . .3H **59**
Knowe. *Dum* . . . . . . . . . . .2A **110**
Knowefield. *Cumb* . . . . . . . . .4F **113**
Knowehead. *Dum* . . . . . . . . .5F **117**
Knowes. *E Lot* . . . . . . . . . . .2C **130**
Knowesgate. *Nmbd* . . . . . . . .1C **114**
Knoweside. *S Ayr* . . . . . . . . . .3B **116**
Knowes of Elrick. *Abers* . . . . . .3D **160**
Knowle. *Bris* . . . . . . . . . . . . .4B **34**
    nr. Braunton . . . . . . . . . .3E **19**
    nr. Budleigh Salterton . . . .4D **12**
    nr. Crediton . . . . . . . . . .2A **12**
**Knowle.** *W Mid* . . . . . . . . . .3F **61**
Knowle Green. *Lanc* . . . . . . . . .1E **91**
Knowle St Giles. *Som* . . . . . . .1G **13**
Knowlesands. *Shrp* . . . . . . . . .1B **60**
Knowl Hill. *Wind* . . . . . . . . . .4G **37**
Knowlton. *Kent* . . . . . . . . . . .5G **41**
Knowsley. *Mers* . . . . . . . . . . .1G **83**
Knowstone. *Devn* . . . . . . . . . .4B **20**
Knucklas. *Powy* . . . . . . . . . . .3E **59**
Knuston. *Nptn* . . . . . . . . . . .4G **63**
**Knutsford.** *Ches E* . . . . . . . . .3B **84**
Knypersley. *Staf* . . . . . . . . . .5C **84**
Krumlin. *W Yor* . . . . . . . . . . .3A **92**
Kuggar. *Corn* . . . . . . . . . . . . .5E **5**
Kyleakin. *High* . . . . . . . . . . .1F **147**
Kyle of Lochalsh. *High* . . . . . . .1F **147**
Kylerhea. *High* . . . . . . . . . . .1F **147**
Kylesku. *High* . . . . . . . . . . .5C **166**
Kyles Lodge. *W Isl* . . . . . . . . .1E **170**
Kylesmorar. *High* . . . . . . . . . .4G **147**
Kylestrome. *High* . . . . . . . . . .5C **166**
Kymin. *Mon* . . . . . . . . . . . . .4A **48**
Kynaston. *Here* . . . . . . . . . . .2B **48**
Kynaston. *Shrp* . . . . . . . . . . .3F **71**
Kynnersley. *Telf* . . . . . . . . . . .4A **72**
Kyre Green. *Worc* . . . . . . . . . .4A **60**
Kyre Park. *Worc* . . . . . . . . . . .4A **60**
Kyrewood. *Worc* . . . . . . . . . . .4A **60**

# L

Labost. *W Isl* . . . . . . . . . . . .3E **171**
Lacasaidh. *W Isl* . . . . . . . . . . .5F **171**
Lacasdail. *W Isl* . . . . . . . . . . .4G **171**
Laceby. *NE Lin* . . . . . . . . . . .4F **95**
Lacey Green. *Buck* . . . . . . . . .5G **51**
Lach Dennis. *Ches W* . . . . . . . .3B **84**
Lache. *Ches W* . . . . . . . . . . . .4F **83**
Lackford. *Suff* . . . . . . . . . . . .3G **65**
Lacock. *Wilts* . . . . . . . . . . . .5E **35**
Ladbroke. *Warw* . . . . . . . . . . .5B **62**
Laddingford. *Kent* . . . . . . . . . .1A **28**
Lade Bank. *Linc* . . . . . . . . . . .5C **88**
Ladock. *Corn* . . . . . . . . . . . . .3C **6**
Lady. *Orkn* . . . . . . . . . . . . .3F **172**
Ladybank. *Fife* . . . . . . . . . . .2F **137**
Ladycross. *Corn* . . . . . . . . . . .4D **10**
Lady Green. *Mers* . . . . . . . . . .4B **90**
Lady Hall. *Cumb* . . . . . . . . . . .1A **96**
Ladykirk. *Bord* . . . . . . . . . . .5E **131**
Ladysford. *Abers* . . . . . . . . . .2G **161**
Ladywood. *W Mid* . . . . . . . . . .2E **61**
Ladywood. *Worc* . . . . . . . . . . .4C **60**
Laga. *High* . . . . . . . . . . . . .2A **140**
Lagavulin. *Arg* . . . . . . . . . . .5C **124**
Lagg. *Arg* . . . . . . . . . . . . .2D **125**
Lagg. *N Ayr* . . . . . . . . . . . .3D **122**

Laggan—Leek Wootton


Laggan. *Arg* 4A **124**
Laggan. *High*
nr. Fort Augustus 4E **149**
nr. Newtonmore 4A **150**
Laggan. *Mor* 5H **159**
Lagganlia. *High* 3C **150**
Lagganulva. *Arg* 4F **139**
Laglingarten. *Arg* 3A **134**
Lagness. *W Sus* 2G **17**
Laid. *High* 3E **166**
Laide. *High* 4C **162**
Laigh Fenwick. *E Ayr* 5F **127**
Laindon. *Essx* 2A **40**
Lairg. *High* 3C **164**
Lairg Muir. *High* 3C **164**
Laithes. *Cumb* 1F **103**
Laithkirk. *Dur* 2C **104**
Lake. *Devn* 3F **19**
Lake. *IOW* 4D **16**
Lake. *Wilts* 3G **23**
Lakenham. *Norf* 5E **79**
Lakenheath. *Suff* 2G **65**
Lakesend. *Norf* 1E **65**
Lakeside. *Cumb* 1C **96**
Laleham. *Surr* 4B **38**
Laleston. *B'end* 3B **32**
Lamancha. *Bord* 4F **129**
Lamarsh. *Essx* 2B **54**
Lamas. *Norf* 3E **79**
Lamb Corner. *Essx* 2D **54**
Lambden. *Bord* 5D **130**
Lamberhead Green. *G Man* 4D **90**
Lamberhurst. *Kent* 2A **28**
Lamberhurst Quarter. *Kent* 2A **28**
Lamberton. *Bord* 4F **131**
**Lambeth**. *G Lon* 3E **39**
Lambfell Moar. *IOM* 3B **108**
Lambhill. *Glas* 3G **127**
Lambley. *Nmbd* 4H **113**
Lambley. *Notts* 1D **74**
Lambourn. *W Ber* 4B **36**
Lambourne End. *Essx* 1F **39**
Lambourn Woodlands.
*W Ber* 4B **36**
Lambs Green. *Dors* 3E **15**
Lambs Green. *W Sus* 2D **26**
Lambston. *Pemb* 3D **42**
Lamellion. *Corn* 2G **7**
Lamerton. *Devn* 5E **11**
Lamesley. *Tyne* 4F **115**
Laminess. *Orkn* 4F **172**
Lamington. *High* 1B **158**
Lamington. *S Lan* 1B **118**
Lamlash. *N Ayr* 2E **123**
Lamonby. *Cumb* 1F **103**
Lamorick. *Corn* 2E **7**
Lamorna. *Corn* 4B **4**
Lamorran. *Corn* 4C **6**
Lampeter. *Cdgn* 1F **45**
Lampeter Velfrey. *Pemb* 3F **43**
Lamphey. *Pemb* 4E **43**
Lamplugh. *Cumb* 2B **102**
Lamport. *Nptn* 3E **63**
Lamyatt. *Som* 3B **22**
Lana. *Devn*
nr. Ashwater 3D **10**
nr. Holsworthy 2D **10**
Lanark. *S Lan* 5B **128**
Lanarth. *Corn* 4E **5**
**Lancaster**. *Lanc* 3D **97**
Lanchester. *Dur* 5E **115**
**Lancing**. *W Sus* 5C **26**
Landbeach. *Cambs* 4D **65**
Landcross. *Devn* 4E **19**
Landerberry. *Abers* 3E **153**
Landford. *Wilts* 1A **16**
Land Gate. *G Man* 4D **90**
Landhallow. *High* 5D **169**
Landimore. *Swan* 3D **30**
Landkey. *Devn* 3F **19**
Landkey Newland. *Devn* 3F **19**
Landore. *Swan* 3F **31**
Landport. *Port* 2E **17**
Landrake. *Corn* 2H **7**
Landscove. *Devn* 2D **9**
Land's End Airport. *Corn* 4A **4**
Landshipping. *Pemb* 3E **43**
Landulph. *Corn* 2A **8**
Landywood. *Staf* 5D **73**
Lane. *Corn* 2C **6**
Laneast. *Corn* 4C **10**
Lane Bottom. *Lanc* 1G **91**
Lane End. *Buck* 2G **37**
Lane End. *Hants* 4D **24**
Lane End. *IOW* 4E **17**
Lane End. *Wilts* 2D **22**
Lane Ends. *Derbs* 2G **73**
Lane Ends. *Dur* 1E **105**
Lane Ends. *Lanc* 4G **97**
Laneham. *Notts* 3F **87**
Lane Head. *Dur*
nr. Hutton Magna 3E **105**
nr. Woodland 2D **105**
Lane Head. *G Man* 1A **84**
Lane Head. *W Yor* 4B **92**
Lanehead. *Dur* 5B **114**
Lanehead. *Nmbd* 1A **114**
Lane Heads. *Lanc* 1C **90**
Lanercost. *Cumb* 3G **113**
Laneshaw Bridge. *Lanc* 5B **98**
Laney Green. *Staf* 5D **72**
Langais. *W Isl* 2D **170**
Langal. *High* 2B **140**
Langar. *Notts* 2E **74**
Langbank. *Ren* 2E **127**
Langbar. *N Yor* 4C **98**
Langburnshiels. *Bord* 4H **119**
Langcliffe. *N Yor* 3H **97**
Langdale End. *N Yor* 5G **107**
Langdon. *Corn* 3C **10**
Langdon Beck. *Dur* 1B **104**
Langdon Cross. *Corn* 4D **10**
Langdon Hills. *Essx* 2A **40**
Langdown. *Hants* 2C **16**
Langdyke. *Fife* 3F **137**
Langenhoe. *Essx* 4D **54**
Langford. *C Beds* 1B **52**
Langford. *Devn* 2D **12**
Langford. *Essx* 5B **54**
Langford. *Notts* 5F **87**
Langford. *Oxon* 5H **49**
Langford. *Som* 4F **21**
Langford Budville. *Som* 4E **20**
Langham. *Dors* 4C **22**
Langham. *Essx* 2D **54**
Langham. *Norf* 1C **78**
Langham. *Rut* 4F **75**
Langham. *Suff* 4B **66**
Langho. *Lanc* 1F **91**
Langholm. *Dum* 1E **113**
Langland. *Swan* 4F **31**
Langleeford. *Nmbd* 2D **120**
Langley. *Ches E* 3D **84**
Langley. *Derbs* 1B **74**
Langley. *Essx* 2E **53**
Langley. *Glos* 3F **49**
Langley. *Hants* 2C **16**
Langley. *Herts* 3C **52**
Langley. *Kent* 5C **40**
Langley. *Nmbd* 3B **114**
Langley. *Slo* 3B **38**
Langley. *Som* 4D **20**
Langley. *Warw* 4F **61**
Langley. *W Sus* 4G **25**
Langley Burrell. *Wilts* 4E **35**
Langleybury. *Herts* 5A **52**
Langley Common. *Derbs* 2G **73**
Langley Green. *Derbs* 2G **73**
Langley Green. *Norf* 5F **79**
Langley Green. *Warw* 4F **61**
Langley Green. *W Sus* 2D **26**
Langley Heath. *Kent* 5C **40**
Langley Marsh. *Som* 4D **20**
Langley Moor. *Dur* 5F **115**
Langley Park. *Dur* 5F **115**
Langley Street. *Norf* 5F **79**
Langney. *E Sus* 5H **27**
Langold. *Notts* 2C **86**
Langore. *Corn* 4C **10**
Langport. *Som* 4H **21**
Langrick. *Linc* 1B **76**
Langridge. *Bath* 5C **34**
Langridgeford. *Devn* 4F **19**
Langrigg. *Cumb* 5C **112**
Langrish. *Hants* 4F **25**
Langsett. *S Yor* 4C **92**
Langshaw. *Bord* 1H **119**
Langstone. *Hants* 2F **17**
Langthorne. *N Yor* 5F **105**
Langthorpe. *N Yor* 3F **99**
Langthwaite. *N Yor* 4D **104**
Langtoft. *E Yor* 3E **101**
Langtoft. *Linc* 4A **76**
Langton. *Dur* 3E **105**
Langton. *Linc*
nr. Horncastle 4B **88**
nr. Spilsby 3C **88**
Langton. *N Yor* 3B **100**
Langton by Wragby. *Linc* 3A **88**
Langton Green. *Kent* 2G **27**
Langton Herring. *Dors* 4B **14**
Langton Long Blandford.
*Dors* 2D **15**
Langton Matravers. *Dors* 5E **15**
Langtree. *Devn* 1E **11**
Langwathby. *Cumb* 1G **103**
Langwith. *Derbs* 3C **86**
Langworth. *Linc* 3H **87**
Lanivet. *Corn* 2E **7**
Lanjeth. *Corn* 3D **6**
Lank. *Corn* 5A **10**
Lanlivery. *Corn* 3E **7**
Lanner. *Corn* 5B **6**
Lanreath. *Corn* 3F **7**
Lansallos. *Corn* 3F **7**
Lansdown. *Bath* 5C **34**
Lansdown. *Glos* 3E **49**
Lanteglos Highway. *Corn* 3F **7**
Lanton. *Nmbd* 1D **120**
Lanton. *Bord* 2A **120**
Lapford. *Devn* 2H **11**
Lapford Cross. *Devn* 2H **11**
Laphroaig. *Arg* 5B **124**
Lapley. *Staf* 4C **72**
Lapworth. *Warw* 3F **61**
Larachbeg. *High* 4A **140**
Larbert. *Falk* 1B **128**
Larden Green. *Ches E* 5H **83**
Larel. *High* 3D **169**
Largie. *Abers* 5D **160**
Largiemore. *Arg* 1H **125**
Largoward. *Fife* 3G **137**
**Largs**. *N Ayr* 4D **126**
Largue. *Abers* 4D **160**
Largybeg. *N Ayr* 3E **123**
Largymeanoch. *N Ayr* 3E **123**
Largymore. *N Ayr* 3E **123**
Larkfield. *Inv* 2D **126**
Larkfield. *Kent* 5B **40**
Larkhall. *Bath* 5C **34**
**Larkhall**. *S Lan* 4A **128**
Larkhill. *Wilts* 2G **23**
Larling. *Norf* 2B **66**
**Larne**. *ME Ant* 2H **175**
Larport. *Here* 2A **48**
Lartington. *Dur* 3D **104**
Lary. *Abers* 3H **151**
Lasham. *Hants* 2E **25**
Lashenden. *Kent* 1C **28**
Lasswade. *Midl* 3G **129**
Lastingham. *N Yor* 5E **107**
Latchford. *Herts* 3D **53**
Latchford. *Oxon* 5E **51**
Latchingdon. *Essx* 5B **54**
Latchley. *Corn* 5E **11**
Latchmere Green. *Hants* 1E **25**
Lathbury. *Mil* 1G **51**
Latheron. *High* 5D **169**
Latheronwheel. *High* 5D **169**
Lathom. *Lanc* 4C **90**
Lathones. *Fife* 3G **137**
Latimer. *Buck* 1B **38**
Latteridge. *S Glo* 3B **34**
Lattiford. *Som* 4B **22**
Latton. *Wilts* 2F **35**
Laudale House. *High* 3B **140**
Lauder. *Bord* 5B **130**
Laugharne. *Carm* 3H **43**
Laughterton. *Linc* 3F **87**
Laughton. *E Sus* 4G **27**
Laughton. *Leics* 2D **62**
Laughton. *Linc*
nr. Gainsborough 1F **87**
nr. Grantham 2H **75**
Laughton Common. *S Yor* 2C **86**
Laughton en le Morthen.
*S Yor* 2C **86**
Launcells. *Corn* 2C **10**
Launceston. *Corn* 4D **10**
Launcherley. *Som* 2A **22**
Launton. *Oxon* 3E **50**
Laurencekirk. *Abers* 1G **145**
Laurieston. *Dum* 3D **111**
Laurieston. *Falk* 2C **128**
Lavendon. *Mil* 5G **63**
Lavenham. *Suff* 1C **54**
Laverhay. *Dum* 5D **118**
Laversdale. *Cumb* 3F **113**
Laverstock. *Wilts* 3G **23**
Laverstoke. *Hants* 2C **24**
Laverton. *Glos* 2F **49**
Laverton. *N Yor* 2E **99**
Laverton. *Som* 1C **22**
Lavister. *Wrex* 5F **83**
Law. *S Lan* 4B **128**
Lawers. *Per* 5D **142**
Lawford. *Essx* 2D **54**
Lawhitton. *Corn* 4D **10**
Lawkland. *N Yor* 3G **97**
Lawley. *Telf* 5A **72**
Lawnhead. *Staf* 3C **72**
Lawrenny. *Pemb* 4E **43**
Lawshall. *Suff* 5A **66**
Lawton. *Here* 5G **59**
Laxey. *IOM* 3D **108**
Laxfield. *Suff* 3E **67**
Laxfirth. *Shet* 6F **173**
Laxo. *Shet* 5F **173**
Laxton. *E Yor* 2A **94**
Laxton. *Nptn* 1G **63**
Laxton. *Notts* 4E **86**
Laycock. *W Yor* 5C **98**
Layer Breton. *Essx* 4C **54**
Layer-de-la-Haye. *Essx* 3C **54**
Layer Marney. *Essx* 4C **54**
Laymore. *Dors* 2G **13**
Laysters Pole. *Here* 4H **59**
Layter's Green. *Buck* 1A **38**
Laytham. *E Yor* 1H **93**
Lazenby. *Red C* 3C **106**
Lazonby. *Cumb* 1G **103**
Lea. *Derbs* 5H **85**
Lea. *Here* 3B **48**
Lea. *Linc* 2F **87**
Lea. *Shrp*
nr. Bishop's Castle 2F **59**
nr. Shrewsbury 5G **71**
Lea. *Wilts* 3E **35**
Leabrooks. *Derbs* 5B **86**
Leac a Li. *W Isl* 8D **171**
Leachd. *Arg* 4H **133**
Leachkin. *High* 4A **158**
Leachpool. *Pemb* 3D **42**
Leadburn. *Midl* 4F **129**
Leadenham. *Linc* 5G **87**
Leaden Roding. *Essx* 4F **53**
Leaderfoot. *Bord* 1H **119**
Leadgate. *Cumb* 5A **114**
Leadgate. *Dur* 4E **115**
Leadgate. *Nmbd* 4E **115**
Leadhills. *S Lan* 3A **118**
Leadingcross Green. *Kent* 5C **40**
Lea End. *Worc* 3E **61**
Leafield. *Oxon* 4B **50**
Leagrave. *Lutn* 3A **52**
Lea Hall. *W Mid* 2F **61**
Lea Heath. *Staf* 3E **73**
Leake. *N Yor* 5B **106**
Leake Common Side. *Linc* 5C **88**
Leake Fold Hill. *Linc* 5D **88**
Leake Hurn's End. *Linc* 1D **76**
Lealholm. *N Yor* 4E **107**
Lealt. *Arg* 4D **132**
Lealt. *High* 2E **155**
Leam. *Derbs* 3G **85**
Lea Marston. *Warw* 1G **61**
Leamington Hastings. *Warw* 4B **62**
**Leamington Spa, Royal**.
*Warw* 4H **61**
Leamonsley. *Staf* 5F **73**
Leamside. *Dur* 5G **115**
Leargybreck. *Arg* 2D **124**
Lease Rigg. *N Yor* 4F **107**
Leasgill. *Cumb* 1D **97**
Leasingham. *Linc* 1H **75**
Leasingthorne. *Dur* 1F **105**
Leasowe. *Mers* 1E **83**
**Leatherhead**. *Surr* 5C **38**
Leathley. *N Yor* 5E **99**
Leaths. *Dum* 3E **111**
Leaton. *Shrp* 4G **71**
Leaton. *Telf* 4A **72**
Lea Town. *Lanc* 1C **90**
Leaveland. *Kent* 5E **40**
Leavenheath. *Suff* 2C **54**
Leavening. *N Yor* 3B **100**
Leaves Green. *G Lon* 4F **39**
Lea Yeat. *Cumb* 1G **97**
Leazes. *Dur* 4E **115**
Lebberston. *N Yor* 1E **101**
Lechlade on Thames. *Glos* 2H **35**
Leck. *Lanc* 2F **97**
Leckford. *Hants* 3B **24**
Leckfurin. *High* 3H **167**
Leckgruinart. *Arg* 3A **124**
Leckhampstead. *Buck* 2F **51**
Leckhampstead. *W Ber* 4C **36**
Leckhampton. *Glos* 4E **49**
Leckmelm. *High* 4F **163**
Leckwith. *V Glam* 4E **33**
Leconfield. *E Yor* 5E **101**
Ledaig. *Arg* 5D **140**
Ledburn. *Buck* 3H **51**
Ledbury. *Here* 2C **48**
Ledgemoor. *Here* 5G **59**
Ledgowan. *High* 3D **156**
Ledicot. *Here* 4G **59**
Ledmore. *High* 2G **163**
Lednabirichen. *High* 4E **165**
Lednagullin. *High* 2A **168**
Ledsham. *Ches W* 3F **83**
Ledsham. *W Yor* 2E **93**
Ledston. *W Yor* 2E **93**
Ledstone. *Devn* 4D **8**
Ledwell. *Oxon* 3C **50**
Lee. *Devn*
nr. Ilfracombe 2E **19**
nr. South Molton 4B **20**
Lee. *G Lon* 3E **39**
Lee. *Hants* 1B **16**
Lee. *Lanc* 4E **97**
Lee. *Shrp* 2G **71**
The Lee. *Buck* 5H **51**
Leeans. *Shet* 7E **173**
Leebotten. *Shet* 9F **173**
Leebotwood. *Shrp* 1G **59**
Lee Brockhurst. *Shrp* 3H **71**
Leece. *Cumb* 3B **96**
Leechpool. *Mon* 3A **34**
Lee Clump. *Buck* 5H **51**
Leeds. *Kent* 5C **40**
**Leeds**. *W Yor* 1C **92**
Leeds Bradford Airport.
*W Yor* 5E **99**
Leedstown. *Corn* 3D **4**
Leegomery. *Telf* 4A **72**
Lee Head. *Derbs* 1E **85**
**Leek**. *Staf* 5D **85**
Leekbrook. *Staf* 5D **85**
Leek Wootton. *Warw* 4G **61**

Lee Mill. Devn . . . . . . . . . . .3B 8
Leeming. N Yor . . . . . . . . . . .1E 99
Leeming Bar. N Yor . . . . . .5F 105
Lee Moor. Devn . . . . . . . . . . .2B 8
Lee Moor. W Yor . . . . . . . . .2D 92
Lee-on-the-Solent. Hants . . . .2D 16
Lees. Derbs . . . . . . . . . . . . . .2G 73
Lees. G Man . . . . . . . . . . . . .4H 91
Lees. W Yor . . . . . . . . . . . . . .1A 92
The Lees. Kent . . . . . . . . . . . .5E 40
Leeswood. Flin . . . . . . . . . . . .4E 83
Leetown. Per . . . . . . . . . . . .1E 136
Leftwich. Ches W . . . . . . . . . .3A 84
Legbourne. Linc . . . . . . . . . . .2C 88
Legburthwaite. Cumb . . . . .3E 102
Legerwood. Bord . . . . . . . . .5B 130
Legsby. Linc . . . . . . . . . . . . . .2A 88
Leicester. Leic . . . . . . . . . . . . .5C 74
Leicester Forest East. Leics . . .5C 74
Leigh. Dors . . . . . . . . . . . . . . .2B 14
Leigh. G Man . . . . . . . . . . . . .4E 91
Leigh. Kent . . . . . . . . . . . . . . .1G 27
Leigh. Shrp . . . . . . . . . . . . . . .5F 71
Leigh. Surr . . . . . . . . . . . . . . .1D 26
Leigh. Wilts . . . . . . . . . . . . . .2F 35
Leigh. Worc . . . . . . . . . . . . . . .5B 60
The Leigh. Glos . . . . . . . . . . .3D 48
Leigham. Plym . . . . . . . . . . . . .3B 8
Leigh Beck. Essx . . . . . . . . . . .2C 40
Leigh Common. Som . . . . . . . .4C 22
Leigh Delamere. Wilts . . . . . .4D 35
Leigh Green. Kent . . . . . . . . . .2D 28
Leighland Chapel. Som . . . . .3D 20
Leigh-on-Sea. S'end . . . . . . . .2C 40
Leigh Park. Hants . . . . . . . . . .2F 17
Leigh Sinton. Worc . . . . . . . . .5B 60
Leighterton. Glos . . . . . . . . . .2D 34
Leighton. N Yor . . . . . . . . . . .2D 98
Leighton. Powy . . . . . . . . . . . .5E 71
Leighton. Shrp . . . . . . . . . . . .5A 72
Leighton. Som . . . . . . . . . . . .2C 22
Leighton Bromswold. Cambs . . .3A 64
**Leighton Buzzard.** C Beds . . .3H 51
Leigh-upon-Mendip. Som . . .2B 22
Leinthall Earls. Here . . . . . . . .4G 59
Leinthall Starkes. Here . . . . . .4G 59
Leintwardine. Here . . . . . . . . .3G 59
Leire. Leics . . . . . . . . . . . . . . .1C 62
Leirinmore. High . . . . . . . . . .2E 166
Leishmore. High . . . . . . . . . .4G 157
Leiston. Suff . . . . . . . . . . . . . .4G 67
Leitfie. Per . . . . . . . . . . . . . . .4B 144
Leith. Edin . . . . . . . . . . . . . .2F 129
Leitholm. Bord . . . . . . . . . . .5D 130
Lelant. Corn . . . . . . . . . . . . . . .3C 4
Lelant Downs. Corn . . . . . . . . . .3C 4
Lelley. E Yor . . . . . . . . . . . . . .1F 95
Lem Hill. Shrp . . . . . . . . . . . . .3B 60
Lemington. Tyne . . . . . . . . . .3E 115
Lempitlaw. Bord . . . . . . . . . .1B 120
Lemsford. Herts . . . . . . . . . . .4C 52
Lenacre. Cumb . . . . . . . . . . . .1F 97
Lenchie. Abers . . . . . . . . . . .5C 160
Lenchwick. Worc . . . . . . . . . . .1F 49
Lendalfoot. S Ayr . . . . . . . . .1G 109
Lendrick. Stir . . . . . . . . . . . .3E 135
Lenham. Kent . . . . . . . . . . . . .5C 40
Lenham Heath. Kent . . . . . . . .1D 28
Lenimore. N Ayr . . . . . . . . . .5G 125
Lennel. Bord . . . . . . . . . . . . .5E 131
Lennoxtown. E Dun . . . . . . .2H 127
Lenton. Linc . . . . . . . . . . . . . .2H 75
Lentran. High . . . . . . . . . . . . .4H 157
Lenwade. Norf . . . . . . . . . . . .4C 78
**Lenzie.** E Dun . . . . . . . . . . .2H 127
Leochel Cushnie. Abers . . . .2C 152
Leogh. Shet . . . . . . . . . . . . . .1B 172
**Leominster.** Here . . . . . . . . .5G 59
Leonard Stanley. Glos . . . . . .5D 48
Lepe. Hants . . . . . . . . . . . . . .3C 16
Lephenstrath. Arg . . . . . . . . .5A 122
Lephin. High . . . . . . . . . . . . .4A 154
Lephinchapel. Arg . . . . . . . . .4G 133
Lephinmore. Arg . . . . . . . . . .4G 133

Leppington. N Yor . . . . . . . .3B 100
Lepton. W Yor . . . . . . . . . . . .3C 92
Lerryn. Corn . . . . . . . . . . . . . . .3F 7
Lerwick. Shet . . . . . . . . . . . .7F 173
Lerwick (Tingwall) Airport.
  Shet . . . . . . . . . . . . . . . . . .7F 173
Lesbury. Nmbd . . . . . . . . . . .3G 121
Leslie. Abers . . . . . . . . . . . . .1C 152
Leslie. Fife . . . . . . . . . . . . . . .3E 137
Lesmahagow. S Lan . . . . . . .1H 117
Lesnewth. Corn . . . . . . . . . . . .3B 10
Lessingham. Norf . . . . . . . . . .3F 79
Lessonhall. Cumb . . . . . . . . .4D 112
Leswalt. Dum . . . . . . . . . . . .3F 109
Letchmore Heath. Herts . . . . .1C 38
Letchworth Garden City.
  Herts . . . . . . . . . . . . . . . . . .2C 52
Letcombe Bassett. Oxon . . . .3B 36
Letcombe Regis. Oxon . . . . . .3B 36
Letham. Ang . . . . . . . . . . . . .4E 145
Letham. Falk . . . . . . . . . . . . .1B 128
Letham. Fife . . . . . . . . . . . . . .2F 137
Lethanhill. E Ayr . . . . . . . . . .3D 116
Letheringham. Suff . . . . . . . . .5E 67
Letheringsett. Norf . . . . . . . . .2C 78
Lettaford. Devn . . . . . . . . . . . .4H 11
Lettan. Orkn . . . . . . . . . . . . .3G 172
Letter. Abers . . . . . . . . . . . . .2E 153
Letterewe. High . . . . . . . . . . .1B 156
Letterfearn. High . . . . . . . . . .1A 148
Letterston. Arg . . . . . . . . . . . .4F 139
Letters. High . . . . . . . . . . . . .5F 163
Letterston. Pemb . . . . . . . . . .2D 42
Letton. Here
  nr. Kington . . . . . . . . . . . .1G 47
  nr. Leintwardine . . . . . .3F 59
Letty Green. Herts . . . . . . . . .4C 52
Letwell. S Yor . . . . . . . . . . . . .2C 86
Leuchars. Fife . . . . . . . . . . . .1G 137
Leumrabhagh. W Isl . . . . . .6F 171
Leusdon. Devn . . . . . . . . . . . . .5H 11
Levaneap. Shet . . . . . . . . . . .5F 173
Levedale. Staf . . . . . . . . . . . . .4C 72
Leven. E Yor . . . . . . . . . . . . .5F 101
Leven. Fife . . . . . . . . . . . . . . .3F 137
Levencorroch. N Ayr . . . . . . .3E 123
Levenhall. E Lot . . . . . . . . . .2G 129
Levens. Cumb . . . . . . . . . . . . .1D 97
Levens Green. Herts . . . . . . . .3D 52
Levenshulme. G Man . . . . . . . .1C 84
Levenwick. Shet . . . . . . . . . .9F 173
Leverburgh. W Isl . . . . . . . .9C 171
Leverington. Cambs . . . . . . . .4D 76
Leverton. Linc . . . . . . . . . . . . .1C 76
Leverton. W Ber . . . . . . . . . . .4B 36
Leverton Lucasgate. Linc . . . .1D 76
Leverton Outgate. Linc . . . . . .1D 76
Levington. Suff . . . . . . . . . . . .2F 55
Levisham. N Yor . . . . . . . . . .5F 107
Levishie. High . . . . . . . . . . . .2G 149
Lew. Oxon . . . . . . . . . . . . . . .5B 50
Lewaigue. IOM . . . . . . . . . . .2D 108
Lewannick. Corn . . . . . . . . . . .4C 10
Lewdown. Devn . . . . . . . . . . . .4E 11
**Lewes.** E Sus . . . . . . . . . . . .4F 27
Leweston. Pemb . . . . . . . . . . .2D 42
**Lewisham.** G Lon . . . . . . . . .3E 39
Lewiston. High . . . . . . . . . . . .1H 149
Lewistown. B'end . . . . . . . . . .3C 32
Lewknor. Oxon . . . . . . . . . . . .2F 37
Leworthy. Devn
  nr. Barnstaple . . . . . . . . .3G 19
  nr. Holsworthy . . . . . . . .2D 10
Lewson Street. Kent . . . . . . . .4D 40
Lewthorn Cross. Devn . . . . . .5A 12
Lewtrenchard. Devn . . . . . . . .4E 11
Ley. Corn . . . . . . . . . . . . . . . . .2F 7
Leybourne. Kent . . . . . . . . . . .5A 40
Leyburn. N Yor . . . . . . . . . . .5E 105
Leycett. Staf . . . . . . . . . . . . . .1B 72
Leyfields. Staf . . . . . . . . . . . . .5G 73
Ley Green. Herts . . . . . . . . . . .3B 52
Ley Hill. Buck . . . . . . . . . . . . .5H 51

**Leyland.** Lanc . . . . . . . . . . . .2D 90
Leylodge. Abers . . . . . . . . . .2E 153
Leymoor. W Yor . . . . . . . . . . .3B 92
Leys. Per . . . . . . . . . . . . . . . .5B 144
Leysdown-on-Sea. Kent . . . . . .3E 41
Leysmill. Ang . . . . . . . . . . . . .4F 145
**Leyton.** G Lon . . . . . . . . . . . .2E 39
Leytonstone. G Lon . . . . . . . .2F 39
Lezant. Corn . . . . . . . . . . . . . .5D 10
Leziate. Norf . . . . . . . . . . . . . .4F 77
Lhanbryde. Mor . . . . . . . . . .2G 159
The Lhen. IOM . . . . . . . . . . .1C 108
Liatrie. High . . . . . . . . . . . . . .5E 157
Libanus. Powy . . . . . . . . . . . .3C 46
Libberton. S Lan . . . . . . . . .5C 128
Libbery. Worc . . . . . . . . . . . . .5D 60
Liberton. Edin . . . . . . . . . . . .3F 129
Liceasto. W Isl . . . . . . . . . . .8D 171
**Lichfield.** Staf . . . . . . . . . . . .5F 73
Lickey. Worc . . . . . . . . . . . . . .3D 61
Lickey End. Worc . . . . . . . . . .3D 60
Lickfold. W Sus . . . . . . . . . . .3A 26
Liddaton. Devn . . . . . . . . . . . .4E 11
Liddington. Swin . . . . . . . . . .3H 35
Lidgate. Suff . . . . . . . . . . . . . .5G 65
Lidgett. Notts . . . . . . . . . . . . .4D 86
Lidham Hill. E Sus . . . . . . . . .4C 28
Lidlington. C Beds . . . . . . . . .2H 51
Lidsey. W Sus . . . . . . . . . . . . .5A 26
Lidstone. Oxon . . . . . . . . . . . .3B 50
Lienassie. High . . . . . . . . . . .1B 148
Liff. Ang . . . . . . . . . . . . . . . .5C 144
Lifford. W Mid . . . . . . . . . . . . .2E 61
Lifton. Devn . . . . . . . . . . . . . .4D 11
Liftondown. Devn . . . . . . . . . .4D 10
Lighthorne. Warw . . . . . . . . . .5H 61
Light Oaks. Stoke . . . . . . . . . .5D 84
Lightwater. Surr . . . . . . . . . . .4A 38
Lightwood. Staf . . . . . . . . . . . .1E 73
Lightwood. Stoke . . . . . . . . . .1D 72
Lightwood Green. Ches E . . . .1A 72
Lightwood Green. Wrex . . . . . .1F 71
Lilbourne. Nptn . . . . . . . . . . . .3C 62
Lilburn Tower. Nmbd . . . . . .2E 121
Lilleshall. Telf . . . . . . . . . . . . .4B 72
Lilley. Herts . . . . . . . . . . . . . . .3B 52
Lilliesleaf. Bord . . . . . . . . . .2H 119
Lillingstone Dayrell. Buck . . . .2F 51
Lillingstone Lovell. Buck . . . . .1F 51
Lillington. Dors . . . . . . . . . . . .1B 14
Lilstock. Som . . . . . . . . . . . . . .2E 21
Lilybank. Inv . . . . . . . . . . . . .2E 126
Lilyhurst. Shrp . . . . . . . . . . . . .4B 72
**Limavady.** Caus . . . . . . . . .1D 174
Limbrick. Lanc . . . . . . . . . . . .3E 90
Limbury. Lutn . . . . . . . . . . . . .3A 52
Limekilnburn. S Lan . . . . . . .4A 128
Limekilns. Fife . . . . . . . . . . . .1D 129
Limerigg. Falk . . . . . . . . . . . .2B 128
Limestone Brae. Nmbd . . . . .5A 114
Lime Street. Worc . . . . . . . . . .2D 48
Limington. Som . . . . . . . . . . . .4A 22
Limpenhoe. Norf . . . . . . . . . . .5F 79
Limpley Stoke. Wilts . . . . . . . .5C 34
Limpsfield. Surr . . . . . . . . . . . .5F 39
Limpsfield Chart. Surr . . . . . . .5F 39
Linburn. W Lot . . . . . . . . . . .3E 129
Linby. Notts . . . . . . . . . . . . . .5C 86
Linchmere. W Sus . . . . . . . . . .3G 25
Lincluden. Dum . . . . . . . . . .2A 112
**Lincoln.** Linc . . . . . . . . . . . . .3G 87
Lincomb. Worc . . . . . . . . . . . .4C 60
Lindale. Cumb . . . . . . . . . . . .1D 96
Lindal in Furness. Cumb . . . . .2B 96
Lindean. Bord . . . . . . . . . . . .1G 119
Linden. Glos . . . . . . . . . . . . . .4D 48
Lindfield. W Sus . . . . . . . . . . .3E 27
Lindford. Hants . . . . . . . . . . . .3G 25
Lindores. Fife . . . . . . . . . . . . .2E 137
Lindridge. Worc . . . . . . . . . . . .4A 60
Lindsell. Essx . . . . . . . . . . . . .3G 53
Lindsey. Suff . . . . . . . . . . . . . .1C 54

Lindsey Tye. Suff . . . . . . . . . . .1C 54
Linford. Hants . . . . . . . . . . . . .2G 15
Linford. Thur . . . . . . . . . . . . . .3A 40
Lingague. IOM . . . . . . . . . . .4B 108
Lingdale. Red C . . . . . . . . . .3D 106
Lingen. Here . . . . . . . . . . . . . .4F 59
Lingfield. Surr . . . . . . . . . . . . .1E 27
Lingreabhagh. W Isl . . . . . .9C 171
Lingwood. Norf . . . . . . . . . . . .5F 79
Linicro. High . . . . . . . . . . . . .2C 154
Linkend. Worc . . . . . . . . . . . . .2D 48
Linkenholt. Hants . . . . . . . . . .1B 24
Linkinhorne. Corn . . . . . . . . . .5D 10
Linklater. Orkn . . . . . . . . . . .9D 172
Linksness. Orkn . . . . . . . . . .6E 172
Linktown. Fife . . . . . . . . . . . .4E 137
Linkwood. Mor . . . . . . . . . . .2G 159
Linley. Shrp
  nr. Bishop's Castle . . . . .1F 59
  nr. Bridgnorth . . . . . . . .1A 60
Linley Green. Here . . . . . . . . .5A 60
**Linlithgow.** W Lot . . . . . . .2C 128
Linlithgow Bridge. Falk . . . .2C 128
Linneraineach. High . . . . . . .3F 163
Linshiels. Nmbd . . . . . . . . . .4C 120
Linsiadar. W Isl . . . . . . . . . .4E 171
Linsidemore. High . . . . . . . .4C 164
Linslade. C Beds . . . . . . . . . .3H 51
Linstead Parva. Suff . . . . . . . .3F 67
Linstock. Cumb . . . . . . . . . . .4F 113
Linthwaite. W Yor . . . . . . . . . .3B 92
Lintlaw. Bord . . . . . . . . . . . .4E 131
Lintmill. Mor . . . . . . . . . . . . .2C 160
Linton. Cambs . . . . . . . . . . . . .1F 53
Linton. Derbs . . . . . . . . . . . . .4G 73
Linton. Here . . . . . . . . . . . . . .3B 48
Linton. Kent . . . . . . . . . . . . . .1B 28
Linton. N Yor . . . . . . . . . . . . . .3B 98
Linton. Bord . . . . . . . . . . . . .2B 120
Linton. W Yor . . . . . . . . . . . . .5F 99
Linton Colliery. Nmbd . . . . . .5G 121
Linton Hill. Here . . . . . . . . . . .3B 48
Linton-on-Ouse. N Yor . . . . . .3G 99
Lintzford. Dur . . . . . . . . . . . .4E 115
Lintzgarth. Dur . . . . . . . . . . .5C 114
Linwood. Hants . . . . . . . . . . . .2G 15
Linwood. Linc . . . . . . . . . . . . .2A 88
**Linwood.** Ren . . . . . . . . . . . .3F 127
Lionacleit. W Isl . . . . . . . . . .4C 170
Lionacro. High . . . . . . . . . . .2C 154
Lionacuidhe. W Isl . . . . . . . .4C 170
Lional. W Isl . . . . . . . . . . . . .1H 171
Liphook. Hants . . . . . . . . . . . .3G 25
Lipley. Shrp . . . . . . . . . . . . . . .2B 72
Lipyeate. Som . . . . . . . . . . . . .1B 22
Liquo. N Lan . . . . . . . . . . . . .4B 128
Lisbellaw. Ferm . . . . . . . . . .5C 174
Liscard. Mers . . . . . . . . . . . . .1F 83
Liscombe. Som . . . . . . . . . . . .3B 20
Liskeard. Corn . . . . . . . . . . . . .2G 7
Lisle Court. Hants . . . . . . . . . .3B 16
Lisnaskea. Ferm . . . . . . . . . .6C 174
Liss. Hants . . . . . . . . . . . . . . .4F 25
Lissett. E Yor . . . . . . . . . . . . .4F 101
Liss Forest. Hants . . . . . . . . . .4F 25
Lissington. Linc . . . . . . . . . . . .2A 88
Liston. Essx . . . . . . . . . . . . . . .1B 54
Lisvane. Card . . . . . . . . . . . . .3E 33
Liswerry. Newp . . . . . . . . . . . .3G 33
Litcham. Norf . . . . . . . . . . . . .4A 78
Litchard. B'end . . . . . . . . . . . .3C 32
Litchborough. Nptn . . . . . . . . .5D 62
Litchfield. Hants . . . . . . . . . . .1C 24
**Litherland.** Mers . . . . . . . . . .1F 83
Litlington. Cambs . . . . . . . . . .1D 52
Litlington. E Sus . . . . . . . . . . .5G 27
Littemill. Nmbd . . . . . . . . . .3G 121
Litterty. Abers . . . . . . . . . . . .3E 161
Little Abington. Cambs . . . . . .1F 53
Little Addington. Nptn . . . . . .3G 63
Little Airmyn. N Yor . . . . . . . .2H 93
Little Alne. Warw . . . . . . . . . .4F 61

Little Ardo. Abers . . . . . . . . .5F 161
Little Asby. Cumb . . . . . . . .4H 103
Little Aston. Staf . . . . . . . . . . .5E 73
Little Atherfield. IOW . . . . . . .4C 16
Little Ayton. N Yor . . . . . . . .3C 106
Little Baddow. Essx . . . . . . . . .5A 54
Little Badminton. S Glo . . . . .3D 34
Little Ballinluig. Per . . . . . . .3G 143
Little Bampton. Cumb . . . . .4D 112
Little Bardfield. Essx . . . . . . . .2G 53
Little Barford. Bed . . . . . . . . . .5A 64
Little Barningham. Norf . . . . .2D 78
Little Barrington. Glos . . . . . .4H 49
Little Barrow. Ches W . . . . . . .4G 83
Little Barugh. N Yor . . . . . . .2B 100
Little Bavington. Nmbd . . . .2C 114
Little Bealings. Suff . . . . . . . . .1F 55
Littlebeck. Cumb . . . . . . . . . .3H 103
Little Bedwyn. Wilts . . . . . . . .5A 36
Little Bentley. Essx . . . . . . . . .3E 54
Little Berkhamsted. Herts . . . .5C 52
Little Billing. Nptn . . . . . . . . . .4F 63
Little Billington. C Beds . . . . .3H 51
Little Birch. Here . . . . . . . . . . .2A 48
Little Bispham. Bkpl . . . . . . . .5C 96
Little Blakenham. Suff . . . . . . .1E 54
Little Blencow. Cumb . . . . . .1F 103
Little Bognor. W Sus . . . . . . . .3B 26
Little Bolas. Shrp . . . . . . . . . . .3A 72
Little Bollington. Ches E . . . . .2B 84
Little Bookham. Surr . . . . . . . .5C 38
**Littleborough.** G Man . . . . . .3H 91
Littleborough. Notts . . . . . . . . .2F 87
Littlebourne. Kent . . . . . . . . . .5G 41
Little Bourton. Oxon . . . . . . . .1C 50
Little Bowden. Leics . . . . . . . .2E 63
Little Bradley. Suff . . . . . . . . . .5F 65
Little Brampton. Shrp . . . . . . .2F 59
Little Brechin. Ang . . . . . . . .2E 145
Littlebredy. Dors . . . . . . . . . . .4A 14
Little Brickhill. Mil . . . . . . . . .2H 51
Little Bridgeford. Staf . . . . . . .3C 72
Little Brington. Nptn . . . . . . . .4D 62
Little Bromley. Essx . . . . . . . . .3D 54
Little Broughton. Cumb . . . .1B 102
Little Budworth. Ches W . . . . .4H 83
Little Burstead. Essx . . . . . . . .1A 40
Little Burton. E Yor . . . . . . . .5F 101
Littlebury. Essx . . . . . . . . . . . .2F 53
Littlebury Green. Essx . . . . . . .2E 53
Little Bytham. Linc . . . . . . . . .4H 75
Little Canfield. Essx . . . . . . . . .3F 53
Little Canford. Dors . . . . . . . . .3F 15
Little Carlton. Linc . . . . . . . . .2C 88
Little Carlton. Notts . . . . . . . . .5E 87
Little Casterton. Rut . . . . . . . .5H 75
Little Catwick. E Yor . . . . . . .5F 101
Little Catworth. Cambs . . . . . .3A 64
Little Cawthorpe. Linc . . . . . . .2C 88
Little Chalfont. Buck . . . . . . . .1A 38
Little Chart. Kent . . . . . . . . . . .1D 28
Little Chesterford. Essx . . . . . .1F 53
Little Cheverell. Wilts . . . . . . .1E 23
Little Chishill. Cambs . . . . . . .2E 53
Little Clacton. Essx . . . . . . . . .4E 55
Little Clanfield. Oxon . . . . . . .5A 50
Little Clifton. Cumb . . . . . . . .2B 102
Little Coates. NE Lin . . . . . . .4F 95
Little Comberton. Worc . . . . . .1E 49
Little Common. E Sus . . . . . . .5B 28
Little Compton. Warw . . . . . . .2A 50
Little Cornard. Suff . . . . . . . . .2B 54
Littlecote. Buck . . . . . . . . . . . .3G 51
Littlecott. Wilts . . . . . . . . . . . .1G 23
Little Cowarne. Here . . . . . . . .5A 60
Little Coxwell. Oxon . . . . . . . .2A 36
Little Crakehall. N Yor . . . . .5F 105
Little Crawley. Mil . . . . . . . . . .1H 51
Little Creich. High . . . . . . . . .5D 164
Little Cressingham. Norf . . . . .5A 78
Little Crosby. Mers . . . . . . . . .4B 90
Little Crosthwaite. Cumb . . .2D 102
Little Cubley. Derbs . . . . . . . .2F 73

Little Dalby. *Leics* . . . . . . . . . . 4E 75
Little Dawley. *Telf* . . . . . . . . . . . 5A 72
Littledean. *Glos* . . . . . . . . . . . . 4B 48
Little Dens. *Abers* . . . . . . . . . . 4H 161
Little Dewchurch. *Here* . . . . . . 2A 48
Little Ditton. *Cambs* . . . . . . . . . 5F 65
Little Down. *Hants* . . . . . . . . . . 1B 24
Little Downham. *Cambs* . . . . . . 2E 65
Little Drayton. *Shrp* . . . . . . . . . 2A 72
Little Driffield. *E Yor* . . . . . . . . 4E 101
Little Dunham. *Norf* . . . . . . . . . 4A 78
Little Dunkeld. *Per* . . . . . . . . . 4H 143
Little Dunmow. *Essx* . . . . . . . . 3G 53
Little Easton. *Essx* . . . . . . . . . . 3G 53
Little Eaton. *Derbs* . . . . . . . . . 1A 74
Little Eccleston. *Lanc* . . . . . . . . 5D 96
Little Ellingham. *Norf* . . . . . . . 1C 66
Little Elm. *Som* . . . . . . . . . . . . 2C 22
Little End. *Essx* . . . . . . . . . . . . 5F 53
Little Everdon. *Nptn* . . . . . . . . 5C 62
Little Eversden. *Cambs* . . . . . . 5C 64
Little Faringdon. *Oxon* . . . . . . 5H 49
Little Fencote. *N Yor* . . . . . . . 5F 105
Little Fenton. *N Yor* . . . . . . . . 1F 93
Littleferry. *High* . . . . . . . . . . 4F 165
Little Fransham. *Norf* . . . . . . . 4B 78
Little Gaddesden. *Herts* . . . . . 4H 51
Little Garway. *Here* . . . . . . . . . 3H 47
Little Gidding. *Cambs* . . . . . . . 2A 64
Little Glemham. *Suff* . . . . . . . . 5F 67
Little Glenshee. *Per* . . . . . . . 5G 143
Little Gransden. *Cambs* . . . . . . 5B 64
Little Green. *Suff* . . . . . . . . . . . 3C 66
Little Green. *Wrex* . . . . . . . . . . 1G 71
Little Grimsby. *Linc* . . . . . . . . . 1C 88
Little Habton. *N Yor* . . . . . . . . 2B 100
Little Hadham. *Herts* . . . . . . . . 3E 53
Little Hale. *Linc* . . . . . . . . . . . 1A 76
Little Hallingbury. *Essx* . . . . . . 4E 53
Littleham. *Devn*
   nr. Bideford . . . . . . . . . . . . 4E 19
   nr. Exmouth . . . . . . . . . . . 4D 12
Littlehampton. *W Sus* . . . . . . . 5B 26
Little Haresfield. *Glos* . . . . . . . 5D 48
Little Harrowden. *Nptn* . . . . . . 3F 63
Little Haseley. *Oxon* . . . . . . . . 5E 51
Little Hatfield. *E Yor* . . . . . . . 5F 101
Little Hautbois. *Norf* . . . . . . . . 3E 79
Little Haven. *Pemb* . . . . . . . . . 3C 42
Little Hay. *Staf* . . . . . . . . . . . . 5F 73
Little Hayfield. *Derbs* . . . . . . . 2E 85
Little Haywood. *Staf* . . . . . . . . 3E 73
Little Heath. *W Mid* . . . . . . . . . 2H 61
Little Heck. *N Yor* . . . . . . . . . . 2F 93
Littlehempston. *Devn* . . . . . . . . 2E 9
Little Herbert's. *Glos* . . . . . . . . 4E 49
Little Hereford. *Here* . . . . . . . . 4H 59
Little Horkesley. *Essx* . . . . . . . 2C 54
Little Hormead. *Herts* . . . . . . . 3D 53
Little Horsted. *E Sus* . . . . . . . . 4F 27
Little Horton. *W Yor* . . . . . . . . 1B 92
Little Horwood. *Buck* . . . . . . . 2F 51
Little Houghton. *Nptn* . . . . . . . 5F 63
Littlehoughton. *Nmbd* . . . . . . 3G 121
Little Hucklow. *Derbs* . . . . . . . 3F 85
Little Hulton. *G Man* . . . . . . . . 4F 91
Little Irchester. *Nptn* . . . . . . . 4G 63
Little Kelk. *E Yor* . . . . . . . . . 3E 101
Little Kimble. *Buck* . . . . . . . . . 5G 51
Little Kineton. *Warw* . . . . . . . . 5H 61
Little Kingshill. *Buck* . . . . . . . . 2G 37
Little Langdale. *Cumb* . . . . . . 4E 102
Little Langford. *Wilts* . . . . . . . 3F 23
Little Laver. *Essx* . . . . . . . . . . 5F 53
Little Lawford. *Warw* . . . . . . . . 3B 62
Little Leigh. *Ches W* . . . . . . . . 3A 84
Little Leighs. *Essx* . . . . . . . . . 4H 53
Little Leven. *E Yor* . . . . . . . . 5E 101
**Little Lever.** *G Man* . . . . . . . 4F 91
Little Linford. *Mil* . . . . . . . . . . 1G 51
Little London. *Buck* . . . . . . . . . 4E 51
Little London. *E Sus* . . . . . . . . 4G 27

Little London. *Hants*
   nr. Andover . . . . . . . . . . . . 2B 24
   nr. Basingstoke . . . . . . . . . 1E 24
Little London. *Linc*
   nr. Long Sutton . . . . . . . . 3D 76
   nr. Spalding . . . . . . . . . . . 3B 76
Little London. *Norf*
   nr. North Walsham . . . . . . 2E 79
   nr. Northwold . . . . . . . . . 1G 65
   nr. Saxthorpe . . . . . . . . . 2D 78
   nr. Southery . . . . . . . . . . 1F 65
Little London. *Powy* . . . . . . . . 2C 58
Little Longstone. *Derbs* . . . . . . 3F 85
Little Malvern. *Worc* . . . . . . . . 1C 48
Little Maplestead. *Essx* . . . . . . 2B 54
Little Marcle. *Here* . . . . . . . . . 2B 48
Little Marlow. *Buck* . . . . . . . . . 3G 37
Little Massingham. *Norf* . . . . . 3G 77
Little Melton. *Norf* . . . . . . . . . 5D 78
Little Mill. *Mon* . . . . . . . . . . . . 5G 47
Little Milton. *Oxon* . . . . . . . . . 5E 50
Little Missenden. *Buck* . . . . . . 1A 38
Littlemoor. *Derbs* . . . . . . . . . . 4A 86
Littlemoor. *Dors* . . . . . . . . . . . 4B 14
Littlemore. *Oxon* . . . . . . . . . . 5D 50
Little Mountain. *Flin* . . . . . . . . 4E 83
Little Musgrave. *Cumb* . . . . . 3A 104
Little Ness. *Shrp* . . . . . . . . . . . 4G 71
Little Neston. *Ches W* . . . . . . . 3F 83
Little Newcastle. *Pemb* . . . . . . 2D 43
Little Newsham. *Dur* . . . . . . . 3E 105
Little Oakley. *Essx* . . . . . . . . . 3F 55
Little Oakley. *Nptn* . . . . . . . . . 2F 63
Little Onn. *Staf* . . . . . . . . . . . . 4C 72
Little Ormside. *Cumb* . . . . . . 3A 104
Little Orton. *Cumb* . . . . . . . . 4E 113
Little Orton. *Leics* . . . . . . . . . 5H 73
Little Ouse. *Cambs* . . . . . . . . . 2H 73
Little Ouseburn. *N Yor* . . . . . . 3G 99
Littleover. *Derb* . . . . . . . . . . . 2H 73
Little Packington. *Warw* . . . . . 2G 61
Little Paxton. *Cambs* . . . . . . . 4A 64
Little Petherick. *Corn* . . . . . . . 1D 6
Little Plumpton. *Lanc* . . . . . . 1B 90
Little Plumstead. *Norf* . . . . . . 4F 79
Little Ponton. *Linc* . . . . . . . . . 2G 75
Littleport. *Cambs* . . . . . . . . . . 2E 65
Little Posbrook. *Hants* . . . . . . 2D 16
Little Potheridge. *Devn* . . . . . . 1F 11
Little Preston. *Nptn* . . . . . . . . 5C 62
Little Raveley. *Cambs* . . . . . . . 3B 64
Little Reynoldston. *Swan* . . . . 4D 31
Little Ribston. *N Yor* . . . . . . . 4F 99
Little Rissington. *Glos* . . . . . . 4G 49
Little Rogart. *High* . . . . . . . . 3E 165
Little Rollright. *Oxon* . . . . . . . 2A 50
Little Ryburgh. *Norf* . . . . . . . . 3B 78
Little Ryle. *Nmbd* . . . . . . . . . 3E 121
Little Ryton. *Shrp* . . . . . . . . . 5G 71
Little Salkeld. *Cumb* . . . . . . 1G 103
Little Sampford. *Essx* . . . . . . . 2G 53
Little Sandhurst. *Brac* . . . . . . . 5G 37
Little Saredon. *Staf* . . . . . . . . 5D 72
Little Saxham. *Suff* . . . . . . . . . 4G 65
Little Scatwell. *High* . . . . . . . 3F 157
Little Shelford. *Cambs* . . . . . . 5D 64
Little Shoddesden. *Hants* . . . . 2A 24
Little Singleton. *Lanc* . . . . . . 1B 90
Little Smeaton. *N Yor* . . . . . . . 3F 93
Little Snoring. *Norf* . . . . . . . . 2B 78
Little Sodbury. *S Glo* . . . . . . . 3C 34
Little Somborne. *Hants* . . . . . . 3B 24
Little Somerford. *Wilts* . . . . . . 3E 35
Little Soudley. *Shrp* . . . . . . . . 3B 72
Little Stainforth. *N Yor* . . . . . . 3H 97
Little Stainton. *Darl* . . . . . . . 3A 106
Little Stanney. *Ches W* . . . . . . 3G 83
Little Staughton. *Bed* . . . . . . . 4A 64
Little Steeping. *Linc* . . . . . . . . 4D 88
Littlester. *Shet* . . . . . . . . . . 3G 173
Little Stoke. *Staf* . . . . . . . . . . 2D 72

Littlestone-on-Sea. *Kent* . . . . . 3E 29
Little Stonham. *Suff* . . . . . . . . 4D 66
Little Stretton. *Leics* . . . . . . . . 5D 74
Little Stretton. *Shrp* . . . . . . . . 1G 59
Little Strickland. *Cumb* . . . . . 3G 103
Little Stukeley. *Cambs* . . . . . . 3B 64
Little Sugnall. *Staf* . . . . . . . . . 2C 72
Little Sutton. *Ches W* . . . . . . . 3F 83
Little Sutton. *Linc* . . . . . . . . . . 3D 76
Little Swinburne. *Nmbd* . . . . 2C 114
Little Tew. *Oxon* . . . . . . . . . . 3B 50
Little Tey. *Essx* . . . . . . . . . . . . 3B 54
Little Thetford. *Cambs* . . . . . . 3E 65
Little Thirkleby. *N Yor* . . . . . . 2G 99
Little Thornage. *Norf* . . . . . . . 2C 78
Little Thornton. *Lanc* . . . . . . . 5C 96
Little Thorpe. *W Yor* . . . . . . . . 2B 92
Littlethorpe. *Leics* . . . . . . . . . 1C 62
Littlethorpe. *N Yor* . . . . . . . . . 3F 99
Little Thurlow. *Suff* . . . . . . . . . 5F 65
Little Thurrock. *Thur* . . . . . . . 3H 39
Littleton. *Ches W* . . . . . . . . . . 4G 83
Littleton. *Hants* . . . . . . . . . . . 3C 24
Littleton. *Som* . . . . . . . . . . . . 3H 21
Littleton. *Surr*
   nr. Guildford . . . . . . . . . . 1A 26
   nr. Staines . . . . . . . . . . . 4B 38
Littleton Drew. *Wilts* . . . . . . . 3D 34
Littleton Pannell. *Wilts* . . . . . . 1F 23
Littleton-upon-Severn.
   *S Glo* . . . . . . . . . . . . . . . . 3A 34
Little Torboll. *High* . . . . . . . . 4E 165
Little Torrington. *Devn* . . . . . . 1E 11
Little Totham. *Essx* . . . . . . . . . 4B 54
Little Town. *Cumb* . . . . . . . . 3D 102
Little Town. *Lanc* . . . . . . . . . . 1E 91
Littletown. *Dur* . . . . . . . . . . . 5G 115
Littletown. *High* . . . . . . . . . . 5E 165
Little Twycross. *Leics* . . . . . . . 5H 73
Little Urswick. *Cumb* . . . . . . . 2B 96
Little Wakering. *Essx* . . . . . . . 2D 40
Little Walden. *Essx* . . . . . . . . . 1F 53
Little Waldingfield. *Suff* . . . . . 1C 54
Little Walsingham. *Norf* . . . . . 2B 78
Little Waltham. *Essx* . . . . . . . . 4H 53
Little Warley. *Essx* . . . . . . . . . 1H 39
Little Weighton. *E Yor* . . . . . . 1C 94
Little Wenham. *Suff* . . . . . . . . 2D 54
Little Wenlock. *Telf* . . . . . . . . 5A 72
Little Whelnetham. *Suff* . . . . . 4A 66
Little Whittingham Green.
   *Suff* . . . . . . . . . . . . . . . . . 3E 67
Littlewick Green. *Wind* . . . . . . 4G 37
Little Wilbraham. *Cambs* . . . . 5E 65
Littlewindsor. *Dors* . . . . . . . . . 2H 13
Little Wisbeach. *Linc* . . . . . . . 2A 76
Little Witcombe. *Glos* . . . . . . . 4E 49
Little Witley. *Worc* . . . . . . . . . 4B 60
Little Wittenham. *Oxon* . . . . . 2D 36
Little Wolford. *Warw* . . . . . . . 2A 50
Littleworth. *Bed* . . . . . . . . . . . 1A 52
Littleworth. *Glos* . . . . . . . . . . 2G 49
Littleworth. *Oxon* . . . . . . . . . . 2B 36
Littleworth. *Staf*
   nr. Cannock . . . . . . . . . . 4E 73
   nr. Eccleshall . . . . . . . . . 3B 72
   nr. Stafford . . . . . . . . . . . 3D 72
Littleworth. *W Sus* . . . . . . . . . 3C 26
Littleworth. *Worc*
   nr. Redditch . . . . . . . . . . 4D 61
   nr. Worcester . . . . . . . . . 5C 60
Little Wratting. *Suff* . . . . . . . . 1G 53
Little Wymondley. *Herts* . . . . . 3C 52
Little Wyrley. *Staf* . . . . . . . . . 5E 73
Little Yeldham. *Essx* . . . . . . . . 2A 54
Littley Green. *Essx* . . . . . . . . . 4G 53
Litton. *Derbs* . . . . . . . . . . . . . 3F 85
Litton. *N Yor* . . . . . . . . . . . . . 2B 98
Litton. *Som* . . . . . . . . . . . . . . 1A 22
Litton Cheney. *Dors* . . . . . . . . 3A 14
Liurbost. *W Isl* . . . . . . . . . . . 5F 171
**Liverpool.** *Mers* . . . . . . . . . . 1F 83
Liverpool John Lennon
   Airport. *Mers* . . . . . . . . 2G 83

**Liversedge.** *W Yor* . . . . . . . . 2B 92
Liverton. *Devn* . . . . . . . . . . . . 5B 12
Liverton. *Red C* . . . . . . . . . . 3E 107
Liverton Mines. *Red C* . . . . . 3E 107
**Livingston.** *W Lot* . . . . . . . . 3D 128
Livingston Village. *W Lot* . . . 3D 128
Lixwm. *Flin* . . . . . . . . . . . . . . 3D 82
Lizard. *Corn* . . . . . . . . . . . . . . 5E 5
Llaingoch. *IOA* . . . . . . . . . . . 2B 80
Llaithddu. *Powy* . . . . . . . . . . . 2C 58
Llampha. *V Glam* . . . . . . . . . . 4C 32
Llan. *Powy* . . . . . . . . . . . . . . 5A 70
Llanaber. *Gwyn* . . . . . . . . . . . 4F 69
Llanaelhaearn. *Gwyn* . . . . . . . 1C 68
Llanaeron. *Cdgn* . . . . . . . . . . 4D 57
Llanafan. *Cdgn* . . . . . . . . . . . 3F 57
Llanafan-fawr. *Powy* . . . . . . . 5B 58
Llanafan-fechan. *Powy* . . . . . 5B 58
Llanallgo. *IOA* . . . . . . . . . . . . 2D 81
Llanandras. *Powy* . . . . . . . . . 4F 59
Llananno. *Powy* . . . . . . . . . . . 3C 58
Llanarmon. *Gwyn* . . . . . . . . . 2D 68
Llanarmon Dyffryn Ceiriog.
   Wrex . . . . . . . . . . . . . . . . 2D 70
Llanarmon-yn-Ial. *Den* . . . . . . 5D 82
Llanarth. *Cdgn* . . . . . . . . . . . . 5D 56
Llanarth. *Mon* . . . . . . . . . . . . 4G 47
Llanarthne. *Carm* . . . . . . . . . . 3F 45
Llanasa. *Flin* . . . . . . . . . . . . . 2D 82
Llanbabo. *IOA* . . . . . . . . . . . . 2C 80
Llanbadarn Fawr. *Cdgn* . . . . . 2F 57
Llanbadarn Fynydd. *Powy* . . . 3D 58
Llanbadarn-y-garreg. *Powy* . . 1E 46
Llanbadoc. *Mon* . . . . . . . . . . 5G 47
Llanbadrig. *IOA* . . . . . . . . . . . 1C 80
Llanbeder. *Gwyn* . . . . . . . . . . 2G 33
Llanbedr. *Gwyn* . . . . . . . . . . . 3E 69
Llanbedr. *Powy*
   nr. Crickhowell . . . . . . . . 3F 47
   nr. Hay-on-Wye . . . . . . . 1E 47
Llanbedr-Dyffryn-Clwyd.
   Den . . . . . . . . . . . . . . . . . 5D 82
Llanbedrgoch. *IOA* . . . . . . . . . 2E 81
Llanbedrog. *Gwyn* . . . . . . . . . 2C 68
Llanbedr Pont Steffan. *Cdgn* . 1F 45
Llanbedr-y-cennin. *Cnwy* . . . 4G 81
Llanberis. *Gwyn* . . . . . . . . . . 4E 81
Llanbethery. *V Glam* . . . . . . . 5D 32
Llanbister. *Powy* . . . . . . . . . . 3D 58
Llanblethian. *V Glam* . . . . . . . 4C 32
Llanboidy. *Carm* . . . . . . . . . . 2G 43
Llanbradach. *Cphy* . . . . . . . . 2E 33
Llanbrynmair. *Powy* . . . . . . . 5A 70
Llanbydderi. *V Glam* . . . . . . . 5D 32
Llancadle. *V Glam* . . . . . . . . . 5D 32
Llancarfan. *V Glam* . . . . . . . . 4D 32
Llancatal. *V Glam* . . . . . . . . . 5D 32
Llancayo. *Mon* . . . . . . . . . . . 5G 47
Llancloudy. *Here* . . . . . . . . . . 3H 47
Llancoch. *Powy* . . . . . . . . . . . 3E 58
Llancynfelyn. *Cdgn* . . . . . . . . 1F 57
Llandaff. *Card* . . . . . . . . . . . . 4E 33
Llandanwg. *Gwyn* . . . . . . . . . 3E 69
Llandarcy. *Neat* . . . . . . . . . . . 3G 31
Llandawke. *Carm* . . . . . . . . . . 3G 43
Llanddaniel Fab. *IOA* . . . . . . . 3D 81
Llanddarog. *Carm* . . . . . . . . . 4F 45
Llanddeiniol. *Cdgn* . . . . . . . . 3E 57
Llanddeiniolen. *Gwyn* . . . . . . 4E 81
Llandderfel. *Gwyn* . . . . . . . . . 2B 70
Llanddeusant. *Carm* . . . . . . . 3A 46
Llanddeusant. *IOA* . . . . . . . . . 2C 80
Llanddew. *Powy* . . . . . . . . . . 2D 46
Llanddewi. *Swan* . . . . . . . . . . 4D 30
Llanddewi Brefi. *Cdgn* . . . . . . 5F 57
Llanddewi'r Cwm. *Powy* . . . . 1D 46
Llanddewi Rhydderch. *Mon* . . 4G 47
Llanddewi Velfrey. *Pemb* . . . . 3F 43
Llanddewi Ystradenni.
   Powy . . . . . . . . . . . . . . . . 4D 58
Llanddoged. *Cnwy* . . . . . . . . 4H 81
Llanddona. *IOA* . . . . . . . . . . . 3E 81
Llanddowror. *Carm* . . . . . . . . 3G 43
Llanddulas. *Cnwy* . . . . . . . . . 3B 82

Llanddwywe. *Gwyn* . . . . . . . . 3E 69
Llanddyfnan. *IOA* . . . . . . . . . . 3E 81
Llandecwyn. *Gwyn* . . . . . . . . 2F 69
Llandefaelog Fach. *Powy* . . . . 2D 46
Llandefaelog-tre'r-graig.
   Powy . . . . . . . . . . . . . . . . 2E 47
Llandefalle. *Powy* . . . . . . . . . 2E 46
Llandegai. *IOA* . . . . . . . . . . . . 3E 81
Llandegfan. *IOA* . . . . . . . . . . . 3E 81
Llandegla. *Den* . . . . . . . . . . . 5D 82
Llandegley. *Powy* . . . . . . . . . . 4D 58
Llandegveth. *Mon* . . . . . . . . . 2G 33
Llandeilo. *Carm* . . . . . . . . . . . 3G 45
Llandeilo Graban. *Powy* . . . . . 1D 46
Llandeilo'r Fan. *Powy* . . . . . . 2B 46
Llandeloy. *Pemb* . . . . . . . . . . 2C 42
Llandenny. *Mon* . . . . . . . . . . 5H 47
Llandevaud. *Newp* . . . . . . . . 2H 33
Llandevenny. *Mon* . . . . . . . . . 3H 33
Llandilo. *Pemb* . . . . . . . . . . . 2F 43
Llandinabo. *Here* . . . . . . . . . . 3A 48
Llandinam. *Powy* . . . . . . . . . . 2C 58
Llandissilio. *Pemb* . . . . . . . . . 2F 43
Llandogo. *Mon* . . . . . . . . . . . 5A 48
Llandough. *V Glam*
   nr. Cowbridge . . . . . . . . 4C 32
   nr. Penarth . . . . . . . . . . 4E 33
Llandovery. *Carm* . . . . . . . . . 2A 46
Llandow. *V Glam* . . . . . . . . . . 4C 32
Llandre. *Cdgn* . . . . . . . . . . . . 2F 57
Llandrillo. *Den* . . . . . . . . . . . . 2C 70
Llandrillo-yn-Rhos. *Cnwy* . . . 2H 81
Llandrindod. *Powy* . . . . . . . . . 4C 58
Llandrindod Wells. *Powy* . . . . 4C 58
Llandrinio. *Powy* . . . . . . . . . . 4E 71
**Llandudno.** *Cnwy* . . . . . . . . 2G 81
Llandudno Junction. *Cnwy* . . . 3G 81
Llandudoch. *Pemb* . . . . . . . . 1B 44
Llandw. *V Glam* . . . . . . . . . . . 4C 32
Llandwrog. *Gwyn* . . . . . . . . . 5D 80
Llandybie. *Carm* . . . . . . . . . . 4G 45
Llandyfaelog. *Carm* . . . . . . . . 4E 45
Llandyfan. *Carm* . . . . . . . . . . 4G 45
Llandyfriog. *Cdgn* . . . . . . . . . 1D 44
Llandyfrydog. *IOA* . . . . . . . . . 2D 80
Llandygai. *Gwyn* . . . . . . . . . . 3F 81
Llandygwydd. *Cdgn* . . . . . . . . 1C 44
Llandynan. *Den* . . . . . . . . . . . 1D 70
Llandyrnog. *Den* . . . . . . . . . . 4D 82
Llandysilio. *Powy* . . . . . . . . . 4E 71
Llandyssil. *Powy* . . . . . . . . . . 1D 58
Llandysul. *Cdgn* . . . . . . . . . . 1E 45
Llanedeyrn. *Card* . . . . . . . . . . 3F 33
Llaneglwys. *Powy* . . . . . . . . . 2D 46
Llanegryn. *Gwyn* . . . . . . . . . . 5F 69
Llanegwad. *Carm* . . . . . . . . . 3F 45
Llaneilian. *IOA* . . . . . . . . . . . . 1D 80
Llaneilian-yn-Rhos. *Cnwy* . . . 3A 82
Llanelian. *Den* . . . . . . . . . . . 5D 82
Llanelieu. *Powy* . . . . . . . . . . . 2E 47
Llanellen. *Mon* . . . . . . . . . . . 4G 47
**Llanelli.** *Carm* . . . . . . . . . . . 3E 31
Llanelltyd. *Gwyn* . . . . . . . . . . 4G 69
Llanelly. *Mon* . . . . . . . . . . . . 4F 47
Llanelly Hill. *Mon* . . . . . . . . . 4F 47
Llanelwedd. *Powy* . . . . . . . . . 5C 58
**Llan-Elwy.** *Den* . . . . . . . . . . 3C 82
Llanenddwyn. *Gwyn* . . . . . . . 3E 69
Llanengan. *Gwyn* . . . . . . . . . 3B 68
Llanerch. *Powy* . . . . . . . . . . . 1F 59
Llanerchymedd. *IOA* . . . . . . . 2D 80
Llanerfyl. *Powy* . . . . . . . . . . . 5C 70
Llaneuddog. *IOA* . . . . . . . . . . 2D 80
Llanfachraeth. *IOA* . . . . . . . . . 2C 80
Llanfachreth. *Gwyn* . . . . . . . . 3G 69
Llanfaelog. *IOA* . . . . . . . . . . . 3C 80
Llanfaelrhys. *Gwyn* . . . . . . . . 3B 68
Llanfaenor. *Mon* . . . . . . . . . . 4H 47
Llanfaes. *IOA* . . . . . . . . . . . . 3F 81
Llanfaes. *Powy* . . . . . . . . . . . 3D 46
Llanfaethlu. *IOA* . . . . . . . . . . 2C 80
Llanfaglan. *Gwyn* . . . . . . . . . 4D 80
Llanfair. *Gwyn* . . . . . . . . . . . 3E 69
Llanfair. *Here* . . . . . . . . . . . . 1F 47
Llanfair Caereinion. *Powy* . . . 5D 70

Llanfair Clydogau. Cdgn . . . . . . . .5F 57
Llanfair Dyffryn Clwyd. Den . . . . .5D 82
Llanfairfechan. Cnwy . . . . . . . . . . .3F 81
Llanfair-Nant-Gwyn. Pemb . . . . .1F 43
Llanfair Pwllgwyngyll. IOA . . . . .3E 81
Llanfair Talhaiarn. Cnwy . . . . . . .3B 82
Llanfair Waterdine. Shrp . . . . . . .3E 59
Llanfair-ym-Muallt. Powy . . . . . .5C 58
Llanfairyneubwll. IOA . . . . . . . . .3C 80
Llanfairynghornwy. IOA . . . . . . .1C 80
Llanfallteg. Carm . . . . . . . . . . . . .3F 43
Llanfallteg West. Carm . . . . . . . .3F 43
Llanfaredd. Powy . . . . . . . . . . . . .5C 58
Llanfarian. Cdgn . . . . . . . . . . . . .3E 57
Llanfechain. Powy . . . . . . . . . . . .3D 70
Llanfechell. IOA . . . . . . . . . . . . . .1C 80
Llanfendigaid. Gwyn . . . . . . . . . .5E 69
Llanferres. Den . . . . . . . . . . . . . .4D 82
Llan Ffestiniog. Gwyn . . . . . . . . .1G 69
Llanfflewyn. IOA . . . . . . . . . . . . .2C 80
Llanfihangel-ar-Arth. Carm . . . . .2E 45
Llanfihangel Glyn Myfyr.
  Cnwy . . . . . . . . . . . . . . . . . . . .1B 70
Llanfihangel Nant Bran.
  Powy . . . . . . . . . . . . . . . . . . . .2C 46
Llanfihangel-Nant-Melan.
  Powy . . . . . . . . . . . . . . . . . . . .5D 58
Llanfihangel near Rogiet.
  Mon . . . . . . . . . . . . . . . . . . . . .3H 33
Llanfihangel Rhydithon.
  Powy . . . . . . . . . . . . . . . . . . . .4D 58
Llanfihangel Tal-y-llyn. Powy . . .3E 46
Llanfihangel-uwch-Gwili.
  Carm . . . . . . . . . . . . . . . . . . . .3E 45
Llanfihangel-y-Creuddyn.
  Cdgn . . . . . . . . . . . . . . . . . . . .3F 57
Llanfihangel-yng-Ngwynfa.
  Powy . . . . . . . . . . . . . . . . . . . .4C 70
Llanfihangel-yn Nhowyn. IOA . . .3C 80
Llanfihangel-y-pennant. Gwyn
  nr. Golan . . . . . . . . . . . . . . . . .1E 69
  nr. Tywyn . . . . . . . . . . . . . . . . .5F 69
Llanfihangel-y-traethau. Gwyn . .2E 69
Llanfilo. Powy . . . . . . . . . . . . . . .2E 46
Llanfleiddan. V Glam . . . . . . . . . .4C 32
Llanfoist. Mon . . . . . . . . . . . . . . .4F 47
Llanfor. Gwyn . . . . . . . . . . . . . . .2B 70
Llanfrechfa. Torf . . . . . . . . . . . . . .2G 33
Llanfrothen. Gwyn . . . . . . . . . . . .1F 69
Llanfrynach. Powy . . . . . . . . . . . .3D 46
Llanfwrog. Den . . . . . . . . . . . . . .5D 82
Llanfwrog. IOA . . . . . . . . . . . . . .2C 80
Llanfyllin. Powy . . . . . . . . . . . . . .4D 70
Llanfynydd. Carm . . . . . . . . . . . .3F 45
Llanfynydd. Flin . . . . . . . . . . . . . .5E 83
Llanfyrnach. Pemb . . . . . . . . . . .1G 43
Llangadfan. Powy . . . . . . . . . . . .4C 70
Llangadog. Carm
  nr. Llandovery . . . . . . . . . . . . . .3H 45
  nr. Llanelli . . . . . . . . . . . . . . . . .5E 45
Llangadwaladr. IOA . . . . . . . . . .4C 80
Llangadwaladr. Powy . . . . . . . . .2D 70
Llangaffo. IOA . . . . . . . . . . . . . .4D 80
Llangain. Carm . . . . . . . . . . . . . .4D 44
Llangammarch Wells. Powy . . . .1C 46
Llangan. V Glam . . . . . . . . . . . . .4C 32
Llangarron. Here . . . . . . . . . . . . .3A 48
Llangasty-Talyllyn. Powy . . . . . . .3E 47
Llangathen. Carm . . . . . . . . . . . .3F 45
Llangattock. Powy . . . . . . . . . . . .4F 47
Llangattock Lingoed. Mon . . . . . .3G 47
Llangattock-Vibon-Avel. Mon . . .4H 47
Llangedwyn. Powy . . . . . . . . . . .3D 70
Llangefni. IOA . . . . . . . . . . . . . . .3D 80
Llangeinor. B'end . . . . . . . . . . . . .3C 32
Llangeitho. Cdgn . . . . . . . . . . . . .5F 57
Llangeler. Carm . . . . . . . . . . . . . .2D 44
Llangelynin. Gwyn . . . . . . . . . . . .5E 69
Llangendeirne. Carm . . . . . . . . . .4E 45
Llangennech. Carm . . . . . . . . . . .5F 45
Llangennith. Swan . . . . . . . . . . . .3D 30
Llangenny. Powy . . . . . . . . . . . . .4F 47
Llangernyw. Cnwy . . . . . . . . . . . .4A 82
Llangian. Gwyn . . . . . . . . . . . . . .3B 68

Llangiwg. Neat . . . . . . . . . . . . . . .5H 45
Llangloffan. Pemb . . . . . . . . . . . .1D 42
Llanglydwen. Carm . . . . . . . . . . .2F 43
Llangoed. IOA . . . . . . . . . . . . . . .3F 81
Llangoedmor. Cdgn . . . . . . . . . .1B 44
Llangollen. Den . . . . . . . . . . . . . .1E 70
Llangolman. Pemb . . . . . . . . . . .2F 43
Llangorse. Powy . . . . . . . . . . . . .3E 47
Llangorwen. Cdgn . . . . . . . . . . . .2F 57
Llangovan. Mon . . . . . . . . . . . . . .5H 47
Llangower. Gwyn . . . . . . . . . . . .2B 70
Llangranog. Cdgn . . . . . . . . . . . .5C 56
Llangristiolus. IOA . . . . . . . . . . . .3D 80
Llangrove. Here . . . . . . . . . . . . . .4A 48
Llangua. Mon . . . . . . . . . . . . . . . .3G 47
Llangunllo. Powy . . . . . . . . . . . . .3E 58
Llangunnor. Carm . . . . . . . . . . . .3E 45
Llangurig. Powy . . . . . . . . . . . . . .3B 58
Llangwm. Cnwy . . . . . . . . . . . . . .1B 70
Llangwm. Mon . . . . . . . . . . . . . . .5H 47
Llangwm. Pemb . . . . . . . . . . . . . .4D 43
Llangwm-isaf. Mon . . . . . . . . . . .5H 47
Llangwnnadl. Gwyn . . . . . . . . . . .2B 68
Llangwyfan. Den . . . . . . . . . . . . .4D 82
Llangwyfan-isaf. IOA . . . . . . . . . .4C 80
Llangwyllog. IOA . . . . . . . . . . . . .3D 80
Llangwyryfon. Cdgn . . . . . . . . . .3F 57
Llangybi. Cdgn . . . . . . . . . . . . . . .5F 57
Llangybi. Gwyn . . . . . . . . . . . . . .1D 68
Llangybi. Mon . . . . . . . . . . . . . . .2G 33
Llangyfelach. Swan . . . . . . . . . . .3F 31
Llangynhafal. Den . . . . . . . . . . . .4D 82
Llangynidr. Powy . . . . . . . . . . . . .4E 47
Llangynin. Carm . . . . . . . . . . . . .3G 43
Llangynog. Carm . . . . . . . . . . . . .3H 43
Llangynog. Powy . . . . . . . . . . . . .3C 70
Llangynwyd. B'end . . . . . . . . . . .3B 32
Llanhamlach. Powy . . . . . . . . . . .3D 46
Llanharan. Rhon . . . . . . . . . . . . .3D 32
Llanharry. Rhon . . . . . . . . . . . . . .3D 32
Llanhennock. Mon . . . . . . . . . . . .2G 33
Llanhilleth. Blae . . . . . . . . . . . . . .5F 47
Llanidloes. Powy . . . . . . . . . . . . .2B 58
Llaniestyn. Gwyn . . . . . . . . . . . . .2B 68
Llanigon. Powy . . . . . . . . . . . . . .1F 47
Llanilar. Cdgn . . . . . . . . . . . . . . .3F 57
Llanilid. Rhon . . . . . . . . . . . . . . . .3C 32
Llanilltud Fawr. V Glam . . . . . . . .5C 32
Llanishen. Card . . . . . . . . . . . . . .3E 33
Llanishen. Mon . . . . . . . . . . . . . .5H 47
Llanllawddog. Carm . . . . . . . . . .3E 45
Llanllechid. Gwyn . . . . . . . . . . . . .4F 81
Llanllowell. Mon . . . . . . . . . . . . .2G 33
Llanllugan. Powy . . . . . . . . . . . . .5C 70
Llanllwch. Carm . . . . . . . . . . . . . .4D 45
Llanllwchaiarn. Powy . . . . . . . . .1D 58
Llanllwni. Carm . . . . . . . . . . . . . .2E 45
Llanllyfni. Gwyn . . . . . . . . . . . . . .5D 80
Llanmadoc. Swan . . . . . . . . . . . .3D 30
Llanmaes. V Glam . . . . . . . . . . . .5C 32
Llanmartin. Newp . . . . . . . . . . . .3G 33
Llanmihangel. V Glam . . . . . . . . .4C 32
Llan-mill. Pemb . . . . . . . . . . . . . .3F 43
Llanmiloe. Carm . . . . . . . . . . . . .4G 43
Llanmorlais. Swan . . . . . . . . . . . .3E 31
Llannefydd. Cnwy . . . . . . . . . . . .3B 82
Llan-non. Cdgn . . . . . . . . . . . . . .4E 57
Llannon. Carm . . . . . . . . . . . . . . .5F 45
Llannor. Gwyn . . . . . . . . . . . . . . .2C 68
Llanover. Mon . . . . . . . . . . . . . . .5G 47
Llanpumsaint. Carm . . . . . . . . . .3E 45
Llanreithan. Pemb . . . . . . . . . . . .2C 42
Llanrhaeadr. Den . . . . . . . . . . . . .4C 82
Llanrhaeadr-ym-Mochnant.
  Powy . . . . . . . . . . . . . . . . . . . .3D 70
Llanrhian. Pemb . . . . . . . . . . . . .1C 42
Llanrhidian. Swan . . . . . . . . . . . .3D 31
Llanrhos. Cnwy . . . . . . . . . . . . . .2G 81
Llanrhyddlad. IOA . . . . . . . . . . . .2C 80
Llanrhystud. Cdgn . . . . . . . . . . . .4E 57
Llanrothal. Here . . . . . . . . . . . . . .4H 47
Llanrug. Gwyn . . . . . . . . . . . . . . .4E 81
Llanrumney. Card . . . . . . . . . . . .3F 33
Llanrwst. Cnwy . . . . . . . . . . . . . .4G 81

Llansadurnen. Carm . . . . . . . . . .3G 43
Llansadwrn. Carm . . . . . . . . . . . .2G 45
Llansadwrn. IOA . . . . . . . . . . . . .3E 81
Llansaint. Carm . . . . . . . . . . . . . .5D 45
Llansamlet. Swan . . . . . . . . . . . .3F 31
Llansanffraid Glan Conwy.
  Cnwy . . . . . . . . . . . . . . . . . . . .3H 81
Llansannan. Cnwy . . . . . . . . . . . .4B 82
Llansannor. V Glam . . . . . . . . . . .4C 32
Llansantffraed. Cdgn . . . . . . . . . .4E 57
Llansantffraed. Powy . . . . . . . . . .3E 46
Llansantffraed
  Cwmdeuddwr. Powy . . . . . . . .4B 58
Llansantffraed-in-Elwel.
  Powy . . . . . . . . . . . . . . . . . . . .5C 58
Llansantffraid-ym-Mechain.
  Powy . . . . . . . . . . . . . . . . . . . .3E 70
Llansawel. Carm . . . . . . . . . . . . .2G 45
Llansawel. Neat . . . . . . . . . . . . . .3G 31
Llansilin. Powy . . . . . . . . . . . . . . .3E 70
Llansoy. Mon . . . . . . . . . . . . . . . .5H 47
Llanspyddid. Powy . . . . . . . . . . . .3D 46
Llanstadwell. Pemb . . . . . . . . . . .4D 42
Llansteffan. Carm . . . . . . . . . . . .4D 44
Llanstephan. Powy . . . . . . . . . . .1E 46
Llantarnam. Torf . . . . . . . . . . . . . .2G 33
Llanteg. Pemb . . . . . . . . . . . . . . .3F 43
Llanthony. Mon . . . . . . . . . . . . . .3F 47
Llantilio Crossenny. Mon . . . . . . .4G 47
Llantilio Pertholey. Mon . . . . . . . .4G 47
Llantood. Pemb . . . . . . . . . . . . . .1B 44
Llantrisant. Mon . . . . . . . . . . . . . .2G 33
Llantrisant. Rhon . . . . . . . . . . . . .3D 32
Llantrithyd. V Glam . . . . . . . . . . .4D 32
Llantwit Fardre. Rhon . . . . . . . . . .3D 32
Llantwit Major. V Glam . . . . . . . .5C 32
Llanuwchllyn. Gwyn . . . . . . . . . .2A 70
Llanvaches. Newp . . . . . . . . . . . .2H 33
Llanvair Discoed. Mon . . . . . . . . .2H 33
Llanvapley. Mon . . . . . . . . . . . . . .4G 47
Llanvetherine. Mon . . . . . . . . . . .4G 47
Llanveynoe. Here . . . . . . . . . . . . .2G 47
Llanvihangel Crucorney.
  Mon . . . . . . . . . . . . . . . . . . . . .3G 47
Llanvihangel Gobion. Mon . . . . .5G 47
Llanvihangel Ystern-
  Llewern. Mon . . . . . . . . . . . . . .4H 47
Llanwarne. Here . . . . . . . . . . . . . .3A 48
Llanwddyn. Powy . . . . . . . . . . . .4C 70
Llanwenarth. Mon . . . . . . . . . . . .4F 47
Llanwenog. Cdgn . . . . . . . . . . . .1E 45
Llanwern. Newp . . . . . . . . . . . . . .3G 33
Llanwinio. Carm . . . . . . . . . . . . . .2G 43
Llanwnda. Gwyn . . . . . . . . . . . . .5D 80
Llanwnda. Pemb . . . . . . . . . . . . .1D 42
Llanwnnen. Cdgn . . . . . . . . . . . .1F 45
Llanwnog. Powy . . . . . . . . . . . . .1C 58
Llanwrda. Carm . . . . . . . . . . . . . .2H 45
Llanwrin. Powy . . . . . . . . . . . . . .5G 69
Llanwrthwl. Powy . . . . . . . . . . . .4B 58
Llanwrtud. Powy . . . . . . . . . . . . .1B 46
Llanwrtyd. Powy . . . . . . . . . . . . .1B 46
Llanwrtyd Wells. Powy . . . . . . . .1B 46
Llanyblodwel. Shrp . . . . . . . . . . .3E 71
Llanybri. Carm . . . . . . . . . . . . . . .3H 43
Llanybydder. Carm . . . . . . . . . . .1F 45
Llanycefn. Pemb . . . . . . . . . . . . .2E 43
Llanychaer. Pemb . . . . . . . . . . . .1D 42
Llanycil. Gwyn . . . . . . . . . . . . . . .2B 70
Llanymawddwy. Gwyn . . . . . . . . .4B 70
Llanymddyfri. Carm . . . . . . . . . . .2A 46
Llanymynech. Powy . . . . . . . . . . .3E 71
Llanynghenedl. IOA . . . . . . . . . . .2C 80
Llanynys. Den . . . . . . . . . . . . . . .4D 82
Llan-y-pwll. Wrex . . . . . . . . . . . . .5F 83
Llanyrafon. Torf . . . . . . . . . . . . . .2G 33
Llanystumdwy. Gwyn . . . . . . . . . .2D 68
Llanwern. Powy . . . . . . . . . . . . . .5A 58
Llanwaden. Pemb . . . . . . . . . . . .3E 43
Llawndy. Flin . . . . . . . . . . . . . . . .2D 82
Llawnt. Shrp . . . . . . . . . . . . . . . . .2E 71
Llawr Dref. Gwyn . . . . . . . . . . . . .3B 68

Llawryglyn. Powy . . . . . . . . . . . . .1B 58
Llay. Wrex . . . . . . . . . . . . . . . . . . .5F 83
Llechfaen. Powy . . . . . . . . . . . . . .3D 46
Llechryd. Cphy . . . . . . . . . . . . . . .5E 46
Llechryd. Cdgn . . . . . . . . . . . . . .1C 44
Llechrydau. Wrex . . . . . . . . . . . . .2E 71
Lledrod. Cdgn . . . . . . . . . . . . . . .3F 57
Llethrid. Swan . . . . . . . . . . . . . . .3E 31
Llidiad-Nenog. Carm . . . . . . . . . .2F 45
Llidiardau. Gwyn . . . . . . . . . . . . .2A 70
Llidiart y Parc. Den . . . . . . . . . . . .1D 70
Llithfaen. Gwyn . . . . . . . . . . . . . .1C 68
Lloc. Flin . . . . . . . . . . . . . . . . . . . .3D 82
Llong. Flin . . . . . . . . . . . . . . . . . . .4E 83
Llowes. Powy . . . . . . . . . . . . . . . .1E 47
Lloyney. Powy . . . . . . . . . . . . . . . .3E 59
Llundain-fach. Cdgn . . . . . . . . . .5E 57
Llwydcoed. Rhon . . . . . . . . . . . . .5C 46
Llwyncelyn. Cdgn . . . . . . . . . . . .5D 56
Llwyndafydd. Cdgn . . . . . . . . . . .5C 56
Llwynderw. Powy . . . . . . . . . . . . .5E 70
Llwyn-du. Mon . . . . . . . . . . . . . . .4F 47
Llwyngwril. Gwyn . . . . . . . . . . . .5E 69
Llwynhendy. Carm . . . . . . . . . . . .3E 31
Llwynmawr. Wrex . . . . . . . . . . . . .2E 71
Llwyn-on Village. Mer T . . . . . . . .4D 46
Llwyn-têg. Carm . . . . . . . . . . . . .5F 45
Llwyn-y-brain. Carm . . . . . . . . . .3F 43
Llwyn-y-groes. Cdgn . . . . . . . . . .5E 57
Llwynygog. Powy . . . . . . . . . . . . .1A 58
Llwynypia. Rhon . . . . . . . . . . . . . .2C 32
Llynclys. Shrp . . . . . . . . . . . . . . . .3E 71
Llynfaes. IOA . . . . . . . . . . . . . . . .3D 80
Llysfaen. Cnwy . . . . . . . . . . . . . . .3A 82
Llyswen. Powy . . . . . . . . . . . . . . .2E 46
Llysworney. V Glam . . . . . . . . . . .4C 32
Llys-y-frân. Pemb . . . . . . . . . . . . .2E 43
Llywel. Powy . . . . . . . . . . . . . . . . .2B 46
Llywernog. Cdgn . . . . . . . . . . . . .2G 57
Loan. Falk . . . . . . . . . . . . . . . . . .2C 128
Loanend. Nmbd . . . . . . . . . . . . .4F 131
Loanhead. Midl . . . . . . . . . . . . . .3F 129
Loaningfoot. Dum . . . . . . . . . . . .4A 112
Loanreoch. High . . . . . . . . . . . . .1A 158
Loans. S Ayr . . . . . . . . . . . . . . . .1C 116
Loansdean. Nmbd . . . . . . . . . . .1E 115
Lobb. Devn . . . . . . . . . . . . . . . . . .3E 19
Lobhillcross. Devn . . . . . . . . . . . .4E 11
Lochaber. Mor . . . . . . . . . . . . . . .3D 159
Loch a Charnain. W Isl . . . . . . . . .4D 170
Loch a Ghainmhich. W Isl . . . . . .5E 171
Lochailort. High . . . . . . . . . . . . . .5F 147
Lochaline. High . . . . . . . . . . . . . .4A 140
Lochans. Dum . . . . . . . . . . . . . . .4F 109
Locharbriggs. Dum . . . . . . . . . . .1A 112
Lochardil. High . . . . . . . . . . . . . .4A 158
Lochassynt Lodge. High . . . . . . .1F 163
Lochavich. Arg . . . . . . . . . . . . . . .2G 133
Lochawe. Arg . . . . . . . . . . . . . . . .1A 134
Loch Baghasdail. W Isl . . . . . . . . .7C 170
Lochboisdale. W Isl . . . . . . . . . . .7C 170
Lochbuie. Arg . . . . . . . . . . . . . . . .1D 132
Lochcarron. High . . . . . . . . . . . . .5A 156
Loch Choire Lodge. High . . . . . . .5G 167
Lochdochart House. Stir . . . . . . .1D 134
Lochdon. Arg . . . . . . . . . . . . . . . .5B 140
Lochearnhead. Stir . . . . . . . . . . .1E 135
Lochee. D'dee . . . . . . . . . . . . . . .5C 144
Lochend. High
  nr. Inverness . . . . . . . . . . . . . . .5H 157
  nr. Thurso . . . . . . . . . . . . . . . . .2E 169
Locherben. Dum . . . . . . . . . . . . .5B 118
Loch Euphort. W Isl . . . . . . . . . . .2D 170
Lochfoot. Dum . . . . . . . . . . . . . . .2F 111
Lochgair. Arg . . . . . . . . . . . . . . . .4G 133
Lochgarthside. High . . . . . . . . . . .2H 149
Lochgelly. Fife . . . . . . . . . . . . . . .4D 136
Lochgilphead. Arg . . . . . . . . . . . .1G 125
Lochgoilhead. Arg . . . . . . . . . . . .3A 134
Loch Head. Dum . . . . . . . . . . . . .5A 110
Lochhill. Mor . . . . . . . . . . . . . . . .2G 159
Lochindorb Lodge. High . . . . . . .5D 158
Lochinver. High . . . . . . . . . . . . . .1E 163

Lochlane. Per . . . . . . . . . . . . . . . .1H 135
Loch Lomond. Arg . . . . . . . . . . . .3C 134
Loch Loyal Lodge. High . . . . . . . .4G 167
Lochluichart. High . . . . . . . . . . . .2F 157
Lochmaben. Dum . . . . . . . . . . . .1B 112
Lochmaddy. W Isl . . . . . . . . . . . .2E 170
Loch nam Madadh. W Isl . . . . . . .2E 170
Lochore. Fife . . . . . . . . . . . . . . . .4D 136
Lochportain. W Isl . . . . . . . . . . . .1E 170
Loch Sgioport. W Isl . . . . . . . . . . .5D 170
Lochside. Abers . . . . . . . . . . . . .2G 145
Lochside. High
  nr. Achentoul . . . . . . . . . . . . . . .5A 168
  nr. Nairn . . . . . . . . . . . . . . . . . .3C 158
Lochslin. High . . . . . . . . . . . . . . .5E 165
Lochton. Abers . . . . . . . . . . . . . .4E 153
Lochty. Fife . . . . . . . . . . . . . . . . .3H 137
Lochuisge. High . . . . . . . . . . . . .3B 140
Lochussie. High . . . . . . . . . . . . . .3G 157
Lochwinnoch. Ren . . . . . . . . . . . .4E 127
Lochyside. High . . . . . . . . . . . . . .1F 141
Lockengate. Corn . . . . . . . . . . . . . .2E 7
Lockerbie. Dum . . . . . . . . . . . . . .1C 112
Lockeridge. Wilts . . . . . . . . . . . . .5G 35
Lockerley. Hants . . . . . . . . . . . . . .4A 24
Lockhills. Cumb . . . . . . . . . . . . .5G 113
Locking. N Som . . . . . . . . . . . . . .1G 21
Lockington. E Yor . . . . . . . . . . . . .5D 101
Lockington. Leics . . . . . . . . . . . .3B 74
Locksgreen. IOW . . . . . . . . . . . . .3C 16
Locks Heath. Hants . . . . . . . . . . .2D 16
Lockton. N Yor . . . . . . . . . . . . . . .5F 107
Loddington. Leics . . . . . . . . . . . .5E 75
Loddington. Nptn . . . . . . . . . . . . .3F 63
Loddiswell. Devn . . . . . . . . . . . . . .4D 8
Loddon. Norf . . . . . . . . . . . . . . . .1F 67
Lode. Cambs . . . . . . . . . . . . . . . .4E 65
Loders. Dors . . . . . . . . . . . . . . . .3H 13
Lodsworth. W Sus . . . . . . . . . . . .3A 26
Lofthouse. N Yor . . . . . . . . . . . . .2D 98
Lofthouse. W Yor . . . . . . . . . . . . .2D 92
Lofthouse Gate. W Yor . . . . . . . . .2D 92
Loftus. Red C . . . . . . . . . . . . . . .3E 107
Logan. E Ayr . . . . . . . . . . . . . . . .2E 117
Loganlea. W Lot . . . . . . . . . . . . .3C 128
Logaston. Here . . . . . . . . . . . . . . .5F 59
Loggerheads. Den . . . . . . . . . . . .4D 82
Loggerheads. Staf . . . . . . . . . . . .2B 72
Loggie. High . . . . . . . . . . . . . . . .4F 163
Logie. Ang . . . . . . . . . . . . . . . . . .2F 145
Logie. Fife . . . . . . . . . . . . . . . . . .1G 137
Logie. Mor . . . . . . . . . . . . . . . . . .3E 159
Logie Coldstone. Abers . . . . . . . .3B 152
Logie Pert. Ang . . . . . . . . . . . . . .2F 145
Logierait. Per . . . . . . . . . . . . . . . .3G 143
Login. Carm . . . . . . . . . . . . . . . . .2F 43
Lolworth. Cambs . . . . . . . . . . . . .4C 64
Lonbain. High . . . . . . . . . . . . . . . .3F 155
Londesborough. E Yor . . . . . . . . .5C 100
London. G Lon . . . . . . . . . . . . . . .2E 39
London Apprentice. Corn . . . . . . . .3E 6
London Ashford Airport. Kent . . .3E 29
London City Airport. G Lon . . . . . .2F 39
London Colney. Herts . . . . . . . . . .5B 52
Londonderry. Derr . . . . . . . . . . . .2C 174
Londonderry. N Yor . . . . . . . . . . .1F 99
London Gatwick Airport.
  W Sus . . . . . . . . . . . . . . . . . . .1D 26
London Heathrow Airport.
  G Lon . . . . . . . . . . . . . . . . . . . .3B 38
London Luton Airport. Lutn . . . . .3B 52
London Southend Airport.
  Essx . . . . . . . . . . . . . . . . . . . . .2C 40
London Stansted Airport.
  Essx . . . . . . . . . . . . . . . . . . . . .3F 53
Londonthorpe. Linc . . . . . . . . . . .2G 75
Londubh. High . . . . . . . . . . . . . . .5C 162
Lone. High . . . . . . . . . . . . . . . . . .4D 166
Lonemore. High
  nr. Dornoch . . . . . . . . . . . . . . . .5E 165
  nr. Gairloch . . . . . . . . . . . . . . . .1G 155

Long Ashton. N Som ....4A 34
Long Bank. Worc ....3B 60
Longbar. N Ayr ....4E 127
Long Bennington. Linc ....1F 75
Longbenton. Tyne ....3F 115
Longborough. Glos ....3G 49
Long Bredy. Dors ....3A 14
Longbridge. Warw ....4G 61
Longbridge. W Mid ....3E 61
Longbridge Deverill. Wilts ....2D 22
Long Buckby. Nptn ....4D 62
Long Buckby Wharf. Nptn ....4D 62
Longburgh. Cumb ....4E 112
Longburton. Dors ....1B 14
Long Clawson. Leics ....3E 74
Longcliffe. Derbs ....5G 85
Long Common. Hants ....1D 16
Long Compton. Staf ....3C 72
Long Compton. Warw ....2A 50
Longcot. Oxon ....2A 36
Long Crendon. Buck ....5E 51
Long Crichel. Dors ....1E 15
Longcroft. Cumb ....4D 112
Longcroft. Falk ....2A 128
Longcross. Surr ....4A 38
Longdale. Cumb ....4H 103
Longdales. Cumb ....5G 113
Longden. Shrp ....5G 71
Longden Common. Shrp ....5G 71
Long Ditton. Surr ....4C 38
Longdon. Staf ....4E 73
Longdon. Worc ....2D 48
Longdon Green. Staf ....4E 73
Longdon on Tern. Telf ....4A 72
Longdown. Devn ....3B 12
Longdowns. Corn ....5B 6
Long Drax. N Yor ....2G 93
Long Duckmanton. Derbs ....3B 86
Long Eaton. Derbs ....2B 74
Longfield. Kent ....4H 39
Longfield. Shet ....10E 173
Longfield Hill. Kent ....4H 39
Longford. Derbs ....2G 73
Longford. Glos ....3D 48
Longford. G Lon ....3B 38
Longford. Shrp ....2A 72
Longford. Telf ....4B 72
Longford. W Mid ....2A 62
Longforgan. Per ....5C 144
Longformacus. Bord ....4C 130
Longframlington. Nmbd ....4F 121
Long Gardens. Essx ....2B 54
Long Green. Ches W ....3G 83
Long Green. Worc ....2D 48
Longham. Dors ....3F 15
Longham. Norf ....4B 78
Long Hanborough. Oxon ....4C 50
Longhedge. Wilts ....2D 22
Longhill. Abers ....3H 161
Longhirst. Nmbd ....1F 115
Longhope. Glos ....4B 48
Longhope. Orkn ....8C 172
Longhorsley. Nmbd ....5F 121
Longhoughton. Nmbd ....3G 121
Long Itchington. Warw ....4B 62
Longlands. Cumb ....1D 102
Long Lane. Telf ....4A 72
Longlane. Derbs ....2G 73
Longlane. W Ber ....4C 36
Long Lawford. Warw ....3B 62
Long Lease. N Yor ....4G 107
Longley Green. Worc ....5B 60
Long Load. Som ....4H 21
Longmanhill. Abers ....2E 161
Long Marston. Herts ....4G 51
Long Marston. N Yor ....4H 99
Long Marston. Warw ....1G 49
Long Marton. Cumb ....2H 103
Long Meadow. Cambs ....4E 65
Long Meadowend. Shrp ....2G 59
Long Melford. Suff ....1B 54
Longmoor Camp. Hants ....3F 25
Longmorn. Mor ....3G 159
Longmoss. Ches E ....3C 84

Long Newton. Glos ....2E 35
Long Newton. Stoc T ....3A 106
Longnewton. Bord ....2H 119
Longney. Glos ....4C 48
Longniddry. E Lot ....2H 129
Longnor. Shrp ....5G 71
Longnor. Staf
  nr. Leek ....4E 85
  nr. Stafford ....4C 72
Longparish. Hants ....2C 24
Longpark. Cumb ....3F 113
Long Preston. N Yor ....4H 97
Longridge. Lanc ....1E 90
Longridge. Staf ....4D 72
Longridge. W Lot ....3C 128
Longriggend. N Lan ....2B 128
Long Riston. E Yor ....5F 101
Longrock. Corn ....3C 4
Longsdon. Staf ....5D 84
Longshaw. G Man ....4D 90
Longshaw. Staf ....1E 73
Longside. Abers ....4H 161
Longslow. Shrp ....2A 72
Longstanton. Cambs ....4C 64
Longstock. Hants ....3B 24
Longstone. Cambs ....5C 64
Long Stratton. Norf ....1D 66
Long Street. Mil ....1F 51
Longstreet. Wilts ....1G 23
Long Sutton. Hants ....2F 25
Long Sutton. Linc ....3D 76
Long Sutton. Som ....4H 21
Longthorpe. Pet ....1A 64
Long Thurlow. Suff ....4C 66
Longthwaite. Cumb ....2F 103
Longton. Lanc ....2C 90
Longton. Stoke ....1D 72
Longtown. Cumb ....3E 113
Longtown. Here ....3G 47
Longville in the Dale. Shrp ....1H 59
Long Whatton. Leics ....3B 74
Longwick. Buck ....5F 51
Long Wittenham. Oxon ....2D 36
Longworth. Nmbd ....1D 115
Longworth. Oxon ....2B 36
Longyester. E Lot ....3B 130
Lonmore. High ....4B 154
Looe. Corn ....3G 7
Loose. Kent ....5B 40
Loosegate. Linc ....3C 76
Loosley Row. Buck ....5G 51
Lopcombe Corner. Wilts ....3A 24
Lopen. Som ....1H 13
Loppington. Shrp ....3G 71
Lorbottle. Nmbd ....4E 121
Lordington. W Sus ....2F 17
Loscoe. Derbs ....1B 74
Loscombe. Dors ....3A 14
Losgaintir. W Isl ....8C 171
Lossiemouth. Mor ....2G 159
Lossit. Arg ....4A 124
Lostock Gralam. Ches W ....3A 84
Lostock Green. Ches W ....3A 84
Lostock Hall. Lanc ....2D 90
Lostock Junction. G Man ....4E 91
Lostwithiel. Corn ....3F 7
Lothbeg. High ....2G 165
Lothersdale. N Yor ....5B 98
Lothianbridge. Midl ....3G 129
Lothianburn. Midl ....3F 129
Lothmore. High ....2G 165
Lottisham. Som ....3A 22
Loudwater. Buck ....1A 38
Loughborough. Leics ....4C 74
Loughor. Swan ....3E 31
Loughton. Essx ....1F 39
Loughton. Mil ....2G 51
Loughton. Shrp ....2A 60
Lound. Linc ....4H 75
Lound. Notts ....2D 86
Lound. Suff ....1H 67
Lount. Leics ....4A 74
Louth. Linc ....2C 88
Love Clough. Lanc ....2G 91

Lovedean. Hants ....1E 17
Lover. Wilts ....4H 23
Loversall. S Yor ....1C 86
Loves Green. Essx ....5G 53
Loveston. Pemb ....4E 43
Lovington. Som ....3A 22
Low Ackworth. W Yor ....3E 93
Low Angerton. Nmbd ....1D 115
Low Ardwell. Dum ....5F 109
Low Ballochdowan. S Ayr ....2F 109
Lowbands. Glos ....2C 48
Low Barlings. Linc ....3H 87
Low Bell End. N Yor ....5E 107
Low Bentham. N Yor ....3F 97
Low Borrowbridge. Cumb ....4H 103
Low Bradfield. S Yor ....1G 85
Low Bradley. N Yor ....5C 98
Low Braithwaite. Cumb ....5F 113
Low Brunton. Nmbd ....2C 114
Low Burnham. N Lin ....4A 94
Lowca. Cumb ....2A 102
Low Catton. E Yor ....4B 100
Low Coniscliffe. Darl ....3F 105
Low Coylton. S Ayr ....3D 116
Low Crosby. Cumb ....4F 113
Low Dalby. N Yor ....1C 100
Lowdham. Notts ....1D 74
Low Dinsdale. Darl ....3A 106
Lowe. Shrp ....2H 71
Low Ellington. N Yor ....1E 98
Lower Amble. Corn ....1D 6
Lower Ansty. Dors ....2C 14
Lower Arboll. High ....5F 165
Lower Arncott. Oxon ....4E 50
Lower Ashton. Devn ....4B 12
Lower Assendon. Oxon ....3F 37
Lower Auchenreath. Mor ....2A 160
Lower Badcall. High ....4B 166
Lower Ballam. Lanc ....1B 90
Lower Basildon. W Ber ....4E 36
Lower Beeding. W Sus ....3D 26
Lower Benefield. Nptn ....2G 63
Lower Bentley. Worc ....4D 61
Lower Beobridge. Shrp ....1B 60
Lower Bockhampton. Dors ....3C 14
Lower Boddington. Nptn ....5B 62
Lower Bordean. Hants ....4E 25
Lower Brailes. Warw ....2B 50
Lower Breakish. High ....1E 147
Lower Broadheath. Worc ....5C 60
Lower Brynamman. Neat ....4H 45
Lower Bullingham. Here ....2A 48
Lower Bullington. Hants ....2C 24
Lower Burgate. Hants ....1G 15
Lower Cam. Glos ....5C 48
Lower Catesby. Nptn ....5C 62
Lower Chapel. Powy ....2D 46
Lower Cheriton. Devn ....2E 12
Lower Chicksgrove. Wilts ....3E 23
Lower Chute. Wilts ....1B 24
Lower Clopton. Warw ....5F 61
Lower Common. Hants ....2E 25
Lower Crossings. Derbs ....2E 85
Lower Cumberworth. W Yor ....4C 92
Lower Darwen. Bkbn ....2E 91
Lower Dean. Bed ....4H 63
Lower Dean. Devn ....2D 8
Lower Diabaig. High ....2G 155
Lower Dicker. E Sus ....4G 27
Lower Dounreay. High ....2B 168
Lower Down. Shrp ....2F 59
Lower Dunsforth. N Yor ....3G 99
Lower East Carleton. Norf ....5D 78
Lower Egleton. Here ....1B 48
Lower Ellastone. Staf ....1F 73
Lower Everleigh. Wilts ....1G 23
Lower Eype. Dors ....3H 13
Lower Failand. N Som ....4A 34
Lower Faintree. Shrp ....2A 60
Lower Farringdon. Hants ....3F 25
Lower Foxdale. IOM ....4B 108
Lower Frankton. Shrp ....2F 71
Lower Froyle. Hants ....2F 25

Lower Gabwell. Devn ....2F 9
Lower Gledfield. High ....4C 164
Lower Godney. Som ....2H 21
Lower Gravenhurst. C Beds ....2B 52
Lower Green. Essx ....2E 53
Lower Green. Norf ....2B 78
Lower Green. W Ber ....5B 36
Lower Halstow. Kent ....4C 40
Lower Hardres. Kent ....5F 41
Lower Hardwick. Here ....5G 59
Lower Hartshay. Derbs ....5A 86
Lower Hawthwaite. Cumb ....1B 96
Lower Haysden. Kent ....1G 27
Lower Hayton. Shrp ....2H 59
Lower Hergest. Here ....5E 59
Lower Heyford. Oxon ....3C 50
Lower Heysham. Lanc ....3D 96
Lower Higham. Kent ....3B 40
Lower Holbrook. Suff ....2E 55
Lower Holditch. Dors ....2G 13
Lower Hordley. Shrp ....3F 71
Lower Horncroft. W Sus ....4B 26
Lower Horsebridge. E Sus ....4G 27
Lower Kilcot. Glos ....3C 34
Lower Killeyan. Arg ....5A 124
Lower Kingcombe. Dors ....3A 14
Lower Kingswood. Surr ....5D 38
Lower Kinnerton. Ches W ....4F 83
Lower Langford. N Som ....5H 33
Lower Largo. Fife ....3G 137
Lower Layham. Suff ....1D 54
Lower Ledwyche. Shrp ....3H 59
Lower Leigh. Staf ....2E 73
Lower Lemington. Glos ....2H 49
Lower Lenie. High ....1H 149
Lower Ley. Glos ....4C 48
Lower Llanfadog. Powy ....4B 58
Lower Lode. Glos ....2D 49
Lower Lovacott. Devn ....4F 19
Lower Loxhore. Devn ....3G 19
Lower Loxley. Staf ....2E 73
Lower Lydbrook. Glos ....4A 48
Lower Lye. Here ....4G 59
Lower Machen. Newp ....3F 33
Lower Maes-coed. Here ....2G 47
Lower Meend. Glos ....5A 48
Lower Midway. Derbs ....3H 73
Lower Milovaig. High ....3A 154
Lower Moor. Worc ....1E 49
Lower Morton. S Glo ....2B 34
Lower Mountain. Flin ....5F 83
Lower Nazeing. Essx ....5D 53
Lower Netchwood. Shrp ....1A 60
Lower Nyland. Dors ....4C 22
Lower Oakfield. Fife ....4D 136
Lower Oddington. Glos ....3H 49
Lower Ollach. High ....5E 155
Lower Penarth. V Glam ....5E 33
Lower Penn. Staf ....1C 60
Lower Pennington. Hants ....3B 16
Lower Peover. Ches W ....3B 84
Lower Pilsley. Derbs ....4B 86
Lower Pitkerrie. High ....1C 158
Lower Place. G Man ....3H 91
Lower Quinton. Warw ....1G 49
Lower Rainham. Medw ....4C 40
Lower Raydon. Suff ....2D 54
Lower Seagry. Wilts ....3E 35
Lower Shelton. C Beds ....1H 51
Lower Shiplake. Oxon ....4F 37
Lower Shuckburgh. Warw ....4B 62
Lower Sketty. Swan ....3F 31
Lower Slade. Devn ....2F 19
Lower Slaughter. Glos ....3G 49
Lower Soudley. Glos ....4B 48
Lower Stanton St Quintin.
  Wilts ....3E 35
Lower Stoke. Medw ....3C 40
Lower Stondon. C Beds ....2B 52
Lower Stonnall. Staf ....5E 73
Lower Stow Bedon. Norf ....1B 66
Lower Street. Norf ....2E 79
Lower Strensham. Worc ....1E 49
Lower Sundon. C Beds ....3A 52

Lower Swanwick. Hants ....2C 16
Lower Swell. Glos ....3G 49
Lower Tale. Devn ....2D 12
Lower Tean. Staf ....2E 73
Lower Thurlton. Norf ....1G 67
Lower Thurnham. Lanc ....4D 96
Lower Thurvaston. Derbs ....2G 73
Lower Town. Here ....1B 48
Lower Town. IOS ....1B 4
Lower Town. Pemb ....1D 42
Lowertown. Corn ....4D 4
Lowertown. Orkn ....8D 172
Lower Tysoe. Warw ....1B 50
Lower Upham. Hants ....1D 16
Lower Upnor. Medw ....3B 40
Lower Vexford. Som ....3E 20
Lower Walton. Warr ....2A 84
Lower Wear. Devn ....4C 12
Lower Weare. Som ....1H 21
Lower Welson. Here ....5E 59
Lower Whatcombe. Dors ....2D 14
Lower Whitley. Ches W ....3A 84
Lower Wield. Hants ....2E 25
Lower Withington. Ches E ....4C 84
Lower Woodend. Buck ....3G 37
Lower Woodford. Wilts ....3G 23
Lower Wraxall. Dors ....2A 14
Lower Wych. Ches W ....1G 71
Lower Wyche. Worc ....1C 48
Lowesby. Leics ....5E 74
Lowestoft. Suff ....1H 67
Loweswater. Cumb ....2C 102
Low Etherley. Dur ....2E 105
Lowfield Heath. W Sus ....1D 26
Lowford. Hants ....1C 16
Low Fulney. Linc ....3B 76
Low Gate. Nmbd ....3C 114
Lowgill. Cumb ....5H 103
Lowgill. Lanc ....3F 97
Low Grantley. N Yor ....2E 99
Low Green. N Yor ....4E 98
Low Habberley. Worc ....3C 60
Low Ham. Som ....4H 21
Low Hameringham. Linc ....4C 88
Low Hawsker. N Yor ....4G 107
Low Hesket. Cumb ....5F 113
Low Hesleyhurst. Nmbd ....5E 121
Lowick. Cumb ....1B 96
Lowick. Nptn ....2G 63
Lowick. Nmbd ....1E 121
Lowick Bridge. Cumb ....1B 96
Lowick Green. Cumb ....1B 96
Low Knipe. Cumb ....2G 103
Low Leighton. Derbs ....2E 85
Low Lorton. Cumb ....2C 102
Low Marishes. N Yor ....2C 100
Low Marnham. Notts ....4F 87
Low Mill. N Yor ....5D 106
Low Moor. Lanc ....5G 97
Low Moor. W Yor ....2B 92
Low Moorsley. Tyne ....5G 115
Low Newton-by-the-Sea.
  Nmbd ....2G 121
Lownie Moor. Ang ....4D 145
Lowood. Bord ....1H 119
Low Row. Cumb
  nr. Brampton ....3G 113
  nr. Wigton ....5C 112
Lowsonford. Warw ....4F 61
Low Street. Norf ....5C 78
Lowther. Cumb ....2G 103
Lowthorpe. E Yor ....3E 101
Lowton. Devn ....2G 11
Lowton. G Man ....1A 84
Lowton. Som ....1E 13
Lowton Common. G Man ....1A 84
Low Torry. Fife ....1D 128
Low Toynton. Linc ....3B 88
Low Valleyfield. Fife ....1C 128
Low Westwood. Dur ....4E 115
Low Whinnow. Cumb ....4E 112
Low Wood. Cumb ....1C 96
Low Worsall. N Yor ....4A 106

Low Wray. *Cumb* . . . . . . . . . .4E 103
Loxbeare. *Devn* . . . . . . . . . . .1C 12
Loxhill. *Surr* . . . . . . . . . . . . . .2B 26
Loxhore. *Devn* . . . . . . . . . . . .3G 19
Loxley. *S Yor* . . . . . . . . . . . . .2H 85
Loxley. *Warw* . . . . . . . . . . . . .5G 61
Loxley Green. *Staf* . . . . . . . . .2E 73
Loxton. *N Som* . . . . . . . . . . . .1G 21
Loxwood. *W Sus* . . . . . . . . . .2B 26
Lubcroy. *High* . . . . . . . . . . . .3A 164
Lubenham. *Leics* . . . . . . . . . .2E 62
Lubinvullin. *High* . . . . . . . . . .2F 167
Luccombe. *Som* . . . . . . . . . . .2C 20
Luccombe Village. *IOW* . . . . . .4D 16
Lucker. *Nmbd* . . . . . . . . . . . .1F 121
Luckett. *Corn* . . . . . . . . . . . . .5D 11
Luckington. *Wilts* . . . . . . . . . .3D 34
Lucklawhill. *Fife* . . . . . . . . . .1G 137
Luckwell Bridge. *Som* . . . . . . .3C 20
Lucton. *Here* . . . . . . . . . . . . .4G 59
Ludag. *W Isl* . . . . . . . . . . . . .7C 170
Ludborough. *Linc* . . . . . . . . . .1B 88
Ludchurch. *Pemb* . . . . . . . . . .3F 43
Luddenden. *W Yor* . . . . . . . . .2A 92
Luddenden Foot. *W Yor* . . . . . .2A 92
Luddenham. *Kent* . . . . . . . . . .4D 40
Ludderburn. *Cumb* . . . . . . . . .5F 103
Luddesdown. *Kent* . . . . . . . . .4A 40
Luddington. *N Lin* . . . . . . . . . .3B 94
Luddington. *Warw* . . . . . . . . . .5F 61
Luddington in the Brook.
        *Nptn* . . . . . . . . . . . . . .2A 64
Ludford. *Linc* . . . . . . . . . . . . .2A 88
Ludford. *Shrp* . . . . . . . . . . . .3H 59
Ludgershall. *Buck* . . . . . . . . . .4E 51
Ludgershall. *Wilts* . . . . . . . . .1A 24
Ludgvan. *Corn* . . . . . . . . . . . . .3C 4
Ludham. *Norf* . . . . . . . . . . . . .4F 79
Ludlow. *Shrp* . . . . . . . . . . . . .3H 59
Ludstone. *Shrp* . . . . . . . . . . . .1C 60
Ludwell. *Wilts* . . . . . . . . . . . . .4E 23
Ludworth. *Dur* . . . . . . . . . . . .5G 115
Luffenhall. *Herts* . . . . . . . . . . .3C 52
Luffincott. *Devn* . . . . . . . . . . .3D 10
Lugar. *E Ayr* . . . . . . . . . . . . .2E 117
Luggate Burn. *E Lot* . . . . . . . .2C 130
Lugg Green. *Here* . . . . . . . . . .4G 59
Luggiebank. *N Lan* . . . . . . . . .2A 128
Lugton. *E Ayr* . . . . . . . . . . . .4F 127
Lugwardine. *Here* . . . . . . . . . .1A 48
Luib. *High* . . . . . . . . . . . . . . .1D 146
Luib. *Stir* . . . . . . . . . . . . . . .1D 135
Lulham. *Here* . . . . . . . . . . . . .1H 47
Lullington. *Derbs* . . . . . . . . . . .4G 73
Lullington. *E Sus* . . . . . . . . . . .5G 27
Lullington. *Som* . . . . . . . . . . . .1C 22
Lulsgate Bottom. *N Som* . . . . . .5A 34
Lulsley. *Worc* . . . . . . . . . . . . .5B 60
Lulworth Camp. *Dors* . . . . . . . .4D 14
Lumb. *Lanc* . . . . . . . . . . . . . .2G 91
Lumby. *N Yor* . . . . . . . . . . . . .1E 93
Lumphanan. *Abers* . . . . . . . . .3C 152
Lumphinnans. *Fife* . . . . . . . . .4D 136
Lumsdaine. *Bord* . . . . . . . . . .3E 131
Lumsden. *Abers* . . . . . . . . . .1B 152
Lunan. *Ang* . . . . . . . . . . . . . .3F 145
Lunanhead. *Ang* . . . . . . . . . .3D 145
Luncarty. *Per* . . . . . . . . . . . .1C 136
Lund. *E Yor* . . . . . . . . . . . . . .5D 100
Lund. *N Yor* . . . . . . . . . . . . . .1G 93
Lundie. *Ang* . . . . . . . . . . . . . .5B 144
Lundin Links. *Fife* . . . . . . . . .3G 137
Lundy Green. *Norf* . . . . . . . . . .1E 67
Lunna. *Shet* . . . . . . . . . . . . .5F 173
Lunning. *Shet* . . . . . . . . . . . .5G 173
Lunnon. *Swan* . . . . . . . . . . . .4E 31
Lunsford. *Kent* . . . . . . . . . . . .5A 40
Lunsford's Cross. *E Sus* . . . . . .4B 28
Lunt. *Mers* . . . . . . . . . . . . . . .4B 90
Luppitt. *Devn* . . . . . . . . . . . . .2E 13
Lupridge. *Devn* . . . . . . . . . . . . .3C 8
Lupset. *W Yor* . . . . . . . . . . . . .3D 92
Lupton. *Cumb* . . . . . . . . . . . . .1E 97
Lurgan. *Arm* . . . . . . . . . . . . .5F 175

Lurgashall. *W Sus* . . . . . . . . . .3A 26
Lurley. *Devn* . . . . . . . . . . . . .1C 12
Lusby. *Linc* . . . . . . . . . . . . . .4C 88
Luscombe. *Devn* . . . . . . . . . . . .3D 9
Luson. *Devn* . . . . . . . . . . . . . . .4C 8
Luss. *Arg* . . . . . . . . . . . . . . .4C 134
Lussagiven. *Arg* . . . . . . . . . .1E 125
Lusta. *High* . . . . . . . . . . . . .3B 154
Lustleigh. *Devn* . . . . . . . . . . .4A 12
Luston. *Here* . . . . . . . . . . . . .4G 59
Luthermuir. *Abers* . . . . . . . . .2F 145
Luthrie. *Fife* . . . . . . . . . . . . .2F 137
Lutley. *Staf* . . . . . . . . . . . . . .2C 60
Luton. *Devn*
        nr. Honiton . . . . . . . . . . .2D 12
        nr. Teignmouth . . . . . . . .5C 12
**Luton.** *Lutn* . . . . . . . . . . . . .3A 52
Luton Airport. *Lutn* . . . . . . . . .3B 52
Lutterworth. *Leics* . . . . . . . . . .2C 62
Lutton. *Devn*
        nr. Ivybridge . . . . . . . . . . .3B 8
        nr. South Brent . . . . . . . . .2C 8
Lutton. *Linc* . . . . . . . . . . . . . .3D 76
Lutton. *Nptn* . . . . . . . . . . . . .2A 64
Lutton Gowts. *Linc* . . . . . . . . .3D 76
Lutworthy. *Devn* . . . . . . . . . . .1A 12
Luxborough. *Som* . . . . . . . . . .3C 20
Luxley. *Glos* . . . . . . . . . . . . . .3B 48
Luxulyan. *Corn* . . . . . . . . . . . . .3E 7
Lybster. *High* . . . . . . . . . . . .5E 169
Lydbury North. *Shrp* . . . . . . . .2F 59
Lydcott. *Devn* . . . . . . . . . . . .3G 19
Lydd. *Kent* . . . . . . . . . . . . . . .3E 29
Lydd Airport. *Kent* . . . . . . . . . .3E 29
Lydden. *Kent*
        nr. Dover . . . . . . . . . . . .1G 29
        nr. Margate . . . . . . . . . . .4H 41
Lyddington. *Rut* . . . . . . . . . . . .1F 63
Lydd-on-Sea. *Kent* . . . . . . . . .3E 29
Lydeard St Lawrence. *Som* . . . .3E 21
Lyde Green. *Hants* . . . . . . . . .1F 25
Lydford. *Devn* . . . . . . . . . . . . .4F 11
Lydford Fair Place. *Som* . . . . . .3A 22
Lydgate. *G Man* . . . . . . . . . . .4H 91
Lydgate. *W Yor* . . . . . . . . . . . .2H 91
Lydham. *Shrp* . . . . . . . . . . . . .1F 59
Lydiard Millicent. *Wilts* . . . . . . .3F 35
Lydiate. *Mers* . . . . . . . . . . . . .4B 90
Lydiate Ash. *Worc* . . . . . . . . . .3D 61
Lydlinch. *Dors* . . . . . . . . . . . .1C 14
Lydmarsh. *Som* . . . . . . . . . . .2G 13
Lydney. *Glos* . . . . . . . . . . . . . .5B 48
Lydstep. *Pemb* . . . . . . . . . . . .5E 43
Lye. *W Mid* . . . . . . . . . . . . . . .2D 60
The Lye. *Shrp* . . . . . . . . . . . . .1A 60
Lye Green. *Buck* . . . . . . . . . . .5H 51
Lye Green. *E Sus* . . . . . . . . . .2G 27
Lye Head. *Worc* . . . . . . . . . . . .3B 60
Lyford. *Oxon* . . . . . . . . . . . . .2B 36
Lyham. *Nmbd* . . . . . . . . . . . .1E 121
Lylestone. *N Ayr* . . . . . . . . . .5E 127
Lymbridge Green. *Kent* . . . . . . .1F 29
Lyme Regis. *Dors* . . . . . . . . . .3G 13
Lyminge. *Kent* . . . . . . . . . . . . .1F 29
**Lymington.** *Hants* . . . . . . . . .3B 16
Lyminster. *W Sus* . . . . . . . . . .5B 26
**Lymm.** *Warr* . . . . . . . . . . . . .2A 84
Lymore. *Hants* . . . . . . . . . . . .3A 16
Lympne. *Kent* . . . . . . . . . . . . .2F 29
Lympsham. *Som* . . . . . . . . . . .1G 21
Lympstone. *Devn* . . . . . . . . . . .4C 12
Lynaberack Lodge. *High* . . . . .4B 150
Lynbridge. *Devn* . . . . . . . . . . .2H 19
Lynch. *Som* . . . . . . . . . . . . . .2C 20
Lynchat. *High* . . . . . . . . . . . .3B 150
Lynch Green. *Norf* . . . . . . . . . .5D 78
Lyndhurst. *Hants* . . . . . . . . . .2B 16
Lyndon. *Rut* . . . . . . . . . . . . . .5G 75
Lyne. *Bord* . . . . . . . . . . . . . .5F 129
Lyne. *Surr* . . . . . . . . . . . . . . .4B 38
Lyneal. *Shrp* . . . . . . . . . . . . .2G 71
Lyne Down. *Here* . . . . . . . . . .2B 48
Lyneham. *Oxon* . . . . . . . . . . . .3A 50
Lyneham. *Wilts* . . . . . . . . . . . .4F 35

Lyneholmeford. *Cumb* . . . . . . .2G 113
Lynemouth. *Nmbd* . . . . . . . . .5G 121
Lyne of Gorthleck. *High* . . . . . .1H 149
Lyne of Skene. *Abers* . . . . . . .2E 153
Lynesack. *Dur* . . . . . . . . . . . .2D 105
Lyness. *Orkn* . . . . . . . . . . . . .8C 172
Lyng. *Norf* . . . . . . . . . . . . . . . .4C 78
Lyngate. *Norf*
        nr. North Walsham . . . . . .2E 79
        nr. Worstead . . . . . . . . . .3F 79
Lynmouth. *Devn* . . . . . . . . . . .2H 19
Lynn. *Staf* . . . . . . . . . . . . . . .5E 73
Lynn. *Telf* . . . . . . . . . . . . . . . .4B 72
Lynsted. *Kent* . . . . . . . . . . . . .4D 40
Lynstone. *Corn* . . . . . . . . . . . .2C 10
Lynton. *Devn* . . . . . . . . . . . . .2H 19
Lynwilg. *High* . . . . . . . . . . . .2C 150
Lyon's Gate. *Dors* . . . . . . . . . .2B 14
Lyonshall. *Here* . . . . . . . . . . . .5F 59
Lytchett Matravers. *Dors* . . . . . .3E 15
Lytchett Minster. *Dors* . . . . . . .3E 15
Lyth. *High* . . . . . . . . . . . . . . .2E 169
Lytham. *Lanc* . . . . . . . . . . . . .2B 90
**Lytham St Anne's.** *Lanc* . . . . .2B 90
Lythe. *N Yor* . . . . . . . . . . . . .3F 107
Lythes. *Orkn* . . . . . . . . . . . . .9D 172
Lythmore. *High* . . . . . . . . . . .2C 168

## M

Mabe Burnthouse. *Corn* . . . . . . . .5B 6
Mabie. *Dum* . . . . . . . . . . . . .2A 112
Mablethorpe. *Linc* . . . . . . . . . .2E 89
Macbiehill. *Bord* . . . . . . . . . . .4E 129
**Macclesfield.** *Ches E* . . . . . . .3D 84
Macclesfield Forest. *Ches E* . . . .3D 84
Macduff. *Abers* . . . . . . . . . . . .2E 160
Machan. *S Lan* . . . . . . . . . . .4A 128
Macharioch. *Arg* . . . . . . . . . .5B 122
Machen. *Cphy* . . . . . . . . . . . . .3F 33
Machrie. *N Ayr* . . . . . . . . . . .2C 122
Machrihanish. *Arg* . . . . . . . . .3A 122
Machroes. *Gwyn* . . . . . . . . . . .3C 68
Machynlleth. *Powy* . . . . . . . . . .5G 69
Mackerye End. *Herts* . . . . . . . .4B 52
Mackworth. *Derb* . . . . . . . . . .2H 73
Macmerry. *E Lot* . . . . . . . . . .2H 129
Madderty. *Per* . . . . . . . . . . . . .1B 136
Maddington. *Wilts* . . . . . . . . . .2F 23
Maddiston. *Falk* . . . . . . . . . .2C 128
Madehurst. *W Sus* . . . . . . . . .4A 26
Madeley. *Staf* . . . . . . . . . . . . .1B 72
Madeley. *Telf* . . . . . . . . . . . . .5A 72
Madeley Heath. *Staf* . . . . . . . . .1B 72
Madeley Heath. *Worc* . . . . . . . .3D 60
Madford. *Devn* . . . . . . . . . . . . .1E 13
Madingley. *Cambs* . . . . . . . . . .4C 64
Madley. *Here* . . . . . . . . . . . . .2H 47
Madresfield. *Worc* . . . . . . . . . .1D 48
Madron. *Corn* . . . . . . . . . . . . . .3B 4
Maenaddwyn. *IOA* . . . . . . . . . .2D 80
Maenclochog. *Pemb* . . . . . . . . .2E 43
Maendy. *V Glam* . . . . . . . . . . .4D 32
Maenporth. *Corn* . . . . . . . . . . . .4E 5
Maentwrog. *Gwyn* . . . . . . . . . .1F 69
Maen-y-groes. *Cdgn* . . . . . . . . .5C 56
Maer. *Staf* . . . . . . . . . . . . . . . .2B 72
Maerdy. *Carm* . . . . . . . . . . . . .3G 45
Maerdy. *Cnwy* . . . . . . . . . . . . .1C 70
Maerdy. *Rhon* . . . . . . . . . . . . .2C 32
Maesbrook. *Shrp* . . . . . . . . . . .3F 71
Maesbury. *Shrp* . . . . . . . . . . . .3F 71
Maesbury Marsh. *Shrp* . . . . . . .3F 71
Maes-glas. *Flin* . . . . . . . . . . . .3D 82
Maesgwyn-Isaf. *Powy* . . . . . . . .4D 70
Maeshafn. *Den* . . . . . . . . . . . .4E 82
Maesllyn. *Cdgn* . . . . . . . . . . . .1D 45
Maesmynis. *Powy* . . . . . . . . . .1D 46
**Maesteg.** *B'end* . . . . . . . . . . .2B 32
Maestir. *Cdgn* . . . . . . . . . . . . .1F 45
Maesybont. *Carm* . . . . . . . . . . .4F 45
Maesycrugiau. *Carm* . . . . . . . . .1E 45
Maesywmmer. *Cphy* . . . . . . . . .2E 33

Maesyrhandir. *Powy* . . . . . . . . .1C 58
Magdalen Laver. *Essx* . . . . . . . .5F 53
Maggieknockater. *Mor* . . . . . . .4H 159
Maghaberry. *Lis* . . . . . . . . . . .4G 175
Magham Down. *E Sus* . . . . . . .4H 27
Maghera. *M Ulst* . . . . . . . . . . .2E 175
Magherafelt. *M Ulst* . . . . . . . . .3E 175
Magheralin. *Arm* . . . . . . . . . . .5G 175
**Maghull.** *Mers* . . . . . . . . . . . .4B 90
Magna Park. *Leics* . . . . . . . . . .2C 62
Magor. *Mon* . . . . . . . . . . . . . .3H 33
Magpie Green. *Suff* . . . . . . . . .3C 66
Magwyr. *Mon* . . . . . . . . . . . . .3H 33
Maidenbower. *W Sus* . . . . . . . .2D 27
Maiden Bradley. *Wilts* . . . . . . . .3D 22
Maidencombe. *Torb* . . . . . . . . . .2F 9
Maidenhayne. *Devn* . . . . . . . . . .3F 13
**Maidenhead.** *Wind* . . . . . . . . .3G 37
Maiden Law. *Dur* . . . . . . . . . .5E 115
Maiden Newton. *Dors* . . . . . . . .3A 14
Maidens. *S Ayr* . . . . . . . . . . .4B 116
Maiden's Green. *Brac* . . . . . . . .4G 37
Maidensgrove. *Oxon* . . . . . . . . .3F 37
Maidenwell. *Corn* . . . . . . . . . . .5B 10
Maidenwell. *Linc* . . . . . . . . . . .3C 88
Maiden Wells. *Pemb* . . . . . . . . .5D 42
Maidford. *Nptn* . . . . . . . . . . . .5D 62
Maids Moreton. *Buck* . . . . . . . .2F 51
**Maidstone.** *Kent* . . . . . . . . . .5B 40
Maidwell. *Nptn* . . . . . . . . . . . .3E 63
Mail. *Shet* . . . . . . . . . . . . . . .9F 173
Mainsbank. *Devn* . . . . . . . . . . .3G 33
Mains of Auchindachy.
        *Mor* . . . . . . . . . . . . . . .4B 160
Mains of Auchnagatt.
        *Abers* . . . . . . . . . . . . .4G 161
Mains of Drum. *Abers* . . . . . . .4F 153
Mains of Edingight. *Mor* . . . . . .3C 160
Mainsriddle. *Dum* . . . . . . . . . .4G 111
Mainstone. *Shrp* . . . . . . . . . . . .2F 59
Maisemore. *Glos* . . . . . . . . . . . .3D 48
Major's Green. *Worc* . . . . . . . . .3F 61
Makeney. *Derbs* . . . . . . . . . . . .1A 74
Makerstoun. *Bord* . . . . . . . . . .1A 120
Malacleit. *W Isl* . . . . . . . . . . .1C 170
Malaig. *High* . . . . . . . . . . . . .4E 147
Malaig Bheag. *High* . . . . . . . . .4E 147
Malborough. *Devn* . . . . . . . . . . .5D 8
Malcoff. *Derbs* . . . . . . . . . . . . .2E 85
Malcolmburn. *Mor* . . . . . . . . .3A 160
Malden Rushett. *G Lon* . . . . . . .4C 38
**Maldon.** *Essx* . . . . . . . . . . . . .5B 54
Malham. *N Yor* . . . . . . . . . . . . .3B 98
Maligar. *High* . . . . . . . . . . . .2D 155
Malinslee. *Telf* . . . . . . . . . . . . .5A 72
Mallaig. *High* . . . . . . . . . . . . .4E 147
Malleny Mills. *Edin* . . . . . . . . .3E 129
Mallows Green. *Essx* . . . . . . . .3E 53
Malltraeth. *IOA* . . . . . . . . . . . .4D 80
Mallwyd. *Gwyn* . . . . . . . . . . . .4A 70
Malmesbury. *Wilts* . . . . . . . . . .3E 35
Malmsmead. *Devn* . . . . . . . . . .2A 20
Malpas. *Ches W* . . . . . . . . . . .1G 71
Malpas. *Corn* . . . . . . . . . . . . . .4C 6
Malpas. *Newp* . . . . . . . . . . . . .2G 33
Malswick. *Glos* . . . . . . . . . . . . .3C 48
**Maltby.** *S Yor* . . . . . . . . . . . .1C 86
Maltby. *Stoc T* . . . . . . . . . . . .3B 106
Maltby le Marsh. *Linc* . . . . . . . .2D 88
Malt Lane. *Arg* . . . . . . . . . . . .3H 133
Maltman's Hill. *Kent* . . . . . . . . .1D 28
Malton. *N Yor* . . . . . . . . . . . .2B 100
Malvern Link. *Worc* . . . . . . . . . .1C 48
Malvern Wells. *Worc* . . . . . . . . .1C 48
Mamble. *Worc* . . . . . . . . . . . . .3A 60
Mamhilad. *Mon* . . . . . . . . . . . .5G 47
Manaccan. *Corn* . . . . . . . . . . . . .4E 5
Manafon. *Powy* . . . . . . . . . . . .5D 70
Manais. *W Isl* . . . . . . . . . . . . .9D 171
Manaton. *Devn* . . . . . . . . . . . .4A 12
Manby. *Linc* . . . . . . . . . . . . . .2C 88
Mancetter. *Warw* . . . . . . . . . . .1H 61
**Manchester.** *G Man* . . . . . . . .1C 84

Manchester Airport. *G Man* . . . . .2C 84
Mancot. *Flin* . . . . . . . . . . . . . .4F 83
Manea. *Cambs* . . . . . . . . . . . .2D 65
Maney. *W Mid* . . . . . . . . . . . . .1F 61
Manfield. *N Yor* . . . . . . . . . . .3F 105
**Mangotsfield.** *S Glo* . . . . . . . .4B 34
Mangurstadh. *W Isl* . . . . . . . .4C 171
Mankinholes. *W Yor* . . . . . . . . .2H 91
Manley. *Ches W* . . . . . . . . . . . .3H 83
Manmoel. *Cphy* . . . . . . . . . . . .5E 47
Mannal. *Arg* . . . . . . . . . . . . . .4A 138
Mannerston. *Falk* . . . . . . . . . .2D 128
Manningford Bohune.
        *Wilts* . . . . . . . . . . . . . .1G 23
Manningford Bruce. *Wilts* . . . . . .1G 23
Manningham. *W Yor* . . . . . . . . .1B 92
Mannings Heath. *W Sus* . . . . . .3D 26
Mannington. *Dors* . . . . . . . . . . .2F 15
Manningtree. *Essx* . . . . . . . . . .2E 54
Mannofield. *Aber* . . . . . . . . . .3G 153
Manorbier. *Pemb* . . . . . . . . . . .5E 43
Manorbier Newton. *Pemb* . . . . . .5E 43
Manordeilo. *Carm* . . . . . . . . . .3G 45
Manorowen. *Pemb* . . . . . . . . . .1D 42
Manor Park. *G Lon* . . . . . . . . . .2F 39
Mansell Gamage. *Here* . . . . . . .1G 47
Mansell Lacy. *Here* . . . . . . . . . .1H 47
Mansergh. *Cumb* . . . . . . . . . . .1F 97
Mansewood. *Glas* . . . . . . . . . .3G 127
**Mansfield.** *Notts* . . . . . . . . . .4C 86
**Mansfield Woodhouse.**
        *Notts* . . . . . . . . . . . . . .4C 86
Mansriggs. *Cumb* . . . . . . . . . .1B 96
Manston. *Dors* . . . . . . . . . . . .1D 14
Manston. *Kent* . . . . . . . . . . . . .4H 41
Manston. *W Yor* . . . . . . . . . . . .1D 92
Manswood. *Dors* . . . . . . . . . . .2E 15
Manthorpe. *Linc*
        nr. Bourne . . . . . . . . . . . .4H 75
        nr. Grantham . . . . . . . . . .2G 75
Manton. *N Lin* . . . . . . . . . . . . .4C 94
Manton. *Notts* . . . . . . . . . . . . .3C 86
Manton. *Rut* . . . . . . . . . . . . . .5F 75
Manton. *Wilts* . . . . . . . . . . . . .5G 35
Manuden. *Essx* . . . . . . . . . . . .3E 53
Maperton. *Som* . . . . . . . . . . . .4B 22
Maplebeck. *Notts* . . . . . . . . . . .4E 86
Maple Cross. *Herts* . . . . . . . . . .1B 38
Mapledurham. *Oxon* . . . . . . . . .4E 37
Mapledurwell. *Hants* . . . . . . . . .1E 25
Maplehurst. *W Sus* . . . . . . . . . .3C 26
Maplescombe. *Kent* . . . . . . . . .4G 39
Mapleton. *Derbs* . . . . . . . . . . . .1F 73
Mapperley. *Derbs* . . . . . . . . . . .1B 74
Mapperley. *Nott* . . . . . . . . . . . .1C 74
Mapperley Park. *Nott* . . . . . . . .1C 74
Mapperton. *Dors*
        nr. Beaminster . . . . . . . . .3A 14
        nr. Poole . . . . . . . . . . . . .3E 15
Mappleborough Green.
        *Warw* . . . . . . . . . . . . . .4E 61
Mappleton. *E Yor* . . . . . . . . . .5G 101
Mapplewell. *S Yor* . . . . . . . . . .4D 92
Mappowder. *Dors* . . . . . . . . . .2C 14
Maraig. *W Isl* . . . . . . . . . . . . .7E 171
Marazion. *Corn* . . . . . . . . . . . . .3C 4
Marbhig. *W Isl* . . . . . . . . . . . .6G 171
Marbury. *Ches E* . . . . . . . . . . . .1H 71
Marcham. *Oxon* . . . . . . . . . . . .2C 36
Marchamley. *Shrp* . . . . . . . . . .3H 71
Marchington. *Staf* . . . . . . . . . . .2F 73
Marchington Woodlands.
        *Staf* . . . . . . . . . . . . . . .3F 73
Marchwiel. *Wrex* . . . . . . . . . . . .1F 71
Marchwood. *Hants* . . . . . . . . . .1B 16
Marcross. *V Glam* . . . . . . . . . . .5C 32
Marden. *Here* . . . . . . . . . . . . .1A 48
Marden. *Kent* . . . . . . . . . . . . .1B 28
Marden. *Wilts* . . . . . . . . . . . . .1F 23
Marden Beech. *Kent* . . . . . . . . .1B 28
Marden Thorn. *Kent* . . . . . . . . .1B 28
Mardu. *Shrp* . . . . . . . . . . . . . .2E 59

Mardy. Mon . . . . . . . . . . . . . . . .4G 47
Marefield. Leics . . . . . . . . . . . . .5E 75
Mareham le Fen. Linc . . . . . . .4B 88
Mareham on the Hill. Linc . . . .4B 88
Marehay. Derbs . . . . . . . . . . . . .1B 74
Marehill. W Sus . . . . . . . . . . . . .4B 26
Maresfield. E Sus . . . . . . . . . . . .3F 27
Marford. Wrex . . . . . . . . . . . . . .5F 83
Margam. Neat . . . . . . . . . . . . . .3A 32
Margaret Marsh. Dors . . . . . . .1D 14
Margaret Roding. Essx . . . . . . .4F 53
Margaretting. Essx . . . . . . . . . .5G 53
Margaretting Tye. Essx . . . . . . .5G 53
Margate. Kent . . . . . . . . . . . . . .3H 41
Margery. Surr . . . . . . . . . . . . . . .5D 38
Margnaheglish. N Ayr . . . . . . .2E 123
Marham. Norf . . . . . . . . . . . . . . .5G 77
Marhamchurch. Corn . . . . . . . .2C 10
Marholm. Pet . . . . . . . . . . . . . . .5A 76
Marian Cwm. Den . . . . . . . . . . .3C 82
Mariandyrys. IOA . . . . . . . . . . . .2F 81
Marian-glas. IOA . . . . . . . . . . . .2E 81
Mariansleigh. Devn . . . . . . . . . .4H 19
Marian-y-de. Gwyn . . . . . . . . . .2C 68
Marian-y-mor. Gwyn . . . . . . . . .2C 68
Marine Town. Kent . . . . . . . . . .3D 40
Marishader. High . . . . . . . . . . .2D 155
Marjoriebanks. Dum . . . . . . . .1B 112
Mark. Dum . . . . . . . . . . . . . . . .4G 109
Mark. Som . . . . . . . . . . . . . . . . .2G 21
Markbeech. Kent . . . . . . . . . . . .1F 27
Markby. Linc . . . . . . . . . . . . . . .3D 89
Mark Causeway. Som . . . . . . . .2G 21
Mark Cross. E Sus . . . . . . . . . . .2G 27
Markeaton. Derb . . . . . . . . . . . .2H 73
Market Bosworth. Leics . . . . . . .5B 74
Market Deeping. Linc . . . . . . . .4A 76
Market Drayton. Shrp . . . . . . . .2A 72
Market End. Warw . . . . . . . . . .2H 61
Market Harborough. Leics . . . .2E 63
Markethill. Arm . . . . . . . . . . . . .6F 175
Markethill. Per . . . . . . . . . . . . .5B 144
Market Lavington. Wilts . . . . . .1F 23
Market Overton. Rut . . . . . . . . .4F 75
Market Rasen. Linc . . . . . . . . . .2A 88
Market Stainton. Linc . . . . . . . .2B 88
Market Weighton. E Yor . . . . . .5C 100
Market Weston. Suff . . . . . . . . .3B 66
Markfield. Leics . . . . . . . . . . . .4B 74
Markham. Cphy . . . . . . . . . . . . .5E 47
Markinch. Fife . . . . . . . . . . . . .3E 137
Markington. N Yor . . . . . . . . . .3E 99
Marksbury. Bath . . . . . . . . . . . .5B 34
Mark's Corner. IOW . . . . . . . . .3C 16
Marks Tey. Essx . . . . . . . . . . . .3C 54
Markwell. Corn . . . . . . . . . . . . .3H 7
Markyate. Herts . . . . . . . . . . . .4A 52
Marlborough. Wilts . . . . . . . . . .5G 35
Marlcliff. Warw . . . . . . . . . . . . .5E 61
Marldon. Devn . . . . . . . . . . . . . .2E 9
Marle Green. E Sus . . . . . . . . . .4G 27
Marlesford. Suff . . . . . . . . . . . .5F 67
Marley Green. Ches E . . . . . . .1H 71
Marley Hill. Tyne . . . . . . . . . . .4F 115
Marlingford. Norf . . . . . . . . . . .5D 78
Mar Lodge. Abers . . . . . . . . . .5E 151
Marloes. Pemb . . . . . . . . . . . . .4B 42
Marlow. Buck . . . . . . . . . . . . . .3G 37
Marlow. Here . . . . . . . . . . . . . .3F 59
Marlow Bottom. Buck . . . . . . . .3G 37
Marlow Common. Buck . . . . . . .3G 37
Marlpit Hill. Kent . . . . . . . . . . .1F 27
Marlpits. E Sus . . . . . . . . . . . . .3F 27
Marlpool. Derbs . . . . . . . . . . . .1B 74
Marnhull. Dors . . . . . . . . . . . . .1C 14
Marnoch. Abers . . . . . . . . . . . .3C 160
Marnock. N Lan . . . . . . . . . . . .3A 128
Marple. G Man . . . . . . . . . . . . .2D 84
Marr. S Yor . . . . . . . . . . . . . . . .4F 93
Marrel. High . . . . . . . . . . . . . .2H 165
Marrick. N Yor . . . . . . . . . . . . .5D 105
Marrister. Shet . . . . . . . . . . . .5G 173
Marros. Carm . . . . . . . . . . . . . .4G 43

Marsden. Tyne . . . . . . . . . . . . .3G 115
Marsden. W Yor . . . . . . . . . . . .3A 92
Marsett. N Yor . . . . . . . . . . . . .1B 98
Marsh. Buck . . . . . . . . . . . . . . .5G 51
Marsh. Devn . . . . . . . . . . . . . . .1F 13
The Marsh. Powy . . . . . . . . . . .1F 59
The Marsh. Shrp . . . . . . . . . . . .3A 72
Marshall Meadows. Nmbd . . .4F 131
Marshalsea. Dors . . . . . . . . . . .2G 13
Marshalswick. Herts . . . . . . . . .5B 52
Marsham. Norf . . . . . . . . . . . . .3D 78
Marshaw. Lanc . . . . . . . . . . . . .4E 97
Marsh Baldon. Oxon . . . . . . . . .2D 36
Marsh Benham. W Ber . . . . . . .5C 36
Marshborough. Kent . . . . . . . .5H 41
Marshbrook. Shrp . . . . . . . . . . .2G 59
Marshchapel. Linc . . . . . . . . . .1C 88
Marshfield. Newp . . . . . . . . . . .3F 33
Marshfield. S Glo . . . . . . . . . . .4C 34
Marshgate. Corn . . . . . . . . . . . .3B 10
Marsh Gibbon. Buck . . . . . . . . .3E 51
Marsh Green. Devn . . . . . . . . . .3D 12
Marsh Green. Kent . . . . . . . . . .1F 27
Marsh Green. Staf . . . . . . . . . . .5C 84
Marsh Green. Telf . . . . . . . . . . .4A 72
Marsh Lane. Derbs . . . . . . . . . .3B 86
Marsh Side. Norf . . . . . . . . . . .1G 77
Marshside. Kent . . . . . . . . . . . .4G 41
Marshside. Mers . . . . . . . . . . . .3B 90
Marsh Street. Som . . . . . . . . . .2C 20
Marshwood. Dors . . . . . . . . . . .3G 13
Marske. N Yor . . . . . . . . . . . . .4E 105
Marske-by-the-Sea.
  Red C . . . . . . . . . . . . . . . .2D 106
Marston. Ches W . . . . . . . . . . .3A 84
Marston. Here . . . . . . . . . . . . . .5F 59
Marston. Linc . . . . . . . . . . . . . .1F 75
Marston. Oxon . . . . . . . . . . . . .5D 50
Marston. Staf
  nr. Stafford . . . . . . . . . . . . .3D 72
  nr. Wheaton Aston . . . . . .4C 72
Marston. Warw . . . . . . . . . . . . .1G 61
Marston. Wilts . . . . . . . . . . . . .1E 23
Marston Doles. Warw . . . . . . . .5B 62
Marston Green. W Mid . . . . . . .2F 61
Marston Hill. Glos . . . . . . . . . . .2G 35
Marston Jabbett. Warw . . . . . .2A 62
Marston Magna. Som . . . . . . . .4A 22
Marston Meysey. Wilts . . . . . . .2G 35
Marston Montgomery.
  Derbs . . . . . . . . . . . . . . . .2F 73
Marston Moretaine. C Beds . .1H 51
Marston on Dove. Derbs . . . . . .3G 73
Marston St Lawrence. Nptn . . .1D 50
Marston Stannett. Here . . . . . .5H 59
Marston Trussell. Nptn . . . . . . .2D 62
Marstow. Here . . . . . . . . . . . . . .4A 48
Marsworth. Buck . . . . . . . . . . . .4H 51
Marten. Wilts . . . . . . . . . . . . . .1A 24
Marthall. Ches E . . . . . . . . . . . .3C 84
Martham. Norf . . . . . . . . . . . . . .4G 79
Marthwaite. Cumb . . . . . . . . . .5H 103
Martin. Hants . . . . . . . . . . . . . .1F 15
Martin. Kent . . . . . . . . . . . . . . .1H 29
Martin. Linc
  nr. Horncastle . . . . . . . . . . .4B 88
  nr. Metheringham . . . . . .5A 88
Martindale. Cumb . . . . . . . . . .3F 103
Martin Dales. Linc . . . . . . . . . . .4A 88
Martin Drove End. Hants . . . . .4F 23
Martinhoe. Devn . . . . . . . . . . . .2G 19
Martinhoe Cross. Devn . . . . . . .2G 19
Martin Hussingtree. Worc . . . . .4C 60
Martin Mill. Kent . . . . . . . . . . . .1H 29
Martinscroft. Warr . . . . . . . . . . .2A 84
Martin's Moss. Ches E . . . . . . .4C 84
Martinstown. Dors . . . . . . . . . .4B 14
Martlesham. Suff . . . . . . . . . . .1F 55
Martlesham Heath. Suff . . . . . .1F 55
Martletwy. Pemb . . . . . . . . . . .3E 43
Martley. Worc . . . . . . . . . . . . . .4B 60
Martock. Som . . . . . . . . . . . . . .1H 13
Marton. Ches E . . . . . . . . . . . . .4C 84
Marton. Cumb . . . . . . . . . . . . . .2B 96

Marton. E Yor
  nr. Bridlington . . . . . . . .3G 101
  nr. Hull . . . . . . . . . . . . . . .1E 95
Marton. Linc . . . . . . . . . . . . . . .2F 87
Marton. Midd . . . . . . . . . . . . . .3C 106
Marton. N Yor
  nr. Boroughbridge . . . . . .3G 99
  nr. Pickering . . . . . . . . . .1B 100
Marton. Shrp
  nr. Myddle . . . . . . . . . . . .3G 71
  nr. Worthen . . . . . . . . . . .5E 71
Marton. Warw . . . . . . . . . . . . . .4B 62
Marton Abbey. N Yor . . . . . . . .3H 99
Marton-le-Moor. N Yor . . . . . . .2F 99
Martyr's Green. Surr . . . . . . . . .5B 38
Martyr Worthy. Hants . . . . . . . .3D 24
Marwick. Orkn . . . . . . . . . . . . .5B 172
Marwood. Devn . . . . . . . . . . . . .3F 19
Marybank. High
  nr. Dingwall . . . . . . . . . .3G 157
  nr. Invergordon . . . . . . . .1B 158
Maryburgh. High . . . . . . . . . . .3H 157
Maryfield. Corn . . . . . . . . . . . . .3A 8
Maryhill. Glas . . . . . . . . . . . . .3G 127
Marykirk. Abers . . . . . . . . . . . .2F 145
Marylebone. G Lon . . . . . . . . . .2D 39
Marylebone. G Man . . . . . . . . .4D 90
Marypark. Mor . . . . . . . . . . . . .5F 159
Maryport. Cumb . . . . . . . . . . . .1B 102
Maryport. Dum . . . . . . . . . . . . .5E 109
Marystow. Devn . . . . . . . . . . . .4E 11
Mary Tavy. Devn . . . . . . . . . . . .5F 11
Maryton. Ang
  nr. Kirriemuir . . . . . . . . .3C 144
  nr. Montrose . . . . . . . . . .3F 145
Marywell. Abers . . . . . . . . . . . .4C 152
Marywell. Ang . . . . . . . . . . . . .4F 145
Masham. N Yor . . . . . . . . . . . . .1E 98
Mashbury. Essx . . . . . . . . . . . . .4G 53
Masongill. N Yor . . . . . . . . . . . .2F 97
Masons Lodge. Abers . . . . . . .3F 153
Mastin Moor. Derbs . . . . . . . . .3B 86
Mastrick. Aber . . . . . . . . . . . . .3G 153
Matching. Essx . . . . . . . . . . . . .4F 53
Matching Green. Essx . . . . . . .4F 53
Matching Tye. Essx . . . . . . . . . .4F 53
Matfen. Nmbd . . . . . . . . . . . . .2D 114
Matfield. Kent . . . . . . . . . . . . . .1A 28
Mathern. Mon . . . . . . . . . . . . . .2A 34
Mathon. Here . . . . . . . . . . . . . .1C 48
Mathry. Pemb . . . . . . . . . . . . . .1C 42
Matlaske. Norf . . . . . . . . . . . . .2D 78
Matlock. Derbs . . . . . . . . . . . . .5G 85
Matlock Bath. Derbs . . . . . . . . .5G 85
Matterdale End. Cumb . . . . . .2E 103
Mattersey. Notts . . . . . . . . . . . .2D 86
Mattersey Thorpe. Notts . . . . . .2D 86
Mattingley. Hants . . . . . . . . . . .1F 25
Mattishall. Norf . . . . . . . . . . . .4C 78
Mattishall Burgh. Norf . . . . . . .4C 78
Mauchline. E Ayr . . . . . . . . . . .2D 117
Maud. Abers . . . . . . . . . . . . . .4G 161
Maugersbury. Glos . . . . . . . . . .3G 49
Maughold. IOM . . . . . . . . . . . .2D 108
Maulden. C Beds . . . . . . . . . . .2A 52
Maulds Meaburn. Cumb . . . . .3H 103
Maunby. N Yor . . . . . . . . . . . . . .1F 99
Maund Bryan. Here . . . . . . . . . .5H 59
Mautby. Norf . . . . . . . . . . . . . . .4G 79
Mavesyn Ridware. Staf . . . . . . .4E 73
Mavis Enderby. Linc . . . . . . . . .4C 88
Mawbray. Cumb . . . . . . . . . . . .5B 112
Mawdesley. Lanc . . . . . . . . . . . .3C 90
Mawdlam. B'end . . . . . . . . . . . .3B 32
Mawgan. Corn . . . . . . . . . . . . . . .4E 5
Mawgan Porth. Corn . . . . . . . . .2C 6
Maw Green. Ches E . . . . . . . . .5B 84
Mawla. Corn . . . . . . . . . . . . . . . .4B 6
Mawnan. Corn . . . . . . . . . . . . . .4E 5
Mawnan Smith. Corn . . . . . . . . .4E 5
Mawsley Village. Nptn . . . . . . .3E 63
Mawthorpe. Linc . . . . . . . . . . . .3D 88
Maxey. Pet . . . . . . . . . . . . . . . .5A 76

Maxstoke. Warw . . . . . . . . . . . .2G 61
Maxted Street. Kent . . . . . . . . .1F 29
Maxton. Kent . . . . . . . . . . . . . . .1G 29
Maxton. Bord . . . . . . . . . . . . . .1A 120
Maxwellheugh. Bord . . . . . . . .1B 120
Maxwelltown. Dum . . . . . . . . .2A 112
Maxworthy. Corn . . . . . . . . . . . .3C 10
Mayals. Swan . . . . . . . . . . . . . . .4F 31
Maybole. S Ayr . . . . . . . . . . . . .3C 116
Maybush. Sotn . . . . . . . . . . . . . .1B 16
Mayes Green. Surr . . . . . . . . . . .2C 26
Mayfield. E Sus . . . . . . . . . . . . .3G 27
Mayfield. Midl . . . . . . . . . . . . .3G 129
Mayfield. Per . . . . . . . . . . . . . .1C 136
Mayfield. Staf . . . . . . . . . . . . . .1F 73
Mayford. Surr . . . . . . . . . . . . . . .5A 38
Mayhill. Swan . . . . . . . . . . . . . . .3F 31
Mayland. Essx . . . . . . . . . . . . . .5C 54
Maylandsea. Essx . . . . . . . . . . .5C 54
Maynard's Green. E Sus . . . . . .4G 27
Maypole. IOS . . . . . . . . . . . . . . .1B 4
Maypole. Kent . . . . . . . . . . . . . .4G 41
Maypole. Mon . . . . . . . . . . . . . .4H 47
Maypole Green. Norf . . . . . . . . .1G 67
Maypole Green. Suff . . . . . . . . .5B 66
Maywick. Shet . . . . . . . . . . . . .9E 173
Mead. Devn . . . . . . . . . . . . . . . .1C 10
Meadgate. Bath . . . . . . . . . . . . .1B 22
Meadle. Buck . . . . . . . . . . . . . . .5G 51
Meadowbank. Ches W . . . . . . .4A 84
Meadowfield. Dur . . . . . . . . . .1F 105
Meadow Green. Here . . . . . . . . .5B 60
Meadowmill. E Lot . . . . . . . . . .2H 129
Meadows. Nott . . . . . . . . . . . . . .2C 74
Meadowtown. Shrp . . . . . . . . . .5F 71
Meadwell. Devn . . . . . . . . . . . . .4E 11
Meaford. Staf . . . . . . . . . . . . . . .2C 72
Mealabost. W Isl nr. Borgh . . .2G 171
  nr. Stornoway . . . . . . . . .4G 171
Mealasta. W Isl . . . . . . . . . . . . .5B 171
Meal Bank. Cumb . . . . . . . . . .5G 103
Mealrigg. Cumb . . . . . . . . . . . .5C 112
Mealsgate. Cumb . . . . . . . . . . .5D 112
Meanwood. W Yor . . . . . . . . . . .1C 92
Mearbeck. N Yor . . . . . . . . . . . .3H 97
Meare. Som . . . . . . . . . . . . . . . .2H 21
Meare Green. Som
  nr. Curry Mallet . . . . . . . .4F 21
  nr. Stoke St Gregory . . . .4G 21
Mears Ashby. Nptn . . . . . . . . . .4F 63
Measham. Leics . . . . . . . . . . . .4H 73
Meath Green. Surr . . . . . . . . . .1D 27
Meathop. Cumb . . . . . . . . . . . .1D 96
Meaux. E Yor . . . . . . . . . . . . . . .1D 94
Meavy. Devn . . . . . . . . . . . . . . . .2B 8
Medbourne. Leics . . . . . . . . . . .1E 63
Medburn. Nmbd . . . . . . . . . . .2E 115
Meddon. Devn . . . . . . . . . . . . . .1C 10
Meden Vale. Notts . . . . . . . . . .4C 86
Medlam. Linc . . . . . . . . . . . . . . .5C 88
Medlicott. Shrp . . . . . . . . . . . . .1G 59
Medmenham. Buck . . . . . . . . . .3G 37
Medomsley. Dur . . . . . . . . . . .4E 115
Medstead. Hants . . . . . . . . . . .3E 25
Medway Towns. Medw . . . . . . .4B 40
Meerbrook. Staf . . . . . . . . . . . .4D 85
Meer End. W Mid . . . . . . . . . . . .3G 61
Meers Bridge. Linc . . . . . . . . . .2D 89
Meesden. Herts . . . . . . . . . . . . .2E 53
Meeson. Telf . . . . . . . . . . . . . . .3A 72
Meeth. Devn . . . . . . . . . . . . . . .2F 11
Meeting Green. Suff . . . . . . . . .5G 65
Meeting House Hill. Norf . . . . . .3F 79
Meidrim. Carm . . . . . . . . . . . . .2G 43
Meifod. Powy . . . . . . . . . . . . . .4D 70
Meigle. Per . . . . . . . . . . . . . . .4B 144
Meikle Earnock. S Lan . . . . . . .4A 128
Meikle Kilchattan Butts. Arg . .4B 126
Meikle Tarty. Abers . . . . . . . . .1G 153
Meikle Wartle. Abers . . . . . . . .5E 160
Meinciau. Carm . . . . . . . . . . . . .4E 45
Meir. Stoke . . . . . . . . . . . . . . . . .1D 72
Meir Heath. Staf . . . . . . . . . . . .1D 72

Melbourn. Cambs . . . . . . . . . . .1D 53
Melbourne. Derbs . . . . . . . . . . .3A 74
Melbourne. E Yor . . . . . . . . . . .5B 100
Melbury Abbas. Dors . . . . . . . .4D 23
Melbury Bubb. Dors . . . . . . . . .2A 14
Melbury Osmond. Dors . . . . . . .2A 14
Melbury Sampford. Dors . . . . .2A 14
Melby. Shet . . . . . . . . . . . . . . .6C 173
Melchbourne. Bed . . . . . . . . . . .4H 63
Melcombe Bingham. Dors . . . .2C 14
Melcombe Regis. Dors . . . . . . .4B 14
Meldon. Devn . . . . . . . . . . . . . . .3F 11
Meldon. Nmbd . . . . . . . . . . . . .1E 115
Meldreth. Cambs . . . . . . . . . . . .1D 53
Melfort. Arg . . . . . . . . . . . . . . .2F 133
Melgarve. High . . . . . . . . . . . . .4G 149
Meliden. Den . . . . . . . . . . . . . . .2C 82
Melinbyrhedyn. Powy . . . . . . . .1H 57
Melincourt. Neat . . . . . . . . . . . .5B 46
Melin-y-coed. Cnwy . . . . . . . . .4H 81
Melin-y-ddol. Powy . . . . . . . . .5C 70
Melin-y-wig. Den . . . . . . . . . . . .1C 70
Melkinthorpe. Cumb . . . . . . . .2G 103
Melkridge. Nmbd . . . . . . . . . .3A 114
Melksham. Wilts . . . . . . . . . . . .5E 35
Mellangaun. High . . . . . . . . . .5C 162
Melldalloch. Arg . . . . . . . . . . .2H 125
Melliguards. Cumb . . . . . . . . . .5F 113
Melling. Lanc . . . . . . . . . . . . . . .2E 97
Melling. Mers . . . . . . . . . . . . . . .4B 90
Melling Mount. Mers . . . . . . . . .4C 90
Mellis. Suff . . . . . . . . . . . . . . . . .3C 66
Mellon Charles. High . . . . . . . .4C 162
Mellon Udrigle. High . . . . . . . .4C 162
Mellor. G Man . . . . . . . . . . . . . .2D 85
Mellor. Lanc . . . . . . . . . . . . . . . .1E 91
Mellor Brook. Lanc . . . . . . . . . .1E 91
Mells. Som . . . . . . . . . . . . . . . .2C 22
Melmerby. Cumb . . . . . . . . . . .1H 103
Melmerby. N Yor
  nr. Middleham . . . . . . . . .1C 98
  nr. Ripon . . . . . . . . . . . . .2F 99
Melplash. Dors . . . . . . . . . . . . .3H 13
Melrose. Bord . . . . . . . . . . . . .1H 119
Melsetter. Orkn . . . . . . . . . . . .9B 172
Melsonby. N Yor . . . . . . . . . . .4E 105
Meltham. W Yor . . . . . . . . . . . . .3B 92
Meltham Mills. W Yor . . . . . . . .3B 92
Melton. E Yor . . . . . . . . . . . . . . .2C 94
Melton. Suff . . . . . . . . . . . . . . . .5E 67
Meltonby. E Yor . . . . . . . . . . . .4B 100
Melton Constable. Norf . . . . . . .2C 78
Melton Mowbray. Leics . . . . . . .4E 75
Melton Ross. N Lin . . . . . . . . . .3D 94
Melvaig. High . . . . . . . . . . . . . .5B 162
Melverley. Shrp . . . . . . . . . . . . .4F 71
Melverley Green. Shrp . . . . . . .4F 71
Melvich. High . . . . . . . . . . . . . .2A 168
Membury. Devn . . . . . . . . . . . . .2F 13
Memsie. Abers . . . . . . . . . . . . .2G 161
Memus. Ang . . . . . . . . . . . . . . .3D 144
Menabilly. Corn . . . . . . . . . . . . .3E 7
Menai Bridge. IOA . . . . . . . . . . .3E 81
Mendham. Suff . . . . . . . . . . . . .2E 67
Mendlesham. Suff . . . . . . . . . . .4D 66
Mendlesham Green. Suff . . . . .4C 66
Menethorpe. N Yor . . . . . . . . .3B 100
Menheniot. Corn . . . . . . . . . . . .2G 7
Menithwood. Worc . . . . . . . . . .4B 60
Mennock. Dum . . . . . . . . . . . . .4H 117
Menston. W Yor . . . . . . . . . . . . .5D 98
Menstrie. Clac . . . . . . . . . . . . .4H 135
Menthorpe. N Yor . . . . . . . . . . .1H 93
Mentmore. Buck . . . . . . . . . . . .4H 51
Meole Brace. Shrp . . . . . . . . . . .4G 71
Meols. Mers . . . . . . . . . . . . . . . .1E 83
Meon. Hants . . . . . . . . . . . . . . . .2D 16
Meonstoke. Hants . . . . . . . . . . .1E 16
Meopham. Kent . . . . . . . . . . . . .4H 39
Meopham Green. Kent . . . . . . .4H 39
Meopham Station. Kent . . . . . .4H 39
Mepal. Cambs . . . . . . . . . . . . . .2D 64

# Meppershall—Milton of Cushnie



Meppershall. C Beds 2B 52
Merbach. Here 1G 47
Mercaston. Derbs 1G 73
Merchiston. Edin 2F 129
Mere. Ches E 2B 84
Mere. Wilts 3D 22
Mere Brow. Lanc 3C 90
Mereclough. Lanc 1G 91
Mere Green. W Mid 1F 61
Mere Green. Worc 4D 60
Mere Heath. Ches W 3A 84
Mereside. Bkpl 1B 90
Meretown. Staf 3B 72
Mereworth. Kent 5A 40
Meriden. W Mid 2G 61
Merkadale. High 5C 154
Merkland. S Ayr 5B 116
Merkland Lodge. High 1A 164
Merley. Pool 3F 15
Merlin's Bridge. Pemb 3D 42
Merridge. Som 3F 21
Merrington. Shrp 3G 71
Merrion. Pemb 5D 42
Merriott. Som 1H 13
Merrivale. Devn 5F 11
Merrow. Surr 5B 38
Merrybent. Darl 3F 105
Merry Lees. Leics 5B 74
Merrymeet. Corn 2G 7
Mersham. Kent 2E 29
Merstham. Surr 5D 39
Merston. W Sus 2G 17
Merstone. IOW 4D 16
Merther. Corn 4C 6
Merthyr. Carm 3D 44
Merthyr Cynog. Powy 2C 46
Merthyr Dyfan. V Glam 4E 32
Merthyr Mawr. B'end 4B 32
**Merthyr Tudful**. Mer T 5D 46
**Merthyr Tydfil**. Mer T 5D 46
Merthyr Vale. Mer T 2D 32
Merton. Devn 1F 11
**Merton**. G Lon 4D 38
Merton. Norf 1B 66
Merton. Oxon 4D 50
Meshaw. Devn 1A 12
Messing. Essx 4B 54
Messingham. N Lin 4B 94
Metcombe. Devn 3D 12
Metfield. Suff 2E 67
Metherell. Corn 2A 8
Metheringham. Linc 4H 87
Methil. Fife 4F 137
Methilhill. Fife 4F 137
Methley. W Yor 2D 93
Methley Junction. W Yor 2D 93
Methlick. Abers 5F 161
Methven. Per 1C 136
Methwold. Norf 1G 65
Methwold Hythe. Norf 1G 65
Mettingham. Suff 2F 67
Metton. Norf 2D 78
Mevagissey. Corn 4E 6
**Mexborough**. S Yor 4E 93
Mey. High 1E 169
Meysey Hampton. Glos 2G 35
Miabhag. W Isl 8D 171
Miabhaig. W Isl
  nr. Cliasmol 7C 171
  nr. Timsgearraidh 4C 171
Mial. High 1G 155
Michaelchurch. Here 3A 48
Michaelchurch Escley. Here 2G 47
Michaelchurch-on-Arrow. Powy 5E 59
Michaelston-le-Pit. V Glam 4E 33
Michaelston-y-Fedw. Newp 3F 33
Michaelstow. Corn 5A 10
Michelcombe. Devn 2C 8
Micheldever. Hants 3D 24
Micheldever Station. Hants 2D 24
Michelmersh. Hants 4B 24
Mickfield. Suff 4D 66
Micklebring. S Yor 1C 86
Mickleby. N Yor 3F 107
Micklefield. W Yor 1E 93
Micklefield Green. Herts 1B 38
Mickleham. Surr 5C 38
Mickleover. Derb 2H 73
Micklethwaite. Cumb 4D 112
Micklethwaite. W Yor 5D 98
Mickleton. Dur 2C 104
Mickleton. Glos 1G 49
Mickletown. W Yor 2D 93
Mickle Trafford. Ches W 4G 83
Mickley. N Yor 2E 99
Mickley Green. Suff 5H 65
Mickley Square. Nmbd 3D 115
Mid Ardlaw. Abers 2G 161
Midbea. Orkn 3D 172
Mid Beltie. Abers 3D 152
Mid Calder. W Lot 3D 129
Mid Clyth. High 5E 169
Middle Assendon. Oxon 3F 37
Middle Aston. Oxon 3C 50
Middle Barton. Oxon 3C 50
Middlebie. Dum 2D 112
Middle Chinnock. Som 1H 13
Middle Claydon. Buck 3F 51
Middlecliffe. S Yor 4E 93
Middlecott. Devn 4H 11
Middle Drums. Ang 3E 145
Middle Duntisbourne. Glos 5E 49
Middle Essie. Abers 3H 161
Middleforth Green. Lanc 2D 90
Middleham. N Yor 1D 98
Middle Handley. Derbs 3B 86
Middle Harling. Norf 2B 66
Middlehope. Shrp 2G 59
Middle Littleton. Worc 1F 49
Middle Maes-coed. Here 2G 47
Middlemarsh. Dors 2B 14
Middle Marwood. Devn 3F 19
Middle Mayfield. Staf 1F 73
Middlemoor. Devn 5E 11
Middlemuir. Abers
  nr. New Deer 4F 161
  nr. Strichen 3G 161
Middle Rainton. Tyne 5G 115
Middle Rasen. Linc 2H 87
The Middles. Dur 4F 115
**Middlesbrough**. Midd 3B 106
Middlesceugh. Cumb 5E 113
Middleshaw. Cumb 1E 97
Middlesmoor. N Yor 2C 98
Middlestone. Dur 1F 105
Middlestone Moor. Dur 1F 105
Middle Stoughton. Som 2H 21
Middlestown. W Yor 3C 92
Middle Street. Glos 5C 48
Middle Taphouse. Corn 2F 7
Middleton. Ang 4E 145
Middleton. Arg 4A 138
Middleton. Cumb 1F 97
Middleton. Derbs
  nr. Bakewell 4F 85
  nr. Wirksworth 5G 85
Middleton. Essx 2B 54
**Middleton**. G Man 4G 91
Middleton. Hants 2C 24
Middleton. Hart 1C 106
Middleton. Here 4H 59
Middleton. IOW 4B 16
Middleton. Lanc 4D 96
Middleton. Midl 4G 129
Middleton. Norf 4F 77
Middleton. Nptn 2F 63
Middleton. Nmbd
  nr. Belford 1F 121
  nr. Morpeth 1D 114
Middleton. N Yor
  nr. Ilkley 5D 98
  nr. Pickering 1B 100
Middleton. Per 3D 136
Middleton. Shrp
  nr. Ludlow 3H 59
  nr. Oswestry 3F 71
Middleton. Suff 4G 67
Middleton. Swan 4D 30
Middleton. Warw 1F 61
Middleton. W Yor 2C 92
Middleton Cheney. Nptn 1D 50
Middleton Green. Staf 2D 73
Middleton-in-Teesdale. Dur 2C 104
Middleton One Row. Darl 3A 106
Middleton-on-Leven. N Yor 4B 106
Middleton-on-Sea. W Sus 5A 26
Middleton on the Hill. Here 4H 59
Middleton-on-the-Wolds. E Yor 5D 100
Middleton Priors. Shrp 1A 60
Middleton Quernhow. N Yor 2F 99
Middleton St George. Darl 3A 106
Middleton Scriven. Shrp 2A 60
Middleton Stoney. Oxon 3D 50
Middleton Tyas. N Yor 4F 105
Middle Town. IOS 1B 4
Middletown. Cumb 4A 102
Middletown. Powy 4F 71
Middle Tysoe. Warw 1B 50
Middle Wallop. Hants 3A 24
**Middlewich**. Ches E 4B 84
Middle Winterslow. Wilts 3H 23
Middlewood. Corn 5C 10
Middlewood. S Yor 1H 85
Middle Woodford. Wilts 3G 23
Middlewood Green. Suff 4C 66
Middleyard. Glos 5D 48
Middlezoy. Som 3G 21
Middridge. Dur 2F 105
Midelney. Som 4H 21
Midfield. High 2F 167
Midford. Bath 5C 34
Mid Garrary. Dum 2C 110
Midge Hall. Lanc 2D 90
Midgeholme. Cumb 4H 113
Midgham. W Ber 5D 36
Midgley. W Yor
  nr. Halifax 2A 92
  nr. Horbury 3C 92
Mid Ho. Shet 2G 173
Midhopestones. S Yor 1G 85
Midhurst. W Sus 4G 25
Mid Kirkton. N Ayr 4C 126
Mid Lambrook. Som 1H 13
Midland. Orkn 7C 172
Mid Lavant. W Sus 2G 17
Midlem. Bord 2H 119
Midney. Som 4A 22
**Midsomer Norton**. Bath 1B 22
Midton. Inv 2D 126
Midtown. High
  nr. Poolewe 5C 162
  nr. Tongue 2F 167
Midville. Linc 5C 88
Mid Walls. Shet 7C 173
Mid Yell. Shet 2G 173
Migdale. High 4D 164
Migvie. Abers 3B 152
Milborne Port. Som 1B 14
Milborne St Andrew. Dors 3D 14
Milborne Wick. Som 4B 22
Milbourne. Nmbd 2E 115
Milbourne. Wilts 3E 35
Milburn. Cumb 2H 103
Milbury Heath. S Glo 2B 34
Milby. N Yor 3G 99
Milcombe. Oxon 2C 50
Milden. Suff 1C 54
**Mildenhall**. Suff 3G 65
Mildenhall. Wilts 5H 35
Milebrook. Powy 3F 59
Milebush. Kent 1B 28
Mile End. Cambs 2F 65
Mile End. Essx 3C 54
Mileham. Norf 4B 78
Mile Oak. Brig 5D 26
Miles Green. Staf 5C 84
Miles Hope. Here 4H 59
Milesmark. Fife 1D 128
Mile Town. Kent 3D 40
Milfield. Nmbd 1D 120
Milford. Derbs 1A 74
Milford. Devn 4C 18
Milford. Powy 1C 58
Milford. Staf 3D 72
Milford. Surr 1A 26
**Milford Haven**. Pemb 4D 42
Milford on Sea. Hants 3A 16
Milkwall. Glos 5A 48
Milkwell. Wilts 4E 23
Milland. W Sus 4G 25
Mill Bank. W Yor 2A 92
Millbank. High 2D 168
Millbeck. Cumb 2D 102
Millbounds. Orkn 4E 172
Millbreck. Abers 4H 161
Millbridge. Surr 2G 25
Millbrook. C Beds 2A 52
Millbrook. Corn 3A 8
Millbrook. G Man 1D 85
Millbrook. Sotn 1B 16
Mill Common. Suff 2G 67
Mill Corner. E Sus 3C 28
Milldale. Staf 5F 85
Millden Lodge. Ang 1E 145
Milldens. Ang 3E 145
Millearn. Per 2B 136
Mill End. Buck 3F 37
Mill End. Cambs 5F 65
Mill End. Glos 4G 49
Mill End. Herts 2D 52
Millend. Glos 2C 34
Millerhill. Midl 3G 129
Miller's Dale. Derbs 3F 85
Millers Green. Derbs 5G 85
Millerston. Glas 3H 127
Millfield. Abers 4B 152
Millfield. Pet 5A 76
Millgate. Lanc 3G 91
Mill Green. Essx 5G 53
Mill Green. Norf 2D 66
Mill Green. Shrp 3A 72
Mill Green. Staf 3E 73
Mill Green. Suff 1C 54
Millhalf. Here 1F 47
Millhall. E Ren 4G 127
Millhayes. Devn
  nr. Honiton 2F 13
  nr. Wellington 1E 13
Millhead. Lanc 2D 97
Millheugh. S Lan 4A 128
Mill Hill. Bkbn 2E 91
Mill Hill. G Lon 1D 38
Millholme. Cumb 5G 103
Millhouse. Arg 2A 126
Millhouse. Cumb 1E 103
Millhousebridge. Dum 1C 112
Millhouses. S Yor 2H 85
Millikenpark. Ren 3F 127
Millington. E Yor 4C 100
Millington Green. Derbs 1G 73
Millisle. Ards 4J 175
Mill Knowe. Arg 3B 122
Mill Lane. Hants 1F 25
Millmeece. Staf 2C 72
Mill of Craigievar. Abers 2C 152
Mill of Fintray. Abers 2F 153
Mill of Haldane. W Dun 1F 127
Millom. Cumb 1A 96
Millow. C Beds 1C 52
Millpool. Corn 5B 10
Millport. N Ayr 4C 126
Mill Side. Cumb 1D 96
Mill Street. Norf
  nr. Lyng 4C 78
  nr. Swanton Morley 4C 78
Millthorpe. Derbs 3H 85
Millthorpe. Linc 2A 76
Millthrop. Cumb 5H 103
Milltimber. Aber 3F 153
Milltown. Abers
  nr. Corgarff 3G 151
  nr. Lumsden 2B 152
Milltown. Corn 3F 7
Milltown. Derbs 4A 86
Milltown. Devn 3F 19
Milltown. Dum 2E 113
Milltown of Aberdalgie. Per 1C 136
Milltown of Auchindoun. Mor 4A 160
Milltown of Campfield. Abers 3D 152
Milltown of Edinvillie. Mor 4G 159
Milltown of Rothiemay. Mor 4C 160
Milltown of Towie. Abers 2B 152
Milnacraig. Ang 3B 144
Milnathort. Per 3D 136
**Milngavie**. E Dun 2G 127
Milnholm. Stir 1A 128
**Milnrow**. G Man 3H 91
Milnthorpe. Cumb 1D 97
Milnthorpe. W Yor 3D 92
Milson. Shrp 3A 60
Milstead. Kent 5D 40
Milston. Wilts 2G 23
Milthorpe. Nptn 1D 50
Milton. Ang 4C 144
Milton. Cambs 4D 65
Milton. Cumb
  nr. Brampton 3G 113
  nr. Crooklands 1E 97
Milton. Derbs 3H 73
Milton. Dum
  nr. Crocketford 2F 111
  nr. Glenluce 4H 109
Milton. Glas 3G 127
Milton. High
  nr. Achnasheen 3F 157
  nr. Applecross 4G 155
  nr. Drumnadrochit 5G 157
  nr. Invergordon 1B 158
  nr. Inverness 4H 157
  nr. Wick 3F 169
Milton. Mor
  nr. Cullen 2C 160
  nr. Tomintoul 2F 151
Milton. N Som 5G 33
Milton. Notts 3E 86
Milton. Oxon
  nr. Bloxham 2C 50
  nr. Didcot 2C 36
Milton. Pemb 4E 43
Milton. Port 3E 17
Milton. Som 4H 21
Milton. S Ayr 2D 116
Milton. Stir
  nr. Aberfoyle 3E 135
  nr. Drymen 4D 134
Milton. Stoke 5D 84
Milton. W Dun 2F 127
Milton Abbas. Dors 2D 14
Milton Abbot. Devn 5E 11
Milton Auchlossan. Abers 3C 152
Milton Bridge. Midl 3F 129
Milton Bryan. C Beds 2H 51
Milton Clevedon. Som 3B 22
Milton Coldwells. Abers 5G 161
Milton Combe. Devn 2A 8
Milton Common. Oxon 5E 51
Milton Damerel. Devn 1D 11
Miltonduff. Mor 2F 159
Milton End. Glos 5G 49
Milton Ernest. Bed 5H 63
Milton Green. Ches W 5G 83
Milton Hill. Devn 5C 12
Milton Hill. Oxon 2C 36
**Milton Keynes**. Mil 2G 51
Milton Keynes Village. Mil 2G 51
Milton Lilbourne. Wilts 5G 35
Milton Malsor. Nptn 5E 63
Milton Morenish. Per 5D 142
Milton of Auchinhove. Abers 3C 152
Milton of Balgonie. Fife 3F 137
Milton of Barras. Abers 1H 145
Milton of Campsie. E Dun 2H 127
Milton of Cultoquhey. Per 1A 136
Milton of Cushnie. Abers 2C 152

Milton of Finavon. Ang ......3D **145**
Milton of Gollanfield. High ...3B **158**
Milton of Lesmore. Abers ....1B **152**
Milton of Leys. High ......4A **158**
Milton on Stour. Dors ......4C **22**
Milton Regis. Kent .........4C **40**
Milton Street. E Sus ........5G **27**
Milton-under-Wychwood.
   Oxon ...................4A **50**
Milverton. Som ...........4E **20**
Milverton. Warw ..........4H **61**
Milwich. Staf ............2D **72**
Mimbridge. Surr ..........4A **38**
Minard. Arg ..............4G **133**
Minchington. Dors ........1E **15**
Minchinhampton. Glos ....5D **48**
Mindrum. Nmbd ..........1C **120**
Minehead. Som ..........2C **20**
Minera. Wrex ............5E **83**
Minety. Wilts ............2F **35**
Minffordd. Gwyn .........2E **69**
Mingarrypark. High .......2A **140**
Mingary. High ...........2G **139**
Mingearraidh. W Isl ......6C **170**
Miningsby. Linc ..........4C **88**
Minions. Corn ...........5C **10**
Minishant. S Ayr .........3C **116**
Minllyn. Gwyn ...........4A **70**
Minnigaff. Dum ..........3B **110**
Minorca. IOM ...........3D **108**
Minskip. N Yor ..........3F **99**
Minstead. Hants .........1A **16**
Minsted. W Sus ..........4G **25**
Minster. Kent
   nr. Ramsgate .........4H **41**
**Minster.** Kent
   nr. Sheerness ........3D **40**
Minsteracres. Nmbd .....4D **114**
Minsterley. Shrp .........5F **71**
Minster Lovell. Oxon ......4B **50**
Minsterworth. Glos .......4C **48**
Minterne Magna. Dors ....2B **14**
Minterne Parva. Dors ....2B **14**
Minting. Linc ............3A **88**
Mintlaw. Abers ..........4H **161**
Minto. Bord .............2H **119**
Minton. Shrp ............1G **59**
Minwear. Pemb ..........3E **43**
Minworth. W Mid .........1F **61**
Miodar. Arg .............4B **138**
Mirbister. Orkn ..........5C **172**
Mirehouse. Cumb ........3A **102**
Mireland. High ...........2F **169**
**Mirfield.** W Yor .........3C **92**
Miserden. Glos ..........5E **49**
Miskin. Rhon ............3D **32**
Misson. Notts ...........1D **86**
Misterton. Leics .........2C **62**
Misterton. Notts .........1E **87**
Misterton. Som ..........2H **13**
Mistley. Essx ............2E **54**
Mistley Heath. Essx ......2E **55**
**Mitcham.** G Lon ........4D **39**
Mitcheldean. Glos .......4B **48**
Mitchell. Corn ...........3C **6**
Mitchel Troy. Mon ........4H **47**
Mitford. Nmbd ..........1E **115**
Mithian. Corn ...........3B **6**
Mitton. Staf ............4C **72**
Mixbury. Oxon ..........2E **50**
Mixenden. W Yor ........2A **92**
Mixon. Staf .............5E **85**
Moaness. Orkn ..........7B **172**
Moarfield. Shet .........1G **173**
Moat. Cumb .............2F **113**
Moats Tye. Suff .........5C **66**
Mobberley. Ches E .......3B **84**
Moccas. Here ...........1G **47**
Mochdre. Cnwy ..........3H **81**
Mochdre. Powy .........2C **58**
Mochrum. Dum ..........5A **110**

Mockbeggar. Hants ......2G **15**
Mockerkin. Cumb ........2B **102**
Modbury. Devn ..........3C **8**
Moddershall. Staf ........2D **72**
Modsarie. High .........2G **167**
Moelfre. Cnwy ..........3B **82**
Moelfre. IOA ............2E **81**
Moelfre. Powy ..........3D **70**
Moffat. Dum ............4C **118**
Moggerhanger. C Beds ...1B **52**
Mogworthy. Devn ........1B **12**
Moira. Leics ............4H **73**
Moira. Lis ..............4G **175**
Molash. Kent ...........5E **41**
Mol-chlach. High ........2C **146**
Mold. Flin ..............4E **83**
Molehill Green. Essx .....3F **53**
Molescroft. E Yor .......5E **101**
Molesden. Nmbd ........1E **115**
Molesworth. Cambs .....3H **63**
Moll. High ..............1D **146**
Molland. Devn ..........4B **20**
Mollington. Ches W ......3F **83**
Mollington. Oxon ........1C **50**
Mollinsburn. N Lan ......2A **128**
Monachty. Cdgn ........4E **57**
Monachyle. Stir .........2D **135**
Monar Lodge. High ......4E **156**
Monaughty. Powy .......4E **59**
Monewden. Suff ........5E **67**
Moneydie. Per ..........1C **136**
Moneymore. M Ulst .....3E **175**
Moneyrow Green. Wind ...4G **37**
Moniaive. Dum ..........5G **117**
Monifieth. Ang .........5E **145**
Monikie. Ang ...........5E **145**
Monimail. Fife ..........2E **137**
Monington. Pemb .......1B **44**
Monk Bretton. S Yor .....4D **92**
Monken Hadley. G Lon ...1D **38**
Monk Fryston. N Yor .....2F **93**
Monk Hesleden. Dur .....1B **106**
Monkhide. Here .........1B **48**
Monkhill. Cumb .........4E **113**
Monkhopton. Shrp .......1A **60**
Monkland. Here .........5G **59**
Monkleigh. Devn .........4E **19**
Monknash. V Glam .......4C **32**
Monkokehampton. Devn ...2F **11**
Monkseaton. Tyne .......2G **115**
Monks Eleigh. Suff .......1C **54**
Monk's Gate. W Sus ......3D **26**
Monk's Heath. Ches E ....3C **84**
Monkshill. Abers .........4E **161**
Monks Kirby. Warw ......2B **62**
Monk Soham. Suff .......4E **66**
Monk Soham Green. Suff ...4E **66**
Monkspath. W Mid ......3F **61**
Monks Risborough. Buck ...5G **51**
Monksthorpe. Linc .......4D **88**
Monk Street. Essx .......3G **53**
Monkswood. Mon ........5G **47**
Monkton. Devn ..........2E **13**
Monkton. Kent ..........4G **41**
Monkton. Pemb ..........4D **42**
Monkton. S Ayr .........2C **116**
Monkton Combe. Bath ...5C **34**
Monkton Deverill. Wilts ...3D **22**
Monkton Farleigh. Wilts ...5D **34**
Monkton Heathfield. Som ...4F **21**
Monktonhill. S Ayr .......2C **116**
Monkton Up Wimborne.
   Dors ..................1F **15**
Monkton Wyld. Dors .....3G **13**
Monkwearmouth. Tyne ...4G **115**
Monkwood. Dors ........3H **13**
Monkwood. Hants ........3E **25**
Monmarsh. Here .........1A **48**
Monmouth. Mon .........4A **48**
Monnington on Wye. Here ...1G **47**
Monreith. Dum ..........5A **110**
Montacute. Som .........1H **13**

Montford. Arg ...........3C **126**
Montford. Shrp ..........4G **71**
Montford Bridge. Shrp ...4G **71**
Montgarrie. Abers .......2C **152**
Montgarswood. E Ayr ....2E **117**
Montgomery. Powy .......1E **58**
Montgreenan. N Ayr .....5E **127**
**Montrose.** Ang .........3G **145**
Monxton. Hants .........2B **24**
Monyash. Derbs .........4F **85**
Monymusk. Abers ........2D **152**
Monzie. Per .............1A **136**
Moodiesburn. N Lan .....2H **127**
Moon's Green. Kent ......3C **28**
Moonzie. Fife ...........2F **137**
Moor. Som .............1H **13**
The Moor. Kent .........3B **28**
Moor Allerton. W Yor ....1C **92**
Moorbath. Dors .........3H **13**
Moorbrae. Shet .........3F **173**
Moorby. Linc ............4B **88**
Moorcot. Here ..........5F **59**
Moor Crichel. Dors .......2E **15**
Moor Cross. Devn ........3C **8**
Moordown. Bour .........3F **15**
Moore. Hal .............2H **83**
Moor End. E Yor .........1B **94**
Moorend. Dum ..........2D **112**
Moorend. Glos
   nr. Dursley ...........5C **48**
   nr. Gloucester .......4D **48**
Moorends. S Yor ........3G **93**
Moorgate. S Yor .........1B **86**
Moor Green. Wilts ........5D **34**
Moorgreen. Hants ........1C **16**
Moorgreen. Notts .......1B **74**
Moorhaigh. Notts .......4C **86**
Moorhall. Derbs ........3H **85**
Moorhampton. Here ......1G **47**
Moorhouse. Cumb
   nr. Carlisle ..........4E **113**
   nr. Wigton ..........4D **112**
Moorhouse. Notts .......4E **87**
Moorhouse. Surr .........5F **39**
Moorhouses. Linc .......5B **88**
Moorland. Som ..........3G **21**
Moorlinch. Som .........3H **21**
Moor Monkton. N Yor ....4H **99**
Moor of Granary. Mor ....3E **159**
Moor Row. Cumb
   nr. Whitehaven ......3B **102**
   nr. Wigton ..........5D **112**
Moorsholm. Red C .......3D **107**
Moorside. Dors .........1C **14**
Moorside. G Man .......4H **91**
Moortown. Devn .........3D **10**
Moortown. Hants ........2G **15**
Moortown. IOW ..........4C **16**
Moortown. Linc .........1H **87**
Moortown. Telf .........4A **72**
Moortown. W Yor ........1D **92**
Morangie. High .........5E **165**
Morar. High .............4E **147**
Morborne. Cambs .......1A **64**
Morchard Bishop. Devn ...2A **12**
Morcombelake. Dors .....3H **13**
Morcott. Rut ...........5G **75**
Morda. Shrp ............3E **71**
**Morden.** G Lon .........4D **38**
Mordiford. Here .........2A **48**
Mordon. Dur ...........2A **106**
More. Shrp .............1F **59**
Morebath. Devn .........4C **20**
Morebattle. Bord ........2B **120**
**Morecambe.** Lanc ......3D **96**
Morefield. High .........4F **163**
Moreleigh. Devn .........3D **9**
Morenish. Per ..........5C **142**
Moresby Parks. Cumb ...3A **102**
Morestead. Hants ........4D **24**
Moreton. Dors ..........4D **14**
Moreton. Essx ..........5F **53**
Moreton. Here ..........4H **59**

**Moreton.** Mers ........1E **83**
Moreton. Oxon ..........5E **51**
Moreton. Staf ..........4B **72**
Moreton Corbet. Shrp ...3H **71**
Moretonhampstead. Devn ...4A **12**
Moreton-in-Marsh. Glos ...2H **49**
Moreton Jeffries. Here ...1B **48**
Moreton on Lugg. Here ...1A **48**
Moreton Pinkney. Nptn ...1D **50**
Moreton Say. Shrp .......2A **72**
Moreton Valence. Glos ...5C **48**
Morfa. Cdgn ............5C **56**
Morfa Bach. Carm .......4D **44**
Morfa Bychan. Gwyn .....2E **69**
Morfa Glas. Neat ........5B **46**
Morfa Nefyn. Gwyn ......1B **68**
Morganstown. Card ......3E **33**
Morgan's Vale. Wilts .....4G **23**
Morham. E Lot ..........2B **130**
Moriah. Cdgn ...........3F **57**
Morland. Cumb ..........2G **103**
Morley. Ches E ..........2C **84**
Morley. Derbs ..........1A **74**
Morley. Dur ............2E **105**
**Morley.** W Yor .........2C **92**
Morley St Botolph. Norf ...1C **66**
Morningside. Edin .......2F **129**
Morningside. N Lan ......4B **128**
Morningthorpe. Norf .....1E **66**
**Morpeth.** Nmbd .......1F **115**
Morrey. Staf ...........4F **73**
Morridge Side. Staf ......5E **85**
Morridge Top. Staf .......4E **85**
Morrington. Dum ........1F **111**
Morris Green. Essx ......2H **53**
Morriston. Swan ........3F **31**
Morston. Norf ..........1C **78**
Mortehoe. Devn .........2E **19**
Morthen. S Yor .........2B **86**
Mortimer. W Ber ........5E **37**
Mortimer's Cross. Here ...4G **59**
Mortimer West End. Hants ...5E **37**
Mortomley. S Yor ........1H **85**
Morton. Cumb
   nr. Calthwaite ......1F **103**
   nr. Carlisle .........4E **113**
Morton. Derbs ..........4B **86**
Morton. Linc
   nr. Bourne .........3H **75**
   nr. Gainsborough ...1F **87**
   nr. Lincoln .........4F **87**
Morton. Norf ...........4D **78**
Morton. Notts ..........5E **87**
Morton. Shrp ...........3E **71**
Morton. S Glo ..........2B **34**
Morton Bagot. Warw .....4F **61**
Morton Mill. Shrp ........3H **71**
Morton-on-Swale. N Yor ...5A **106**
Morton Tinmouth. Dur ...2E **105**
Morvah. Corn ...........3B **4**
Morval. Corn ...........3G **7**
Morvich. High
   nr. Golspie .........3E **165**
   nr. Shiel Bridge .....1B **148**
Morvil. Pemb ...........1E **43**
Morville. Shrp ..........1A **60**
Morwenstow. Corn ......1C **10**
Morwick. Nmbd .........4G **121**
**Mosborough.** S Yor .....2B **86**
Moscow. E Ayr .........5F **127**
Mose. Shrp ............1B **60**
Mosedale. Cumb ........1E **103**
Moseley. W Mid
   nr. Birmingham ......2E **61**
   nr. Wolverhampton ...5D **72**
Moseley. Worc ..........5C **60**
Moss. Arg .............4A **138**
Moss. High .............2A **140**
Moss. S Yor ............3F **93**
Moss. Wrex ............5F **83**
Mossat. Abers ..........2B **152**
Moss Bank. Mers ........1H **83**
Mossbank. Shet ........4F **173**

Mossblown. S Ayr .......2D **116**
Mossbrow. G Man .......2B **84**
Mossburnford. Bord .....3A **120**
Mossdale. Dum .........2D **110**
Mossedge. Cumb ........3F **113**
Mossend. N Lan ........3A **128**
Mossgate. Staf .........2D **72**
Moss Lane. Ches E ......3D **84**
Mossley. Ches E .........4C **84**
**Mossley.** G Man ........4H **91**
Mossley Hill. Mers ......2F **83**
Moss of Barmuckity. Mor ...2G **159**
Mosspark. Glas .........3G **127**
Mosspaul. Bord ........5G **119**
Moss Side. Cumb ........4C **112**
Moss Side. G Man .......1C **84**
Moss Side. Lanc
   nr. Blackpool ........1B **90**
   nr. Preston .........2D **90**
Moss Side. Mers ........4B **90**
Moss-side. High .........3C **158**
Moss-side of Cairness.
   Abers .................2H **161**
Mosstodloch. Mor ......2H **159**
Mosswood. Nmbd .......4D **114**
Mossy Lea. Lanc ........3D **90**
Mosterton. Dors .........2H **13**
Moston. Shrp ...........3H **71**
Moston Green. Ches E ...4B **84**
Mostyn. Flin ...........2D **82**
Mostyn Quay. Flin .......2D **82**
Motcombe. Devn ........4C **8**
Motherby. Cumb ........2F **103**
**Motherwell.** N Lan ......4A **128**
Mottingham. G Lon ......3F **39**
Mottisfont. Hants .......4B **24**
Mottistone. IOW ........4C **16**
**Mottram in Longdendale.**
   G Man ...............1D **85**
Mottram St Andrew. Ches E ...3C **84**
Mott's Mill. E Sus ........2G **27**
Mouldsworth. Ches W ...3H **83**
Moulin. Per ............3G **143**
Moulsecoomb. Brig ......5E **27**
Moulsford. Oxon ........3D **36**
Moulsoe. Mil ...........1H **51**
Moulton. Ches W ........4A **84**
Moulton. Linc ..........3C **76**
Moulton. Nptn ..........4E **63**
Moulton. N Yor .........4F **105**
Moulton. Suff ..........4F **65**
Moulton. V Glam ........4D **32**
Moulton Chapel. Linc ....4B **76**
Moulton Eaugate. Linc ...4C **76**
Moulton St Mary. Norf ...5F **79**
Moulton Seas End. Linc ...3C **76**
Mount. Corn
   nr. Bodmin ..........2F **7**
   nr. Newquay ........3B **6**
**Mountain Ash.** Rhon ....2D **32**
Mountain Cross. Bord ...5E **129**
Mountain Street. Kent ...5E **41**
Mount Ambrose. Corn ....4B **6**
Mountbenger. Bord .....2F **119**
**Mountblow.** W Dun .....2F **127**
Mount Bures. Essx ......2C **54**
Mountfield. E Sus .......3B **28**
Mountgerald. High ......2H **157**
Mount Hawke. Corn ......4B **6**
Mount High. High ........2A **158**
Mountjoy. Corn .........2C **6**
Mount Lothian. Midl .....4F **129**
Mountnessing. Essx .....1H **39**
Mounton. Mon ..........2A **34**
Mount Pleasant. Buck ...2E **51**
Mount Pleasant. Ches E ...5C **84**
Mount Pleasant. Derbs
   nr. Derby ...........1H **73**
   nr. Swadlincote .....4G **73**
Mount Pleasant. E Sus ...4F **27**
Mount Pleasant. Hants ...3A **16**
Mount Pleasant. Norf ....1B **66**

Mount Skippett—Newbiggin


Mount Skippett. Oxon 4B 50
Mountsorrel. Leics 4C 74
Mount Stuart. Arg 4C 126
Mousehole. Corn 4B 4
Mouswald. Dum 2B 112
Mow Cop. Ches E 5C 84
Mowden. Darl 3F 105
Mowhaugh. Bord 2C 120
Mowmacre Hill. Leic 5C 74
Mowsley. Leics 2D 62
Moy. High 5B 158
Moy. M Ulst 5E 175
Moygashel. M Ulst 4E 175
Moylgrove. Pemb 1B 44
Moy Lodge. High 5G 149
Muasdale. Arg 5E 125
Muchalls. Abers 4G 153
Much Birch. Here 2A 48
Much Cowarne. Here 1B 48
Much Dewchurch. Here 2H 47
Muchelney. Som 4H 21
Muchelney Ham. Som 4H 21
Much Hadham. Herts 4E 53
Much Hoole. Lanc 2C 90
Muchlarnick. Corn 3G 7
Much Marcle. Here 2B 48
Muchrachd. High 5E 157
Much Wenlock. Shrp 5A 72
Mucking. Thur 2A 40
Muckle Breck. Shet 5G 173
Muckleford. Dors 3B 14
Mucklestone. Staf 2B 72
Muckleton. Norf 2H 77
Muckleton. Shrp 3H 71
Muckley. Shrp 1A 60
Muckley Corner. Staf 5E 73
Muckton. Linc 2C 88
Mudale. High 5F 167
Muddiford. Devn 3F 19
Mudeford. Dors 3G 15
Mudford. Som 1A 14
Mudgley. Som 2H 21
Mugdock. Stir 2G 127
Mugeary. High 5D 154
Muggington. Derbs 1G 73
Muggintonlane End. Derbs 1G 73
Muggleswick. Dur 4D 114
Mugswell. Surr 5D 38
Muie. High 3D 164
Muirden. Abers 3E 160
Muirdrum. Ang 5E 145
Muiredge. Per 1E 137
Muirend. Glas 3G 127
Muirhead. Ang 5C 144
Muirhead. Fife 3E 137
Muirhead. N Lan 3H 127
Muirhouses. Falk 1D 128
Muirkirk. E Ayr 2F 117
Muir of Alford. Abers 2C 152
Muir of Fairburn. High 3G 157
Muir of Fowlis. Abers 2C 152
Muir of Miltonduff. Mor 3F 159
Muir of Ord. High 3H 157
Muir of Tarradale. High 3H 157
Muirshearlich. High 5D 148
Muirtack. Abers 5G 161
Muirton. High 2B 158
Muirton. Per 1D 136
Muirton of Ardblair. Per 4A 144
Muirtown. Per 2B 136
Muiryfold. Abers 3E 161
Muker. N Yor 5C 104
Mulbarton. Norf 5D 78
Mulben. Mor 3A 160
Mulindry. Arg 4B 124
Mulla. Shet 5F 173
Mullach Charlabhaigh. W Isl 3E 171
Mullacott. Devn 2F 19
Mullion. Corn 5D 5
Mullion Cove. Corn 5D 4
Mumbles. Swan 4F 31
Mumby. Linc 3E 89
Munderfield Row. Here 5A 60
Munderfield Stocks. Here 5A 60
Mundesley. Norf 2F 79
Mundford. Norf 1H 65
Mundham. Norf 1F 67
Mundon. Essx 5B 54
Munerigie. High 3E 149
Muness. Shet 1H 173
Mungasdale. High 4D 162
Mungrisdale. Cumb 1E 103
Munlochy. High 3A 158
Munsley. Here 1B 48
Munslow. Shrp 2H 59
Murchington. Devn 4G 11
Murcot. Worc 1F 49
Murcott. Oxon 4D 50
Murdishaw. Hal 2H 83
Murieston. W Lot 3D 128
Murkle. High 2D 168
Murlaggan. High 4C 148
Murra. Orkn 7B 172
The Murray. S Lan 4H 127
Murrayfield. Edin 2F 129
Murrell Green. Hants 1F 25
Murroes. Ang 5D 144
Murrow. Cambs 5C 76
Mursley. Buck 3G 51
Murthly. Per 5H 143
Murton. Cumb 2A 104
Murton. Dur 5G 115
Murton. Nmbd 5F 131
Murton. Swan 4E 31
Murton. York 4A 100
Musbury. Devn 3F 13
Muscoates. N Yor 1A 100
Muscott. Nptn 4D 62
**Musselburgh**. E Lot 2G 129
Muston. Leics 2F 75
Muston. N Yor 2E 101
Mustow Green. Worc 3C 60
Muswell Hill. G Lon 2D 39
Mutehill. Dum 5D 111
Mutford. Suff 2G 67
Muthill. Per 2A 136
Mutterton. Devn 2D 12
Muxton. Telf 4B 72
Mwmbwls. Swan 4F 31
Mybster. High 3D 168
Myddfai. Carm 2A 46
Myddle. Shrp 3G 71
Mydroilyn. Cdgn 5D 56
Myerscough. Lanc 1C 90
Mylor Bridge. Corn 5C 6
Mylor Churchtown. Corn 5C 6
Mynachlog-ddu. Pemb 1F 43
Mynydd-bach. Mon 2H 33
Mynydd Isa. Flin 4E 83
Mynyddislwyn. Cphy 2E 33
Mynydd Llandegai. Gwyn 4F 81
Mynydd Mechell. IOA 1C 80
Mynydd-y-briw. Powy 3D 70
Mynyddygarreg. Carm 5E 45
Mynytho. Gwyn 2C 68
Myrebird. Abers 4E 153
Myrelandhorn. High 3E 169
Mytchett. Surr 1G 25
The Mythe. Glos 2D 49
Mytholmroyd. W Yor 2A 92
Myton-on-Swale. N Yor 3G 99
Mytton. Shrp 4G 71


## N


Naast. High 5C 162
Na Buirgh. W Isl 8C 171
Naburn. York 5H 99
Nab Wood. W Yor 1B 92
Nackington. Kent 5F 41
Nacton. Suff 1F 55
Nafferton. E Yor 4E 101
Na Gearrannan. W Isl 3D 171
Nailbridge. Glos 4B 48
Nailsbourne. Som 4F 21
**Nailsea**. N Som 4H 33
Nailstone. Leics 5B 74
Nailsworth. Glos 2D 34
Nairn. High 3C 158
Nalderswood. Surr 1D 26
Nancegollan. Corn 3D 4
Nancledra. Corn 3B 4
Nangreaves. G Man 3G 91
Nanhyfer. Pemb 1E 43
Nannerch. Flin 4D 82
Nanpantan. Leics 4C 74
Nanpean. Corn 3D 6
Nanstallon. Corn 2E 7
Nant-ddu. Powy 4D 46
Nanternis. Cdgn 5C 56
Nantgaredig. Carm 3E 45
Nantgarw. Rhon 3E 33
Nant Glas. Powy 4B 58
Nantglyn. Den 4C 82
Nantgwyn. Powy 3B 58
Nantlle. Gwyn 5E 81
Nantmawr. Shrp 3E 71
Nantmel. Powy 4C 58
Nantmor. Gwyn 1F 69
Nant Peris. Gwyn 5F 81
**Nantwich**. Ches E 5A 84
Nant-y-bai. Carm 1A 46
Nant-y-bwch. Blae 4E 47
Nant-y-Derry. Mon 5G 47
Nant-y-dugoed. Powy 4B 70
Nant-y-felin. Cnwy 3F 81
Nantyffyllon. B'end 2B 32
Nantyglo. Blae 4E 47
Nant-y-meichiaid. Powy 4D 70
Nant-y-moel. B'end 2C 32
Nant-y-pandy. Cnwy 3F 81
Naphill. Buck 2G 37
Nappa. N Yor 4A 98
Napton on the Hill. Warw 4B 62
Narberth. Pemb 3F 43
Narberth Bridge. Pemb 3F 43
Narborough. Leics 1C 62
Narborough. Norf 4G 77
Narkurs. Corn 3H 7
The Narth. Mon 5A 48
Narthwaite. Cumb 5A 104
Nasareth. Gwyn 5D 80
Naseby. Nptn 3D 62
Nash. Buck 2F 51
Nash. Here 4F 59
Nash. Kent 5G 41
Nash. Newp 3G 33
Nash. Shrp 3A 60
Nash Lee. Buck 5G 51
Nassington. Nptn 1H 63
Nasty. Herts 3D 52
Natcott. Devn 4C 18
Nateby. Cumb 4A 104
Nateby. Lanc 5D 96
Nately Scures. Hants 1F 25
Natland. Cumb 1E 97
Naughton. Suff 1D 54
Naunton. Glos 3G 49
Naunton. Worc 2D 49
Naunton Beauchamp. Worc 5D 60
Navenby. Linc 5G 87
Navestock. Essx 1G 39
Navestock Side. Essx 1G 39
Navidale. High 2H 165
Nawton. N Yor 1A 100
Nayland. Suff 2C 54
Nazeing. Essx 5E 53
Neacroft. Hants 3G 15
Nealhouse. Cumb 4E 113
Neal's Green. Warw 2H 61
Near Sawrey. Cumb 5E 103
Neasden. G Lon 2D 38
Neasham. Darl 3A 106
**Neath**. Neat 2A 32
Neath Abbey. Neat 3G 31
Neatishead. Norf 3F 79
Neaton. Norf 5B 78
Nebo. Cdgn 4E 57
Nebo. Cnwy 5H 81
Nebo. Gwyn 5D 81
Nebo. IOA 1D 80
Necton. Norf 5A 78
Nedd. High 5B 166
Nedderton. Nmbd 1F 115
Nedging. Suff 1D 54
Nedging Tye. Suff 1D 54
Needham. Norf 2E 67
Needham Market. Suff 5C 66
Needham Street. Suff 4G 65
Needingworth. Cambs 3C 64
Needwood. Staf 3F 73
Neen Savage. Shrp 3A 60
Neen Sollars. Shrp 3A 60
Neenton. Shrp 2A 60
Nefyn. Gwyn 1C 68
Neilston. E Ren 4F 127
Neithrop. Oxon 1C 50
Nelly Andrews Green. Powy 5E 71
Nelson. Cphy 2E 32
**Nelson**. Lanc 1G 91
Nelson Village. Nmbd 2F 115
Nemphlar. S Lan 5B 128
Nempnett Thrubwell. Bath 5A 34
Nene Terrace. Linc 5B 76
Nenthall. Cumb 5A 114
Nenthead. Cumb 5A 114
Nenthorn. Bord 1A 120
Nercwys. Flin 4E 83
Neribus. Arg 4A 124
Nerston. S Lan 4H 127
Nesbit. Nmbd 1D 121
Nesfield. N Yor 5C 98
Ness. Ches W 3F 83
Nesscliffe. Shrp 4F 71
Ness of Tenston. Orkn 6B 172
**Neston**. Ches W 3E 83
Neston. Wilts 5D 34
Nethanfoot. S Lan 5B 128
Nether Alderley. Ches E 3C 84
Netheravon. Wilts 2G 23
Nether Blainslie. Bord 5B 130
Netherbrae. Abers 3E 161
Netherbrough. Orkn 6C 172
Nether Broughton. Leics 3D 74
Netherburn. S Lan 5B 128
Nether Burrow. Lanc 2F 97
Netherbury. Dors 3H 13
Netherby. Cumb 2E 113
Nether Careston. Ang 3E 145
Nether Cerne. Dors 3B 14
Nether Compton. Dors 1A 14
Nethercote. Glos 3G 49
Nethercote. Warw 4C 62
Nethercott. Devn 3E 19
Nethercott. Oxon 3C 50
Nether Dallachy. Mor 2A 160
Nether Durdie. Per 1E 136
Nether End. Derbs 3G 85
Netherend. Glos 5A 48
Nether Exe. Devn 2C 12
Netherfield. E Sus 4B 28
Netherfield. Notts 1D 74
Nethergate. Norf 3C 78
Netherhampton. Wilts 4G 23
Nether Handley. Derbs 3B 86
Nether Haugh. S Yor 1B 86
Nether Heage. Derbs 5A 86
Nether Heyford. Nptn 5D 62
Netherhouses. Cumb 1B 96
Nether Howcleugh. S Lan 3C 118
Nether Kellet. Lanc 3E 97
Nether Kinmundy. Abers 4H 161
Netherland Green. Staf 2F 73
Nether Langwith. Notts 3C 86
Netherlaw. Dum 5E 111
Netherley. Abers 4F 153
Nethermill. Dum 1B 112
Nethermills. Mor 3C 160
Nether Moor. Derbs 4A 86
Nether Padley. Derbs 3G 85
Netherplace. E Ren 4G 127
Nether Poppleton. York 4H 99
Netherseal. Derbs 4G 73
Nether Silton. N Yor 5B 106
Nether Stowey. Som 3E 21
Nether Street. Essx 4F 53
Netherstreet. Wilts 5E 35
Netherthird. E Ayr 3E 117
Netherthong. W Yor 4B 92
Netherton. Ang 3E 145
Netherton. Cumb 1B 102
Netherton. Devn 5B 12
Netherton. Hants 1B 24
Netherton. Here 3A 48
Netherton. Mers 1F 83
Netherton. N Lan 4A 128
Netherton. Nmbd 4D 121
Netherton. Per 3A 144
Netherton. Shrp 2B 60
Netherton. Stir 2G 127
Netherton. W Mid 2D 60
Netherton. W Yor
nr. Armitage Bridge 3B 92
nr. Horbury 3C 92
Netherton. Worc 1E 49
Nethertown. Cumb 4A 102
Nethertown. High 1F 169
Nethertown. Staf 4F 73
Nether Urquhart. Fife 3D 136
Nether Wallop. Hants 3B 24
Nether Wasdale. Cumb 4C 102
Nether Welton. Cumb 5E 113
Nether Westcote. Glos 3H 49
Nether Whitacre. Warw 1G 61
Nether Winchendon. Buck 4F 51
Netherwitton. Nmbd 5F 121
Nether Worton. Oxon 2C 50
Nethy Bridge. High 1E 151
Netley. Shrp 5G 71
Netley Abbey. Hants 2C 16
Netley Marsh. Hants 1B 16
Nettlebed. Oxon 3F 37
Nettlebridge. Som 2B 22
Nettlecombe. Dors 3A 14
Nettlecombe. IOW 5D 16
Nettleden. Herts 4A 52
Nettleham. Linc 3H 87
Nettlestead. Kent 5A 40
Nettlestead Green. Kent 5A 40
Nettlestone. IOW 3E 16
Nettlesworth. Dur 5F 115
Nettleton. Linc 4E 94
Nettleton. Wilts 4D 34
Netton. Devn 4B 8
Netton. Wilts 3G 23
Neuadd. Powy 5C 70
The Neuk. Abers 4E 153
Nevendon. Essx 1B 40
Nevern. Pemb 1E 43
New Abbey. Dum 3A 112
New Aberdour. Abers 2F 161
**New Addington**. G Lon 4E 39
Newall. W Yor 5E 98
New Alresford. Hants 3D 24
New Alyth. Per 4B 144
Newark. Orkn 3G 172
Newark. Pet 5B 76
**Newark-on-Trent**. Notts 5E 87
New Arley. Warw 2G 61
Newarthill. N Lan 4A 128
New Ash Green. Kent 4H 39
New Balderton. Notts 5F 87
New Barn. Kent 4H 39
New Barnetby. N Lin 3D 94
Newbattle. Midl 3G 129
New Bewick. Nmbd 2E 121
Newbie. Dum 3C 112
Newbiggin. Cumb
nr. Appleby 2H 103
nr. Barrow-in-Furness 3B 96
nr. Cumrew 5G 113
nr. Penrith 2F 103
nr. Seascale 5B 102
Newbiggin. Dur
nr. Consett 5E 115
nr. Holwick 2C 104
Newbiggin. Nmbd 5C 114

Newbiggin—Newtown

Newbiggin. *N Yor*
nr. Askrigg 5C 104
nr. Filey 1F 101
nr. Thoralby 1B 98
Newbiggin-by-the-Sea. *Nmbd* 1G 115
Newbigging. *Ang*
nr. Monikie 5D 145
nr. Newtyle 4B 144
nr. Tealing 5D 144
Newbigging. *Edin* 2E 129
Newbigging. *S Lan* 5D 128
Newbiggin-on-Lune. *Cumb* 4A 104
Newbold. *Derbs* 3A 86
Newbold. *Leics* 4B 74
Newbold on Avon. *Warw* 3B 62
Newbold on Stour. *Warw* 1H 49
Newbold Pacey. *Warw* 5G 61
Newbold Verdon. *Leics* 5B 74
New Bolingbroke. *Linc* 5C 88
Newborough. *IOA* 4D 80
Newborough. *Pet* 5B 76
Newborough. *Staf* 3F 73
Newbottle. *Nptn* 2D 50
Newbottle. *Tyne* 4G 115
New Boultham. *Linc* 3G 87
Newbourne. *Suff* 1F 55
New Brancepeth. *Dur* 5F 115
New Bridge. *Dum* 2G 111
Newbridge. *Cphy* 2F 33
Newbridge. *Cdgn* 5E 57
Newbridge. *Corn* 3B 4
Newbridge. *Edin* 2E 129
Newbridge. *Hants* 1A 16
Newbridge. *IOW* 4C 16
Newbridge. *N Yor* 1C 100
Newbridge. *Pemb* 1D 42
Newbridge. *Wrex* 1E 71
Newbridge Green. *Worc* 2D 48
Newbridge-on-Usk. *Mon* 2G 33
Newbridge on Wye. *Powy* 5C 58
New Brighton. *Flin* 4E 83
New Brighton. *Hants* 2F 17
New Brighton. *Mers* 1F 83
New Brinsley. *Notts* 5B 86
Newbrough. *Nmbd* 3B 114
New Broughton. *Wrex* 5F 83
New Buckenham. *Norf* 1C 66
New Buildings. *Derr* 2C 174
Newbuildings. *Devn* 2A 12
Newburgh. *Abers* 1G 153
Newburgh. *Fife* 2E 137
Newburgh. *Lanc* 3C 90
**Newburn**. *Tyne* 3E 115
**Newbury**. *W Ber* 5C 36
Newbury. *Wilts* 2D 22
Newby. *Cumb* 2G 103
Newby. *N Yor*
nr. Ingleton 2G 97
nr. Scarborough 1E 101
nr. Stokesley 3C 106
Newby Bridge. *Cumb* 1C 96
Newby Cote. *N Yor* 2G 97
Newby East. *Cumb* 4F 113
Newby Head. *Cumb* 2G 103
New Byth. *Abers* 3F 161
Newby West. *Cumb* 4E 113
Newby Wiske. *N Yor* 1F 99
Newcastle. *B'end* 3B 32
Newcastle. *Mon* 4H 47
Newcastle. *New M* 6H 175
Newcastle. *Shrp* 2E 59
Newcastle Emlyn. *Carm* 1D 44
Newcastle International Airport. *Tyne* 2E 115
Newcastleton. *Bord* 1F 113
**Newcastle-under-Lyme**. *Staf* 1C 72
**Newcastle upon Tyne**. *Tyne* 3F 115
Newchapel. *Pemb* 1G 43
Newchapel. *Powy* 2B 58
Newchapel. *Staf* 5C 84
Newchapel. *Surr* 1E 27
New Cheriton. *Hants* 4D 24
Newchurch. *Carm* 3D 45
Newchurch. *Here* 5F 59
Newchurch. *IOW* 4D 16
Newchurch. *Kent* 2E 29
Newchurch. *Lanc* 2G 91
Newchurch. *Mon* 2H 33
Newchurch. *Powy* 5E 58
Newchurch. *Staf* 3F 73
Newchurch in Pendle. *Lanc* 1G 91
New Costessey. *Norf* 4D 78
Newcott. *Devn* 2F 13
New Cowper. *Cumb* 5C 112
Newcraighall. *Edin* 2G 129
New Crofton. *W Yor* 3D 93
New Cross. *Cdgn* 3F 57
New Cross. *Som* 1H 13
New Cumnock. *E Ayr* 3F 117
New Deer. *Abers* 4F 161
New Denham. *Buck* 2B 38
Newdigate. *Surr* 1C 26
New Duston. *Nptn* 4E 62
New Earswick. *York* 4A 100
New Edlington. *S Yor* 1C 86
New Elgin. *Mor* 2G 159
New Ellerby. *E Yor* 1E 95
Newell Green. *Brac* 4G 37
New Eltham. *G Lon* 3F 39
New End. *Warw* 4F 61
New End. *Worc* 5E 61
Newenden. *Kent* 3C 28
New England. *Essx* 1H 53
New England. *Pet* 5A 76
Newent. *Glos* 3C 48
New Ferry. *Mers* 2F 83
Newfield. *Dur*
nr. Chester-le-Street 4F 115
nr. Willington 1F 105
Newfound. *Hants* 1D 24
New Fryston. *W Yor* 2E 93
Newgale. *Pemb* 2C 42
New Galloway. *Dum* 2D 110
Newgate. *Norf* 1C 78
Newgate Street. *Herts* 5D 52
New Greens. *Herts* 5B 52
New Grimsby. *IOS* 1A 4
New Hainford. *Norf* 4E 78
Newhall. *Ches E* 1A 72
Newhall. *Derbs* 3G 73
Newham. *Nmbd* 2F 121
New Hartley. *Nmbd* 2G 115
Newhaven. *Derbs* 4F 85
**Newhaven**. *E Sus* 5F 27
Newhaven. *Edin* 2F 129
New Haw. *Surr* 4B 38
New Hedges. *Pemb* 4F 43
New Herrington. *Tyne* 4G 115
Newhey. *G Man* 3H 91
New Holkham. *Norf* 2A 78
New Holland. *N Lin* 2D 94
Newholm. *N Yor* 3F 107
New Houghton. *Derbs* 4C 86
New Houghton. *Norf* 3G 77
Newhouse. *N Lan* 3A 128
New Houses. *N Yor* 2H 97
New Hutton. *Cumb* 5G 103
New Hythe. *Kent* 5B 40
Newick. *E Sus* 3F 27
Newingreen. *Kent* 2F 29
Newington. *Edin* 2F 129
Newington. *Kent*
nr. Folkestone 2F 29
nr. Sittingbourne 4C 40
Newington. *Notts* 1D 86
Newington. *Oxon* 2E 36
Newington Bagpath. *Glos* 2D 34
New Inn. *Carm* 2E 45
New Inn. *Mon* 5H 47
New Inn. *N Yor* 2H 97
New Inn. *Torf* 2G 33
New Invention. *Shrp* 3E 59
New Kelso. *High* 4B 156
New Lanark. *S Lan* 5B 128
Newland. *Glos* 5A 48
Newland. *Hull* 1D 94
Newland. *N Yor* 2G 93
Newland. *Som* 3B 20
Newland. *Worc* 1C 48
Newlandrig. *Midl* 3G 129
Newlands. *Cumb* 1E 103
Newlands. *High* 4B 158
Newlands. *Nmbd* 4D 115
Newlands. *Staf* 3E 73
Newlands of Geise. *High* 2C 168
Newlands of Tynet. *Mor* 2A 160
Newlands Park. *IOA* 2B 80
New Lane. *Lanc* 3C 90
New Lane End. *Warr* 1A 84
New Langholm. *Dum* 1E 113
New Leake. *Linc* 5D 88
New Leeds. *Abers* 3G 161
New Lenton. *Nott* 2C 74
New Longton. *Lanc* 2D 90
Newlot. *Orkn* 6E 172
New Luce. *Dum* 3G 109
Newlyn. *Corn* 4B 4
Newmachar. *Abers* 2F 153
Newmains. *N Lan* 4B 128
New Mains of Ury. *Abers* 5F 153
**New Malden**. *G Lon* 4D 38
Newman's Green. *Suff* 1B 54
**Newmarket**. *Suff* 4F 65
Newmarket. *W Isl* 4G 171
New Marske. *Red C* 2D 106
New Marton. *Shrp* 2F 71
New Micklefield. *W Yor* 1E 93
New Mill. *Abers* 4E 160
New Mill. *Corn* 3B 4
New Mill. *Herts* 4H 51
New Mill. *W Yor* 4B 92
New Mill. *Wilts* 5G 35
Newmill. *Mor* 3B 160
Newmill. *Bord* 3G 119
Newmillerdam. *W Yor* 3D 92
New Mills. *Corn* 3C 6
New Mills. *Derbs* 2E 85
New Mills. *Mon* 5A 48
New Mills. *Powy* 5C 70
Newmills. *Fife* 1D 128
Newmills. *High* 2A 158
Newmiln. *Per* 5A 144
Newmilns. *E Ayr* 1E 117
**New Milton**. *Hants* 3H 15
New Mistley. *Essx* 2E 54
New Moat. *Pemb* 2E 43
Newmore. *High*
nr. Dingwall 3H 157
nr. Invergordon 1A 158
Newnham. *Cambs* 5D 64
Newnham. *Glos* 4B 48
Newnham. *Hants* 1F 25
Newnham. *Herts* 2C 52
Newnham. *Kent* 5D 40
Newnham. *Nptn* 5C 62
Newnham. *Warw* 4F 61
Newnham Bridge. *Worc* 4A 60
New Ollerton. *Notts* 4D 86
New Oscott. *W Mid* 1E 61
New Park. *N Yor* 4E 99
Newpark. *Fife* 2G 137
New Pitsligo. *Abers* 3F 161
New Polzeath. *Corn* 1D 6
Newport. *Corn* 4D 10
Newport. *Devn* 3F 19
Newport. *E Yor* 1B 94
Newport. *Essx* 2F 53
Newport. *Glos* 2B 34
Newport. *High* 1H 165
**Newport**. *IOW* 4D 16
**Newport**. *Newp* 3G 33
Newport. *Norf* 4H 79
Newport. *Pemb* 1E 43
Newport. *Som* 4G 21
**Newport**. *Telf* 4B 72
Newport-on-Tay. *Fife* 1G 137
**Newport Pagnell**. *Mil* 1G 51
Newpound Common. *W Sus* 3B 26
New Prestwick. *S Ayr* 2C 116
New Quay. *Cdgn* 5C 56
**Newquay**. *Corn* 2C 6
Newquay Cornwall Airport. *Corn* 2C 6
New Rackheath. *Norf* 4E 79
New Radnor. *Powy* 4E 58
New Rent. *Cumb* 1F 103
New Ridley. *Nmbd* 4D 114
New Romney. *Kent* 3E 29
**New Rossington**. *S Yor* 1D 86
New Row. *Cdgn* 3G 57
**Newry**. *New M* 6F 175
New Sauchie. *Clac* 4A 136
Newsbank. *Ches E* 4C 84
Newseat. *Abers* 5E 160
Newsham. *Lanc* 1D 90
Newsham. *Nmbd* 2G 115
Newsham. *N Yor*
nr. Richmond 3E 105
nr. Thirsk 1F 99
New Sharlston. *W Yor* 2D 93
Newsholme. *E Yor* 2H 93
Newsholme. *Lanc* 4H 97
New Shoreston. *Nmbd* 1F 121
New Springs. *G Man* 4D 90
Newstead. *Notts* 5C 86
Newstead. *Bord* 1H 119
New Stevenston. *N Lan* 4A 128
New Street. *Here* 5F 59
Newstreet Lane. *Shrp* 2A 72
New Swanage. *Dors* 4F 15
New Swannington. *Leics* 4B 74
Newthorpe. *N Yor* 1E 93
Newthorpe. *Notts* 1B 74
Newton. *Arg* 4H 133
Newton. *B'end* 4B 32
Newton. *Cambs*
nr. Cambridge 1E 53
nr. Wisbech 4D 76
Newton. *Ches W*
nr. Chester 4G 83
nr. Tattenhall 5H 83
Newton. *Cumb* 2B 96
Newton. *Derbs* 5B 86
Newton. *Dors* 1C 14
Newton. *Dum*
nr. Annan 2D 112
nr. Moffat 5D 118
Newton. *G Man* 1D 84
Newton. *Here*
nr. Ewyas Harold 2G 47
nr. Leominster 5H 59
Newton. *High*
nr. Cromarty 2B 158
nr. Inverness 4B 158
nr. Kylestrome 5C 166
nr. Wick 4F 169
Newton. *Lanc*
nr. Blackpool 1B 90
nr. Carnforth 2E 97
nr. Clitheroe 4F 97
Newton. *Linc* 2H 75
Newton. *Mers* 2E 83
Newton. *Mor* 2F 159
Newton. *Norf* 4H 77
Newton. *Nptn* 2F 63
Newton. *Nmbd* 3D 114
Newton. *Notts* 1D 74
Newton. *Bord* 2A 120
Newton. *Shet* 8E 173
Newton. *Shrp*
nr. Bridgnorth 1B 60
nr. Wem 2G 71
Newton. *Som* 3E 20
Newton. *S Lan*
nr. Glasgow 3H 127
nr. Lanark 1B 118
Newton. *Staf* 3E 73
Newton. *Suff* 1C 54
Newton. *Swan* 4F 31
Newton. *Warw* 3C 62
Newton. *W Lot* 2D 129
Newton. *Wilts* 4H 23
**Newton Abbot**. *Devn* 5B 12
Newtonairds. *Dum* 1F 111
Newton Arlosh. *Cumb* 4D 112
**Newton Aycliffe**. *Dur* 2F 105
Newton Bewley. *Hart* 2B 106
Newton Blossomville. *Mil* 5G 63
Newton Bromswold. *Nptn* 4G 63
Newton Burgoland. *Leics* 5A 74
Newton by Toft. *Linc* 2H 87
Newton Ferrers. *Devn* 4B 8
Newton Flotman. *Norf* 1E 66
Newtongrange. *Midl* 3G 129
Newton Green. *Mon* 2A 34
Newton Hall. *Dur* 5F 115
Newton Hall. *Nmbd* 3D 114
Newton Harcourt. *Leics* 1D 62
Newton Heath. *G Man* 4G 91
Newton Hill. *W Yor* 2D 92
Newtonhill. *Abers* 4G 153
Newtonhill. *High* 4H 157
Newton Ketton. *Darl* 2A 106
Newton Kyme. *N Yor* 5G 99
**Newton-le-Willows**. *Mers* 1H 83
Newton-le-Willows. *N Yor* 1E 98
Newton Longville. *Buck* 2G 51
**Newton Mearns**. *E Ren* 4G 127
Newtonmore. *High* 4B 150
Newton Morrell. *N Yor* 4F 105
Newton Mulgrave. *N Yor* 3E 107
Newton of Ardtoe. *High* 1A 140
Newton of Balcanquhal. *Per* 2D 136
Newton of Beltrees. *Ren* 4E 127
Newton of Falkland. *Fife* 3E 137
Newton of Mountblairy. *Abers* 3D 160
Newton of Pitcairns. *Per* 2C 136
Newton-on-Ouse. *N Yor* 4H 99
Newton-on-Rawcliffe. *N Yor* 5F 107
Newton on the Hill. *Shrp* 3G 71
Newton-on-the-Moor. *Nmbd* 4F 121
Newton on Trent. *Linc* 3F 87
Newton Poppleford. *Devn* 4D 12
Newton Purcell. *Oxon* 2E 51
Newton Regis. *Warw* 5G 73
Newton Reigny. *Cumb* 1F 103
Newton Rigg. *Cumb* 1F 103
Newton St Cyres. *Devn* 3B 12
Newton St Faith. *Norf* 4E 78
Newton St Loe. *Bath* 5C 34
Newton St Petrock. *Devn* 1E 11
Newton Solney. *Derbs* 3G 73
Newton Stacey. *Hants* 2C 24
Newton Stewart. *Dum* 3B 110
Newton Toney. *Wilts* 2H 23
Newton Tony. *Wilts* 2H 23
Newton Tracey. *Devn* 4F 19
Newton under Roseberry. *Red C* 3C 106
Newton upon Ayr. *S Ayr* 2C 116
Newton upon Derwent. *E Yor* 5B 100
Newton Valence. *Hants* 3F 25
Newton-with-Scales. *Lanc* 1C 90
New Town. *Dors* 1E 15
New Town. *E Lot* 2H 129
New Town. *Lutn* 3A 52
New Town. *W Yor* 2E 93
Newtown. *Abers* 2E 160
Newtown. *Cambs* 4H 63
Newtown. *Corn* 5C 10
Newtown. *Cumb*
nr. Aspatria 5B 112
nr. Brampton 3G 113
nr. Penrith 2G 103
Newtown. *Derbs* 2D 85
Newtown. *Devn* 4A 20
Newtown. *Dors* 2H 13
Newtown. *Falk* 1C 128
Newtown. *Glos*
nr. Lydney 5B 48
nr. Tewkesbury 2E 49

Newtown—Norton


Newtown. *Hants*
nr. Bishop's Waltham 1D **16**
nr. Liphook 3G **25**
nr. Lyndhurst 1A **16**
nr. Newbury 5C **36**
nr. Romsey 4B **24**
nr. Warsash 2C **16**
nr. Wickham 1E **16**
Newtown. *Here*
nr. Little Dewchurch 2A **48**
nr. Stretton Grandison 1B **48**
Newtown. *High* 3F **149**
Newtown. *IOM* 4C **108**
Newtown. *IOW* 3C **16**
Newtown. *Lanc* 3D **90**
Newtown. *Nmbd*
nr. Rothbury 4E **121**
nr. Wooler 2E **121**
Newtown. *Pool* 3F **15**
**Newtown**. *Powy* 1D **58**
Newtown. *Rhon* 2D **32**
Newtown. *Shet* 3F **173**
Newtown. *Shrp* 2G **71**
Newtown. *Som* 1F **13**
Newtown. *Staf*
nr. Biddulph 4D **84**
nr. Cannock 5D **73**
nr. Longnor 4E **85**
Newtown. *Wilts* 4E **23**
**Newtownabbey**. *Ant* 3H **175**
**Newtownards**. *Ards* 4H **175**
Newtown-in-St Martin. *Corn* 4E **5**
Newtown Linford. *Leics* 5C **74**
Newtown St Boswells. *Bord* 1H **119**
Newtownstewart. *Derr* 3C **174**
Newtown Unthank. *Leics* 5B **74**
New Tredegar. *Cphy* 5E **47**
Newtyle. *Ang* 4B **144**
New Village. *E Yor* 1D **94**
New Village. *S Yor* 4F **93**
New Walsoken. *Cambs* 5D **76**
New Waltham. *NE Lin* 4F **95**
New Winton. *E Lot* 2H **129**
New World. *Cambs* 1C **64**
New Yatt. *Oxon* 4B **50**
Newyears Green. *G Lon* 2B **38**
New York. *Linc* 5B **88**
New York. *Tyne* 2G **115**
Nextend. *Here* 5F **59**
Neyland. *Pemb* 4D **42**
Nib Heath. *Shrp* 4G **71**
Nicholashayne. *Devn* 1E **12**
Nicholaston. *Swan* 4E **31**
Nidd. *N Yor* 3F **99**
Niddrie. *Edin* 2G **129**
Niddry. *W Lot* 2D **129**
Nigg. *Aber* 3G **153**
Nigg. *High* 1C **158**
Nigg Ferry. *High* 2B **158**
Nightcott. *Som* 4B **20**
Nimmer. *Som* 1G **13**
Nine Ashes. *Essx* 5F **53**
Ninebanks. *Nmbd* 4A **114**
Nine Elms. *Swin* 3G **35**
Ninemile Bar. *Dum* 2F **111**
Nine Mile Burn. *Midl* 4E **129**
Ninfield. *E Sus* 4B **28**
Ningwood. *IOW* 4C **16**
Nisbet. *Bord* 2A **120**
Nisbet Hill. *Bord* 4D **130**
Niton. *IOW* 5D **16**
Nitshill. *Glas* 3G **127**
Niwbwrch. *IOA* 4D **80**
Noak Hill. *G Lon* 1G **39**
Nobold. *Shrp* 4G **71**
Nobottle. *Nptn* 4D **62**
Nocton. *Linc* 4H **87**
Nogdam End. *Norf* 5F **79**
Noke. *Oxon* 4D **50**
Nolton. *Pemb* 3C **42**
Nolton Haven. *Pemb* 3C **42**
No Man's Heath. *Ches W* 1H **71**
No Man's Heath. *Warw* 5G **73**
Nomansland. *Devn* 1B **12**
Nomansland. *Wilts* 1A **16**
Noneley. *Shrp* 3G **71**
Noness. *Shet* 9F **173**
Nonikiln. *High* 1A **158**
Nonington. *Kent* 5G **41**
Nook. *Cumb*
nr. Longtown 2F **113**
nr. Milnthorpe 1E **97**
Noranside. *Ang* 2D **144**
Norbreck. *Bkpl* 5C **96**
Norbridge. *Here* 1C **48**
Norbury. *Ches E* 1H **71**
Norbury. *Derbs* 1F **73**
Norbury. *Shrp* 1F **59**
Norbury. *Staf* 3B **72**
Norby. *N Yor* 1G **99**
Norby. *Shet* 6C **173**
Norcross. *Lanc* 5C **96**
Nordelph. *Norf* 5E **77**
Norden. *G Man* 3G **91**
Nordley. *Shrp* 1A **60**
Norham. *Nmbd* 5F **131**
Norland Town. *W Yor* 2A **92**
Norley. *Ches W* 3H **83**
Norleywood. *Hants* 3B **16**
Normanby. *N Lin* 3B **94**
Normanby. *N Yor* 1B **100**
Normanby. *Red C* 3C **106**
Normanby-by-Spital. *Linc* 2H **87**
Normanby le Wold. *Linc* 1A **88**
Norman Cross. *Cambs* 1A **64**
Normandy. *Surr* 5A **38**
Norman's Bay. *E Sus* 5A **28**
Norman's Green. *Devn* 2D **12**
Normanton. *Derb* 2H **73**
Normanton. *Leics* 1F **75**
Normanton. *Notts* 5E **86**
**Normanton**. *W Yor* 2D **93**
Normanton le Heath. *Leics* 4A **74**
Normanton-on-Cliffe. *Linc* 1G **75**
Normanton on Soar. *Notts* 3C **74**
Normanton-on-the-Wolds. *Notts* 2D **74**
Normanton on Trent. *Notts* 4E **87**
Normoss. *Lanc* 1B **90**
Norrington Common. *Wilts* 5D **35**
Norris Green. *Mers* 1F **83**
Norris Hill. *Leics* 4H **73**
Norristhorpe. *W Yor* 2C **92**
Northacre. *Norf* 1B **66**
Northall. *Buck* 3H **51**
**Northallerton**. *N Yor* 5A **106**
Northam. *Devn* 4E **19**
Northam. *Sotn* 1C **16**
**Northampton**. *Nptn* 4E **63**
North Anston. *S Yor* 2C **86**
North Ascot. *Brac* 4A **38**
North Aston. *Oxon* 3C **50**
Northaw. *Herts* 5C **52**
Northay. *Som* 1F **13**
North Baddesley. *Hants* 4B **24**
North Balfern. *Dum* 4B **110**
North Ballachulish. *High* 2E **141**
North Barrow. *Som* 4B **22**
North Barsham. *Norf* 2B **78**
Northbeck. *Linc* 1H **75**
North Benfleet. *Essx* 2B **40**
North Bersted. *W Sus* 5A **26**
North Berwick. *E Lot* 1B **130**
North Bitchburn. *Dur* 1E **105**
North Blyth. *Nmbd* 1G **115**
North Boarhunt. *Hants* 1E **16**
North Bockhampton. *Dors* 3G **15**
Northborough. *Pet* 5A **76**
Northbourne. *Kent* 5H **41**
Northbourne. *Oxon* 3D **36**
North Bovey. *Devn* 4H **11**
North Bowood. *Dors* 3H **13**
North Bradley. *Wilts* 1D **22**
North Brentor. *Devn* 4E **11**
North Brewham. *Som* 3C **22**
Northbrook. *Oxon* 3C **50**
North Brook End. *Cambs* 1C **52**
North Broomhill. *Nmbd* 4G **121**
North Buckland. *Devn* 2E **19**
North Burlingham. *Norf* 4F **79**
North Cadbury. *Som* 4B **22**
North Carlton. *Linc* 3G **87**
North Cave. *E Yor* 1B **94**
North Cerney. *Glos* 5F **49**
North Chailey. *E Sus* 3E **27**
Northchapel. *W Sus* 3A **26**
North Charford. *Hants* 1G **15**
North Charlton. *Nmbd* 2F **121**
North Cheriton. *Som* 4B **22**
North Chideock. *Dors* 3H **13**
Northchurch. *Herts* 5H **51**
North Cliffe. *E Yor* 1B **94**
North Clifton. *Notts* 3F **87**
North Close. *Dur* 1F **105**
North Cockerington. *Linc* 1C **88**
North Coker. *Som* 1A **14**
North Collafirth. *Shet* 3E **173**
North Common. *E Sus* 3E **27**
North Commonty. *Abers* 4F **161**
North Coombe. *Devn* 1B **12**
North Cornelly. *B'end* 3B **32**
North Cotes. *Linc* 4G **95**
Northcott. *Devn*
nr. Boyton 3D **10**
nr. Culmstock 1D **12**
Northcourt. *Oxon* 2D **36**
North Cove. *Suff* 2G **67**
North Cowton. *N Yor* 4F **105**
North Craigo. *Ang* 2F **145**
North Crawley. *Mil* 1H **51**
North Cray. *G Lon* 3F **39**
North Creake. *Norf* 2A **78**
North Curry. *Som* 4G **21**
North Dalton. *E Yor* 4D **100**
North Deighton. *N Yor* 4F **99**
North Dronley. *Ang* 5C **144**
North Duffield. *N Yor* 1G **93**
Northdyke. *Orkn* 5B **172**
Northedge. *Derbs* 4A **86**
North Elkington. *Linc* 1B **88**
North Elmham. *Norf* 3B **78**
North Elmsall. *W Yor* 3E **93**
North End. *E Yor* 1F **95**
North End. *Essx*
nr. Great Dunmow 4G **53**
nr. Great Yeldham 2A **54**
North End. *Hants* 5C **36**
North End. *Leics* 4C **74**
North End. *Linc* 1B **76**
North End. *Norf* 1B **66**
North End. *N Som* 5H **33**
North End. *Port* 2E **17**
North End. *W Sus* 5C **26**
North End. *Wilts* 2F **35**
Northend. *Buck* 2F **37**
Northend. *Warw* 5A **62**
North Erradale. *High* 5B **162**
North Evington. *Leic* 5D **74**
North Fambridge. *Essx* 1C **40**
North Fearns. *High* 5E **155**
North Featherstone. *W Yor* 2E **93**
North Feorline. *N Ayr* 3D **122**
North Ferriby. *E Yor* 2C **94**
Northfield. *Aber* 3F **153**
Northfield. *E Yor* 2D **94**
Northfield. *Som* 3F **21**
Northfield. *W Mid* 3E **61**
**Northfleet**. *Kent* 3H **39**
North Frodingham. *E Yor* 4F **101**
Northgate. *Linc* 3A **76**
North Gluss. *Shet* 4E **173**
North Gorley. *Hants* 1G **15**
North Green. *Norf* 2E **66**
North Green. *Suff*
nr. Framlingham 4F **67**
nr. Halesworth 3F **67**
nr. Saxmundham 4F **67**
North Greetwell. *Linc* 3H **87**
North Grimston. *N Yor* 3C **100**
North Halling. *Medw* 4B **40**
North Hayling. *Hants* 2F **17**
North Hazelrigg. *Nmbd* 1E **121**
North Heasley. *Devn* 3H **19**
North Heath. *W Sus* 3B **26**
North Hill. *Corn* 5C **10**
North Holmwood. *Surr* 1C **26**
North Huish. *Devn* 3D **8**
North Hykeham. *Linc* 4G **87**
Northiam. *E Sus* 3C **28**
Northill. *C Beds* 1B **52**
Northington. *Hants* 3D **24**
North Kelsey. *Linc* 4D **94**
North Kelsey Moor. *Linc* 4D **94**
North Kessock. *High* 4A **158**
North Killingholme. *N Lin* 3E **95**
North Kilvington. *N Yor* 1G **99**
North Kilworth. *Leics* 2D **62**
North Kyme. *Linc* 5A **88**
North Lancing. *W Sus* 5C **26**
Northlands. *Linc* 5C **88**
Northleach. *Glos* 4G **49**
North Lee. *Buck* 5G **51**
North Lees. *N Yor* 2E **99**
North Leigh. *Kent* 1F **29**
North Leigh. *Oxon* 4B **50**
Northleigh. *Devn*
nr. Barnstaple 3G **19**
nr. Honiton 3E **13**
North Leverton. *Notts* 2E **87**
Northlew. *Devn* 3F **11**
North Littleton. *Worc* 1F **49**
North Lopham. *Norf* 2C **66**
North Luffenham. *Rut* 5G **75**
North Marden. *W Sus* 1G **17**
North Marston. *Buck* 3F **51**
North Middleton. *Midl* 4G **129**
North Middleton. *Nmbd* 2E **121**
North Molton. *Devn* 4H **19**
North Moor. *N Yor* 1D **100**
Northmoor. *Oxon* 5C **50**
Northmoor Green. *Som* 3G **21**
North Moreton. *Oxon* 3D **36**
Northmuir. *Ang* 3C **144**
North Mundham. *W Sus* 2G **17**
North Murie. *Per* 1E **137**
North Muskham. *Notts* 5E **87**
North Ness. *Orkn* 8C **172**
North Newbald. *E Yor* 1C **94**
North Newington. *Oxon* 2C **50**
North Newnton. *Wilts* 1G **23**
North Newton. *Som* 3F **21**
Northney. *Hants* 2F **17**
North Nibley. *Glos* 2C **34**
North Oakley. *Hants* 1D **24**
North Ockendon. *G Lon* 2G **39**
**Northolt**. *G Lon* 2C **38**
Northop. *Flin* 4E **83**
Northop Hall. *Flin* 4E **83**
North Ormesby. *Midd* 3C **106**
North Ormsby. *Linc* 1B **88**
Northorpe. *Linc*
nr. Bourne 4H **75**
nr. Donington 2B **76**
nr. Gainsborough 1F **87**
North Otterington. *N Yor* 1F **99**
Northover. *Som*
nr. Glastonbury 3H **21**
nr. Yeovil 4A **22**
North Owersby. *Linc* 1H **87**
Northowram. *W Yor* 2B **92**
North Perrott. *Som* 2H **13**
North Petherton. *Som* 3F **21**
North Petherwin. *Corn* 4C **10**
North Pickenham. *Norf* 5A **78**
North Piddle. *Worc* 5D **60**
North Poorton. *Dors* 3A **14**
North Port. *Arg* 1H **133**
Northport. *Dors* 4E **15**
North Queensferry. *Fife* 1E **129**
North Radworthy. *Devn* 3A **20**
North Rauceby. *Linc* 1H **75**
Northrepps. *Norf* 2E **79**
North Rigton. *N Yor* 5E **99**
North Rode. *Ches E* 4C **84**
North Roe. *Shet* 3E **173**
North Ronaldsay Airport. *Orkn* 2G **172**
North Row. *Cumb* 1D **102**
North Runcton. *Norf* 4F **77**
North Sannox. *N Ayr* 5B **126**
North Scale. *Cumb* 2A **96**
North Scarle. *Linc* 4F **87**
North Seaton. *Nmbd* 1F **115**
North Seaton Colliery. *Nmbd* 1F **115**
North Sheen. *G Lon* 3C **38**
North Shian. *Arg* 4D **140**
**North Shields**. *Tyne* 3G **115**
North Shoebury. *S'end* 2D **40**
North Shore. *Bkpl* 1B **90**
North Side. *Cumb* 2B **102**
North Skelton. *Red C* 3D **106**
North Somercotes. *Linc* 1D **88**
North Stainley. *N Yor* 2E **99**
North Stainmore. *Cumb* 3B **104**
North Stifford. *Thur* 2H **39**
North Stoke. *Bath* 5C **34**
North Stoke. *Oxon* 3E **36**
North Stoke. *W Sus* 4B **26**
Northstowe. *Cambs* 4D **64**
North Street. *Hants* 3E **25**
North Street. *Kent* 5E **40**
North Street. *Medw* 3C **40**
North Street. *W Ber* 4E **37**
North Sunderland. *Nmbd* 1G **121**
North Tamerton. *Corn* 3D **10**
North Tawton. *Devn* 2G **11**
North Thoresby. *Linc* 1B **88**
North Tidworth. *Wilts* 2H **23**
North Town. *Devn* 2F **11**
North Town. *Shet* 10E **173**
Northtown. *Orkn* 8D **172**
North Tuddenham. *Norf* 4C **78**
North Walbottle. *Tyne* 3E **115**
Northwall. *Orkn* 3G **172**
North Walney. *Cumb* 3A **96**
**North Walsham**. *Norf* 2E **79**
North Waltham. *Hants* 2D **24**
North Warnborough. *Hants* 1F **25**
North Water Bridge. *Ang* 2F **145**
North Watten. *High* 3E **169**
Northway. *Glos* 2E **49**
Northway. *Swan* 4E **31**
North Weald Bassett. *Essx* 5F **53**
North Weston. *N Som* 4H **33**
North Weston. *Oxon* 5E **51**
North Wheatley. *Notts* 2E **87**
North Whilborough. *Devn* 2E **9**
**Northwich**. *Ches W* 3A **84**
North Wick. *Bath* 5A **34**
Northwick. *Som* 2G **21**
Northwick. *S Glo* 3A **34**
North Widcombe. *Bath* 1A **22**
North Willingham. *Linc* 2A **88**
**North Wingfield**. *Derbs* 4B **86**
North Witham. *Linc* 3G **75**
Northwold. *Norf* 1G **65**
Northwood. *Derbs* 4G **85**
**Northwood**. *G Lon* 1B **38**
Northwood. *IOW* 3C **16**
Northwood. *Kent* 4H **41**
Northwood. *Shrp* 2G **71**
Northwood. *Stoke* 1C **72**
Northwood Green. *Glos* 4C **48**
North Wootton. *Dors* 1B **14**
North Wootton. *Norf* 3F **77**
North Wootton. *Som* 2A **22**
North Wraxall. *Wilts* 4D **34**
North Wroughton. *Swin* 3G **35**
North Yardhope. *Nmbd* 4D **120**
Norton. *Devn* 3E **9**
Norton. *Glos* 3D **48**
Norton. *Hal* 2H **83**
Norton. *Herts* 2C **52**
Norton. *IOW* 4B **16**
Norton. *Mon* 3H **47**
Norton. *Nptn* 4D **62**
Norton. *Notts* 3C **86**
Norton. *Powy* 4F **59**

Norton. *Shrp*
  nr. Ludlow ............2G 59
  nr. Madeley ...........5B 72
  nr. Shrewsbury .......5H 71
Norton. *S Yor*
  nr. Askern ............3F 93
  nr. Sheffield .........2A 86
Norton. *Stoc T* ...........2B 106
Norton. *Suff* ...............4B 66
Norton. *Swan* ..............4F 31
Norton. *W Sus*
  nr. Selsey ............3G 17
  nr. Westergate .......5A 26
Norton. *Wilts* .............3D 35
Norton. *Worc*
  nr. Evesham ..........1F 49
  nr. Worcester ........5C 60
Norton Bavant. *Wilts* .....2E 23
Norton Bridge. *Staf* ......2C 72
Norton Canes. *Staf* .......5E 73
Norton Canon. *Here* .......1G 47
Norton Corner. *Norf* ......3C 78
Norton Disney. *Linc* ......5F 87
Norton East. *Staf* ........5E 73
Norton Ferris. *Wilts* .....3C 22
Norton Fitzwarren. *Som* ...4F 21
Norton Green. *IOW* ........4B 16
Norton Green. *Stoke* ......5D 84
Norton Hawkfield. *Bath* ...5A 34
Norton Heath. *Essx* .......5F 53
Norton in Hales. *Shrp* ....2B 72
Norton in the Moors. *Stoke* .5C 84
Norton-Juxta-Twycross.
  *Leics* ...............5H 73
Norton-le-Clay. *N Yor* ....2G 99
Norton Lindsey. *Warw* .....4G 61
Norton Little Green. *Suff* .4B 66
Norton Malreward. *Bath* ...5B 34
Norton Mandeville. *Essx* ..5F 53
Norton-on-Derwent. *N Yor* ..2B 100
Norton St Philip. *Som* ....1C 22
Norton Subcourse. *Norf* ...1G 67
Norton sub Hamdon. *Som* ...1H 13
Norton Woodseats. *S Yor* ..2A 86
Norwell. *Notts* ...........4E 87
Norwell Woodhouse. *Notts* .4E 87
**Norwich.** *Norf* .........5E 79
Norwich Airport. *Norf* ....4E 79
Norwick. *Shet* ...........1H 173
Norwood. *Derbs* ..........2B 86
Norwood Green. *W Yor* .....2B 92
Norwood Hill. *Surr* .......1D 26
Norwood Park. *Som* ........3A 22
Norwoodside. *Cambs* .......1D 64
Noseley. *Leics* ...........1E 63
Noss. *Shet* .............10E 173
Noss Mayo. *Devn* ...........4B 8
Nosterfield. *N Yor* .......1E 99
Nostie. *High* ............1A 148
Notgrove. *Glos* ...........3G 49
**Nottingham.** *Nott* ......1C 74
Nottington. *Dors* .........4B 14
Notton. *Dors* .............3B 14
Notton. *W Yor* ............3D 92
Notton. *Wilts* ............5E 35
Nounsley. *Essx* ...........4A 54
Noutard's Green. *Worc* ....4B 60
Nox. *Shrp* ................4G 71
Noyadd Trefawr. *Cdgn* .....1C 44
Nuffield. *Oxon* ...........3E 37
Nunburnholme. *E Yor* ......5C 100
Nuncargate. *Notts* ........5C 86
Nunclose. *Cumb* ..........5F 113
**Nuneaton.** *Warw* ........1A 62
Nuneham Courtenay. *Oxon* ..2D 36
Nun Monkton. *N Yor* .......4H 99
Nunnerie. *S Lan* .........3B 118
Nunney. *Som* ..............2C 22
Nunnington. *N Yor* .......2A 100
Nunnykirk. *Nmbd* ..........5E 121
Nunsthorpe. *NE Lin* .......4F 95
Nunthorpe. *Midd* .........3C 106
Nunthorpe. *York* ..........4H 99

Nunton. *Wilts* .............4G 23
Nunwick. *Nmbd* ...........2B 114
Nunwick. *N Yor* ...........2F 99
Nupend. *Glos* .............5C 48
Nursling. *Hants* ..........1B 16
Nursted. *Hants* ...........4F 25
Nursted. *Wilts* ...........5F 35
Nurston. *V Glam* ..........5D 32
Nutbourne. *W Sus*
  nr. Chichester .......2F 17
  nr. Pulborough .......4B 26
Nutfield. *Surr* ...........5E 39
Nuthall. *Notts* ...........1C 74
Nuthampstead. *Herts* ......2E 53
Nuthurst. *Warw* ...........3F 61
Nuthurst. *W Sus* ..........3C 26
Nutley. *E Sus* ............3F 27
Nuttall. *G Man* ...........3F 91
Nutwell. *S Yor* ...........4G 93
Nybster. *High* ...........2F 169
Nyetimber. *W Sus* .........3G 17
Nyewood. *W Sus* ...........4G 25
Nymet Rowland. *Devn* ......2H 11
Nymet Tracey. *Devn* .......2H 11
Nympsfield. *Glos* .........5D 48
Nynehead. *Som* ............4E 21
Nyton. *W Sus* .............5A 26

# O

**Oadby.** *Leics* ...........5D 74
Oad Street. *Kent* .........4C 40
Oakamoor. *Staf* ...........1E 73
Oakbank. *Arg* ............5B 140
Oakbank. *W Lot* ..........3D 129
Oakdale. *Cphy* ............2E 33
Oakdale. *Pool* ............3F 15
Oake. *Som* ................4E 21
Oaken. *Staf* ..............5C 72
Oakenclough. *Lanc* ........5E 97
Oakengates. *Telf* .........4A 72
Oakenholt. *Flin* ..........3E 83
Oakenshaw. *Dur* ..........1F 105
Oakenshaw. *W Yor* .........2B 92
Oakerthorpe. *Derbs* .......5A 86
Oakford. *Cdgn* ............5D 56
Oakford. *Devn* ............4C 20
Oakfordbridge. *Devn* ......4C 20
Oakgrove. *Ches E* .........4D 84
Oakham. *Rut* ..............5F 75
Oakhanger. *Ches E* ........5B 84
Oakhanger. *Hants* .........3F 25
Oakhill. *Som* .............2B 22
Oakington. *Cambs* .........4D 64
Oaklands. *Powy* ...........5C 58
Oakle Street. *Glos* .......4C 48
Oakley. *Bed* ..............5H 63
Oakley. *Buck* .............4E 51
Oakley. *Fife* ............1D 128
Oakley. *Hants* ............1D 24
Oakley. *Suff* .............3D 66
Oakley Green. *Wind* .......3A 38
Oakley Park. *Powy* ........2B 58
Oakmere. *Ches W* ..........4H 83
Oakridge Lynch. *Glos* .....5E 49
Oaks. *Shrp* ...............5G 71
Oaksey. *Wilts* ............2E 35
Oaks Green. *Derbs* ........2F 73
Oakshaw Ford. *Cumb* ......2G 113
Oakshott. *Hants* ..........4F 25
Oakthorpe. *Leics* .........4H 73
Oak Tree. *Darl* ..........3A 106
Oakwood. *Derb* ............2A 74
Oakwood. *W Yor* ...........1D 92
Oakwoodhill. *Surr* ........2C 26
Oakworth. *W Yor* ..........1A 92
Oape. *High* ..............3C 164
Oare. *Kent* ...............4E 40
Oare. *Som* ................2B 20
Oare. *W Ber* ..............4D 36
Oare. *Wilts* ..............5G 35
Oareford. *Som* ............2B 20
Oasby. *Linc* ..............2H 75

Oath. *Som* ................4G 21
Oathlaw. *Ang* ............3D 145
Oatlands. *N Yor* ..........4F 99
**Oban.** *Arg* ............1F 133
Oban. *W Isl* .............7D 171
Oborne. *Dors* .............1B 14
Obsdale. *High* ...........2A 158
Obthorpe. *Linc* ...........4H 75
Occlestone Green. *Ches W* .4A 84
Occold. *Suff* .............3D 66
Ochiltree. *E Ayr* ........2E 117
Ochtermuthill. *Per* ......2H 135
Ochtertyre. *Per* .........1H 135
Ockbrook. *Derbs* ..........2B 74
Ockeridge. *Worc* ..........4B 60
Ockham. *Surr* .............5B 38
Ockle. *High* .............1G 139
Ockley. *Surr* .............1C 26
Ocle Pychard. *Here* .......1A 48
Octofad. *Arg* ............4A 124
Octomore. *Arg* ...........4A 124
Octon. *E Yor* ............3E 101
Odcombe. *Som* .............1A 14
Odd Down. *Bath* ...........5C 34
Oddingley. *Worc* ..........5D 60
Oddington. *Oxon* ..........4D 50
Oddsta. *Shet* ............2G 173
Odell. *Bed* ...............5G 63
Odie. *Orkn* ..............5F 172
Odiham. *Hants* ............1F 25
Odsey. *Cambs* .............2C 52
Odstock. *Wilts* ...........4G 23
Odstone. *Leics* ...........5A 74
Offchurch. *Warw* .........4A 62
Offenham. *Worc* ...........1F 49
Offenham Cross. *Worc* .....1F 49
Offerton. *G Man* ..........2D 84
Offerton. *Tyne* ..........4G 115
Offham. *E Sus* ............4E 27
Offham. *Kent* .............5A 40
Offham. *W Sus* ............5B 26
Offleyhay. *Staf* ..........3C 72
Offley Hoo. *Herts* ........3B 52
Offleymarsh. *Staf* ........3B 72
Offord Cluny. *Cambs* ......4B 64
Offord D'Arcy. *Cambs* .....4B 64
Offton. *Suff* .............1D 54
Offwell. *Devn* ............3E 13
Ogbourne Maizey. *Wilts* ...4G 35
Ogbourne St Andrew. *Wilts* .4G 35
Ogbourne St George. *Wilts* .4H 35
Ogden. *G Man* .............3H 91
Ogle. *Nmbd* .............2E 115
Ogmore. *V Glam* ...........4B 32
Ogmore-by-Sea. *V Glam* ....4B 32
Ogmore Vale. *B'end* .......2C 32
Okeford Fitzpaine. *Dors* ..1D 14
Okehampton. *Devn* .........3F 11
Okehampton Camp. *Devn* ....3F 11
Okraquoy. *Shet* ..........8F 173
Okus. *Swin* ...............3G 35
Old. *Nptn* ................3E 63
Old Aberdeen. *Aber* ......3G 153
Old Alresford. *Hants* .....3D 24
Oldany. *High* ............5B 166
Old Arley. *Warw* ..........1G 61
Old Basford. *Nott* ........1C 74
Old Basing. *Hants* ........1E 25
Oldberrow. *Warw* ..........4F 61
Old Bewick. *Nmbd* ........2E 121
Old Bexley. *G Lon* ........3F 39
Old Blair. *Per* ..........2F 143
Old Bolingbroke. *Linc* ....4C 88
Old Brampton. *Derbs* ......3H 85
Old Bridge of Tilt. *Per* ..2F 143
Old Bridge of Urr. *Dum* ...3E 111
Old Brumby. *N Lin* ........4B 94
Old Buckenham. *Norf* .....1C 66
Old Burghclere. *Hants* ....1C 24
Oldbury. *Shrp* ............1B 60
Oldbury. *Warw* ............1H 61
**Oldbury.** *W Mid* ........2D 61
Oldbury-on-Severn. *S Glo* ..2B 34

Oldbury on the Hill. *Glos* ..3D 34
Old Byland. *N Yor* ........1H 99
Old Cassop. *Dur* .........1A 106
Oldcastle. *Mon* ...........3G 47
Oldcastle Heath. *Ches W* ..1G 71
Old Catton. *Norf* .........4E 79
Old Clee. *NE Lin* .........4F 95
Old Cleeve. *Som* ..........2D 20
Old Colwyn. *Cnwy* .........3A 82
Oldcotes. *Notts* ..........2C 86
Old Coulsdon. *G Lon* ......5E 39
Old Dailly. *S Ayr* .......5B 116
Old Dalby. *Leics* .........3D 74
Old Dam. *Derbs* ...........3F 85
Old Deer. *Abers* .........4G 161
Old Dilton. *Wilts* ........2D 22
Old Down. *S Glo* ..........3B 34
Oldeamere. *Cambs* .........1C 64
Old Edlington. *S Yor* .....1C 86
Old Eldon. *Dur* ..........2F 105
Old Ellerby. *E Yor* .......1E 95
Old Fallings. *W Mid* ......5D 72
Oldfallow. *Staf* ..........4D 73
Old Felixstowe. *Suff* .....2G 55
Oldfield. *Shrp* ...........2A 60
Oldfield. *Worc* ...........4C 60
Old Fletton. *Pet* ........1A 64
Oldford. *Som* .............1C 22
Old Forge. *Here* ..........4A 48
Old Glossop. *Derbs* .......1E 85
Old Goole. *E Yor* .........2H 93
Old Gore. *Here* ...........3B 48
Old Graitney. *Dum* .......3E 112
Old Grimsby. *IOS* ..........1A 4
Old Hall, The. *Norf* ......1C 64
Oldhall. *High* ...........3E 169
Old Hall Street. *Norf* ....2F 79
**Oldham.** *G Man* .........4H 91
Oldhamstocks. *E Lot* .....2D 130
Old Heathfield. *E Sus* ....3G 27
Old Hill. *W Mid* ..........2D 60
Old Hunstanton. *Norf* .....1F 77
Oldhurst. *Cambs* ..........3B 64
Old Hutton. *Cumb* ........1E 97
Old Kea. *Corn* .............4C 6
Old Kilpatrick. *W Dun* ...2F 127
Old Kinnernie. *Abers* ....3E 152
Old Knebworth. *Herts* .....3C 52
Oldland. *S Glo* ...........4B 34
Old Laxey. *IOM* ..........3D 108
Old Leake. *Linc* ..........5D 88
Old Lenton. *Nott* .........2C 74
Old Llanberis. *Gwyn* ......5F 81
Old Malton. *N Yor* .......2B 100
Oldmeldrum. *Abers* .......1F 153
Old Micklefield. *W Yor* ...1E 93
Old Mill. *Corn* ...........5D 10
Oldmixon. *N Som* .........1G 21
Old Monkland. *N Lan* .....3A 128
Old Newton. *Suff* .........4C 66
Old Park. *Telf* ...........5A 72
Old Pentland. *Midl* ......3F 129
Old Philpstoun. *W Lot* ...2D 128
Old Quarrington. *Dur* ....1A 106
Old Radnor. *Powy* .........5E 59
Old Rayne. *Abers* ........1D 152
Oldridge. *Devn* ...........3B 12
Old Romney. *Kent* .........3E 29
Old Scone. *Per* ..........1D 136
Oldshore Beg. *High* ......3B 166
Oldshoremore. *High* ......3C 166
Old Snydale. *W Yor* .......2E 93
Old Sodbury. *S Glo* .......3C 34
Old Somerby. *Linc* ........2G 75
Old Spital. *Dur* .........3C 104
Oldstead. *N Yor* .........1H 99
Old Stratford. *Nptn* ......1F 51
Old Swan. *Mers* ...........1F 83
Old Swarland. *Nmbd* ......4F 121
Old Tebay. *Cumb* .........4H 103
Old Town. *Cumb* ..........5F 113
Old Town. *E Sus* ..........5G 27
Old Town. *IOS* .............1B 4
Old Town. *Nmbd* ..........5C 120
Oldtown. *High* ...........5C 164

Old Trafford. *G Man* .......1C 84
Old Tupton. *Derbs* ........4A 86
Oldwall. *Cumb* ...........3F 113
Oldwalls. *Swan* ...........3D 31
Old Warden. *C Beds* .......1B 52
Oldways End. *Som* .........4B 20
Old Westhall. *Abers* .....1D 152
Old Weston. *Cambs* ........3H 63
Oldwhat. *Abers* ..........3F 161
Old Windsor. *Wind* ........3A 38
Old Wives Lees. *Kent* .....5E 41
Old Woking. *Surr* .........5B 38
Oldwood Common. *Worc* .....4H 59
Old Woodstock. *Oxon* ......4C 50
Olgrinmore. *High* ........3C 168
Oliver's Battery. *Hants* ...4C 24
Ollaberry. *Shet* .........3E 173
Ollerton. *Ches E* .........3B 84
Ollerton. *Notts* ..........4D 86
Ollerton. *Shrp* ...........3A 72
Olmarch. *Cdgn* ............5F 57
Olmstead Green. *Cambs* ...1G 53
Olney. *Mil* ...............5F 63
Olrig. *High* .............2D 169
Olton. *W Mid* .............2F 61
Olveston. *S Glo* ..........3B 34
**Omagh.** *Ferm* ..........4C 174
Ombersley. *Worc* .........4C 60
Ompton. *Notts* ............4D 86
Omunsgarth. *Shet* ........7E 173
Onchan. *IOM* .............4D 108
Onecote. *Staf* ............5E 85
Onehouse. *Suff* ...........5C 66
Onen. *Mon* ................4H 47
Ongar Hill. *Norf* .........3E 77
Ongar Street. *Here* .......4F 59
Onibury. *Shrp* ............3G 59
Onich. *High* .............2E 141
Onllwyn. *Neat* ............4B 46
Onneley. *Staf* ............1B 72
Onslow Green. *Essx* .......4G 53
Onslow Village. *Surr* .....1A 26
Onthank. *E Ayr* ..........1D 116
Openwoodgate. *Derbs* .....1A 74
Opinan. *High*
  nr. Gairloch .........1G 155
  nr. Laide ............4C 162
Orasaigh. *W Isl* .........6F 171
Orbost. *High* ............4B 154
Orby. *Linc* ...............4D 89
Orchard Hill. *Devn* .......4E 19
Orchard Portman. *Som* .....4F 21
Orcheston. *Wilts* .........2F 23
Orcop. *Here* ..............3H 47
Orcop Hill. *Here* .........3H 47
Ord. *High* ...............2E 147
Ordale. *Shet* ...........1H 173
Ordhead. *Abers* ..........2D 152
Ordie. *Abers* ............3B 152
Ordiequish. *Mor* .........3H 159
Ordley. *Nmbd* ............4C 114
Ordsall. *Notts* ...........3E 86
Ore. *E Sus* ...............4C 28
Oreton. *Shrp* .............2A 60
Orford. *Suff* .............1H 55
Orford. *Warr* .............1A 84
Organford. *Dors* ..........3E 15
Orgil. *Orkn* .............7B 172
Orgreave. *Staf* ...........4F 73
Oridge Street. *Glos* ......3C 48
Orlestone. *Kent* .........2D 28
Orleton. *Here* ...........4G 59
Orleton. *Worc* ............4A 60
Orleton Common. *Here* .....4G 59
Orlingbury. *Nptn* .........3F 63
Ormacleit. *W Isl* ........5C 170
Ormathwaite. *Cumb* .......2D 102
Ormesby. *Red C* ..........3C 106
Ormesby St Margaret. *Norf* .4G 79
Ormesby St Michael. *Norf* .4G 79
Ormiscaig. *High* .........4C 162
Ormiston. *E Lot* .........3H 129
Ormsaigbeg. *High* ........2F 139
Ormsaigmore. *High* .......2F 139

**Ormsary**. Arg .....2F 125
Ormsgill. Cumb .....2A 96
**Ormskirk**. Lanc .....4C 90
Orphir. Orkn .....7C 172
**Orpington**. G Lon .....4F 39
**Orrell**. G Man .....4D 90
Orrell. Mers .....1F 83
Orrisdale. IOM .....2C 108
Orsett. Thur .....2H 39
Orslow. Staf .....4C 72
Orston. Notts .....1E 75
Orthwaite. Cumb .....1D 102
Orton. Cumb .....4H 103
Orton. Mor .....3H 159
Orton. Nptn .....3F 63
Orton. Staf .....1C 60
Orton Longueville. Pet .....1A 64
Orton-on-the-Hill. Leics .....5H 73
Orton Waterville. Pet .....1A 64
Orton Wistow. Pet .....1A 64
Orwell. Cambs .....5C 64
Osbaldeston. Lanc .....1E 91
Osbaldwick. York .....4A 100
Osbaston. Leics .....5B 74
Osbaston. Shrp .....3F 71
Osbournby. Linc .....2H 75
Osclay. High .....5E 169
Oscroft. Ches W .....4H 83
Ose. High .....4C 154
Osgathorpe. Leics .....4B 74
Osgodby. Linc .....1H 87
Osgodby. N Yor
  nr. Scarborough .....1E 101
  nr. Selby .....1G 93
Oskaig. High .....5E 155
Oskamull. Arg .....5F 139
Osleston. Derbs .....2G 73
Osmaston. Derb .....2A 74
Osmaston. Derbs .....1G 73
Osmington. Dors .....4C 14
Osmington Mills. Dors .....4C 14
Osmondthorpe. W Yor .....1D 92
Osmondwall. Orkn .....9C 172
Osmotherley. N Yor .....5B 106
Osnaburgh. Fife .....2G 137
Ospisdale. High .....5E 164
Ospringe. Kent .....4E 40
**Ossett**. W Yor .....2C 92
Ossington. Notts .....4E 87
Ostend. Essx .....1D 40
Ostend. Norf .....2F 79
Osterley. G Lon .....3C 38
Oswaldkirk. N Yor .....2A 100
**Oswaldtwistle**. Lanc .....2F 91
**Oswestry**. Shrp .....3E 71
Otby. Linc .....1A 88
Otford. Kent .....5G 39
Otham. Kent .....5B 40
Otherton. Staf .....4D 72
Othery. Som .....3G 21
**Otley**. W Yor .....5E 98
Otterbourne. Hants .....4C 24
Otterburn. Nmbd .....5C 120
Otterburn. N Yor .....4A 98
Otterburn Camp. Nmbd .....5C 120
Otterburn Hall. Nmbd .....5C 120
Otter Ferry. Arg .....1H 125
Otterford. Som .....1F 13
Otterham. Corn .....3B 10
Otterhampton. Som .....2F 21
Otterham Quay. Medw .....4C 40
Ottershaw. Surr .....4B 38
Otterspool. Mers .....2F 83
Otterswick. Shet .....3G 173
Otterton. Devn .....4D 12
Otterwood. Hants .....2C 16
Ottery St Mary. Devn .....3D 12
Ottinge. Kent .....1F 29
Ottringham. E Yor .....2F 95
Oughterby. Cumb .....4D 112
Oughtershaw. N Yor .....1A 98
Oughterside. Cumb .....5C 112
Oughtibridge. S Yor .....1H 85

Oughtrington. Warr .....2A 84
Oulston. N Yor .....2H 99
Oulton. Cumb .....4D 112
Oulton. Norf .....3D 78
Oulton. Staf
  nr. Gnosall Heath .....3B 72
  nr. Stone .....2D 72
Oulton. Suff .....1H 67
Oulton. W Yor .....2D 92
Oulton Broad. Suff .....1H 67
Oulton Street. Norf .....3D 78
Oundle. Nptn .....2H 63
Ousby. Cumb .....1H 103
Ousdale. High .....2H 165
Ousden. Suff .....5G 65
Ousefleet. E Yor .....2B 94
Ouston. Dur .....4F 115
Ouston. Nmbd
  nr. Bearsbridge .....4A 114
  nr. Stamfordham .....2D 114
Outer Hope. Devn .....4C 8
Outertown. Orkn .....6B 172
Outgate. Cumb .....5E 103
Outhgill. Cumb .....4A 104
Outlands. Staf .....2B 72
Outlane. W Yor .....3A 92
Out Newton. E Yor .....2G 95
Out Rawcliffe. Lanc .....5D 96
Outwell. Norf .....5E 77
Outwick. Hants .....1G 15
Outwood. Surr .....1E 27
Outwood. W Yor .....2D 92
Outwood. Worc .....3D 60
Outwoods. Leics .....4B 74
Outwoods. Staf .....4B 72
Ouzlewell Green. W Yor .....2D 92
Ovenden. W Yor .....2A 92
Over. Cambs .....3C 64
Over. Ches W .....4A 84
Over. Glos .....4D 48
Over. S Glo .....3A 34
Overbister. Orkn .....3F 172
Over Burrows. Derbs .....2G 73
Overbury. Worc .....2E 49
Overcombe. Dors .....4B 14
Over Compton. Dors .....1A 14
Over End. Cambs .....1H 63
Over Finlarg. Ang .....4D 144
Over Green. Warw .....1F 61
Overgreen. Derbs .....3H 85
Over Haddon. Derbs .....4G 85
Over Hulton. G Man .....4E 91
Over Kellet. Lanc .....2E 97
Over Kiddington. Oxon .....3C 50
Overleigh. Som .....3H 21
Overley. Staf .....4F 73
Over Monnow. Mon .....4A 48
Over Norton. Oxon .....3B 50
Over Peover. Ches E .....3B 84
Overpool. Ches W .....3F 83
Overscaig. High .....1B 164
Overseal. Derbs .....4G 73
Over Silton. N Yor .....5B 106
Oversland. Kent .....5E 41
Overstone. Nptn .....4F 63
Over Stowey. Som .....3E 21
Overstrand. Norf .....1E 79
Over Stratton. Som .....1H 13
Over Street. Wilts .....3F 23
Overthorpe. Nptn .....1C 50
Overton. Aber .....2F 153
Overton. Ches W .....3H 83
Overton. Hants .....2D 24
Overton. High .....5E 169
Overton. Lanc .....4D 96
Overton. N Yor .....4H 99
Overton. Shrp
  nr. Bridgnorth .....2A 60
  nr. Ludlow .....3H 59
Overton. Swan .....4D 30
Overton. W Yor .....3C 92
Overton. Wrex .....1F 71
Overtown. Lanc .....2E 97
Overtown. N Lan .....4B 128

Overtown. Swin .....4G 35
Over Wallop. Hants .....3A 24
Over Whitacre. Warw .....1G 61
Over Worton. Oxon .....3C 50
Oving. Buck .....3F 51
Oving. W Sus .....5A 26
Ovingdean. Brig .....5E 27
Ovingham. Nmbd .....3D 115
Ovington. Dur .....3E 105
Ovington. Essx .....1A 54
Ovington. Hants .....3D 24
Ovington. Norf .....5B 78
Ovington. Nmbd .....3D 114
Owen's Bank. Staf .....3G 73
Ower. Hants
  nr. Holbury .....2C 16
  nr. Totton .....1B 16
Owermoigne. Dors .....4C 14
Owlbury. Shrp .....1F 59
Owler Bar. Derbs .....3G 85
Owlerton. S Yor .....1H 85
Owlsmoor. Brac .....5G 37
Owlswick. Buck .....5F 51
Owmby. Linc .....4D 94
Owmby-by-Spital. Linc .....2H 87
Ownham. W Ber .....4C 36
Owrytn. Wrex .....1F 71
Owslebury. Hants .....4D 24
Owston. Leics .....5E 75
Owston. S Yor .....3F 93
Owston Ferry. N Lin .....4B 94
Owstwick. E Yor .....1F 95
Owthorne. E Yor .....2G 95
Owthorpe. Notts .....2D 74
Oxborough. Norf .....5G 77
Oxbridge. Dors .....3H 13
Oxcombe. Linc .....3C 88
Oxen End. Essx .....3G 53
Oxenhall. Glos .....3C 48
Oxenholme. Cumb .....5G 103
Oxenhope. W Yor .....1A 92
Oxen Park. Cumb .....1C 96
Oxenpill. Som .....2H 21
Oxenton. Glos .....2E 49
Oxenwood. Wilts .....1B 24
**Oxford**. Oxon .....5D 50
Oxgangs. Edin .....3F 129
Oxhey. Herts .....1C 38
Oxhill. Warw .....1B 50
Oxley. W Mid .....5D 72
Oxley Green. Essx .....4C 54
Oxley's Green. E Sus .....3A 28
Oxlode. Cambs .....2D 65
Oxnam. Bord .....3B 120
Oxnead. Norf .....3E 79
Oxshott. Surr .....4C 38
Oxspring. S Yor .....4C 92
**Oxted**. Surr .....5E 39
Oxton. Mers .....2F 83
Oxton. N Yor .....5H 99
Oxton. Notts .....5D 86
Oxton. Bord .....4A 130
Oxwich. Swan .....4D 31
Oxwich Green. Swan .....4D 31
Oxwick. Norf .....3B 78
Oykel Bridge. High .....3A 164
Oyne. Abers .....1D 152
Oystermouth. Swan .....4F 31
Ozleworth. Glos .....2C 34

# P

**Paddington**. G Lon .....2D 38
Paddington. Warr .....2A 84
Paddlesworth. Kent .....2F 29
Paddock. Kent .....5D 40
Paddockhole. Dum .....1D 112
Paddock Wood. Kent .....1A 28
Padeswood. Flin .....4E 83
**Padiham**. Lanc .....1F 91
Padside. N Yor .....4D 98
Padson. Devn .....3F 11
Padstow. Corn .....1D 6
Padworth. W Ber .....5E 36
Page Bank. Dur .....1F 105
Pagham. W Sus .....3G 17
Paglesham Churchend. Essx .....1D 40
Paglesham Eastend. Essx .....1D 40
Paibeil. W Isl
  on North Uist .....2C 170
  on Taransay .....8C 171
Paiblesgearraidh. W Isl .....2C 170
**Paignton**. Torb .....2E 9
Pailton. Warw .....2B 62
Paine's Corner. E Sus .....3H 27
Painleyhill. Staf .....2E 73
Painscastle. Powy .....1E 47
Painshawfield. Nmbd .....3D 114
Painsthorpe. E Yor .....4C 100
Painswick. Glos .....5D 48
Painter's Forstal. Kent .....5D 40
Painthorpe. W Yor .....3D 92
Pairc Shiabost. W Isl .....3E 171
**Paisley**. Ren .....3F 127
Pakefield. Suff .....1H 67
Pakenham. Suff .....4B 66
Pale. Gwyn .....2B 70
Palehouse Common. E Sus .....4F 27
Palestine. Hants .....2A 24
Paley Street. Wind .....4G 37
Palgowan. Dum .....1A 110
Palgrave. Suff .....3D 66
Pallington. Dors .....3C 14
Palmarsh. Kent .....2F 29
Palmer Moor. Derbs .....2F 73
Palmers Cross. W Mid .....5C 72
Palmerstown. V Glam .....5E 33
Palnackie. Dum .....4F 111
Palnure. Dum .....3B 110
Palterton. Derbs .....4B 86
Pamber End. Hants .....1E 24
Pamber Green. Hants .....1E 24
Pamber Heath. Hants .....5E 36
Pamington. Glos .....2E 49
Pamphill. Dors .....2E 15
Pampisford. Cambs .....1E 53
Panborough. Som .....2H 21
Panbride. Ang .....5E 145
Pancrasweek. Devn .....2C 10
Pandy. Gwyn
  nr. Bala .....2A 70
  nr. Tywyn .....5F 69
Pandy. Mon .....3G 47
Pandy. Powy .....5B 70
Pandy. Wrex .....2D 70
Pandy Tudur. Cnwy .....4A 82
Panfield. Essx .....3H 53
Pangbourne. W Ber .....4E 37
Pannal. N Yor .....4F 99
Pannal Ash. N Yor .....4E 99
Pannanich. Abers .....4A 152
Pant. Shrp .....3E 71
Pant. Wrex .....1E 71
Pantasaph. Flin .....3D 82
Pant Glas. Gwyn .....1D 68
Pant-glas. Shrp .....2E 71
Pantgwyn. Carm .....3F 45
Pantgwyn. Cdgn .....1C 44
Pant-lasau. Swan .....5G 45
Panton. Linc .....3A 88
Pant-pastynog. Den .....4C 82
Pantperthog. Gwyn .....5G 69
Pant-teg. Carm .....3E 45
Pant-y-Caws. Carm .....2F 43
Pant-y-dwr. Powy .....3B 58

Pant-y-ffridd. Powy .....5D 70
Pantyffynnon. Carm .....4G 45
Pantygasseg. Torf .....5F 47
Pant-y-llyn. Carm .....4G 45
Pant-yr-awel. B'end .....3C 32
Panxworth. Norf .....4F 79
Papa Stour Airport. Shet .....6C 173
Papa Westray Airport.
  Orkn .....2D 172
Papcastle. Cumb .....1C 102
Papigoe. High .....3F 169
Papil. Shet .....8E 173
Papple. E Lot .....2B 130
Papplewick. Notts .....5C 86
Papworth Everard. Cambs .....4B 64
Papworth St Agnes. Cambs .....4B 64
Par. Corn .....3E 7
Paramour Street. Kent .....4G 41
Parbold. Lanc .....3C 90
Parbrook. Som .....3A 22
Parbrook. W Sus .....3B 26
Parc. Gwyn .....2A 70
Parcllyn. Cdgn .....5B 56
Parc-Seymour. Newp .....2H 33
Pardown. Hants .....2D 24
Pardshaw. Cumb .....2B 102
Parham. Suff .....4F 67
Park. Abers .....4E 153
Park. Arg .....4D 140
Park Bottom. Corn .....4A 6
Parkburn. Abers .....5E 161
Park Corner. E Sus .....2G 27
Park Corner. Oxon .....3E 37
Park End. Nmbd .....2B 114
Parkend. Glos .....5B 48
Parkeston. Essx .....2F 55
Parkfield. Corn .....2H 7
Park Gate. Hants .....2D 16
Park Gate. Worc .....3D 60
Park Gate. Surr .....3D 60
Parkgate. Ches W .....3E 83
Parkgate. Cumb .....5D 112
Parkgate. Dum .....1B 112
Parkgate. Surr .....1D 26
Parkhall. W Dun .....2F 127
Parkham. Devn .....4D 19
Parkham Ash. Devn .....4D 18
Parkhead. Cumb .....5E 113
Parkhead. Glas .....3H 127
Park Hill. Mers .....4C 90
Parkhouse. Mon .....5A 48
Parkhurst. IOW .....3C 16
Park Lane. G Man .....4F 91
Park Lane. Staf .....5C 72
Park Mill. W Yor .....3C 92
Parkmill. Swan .....4E 31
Parkneuk. Abers .....1G 145
Parkside. N Lan .....4B 128
Parkstone. Pool .....3F 15
Park Street. Herts .....5B 52
Park Street. W Sus .....2C 26
Park Town. Oxon .....5D 50
Park Village. Nmbd .....3H 113
Parkway. Here .....2C 48
Parley Cross. Dors .....3F 15
Parmoor. Buck .....3F 37
Parr. Mers .....1H 83
Parracombe. Devn .....2G 19
Parrog. Pemb .....1E 43
Parsonage Green. Essx .....4H 53
Parsonby. Cumb .....1C 102
Parson Cross. S Yor .....1H 85
Parson Drove. Cambs .....5C 76
Partick. Glas .....3G 127
Partington. G Man .....1B 84
Partney. Linc .....4D 88
Parton. Cumb
  nr. Whitehaven .....2A 102
  nr. Wigton .....4D 112
Parton. Dum .....2D 111
Partridge Green. W Sus .....4C 26
Parwich. Derbs .....5F 85
Passenham. Nptn .....2F 51

Passfield. Hants . . . . . . . . . . . . . .3G 25
Passingford Bridge. Essx . . . . . .1G 39
Paston. Norf . . . . . . . . . . . . . . . .2F 79
Pasturefields. Staf . . . . . . . . . . . .3D 73
Patchacott. Devn . . . . . . . . . . . . .3E 11
Patcham. Brig . . . . . . . . . . . . . . .5E 27
Patchetts Green. Herts . . . . . . . .1C 38
Patching. W Sus . . . . . . . . . . . . .5B 26
Patchole. Devn . . . . . . . . . . . . . .2G 19
Patchway. S Glo . . . . . . . . . . . . .3B 34
Pateley Bridge. N Yor . . . . . . . . .3D 98
Pathe. Som . . . . . . . . . . . . . . . . .3G 21
Pathfinder Village. Devn . . . . . . .3B 12
Pathhead. Abers . . . . . . . . . . . .2G 145
Pathhead. E Ayr . . . . . . . . . . . . .3F 117
Pathhead. Fife . . . . . . . . . . . . . .4E 137
Pathhead. Midl . . . . . . . . . . . . . .3G 129
Pathlow. Warw . . . . . . . . . . . . . .5F 61
Path of Condie. Per . . . . . . . . . . .2C 136
Pathstruie. Per . . . . . . . . . . . . . .2C 136
Patmore Heath. Herts . . . . . . . . .3E 53
Patna. E Ayr . . . . . . . . . . . . . . .3D 116
Patney. Wilts . . . . . . . . . . . . . . .1F 23
Patrick. IOM . . . . . . . . . . . . . . . .3B 108
Patrick Brompton. N Yor . . . . . . .5F 105
Patrington. E Yor . . . . . . . . . . . .2G 95
Patrington Haven. E Yor . . . . . . .2G 95
Patrixbourne. Kent . . . . . . . . . . .5F 41
Patterdale. Cumb . . . . . . . . . . .3E 103
Pattiesmuir. Fife . . . . . . . . . . . .1D 129
Pattingham. Staf . . . . . . . . . . . . .1C 60
Pattishall. Nptn . . . . . . . . . . . . .5D 62
Pattiswick. Essx . . . . . . . . . . . . .3B 54
Patton Bridge. Cumb . . . . . . . .5G 103
Paul. Corn . . . . . . . . . . . . . . . . . .4B 4
Paulerspury. Nptn . . . . . . . . . . . .1F 51
Paull. E Yor . . . . . . . . . . . . . . . .2E 95
Paulton. Bath . . . . . . . . . . . . . . .1B 22
Pauperhaugh. Nmbd . . . . . . . . .5F 121
Pave Lane. Telf . . . . . . . . . . . . . .4B 72
Pavenham. Bed . . . . . . . . . . . . .5G 63
Pawlett. Som . . . . . . . . . . . . . . .2F 21
Pawston. Nmbd . . . . . . . . . . . . .1C 120
Paxford. Glos . . . . . . . . . . . . . . .2G 49
Paxton. Bord . . . . . . . . . . . . . . .4F 131
Payhembury. Devn . . . . . . . . . . .2D 12
Paythorne. Lanc . . . . . . . . . . . . .4H 97
Payton. Som . . . . . . . . . . . . . . .4E 20
Peacehaven. E Sus . . . . . . . . . . .5F 27
Peak Dale. Derbs . . . . . . . . . . . .3E 85
Peak Forest. Derbs . . . . . . . . . . .3F 85
Peak Hill. Linc . . . . . . . . . . . . . .4B 76
Peakirk. Pet . . . . . . . . . . . . . . . .5A 76
Pearsie. Ang . . . . . . . . . . . . . . .3C 144
Peasedown St John. Bath . . . . . .1C 22
Peaseland Green. Norf . . . . . . . .4C 78
Peasemore. W Ber . . . . . . . . . . .4C 36
Peasenhall. Suff . . . . . . . . . . . . .4F 67
Pease Pottage. W Sus . . . . . . . .2D 26
Peaslake. Surr . . . . . . . . . . . . . .1B 26
Peasley Cross. Mers . . . . . . . . . .1H 83
Peasmarsh. E Sus . . . . . . . . . . .3C 28
Peasmarsh. Som . . . . . . . . . . . .1G 13
Peasmarsh. Surr . . . . . . . . . . . .1A 26
Peaston. E Lot . . . . . . . . . . . . . .3H 129
Peastonbank. E Lot . . . . . . . . . .3H 129
Peathill. Abers . . . . . . . . . . . . .2G 161
Peat Inn. Fife . . . . . . . . . . . . . . .3G 137
Peatling Magna. Leics . . . . . . . . .1C 62
Peatling Parva. Leics . . . . . . . . .2C 62
Peaton. Arg . . . . . . . . . . . . . . . .1D 126
Peaton. Shrp . . . . . . . . . . . . . . .2H 59
Peats Corner. Suff . . . . . . . . . . .4D 66
Pebmarsh. Essx . . . . . . . . . . . . .2B 54
Pebworth. Worc . . . . . . . . . . . . .1G 49
Pecket Well. W Yor . . . . . . . . . . .2H 91
Peckforton. Ches E . . . . . . . . . . .5H 83
Peckham Bush. Kent . . . . . . . . .5A 40
Peckleton. Leics . . . . . . . . . . . . .5B 74
Pedair-ffordd. Powy . . . . . . . . . .3D 70
Pedham. Norf . . . . . . . . . . . . . . .4F 79
Pedlinge. Kent . . . . . . . . . . . . . .2F 29
Pedmore. W Mid . . . . . . . . . . . .2D 60
Pedwell. Som . . . . . . . . . . . . . . .3H 21

Peebles. Bord . . . . . . . . . . . . . .5F 129
Peel. IOM . . . . . . . . . . . . . . . . .3B 108
Peel. Bord . . . . . . . . . . . . . . . . .1G 119
Peel Common. Hants . . . . . . . . .2D 16
Peening Quarter. Kent . . . . . . . .3C 28
Peggs Green. Leics . . . . . . . . . . .4B 74
Pegsdon. C Beds . . . . . . . . . . . .2B 52
Pegswood. Nmbd . . . . . . . . . . .1F 115
Peinchorran. High . . . . . . . . . . .5E 155
Peinlich. High . . . . . . . . . . . . . .3D 154
Pelaw. Tyne . . . . . . . . . . . . . . .3F 115
Pelcomb Bridge. Pemb . . . . . . . .3D 42
Pelcomb Cross. Pemb . . . . . . . .3D 42
Peldon. Essx . . . . . . . . . . . . . . .4C 54
Pelsall. W Mid . . . . . . . . . . . . . .5E 73
Pelton. Dur . . . . . . . . . . . . . . . .4F 115
Pelutho. Cumb . . . . . . . . . . . . .5C 112
Pelynt. Corn . . . . . . . . . . . . . . . . .3G 7
Pemberton. Carm . . . . . . . . . . . .5F 45
Pembrey. Carm . . . . . . . . . . . . .5E 45
Pembridge. Here . . . . . . . . . . . . .5F 59
Pembroke. Pemb . . . . . . . . . . . .4D 43
Pembroke Dock. Pemb . . . . . . . .4D 42
Pembroke Ferry. Pemb . . . . . . . .4D 42
Pembury. Kent . . . . . . . . . . . . . .1H 27
Penallt. Mon . . . . . . . . . . . . . . . .4A 48
Penally. Pemb . . . . . . . . . . . . . .5F 43
Penalt. Here . . . . . . . . . . . . . . . .3A 48
Penalum. Pemb . . . . . . . . . . . . .5F 43
Penare. Corn . . . . . . . . . . . . . . . .4D 6
Penarth. V Glam . . . . . . . . . . . . .4E 33
Penbeagle. Corn . . . . . . . . . . . . . .3C 4
Penberth. Corn . . . . . . . . . . . . . . .4B 4
Pen-bont Rhydybeddau.
  Cdgn . . . . . . . . . . . . . . . . . . .2F 57
Penbryn. Cdgn . . . . . . . . . . . . . .5B 56
Pencader. Carm . . . . . . . . . . . . .2E 45
Pen-cae. Cdgn . . . . . . . . . . . . . .5D 56
Pencaenewydd. Gwyn . . . . . . . .1D 68
Pencaerau. Neat . . . . . . . . . . . .3G 31
Pencaitland. E Lot . . . . . . . . . . .3H 129
Pencarnisiog. IOA . . . . . . . . . . .3C 80
Pencarreg. Carm . . . . . . . . . . . .1F 45
Pencarrow. Corn . . . . . . . . . . . .4B 10
Pencelli. Powy . . . . . . . . . . . . . .3D 46
Pen-clawdd. Swan . . . . . . . . . . .3E 31
Pencoed. B'end . . . . . . . . . . . . .3C 32
Pencombe. Here . . . . . . . . . . . . .5H 59
Pencraig. Here . . . . . . . . . . . . . .3A 48
Pencraig. Powy . . . . . . . . . . . . .3C 70
Pendeen. Corn . . . . . . . . . . . . . . .3A 4
Pendeford. W Mid . . . . . . . . . . .5C 72
Penderyn. Rhon . . . . . . . . . . . . .5C 46
Pendine. Carm . . . . . . . . . . . . . .4G 43
Pendlebury. G Man . . . . . . . . . . .4F 91
Pendleton. G Man . . . . . . . . . . .1C 84
Pendleton. Lanc . . . . . . . . . . . . .1F 91
Pendock. Worc . . . . . . . . . . . . . .2C 48
Pendoggett. Corn . . . . . . . . . . . .5A 10
Pendomer. Som . . . . . . . . . . . . .1A 14
Pendoylan. V Glam . . . . . . . . . . .4D 32
Pendre. B'end . . . . . . . . . . . . . .3C 32
Penegoes. Powy . . . . . . . . . . . .5G 69
Penelewey. Corn . . . . . . . . . . . . .4C 6
Penffordd. Pemb . . . . . . . . . . . .2E 43
Penffordd-Lâs. Powy . . . . . . . . .1A 58
Penfro. Pemb . . . . . . . . . . . . . .4D 43
Pengam. Cphy . . . . . . . . . . . . . .2E 33
Pengam. Card . . . . . . . . . . . . . .4F 33
Penge. G Lon . . . . . . . . . . . . . . .4E 39
Pengelly. Corn . . . . . . . . . . . . . .4A 10
Pengenffordd. Powy . . . . . . . . . .2E 47
Pengersick. Corn . . . . . . . . . . . . .4C 4
Pengorffwysfa. IOA . . . . . . . . . .1D 80
Pengover Green. Corn . . . . . . . . . .2G 7
Pengwern. Den . . . . . . . . . . . . .3C 82
Penhale. Corn
  nr. Mullion . . . . . . . . . . . . . . .5D 5
  nr. St Austell . . . . . . . . . . . . . .3D 6
Penhale Camp. Corn . . . . . . . . . .3B 6
Penhallow. Corn . . . . . . . . . . . . .3B 6
Penhalvean. Corn . . . . . . . . . . . .5B 6
Penhelig. Gwyn . . . . . . . . . . . . .1F 57
Penhill. Swin . . . . . . . . . . . . . . .3G 35

Penhow. Newp . . . . . . . . . . . . . .2H 33
Penhurst. E Sus . . . . . . . . . . . . .4A 28
Peniarth. Gwyn . . . . . . . . . . . . . .5F 69
Penicuik. Midl . . . . . . . . . . . . . .3F 129
Peniel. Carm . . . . . . . . . . . . . . . .3E 45
Penifiler. High . . . . . . . . . . . . . .4D 155
Peninver. Arg . . . . . . . . . . . . . . .3B 122
Penisa'r Waun. Gwyn . . . . . . . . .4E 81
Penistone. S Yor . . . . . . . . . . . . .4C 92
Penketh. Warr . . . . . . . . . . . . . .2H 83
Penkill. S Ayr . . . . . . . . . . . . . . .5B 116
Penkridge. Staf . . . . . . . . . . . . . .4D 72
Penley. Wrex . . . . . . . . . . . . . . .2G 71
Penllech. Gwyn . . . . . . . . . . . . .2B 68
Penllergaer. Swan . . . . . . . . . . . .3F 31
Pen-llyn. IOA . . . . . . . . . . . . . . .2C 80
Penmachno. Cnwy . . . . . . . . . . .5G 81
Penmaen. Swan . . . . . . . . . . . . .4E 31
Penmaenmawr. Cnwy . . . . . . . . .3G 81
Penmaenpool. Gwyn . . . . . . . . . .4F 69
Penmaen Rhos. Cnwy . . . . . . . . .3A 82
Pen-marc. V Glam . . . . . . . . . . .5D 32
Penmark. V Glam . . . . . . . . . . . .5D 32
Penmarth. Corn . . . . . . . . . . . . . .5B 6
Penmon. IOA . . . . . . . . . . . . . . .2F 81
Penmorfa. Gwyn . . . . . . . . . . . .1E 69
Penmynydd. IOA . . . . . . . . . . . .3E 81
Penn. Buck . . . . . . . . . . . . . . . . .1A 38
Penn. Dors . . . . . . . . . . . . . . . .3G 13
Penn. W Mid . . . . . . . . . . . . . . .1C 60
Pennal. Gwyn . . . . . . . . . . . . . .5G 69
Pennan. Abers . . . . . . . . . . . . .2F 161
Pennant. Cdgn . . . . . . . . . . . . . .4E 57
Pennant. Den . . . . . . . . . . . . . . .2C 70
Pennant. Gwyn . . . . . . . . . . . . .3B 70
Pennant. Powy . . . . . . . . . . . . . .1A 58
Pennant Melangell. Powy . . . . . .3C 70
Pennar. Pemb . . . . . . . . . . . . . .4D 42
Pennard. Swan . . . . . . . . . . . . . .4E 31
Pennerley. Shrp . . . . . . . . . . . . .1F 59
Pennington. Cumb . . . . . . . . . . .2B 96
Pennington. G Man . . . . . . . . . . .1A 84
Pennington. Hants . . . . . . . . . . .3B 16
Pennorth. Powy . . . . . . . . . . . . .3E 46
Penn Street. Buck . . . . . . . . . . . .1A 38
Pennsylvania. Devn . . . . . . . . . .3C 12
Pennsylvania. S Glo . . . . . . . . . .4C 34
Penny Bridge. Cumb . . . . . . . . .1C 96
Pennycross. Plym . . . . . . . . . . . . .3A 8
Pennygate. Norf . . . . . . . . . . . . .3F 79
Pennyghael. Arg . . . . . . . . . . . .1C 132
Penny Hill. Linc . . . . . . . . . . . . .3C 76
Pennylands. Lanc . . . . . . . . . . . .4C 90
Pennymoor. Devn . . . . . . . . . . . .1B 12
Pennyvenie. E Ayr . . . . . . . . . . .4D 117
Pennywell. Tyne . . . . . . . . . . . .4G 115
Penparc. Cdgn . . . . . . . . . . . . . .1C 44
Penparcau. Cdgn . . . . . . . . . . . .2E 57
Pen-pedair-heol. Cphy . . . . . . . .2E 33
Penperlleni. Mon . . . . . . . . . . . .5G 47
Penpillick. Corn . . . . . . . . . . . . . .3E 7
Penpol. Corn . . . . . . . . . . . . . . . .5C 6
Penpoll. Corn . . . . . . . . . . . . . . . .3F 7
Penponds. Corn . . . . . . . . . . . . . .3D 4
Penpont. Corn . . . . . . . . . . . . . .5A 10
Penpont. Dum . . . . . . . . . . . . . .5H 117
Penprysg. B'end . . . . . . . . . . . .3C 32
Penquit. Devn . . . . . . . . . . . . . . .3C 8
Penrherber. Carm . . . . . . . . . . . .1G 43
Penrhiw. Pemb . . . . . . . . . . . . . .1C 44
Penrhiwceiber. Rhon . . . . . . . . .2D 32
Pen-Rhiw-fawr. Neat . . . . . . . . .4H 45
Penrhiw-llan. Cdgn . . . . . . . . . . .1D 44
Penrhiw-pal. Cdgn . . . . . . . . . . .1D 44
Penrhos. Gwyn . . . . . . . . . . . . .2C 68
Penrhos. Here . . . . . . . . . . . . . . .5F 59
Penrhos. IOA . . . . . . . . . . . . . . .2B 80
Penrhos. Mon . . . . . . . . . . . . . .4H 47
Penrhos. Powy . . . . . . . . . . . . . .4B 46
Penrhos Garnedd. Gwyn . . . . . . .3E 81
Penrhyn. IOA . . . . . . . . . . . . . . .1C 80
Penrhyn Bay. Cnwy . . . . . . . . . .2H 81
Penrhyn-coch. Cdgn . . . . . . . . . .2F 57

Penrhyndeudraeth. Gwyn . . . . . .2F 69
Penrhyn-side. Cnwy . . . . . . . . . .2H 81
Penrice. Swan . . . . . . . . . . . . . .4D 31
Penrith. Cumb . . . . . . . . . . . . .2G 103
Penrose. Corn . . . . . . . . . . . . . . .1C 6
Penruddock. Cumb . . . . . . . . . .2F 103
Penryn. Corn . . . . . . . . . . . . . . . .5B 6
Pen-sarn. Carm . . . . . . . . . . . . .4E 45
Pen-sarn. Gwyn . . . . . . . . . . . . .3E 69
Pensax. Worc . . . . . . . . . . . . . . .4B 60
Pensby. Mers . . . . . . . . . . . . . . .2E 83
Penselwood. Som . . . . . . . . . . . .3C 22
Pensford. Bath . . . . . . . . . . . . . .5B 34
Pensham. Worc . . . . . . . . . . . . .1E 49
Penshaw. Tyne . . . . . . . . . . . . .4G 115
Penshurst. Kent . . . . . . . . . . . . .1G 27
Pensilva. Corn . . . . . . . . . . . . . . .2G 7
Pennsett. W Mid . . . . . . . . . . . . .2D 60
Penston. E Lot . . . . . . . . . . . . . .2H 129
Penstone. Devn . . . . . . . . . . . . .2A 12
Pentewan. Corn . . . . . . . . . . . . . .4E 6
Pentir. Gwyn . . . . . . . . . . . . . . .4E 81
Pentire. Corn . . . . . . . . . . . . . . . .2B 6
Pentlepoir. Pemb . . . . . . . . . . . .4F 43
Pentlow. Essx . . . . . . . . . . . . . .1B 54
Pentney. Norf . . . . . . . . . . . . . . .4G 77
Penton Mewsey. Hants . . . . . . . .2B 24
Pentraeth. IOA . . . . . . . . . . . . . .3E 81
Pentre. Powy
  nr. Church Stoke . . . . . . . . . . .1E 59
  nr. Kerry . . . . . . . . . . . . . . . . .2D 58
  nr. Mochdre . . . . . . . . . . . . . .2C 58
Pentre. Rhon . . . . . . . . . . . . . . .2C 32
Pentre. Shrp . . . . . . . . . . . . . . . .4F 71
Pentre. Wrex
  nr. Chirk . . . . . . . . . . . . . . . . .2E 71
  nr. Llanarmon Dyffryn Ceiriog
  . . . . . . . . . . . . . . . . . . . . . . . . .2D 70
Pentre-bach. Cdgn . . . . . . . . . . .1F 45
Pentre-bach. Powy . . . . . . . . . . .2C 46
Pentrebach. Carm . . . . . . . . . . . .2B 46
Pentrebach. Mer T . . . . . . . . . . .5D 46
Pentre-bont. Cnwy . . . . . . . . . . .5G 81
Pentre Berw. IOA . . . . . . . . . . . .3D 80
Pentre-bont. Cnwy . . . . . . . . . . .5G 81
Pentrecagal. Carm . . . . . . . . . . .1D 44
Pentre-celyn. Den . . . . . . . . . . .5D 82
Pentre-clawdd. Shrp . . . . . . . . . .2E 71
Pentreclwydau. Neat . . . . . . . . . .5B 46
Pentre-cwrt. Carm . . . . . . . . . . .2D 45
Pentre Dolau Honddu.
  Powy . . . . . . . . . . . . . . . . . . .1C 46
Pentre-dwr. Swan . . . . . . . . . . . .3F 31
Pentrefelin. Carm . . . . . . . . . . . .3F 45
Pentrefelin. Cdgn . . . . . . . . . . . .1G 45
Pentrefelin. Cnwy . . . . . . . . . . . .3H 81
Pentrefelin. Gwyn . . . . . . . . . . . .2E 69
Pentrefoelas. Cnwy . . . . . . . . . .5A 82
Pentre Galar. Pemb . . . . . . . . . .1F 43
Pentregat. Cdgn . . . . . . . . . . . . .5C 56
Pentre Gwenlais. Carm . . . . . . . .4G 45
Pentre Gwynfryn. Gwyn . . . . . . .3E 69
Pentre Halkyn. Flin . . . . . . . . . . .3E 82
Pentre Hodre. Shrp . . . . . . . . . . .3F 59
Pentre-Llanrhaeadr. Den . . . . . . .4C 82
Pentre Llifior. Powy . . . . . . . . . . .1D 58
Pentrellwyn. IOA . . . . . . . . . . . .2E 81
Pentre-llwyn-llwyd. Powy . . . . . .5B 58
Pentre-llyn-cymmer. Cnwy . . . . .5B 82
Pentre Meyrick. V Glam . . . . . . .4C 32
Pentre-piod. Gwyn . . . . . . . . . . .2A 70
Pentre-poeth. Newp . . . . . . . . . .3F 33
Pentre'r beirdd. Powy . . . . . . . . .4D 70
Pentre'r-felin. Powy . . . . . . . . . .2C 46
Pentre-tafarn-y-fedw.
  Cnwy . . . . . . . . . . . . . . . . . . .4H 81
Pentre-ty-gwyn. Carm . . . . . . . .2B 46
Pentre-uchaf. Gwyn . . . . . . . . . .2C 68
Pentrich. Derbs . . . . . . . . . . . . . .5A 86
Pentridge. Dors . . . . . . . . . . . . .1F 15
Pen-twyn. Cphy . . . . . . . . . . . . .5F 47
Pen-twyn. Mon . . . . . . . . . . . . .5A 48
Pentwyn. Card . . . . . . . . . . . . . .3E 33
Pentyrch. Card . . . . . . . . . . . . . .3E 32

Pentywyn. Carm . . . . . . . . . . . . .4G 43
Penuwch. Cdgn . . . . . . . . . . . . .4E 57
Penwithick. Corn . . . . . . . . . . . . .3E 7
Penwyllt. Powy . . . . . . . . . . . . . .4B 46
Pen-y-banc. Carm . . . . . . . . . . . .3G 45
Penybanc. Carm . . . . . . . . . . . . .4G 45
Pen-y-bont. Carm . . . . . . . . . . . .2H 43
Pen-y-bont. Powy . . . . . . . . . . . .3E 70
Penybont. Powy . . . . . . . . . . . . .4D 58
Pen-y-Bont Ar Ogwr.
  B'end . . . . . . . . . . . . . . . . . . .3C 32
Penybontfawr. Powy . . . . . . . . . .3C 70
Pen-y-bryn. Pemb . . . . . . . . . . . .1B 44
Pen-y-bryn. Wrex . . . . . . . . . . . .1E 71
Penybryn. Cphy . . . . . . . . . . . . .2E 33
Pen-y-cae. Powy . . . . . . . . . . . . .4B 46
Pencyae. Wrex . . . . . . . . . . . . . .1E 71
Pen-y-cae mawr. Mon . . . . . . . . .2H 33
Pencyaerau. Swan . . . . . . . . . . . .3A 68
Pen-y-cefn. Flin . . . . . . . . . . . . .3D 82
Pen-y-clawdd. Mon . . . . . . . . . .5H 47
Pen-y-coedcae. Rhon . . . . . . . . .3D 32
Pencywm. Pemb . . . . . . . . . . . . .2C 42
Pen-y-Darren. Mer T . . . . . . . . . .5D 46
Pen-y-fai. B'end . . . . . . . . . . . . .3B 32
Pen-y-ffordd. Flin . . . . . . . . . . . .2D 82
Penyffordd. Flin . . . . . . . . . . . . . .4F 83
Penyffridd. Gwyn . . . . . . . . . . . .5E 81
Pen-y-garn. Cdgn . . . . . . . . . . . .2F 57
Pen-y-garnedd. IOA . . . . . . . . . .3E 81
Penygarnedd. Powy . . . . . . . . . .3D 70
Pen-y-graig. Gwyn . . . . . . . . . . .2B 68
Penygraig. Rhon . . . . . . . . . . . . .2C 32
Pen-y-graigwen. IOA . . . . . . . . . .2D 80
Pen-y-groes. Carm . . . . . . . . . . .4F 45
Penygroes. Gwyn . . . . . . . . . . . .5D 80
Penygroes. Pemb . . . . . . . . . . . .1F 43
Pen-y-Mynydd. Carm . . . . . . . . .5E 45
Penymynydd. Flin . . . . . . . . . . . .4F 83
Pen-yr-heol. Mon . . . . . . . . . . . .4H 47
Penyrheol. Cphy . . . . . . . . . . . . .3E 33
Penyrheol. Swan . . . . . . . . . . . . .3E 31
Penysarn. IOA . . . . . . . . . . . . . .1D 80
Pen-y-stryt. Den . . . . . . . . . . . . .5D 82
Penywaun. Rhon . . . . . . . . . . . . .5C 46
Penzance. Corn . . . . . . . . . . . . . .3B 4
Peopleton. Worc . . . . . . . . . . . . .5D 60
Peover Heath. Ches E . . . . . . . . .3B 84
Peper Harow. Surr . . . . . . . . . . .1A 26
Peplow. Shrp . . . . . . . . . . . . . . .3A 72
Pepper Arden. N Yor . . . . . . . . .4F 105
Perceton. N Ayr . . . . . . . . . . . . .5E 127
Percyhorner. Abers . . . . . . . . . .2G 161
Perham Down. Wilts . . . . . . . . . .2A 24
Periton. Som . . . . . . . . . . . . . . . .2C 20
Perkinsville. Dur . . . . . . . . . . . .4F 115
Perry Green. Essx . . . . . . . . . . . .3B 54
Perry Green. Herts . . . . . . . . . . .4E 53
Perry Green. Wilts . . . . . . . . . . .3E 35
Perry Street. Kent . . . . . . . . . . . .3H 39
Perry Street. Som . . . . . . . . . . . .2G 13
Perrywood. Kent . . . . . . . . . . . . .5E 41
Pershall. Staf . . . . . . . . . . . . . . .3C 72
Pershore. Worc . . . . . . . . . . . . . .1E 49
Pertenhall. Bed . . . . . . . . . . . . . .4H 63
Perth. Per . . . . . . . . . . . . . . . . .1D 136
Perthy. Shrp . . . . . . . . . . . . . . . .2F 71
Perton. Staf . . . . . . . . . . . . . . . .1C 60
Pertwood. Wilts . . . . . . . . . . . . .3D 23
Peterborough. Pet . . . . . . . . . . .1A 64
Peterburn. High . . . . . . . . . . . . .5B 162
Peterchurch. Here . . . . . . . . . . . .2G 47
Peterculter. Aber . . . . . . . . . . . .3F 153
Peterhead. Abers . . . . . . . . . . . .4H 161

Peterlee. Dur .....5H 115
**Petersfield.** Hants .....4F 25
Petersfinger. Wilts .....4G 23
Peters Green. Herts .....4B 52
Peters Marland. Devn .....1E 11
Peterstone Wentlooge.
   Newp .....3F 33
Peterston-super-Ely.
   V Glam .....4D 32
Peterstow. Here .....3A 48
Peters Village. Kent .....4B 40
Peter Tavy. Devn .....5F 11
Petertown. Orkn .....7C 172
Petham. Kent .....5F 41
Petherwin Gate. Corn .....4C 10
Petrockstowe. Devn .....2F 11
Petsoe End. Mil .....1G 51
Pett. E Sus .....4C 28
Pettaugh. Suff .....5D 66
Pett Bottom. Kent .....5F 41
Petteridge. Kent .....1A 28
Pettinain. S Lan .....5C 128
Pettistree. Suff .....5E 67
Petton. Devn .....4D 20
Petton. Shrp .....3G 71
Petts Wood. G Lon .....4F 39
Pettycur. Fife .....1F 129
Pettywell. Norf .....3C 78
Petworth. W Sus .....3A 26
Pevensey. E Sus .....5H 27
Pevensey Bay. E Sus .....5A 28
Pewsey. Wilts .....5G 35
Pheasants Hill. Buck .....3F 37
Philadelphia. Tyne .....4G 115
Philham. Devn .....4C 18
Philiphaugh. Bord .....2G 119
Phillack. Corn .....3C 4
Philleigh. Corn .....5C 6
Philpstoun. W Lot .....2D 128
Phocle Green. Here .....3B 48
Phoenix Green. Hants .....1F 25
Pibsbury. Som .....4H 21
Pibwrlwyd. Carm .....4E 45
Pica. Cumb .....2B 102
Piccadilly. Warw .....1G 61
Piccadilly Corner. Norf .....2E 67
Piccotts End. Herts .....5A 52
Pickering. N Yor .....1B 100
Picket Piece. Hants .....2B 24
Picket Post. Hants .....2G 15
Pickford. W Mid .....2G 61
Pickhill. N Yor .....1F 99
Picklenash. Glos .....3C 48
Picklescott. Shrp .....1G 59
Pickletillem. Fife .....1G 137
Pickmere. Ches E .....3A 84
Pickstock. Telf .....3B 72
Pickwell. Devn .....2E 19
Pickwell. Leics .....4E 75
Pickworth. Linc .....2H 75
Pickworth. Rut .....4G 75
Picton. Ches W .....3G 83
Picton. Flin .....2D 82
Picton. N Yor .....4B 106
Pict's Hill. Som .....4H 21
Piddinghoe. E Sus .....5F 27
Piddington. Buck .....2G 37
Piddington. Nptn .....5F 63
Piddington. Oxon .....4E 51
Piddlehinton. Dors .....3C 14
Piddletrenthide. Dors .....2C 14
Pidley. Cambs .....3C 64
Pidney. Dors .....2C 14
Pie Corner. Here .....4A 60
Piercebridge. Darl .....3F 105
Pierowall. Orkn .....3D 172
Pigdon. Nmbd .....1E 115
Pightley. Som .....3F 21
Pikehall. Derbs .....5F 85
Pikeshill. Hants .....2A 16
Pilford. Dors .....2F 15
Pilgrims Hatch. Essx .....1G 39
Pilham. Linc .....1F 87
Pill. N Som .....4A 34


The Pill. Mon .....3H 33
Pillaton. Corn .....2H 7
Pillaton. Staf .....4D 72
Pillerton Hersey. Warw .....1B 50
Pillerton Priors. Warw .....1A 50
Pilleth. Powy .....4E 59
Pilley. Hants .....3B 16
Pilley. S Yor .....4D 92
Pillgwenlly. Newp .....3G 33
Pilling. Lanc .....5D 96
Pilling Lane. Lanc .....5D 96
Pillowell. Glos .....5B 48
Pillwell. Dors .....1C 14
Pilning. S Glo .....3A 34
Pilsbury. Derbs .....4F 85
Pilsdon. Dors .....3H 13
Pilsgate. Pet .....5H 75
Pilsley. Derbs
   nr. Bakewell .....3G 85
   nr. Clay Cross .....4B 86
Pilson Green. Norf .....4F 79
Piltdown. E Sus .....3F 27
Pilton. Edin .....2F 129
Pilton. Nptn .....2H 63
Pilton. Rut .....5G 75
Pilton. Som .....2A 22
Pilton Green. Swan .....4D 30
Pimperne. Dors .....2E 15
Pinchbeck. Linc .....3B 76
Pinchbeck Bars. Linc .....3A 76
Pinchbeck West. Linc .....3B 76
Pinfold. Lanc .....3B 90
Pinford End. Suff .....5H 65
Pinged. Carm .....5E 45
Pinhoe. Devn .....3C 12
Pinkerton. E Lot .....2D 130
Pinkneys Green. Wind .....3G 37
Pinley. W Mid .....3A 62
Pinley Green. Warw .....4G 61
Pinmill. Suff .....2F 55
Pinmore. S Ayr .....5B 116
**Pinner.** G Lon .....2C 38
Pins Green. Worc .....1C 48
Pinsley Green. Ches E .....1H 71
Pinvin. Worc .....1E 49
Pinwherry. S Ayr .....1G 109
Pinxton. Derbs .....5B 86
Pipe and Lyde. Here .....1A 48
Pipe Aston. Here .....3G 59
Pipe Gate. Shrp .....1B 72
Pipehill. Staf .....5E 73
Piperhill. High .....3C 158
Pipe Ridware. Staf .....4E 73
Pipers Pool. Corn .....4C 10
Pipewell. Nptn .....2F 63
Pippacott. Devn .....3F 19
Pipton. Powy .....2E 47
Pirbright. Surr .....5A 38
Pirnmill. N Ayr .....5G 125
Pirton. Herts .....2B 52
Pirton. Worc .....1D 49
Pisgah. Stir .....3G 135
Pishill. Oxon .....3F 37
Pistyll. Gwyn .....1C 68
Pitagowan. Per .....2F 143
Pitcairn. Per .....3F 143
Pitcairngreen. Per .....1C 136
Pitcalnie. High .....1C 158
Pitcaple. Abers .....1E 152
Pitchcombe. Glos .....5D 48
Pitchcott. Buck .....3F 51
Pitchford. Shrp .....5H 71
Pitch Green. Buck .....5F 51
Pitch Place. Surr .....5A 38
Pitcombe. Som .....3B 22
Pitcox. E Lot .....2C 130
Pitcur. Per .....5B 144
Pitfichie. Abers .....2D 152
Pitgrudy. High .....4E 165
Pitkennedy. Ang .....3E 145
Pitlessie. Fife .....3F 137
Pitlochry. Per .....3G 143
Pitmachie. Abers .....1D 152
Pitmaduthy. High .....1B 158


Pitmedden. Abers .....1F 153
Pitminster. Som .....1F 13
Pitnacree. Per .....3G 143
Pitney. Som .....4H 21
Pitroddie. Per .....1E 136
Pitscottie. Fife .....2G 137
Pitsea. Essx .....2B 40
Pitsford. Nptn .....4E 63
Pitsford Hill. Som .....3E 20
Pitsmoor. S Yor .....2A 86
Pitstone. Buck .....4H 51
Pitt. Hants .....4C 24
Pitt Court. Glos .....2C 34
Pittentrail. High .....3E 164
Pittenweem. Fife .....3H 137
Pittington. Dur .....5G 115
Pitton. Swan .....4D 30
Pitton. Wilts .....3H 23
Pittswood. Kent .....1H 27
Pittulie. Abers .....2G 161
Pittville. Glos .....3E 49
Pitversie. Per .....2D 136
Pity Me. Dur .....5F 115
Pityme. Corn .....1D 6
Pixey Green. Suff .....3E 67
Pixley. Here .....2B 48
Place Newton. N Yor .....2C 100
Plaidy. Abers .....3E 161
Plaidy. Corn .....3G 7
Plain Dealings. Pemb .....3E 43
Plains. N Lan .....3A 128
Plaish. Shrp .....1H 59
Plaistow. Here .....2B 48
Plaistow. W Sus .....2B 26
Plaitford. Wilts .....1A 16
Plastow Green. Hants .....5D 36
Plas yn Cefn. Den .....3C 82
The Platt. E Sus .....2G 27
Platt Bridge. G Man .....4E 90
Platt Lane. Shrp .....2H 71
Platts Common. S Yor .....4D 92
Platt's Heath. Kent .....5C 40
Plawsworth. Dur .....5F 115
Plaxtol. Kent .....5H 39
Playden. E Sus .....3D 28
Playford. Suff .....1F 55
Play Hatch. Oxon .....4F 37
Playing Place. Corn .....4C 6
Playley Green. Glos .....2C 48
Plealey. Shrp .....5G 71
Plean. Stir .....1B 128
Pleasington. Bkbn .....2E 91
Pleasley. Derbs .....4C 86
Pledgdon Green. Essx .....3F 53
Plenmeller. Nmbd .....3A 114
Pleshey. Essx .....4G 53
Plockton. High .....5H 155
Plocrapol. W Isl .....8D 171
Ploughfield. Here .....1G 47
Plowden. Shrp .....2F 59
Ploxgreen. Shrp .....5F 71
Pluckley. Kent .....1D 28
Plucks Gutter. Kent .....4G 41
Plumbland. Cumb .....1C 102
Plumgarths. Cumb .....5F 103
Plumley. Ches E .....3B 84
Plummers Plain. W Sus .....3D 26
Plumpton. Cumb .....1F 103
Plumpton. E Sus .....4E 27
Plumpton. Nptn .....1D 50
Plumpton Foot. Cumb .....1F 103
Plumpton Green. E Sus .....4E 27
Plumpton Head. Cumb .....1G 103
Plumstead. G Lon .....3F 39
Plumstead. Norf .....2D 78
Plumtree. Notts .....2D 74
Plumtree Park. Notts .....2D 74
Plungar. Leics .....2E 75
Plush. Dors .....2C 14
Plushabridge. Corn .....5D 10
Plwmp. Cdgn .....5C 56
**Plymouth.** Plym .....3A 8
Plympton. Plym .....3B 8


Plymstock. Plym .....3B 8
Plymtree. Devn .....2D 12
Pockley. N Yor .....1A 100
Pocklington. E Yor .....5C 100
Pode Hole. Linc .....3B 76
Podimore. Som .....4A 22
Podington. Bed .....4G 63
Podmore. Staf .....2B 72
Poffley End. Oxon .....4B 50
Point Clear. Essx .....4D 54
Pointon. Linc .....2A 76
Pokesdown. Bour .....3G 15
Polbae. Dum .....2H 109
Polbain. High .....3E 163
Polbathic. Corn .....3H 7
Polbeth. W Lot .....3D 128
Polbrock. Corn .....2E 6
Polchar. High .....3C 150
Polebrook. Nptn .....2H 63
Pole Elm. Worc .....1D 48
Polegate. E Sus .....5G 27
Pole Moor. W Yor .....3A 92
Poles. High .....4E 165
Polesworth. Warw .....5G 73
Polglass. High .....3E 163
Polgooth. Corn .....3D 6
Poling. W Sus .....5B 26
Poling Corner. W Sus .....5B 26
Polio. High .....1B 158
Polkerris. Corn .....3E 7
Polla. High .....3D 166
Pollard Street. Norf .....2F 79
Pollicott. Buck .....4F 51
Pollington. E Yor .....3G 93
Polloch. High .....2B 140
Pollok. Glas .....3G 127
Pollokshaws. Glas .....3G 127
Pollokshields. Glas .....3G 127
Polmaily. High .....5G 157
Polmassick. Corn .....4D 6
**Polmont.** Falk .....2C 128
Polnessan. E Ayr .....3D 116
Polnish. High .....5F 147
Polperro. Corn .....3G 7
Polruan. Corn .....3F 7
Polscoe. Corn .....2F 7
Polsham. Som .....2A 22
Polskeoch. Dum .....4F 117
Polstead. Suff .....2C 54
Polstead Heath. Suff .....1C 54
Poltesco. Corn .....5E 5
Poltimore. Devn .....3C 12
Polton. Midl .....3F 129
Polwarth. Bord .....4D 130
Polyphant. Corn .....4C 10
Polzeath. Corn .....1D 6
Ponde. Powy .....2E 46
Pondersbridge. Cambs .....1B 64
Ponders End. G Lon .....1E 39
Pond Street. Essx .....2E 53
Pondtail. Hants .....1G 25
Ponsanooth. Corn .....5B 6
Ponsongath. Corn .....5E 5
Ponsworthy. Devn .....5H 11
Pontamman. Carm .....4G 45
Pontantwn. Carm .....4E 45
Pontardawe. Neat .....5H 45
Pontarddulais. Swan .....5F 45
Pontarfynach. Cdgn .....3G 57
Pont-ar-gothi. Carm .....3F 45
Pont ar Hydfer. Powy .....3B 46
Pontarllechau. Carm .....3H 45
Pontarsais. Carm .....3E 45
Pontblyddyn. Flin .....4E 83
Pontbren Llwyd. Rhon .....5C 46
Pont-Cyfyng. Cnwy .....5G 81
Pontdolgoch. Powy .....1C 58
**Pontefract.** W Yor .....2E 93
**Ponteland.** Nmbd .....2E 115
Ponterwyd. Cdgn .....2G 57
Pontesbury. Shrp .....5G 71
Pontesford. Shrp .....5G 71
Pontfadog. Wrex .....2E 71
Pont-Faen. Shrp .....2E 71


Pont-faen. Powy .....2C 46
Pontfaen. Pemb .....1E 43
Pontgarreg. Cdgn .....5C 56
Pont-Henri. Carm .....5E 45
Ponthir. Torf .....2G 33
Ponthirwaun. Cdgn .....1C 44
Pont-iets. Carm .....5E 45
Pontllanfraith. Cphy .....2E 33
Pontlliw. Swan .....5G 45
Pont Llogel. Powy .....4C 70
Pontlyfni. Gwyn .....5D 80
Pontlottyn. Cphy .....5E 46
Pontneddfechan. Powy .....5C 46
Pont-newydd. Carm .....5E 45
Pont-newydd. Flin .....4D 82
Pontnewynydd. Torf .....2F 33
Ponton. Shet .....6E 173
Pont Pen-y-benglog. Gwyn .....4F 81
Pontrhydfendigaid. Cdgn .....4G 57
Pont Rhyd-y-cyff. B'end .....3B 32
Pontrhydyfen. Neat .....2A 32
Pont-rhyd-y-groes. Cdgn .....3G 57
Pontrhydyrun. Torf .....2F 33
Pont-Rhythall. Gwyn .....4E 81
Pontrilas. Here .....3G 47
Pontrilas Road. Here .....3G 47
Pontrobert. Powy .....4D 70
Pont-rug. Gwyn .....4E 81
Ponts Green. E Sus .....4A 28
Pontshill. Here .....3B 48
Pont-Sian. Cdgn .....1E 45
Pontsticill. Mer T .....4D 46
Pont-Walby. Neat .....5B 46
Pontwelly. Carm .....2E 45
Pontwgan. Cnwy .....3G 81
Pontyates. Carm .....5E 45
Pontyberem. Carm .....4F 45
Pontybodkin. Flin .....5E 83
Pontyclun. Rhon .....3D 32
Pontycymer. B'end .....2C 32
Pontyglazier. Pemb .....1F 43
Pontygwaith. Rhon .....2D 32
Pont-y-pant. Cnwy .....5G 81
**Pontypool.** Torf .....2F 33
**Pontypridd.** Rhon .....3D 32
**Pontywl.** Torf .....2F 33
Pontywaun. Cphy .....2F 33
Pooksgreen. Hants .....1B 16
Pool. Corn .....4A 6
Pool. W Yor .....5E 99
Poole. N Yor .....2E 93
**Poole.** Pool .....3F 15
Poole. Som .....4E 21
Poole Keynes. Glos .....2E 35
Poolend. Staf .....5D 84
Poolewe. High .....5C 162
Pooley Bridge. Cumb .....2F 103
Poolfold. Staf .....5C 84
Pool Head. Here .....5H 59
Pool Hey. Lanc .....3B 90
Poolhill. Glos .....3C 48
Poolmill. Here .....3A 48
Pool o' Muckhart. Clac .....3C 136
Pool Quay. Powy .....4E 71
Poolsbrook. Derbs .....3B 86
Pool Street. Essx .....2A 54
Pootings. Kent .....1F 27
Pope Hill. Pemb .....3D 42
Pope's Hill. Glos .....4B 48
Popeswood. Brac .....5G 37
Popham. Hants .....2D 24
**Poplar.** G Lon .....2E 39
Popley. Hants .....1E 25
Porchfield. IOW .....3C 16
Porin. High .....3F 157
Poringland. Norf .....5E 79
Porkellis. Corn .....5A 6
Porlock. Som .....2B 20
Porlock Weir. Som .....2B 20
Portachoillan. Arg .....4F 125
Port Adhair Bheinn na
   Faoghla. W Isl .....3C 170
Port Adhair Thirilodh. Arg .....4B 138
**Portadown.** Arm .....5F 175

Portaferry. Ards ....5J 175
Port Ann. Arg ....1H 125
Port Appin. Arg ....4D 140
Port Asgaig. Arg ....3C 124
Port Askaig. Arg ....3C 124
Portavadie. Arg ....3H 125
Portavogie. Ards ....4J 175
Portballintrae. Caus ....1F 175
Port Bannatyne. Arg ....3B 126
Portbury. N Som ....4A 34
Port Carlisle. Cumb ....3D 112
Port Charlotte. Arg ....4A 124
Portchester. Hants ....2E 16
Port Clarence. Stoc T ....2B 106
Port Driseach. Arg ....2A 126
Port Dundas. Glas ....3G 127
Port Ellen. Arg ....5B 124
Port Elphinstone. Abers ....1E 153
Portencalzie. Dum ....2F 109
Portencross. N Ayr ....5C 126
Port Erin. IOM ....5A 108
Port Erroll. Abers ....5H 161
Porter's Fen Corner. Norf ....5E 77
Portesham. Dors ....4B 14
Portessie. Mor ....2B 160
Port e Vullen. IOM ....2D 108
Port-Eynon. Swan ....4D 30
Portfield. Som ....4H 21
Portfield Gate. Pemb ....3D 42
Portgate. Devn ....4E 11
Port Glasgow. Inv ....2E 127
Portglenone. ME Ant ....2F 175
Portgordon. Mor ....2A 160
Portgower. High ....2H 165
Porth. Corn ....2C 6
Porth. Rhon ....2D 32
Porthaethwy. IOA ....3E 81
Porthallow. Corn
  nr. Looe ....3G 7
  nr. St Keverne ....4E 5
Porthcawl. B'end ....4B 32
Porthceri. V Glam ....5D 32
Porthcothan. Corn ....1C 6
Porthcurno. Corn ....4A 4
Port Henderson. High ....1G 155
Porthgain. Pemb ....1C 42
Porthgwarra. Corn ....4A 4
Porthill. Shrp ....4G 71
Porthkerry. V Glam ....5D 32
Porthleven. Corn ....4D 4
Porthllechog. IOA ....1D 80
Porthmadog. Gwyn ....2E 69
Porthmeor. Corn ....3B 4
Porth Navas. Corn ....4E 5
Portholland. Corn ....4D 6
Porthoustock. Corn ....4E 5
Porthtowan. Corn ....4A 6
Porth Tywyn. Carm ....5E 45
Porth-y-felin. IOA ....2B 80
Porthyrhyd. Carm
  nr. Carmarthen ....4F 45
  nr. Llandovery ....2H 45
Porth-y-waen. Shrp ....3E 71
Portincaple. Arg ....4B 134
Portington. E Yor ....1A 94
Portinnisherrich. Arg ....2G 133
Portinscale. Cumb ....2D 102
Port Isaac. Corn ....1D 6
Portishead. N Som ....4H 33
Portknockie. Mor ....2B 160
Port Lamont. Arg ....2B 126
Portlethen. Abers ....4G 153
Portlethen Village. Abers ....4G 153
Portling. Dum ....4F 111
Port Lion. Pemb ....4D 43
Portloe. Corn ....5D 6
Port Logan. Dum ....5F 109
Portmahomack. High ....5G 165
Portmead. Swan ....3F 31
Portmeirion. Gwyn ....2E 69
Portmellon. Corn ....4E 6
Port Mholair. W Isl ....4H 171
Port Mor. High ....1F 139

Portmore. Hants ....3B 16
Port Mulgrave. N Yor ....3E 107
Portnacroish. Arg ....4D 140
Portnahaven. Arg ....4A 124
Portnalong. High ....5C 154
Portnaluchaig. High ....5E 147
Portnancon. High ....2E 167
Port Nan Giuran. W Isl ....4H 171
Port nan Long. W Isl ....1D 170
Port Nis. W Isl ....1H 171
Portobello. Edin ....2G 129
Portobello. W Yor ....3D 92
Porton. Wilts ....3G 23
Portormin. High ....5D 168
Portpatrick. Dum ....4F 109
Port Quin. Corn ....1D 6
Port Ramsay. Arg ....4C 140
Portreath. Corn ....4A 6
Portree. High ....4D 155
Port Righ. High ....4D 155
Portrush. Caus ....1E 175
Port St Mary. IOM ....5B 108
Portscatho. Corn ....5C 6
Portsea. Port ....2E 17
Port Seton. E Lot ....2H 129
Portskerra. High ....2A 168
Portskewett. Mon ....3A 34
Portslade-by-Sea. Brig ....5D 26
Portsmouth. Port ....2E 17
Portsmouth. W Yor ....2H 91
Port Soderick. IOM ....4C 108
Port Solent. Port ....2E 17
Portsonachan. Arg ....1H 133
Portsoy. Abers ....2C 160
Portstewart. Caus ....1E 175
Port Sunlight. Mers ....2F 83
Portswood. Sotn ....1C 16
Port Talbot. Neat ....3A 32
Porttannachy. Mor ....2A 160
Port Tennant. Swan ....3F 31
Portuairk. High ....2F 139
Portway. Here ....1H 47
Portway. Worc ....3E 61
Port Wemyss. Arg ....4A 124
Port William. Dum ....5A 110
Portwrinkle. Corn ....3H 7
Poslingford. Suff ....1A 54
Postbridge. Devn ....5G 11
Postcombe. Oxon ....2F 37
Post Green. Dors ....3E 15
Postling. Kent ....2F 29
Postlip. Glos ....3F 49
Post-Mawr. Cdgn ....5D 56
Postwick. Norf ....5E 79
Potarch. Abers ....4D 152
Potsgrove. C Beds ....3H 51
Potten End. Herts ....5A 52
Potter Brompton. N Yor ....2D 101
Pottergate Street. Norf ....1D 66
Potterhanworth. Linc ....4H 87
Potterhanworth Booths.
  Linc ....4H 87
Potter Heigham. Norf ....4G 79
Potter Hill. Leics ....3E 75
The Potteries. Stoke ....1C 72
Potterne. Wilts ....1E 23
Potterne Wick. Wilts ....1F 23
Potternewton. W Yor ....1D 92
Potters Bar. Herts ....5C 52
Potters Brook. Lanc ....4D 97
Potter's Cross. Staf ....2C 60
Potter Somersal. Derbs ....2F 73
Potterspury. Nptn ....1F 51
Potter Street. Essx ....5E 53
Potterton. Abers ....2G 153
Potthorpe. Norf ....3B 78
Pottle Street. Wilts ....2D 22
Potto. N Yor ....4B 106
Potton. C Beds ....1C 52
Pott Row. Norf ....3G 77
Pott Shrigley. Ches E ....3D 84
Poughill. Corn ....2C 10

Poughill. Devn ....2B 12
Poulner. Hants ....2G 15
Poulshot. Wilts ....1E 23
Poulton. Glos ....5G 49
Poulton-le-Fylde. Lanc ....1B 90
Pound Bank. Worc ....3B 60
Poundbury. Dors ....3B 14
Pound Green. E Sus ....3G 27
Pound Green. Suff ....5G 65
Pound Hill. W Sus ....2D 27
Poundland. S Ayr ....1G 109
Poundon. Buck ....3E 51
Poundsgate. Devn ....5H 11
Poundstock. Corn ....3C 10
Pound Street. Hants ....5C 36
Pounsley. E Sus ....3G 27
Powburn. Nmbd ....3E 121
Powderham. Devn ....4C 12
Powerstock. Dors ....3A 14
Powfoot. Dum ....3C 112
Powick. Worc ....5C 60
Powmill. Per ....4C 136
Poxwell. Dors ....4C 14
Poyle. Slo ....3B 38
Poynings. W Sus ....4D 26
Poyntington. Dors ....4B 22
Poynton. Ches E ....2D 84
Poynton. Telf ....4H 71
Poynton Green. Telf ....4H 71
Poystreet Green. Suff ....5B 66
Praa Sands. Corn ....4C 4
Pratt's Bottom. G Lon ....4F 39
Praze-an-Beeble. Corn ....3D 4
Prees. Shrp ....2H 71
Preesall. Lanc ....5C 96
Preesall Park. Lanc ....5C 96
Prees Green. Shrp ....2H 71
Prees Higher Heath. Shrp ....2H 71
Prendergast. Pemb ....3D 42
Prendwick. Nmbd ....3E 121
Pren-gwyn. Cdgn ....1E 45
Prenteg. Gwyn ....1E 69
Prenton. Mers ....2F 83
Prescot. Mers ....1G 83
Prescott. Devn ....1D 12
Prescott. Shrp ....3G 71
Preshute. Wilts ....5G 35
Pressen. Nmbd ....1C 120
Prestatyn. Den ....2C 82
Prestbury. Ches E ....3D 84
Prestbury. Glos ....3E 49
Presteigne. Powy ....4F 59
Presthope. Shrp ....1H 59
Prestleigh. Som ....2B 22
Preston. Brig ....5E 27
Preston. Devn ....5B 12
Preston. Dors ....4C 14
Preston. E Lot
  nr. East Linton ....2B 130
  nr. Prestonpans ....2G 129
Preston. E Yor ....1E 95
Preston. Glos ....5F 49
Preston. Herts ....3B 52
Preston. Kent
  nr. Canterbury ....4G 41
  nr. Faversham ....4E 41
Preston. Lanc ....2D 90
Preston. Nmbd ....2F 121
Preston. Rut ....5F 75
Preston. Bord ....4D 130
Preston. Shrp ....4H 71
Preston. Suff ....5B 66
Preston. Wilts
  nr. Aldbourne ....4A 36
  nr. Lyneham ....4F 35
Preston Bagot. Warw ....4F 61
Preston Bissett. Buck ....3E 51
Preston Bowyer. Som ....4E 21
Preston Brockhurst. Shrp ....3H 71
Preston Brook. Hal ....2H 83
Preston Candover. Hants ....2E 24
Preston Capes. Nptn ....5C 62

Preston Cross. Glos ....2B 48
Preston Gubbals. Shrp ....4G 71
Preston-le-Skerne. Dur ....2A 106
Preston Marsh. Here ....1A 48
Prestonmill. Dum ....4A 112
Preston on Stour. Warw ....1H 49
Preston on the Hill. Hal ....2H 83
Preston on Wye. Here ....1G 47
Prestonpans. E Lot ....2G 129
Preston Plucknett. Som ....1A 14
Preston-under-Scar. N Yor ....5D 104
Preston upon the Weald
  Moors. Telf ....4A 72
Preston Wynne. Here ....1A 48
Prestwich. G Man ....4G 91
Prestwick. Nmbd ....2E 115
Prestwick. S Ayr ....2C 116
Prestwold. Leics ....3C 74
Prestwood. Buck ....5G 51
Prestwood. Staf ....1F 73
Price Town. B'end ....2C 32
Prickwillow. Cambs ....2E 65
Priddy. Som ....1A 22
Priestcliffe. Derbs ....3F 85
Priesthill. Glas ....3G 127
Priest Hutton. Lanc ....2E 97
Priestland. E Ayr ....1E 117
Priest Weston. Shrp ....1E 59
Priestwood. Brac ....4G 37
Priestwood. Kent ....4A 40
Primethorpe. Leics ....1C 62
Primrose Green. Norf ....4C 78
Primrose Hill. Glos ....5B 48
Primrose Hill. Lanc ....4B 90
Primrose Valley. N Yor ....2F 101
Primsidemill. Bord ....2C 120
Princes Gate. Pemb ....3F 43
Princes Risborough. Buck ....5G 51
Princethorpe. Warw ....3B 62
Princetown. Devn ....5F 11
Prinsted. W Sus ....2F 17
Prion. Den ....4C 82
Prior Muir. Fife ....2H 137
Prior's Frome. Here ....2A 48
Priors Halton. Shrp ....3G 59
Priors Hardwick. Warw ....5B 62
Priorslee. Telf ....4B 72
Priors Marston. Warw ....5B 62
Prior's Norton. Glos ....3D 48
The Priory. W Ber ....5B 36
Priory Wood. Here ....1F 47
Priston. Bath ....5B 34
Pristow Green. Norf ....2D 66
Prittlewell. S'end ....2C 40
Privett. Hants ....4E 25
Prixford. Devn ....3F 19
Probus. Corn ....4C 6
Prospect. Cumb ....5C 112
Prospect Village. Staf ....4E 73
Provanmill. Glas ....3H 127
Prudhoe. Nmbd ....3D 115
Publow. Bath ....5B 34
Puckeridge. Herts ....3D 53
Puckington. Som ....1G 13
Pucklechurch. S Glo ....4B 34
Puckrup. Glos ....2D 49
Puddinglake. Ches W ....4B 84
Puddington. Ches W ....3F 83
Puddington. Devn ....1B 12
Puddlebrook. Glos ....4B 48
Puddledock. Norf ....1C 66
Puddletown. Dors ....3C 14
Pudleston. Here ....5H 59
Pudsey. W Yor ....1C 92
Pulborough. W Sus ....4B 26
Puleston. Telf ....3B 72
Pulford. Ches W ....5F 83
Pulham. Dors ....2C 14
Pulham Market. Norf ....2D 66
Pulham St Mary. Norf ....2E 66
Pulley. Shrp ....5G 71
Pulloxhill. C Beds ....2A 52
Pulpit Hill. Arg ....1F 133
Pulverbatch. Shrp ....5G 71

Pumpherston. W Lot ....3D 128
Pumsaint. Carm ....1G 45
Puncheston. Pemb ....2E 43
Puncknowle. Dors ....4A 14
Punnett's Town. E Sus ....3H 27
Purbrook. Hants ....2E 17
Purfleet. Thur ....3G 39
Puriton. Som ....2G 21
Purleigh. Essx ....5B 54
Purley. G Lon ....4E 39
Purley on Thames. W Ber ....4E 37
Purlogue. Shrp ....3F 59
Purl's Bridge. Cambs ....2D 65
Purse Caundle. Dors ....1B 14
Purslow. Shrp ....2F 59
Purston Jaglin. W Yor ....3E 93
Purtington. Som ....2G 13
Purton. Glos
  nr. Lydney ....5B 48
  nr. Sharpness ....5B 48
Purton. Wilts ....3F 35
Purton Stoke. Wilts ....2F 35
Pury End. Nptn ....1F 51
Pusey. Oxon ....2B 36
Putley. Here ....2B 48
Putney. G Lon ....3D 38
Puttenham. Herts ....4G 51
Puttenham. Surr ....1A 26
Puttock End. Essx ....1B 54
Puttock's End. Essx ....4F 53
Puxey. Dors ....1C 14
Puxton. N Som ....5H 33
Pwll. Carm ....5E 45
Pwll. Powy ....5D 70
Pwllcrochan. Pemb ....4D 42
Pwll-glas. Den ....5D 82
Pwllgloyw. Powy ....2D 46
Pwllheli. Gwyn ....2C 68
Pwllmeyric. Mon ....2A 34
Pwll-trap. Carm ....3G 43
Pwll-y-glaw. Neat ....2A 32
Pyecombe. W Sus ....4D 27
Pye Corner. Herts ....4E 53
Pye Corner. Newp ....3G 33
Pye Green. Staf ....4D 73
Pyewipe. NE Lin ....3F 95
Pyle. B'end ....3B 32
Pyle. IOW ....5C 16
Pyle Hill. Surr ....5A 38
Pylle. Som ....3B 22
Pymoor. Cambs ....2D 65
Pymore. Dors ....3H 13
Pyrford. Surr ....5B 38
Pyrford Village. Surr ....5B 38
Pyrton. Oxon ....2E 37
Pytchley. Nptn ....3F 63
Pyworthy. Devn ....2D 10

# Q

Quabbs. Shrp ....2E 58
Quadring. Linc ....2B 76
Quadring Eaudike. Linc ....2B 76
Quainton. Buck ....3F 51
Quaking Houses. Dur ....4E 115
Quarley. Hants ....2A 24
Quarndon. Derbs ....1H 73
Quarrendon. Buck ....4G 51
Quarrier's Village. Inv ....3E 127
Quarrington. Linc ....1H 75
Quarrington Hill. Dur ....1A 106
The Quarry. Glos ....2C 34
Quarry Bank. W Mid ....2D 60
Quarrywood. Mor ....2F 159
Quartalehouse. Abers ....4G 161
Quarter. N Ayr ....3C 126
Quarter. S Lan ....4A 128
Quatford. Shrp ....1B 60
Quatt. Shrp ....2B 60
Quebec. Dur ....5E 115
Quedgeley. Glos ....4D 48
Queen Adelaide. Cambs ....2E 65

Queenborough—Rhondda

Queenborough. Kent 3D 40
Queen Camel. Som 4A 22
Queen Charlton. Bath 5B 34
Queen Dart. Devn 1B 12
Queenhill. Worc 2D 48
Queen Oak. Dors 3C 22
Queensbury. W Yor 1B 92
Queensferry. Flin 4F 83
**Queensferry Crossing**. Edin 2E 129
Queenstown. Bkpl 1B 90
Queen Street. Kent 1A 28
Queenzieburn. N Lan 2H 127
Quemerford. Wilts 5F 35
Quendale. Shet 10E 173
Quendon. Essx 2F 53
Queniborough. Leics 4D 74
Quenington. Glos 5G 49
Quernmore. Lanc 3E 97
Quethiock. Corn 2H 7
Quholm. Orkn 6B 172
Quick's Green. W Ber 4D 36
Quidenham. Norf 2C 66
Quidhampton. Hants 1D 24
Quidhampton. Wilts 3G 23
Quilquox. Abers 5G 161
Quina Brook. Shrp 2H 71
Quindry. Orkn 8D 172
Quine's Hill. IOM 4C 108
Quinton. Nptn 5E 63
Quinton. W Mid 2D 61
Quintrell Downs. Corn 2C 6
Quixhill. Staf 1F 73
Quoditch. Devn 3E 11
Quorn. Leics 4C 74
Quorndon. Leics 4C 74
Quothquan. S Lan 1B 118
Quoyloo. Orkn 5B 172
Quoyness. Orkn 7B 172
Quoys. Shet
on Mainland 5F 173
on Unst 1H 173

## R

Rableyheath. Herts 4C 52
Raby. Cumb 4C 112
Raby. Mers 3F 83
Rachan Mill. Bord 1D 118
Rachub. Gwyn 4F 81
Rack End. Oxon 5C 50
Rackenford. Devn 1B 12
Rackham. W Sus 4B 26
Rackheath. Norf 4E 79
Racks. Dum 2B 112
Rackwick. Orkn
on Hoy 8B 172
on Westray 3D 172
Radbourne. Derbs 2G 73
**Radcliffe**. G Man 4F 91
Radcliffe. Nmbd 4G 121
Radcliffe on Trent. Notts 2D 74
Radclive. Buck 2E 51
Radernie. Fife 3G 137
Radfall. Kent 4F 41
Radford. Bath 1B 22
Radford. Nott 1C 74
Radford. Oxon 3C 50
Radford. W Mid 2H 61
Radford. Worc 5E 61
Radford Semele. Warw 4H 61
Radipole. Dors 4B 14
Radlett. Herts 1C 38
Radley. Oxon 2D 36
Radnage. Buck 2F 37
**Radstock**. Bath 1B 22
Radstone. Nptn 1D 50
Radway. Warw 1B 50
Radway Green. Ches E 5B 84
Radwell. Bed 5H 63
Radwell. Herts 2C 52
Radwinter. Essx 2G 53
Radyr. Card 3E 33
RAF Coltishall. Norf 3E 79
Rafford. Mor 3E 159
Ragdale. Leics 4D 74
Ragdon. Shrp 1G 59
Ragged Appleshaw. Hants 2B 24
Raggra. High 4F 169
Raglan. Mon 5H 47
Ragnall. Notts 3F 87
Raigbeg. High 1C 150
Rainford. Mers 4C 90
Rainford Junction. Mers 4C 90
**Rainham**. G Lon 2G 39
Rainham. Medw 4C 40
Rainhill. Mers 1G 83
Rainow. Ches E 3D 84
Rainton. N Yor 2F 99
Rainworth. Notts 5C 86
Raisbeck. Cumb 4H 103
Raise. Cumb 5A 114
Rait. Per 1E 137
Raithby. Linc 2C 88
Raithby by Spilsby. Linc 4C 88
Raithwaite. N Yor 3F 107
Rake. W Sus 4G 25
Rake End. Staf 4E 73
Rakeway. Staf 1E 73
Rakewood. G Man 3H 91
Ralia. High 4B 150
Ram Alley. Wilts 5H 35
Ramasaig. High 4A 154
Rame. Corn
nr. Millbrook 4A 8
nr. Penryn 5B 6
Ram Lane. Kent 1D 28
Ramnageo. Shet 1H 173
Rampisham. Dors 2A 14
Rampside. Cumb 3B 96
Rampton. Cambs 4D 64
Rampton. Notts 3E 87
**Ramsbottom**. G Man 3F 91
Ramsburn. Mor 3C 160
Ramsbury. Wilts 4A 36
Ramscraigs. High 1H 165
Ramsdean. Hants 4F 25
Ramsdell. Hants 1D 24
Ramsden. Oxon 4B 50
Ramsden. Worc 1E 49
Ramsden Bellhouse. Essx 1B 40
Ramsden Heath. Essx 1B 40
Ramsey. Cambs 2B 64
Ramsey. Essx 2F 55
Ramsey. IOM 2D 108
Ramsey Forty Foot. Cambs 2C 64
Ramsey Heights. Cambs 2B 64
Ramsey Island. Essx 5C 54
Ramsey Mereside. Cambs 2B 64
Ramsey St Mary's. Cambs 2B 64
**Ramsgate**. Kent 4H 41
Ramsgill. N Yor 2D 98
Ramshaw. Dur 5C 114
Ramshorn. Staf 1E 73
Ramsley. Devn 3G 11
Ramsnest Common. Surr 2A 26
Ramstone. Abers 2D 152
Ranais. W Isl 5G 171
Ranby. Linc 3B 88
Ranby. Notts 2D 86
Rand. Linc 3A 88
Randalstown. Ant 3F 175
Randwick. Glos 5D 48
Ranfurly. Ren 3E 127
Rangag. High 4D 169
Rangemore. Staf 3F 73
Rangeworthy. S Glo 3B 34
Rankinston. E Ayr 3D 116
Rank's Green. Essx 4H 53
Ranmore Common. Surr 5C 38
Rannoch Station. Per 3B 142
Ranochan. High 5G 147
Ranskill. Notts 2D 86
Ranton. Staf 3C 72
Ranton Green. Staf 3C 72
Ranworth. Norf 4F 79
Raploch. Stir 4G 135
Rapness. Orkn 3E 172
Rapps. Som 1G 13
Rascal Moor. E Yor 1B 94
Rascarrel. Dum 5E 111
Rasharkin. Caus 2F 175
Rashfield. Arg 1C 126
Rashwood. Worc 4D 60
Raskelf. N Yor 2G 99
Rassau. Blae 4E 47
Rastrick. W Yor 2B 92
Ratagan. High 2B 148
Ratby. Leics 5C 74
Ratcliffe Culey. Leics 1H 61
Ratcliffe on Soar. Notts 3B 74
Ratcliffe on the Wreake. Leics 4D 74
Rathen. Abers 2H 161
Rathfriland. Arm 6G 175
Rathillet. Fife 1F 137
Rathmell. N Yor 3H 97
Ratho. Edin 2E 129
Ratho Station. Edin 2E 129
Rathven. Mor 2B 160
Ratley. Hants 4B 24
Ratley. Warw 1B 50
Ratlinghope. Shrp 1G 59
Rattar. High 1E 169
Ratten Row. Cumb 5E 113
Ratten Row. Lanc 5D 96
Rattery. Devn 2D 8
Rattlesden. Suff 5B 66
Ratton Village. E Sus 5G 27
Rattray. Abers 3H 161
Rattray. Per 4A 144
Raughton. Cumb 5E 113
Raughton Head. Cumb 5E 113
Raunds. Nptn 3G 63
Ravenfield. S Yor 1B 86
Ravenfield Common. S Yor 1B 86
Ravenglass. Cumb 5B 102
Ravenhills Green. Worc 5B 60
Raveningham. Norf 1F 67
Ravenscar. N Yor 4G 107
Ravensdale. IOM 2C 108
Ravensden. Bed 5H 63
Ravenseat. N Yor 4B 104
Ravenshead. Notts 5C 86
Ravensmoor. Ches E 5A 84
Ravensthorpe. Nptn 3D 62
Ravensthorpe. W Yor 2C 92
Ravenstone. Leics 4B 74
Ravenstone. Mil 5F 63
Ravenstonedale. Cumb 4A 104
Ravenstown. Cumb 2C 96
Ravenstruther. S Lan 5C 128
Ravensworth. N Yor 4E 105
Raw. N Yor 4G 107
Rawcliffe. E Yor 2G 93
Rawcliffe. York 4H 99
Rawcliffe Bridge. E Yor 2G 93
Rawdon. W Yor 1C 92
Rawgreen. Nmbd 4C 114
**Rawmarsh**. S Yor 1B 86
Rawnsley. Staf 4E 73
Rawreth. Essx 1B 40
Rawridge. Devn 2F 13
Rawson Green. Derbs 1A 74
**Rawtenstall**. Lanc 2G 91
Raydon. Suff 2D 54
Raylees. Nmbd 5D 120
**Rayleigh**. Essx 1C 40
Raymond's Hill. Devn 3G 13
Rayne. Essx 3H 53
Rayners Lane. G Lon 2C 38
Reach. Cambs 4E 65
Read. Lanc 1F 91
**Reading**. Read 4F 37
Reading Green. Suff 3D 66
Reading Street. Kent 2D 28
Readymoney. Corn 3F 7
Reagill. Cumb 3H 103
Rearquhar. High 4E 165
Rearsby. Leics 4D 74
Reasby. Linc 3H 87
Reaseheath. Ches E 5A 84
Reaster. High 2E 169
Reawick. Shet 7E 173
Reay. High 2B 168
Rechullin. High 3A 156
Reculver. Kent 4G 41
Redberth. Pemb 4E 43
Redbourn. Herts 4B 52
Redbourne. N Lin 4C 94
Redbrook. Glos 5A 48
Redbrook. Wrex 1H 71
Redburn. High 4D 158
Redburn. Nmbd 3A 114
**Redcar**. Red C 2D 106
Redcastle. High 4H 157
Redcliffe Bay. N Som 4H 33
Red Dial. Cumb 5D 112
Redding. Falk 2C 128
Reddingmuirhead. Falk 2C 128
The Reddings. Glos 3E 49
Reddish. G Man 1C 84
**Redditch**. Worc 4E 61
Rede. Suff 5H 65
Redenhall. Norf 2E 67
Redesdale Camp. Nmbd 5C 120
Redesmouth. Nmbd 1B 114
Redford. Ang 4E 145
Redford. Dur 1D 105
Redford. W Sus 4G 25
Redfordgreen. Bord 3F 119
Redgate. Corn 2G 7
Redgrave. Suff 3C 66
Red Hill. Warw 5F 61
Red Hill. W Yor 2E 93
Redhill. Abers 3E 153
Redhill. Herts 2C 52
Redhill. N Som 5A 34
Redhill. Shrp 4B 72
**Redhill**. Surr 5D 39
Redhouses. Arg 3B 124
Redisham. Suff 2G 67
Redland. Bris 4A 34
Redland. Orkn 5C 172
Redlingfield. Suff 3D 66
Red Lodge. Suff 3F 65
Redlynch. Som 3C 22
Redlynch. Wilts 4H 23
Redmain. Cumb 1C 102
Redmarley. Worc 4B 60
Redmarley D'Abitot. Glos 2C 48
Redmarshall. Stoc T 2A 106
Redmile. Leics 2E 75
Redmire. N Yor 5D 104
Rednal. Shrp 3F 71
Redpath. Bord 1H 119
Redpoint. High 2G 155
Red Post. Corn 2C 10
Red Rock. G Man 4D 90
Red Roses. Carm 3G 43
Red Row. Nmbd 5G 121
**Redruth**. Corn 4B 6
Red Street. Staf 5C 84
Redvales. G Man 4G 91
Red Wharf Bay. IOA 2E 81
Redwick. Newp 3H 33
Redwick. S Glo 3A 34
Redworth. Darl 2F 105
Reed. Herts 2D 52
Reed End. Herts 2D 52
Reedham. Linc 5B 88
Reedham. Norf 5G 79
Reedness. E Yor 2B 94
Reeds Beck. Linc 4B 88
Reemshill. Abers 4E 161
Reepham. Linc 3H 87
Reepham. Norf 3C 78
Reeth. N Yor 5D 104
Regaby. IOM 2D 108
Regil. N Som 5A 34
Regoul. High 3C 158
Reiff. High 2D 162
**Reigate**. Surr 5D 38
Reighton. N Yor 2F 101
Reilth. Shrp 2E 59
Reinigeadal. W Isl 7E 171
Reisque. Abers 2F 153
Reiss. High 3F 169
Rejerrah. Corn 3B 6
Releath. Corn 5A 6
Relubbus. Corn 3C 4
Relugas. Mor 4D 159
Remenham. Wok 3F 37
Remenham Hill. Wok 3F 37
Rempstone. Notts 3C 74
Rendcomb. Glos 5F 49
Rendham. Suff 4F 67
Rendlesham. Suff 5F 67
**Renfrew**. Ren 3G 127
Renhold. Bed 5H 63
Renishaw. Derbs 3B 86
Rennington. Nmbd 3G 121
Renton. W Dun 2E 127
Renwick. Cumb 5G 113
Repps. Norf 4G 79
Repton. Derbs 3H 73
Rescassa. Corn 4D 6
Rescobie. Ang 3E 145
Rescorla. Corn
nr. Penwithick 3E 7
nr. Sticker 4D 6
Resipole. High 2B 140
Resolfen. Neat 5B 46
Resolis. High 2A 158
Resolven. Neat 5B 46
Rest and be thankful. Arg 3B 134
Reston. Bord 3E 131
Restrop. Wilts 3F 35
**Retford**. Notts 2E 86
Retire. Corn 2E 6
Rettendon. Essx 1B 40
Revesby. Linc 4B 88
Rew. Devn 5D 8
Rewe. Devn 3C 12
Rew Street. IOW 3C 16
Rexon. Devn 4E 11
Reybridge. Wilts 5E 35
Reydon. Suff 3H 67
Reymerston. Norf 5C 78
Reynalton. Pemb 4E 43
Reynoldston. Swan 4D 31
Rezare. Corn 5D 10
Rhadyr. Mon 5G 47
Rhaeadr Gwy. Powy 4B 58
Rhandirmwyn. Carm 1A 46
Rhayader. Powy 4B 58
Rheindown. High 4H 157
Rhemore. High 3G 139
Rhenetra. High 3D 154
Rhewl. Den
nr. Llangollen 1D 70
nr. Ruthin 4D 82
Rhewl. Shrp 2F 71
Rhewl-Mostyn. Flin 2D 82
Rhian. High 2C 164
Rhian Breck. High 3C 164
Rhicarn. High 1E 163
Rhiconich. High 3C 166
Rhicullen. High 1A 158
Rhidorroch. High 4F 163
Rhifail. High 4H 167
Rhigos. Rhon 5C 46
Rhilochan. High 3E 165
Rhiroy. High 5F 163
Rhitongue. High 3G 167
Rhiw. Gwyn 3B 68
Rhiwabon. Wrex 1F 71
Rhiwbina. Card 3E 33
Rhiwbryfdir. Gwyn 1F 69
Rhiwderin. Newp 3F 33
Rhiwlas. Gwyn
nr. Bala 2B 70
nr. Bangor 4E 81
Rhiwlas. Powy 2D 70
Rhodes. G Man 4G 91
Rhodesia. Notts 2C 86
Rhodes Minnis. Kent 1F 29
Rhodiad-y-Brenin. Pemb 2B 42
**Rhondda**. Rhon 2C 32

Rhonehouse. Dum ....4E 111
Rhoose. V Glam ....5D 32
Rhos. Carm ....2D 45
Rhos. Neat ....5H 45
The Rhos. Pemb ....3E 43
Rhosaman. Carm ....4H 45
Rhoscefnhir. IOA ....3E 81
Rhoscolyn. IOA ....3B 80
Rhos Common. Powy ....4E 71
Rhoscrowther. Pemb ....4D 42
Rhos-ddu. Gwyn ....2B 68
Rhosdylluan. Gwyn ....3A 70
Rhosesmor. Flin ....4E 82
Rhos-fawr. Gwyn ....2C 68
Rhosgadfan. Gwyn ....5E 81
Rhosgoch. IOA ....2D 80
Rhosgoch. Powy ....1E 47
Rhos Haminiog. Cdgn ....4E 57
Rhos-hill. Pemb ....1B 44
Rhoshirwaun. Gwyn ....3A 68
Rhoslan. Gwyn ....1D 69
Rhoslefain. Gwyn ....5E 69
Rhosllanerchrugog. Wrex ....1E 71
Rhôs Lligwy. IOA ....2D 81
Rhosmaen. Carm ....3G 45
Rhosmeirch. IOA ....3D 80
Rhosneigr. IOA ....3C 80
Rhôs-on-Sea. Cnwy ....2H 81
Rhossili. Swan ....4D 30
Rhosson. Pemb ....2B 42
Rhostrenwfa. IOA ....3D 80
Rhostryfan. Gwyn ....5D 81
Rhostyllen. Wrex ....1F 71
Rhoswiel. Shrp ....2E 71
Rhosybol. IOA ....2D 80
Rhos-y-brithdir. Powy ....3D 70
Rhos-y-garth. Cdgn ....3F 57
Rhos-y-gwaliau. Gwyn ....2B 70
Rhos-y-llan. Gwyn ....2B 68
Rhos-y-meirch. Powy ....4E 59
Rhu. Arg ....1D 126
Rhuallt. Den ....3C 82
Rhubha Stoer. High ....1E 163
Rhudbach. Arg ....2B 126
Rhuddall Heath. Ches W ....4H 83
Rhuddlan. Cdgn ....1E 45
Rhuddlan. Den ....3C 82
Rhue. High ....4E 163
Rhulen. Powy ....1E 47
Rhunahaorine. Arg ....5F 125
Rhuthun. Den ....5D 82
Rhuvoult. High ....3C 166
Y Rhws. V Glam ....5D 32
Rhyd. Gwyn ....1F 69
Rhydaman. Carm ....4G 45
Rhydargaeau. Carm ....3E 45
Rhydcymerau. Carm ....2F 45
Rhydd. Worc ....1D 48
Rhyd-Ddu. Gwyn ....5E 81
Rhydding. Neat ....3G 31
Rhydfudr. Cdgn ....4E 57
Rhydlanfair. Cnwy ....5H 81
Rhydlewis. Cdgn ....1D 44
Rhydlios. Gwyn ....2A 68
Rhydlydan. Cnwy ....5A 82
Rhyd-meirionydd. Cdgn ....2F 57
Rhydowen. Cdgn ....1E 45
Rhyd-Rosser. Cdgn ....4E 57
Rhydspence. Here ....1F 47
Rhydtalog. Flin ....5E 83
Rhyd-uchaf. Gwyn ....2B 70
Rhydwyn. IOA ....2C 80
Rhyd-y-clafdy. Gwyn ....2C 68
Rhydycroesau. Powy ....2E 71
Rhydyfelin. Cdgn ....3E 57
Rhydyfelin. Rhon ....3D 32
Rhyd-y-foel. Cnwy ....3B 82
Rhyd-y-fro. Neat ....5H 45
Rhydymain. Gwyn ....3H 69
Rhyd-y-meudwy. Den ....5D 82
Rhydymwyn. Flin ....4E 82
Rhyd-yr-onen. Gwyn ....5F 69
Rhyd-y-sarn. Gwyn ....1F 69
Rhyl. Den ....2C 82

Rhymney. Cphy ....5E 46
Rhymni. Cphy ....5E 46
Rhynd. Per ....1D 136
Rhynie. Abers ....1B 152
Ribbesford. Worc ....3B 60
Ribbleton. Lanc ....1D 90
Ribby. Lanc ....1C 90
Ribchester. Lanc ....1E 91
Riber. Derbs ....5H 85
Ribigill. High ....3F 167
Riby. Linc ....4E 95
Riccall. N Yor ....1G 93
Ricarton. E Ayr ....1D 116
Richards Castle. Here ....4G 59
Richborough Port. Kent ....4H 41
Richhill. Arm ....5F 175
Richings Park. Buck ....3B 38
Richmond. G Lon ....3C 38
Richmond. N Yor ....4E 105
Richmond. Abers ....5F 153
Rickerby. Cumb ....4F 113
Rickerscote. Staf ....3D 72
Rickford. N Som ....1H 21
Rickham. Devn ....5D 8
Rickinghall. Suff ....3C 66
Rickleton. Tyne ....4F 115
Rickling. Essx ....2E 53
Rickling Green. Essx ....3F 53
Rickmansworth. Herts ....1B 38
Riddings. Derbs ....5B 86
Riddlecombe. Devn ....1G 11
Riddlesden. W Yor ....5C 98
Ridge. Dors ....4E 15
Ridge. Herts ....5C 52
Ridge. Wilts ....3E 23
Ridgebourne. Powy ....4C 58
Ridge Lane. Warw ....1G 61
Ridgeway. Derbs
  nr. Alfreton ....5A 86
  nr. Sheffield ....2B 86
Ridgeway. Staf ....5C 84
Ridgeway Cross. Here ....1C 48
Ridgeway Moor. Derbs ....2B 86
Ridgewell. Essx ....1H 53
Ridgewood. E Sus ....3F 27
Ridgmont. C Beds ....2H 51
Ridgwardine. Shrp ....2A 72
Riding Mill. Nmbd ....3D 114
Ridley. Kent ....4H 39
Ridley. Nmbd ....3A 114
Ridlington. Norf ....2F 79
Ridlington. Rut ....5F 75
Ridsdale. Nmbd ....1C 114
Riemore Lodge. Per ....4H 143
Rievaulx. N Yor ....1H 99
Rift House. Hart ....1B 106
Rigg. Dum ....3D 112
Riggend. N Lan ....2A 128
Rigsby. Linc ....3D 88
Rigside. S Lan ....1A 118
Riley Green. Lanc ....2E 90
Rileyhill. Staf ....4F 73
Rilla Mill. Corn ....5C 10
Rillington. N Yor ....2C 100
Rimington. Lanc ....5H 97
Rimpton. Som ....4B 22
Rimside. High ....4H 167
Rimswell. E Yor ....2G 95
Ringasta. Shet ....10E 173
Ringford. Dum ....4D 111
Ringing Hill. Leics ....4B 74
Ringinglow. S Yor ....2G 85
Ringland. Norf ....4D 78
Ringlestone. Kent ....5C 40
Ringmer. E Sus ....4F 27
Ringmore. Devn
  nr. Kingsbridge ....4C 8
  nr. Teignmouth ....5C 12
Ring o' Bells. Lanc ....3C 90
Ring's End. Cambs ....5C 76
Ringsfield. Suff ....2G 67
Ringsfield Corner. Suff ....2G 67
Ringshall. Buck ....4H 51
Ringshall. Suff ....5C 66

Ringshall Stocks. Suff ....5C 66
Ringstead. Norf ....1G 77
Ringstead. Nptn ....3G 63
Ringwood. Hants ....2G 15
Ringwould. Kent ....1H 29
Rinmore. Abers ....2B 152
Rinnigill. Orkn ....8C 172
Rinsey. Corn ....4C 4
Riof. W Isl ....4D 171
Ripe. E Sus ....4G 27
Ripley. Derbs ....5B 86
Ripley. Hants ....3G 15
Ripley. N Yor ....3E 99
Ripley. Surr ....5B 38
Riplingham. E Yor ....1C 94
Ripon. N Yor ....2F 99
Rippingale. Linc ....3H 75
Ripple. Kent ....1H 29
Ripple. Worc ....2D 48
Rippondon. W Yor ....3A 92
Rireavach. High ....4E 163
Risabus. Arg ....5B 124
Risbury. Here ....5H 59
Risby. E Yor ....1D 94
Risby. N Lin ....3C 94
Risby. Suff ....4G 65
Risca. Cphy ....2F 33
Rise. E Yor ....5F 101
Riseden. E Sus ....2H 27
Riseden. Kent ....2B 28
Rise End. Derbs ....5G 85
Riseholme. Linc ....3G 87
Riseley. Bed ....4H 63
Riseley. Wok ....5F 37
Rishangles. Suff ....4D 66
Rishton. Lanc ....1F 91
Rishworth. W Yor ....3A 92
Risley. Derbs ....2B 74
Risley. Warr ....1A 84
Risplith. N Yor ....3E 99
Rispond. High ....2E 167
Rivar. Wilts ....5B 36
Rivenhall. Essx ....4B 54
Rivenhall End. Essx ....4B 54
River. Kent ....1G 29
River. W Sus ....3A 26
River Bank. Cambs ....4E 65
Riverhead. Kent ....5G 39
Rivington. Lanc ....3E 91
Roach Bridge. Lanc ....2D 90
Roachill. Devn ....4B 20
Roade. Nptn ....5E 63
Road Green. Norf ....1E 67
Roadhead. Cumb ....2G 113
Roadmeetings. S Lan ....5B 128
Roadside. High ....2D 168
Roadside of Catterline.
  Abers ....1H 145
Roadside of Kinneff. Abers ....1H 145
Roadwater. Som ....3D 20
Road Weedon. Nptn ....5D 62
Roag. High ....4B 154
Roa Island. Cumb ....3B 96
Roath. Card ....4E 33
Roberton. Bord ....3G 119
Roberton. S Lan ....2B 118
Robertsbridge. E Sus ....3B 28
Robertstown. Mor ....4G 159
Robertstown. Rhon ....5C 46
Roberttown. W Yor ....2B 92
Robeston Back. Pemb ....3E 43
Robeston Wathen. Pemb ....3E 43
Robeston West. Pemb ....4C 42
Robin Hood. Lanc ....3D 90
Robin Hood. W Yor ....2D 92
Robinhood End. Essx ....2H 53
Robin Hood's Bay. N Yor ....4G 107
Roborough. Devn
  nr. Great Torrington ....1F 11
  nr. Plymouth ....2B 8
Rob Roy's House. Arg ....2A 134
Roby Mill. Lanc ....4D 90
Rocester. Staf ....2F 73

Roch. Pemb ....2C 42
Rochdale. G Man ....3G 91
Roche. Corn ....2D 6
Rochester. Medw ....4B 40
Rochester. Nmbd ....5C 120
Rochford. Essx ....1C 40
Rock. Corn ....1D 6
Rock. Nmbd ....2G 121
Rock. W Sus ....4C 26
Rock. Worc ....3B 60
Rockbeare. Devn ....3D 12
Rockbourne. Hants ....1G 15
Rockcliffe. Cumb ....3E 113
Rockcliffe. Dum ....4F 111
Rockcliffe Cross. Cumb ....3E 113
Rock Ferry. Mers ....2F 83
Rockfield. High ....5G 165
Rockfield. Mon ....4H 47
Rockford. Hants ....2G 15
Rockgreen. Shrp ....3H 59
Rockhampton. S Glo ....2B 34
Rockhead. Corn ....4A 10
Rockingham. Nptn ....1F 63
Rockland All Saints. Norf ....1B 66
Rockland St Mary. Norf ....5F 79
Rockland St Peter. Norf ....1B 66
Rockley. Wilts ....4G 35
Rockwell End. Buck ....3F 37
Rockwell Green. Som ....1E 13
Rodborough. Glos ....5D 48
Rodbourne. Wilts ....3E 35
Rodd. Here ....4F 59
Roddam. Nmbd ....2E 121
Rodden. Dors ....4B 14
Roddenloft. E Ayr ....2D 117
Roddymoor. Dur ....1E 105
Rode. Som ....1D 22
Rode Heath. Ches E ....5C 84
Rodeheath. Ches E ....4C 84
Rodel. W Isl ....9C 171
Roden. Telf ....4H 71
Rodhuish. Som ....3D 20
Rodington. Telf ....4H 71
Rodington Heath. Telf ....4H 71
Rodley. Glos ....4C 48
Rodmarton. Glos ....2E 35
Rodmell. E Sus ....5F 27
Rodmersham. Kent ....4D 40
Rodmersham Green. Kent ....4D 40
Rodney Stoke. Som ....2H 21
Rodsley. Derbs ....1G 73
Rodway. Som ....3F 21
Rodway. Telf ....4A 72
Rodwell. Dors ....5B 14
Roecliffe. N Yor ....3F 99
Roe Green. Herts ....2D 52
Roehampton. G Lon ....3D 38
Roesound. Shet ....5E 173
Roffey. W Sus ....2C 26
Rogart. High ....3E 165
Rogate. W Sus ....4G 25
Roger Ground. Cumb ....5E 103
Rogerstone. Newp ....3F 33
Rogiet. Mon ....3H 33
Rogue's Alley. Cambs ....5C 76
Roke. Oxon ....2E 37
Rokemarsh. Oxon ....2E 36
Roker. Tyne ....4H 115
Rollesby. Norf ....4G 79
Rolleston. Leics ....5E 75
Rolleston. Notts ....5E 87
Rolleston on Dove. Staf ....3G 73
Rolston. E Yor ....5G 101
Rolvenden. Kent ....2C 28
Rolvenden Layne. Kent ....2C 28
Romaldkirk. Dur ....2C 104
Roman Bank. Shrp ....1H 59
Romanby. N Yor ....5A 106
Romannobridge. Bord ....5E 129
Romansleigh. Devn ....4H 19
Romers Common. Worc ....4H 59
Romesdal. High ....3D 154
Romford. Dors ....2F 15
Romford. G Lon ....2G 39

Romiley. G Man ....1D 84
Romsey. Hants ....4B 24
Romsley. Shrp ....2B 60
Romsley. Worc ....3D 60
Ronague. IOM ....4B 108
Ronaldsvoe. Orkn ....8D 172
Rookby. Cumb ....3B 104
Rookhope. Dur ....5C 114
Rooking. Cumb ....3F 103
Rookley. IOW ....4D 16
Rooks Bridge. Som ....1G 21
Rooksey Green. Suff ....5B 66
Rook's Nest. Som ....3D 20
Rookwood. W Sus ....3F 17
Roos. E Yor ....1F 95
Roosebeck. Cumb ....3B 96
Roosecote. Cumb ....3B 96
Rootfield. High ....3H 157
Rootham's Green. Bed ....5A 64
Rootpark. S Lan ....4C 128
Ropley. Hants ....3E 25
Ropley Dean. Hants ....3E 25
Ropsley. Linc ....2G 75
Rora. Abers ....3H 161
Rorandle. Abers ....2D 152
Rorrington. Shrp ....5F 71
Rose. Corn ....3B 6
Roseacre. Lanc ....1C 90
Rose Ash. Devn ....4A 20
Rosebank. S Lan ....5B 128
Rosebush. Pemb ....2E 43
Rosedale Abbey. N Yor ....5E 107
Roseden. Nmbd ....2E 121
Rose Green. Essx ....3B 54
Rose Green. Suff ....1C 54
Rosehall. High ....3B 164
Rosehearty. Abers ....2G 161
Rose Hill. E Sus ....4F 27
Rose Hill. Lanc ....1G 91
Rosehill. Shrp
  nr. Market Drayton ....2A 72
  nr. Shrewsbury ....4G 71
Roseisle. Mor ....2F 159
Rosemarket. Pemb ....4D 42
Rosemarkie. High ....3B 158
Rosemary Lane. Devn ....1E 13
Rosemount. Per ....4A 144
Rosenannon. Corn ....2D 6
Roser's Cross. E Sus ....3G 27
Rosevean. Corn ....3E 6
Rosewell. Midl ....3F 129
Roseworth. Stoc T ....2B 106
Roseworthy. Corn ....3D 4
Rosgill. Cumb ....3G 103
Roshven. High ....1B 140
Roskhill. High ....4B 154
Rockorwell. Corn ....4E 5
Rosley. Cumb ....5E 112
Roslin. Midl ....3F 129
Rosliston. Derbs ....4G 73
Rosneath. Arg ....1D 126
Ross. Dum ....5D 110
Ross. Nmbd ....1F 121
Ross. Per ....1G 135
Ross. Bord ....3F 131
Rossendale. Lanc ....2F 91
Rossett. Wrex ....5F 83
Rossington. S Yor ....1D 86
Rosskeen. High ....2A 158
Rossland. Ren ....2F 127
Ross-on-Wye. Here ....3B 48
Roster. High ....5E 169
Rostherne. Ches E ....2B 84
Rostholme. S Yor ....4F 93
Rosthwaite. Cumb ....3D 102
Roston. Derbs ....1F 73
Rostrevor. New M ....6G 175
Rosudgeon. Corn ....4C 4
Rosyth. Fife ....1E 129
Rothbury. Nmbd ....4E 121
Rotherby. Leics ....4D 74
Rotherfield. E Sus ....3G 27
Rotherfield Greys. Oxon ....3F 37
Rotherfield Peppard. Oxon ....3F 37

Rotherham. S Yor ...1B 86
Rothersthorpe. Nptn ...5E 62
Rotherwick. Hants ...1F 25
Rothes. Mor ...4G 159
Rothesay. Arg ...3B 126
Rothienorman. Abers ...5E 160
Rothiesholm. Orkn ...5F 172
Rothley. Leics ...4C 74
Rothley. Nmbd ...1D 114
Rothwell. Linc ...1A 88
Rothwell. Nptn ...2F 63
Rothwell. W Yor ...2D 92
Rotsea. E Yor ...4E 101
Rottal. Ang ...2C 144
Rotten End. Suff ...4F 67
Rotten Row. Norf ...4C 78
Rotten Row. W Ber ...4D 36
Rotten Row. W Mid ...3F 61
Rottingdean. Brig ...5E 27
Rottington. Cumb ...3A 102
Roud. IOW ...4D 16
Rougham. Norf ...3H 77
Rougham. Suff ...4B 66
Rough Close. Staf ...2D 72
Rough Common. Kent ...5F 41
Roughcote. Staf ...1D 72
Rough Haugh. High ...4H 167
Rough Hay. Staf ...3G 73
Roughlee. Lanc ...5H 97
Roughley. W Mid ...1F 61
Roughsike. Cumb ...2G 113
Roughton. Linc ...4B 88
Roughton. Norf ...2E 78
Roughton. Shrp ...1B 60
Roundbush Green. Essx ...4F 53
Roundham. Som ...2H 13
Roundhay. W Yor ...1D 92
Round Hill. Torb ...2E 9
Roundhurst. W Sus ...2A 26
Round Maple. Suff ...1C 54
Round Oak. Shrp ...2F 59
Roundstreet Common. W Sus ...3B 26
Roundthwaite. Cumb ...4H 103
Roundway. Wilts ...5F 35
Roundyhill. Ang ...3C 144
Rousdon. Dor ...3F 13
Rousham. Oxon ...3C 50
Rous Lench. Worc ...5E 61
Routh. E Yor ...5E 101
Rout's Green. Buck ...2F 37
Row. Corn ...5A 10
Row. Cumb
  nr. Kendal ...1D 96
  nr. Penrith ...1H 103
The Row. Lanc ...2D 96
Rowanburn. Dum ...2F 113
Rowanhill. Abers ...3H 161
Rowardennan. Stir ...4C 134
Rowarth. Derbs ...2E 85
Row Ash. Hants ...1D 16
Rowberrow. Som ...1H 21
Rowde. Wilts ...5E 35
Rowden. Devn ...3G 11
Rowen. Cnwy ...3G 81
Rowfoot. Nmbd ...3H 113
Row Green. Essx ...3H 53
Row Heath. Essx ...4E 55
Rowhedge. Essx ...3D 54
Rowhook. W Sus ...2C 26
Rowington. Warw ...4G 61
Rowland. Derbs ...3G 85
Rowlands Castle. Hants ...1F 17
Rowlands Gill. Tyne ...4E 115
Rowledge. Hants ...2G 25
Rowley. Dur ...5D 115
Rowley. E Yor ...1C 94
Rowley. Shrp ...5F 71
Rowley Hill. W Yor ...3B 92
Rowley Regis. W Mid ...2D 60
Rowlstone. Here ...3G 47
Rowly. Surr ...1B 26
Rowner. Hants ...2D 16
Rowney Green. Worc ...3E 61
Rownhams. Hants ...1B 16

Rowrah. Cumb ...3B 102
Rowsham. Buck ...4G 51
Rowsley. Derbs ...4G 85
Rowstock. Oxon ...3C 36
Rowston. Linc ...5H 87
Rowthorne. Derbs ...4B 86
Rowton. Ches W ...4G 83
Rowton. Shrp
  nr. Ludlow ...2G 59
  nr. Shrewsbury ...4F 71
Rowton. Telf ...4A 72
Row Town. Surr ...4B 38
Roxburgh. Bord ...1B 120
Roxby. N Lin ...3C 94
Roxby. N Yor ...3E 107
Roxton. Bed ...5A 64
Roxwell. Essx ...5G 53
Royal Leamington Spa.
  Warw ...4H 61
Royal Oak. Darl ...2F 105
Royal Oak. Lanc ...4C 90
Royal Oak. N Yor ...2F 101
Royal's Green. Ches E ...1A 72
Royal Sutton Coldfield.
  W Mid ...1F 61
Royal Tunbridge Wells.
  Kent ...2G 27
Royal Wootton Bassett.
  Wilts ...3F 35
Roybridge. High ...5E 149
Roydon. Essx ...4E 53
Roydon. Norf
  nr. Diss ...2C 66
  nr. King's Lynn ...3G 77
Roydon Hamlet. Essx ...5E 53
Royston. Herts ...1D 52
Royston. S Yor ...3D 92
Royston Water. Som ...1F 13
Ruabon. Wrex ...1F 71
Ruaig. Arg ...4B 138
Ruan High Lanes. Corn ...5D 6
Ruan Lanihorne. Corn ...4C 6
Ruan Major. Corn ...5E 5
Ruan Minor. Corn ...5E 5
Ruarach. High ...1B 148
Ruardean. Glos ...4B 48
Ruardean Hill. Glos ...4B 48
Ruardean Woodside. Glos ...4B 48
Rubery. Worc ...3D 61
Ruchazie. Glas ...3H 127
Ruckcroft. Cumb ...5G 113
Ruckinge. Kent ...2E 29
Ruckland. Linc ...3C 88
Rucklers Lane. Herts ...5A 52
Ruckley. Shrp ...5H 71
Rudbaxton. Pemb ...2D 42
Rudby. N Yor ...4B 106
Ruddington. Notts ...2C 74
Rudford. Glos ...3C 48
Rudge. Shrp ...1C 60
Rudge. Wilts ...1D 22
Rudge Heath. Shrp ...1B 60
Rudgeway. S Glo ...3B 34
Rudgwick. W Sus ...2B 26
Rudhall. Here ...3B 48
Rudheath. Ches W ...3A 84
Rudley Green. Essx ...5B 54
Rudloe. Wilts ...4D 34
Rudry. Cphy ...3F 33
Rudston. E Yor ...3E 101
Rudyard. Staf ...5D 84
Rufford. Lanc ...3C 90
Rufforth. York ...4H 99
Rugby. Warw ...3C 62
Rugeley. Staf ...4E 73
Ruglen. S Ayr ...4B 116
Ruilick. High ...4H 157
Ruisaurie. High ...4G 157
Ruishton. Som ...4F 21
Ruisigearraidh. W Isl ...1E 170
Ruislip. G Lon ...2B 38
Ruislip Common. G Lon ...2B 38
Rumbling Bridge. Per ...4C 136

Rumburgh. Suff ...2F 67
Rumford. Corn ...1C 6
Rumford. Falk ...2C 128
Rumney. Card ...4F 33
Rumwell. Som ...4E 21
Runcorn. Hal ...2H 83
Runcton. W Sus ...2G 17
Runcton Holme. Norf ...5F 77
Rundlestone. Devn ...5F 11
Runfold. Surr ...2G 25
Runhall. Norf ...5C 78
Runham. Norf ...4G 79
Runnington. Som ...4E 20
Runshaw Moor. Lanc ...3D 90
Runswick. N Yor ...3F 107
Runtaleave. Ang ...2B 144
Runwell. Essx ...1B 40
Ruscombe. Wok ...4F 37
Rushall. Here ...2B 48
Rushall. Norf ...2D 66
Rushall. W Mid ...5E 73
Rushall. Wilts ...1G 23
Rushbrooke. Suff ...4A 66
Rushbury. Shrp ...1H 59
Rushden. Herts ...2D 52
Rushden. Nptn ...4G 63
Rushenden. Kent ...3D 40
Rushford. Devn ...5E 11
Rushford. Suff ...2B 66
Rush Green. Herts ...3C 52
Rushlake Green. E Sus ...4H 27
Rushmere. Suff ...2G 67
Rushmere St Andrew. Suff ...1F 55
Rushmoor. Surr ...2G 25
Rushock. Worc ...3C 60
Rusholme. G Man ...1C 84
Rushton. Ches W ...4H 83
Rushton. Nptn ...2F 63
Rushton. Shrp ...5A 72
Rushton Spencer. Staf ...4D 84
Rushwick. Worc ...5C 60
Rushyford. Dur ...2F 105
Ruskie. Stir ...3F 135
Ruskington. Linc ...5H 87
Rusland. Cumb ...1C 96
Rusper. W Sus ...2D 26
Ruspidge. Glos ...4B 48
Russell's Water. Oxon ...3F 37
Russel's Green. Suff ...3E 67
Russ Hill. Surr ...1D 26
Russland. Orkn ...6C 172
Rusthall. Kent ...2G 27
Rustington. W Sus ...5B 26
Ruston. N Yor ...1D 100
Ruston Parva. E Yor ...3E 101
Ruswarp. N Yor ...4F 107
Rutherglen. S Lan ...3H 127
Ruthernbridge. Corn ...2E 6
Ruthin. Den ...5D 82
Ruthin. V Glam ...4C 32
Ruthrieston. Aber ...3G 153
Ruthven. Abers ...4C 160
Ruthven. Ang ...4B 144
Ruthven. High
  nr. Inverness ...5C 158
  nr. Kingussie ...4B 150
Ruthvoes. Corn ...2D 6
Ruthwaite. Cumb ...1D 102
Ruthwell. Dum ...3C 112
Ruxton Green. Here ...4A 48
Ruyton-XI-Towns. Shrp ...3F 71
Ryal. Nmbd ...2D 114
Ryall. Dors ...3H 13
Ryall. Worc ...1D 48
Ryarsh. Kent ...5A 40
Rychraggan. High ...5G 157
Rydal. Cumb ...4E 103
Ryde. IOW ...3D 16
Rye. E Sus ...3D 28
Ryecroft Gate. Staf ...4D 84
Ryeford. Here ...3B 48
Rye Foreign. E Sus ...3C 28
Rye Harbour. E Sus ...4D 28
Ryehill. E Yor ...2F 95

Rye Street. Worc ...2C 48
Ryhall. Rut ...4H 75
Ryhill. W Yor ...3D 93
Ryhope. Tyne ...4H 115
Ryhope Colliery. Tyne ...4H 115
Rylands. Notts ...2C 74
Rylstone. N Yor ...4B 98
Ryme Intrinseca. Dors ...1A 14
Ryther. N Yor ...1F 93
Ryton. Glos ...2C 48
Ryton. N Yor ...2B 100
Ryton. Shrp ...5B 72
Ryton. Tyne ...3E 115
Ryton. Warw ...2B 62
Ryton-on-Dunsmore. Warw ...3A 62
Ryton Woodside. Tyne ...3E 115

## S

Saasaig. High ...3E 147
Sabden. Lanc ...1F 91
Sacombe. Herts ...4D 52
Sacriston. Dur ...5F 115
Sadberge. Darl ...3A 106
Saddell. Arg ...2B 122
Saddington. Leics ...1D 62
Saddle Bow. Norf ...4F 77
Saddlescombe. W Sus ...4D 26
Sadgill. Cumb ...4F 103
Saffron Walden. Essx ...2F 53
Sageston. Pemb ...4E 43
Saham Hills. Norf ...5B 78
Saham Toney. Norf ...5A 78
Saighdinis. W Isl ...2D 170
Saighton. Ches W ...4G 83
Sain Dunwyd. V Glam ...5C 32
Sain Hilari. V Glam ...4D 32
St Abbs. Bord ...3F 131
St Agnes. Corn ...3B 6
St Albans. Herts ...5B 52
St Allen. Corn ...3C 6
St Andrews. Fife ...2H 137
St Andrews Major. V Glam ...4E 33
St Anne's. Lanc ...2B 90
St Ann's. Dum ...5C 118
St Ann's Chapel. Corn ...5E 11
St Ann's Chapel. Devn ...4C 8
St Anthony. Corn ...5C 6
St Anthony-in-Meneage.
  Corn ...4E 5
St Arvans. Mon ...2A 34
St Asaph. Den ...3C 82
Sain Tathan. V Glam ...5D 32
St Athan. V Glam ...5D 32
St Austell. Corn ...3E 6
St Bartholomew's Hill. Wilts ...4E 23
St Bees. Cumb ...3A 102
St Blazey. Corn ...3E 7
St Blazey Gate. Corn ...3E 7
St Boswells. Bord ...1H 119
St Breock. Corn ...1D 6
St Breward. Corn ...5A 10
St Briavels. Glos ...5A 48
St Brides. Pemb ...3B 42
St Brides Major. V Glam ...4B 32
St Bride's Netherwent. Mon ...3H 33
St Bride's-super-Ely. V Glam ...4D 32
St Brides Wentlooge. Newp ...3F 33
St Budeaux. Plym ...3A 8
Saintbury. Glos ...2G 49
St Buryan. Corn ...4B 4
St Catherine. Bath ...4C 34
St Catherines. Arg ...3A 134
St Clears. Carm ...3G 43
St Cleer. Corn ...2G 7
St Clement. Corn ...4C 6
St Clether. Corn ...4C 10
St Colmac. Arg ...3B 126
St Columb Major. Corn ...2D 6
St Columb Minor. Corn ...2C 6
St Columb Road. Corn ...3D 6
St Combs. Abers ...2H 161

St Cross. Hants ...4C 24
St Cross South Elmham.
  Suff ...2E 67
St Cyrus. Abers ...2G 145
St David's. Pemb ...1B 136
St David's. Per ...1B 136
St Day. Corn ...4B 6
St Dennis. Corn ...3D 6
St Dogmaels. Pemb ...1B 44
St Dominick. Corn ...2H 7
St Donat's. V Glam ...5C 32
St Edith's Marsh. Wilts ...5E 35
St Endellion. Corn ...1D 6
St Enoder. Corn ...3C 6
St Erme. Corn ...4C 6
St Erney. Corn ...3H 7
St Erth. Corn ...3C 4
St Erth Praze. Corn ...3C 4
St Ervan. Corn ...1C 6
St Eval. Corn ...2C 6
St Ewe. Corn ...4D 6
St Fagans. Card ...4E 32
St Fergus. Abers ...3H 161
Saintfield. New M ...5H 175
St Fillans. Per ...1F 135
St Florence. Pemb ...4E 43
St Gennys. Corn ...3B 10
St George. Cnwy ...3B 82
St George's. N Som ...5G 33
St Georges. V Glam ...4D 32
St George's Hill. Surr ...4B 38
St Germans. Corn ...3H 7
St Giles in the Wood. Devn ...1F 11
St Giles on the Heath. Devn ...3D 10
St Giles's Hill. Hants ...4C 24
St Gluvias. Corn ...5B 6
St Harmon. Powy ...3B 58
St Helena. Warw ...5G 73
St Helen Auckland. Dur ...2E 105
St Helen's. E Sus ...4C 28
St Helens. Cumb ...1B 102
St Helens. IOW ...4E 17
St Helens. Mers ...1H 83
St Hilary. Corn ...3C 4
St Hilary. V Glam ...4D 32
Saint Hill. Devn ...2D 12
Saint Hill. W Sus ...2E 27
St Illtyd. Blae ...5F 47
St Ippolyts. Herts ...3B 52
St Ishmael. Carm ...5D 44
St Ishmael's. Pemb ...4C 42
St Issey. Corn ...1D 6
St Ive. Corn ...2H 7
St Ives. Cambs ...3C 64
St Ives. Corn ...2C 4
St Ives. Dors ...2G 15
St James' End. Nptn ...4E 63
St James South Elmham.
  Suff ...2F 67
St Jidgey. Corn ...2D 6
St John. Corn ...3A 8
St John's. IOM ...3B 108
St John's. Worc ...5C 60
St John's Chapel. Devn ...4F 19
St John's Chapel. Dur ...1B 104
St John's Fen End. Norf ...4E 77
St John's Town of Dalry.
  Dum ...1D 110
St Judes. IOM ...2C 108
St Just. Corn ...3A 4
St Just in Roseland. Corn ...5C 6
St Katherines. Abers ...5E 161
St Keverne. Corn ...4E 5
St Kew. Corn ...5A 10
St Kew Highway. Corn ...5A 10
St Keyne. Corn ...2G 7
St Lawrence. Corn ...2E 7
St Lawrence. Essx ...5C 54
St Lawrence. IOW ...5D 16
St Leonards. Buck ...5H 51
St Leonards. Dors ...2G 15
St Leonards. E Sus ...5B 28
St Levan. Corn ...4A 4
St Lythans. V Glam ...4E 32

St Mabyn—Scopwick


St Mabyn. *Corn* 5A **10**
St Madoes. *Per* 1D **136**
St Margaret's. *Herts* 4A **52**
St Margaret's. *Wilts* 5H **35**
St Margarets. *Here* 2G **47**
St Margarets. *Herts* 4D **53**
St Margaret's at Cliffe. *Kent* 1H **29**
St Margaret's Hope. *Orkn* 8D **172**
St Margaret South Elmham.
*Suff* 2F **67**
St Mark's. *IOM* 4B **108**
St Martin. *Corn*
nr. Helston 4E **5**
nr. Looe 3G **7**
St Martin's. *Shrp* 2F **71**
St Martins. *Per* 5A **144**
St Mary Bourne. *Hants* 1C **24**
St Mary Church. *V Glam* 4D **32**
St Marychurch. *Torb* 2F **9**
St Mary Cray. *G Lon* 4F **39**
St Mary Hill. *V Glam* 4C **32**
St Mary Hoo. *Medw* 3C **40**
St Mary in the Marsh. *Kent* 3E **29**
St Mary's. *Orkn* 7D **172**
St Mary's Airport. *IOS* 1B **4**
St Mary's Bay. *Kent* 3E **29**
St Marys Platt. *Kent* 5H **39**
St Maughan's Green. *Mon* 4H **47**
St Mawes. *Corn* 5C **6**
St Mawgan. *Corn* 2C **6**
St Mellion. *Corn* 2H **7**
St Mellons. *Card* 3F **33**
St Merryn. *Corn* 1C **6**
St Mewan. *Corn* 3D **6**
St Michael Caerhays. *Corn* 4D **6**
St Michael Penkevil. *Corn* 4C **6**
St Michaels. *Kent* 2C **28**
St Michaels. *Torb* 3E **9**
St Michaels. *Worc* 4H **59**
St Michael's on Wyre. *Lanc* 5D **96**
St Michael South Elmham.
*Suff* 2F **67**
St Minver. *Corn* 1D **6**
St Monans. *Fife* 3H **137**
St Neot. *Corn* 2F **7**
**St Neots**. *Cambs* 4A **64**
St Newlyn East. *Corn* 3C **6**
St Nicholas. *Pemb* 1C **42**
St Nicholas. *V Glam* 4D **32**
St Nicholas at Wade. *Kent* 4G **41**
St Nicholas South Elmham.
*Suff* 2F **67**
St Ninians. *Stir* 4G **135**
St Olaves. *Norf* 1G **67**
St Osyth. *Essx* 4E **54**
St Osyth Heath. *Essx* 4E **55**
St Owen's Cross. *Here* 3A **48**
St Paul's Cray. *G Lon* 4F **39**
St Paul's Walden. *Herts* 3B **52**
St Peter's. *Kent* 4H **41**
St Peter The Great. *Worc* 5C **60**
St Petrox. *Pemb* 5D **42**
St Pinnock. *Corn* 2G **7**
St Quivox. *S Ayr* 2C **116**
St Ruan. *Corn* 5E **5**
St Stephen. *Corn* 3D **6**
St Stephens. *Corn*
nr. Launceston 4D **10**
nr. Saltash 3A **8**
St Teath. *Corn* 4A **10**
St Thomas. *Devn* 3C **12**
St Thomas. *Swan* 3F **31**
St Tudy. *Corn* 5A **10**
St Twynnells. *Pemb* 5D **42**
St Veep. *Corn* 3F **7**
St Vigeans. *Ang* 4F **145**
St Wenn. *Corn* 2D **6**
St Weonards. *Here* 3H **47**
St Winnolls. *Corn* 3H **7**
St Winnow. *Corn* 3F **7**
Salcombe. *Devn* 5D **8**
Salcombe Regis. *Devn* 4E **13**
Salcott. *Essx* 4C **54**
**Sale**. *G Man* 1B **84**
Saleby. *Linc* 3D **88**
Sale Green. *Worc* 5D **60**
Salehurst. *E Sus* 3B **28**
Salem. *Carm* 3G **45**
Salem. *Cdgn* 2F **57**
Salen. *Arg* 4G **139**
Salen. *High* 2A **140**
Salesbury. *Lanc* 1E **91**
Saleway. *Worc* 5D **60**
Salford. *C Beds* 2H **51**
**Salford**. *G Man* 1C **84**
Salford. *Oxon* 3A **50**
Salford Priors. *Warw* 5E **61**
Salfords. *Surr* 1D **27**
Salhouse. *Norf* 4F **79**
Saligo. *Arg* 3A **124**
Saline. *Fife* 4C **136**
**Salisbury**. *Wilts* 3G **23**
Salkeld Dykes. *Cumb* 1G **103**
Sallachan. *High* 2D **141**
Sallachy. *High*
nr. Lairg 3C **164**
nr. Stromeferry 5B **156**
Salle. *Norf* 3D **78**
Salmonby. *Linc* 3C **88**
Salmond's Muir. *Ang* 5E **145**
Salperton. *Glos* 3F **49**
Salph End. *Bed* 5H **63**
Salsburgh. *N Lan* 3B **128**
Salt. *Staf* 3D **72**
Salta. *Cumb* 5B **112**
Saltaire. *W Yor* 1B **92**
**Saltash**. *Corn* 3A **8**
Saltburn. *High* 2B **158**
Saltburn-by-the-Sea. *Red C* 2D **106**
Saltby. *Leics* 3F **75**
Saltcoats. *Cumb* 5B **102**
**Saltcoats**. *N Ayr* 5D **126**
**Saltdean**. *Brig* 5E **27**
Salt End. *E Yor* 2E **95**
Salter. *Lanc* 3F **97**
Salterforth. *Lanc* 5A **98**
Salters Lode. *Norf* 5E **77**
Salterswall. *Ches W* 4A **84**
Salterton. *Wilts* 3G **23**
Saltfleet. *Linc* 1D **88**
Saltfleetby All Saints. *Linc* 1D **88**
Saltfleetby St Clements. *Linc* 1D **88**
Saltfleetby St Peter. *Linc* 2D **88**
Saltford. *Bath* 5B **34**
Salthouse. *Norf* 1C **78**
Saltmarshe. *E Yor* 2A **94**
Saltness. *Orkn* 9B **172**
Saltness. *Shet* 7D **173**
Saltney. *Flin* 4F **83**
Salton. *N Yor* 2B **100**
Saltrens. *Devn* 4E **19**
Saltwick. *Nmbd* 2E **115**
Saltwood. *Kent* 2F **29**
Salum. *Arg* 4B **138**
Salwarpe. *Worc* 4C **60**
Salwayash. *Dors* 3H **13**
Samalaman. *High* 1A **140**
Sambourne. *Warw* 4E **61**
Sambourne. *Wilts* 2D **22**
Sambrook. *Telf* 3B **72**
Samhia. *W Isl* 2C **170**
Samlesbury. *Lanc* 1D **90**
Samlesbury Bottoms. *Lanc* 2E **90**
Sampford Arundel. *Som* 1E **12**
Sampford Brett. *Som* 2D **20**
Sampford Courtenay. *Devn* 2G **11**
Sampford Peverell. *Devn* 1D **12**
Sampford Spiney. *Devn* 5F **11**
Samsonslane. *Orkn* 5F **172**
Samuelston. *E Lot* 2A **130**
Sanaigmore. *Arg* 2A **124**
Sancreed. *Corn* 4B **4**
Sancton. *E Yor* 1C **94**
Sand. *High* 4D **162**
Sand. *Shet* 7E **173**
Sand. *Som* 2H **21**
Sandaig. *Arg* 4A **138**
Sandaig. *High* 3F **147**
Sandale. *Cumb* 5D **112**
Sandal Magna. *W Yor* 3D **92**
Sandavore. *High* 5C **146**
Sanday Airport. *Orkn* 3F **172**
**Sandbach**. *Ches E* 4B **84**
Sandbank. *Arg* 1C **126**
Sandbanks. *Pool* 4F **15**
Sandend. *Abers* 2C **160**
Sanderstead. *G Lon* 4E **39**
Sandfields. *Neat* 3G **31**
Sandford. *Cumb* 3A **104**
Sandford. *Devn* 2B **12**
Sandford. *Dors* 4E **15**
Sandford. *Hants* 2G **15**
Sandford. *IOW* 4D **16**
Sandford. *N Som* 1H **21**
Sandford. *Shrp*
nr. Oswestry 3F **71**
nr. Whitchurch 2H **71**
Sandford. *S Lan* 5A **128**
Sandfordhill. *Abers* 4H **161**
Sandford-on-Thames. *Oxon* 5D **50**
Sandford Orcas. *Dors* 4B **22**
Sandford St Martin. *Oxon* 3C **50**
Sandgate. *Kent* 2F **29**
Sandgreen. *Dum* 4C **110**
Sandhaven. *Abers* 2G **161**
Sandhead. *Dum* 4F **109**
Sandhill. *Cambs* 2E **65**
Sandhills. *Dors* 1B **14**
Sandhills. *Oxon* 5D **50**
Sandhills. *Surr* 2A **26**
Sandhoe. *Nmbd* 3C **114**
Sand Hole. *E Yor* 1B **94**
Sandholme. *E Yor* 1B **94**
Sandholme. *Linc* 2C **76**
**Sandhurst**. *Brac* 5G **37**
Sandhurst. *Glos* 3D **48**
Sandhurst. *Kent* 3B **28**
Sandhurst Cross. *Kent* 3B **28**
Sand Hutton. *N Yor* 4A **100**
Sandhutton. *N Yor* 1F **99**
Sandiacre. *Derbs* 2B **74**
Sandilands. *Linc* 2E **89**
Sandiway. *Ches W* 3A **84**
Sandleheath. *Hants* 1G **15**
Sandling. *Kent* 5B **40**
Sandlow Green. *Ches E* 4B **84**
Sandness. *Shet* 6C **173**
Sandon. *Essx* 5H **53**
Sandon. *Herts* 2D **52**
Sandon. *Staf* 3D **72**
Sandonbank. *Staf* 3D **72**
**Sandown**. *IOW* 4D **16**
Sandplace. *Corn* 3G **7**
Sandridge. *Herts* 4B **52**
Sandringham. *Norf* 3F **77**
The Sands. *Surr* 2G **25**
Sandsend. *N Yor* 3F **107**
Sandside. *Cumb* 2C **96**
Sandsound. *Shet* 7E **173**
Sandtoft. *N Lin* 4H **93**
Sandvoe. *Shet* 2E **173**
Sandway. *Kent* 5C **40**
Sandwich. *Kent* 5H **41**
Sandwick. *Cumb* 3F **103**
Sandwick. *Orkn*
on Mainland 6B **172**
on South Ronaldsay 9D **172**
Sandwick. *Shet*
on Mainland 9F **173**
on Whalsay 5G **173**
Sandwith. *Cumb* 3A **102**
Sandy. *Carm* 5E **45**
Sandy. *C Beds* 1B **52**
Sandy Bank. *Linc* 5B **88**
Sandycroft. *Flin* 4F **83**
Sandy Cross. *Here* 5A **60**
Sandygate. *Devn* 5B **12**
Sandygate. *IOM* 2C **108**
Sandy Haven. *Pemb* 4C **42**
Sandyhills. *Dum* 4F **111**
Sandylands. *Lanc* 3D **96**
Sandy Lane. *Wilts* 5E **35**
Sandylane. *Swan* 4E **31**
Sandystones. *Bord* 2H **119**
Sandyway. *Here* 3H **47**
Sangobeg. *High* 2E **167**
Sangomore. *High* 2E **166**
Sankyn's Green. *Worc* 4B **60**
Sanna. *High* 2F **139**
Sanndabhaig. *W Isl*
on Isle of Lewis 4G **171**
on South Uist 4D **170**
Sannox. *N Ayr* 5B **126**
Sanquhar. *Dum* 3G **117**
Santon. *Cumb* 4B **102**
Santon Bridge. *Cumb* 4C **102**
Santon Downham. *Suff* 2H **65**
Sapcote. *Leics* 1B **62**
Sapey Common. *Here* 4B **60**
Sapiston. *Suff* 3B **66**
Sapley. *Cambs* 3B **64**
Sapperton. *Derbs* 2F **73**
Sapperton. *Glos* 5E **49**
Sapperton. *Linc* 2H **75**
Saracen's Head. *Linc* 3C **76**
Sarclet. *High* 4F **169**
Sardis. *Carm* 5F **45**
Sardis. *Pemb*
nr. Milford Haven 4D **42**
nr. Tenby 4F **43**
Sarisbury Green. *Hants* 2D **16**
Sarn. *B'end* 3C **32**
Sarn. *Powy* 1E **58**
Sarnau. *Carm* 3E **45**
Sarnau. *Cdgn* 5C **56**
Sarnau. *Gwyn* 2B **70**
Sarnau. *Powy*
nr. Brecon 2D **46**
nr. Welshpool 4E **71**
Sarn Bach. *Gwyn* 3C **68**
Sarnesfield. *Here* 5F **59**
Sarn Meyllteyrn. *Gwyn* 2B **68**
Saron. *Carm*
nr. Ammanford 4G **45**
nr. Newcastle Emlyn 2D **45**
Saron. *Gwyn*
nr. Bethel 4E **81**
nr. Bontnewydd 5D **80**
Sarratt. *Herts* 1B **38**
Sarre. *Kent* 4G **41**
Sarsden. *Oxon* 3A **50**
Satley. *Dur* 5E **115**
Satron. *N Yor* 5C **104**
Satterleigh. *Devn* 4G **19**
Satterthwaite. *Cumb* 5E **103**
Satwell. *Oxon* 3F **37**
Sauchen. *Abers* 2D **152**
Saucher. *Per* 5A **144**
Saughall. *Ches W* 3F **83**
Saughtree. *Bord* 5H **119**
Saul. *Glos* 5C **48**
Saundby. *Notts* 2E **87**
Saundersfoot. *Pemb* 4F **43**
Saunderton. *Buck* 5F **51**
Saunderton Lee. *Buck* 2G **37**
Saunton. *Devn* 3E **19**
Sausthorpe. *Linc* 4C **88**
Saval. *High* 3C **164**
Saverley Green. *Staf* 2D **72**
Sawbridge. *Warw* 4C **62**
**Sawbridgeworth**. *Herts* 4E **53**
Sawdon. *N Yor* 1D **100**
Sawley. *Derbs* 2B **74**
Sawley. *Lanc* 5G **97**
Sawley. *N Yor* 3E **99**
Sawston. *Cambs* 1E **53**
Sawtry. *Cambs* 2A **64**
Saxby. *Leics* 3F **75**
Saxby. *Linc* 2H **87**
Saxby All Saints. *N Lin* 3C **94**
Saxelby. *Leics* 3D **74**
Saxelbye. *Leics* 3D **74**
Saxham Street. *Suff* 4C **66**
Saxilby. *Linc* 3F **87**
Saxlingham. *Norf* 2C **78**
Saxlingham Green. *Norf* 1E **67**
Saxlingham Nethergate. *Norf* 1E **67**
Saxlingham Thorpe. *Norf* 1E **66**
Saxmundham. *Suff* 4F **67**
Saxondale. *Notts* 1D **74**
Saxon Street. *Cambs* 5F **65**
Saxtead. *Suff* 4E **67**
Saxtead Green. *Suff* 4E **67**
Saxthorpe. *Norf* 2D **78**
Saxton. *N Yor* 1E **93**
Sayers Common. *W Sus* 4D **26**
Scackleton. *N Yor* 2A **100**
Scadabhagh. *W Isl* 8D **171**
Scaftworth. *Notts* 1D **86**
Scagglethorpe. *N Yor* 2C **100**
Scaitcliffe. *Lanc* 2F **91**
Scaladal. *W Isl* 6D **171**
Scalasaig. *Arg* 4A **132**
Scalby. *E Yor* 2B **94**
Scalby. *N Yor* 5H **107**
Scalby Mills. *N Yor* 5H **107**
Scaldwell. *Nptn* 3E **63**
Scaleby. *Cumb* 3F **113**
Scaleby Hill. *Cumb* 3F **113**
Scale Houses. *Cumb* 5G **113**
Scales. *Cumb*
nr. Barrow-in-Furness 2B **96**
nr. Keswick 2E **103**
Scalford. *Leics* 3E **75**
Scaling. *N Yor* 3E **107**
Scaling Dam. *Red C* 3E **107**
Scalloway. *Shet* 8F **173**
Scalpaigh. *W Isl* 8E **171**
Scalpay House. *High* 1E **147**
Scamblesby. *Linc* 3B **88**
Scamodale. *High* 1C **140**
Scampston. *N Yor* 2C **100**
Scampton. *Linc* 3G **87**
Scaniport. *High* 5A **158**
Scapa. *Orkn* 7D **172**
Scapegoat Hill. *W Yor* 3A **92**
Scar. *Orkn* 3F **172**
Scarasta. *W Isl* 8C **171**
**Scarborough**. *N Yor* 1E **101**
Scarcliffe. *Derbs* 4B **86**
Scarcroft. *W Yor* 5F **99**
Scardroy. *High* 3E **156**
Scarfskerry. *High* 1E **169**
Scargill. *Dur* 3D **104**
Scarinish. *Arg* 4B **138**
Scarisbrick. *Lanc* 3B **90**
Scarning. *Norf* 4B **78**
Scarrington. *Notts* 1E **75**
Scarth Hill. *Lanc* 4C **90**
Scartho. *NE Lin* 4F **95**
Scarvister. *Shet* 7E **173**
Scatness. *Shet* 10E **173**
Scatwell. *High* 3F **157**
Scaur. *Dum* 4F **111**
Scawby. *N Lin* 4C **94**
Scawby Brook. *N Lin* 4C **94**
Scawsby. *S Yor* 4F **93**
Scawton. *N Yor* 1H **99**
Scaynes Hill. *W Sus* 3E **27**
Scethrog. *Powy* 3E **46**
Scholar Green. *Ches E* 5C **84**
Scholes. *G Man* 4D **90**
Scholes. *W Yor*
nr. Bradford 2B **92**
nr. Holmfirth 4B **92**
nr. Leeds 1D **93**
Scholey Hill. *W Yor* 2D **93**
School Aycliffe. *Darl* 2F **105**
School Green. *Ches W* 4A **84**
School Green. *Essx* 2H **53**
Scissett. *W Yor* 3C **92**
Scleddau. *Pemb* 1D **42**
Scofton. *Notts* 2D **86**
Scole. *Norf* 3D **66**
Scolpaig. *W Isl* 1C **170**
Scolton. *Pemb* 2D **43**
Scone. *Per* 1D **136**
Sconser. *High* 5E **155**
Scoonie. *Fife* 3F **137**
Scopwick. *Linc* 5H **87**

| | | | | |
|---|---|---|---|---|
| Scoraig. *High* ..............4E **163** | Seamer. *N Yor* | Selsdon. *G Lon* ..............4E **39** | Shapwick. *Som* ..............3H **21** | Shelsley Beauchamp. *Worc* ...4B **60** |
| Scorborough. *E Yor* .......5E **101** | nr. Scarborough ........1E **101** | Selsey. *W Sus* ..............3G **17** | Sharcott. *Wilts* ..............1G **23** | Shelsley Walsh. *Worc* ......4B **60** |
| Scorrier. *Corn* ..............4B **6** | nr. Stokesley ..........3B **106** | Selsfield Common. *W Sus* ...2E **27** | Shardlow. *Derbs* ..............2B **74** | Shelthorpe. *Leics* ...........4C **74** |
| Scorriton. *Devn* ..............2D **8** | Seamill. *N Ayr* ..........5D **126** | Selside. *Cumb* ..............5G **103** | Shareshill. *Staf* ..............5D **72** | Shelton. *Bed* ..............4H **63** |
| Scorton. *Lanc* ..............5E **97** | Sea Mills. *Bris* ..........4A **34** | Selside. *N Yor* ..............2G **97** | Sharlston. *W Yor* ..............3D **93** | Shelton. *Norf* ..............1E **67** |
| Scorton. *N Yor* ..............4F **105** | Sea Palling. *Norf* ........3G **79** | Selsley. *Glos* ..............5D **48** | Sharlston Common. *W Yor* ...3D **93** | Shelton. *Notts* ..............1E **75** |
| Sco Ruston. *Norf* ..............3E **79** | Searby. *Linc* ..............4D **94** | Selsted. *Kent* ..............1G **29** | Sharnal Street. *Medw* ....3B **40** | Shelton. *Shrp* ..............4G **71** |
| Scotbheinn. *W Isl* ..........3D **170** | Seasalter. *Kent* ..............4E **41** | Selston. *Notts* ..............5B **86** | Sharnbrook. *Bed* ..............5G **63** | Shelton Green. *Norf* ......1E **67** |
| Scotby. *Cumb* ..............4F **113** | Seascale. *Cumb* ..........4B **102** | Selworthy. *Som* ..............2C **20** | Sharneyford. *Lanc* ......2G **91** | Shelton Lock. *Derb* ......2A **74** |
| **Scotch Corner**. *N Yor* .....4F **105** | Seaside. *Per* ..............1E **137** | Semblister. *Shet* ..............6E **173** | Sharnford. *Leics* ..............1B **62** | Shelve. *Shrp* ..............1F **59** |
| Scotforth. *Lanc* ..............3D **97** | Seater. *High* ..............1F **169** | Semer. *Suff* ..............1D **54** | Sharnhill Green. *Dors* ....2C **14** | Shelwick. *Here* ..............1A **48** |
| Scot Hay. *Staf* ..............1C **72** | Seathorne. *Linc* ..............4E **89** | Semington. *Wilts* ...........5D **35** | Sharoe Green. *Lanc* ......1D **90** | Shelwick Green. *Here* ......1A **48** |
| Scothern. *Linc* ..............3H **87** | Seathwaite. *Cumb* | Semley. *Wilts* ..............4D **23** | Sharow. *N Yor* ..............2F **99** | Shenfield. *Essx* ..............1H **39** |
| Scotland End. *Oxon* ......2B **50** | nr. Buttermere ......3D **102** | Send. *Surr* ..............5B **38** | Sharpenhoe. *C Beds* ......2A **52** | Shenington. *Oxon* ......1B **50** |
| Scotlandwell. *Per* ..........3D **136** | nr. Ulpha ..........5D **102** | Send Marsh. *Surr* ......5B **38** | Sharperton. *Nmbd* ......4D **120** | Shenley. *Herts* ..............5B **52** |
| Scot Lane End. *G Man* ......4E **91** | Seatle. *Cumb* ..............1C **96** | Senghenydd. *Cphy* ......2E **32** | Sharpness. *Glos* ..............5B **48** | Shenley Brook End. *Mil* ....2G **51** |
| Scotsburn. *High* ..............1B **158** | Seatoller. *Cumb* ..........3D **102** | Sennen. *Corn* ..............4A **4** | Sharp Street. *Norf* ......3F **79** | Shenleybury. *Herts* ......5B **52** |
| Scotsburn. *Mor* ..............2G **159** | Seaton. *Corn* ..............3H **7** | Sennen Cove. *Corn* ......4A **4** | Sharpthorne. *W Sus* ......2E **27** | Shenley Church End. *Mil* ..2G **51** |
| Scotsdike. *Cumb* ..............2E **113** | Seaton. *Cumb* ..............1B **102** | Sennybridge. *Powy* ......3C **46** | Sharrington. *Norf* ......2C **78** | Shenmore. *Here* ..............2G **47** |
| Scot's Gap. *Nmbd* ..........1D **114** | Seaton. *Devn* ..............3F **13** | Serlby. *Notts* ..............2D **86** | Shatterford. *Worc* ......2B **60** | Shennanton. *Dum* ......3A **110** |
| Scotstoun. *Glas* ..............3G **127** | Seaton. *Dur* ..............4G **115** | Sessay. *N Yor* ..............2G **99** | Shatton. *Derbs* ..............2F **85** | Shenstone. *Staf* ..............5F **73** |
| Scotstown. *High* ..............2C **140** | Seaton. *E Yor* ..............5F **101** | Setchey. *Norf* ..............4F **77** | Shaugh Prior. *Devn* ......2B **8** | Shenstone. *Worc* ..............3C **60** |
| Scotswood. *Tyne* ..............3F **115** | Seaton. *Nmbd* ..............2G **115** | Setley. *Hants* ..............2B **16** | Shavington. *Ches E* ......5B **84** | Shenstone Woodend. *Staf* ..5F **73** |
| Scottas. *High* ..............3F **147** | Seaton. *Rut* ..............1G **63** | Setter. *Shet* ..............3F **173** | **Shaw**. *G Man* ..............4H **91** | Shenton. *Leics* ..............5A **74** |
| Scotter. *Linc* ..............4B **94** | Seaton Burn. *Tyne* ......2F **115** | Settiscarth. *Orkn* ......6C **172** | Shaw. *W Ber* ..............5C **36** | Shenval. *Mor* ..............1G **151** |
| Scotterthorpe. *Linc* ......4B **94** | Seaton Carew. *Hart* ......2C **106** | Settle. *N Yor* ..............3H **97** | Shaw. *Wilts* ..............5D **35** | Shepeau Stow. *Linc* ......4C **76** |
| Scottlethorpe. *Linc* ......3H **75** | Seaton Delaval. *Nmbd* ....2G **115** | Settrington. *N Yor* ......2C **100** | Shawbirch. *Telf* ..............4A **72** | Shephall. *Herts* ..............3C **52** |
| Scotton. *Linc* ..............1F **87** | Seaton Junction. *Devn* ....3F **13** | Seven Ash. *Som* ..............3E **21** | Shawbury. *Shrp* ..............3H **71** | Shepherd's Bush. *G Lon* ..2D **38** |
| Scotton. *N Yor* | Seaton Ross. *E Yor* ......5B **100** | Sevenhampton. *Glos* ......3F **49** | Shawell. *Leics* ..............2C **62** | Shepherd's Gate. *Norf* ....4E **77** |
| nr. Catterick Garrison ...5E **105** | Seaton Sluice. *Nmbd* ....2G **115** | Sevenhampton. *Swin* ......2H **35** | Shawford. *Hants* ..............4C **24** | Shepherd's Green. *Oxon* ..3F **37** |
| nr. Harrogate ..........4F **99** | Seatown. *Abers* ..........2C **160** | Sevenoaks. *Kent* ..............5G **39** | Shawforth. *Lanc* ..............2G **91** | Shepherd's Port. *Norf* ....2F **77** |
| Scottow. *Norf* ..............3E **79** | Seatown. *Dors* ..........3H **13** | Sevenoaks Weald. *Kent* ....5G **39** | Shaw Green. *Lanc* ......3D **90** | Shepherdswell. *Kent* ....1G **29** |
| Scoulton. *Norf* ..............5B **78** | Seatown. *Mor* | Seven Sisters. *Neat* ......5B **46** | Shawhead. *Dum* ..............2F **111** | Shepley. *W Yor* ..............4B **92** |
| Scounslow Green. *Staf* ....3E **73** | nr. Cullen ..........2C **160** | Seven Springs. *Glos* ......4E **49** | Shaw Mills. *N Yor* ......3E **99** | Shepperdstown. *High* ....4D **169** |
| Scourie. *High* ..............4B **166** | nr. Lossiemouth ......1G **159** | Severn Beach. *S Glo* ......3A **34** | Shawwood. *E Ayr* ......2E **117** | Shepperdine. *S Glo* ......2B **34** |
| Scourie More. *High* ......4B **166** | Seave Green. *N Yor* ......4C **106** | Severn Stoke. *Worc* ......1D **48** | Shearsby. *Leics* ..............1D **62** | Shepperton. *Surr* ..........4B **38** |
| Scousburgh. *Shet* ......10E **173** | Seaview. *IOW* ..............3E **17** | Sevington. *Kent* ..............1E **29** | Shearston. *Som* ..............3F **21** | Shepreth. *Cambs* ..............1D **53** |
| Scout Green. *Cumb* ......4G **103** | Seaville. *Cumb* ..............4C **112** | Sewards End. *Essx* ......2F **53** | Shebbear. *Devn* ..............2E **11** | **Shepshed**. *Leics* ..............4B **74** |
| Scouthead. *G Man* ..........4H **91** | Seavington St Mary. *Som* ..1H **13** | Sewardstone. *Essx* ......1E **39** | Shebdon. *Staf* ..............3B **72** | Shepton Beauchamp. *Som* ..1H **13** |
| Scrabster. *High* ..............1C **168** | Seavington St Michael. *Som* ..1H **13** | Sewell. *C Beds* ..........3H **51** | Shebster. *High* ..............2C **168** | Shepton Mallet. *Som* ......2B **22** |
| Scrafield. *Linc* ..............4C **88** | Sebastopol. *Torf* ..........2F **33** | Sewerby. *E Yor* ..............3G **101** | Sheddocksley. *Aber* ......3F **153** | Shepton Montague. *Som* ..3B **22** |
| Scrainwood. *Nmbd* ......4D **121** | Sebergham. *Cumb* ......5E **113** | Seworgan. *Corn* ..............5B **6** | Shedfield. *Hants* ..............1D **16** | Shepway. *Kent* ..............5B **40** |
| Scrane End. *Linc* ..............1C **76** | Seckington. *Warw* ......5G **73** | Sewstern. *Leics* ..............3F **75** | Shedog. *N Ayr* ..............2D **122** | Sheraton. *Dur* ..............1B **106** |
| Scraptoft. *Leics* ..............5D **74** | Second Coast. *High* ......4D **162** | Sgallairidh. *W Isl* ......9B **170** | Sheen. *Staf* ..............4F **85** | Sherborne. *Dors* ..........1B **14** |
| Scratby. *Norf* ..............4H **79** | Sedbergh. *Cumb* ..........5H **103** | Sgarasta Mhor. *W Isl* ....8C **171** | Sheepbridge. *Derbs* ......3A **86** | Sherborne. *Glos* ..........4G **49** |
| Scrayingham. *N Yor* ......3B **100** | Sedbury. *Glos* ..............2A **34** | Sgiogarstaigh. *W Isl* ....1H **171** | Sheep Hill. *Dur* ..............4E **115** | Sherborne. *Som* ..........1A **22** |
| Scredington. *Linc* ......1H **75** | Sedbusk. *N Yor* ..............5B **104** | Sgreadan. *Arg* ..............4A **132** | Sheepscar. *W Yor* ......1D **92** | Sherborne Causeway. *Dors* ..4D **22** |
| Scremby. *Linc* ..............4D **88** | Sedgeberrow. *Worc* ......2F **49** | Shabbington. *Buck* ......5E **51** | Sheepscombe. *Glos* ......4D **49** | Sherborne St John. *Hants* ..1E **24** |
| Scremerston. *Nmbd* ......5G **131** | Sedgebrook. *Linc* ..........2F **75** | Shackerley. *Shrp* ..........5C **72** | Sheepstor. *Devn* ..............2B **8** | Sherbourne. *Warw* ......4G **61** |
| Screveton. *Notts* ..............1E **75** | Sedgefield. *Dur* ..............2A **106** | Shackerstone. *Leics* ......5A **74** | Sheepwash. *Devn* ..............2E **11** | Sherburn. *Dur* ..........5G **115** |
| Scrivelsby. *Linc* ..............4B **88** | Sedgeford. *Norf* ..............2G **77** | Shackleford. *Surr* ......1A **26** | Sheepwash. *Nmbd* ......1F **115** | Sherburn. *N Yor* ..........2D **100** |
| Scriven. *N Yor* ..............4F **99** | Sedgehill. *Wilts* ..............4D **22** | Shadforth. *Dur* ..............5G **115** | Sheepway. *N Som* ......4H **33** | Sherburn Hill. *Dur* ......5G **115** |
| Scronkey. *Lanc* ..............5D **96** | Sedgley. *W Mid* ..............1D **60** | Shadingfield. *Suff* ......2G **67** | Sheepy Magna. *Leics* ....5H **73** | Sherburn in Elmet. *N Yor* ..1E **93** |
| Scrooby. *Notts* ..............1D **86** | Sedgwick. *Cumb* ..............1E **97** | Shadoxhurst. *Kent* ......2D **28** | Sheepy Parva. *Leics* ....5H **73** | Shere. *Surr* ..............1B **26** |
| Scropton. *Derbs* ..............2F **73** | Sedlescombe. *E Sus* ......4B **28** | Shadsworth. *Bkbn* ......2F **91** | Sheering. *Essx* ..............4F **53** | Shereford. *Norf* ..........3A **78** |
| Scrub Hill. *Linc* ..............5B **88** | Seend. *Wilts* ..............5E **35** | Shadwell. *Norf* ..............2B **66** | **Sheerness**. *Kent* ..............3D **40** | Sherfield English. *Hants* ..4A **24** |
| Scruton. *N Yor* ..............5F **105** | Seend Cleeve. *Wilts* ......5E **35** | Shadwell. *W Yor* ..............1D **92** | Sheerwater. *Surr* ......4B **38** | Sherfield on Loddon. *Hants* ..1E **25** |
| Scuggate. *Cumb* ..............2F **113** | Seer Green. *Buck* ..........1A **38** | Shaftesbury. *Dors* ......4D **22** | Sheet. *Hants* ..............4F **25** | Sherford. *Devn* ..............4D **9** |
| Sculamus. *High* ..............1E **147** | Seething. *Norf* ..............1F **67** | Shafton. *S Yor* ..............3D **93** | **Sheffield**. *S Yor* ..............2A **86** | Sherford. *Dors* ..............3E **15** |
| Sculcoates. *Hull* ..............1D **94** | Sefster. *Shet* ..............6E **173** | Shafton Two Gates. *S Yor* ..3D **93** | Sheffield Bottom. *W Ber* ..5E **37** | Sheriffhales. *Shrp* ......4B **72** |
| Sculthorpe. *Norf* ..............2B **78** | Sefton. *Mers* ..............4B **90** | Shaggs. *Dors* ..............4D **14** | Sheffield Green. *E Sus* ....3F **27** | Sheriff Hutton. *N Yor* ....3A **100** |
| **Scunthorpe**. *N Lin* ......3B **94** | Sefton Park. *Mers* ......2F **83** | Shakesfield. *Glos* ......2B **48** | Shefford. *C Beds* ..........2B **52** | Sheriffston. *Mor* ..........2G **159** |
| Scurlage. *Swan* ..............4D **30** | Segensworth. *Hants* ......2D **16** | Shalbourne. *Wilts* ......5B **36** | Shefford Woodlands. *W Ber* ..4B **36** | Sheringham. *Norf* ......1D **78** |
| Sea. *Som* ..............1G **13** | Seggat. *Abers* ..........4E **161** | Shalcombe. *IOW* ..........4B **16** | Sheigra. *High* ..........3B **166** | Sherington. *Mil* ..........1G **51** |
| Seaborough. *Dors* ......2H **13** | Seghill. *Nmbd* ..............2F **115** | Shalden. *Hants* ..............2E **25** | Sheinton. *Shrp* ..............5A **72** | Shermanbury. *W Sus* ....4D **26** |
| Seabridge. *Staf* ..............1C **72** | Seifton. *Shrp* ..............2G **59** | Shaldon. *Devn* ..............5C **12** | Shelderton. *Shrp* ..........3G **59** | Shernal Green. *Worc* ....4D **60** |
| Seabrook. *Kent* ..............2F **29** | Seighford. *Staf* ..............3C **72** | Shalfleet. *IOW* ..............4C **16** | Sheldon. *Derbs* ..............4F **85** | Shernborne. *Norf* ......2G **77** |
| Seaburn. *Tyne* ..............3H **115** | Seilebost. *W Isl* ..............8C **171** | Shalford. *Essx* ..............3H **53** | Sheldon. *Devn* ..............2E **13** | Sherrington. *Wilts* ......3E **23** |
| Seacombe. *Mers* ..............1F **83** | Seisdon. *Staf* ..............1C **60** | Shalford. *Surr* ..............1B **26** | Sheldon. *W Mid* ..............2F **61** | Sherston. *Wilts* ..........3D **34** |
| Seacroft. *W Yor* ..............1D **92** | Seisiadar. *W Isl* ..............4H **171** | Shalford Green. *Essx* ....3H **53** | Sheldwich. *Kent* ..............5E **40** | Sherwood. *Nott* ..........1C **74** |
| Seadyke. *Linc* ..............2C **76** | Selattyn. *Shrp* ..............2E **71** | Shallowford. *Devn* ......2H **19** | Sheldwich Lees. *Kent* ....5E **40** | Sherwood Green. *Devn* ....4F **19** |
| Seafield. *High* ..............5G **165** | Selborne. *Hants* ..............3F **25** | Shallowford. *Staf* ......3C **72** | Shelf. *W Yor* ..............2B **92** | Shettleston. *Glas* ......3H **127** |
| Seafield. *Midl* ..............3F **129** | **Selby**. *N Yor* ..............1G **93** | Shalmsford Street. *Kent* ..5E **41** | Shelfanger. *Norf* ..........2D **66** | Shevington. *G Man* ......4D **90** |
| Seafield. *S Ayr* ..............2C **116** | Selham. *W Sus* ..............3A **26** | Shalstone. *Buck* ..........2E **51** | Shelfield. *Warw* ..........4F **61** | Shevington Moor. *G Man* ..3D **90** |
| Seafield. *W Lot* ..............3D **128** | Selkirk. *Bord* ..............2G **119** | Shamley Green. *Surr* ....1B **26** | Shelfield. *W Mid* ..............5E **73** | Shevington Vale. *G Man* ..4D **90** |
| **Seaford**. *E Sus* ..............5F **27** | Sellack. *Here* ..............3A **48** | Shandon. *Arg* ..............1D **126** | Shelford. *Notts* ..............1D **74** | Sheviock. *Corn* ..........3H **7** |
| Seaforth. *Mers* ..............1F **83** | Sellafirth. *Shet* ..............2G **173** | Shandwick. *High* ......1C **158** | Shelford. *Warw* ..............2B **62** | Shide. *IOW* ..........4C **16** |
| Seagrave. *Leics* ..............4D **74** | Sellick's Green. *Som* ......1F **13** | Shangton. *Leics* ..............1E **62** | Shell. *Worc* ..........5D **60** | Shiel Bridge. *High* ......2B **148** |
| **Seaham**. *Dur* ..............5H **115** | Sellindge. *Kent* ..............2F **29** | Shankhouse. *Nmbd* ......2F **115** | Shelley. *Suff* ..........2D **54** | Shieldaig. *High* |
| Seahouses. *Nmbd* ......1G **121** | Selling. *Kent* ..............5E **41** | **Shanklin**. *IOW* ..........4D **16** | Shelley. *W Yor* ..........3C **92** | nr. Charlestown ......1H **155** |
| Seal. *Kent* ..........5G **39** | Sells Green. *Wilts* ......5E **35** | Shannochie. *N Ayr* ......3D **123** | Shell Green. *Hal* ..........2H **83** | nr. Torridon ..........3H **155** |
| Sealand. *Flin* ..........4F **83** | Selly Oak. *W Mid* ......2E **61** | Shap. *Cumb* ..........3G **103** | Shellingford. *Oxon* ......2B **36** | Shieldhill. *Dum* ..........1B **112** |
| Seale. *Surr* ..............2G **25** | Selmeston. *E Sus* ......5G **27** | Shapwick. *Dors* ..............2E **15** | Shellow Bowells. *Essx* ....5G **53** | Shieldhill. *Falk* ..........2B **128** |
| | | | | Shieldhill. *S Lan* ..........5D **128** |

Shieldmuir. N Lan ....4A 128
Shielfoot. High ....1A 140
Shielhill. Abers ....3H 161
Shielhill. Ang ....3D 144
Shifnal. Shrp ....5B 72
Shilbottle. Nmbd ....4F 121
Shilbottle Grange. Nmbd ....4G 121
Shildon. Dur ....2F 105
Shillford. E Ren ....4F 127
Shillingford. Devn ....4C 20
Shillingford. Oxon ....2D 36
Shillingford St George. Devn ....4C 12
Shillingstone. Dors ....1D 14
Shillington. C Beds ....2B 52
Shillmoor. Nmbd ....4C 120
Shilton. Oxon ....5A 50
Shilton. Warw ....2B 62
Shilvinghampton. Dors ....4B 14
Shilvington. Nmbd ....1E 115
Shimpling. Norf ....2D 66
Shimpling. Suff ....5A 66
Shimpling Street. Suff ....5A 66
Shincliffe. Dur ....5F 115
Shiney Row. Tyne ....4G 115
Shinfield. Wok ....5F 37
Shingay. Cambs ....1D 52
Shingham. Norf ....5G 77
Shingle Street. Suff ....1G 55
Shinner's Bridge. Devn ....2D 9
Shinness. High ....2C 164
Shipbourne. Kent ....5G 39
Shipham. Norf ....5B 78
Shipham. Som ....1H 21
Shiphay. Torb ....2E 9
Shiplake. Oxon ....4F 37
Shipley. Derbs ....1B 74
Shipley. Nmbd ....3F 121
Shipley. Shrp ....1C 60
Shipley. W Sus ....3C 26
Shipley. W Yor ....1B 92
Shipley Bridge. Surr ....1E 27
Shipmeadow. Suff ....2F 67
Shippon. Oxon ....2C 36
Shipston-on-Stour. Warw ....1A 50
Shipton. Buck ....3F 51
Shipton. Glos ....4F 49
Shipton. N Yor ....4H 99
Shipton. Shrp ....1H 59
Shipton Bellinger. Hants ....2H 23
Shipton Gorge. Dors ....3H 13
Shipton Green. W Sus ....3G 17
Shipton Moyne. Glos ....3D 35
Shipton-on-Cherwell. Oxon ....4C 50
Shiptonthorpe. E Yor ....5C 100
Shipton-under-Wychwood.
  Oxon ....4A 50
Shirburn. Oxon ....2E 37
Shirdley Hill. Lanc ....3B 90
Shire. Cumb ....1H 103
Shirebrook. Derbs ....4C 86
Shiregreen. S Yor ....1A 86
Shirehampton. Bris ....4A 34
Shiremoor. Tyne ....2G 115
Shirenewton. Mon ....2H 33
Shireoaks. Notts ....2C 86
Shires Mill. Fife ....1D 128
Shirkoak. Kent ....2D 28
Shirland. Derbs ....5A 86
Shirley. Derbs ....1G 73
Shirley. Sotn ....1B 16
Shirley. W Mid ....3F 61
Shirleywich. Staf ....3D 73
Shirl Heath. Here ....5G 59
Shirrell Heath. Hants ....1D 16
Shirwell. Devn ....3F 19
Shiskine. N Ayr ....3D 122
Shobdon. Here ....4F 59
Shobnall. Staf ....3G 73
Shobrooke. Devn ....2B 12
Shoby. Leics ....3D 74
Shocklach. Ches W ....1G 71
Shoeburyness. S'end ....2D 40
Sholden. Kent ....5H 41
Sholing. Sotn ....1C 16

Sholver. G Man ....4H 91
Shoot Hill. Shrp ....4G 71
Shop. Corn
  nr. Bude ....1C 10
  nr. Padstow ....1C 6
Shop. Devn ....1D 11
Shopford. Cumb ....2G 113
Shoreditch. G Lon ....2E 39
Shoreditch. Som ....4F 21
Shoregill. Cumb ....4A 104
Shoreham. Kent ....4G 39
Shoreham-by-Sea. W Sus ....5D 26
Shoresdean. Nmbd ....5F 131
Shoreswood. Nmbd ....5F 131
Shorncote. Glos ....2F 35
Shorne. Kent ....3A 40
Shorne Ridgeway. Kent ....3A 40
Shortacombe. Devn ....4F 11
Shortbridge. E Sus ....3F 27
Shortgate. E Sus ....4F 27
Short Green. Norf ....2C 66
Short Heath. Derbs ....3B 50
Short Heath. Derbs ....4H 73
Short Heath. W Mid
  nr. Erdington ....1E 61
  nr. Wednesfield ....5D 73
Shortlanesend. Corn ....4C 6
Shorton. Torb ....2E 9
Shortstown. Bed ....1A 52
Shortwood. S Glo ....4B 34
Shorwell. IOW ....4C 16
Shoscombe. Bath ....1C 22
Shotesham. Norf ....1E 67
Shotgate. Essx ....1B 40
Shotley. Suff ....2F 55
Shotley Bridge. Dur ....4D 115
Shotleyfield. Nmbd ....4D 114
Shotley Gate. Suff ....2F 55
Shottenden. Kent ....5E 41
Shottermill. Surr ....3G 25
Shottery. Warw ....5F 61
Shotteswell. Warw ....1C 50
Shottisham. Suff ....1G 55
Shottle. Derbs ....1H 73
Shotton. Dur
  nr. Peterlee ....1B 106
  nr. Sedgefield ....2A 106
Shotton. Flin ....4F 83
Shotton. Nmbd
  nr. Morpeth ....2F 115
  nr. Town Yetholm ....1C 120
Shotton Colliery. Dur ....5G 115
Shotts. N Lan ....3B 128
Shotwick. Ches W ....3F 83
Shouldham. Norf ....5F 77
Shouldham Thorpe. Norf ....5F 77
Shoulton. Worc ....5C 60
Shrawardine. Shrp ....4G 71
Shrawley. Worc ....4C 60
Shreding Green. Buck ....2B 38
Shrewley. Warw ....4G 61
Shrewsbury. Shrp ....4G 71
Shrewton. Wilts ....2F 23
Shripney. W Sus ....5A 26
Shrivenham. Oxon ....3H 35
Shropham. Norf ....1B 66
Shroton. Dors ....1D 14
Shrub End. Essx ....3C 54
Shucknall. Here ....1A 48
Shudy Camps. Cambs ....1G 53
Shulishadermor. High ....4D 155
Shulista. High ....1D 154
Shurdington. Glos ....4E 49
Shurlock Row. Wind ....4G 37
Shurrery. High ....3C 168
Shurton. Som ....2F 21
Shustoke. Warw ....1G 61
Shute. Devn
  nr. Axminster ....3F 13
  nr. Crediton ....2B 12
Shutford. Oxon ....1B 50
Shut Heath. Staf ....3C 72
Shuthonger. Glos ....2D 49
Shutlanehead. Staf ....1C 72

Shutlanger. Nptn ....1F 51
Shutt Green. Staf ....5C 72
Shuttington. Warw ....5G 73
Shuttlewood. Derbs ....3B 86
Shuttleworth. G Man ....3G 91
Siabost. W Isl ....3E 171
Siabost bho Dheas. W Isl ....3E 171
Siabost bho Thuath. W Isl ....3E 171
Siadar. W Isl ....2F 171
Siadar Uarach. W Isl ....2F 171
Sibbaldbie. Dum ....1C 112
Sibbertoft. Nptn ....2D 62
Sibdon Carwood. Shrp ....2G 59
Sibertswold. Kent ....1G 29
Sibford Ferris. Oxon ....2B 50
Sibford Gower. Oxon ....2B 50
Sible Hedingham. Essx ....2A 54
Sibsey. Linc ....5C 88
Sibsey Fen Side. Linc ....5C 88
Sibson. Cambs ....1H 63
Sibson. Leics ....5A 74
Sibster. High ....3F 169
Sibthorpe. Notts ....1E 75
Sibton. Suff ....4F 67
Sicklesmere. Suff ....4A 66
Sicklinghall. N Yor ....5F 99
Sid. Devn ....4E 13
Sidbury. Devn ....3E 13
Sidbury. Shrp ....2A 60
Sidcot. N Som ....1H 21
Sidcup. G Lon ....3F 39
Siddick. Cumb ....1B 102
Siddington. Ches E ....3C 84
Siddington. Glos ....2F 35
Side of the Moor. G Man ....3F 91
Sidestrand. Norf ....2E 79
Sidford. Devn ....3E 13
Sidlesham. W Sus ....3G 17
Sidley. E Sus ....5B 28
Sidlow. Surr ....1D 26
Sidmouth. Devn ....4E 13
Sigford. Devn ....5A 12
Sigglesthorne. E Yor ....5F 101
Sighthill. Edin ....2E 129
Sigingstone. V Glam ....4C 32
Signet. Oxon ....4H 49
Silchester. Hants ....5E 37
Sildinis. W Isl ....6E 171
Sileby. Leics ....4D 74
Silecroft. Cumb ....1A 96
Silfield. Norf ....1D 66
Silian. Cdgn ....5E 57
Silkstone. S Yor ....4C 92
Silkstone Common. S Yor ....4C 92
Silksworth. Tyne ....4G 115
Silk Willoughby. Linc ....1H 75
Silloth. Cumb ....4C 112
Sills. Nmbd ....4C 120
Sillyearn. Mor ....3C 160
Silpho. N Yor ....5G 107
Silsden. W Yor ....5C 98
Silsoe. C Beds ....2A 52
Silverbank. Abers ....4E 152
Silverburn. Midl ....3F 129
Silverdale. Lanc ....2D 96
Silverdale. Staf ....1C 72
Silverdale Green. Lanc ....2D 96
Silver End. Essx ....4B 54
Silver End. W Mid ....2D 60
Silvergate. Norf ....3D 78
Silver Green. Norf ....1E 67
Silverhillocks. Abers ....2E 161
Silverley's Green. Suff ....3E 67
Silverstone. Nptn ....1E 51
Silverton. Devn ....2C 12
Silverton. W Dun ....2F 127
Silvington. Shrp ....3A 60
Simm's Cross. Hal ....2H 83
Simm's Lane End. Mers ....4D 90
Simonburn. Nmbd ....2B 114
Simonsbath. Som ....3A 20
Simonstone. Lanc ....1F 91
Simprim. Bord ....5E 131
Simpson. Pemb ....3C 42

Simpson Cross. Pemb ....3C 42
Sinclairston. E Ayr ....3D 116
Sinclairtown. Fife ....4E 137
Sinderby. N Yor ....1F 99
Sinderhope. Nmbd ....4B 114
Sindlesham. Wok ....5F 37
Sinfin. Derb ....2H 73
Singleborough. Buck ....2F 51
Singleton. Kent ....1D 28
Singleton. Lanc ....1B 90
Singleton. W Sus ....1G 17
Singlewell. Kent ....3A 40
Sinkhurst Green. Kent ....1C 28
Sinnahard. Abers ....2B 152
Sinnington. N Yor ....1B 100
Sinton Green. Worc ....4C 60
Sion Mills. Derr ....3C 174
Sipson. G Lon ....3B 38
Sirhowy. Blae ....4E 47
Sisland. Norf ....1F 67
Sissinghurst. Kent ....2B 28
Siston. S Glo ....4B 34
Sithney. Corn ....4D 4
Sittingbourne. Kent ....4D 40
Six Ashes. Staf ....2B 60
Six Bells. Blae ....5F 47
Six Hills. Leics ....3D 74
Sixhills. Linc ....2A 88
Six Mile Bottom. Cambs ....5E 65
Sixpenny Handley. Dors ....1E 15
Sizewell. Suff ....4G 67
Skail. High ....4H 167
Skaill. Orkn ....6B 172
Skaills. Orkn ....7E 172
Skares. E Ayr ....3E 117
Skateraw. E Lot ....2D 130
Skaw. Shet ....5G 173
Skeabost. High ....4D 154
Skeabrae. Orkn ....5B 172
Skeeby. N Yor ....4E 105
Skeffington. Leics ....5E 75
Skeffling. E Yor ....3G 95
Skegby. Notts
  nr. Mansfield ....4B 86
  nr. Tuxford ....3E 87
Skegness. Linc ....4E 89
Skelberry. Shet
  nr. Boddam ....10E 173
  nr. Housetter ....3E 173
Skelbo. High ....4E 165
Skelbo Street. High ....4E 165
Skelbrooke. S Yor ....3F 93
Skeldyke. Linc ....2C 76
Skelfhill. Bord ....4G 119
Skellingthorpe. Linc ....3G 87
Skellister. Shet ....6F 173
Skellorn Green. Ches E ....2D 84
Skellow. S Yor ....3F 93
Skelmanthorpe. W Yor ....3C 92
Skelmersdale. Lanc ....4C 90
Skelmorlie. N Ayr ....3C 126
Skelpick. High ....3H 167
Skelton. Cumb ....1F 103
Skelton. E Yor ....2A 94
Skelton. N Yor
  nr. Richmond ....4D 105
  nr. Ripon ....3F 99
Skelton. Red C ....3D 106
Skelton. York ....4H 99
Skelton Green. Red C ....3D 106
Skelwick. Orkn ....3D 172
Skelwith Bridge. Cumb ....4E 103
Skendleby. Linc ....4D 88
Skendleby Psalter. Linc ....3D 88
Skenfrith. Mon ....3H 47
Skerne. E Yor ....4E 101
Skeroblingarry. Arg ....3B 122
Skerray. High ....2G 167
Skerricha. High ....3C 166
Skerries Airport. Shet ....4H 173
Skerton. Lanc ....3D 97
Sketchley. Leics ....1B 62
Sketty. Swan ....3F 31
Skewen. Neat ....3G 31

Skewsby. N Yor ....2A 100
Skeyton. Norf ....3E 79
Skeyton Corner. Norf ....3E 79
Skiall. High ....2C 168
Skidbrooke. Linc ....1D 88
Skidbrooke North End. Linc ....1D 88
Skidby. E Yor ....1D 94
Skilgate. Som ....4C 20
Skillington. Linc ....3F 75
Skinburness. Cumb ....4C 112
Skinflats. Falk ....1C 128
Skinidin. High ....4B 154
Skinnet. High ....2F 167
Skinningrove. Red C ....3E 107
Skipness. Arg ....4G 125
Skippool. Lanc ....5C 96
Skiprigg. Cumb ....5E 113
Skipsea. E Yor ....4F 101
Skipsea Brough. E Yor ....4F 101
Skipton. N Yor ....4B 98
Skipton-on-Swale. N Yor ....2F 99
Skipwith. N Yor ....1G 93
Skirbeck. Linc ....1C 76
Skirbeck Quarter. Linc ....1C 76
Skirlaugh. E Yor ....1E 95
Skirling. Bord ....1C 118
Skirmett. Buck ....2F 37
Skirpenbeck. E Yor ....4B 100
Skirwith. Cumb ....1H 103
Skirwith. N Yor ....2G 97
Skirza. High ....1F 169
Skitby. Cumb ....3F 113
Skitham. Lanc ....5D 96
Skittle Green. Buck ....5F 51
Skroo. Shet ....1B 172
Skulamus. High ....1E 147
Skullomie. High ....2G 167
Skyborry Green. Shrp ....3E 59
Skye Green. Essx ....3B 54
Skye of Curr. High ....1D 151
Slack. W Yor ....2H 91
The Slack. Dur ....2E 105
Slackhall. Derbs ....2E 85
Slack Head. Cumb ....2D 97
Slackhead. Mor ....2B 160
Slackholme End. Linc ....3E 89
Slacks of Cairnbanno.
  Abers ....4F 161
Slad. Glos ....5D 48
Slade. Swan ....4D 31
The Slade. W Ber ....5D 36
Slade End. Oxon ....2D 36
Slade Field. Cambs ....2C 64
Slade Green. G Lon ....3G 39
Slade Heath. Staf ....5D 72
Slade Hooton. S Yor ....2C 86
Sladesbridge. Corn ....5A 10
Slaggyford. Nmbd ....4H 113
Slaidburn. Lanc ....4G 97
Slaid Hill. W Yor ....5F 99
Slaithwaite. W Yor ....3A 92
Slaley. Derbs ....5G 85
Slaley. Nmbd ....4C 114
Slamannan. Falk ....2B 128
Slapton. Buck ....3H 51
Slapton. Devn ....4E 9
Slapton. Nptn ....1E 51
Slattocks. G Man ....4G 91
Slaugham. W Sus ....3D 26
Slaughterbridge. Corn ....4B 10
Slaughterford. Wilts ....4D 34
Slawston. Leics ....1E 63
Sleaford. Hants ....3G 25
Sleaford. Linc ....1H 75
Sleagill. Cumb ....3G 103
Sleap. Shrp ....3G 71
Sledmere. E Yor ....3D 100
Sleightholme. Dur ....3C 104
Sleights. N Yor ....4F 107
Slepe. Dors ....3E 15
Slickly. High ....2E 169
Sliddery. N Ayr ....3D 122
Sligachan. High ....1C 146
Slimbridge. Glos ....5C 48

## Slindon—South Zeal

Slindon. *Staf* 2C **72**
Slindon. *W Sus* 5A **26**
Slinfold. *W Sus* 2C **26**
Slingsby. *N Yor* 2A **100**
Slip End. *C Beds* 4A **52**
Slipton. *Nptn* 3G **63**
Slitting Mill. *Staf* 4E **73**
Slochd. *High* 1C **150**
Slockavullin. *Arg* 4F **133**
Sloley. *Norf* 3E **79**
Sloncombe. *Devn* 4H **11**
Sloothby. *Linc* 3D **89**
**Slough**. *Slo* 3A **38**
Slough Green. *Som* 4F **21**
Slough Green. *W Sus* 3D **27**
Sluggan. *High* 1C **150**
Slyne. *Lanc* 3D **97**
Smailholm. *Bord* 1A **120**
Smallbridge. *G Man* 3H **91**
Smallbrook. *Devn* 3B **12**
Smallburgh. *Norf* 3F **79**
Smallburn. *E Ayr* 2F **117**
Smalldale. *Derbs* 3E **85**
Small Dole. *W Sus* 4D **26**
Smalley. *Derbs* 1B **74**
Smallfield. *Surr* 1E **27**
Small Heath. *W Mid* 2E **61**
Smallholm. *Dum* 2C **112**
Small Hythe. *Kent* 2C **28**
Smallrice. *Staf* 2D **72**
Smallridge. *Devn* 2G **13**
Smallwood Hey. *Lanc* 5C **96**
Smallworth. *Norf* 2C **66**
Smannell. *Hants* 2B **24**
Smardale. *Cumb* 4A **104**
Smarden. *Kent* 1C **28**
Smarden Bell. *Kent* 1C **28**
Smart's Hill. *Kent* 1G **27**
Smeatharpe. *Devn* 1F **13**
Smeeth. *Kent* 2E **29**
The Smeeth. *Norf* 4E **77**
Smeeton Westerby. *Leics* 1D **62**
Smeircleit. *W Isl* 7C **170**
Smerral. *High* 5D **168**
Smestow. *Staf* 1C **60**
**Smethwick**. *W Mid* 2E **61**
Smirisary. *High* 1A **140**
Smisby. *Derbs* 4H **73**
Smitham Hill. *Bath* 1A **22**
Smith End Green. *Worc* 5B **60**
Smithfield. *Cumb* 3F **113**
Smith Green. *Lanc* 4D **97**
The Smithies. *Shrp* 1A **60**
Smithincott. *Devn* 1D **12**
Smith's Green. *Essx* 3F **53**
Smithstown. *High* 1G **155**
Smithton. *High* 4B **158**
Smithwood Green. *Suff* 5B **66**
Smithy Bridge. *G Man* 3H **91**
Smithy Green. *Ches E* 3B **84**
Smithy Lane Ends. *Lanc* 3C **90**
Smockington. *Leics* 2B **62**
Smoogro. *Orkn* 7C **172**
Smythe's Green. *Essx* 4C **54**
Snaigow House. *Per* 4H **143**
Snailbeach. *Shrp* 5F **71**
Snailwell. *Cambs* 4F **65**
Snainton. *N Yor* 1D **100**
Snaith. *E Yor* 2G **93**
Snape. *N Yor* 1E **99**
Snape. *Suff* 5F **67**
Snape Green. *Lanc* 3B **90**
Snapper. *Devn* 3F **19**
Snarestone. *Leics* 5H **73**
Snarford. *Linc* 2H **87**
Snargate. *Kent* 3D **28**
Snave. *Kent* 3E **28**
Sneachill. *Worc* 5D **60**
Snead. *Powy* 1F **59**
Snead Common. *Worc* 4B **60**
Sneaton. *N Yor* 4F **107**
Sneatonthorpe. *N Yor* 4G **107**
Snelland. *Linc* 2H **87**
Snelston. *Derbs* 1F **73**
Snetterton. *Norf* 1B **66**
Snettisham. *Norf* 2F **77**
Snibston. *Leics* 4B **74**
Sniseabhal. *W Isl* 5C **170**
Snitter. *Nmbd* 4E **121**
Snitterby. *Linc* 1G **87**
Snitterfield. *Warw* 5G **61**
Snitton. *Shrp* 3H **59**
Snodhill. *Here* 1G **47**
Snodland. *Kent* 4B **40**
Snods Edge. *Nmbd* 4D **114**
Snowshill. *Glos* 2F **49**
Snow Street. *Norf* 2C **66**
Snydale. *W Yor* 2E **93**
Soake. *Hants* 1E **17**
Soar. *Carm* 3G **45**
Soar. *Gwyn* 2F **69**
Soar. *IOA* 3C **80**
Soar. *Powy* 2C **46**
Soberton. *Hants* 1E **16**
Soberton Heath. *Hants* 1E **16**
Sockbridge. *Cumb* 2G **103**
Sockburn. *Darl* 4A **106**
Sodom. *Den* 3C **82**
Sodom. *Shet* 5G **173**
Soham. *Cambs* 3E **65**
Soham Cotes. *Cambs* 3E **65**
Solas. *W Isl* 1D **170**
Soldon Cross. *Devn* 1D **10**
Soldridge. *Hants* 3E **25**
Solent Breezes. *Hants* 2D **16**
Sole Street. *Kent*
nr. Meopham 4A **40**
nr. Waltham 1E **29**
**Solihull**. *W Mid* 2F **61**
Sollers Dilwyn. *Here* 5G **59**
Sollers Hope. *Here* 2B **48**
Sollom. *Lanc* 3C **90**
Solva. *Pemb* 2B **42**
Somerby. *Leics* 4E **75**
Somerby. *Linc* 4D **94**
Somercotes. *Derbs* 5B **86**
Somerford. *Dors* 3G **15**
Somerford. *Staf* 5C **72**
Somerford Keynes. *Glos* 2F **35**
Somerley. *W Sus* 3G **17**
Somerleyton. *Suff* 1G **67**
Somersal Herbert. *Derbs* 2F **73**
Somersby. *Linc* 3C **88**
Somersham. *Cambs* 3C **64**
Somersham. *Suff* 1D **54**
Somerton. *Oxon* 3C **50**
Somerton. *Som* 4H **21**
Somerton. *Suff* 5H **65**
**Sompting**. *W Sus* 5C **26**
Sonning. *Wok* 4F **37**
Sonning Common. *Oxon* 3F **37**
Sonning Eye. *Oxon* 4F **37**
Sookholme. *Notts* 4C **86**
Sopley. *Hants* 3G **15**
Sopworth. *Wilts* 3D **34**
Sorbie. *Dum* 5B **110**
Sordale. *High* 2D **168**
Sorisdale. *Arg* 2D **138**
Sorn. *E Ayr* 2E **117**
Sornhill. *E Ayr* 1E **117**
Sortat. *High* 2E **169**
Sotby. *Linc* 3B **88**
Sots Hole. *Linc* 4A **88**
Sotterley. *Suff* 2G **67**
Soudley. *Shrp*
nr. Church Stretton 1G **59**
nr. Market Drayton 3B **72**
Soughton. *Flin* 4E **83**
Soulbury. *Buck* 3G **51**
Soulby. *Cumb*
nr. Appleby 3A **104**
nr. Penrith 2F **103**
Souldern. *Oxon* 2D **50**
Souldrop. *Bed* 4G **63**
Sound. *Ches E* 1A **72**
Sound. *Shet*
nr. Lerwick 7F **173**
nr. Tresta 6E **173**
Soundwell. *S Glo* 4B **34**
Sourhope. *Bord* 2C **120**
Sourin. *Orkn* 4D **172**
Sour Nook. *Cumb* 5E **113**
Sourton. *Devn* 3F **11**
Soutergate. *Cumb* 1B **96**
South Acre. *Norf* 4H **77**
**Southall**. *G Lon* 3C **38**
South Allington. *Devn* 5D **9**
South Alloa. *Falk* 4A **136**
Southam. *Glos* 3E **49**
Southam. *Warw* 4B **62**
South Ambersham. *W Sus* 3A **26**
**Southampton**. *Sotn* 1C **16**
Southampton Airport. *Hants* 1C **16**
Southannan. *N Ayr* 4D **126**
South Anston. *S Yor* 2C **86**
South Ascot. *Wind* 4A **38**
South Baddesley. *Hants* 3B **16**
South Balfern. *Dum* 4B **110**
South Ballachulish. *High* 3E **141**
**South Bank**. *Red C* 2C **106**
South Barrow. *Som* 4B **22**
**South Benfleet**. *Essx* 2B **40**
South Bents. *Tyne* 3H **115**
South Bersted. *W Sus* 5A **26**
Southborough. *Kent* 1G **27**
Southbourne. *Bour* 3G **15**
Southbourne. *W Sus* 2F **17**
South Bowood. *Dors* 3H **13**
South Brent. *Devn* 3C **8**
South Brewham. *Som* 3C **22**
South Broomage. *Falk* 1B **128**
South Broomhill. *Nmbd* 5G **121**
Southburgh. *Norf* 5B **78**
South Burlingham. *Norf* 5F **79**
Southburn. *E Yor* 4D **101**
South Cadbury. *Som* 4B **22**
South Carlton. *Linc* 3G **87**
South Cave. *E Yor* 1C **94**
South Cerney. *Glos* 2F **35**
South Chailey. *E Sus* 4E **27**
South Chard. *Som* 2G **13**
South Charlton. *Nmbd* 2F **121**
South Cheriton. *Som* 4B **22**
South Church. *Dur* 2F **105**
Southchurch. *S'end* 2D **40**
South Cleatlam. *Dur* 3E **105**
South Cliffe. *E Yor* 1B **94**
South Clifton. *Notts* 3F **87**
South Clunes. *High* 4H **157**
South Cockerington. *Linc* 2C **88**
South Common. *Devn* 2G **13**
South Cornelly. *B'end* 3B **32**
Southcott. *Devn*
nr. Great Torrington 1E **11**
nr. Okehampton 3F **11**
Southcott. *Wilts* 1G **23**
Southcourt. *Buck* 4G **51**
South Cove. *Suff* 2G **67**
South Creagan. *Arg* 4D **141**
South Creake. *Norf* 2A **78**
South Crosland. *W Yor* 3B **92**
South Croxton. *Leics* 4D **74**
South Dalton. *E Yor* 5D **100**
South Darenth. *Kent* 4G **39**
Southdean. *Bord* 4A **120**
Southdown. *Bath* 5C **34**
South Duffield. *N Yor* 1G **93**
Southease. *E Sus* 5F **27**
South Elkington. *Linc* 2B **88**
South Elmsall. *W Yor* 3E **93**
South End. *Cumb* 3B **96**
South End. *N Lin* 2E **94**
Southend. *Arg* 5A **122**
Southend. *Glos* 2C **34**
Southend. *W Ber* 4D **36**
Southend Airport. *Essx* 2C **40**
**Southend-on-Sea**. *S'end* 2C **40**
Southerfield. *Cumb* 5C **112**
Southerhouse. *Shet* 8E **173**
Southerly. *Devn* 4F **11**
Southernden. *Kent* 1C **28**
Southerndown. *V Glam* 4B **32**
Southerness. *Dum* 4A **112**
South Erradale. *High* 1G **155**
Southerton. *Devn* 3D **12**
Southery. *Norf* 1F **65**
Southey Green. *Essx* 2A **54**
South Fambridge. *Essx* 1C **40**
South Fawley. *W Ber* 3B **36**
South Feorline. *N Ayr* 3D **122**
South Ferriby. *N Lin* 2C **94**
South Field. *E Yor* 2D **94**
Southfleet. *Kent* 3H **39**
South Garvan. *High* 1D **141**
Southgate. *Cdgn* 2E **57**
**Southgate**. *G Lon* 1E **39**
Southgate. *Norf*
nr. Aylsham 3D **78**
nr. Fakenham 2A **78**
Southgate. *Swan* 4E **31**
South Gluss. *Shet* 4E **173**
South Godstone. *Surr* 1E **27**
South Gorley. *Hants* 1G **15**
South Green. *Essx*
nr. Billericay 1A **40**
nr. Colchester 4D **54**
South Green. *Kent* 4C **40**
South Hanningfield. *Essx* 1B **40**
South Harting. *W Sus* 1F **17**
South Hayling. *Hants* 3F **17**
South Hazelrigg. *Nmbd* 1E **121**
South Heath. *Buck* 5H **51**
South Heath. *Essx* 4E **54**
South Heighton. *E Sus* 5F **27**
South Hetton. *Dur* 5G **115**
South Hiendley. *W Yor* 3D **93**
South Hill. *Corn* 5D **10**
South Hill. *Som* 4H **21**
South Hinksey. *Oxon* 5D **50**
South Hole. *Devn* 4C **18**
South Holme. *N Yor* 2B **100**
South Holmwood. *Surr* 1C **26**
South Hornchurch. *G Lon* 2G **39**
South Huish. *Devn* 4C **8**
South Hykeham. *Linc* 4G **87**
South Hylton. *Tyne* 4G **115**
Southill. *C Beds* 1B **52**
Southington. *Hants* 2D **24**
South Kelsey. *Linc* 1H **87**
South Kessock. *High* 4A **158**
South Killingholme. *N Lin* 3E **95**
South Kilvington. *N Yor* 1G **99**
South Kilworth. *Leics* 2D **62**
South Kirkby. *W Yor* 3E **93**
South Kirkton. *Abers* 3E **153**
South Knighton. *Devn* 5B **12**
South Kyme. *Linc* 1A **76**
South Lancing. *W Sus* 5C **26**
South Ledaig. *Arg* 5D **140**
South Leigh. *Oxon* 5B **50**
Southleigh. *Devn* 3F **13**
South Leverton. *Notts* 2E **87**
South Littleton. *Worc* 1F **49**
South Lopham. *Norf* 2C **66**
South Luffenham. *Rut* 5G **75**
South Malling. *E Sus* 4F **27**
South Marston. *Swin* 3G **35**
South Middleton. *Nmbd* 2D **121**
South Milford. *N Yor* 1E **93**
South Milton. *Devn* 4D **8**
South Mimms. *Herts* 5C **52**
Southminster. *Essx* 1D **40**
South Molton. *Devn* 4H **19**
South Moor. *Dur* 4E **115**
Southmoor. *Oxon* 2B **36**
South Moreton. *Oxon* 3D **36**
South Mundham. *W Sus* 2G **17**
South Muskham. *Notts* 5E **87**
South Newbald. *E Yor* 1C **94**
South Newington. *Oxon* 2C **50**
South Newsham. *Nmbd* 2G **115**
South Newton. *N Ayr* 4H **125**
South Newton. *Wilts* 3F **23**
South Normanton. *Derbs* 5B **86**
South Norwood. *G Lon* 4E **39**
South Nutfield. *Surr* 1E **27**
**South Ockendon**. *Thur* 2G **39**
Southoe. *Cambs* 4A **64**
Southolt. *Suff* 4D **66**
South Ormsby. *Linc* 3C **88**
Southorpe. *Pet* 5H **75**
South Otterington. *N Yor* 1F **99**
South Owersby. *Linc* 1H **87**
Southowram. *W Yor* 2B **92**
**South Oxhey**. *Herts* 1C **38**
South Perrott. *Dors* 2H **13**
South Petherton. *Som* 1H **13**
South Petherwin. *Corn* 4D **10**
South Pickenham. *Norf* 5A **78**
South Pool. *Devn* 4D **9**
South Poorton. *Dors* 3A **14**
South Port. *Arg* 1H **133**
**Southport**. *Mers* 3B **90**
Southpunds. *Shet* 10F **173**
South Queensferry. *Edin* 2E **129**
South Radworthy. *Devn* 3A **20**
South Rauceby. *Linc* 1H **75**
South Raynham. *Norf* 3A **78**
Southrepps. *Norf* 2E **79**
South Reston. *Linc* 2D **88**
Southrey. *Linc* 4A **88**
Southrop. *Glos* 5G **49**
Southrope. *Hants* 2E **25**
South Runcton. *Norf* 5F **77**
South Scarle. *Notts* 4F **87**
Southsea. *Port* 3E **17**
**South Shields**. *Tyne* 3G **115**
South Shore. *Bkpl* 1B **90**
Southside. *Orkn* 5E **172**
South Somercotes. *Linc* 1D **88**
South Stainley. *N Yor* 3F **99**
South Stainmore. *Cumb* 3B **104**
South Stifford. *Thur* 3G **39**
South Stoke. *Bath* 5C **34**
South Stoke. *Oxon* 3D **36**
South Stoke. *W Sus* 5B **26**
South Street. *E Sus* 4E **27**
South Street. *Kent*
nr. Faversham 5E **41**
nr. Whitstable 4F **41**
South Tawton. *Devn* 3G **11**
South Thoresby. *Linc* 3D **88**
South Tidworth. *Wilts* 2H **23**
South Town. *Devn* 4C **12**
South Town. *Hants* 3E **25**
Southtown. *Norf* 5H **79**
Southtown. *Orkn* 8D **172**
South View. *Shet* 7E **173**
Southwaite. *Cumb* 5F **113**
South Walsham. *Norf* 4F **79**
South Warnborough. *Hants* 2F **25**
Southwater. *W Sus* 3C **26**
Southwater Street. *W Sus* 3C **26**
Southway. *Som* 2A **22**
South Weald. *Essx* 1G **39**
South Weirs. *Hants* 2A **16**
Southwell. *Dors* 5B **14**
Southwell. *Notts* 5E **86**
South Weston. *Oxon* 2F **37**
South Wheatley. *Corn* 3C **10**
South Wheatley. *Notts* 2E **87**
Southwick. *Hants* 2E **17**
Southwick. *Nptn* 1H **63**
Southwick. *Tyne* 4G **115**
**Southwick**. *W Sus* 5D **26**
Southwick. *Wilts* 1D **22**
South Widcombe. *Bath* 1A **22**
South Wigston. *Leics* 1C **62**
South Willingham. *Linc* 2A **88**
South Wingfield. *Derbs* 5A **86**
South Witham. *Linc* 4G **75**
Southwold. *Suff* 3H **67**
South Wonston. *Hants* 3C **24**
Southwood. *Norf* 5F **79**
Southwood. *Som* 3A **22**
**South Woodham Ferrers**.
*Essx* 1C **40**
South Wootton. *Norf* 3F **77**
South Wraxall. *Wilts* 5D **34**
South Zeal. *Devn* 3G **11**

Soval Lodge. *W Isl* . . . . . . . . . .5F **171**
Sowerby. *N Yor* . . . . . . . . . . . .1G **99**
Sowerby. *W Yor* . . . . . . . . . . .2A **92**
Sowerby Bridge. *W Yor* . . . . . .2A **92**
Sowerby Row. *Cumb* . . . . . . . .5E **113**
Sower Carr. *Lanc* . . . . . . . . . . .5C **96**
Sowley Green. *Suff* . . . . . . . . . .5G **65**
Sowood. *W Yor* . . . . . . . . . . . .3A **92**
Sowton. *Devn* . . . . . . . . . . . . .3C **12**
Soyal. *High* . . . . . . . . . . . . . .4C **164**
Soyland Town. *W Yor* . . . . . . .2A **92**
Spacey Houses. *N Yor* . . . . . . .4F **99**
Spa Common. *Norf* . . . . . . . . .2E **79**
**Spalding.** *Linc* . . . . . . . . . . .3B **76**
Spaldington. *E Yor* . . . . . . . . .1A **94**
Spaldwick. *Cambs* . . . . . . . . . .3A **64**
Spalford. *Notts* . . . . . . . . . . . .4F **87**
Spanby. *Linc* . . . . . . . . . . . . . .2H **75**
Sparham. *Norf* . . . . . . . . . . . .4C **78**
Sparhamhill. *Norf* . . . . . . . . . .4C **78**
Spark Bridge. *Cumb* . . . . . . . . .1C **96**
Sparket. *Cumb* . . . . . . . . . . . .2F **103**
Sparkford. *Som* . . . . . . . . . . . .4B **22**
Sparkwell. *Devn* . . . . . . . . . . . .3B **8**
Sparrow Green. *Norf* . . . . . . . .4B **78**
Sparrowpit. *Derbs* . . . . . . . . . .2E **85**
Sparrow's Green. *E Sus* . . . . . .2H **27**
Sparsholt. *Hants* . . . . . . . . . . .3C **24**
Sparsholt. *Oxon* . . . . . . . . . . .3B **36**
Spartylea. *Nmbd* . . . . . . . . . .5B **114**
Spath. *Staf* . . . . . . . . . . . . . . .2E **73**
Spaunton. *N Yor* . . . . . . . . . .1B **100**
Spaxton. *Som* . . . . . . . . . . . . .3F **21**
Spean Bridge. *High* . . . . . . . . .5E **149**
Spear Hill. *W Sus* . . . . . . . . . . .4C **26**
Speen. *Buck* . . . . . . . . . . . . . .2G **37**
Speen. *W Ber* . . . . . . . . . . . . .5C **36**
Speeton. *N Yor* . . . . . . . . . . . .2F **101**
Speke. *Mers* . . . . . . . . . . . . . .2G **83**
Speldhurst. *Kent* . . . . . . . . . . .1G **27**
Spellbrook. *Herts* . . . . . . . . . .4E **53**
Spelsbury. *Oxon* . . . . . . . . . . .3B **50**
Spencers Wood. *Wok* . . . . . . . .5F **37**
Spennithorne. *N Yor* . . . . . . . .1D **98**
**Spennymoor.** *Dur* . . . . . . . .1F **105**
Spernall. *Warw* . . . . . . . . . . . .4E **61**
Spetchley. *Worc* . . . . . . . . . . . .5C **60**
Spetisbury. *Dors* . . . . . . . . . . .2E **15**
Spexhall. *Suff* . . . . . . . . . . . . .2F **67**
Speybank. *High* . . . . . . . . . . .3C **150**
Spey Bay. *Mor* . . . . . . . . . . . .2A **160**
Speybridge. *High* . . . . . . . . . .1E **151**
Speyview. *Mor* . . . . . . . . . . . .4G **159**
Spilsby. *Linc* . . . . . . . . . . . . . .4D **88**
Spindlestone. *Nmbd* . . . . . . . .1F **121**
Spinkhill. *Derbs* . . . . . . . . . . . .3B **86**
Spinney Hills. *Leic* . . . . . . . . . .5D **74**
Spinningdale. *High* . . . . . . . . .5D **164**
Spital. *Mers* . . . . . . . . . . . . . . .2F **83**
Spitalhill. *Derbs* . . . . . . . . . . . .1F **73**
Spital in the Street. *Linc* . . . . .1G **87**
Spithurst. *E Sus* . . . . . . . . . . . .4F **27**
Spittal. *Dum* . . . . . . . . . . . . .4A **110**
Spittal. *E Lot* . . . . . . . . . . . . .2A **130**
Spittal. *High* . . . . . . . . . . . . . .3D **168**
Spittal. *Nmbd* . . . . . . . . . . . .4G **131**
Spittal. *Pemb* . . . . . . . . . . . . .2D **43**
Spittalfield. *Per* . . . . . . . . . . .4A **144**
Spittal of Glenmuick. *Abers* . . .5H **151**
Spittal of Glenshee. *Per* . . . . .1A **144**
Spittal-on-Rule. *Bord* . . . . . . .2H **119**
Spixworth. *Norf* . . . . . . . . . . . .4E **79**
Splatt. *Corn* . . . . . . . . . . . . . .4C **10**
Spofforth. *N Yor* . . . . . . . . . . .4F **99**
Spondon. *Derb* . . . . . . . . . . . .2B **74**
Spon End. *W Mid* . . . . . . . . . . .3H **61**
Spooner Row. *Norf* . . . . . . . . .1C **66**
Sporle. *Norf* . . . . . . . . . . . . . .4H **77**
Spott. *E Lot* . . . . . . . . . . . . . .2C **130**
Spratton. *Nptn* . . . . . . . . . . . .3E **62**
Spreakley. *Surr* . . . . . . . . . . . .2G **25**
Spreyton. *Devn* . . . . . . . . . . . .3H **11**
Spridlington. *Linc* . . . . . . . . . . .2H **87**
Springburn. *Glas* . . . . . . . . . .3H **127**

Springfield. *Dum* . . . . . . . . . . .3E **113**
Springfield. *Fife* . . . . . . . . . . . .2F **137**
Springfield. *High* . . . . . . . . . .2A **158**
Springfield. *W Mid* . . . . . . . . . .2E **61**
Spring Hill. *W Mid* . . . . . . . . . .1C **60**
Springhill. *Staf* . . . . . . . . . . . .5D **72**
Springholm. *Dum* . . . . . . . . . .3F **111**
Springside. *N Ayr* . . . . . . . . . .1C **116**
Springthorpe. *Linc* . . . . . . . . . .2F **87**
Spring Vale. *IOW* . . . . . . . . . . .3E **16**
Spring Valley. *IOM* . . . . . . . . .4C **108**
Springwell. *Tyne* . . . . . . . . . . .4F **115**
Sproatley. *E Yor* . . . . . . . . . . . .1E **95**
Sproston Green. *Ches W* . . . . . .4B **84**
Sprotbrough. *S Yor* . . . . . . . . .4F **93**
Sproughton. *Suff* . . . . . . . . . . .1E **54**
Sprouston. *Bord* . . . . . . . . . . .1B **120**
Sprowston. *Norf* . . . . . . . . . . .4E **79**
Sproxton. *Leics* . . . . . . . . . . . .3F **75**
Sproxton. *N Yor* . . . . . . . . . .1A **100**
Sprunston. *Cumb* . . . . . . . . . .5F **113**
Spurstow. *Ches E* . . . . . . . . . . .5H **83**
Sparkford. *Staf* . . . . . . . . . . . .5D **72**
Squires Gate. *Bkpl* . . . . . . . . . .1B **90**
Sraid Ruadh. *Arg* . . . . . . . . . .4A **138**
Srannda. *W Isl* . . . . . . . . . . . . .9C **171**
Sron an t-Sithein. *High* . . . . . .2C **140**
Sronphadruig Lodge. *Per* . . . .1E **142**
Sruth Mor. *W Isl* . . . . . . . . . .2E **170**
Stableford. *Shrp* . . . . . . . . . . .1B **60**
Stackhouse. *N Yor* . . . . . . . . . .3H **97**
Stackpole. *Pemb* . . . . . . . . . . .5D **43**
Stackpole Elidor. *Pemb* . . . . . .5D **43**
Stacksford. *Norf* . . . . . . . . . . .1C **66**
Stacksteads. *Lanc* . . . . . . . . . .2G **91**
Staddiscombe. *Plym* . . . . . . . . . .3B **8**
Staddlethorpe. *E Yor* . . . . . . . .2B **94**
Staddon. *Devn* . . . . . . . . . . . .2D **10**
Stadhampton. *Oxon* . . . . . . . . .2E **36**
Stadhlaigearraidh. *W Isl* . . . . .5C **170**
Stafainn. *High* . . . . . . . . . . . .2D **155**
Staffield. *Cumb* . . . . . . . . . . .5G **113**
Staffin. *High* . . . . . . . . . . . . .2D **155**
**Stafford.** *Staf* . . . . . . . . . . .3D **72**
Stafford Park. *Telf* . . . . . . . . . .5B **72**
Stagden Cross. *Essx* . . . . . . . . .4G **53**
Stagsden. *Bed* . . . . . . . . . . . . .1H **51**
Stag's Head. *Devn* . . . . . . . . . .4G **19**
Stainburn. *Cumb* . . . . . . . . . .2B **102**
Stainburn. *N Yor* . . . . . . . . . . .5E **99**
Stainby. *Linc* . . . . . . . . . . . . . .3G **75**
Staincliffe. *W Yor* . . . . . . . . . . .2C **92**
Staincross. *S Yor* . . . . . . . . . . .3D **92**
Staindrop. *Dur* . . . . . . . . . . . .2E **105**
**Staines-upon-Thames.** *Surr* .3B **38**
Stainfield. *Linc*
    nr. Bourne . . . . . . . . . . .3H **75**
    nr. Lincoln . . . . . . . . . . .3A **88**
Stainforth. *N Yor* . . . . . . . . . . .3H **97**
Stainforth. *S Yor* . . . . . . . . . . .3G **93**
Staining. *Lanc* . . . . . . . . . . . .1B **90**
Stainland. *W Yor* . . . . . . . . . . .3A **92**
Stainsacre. *N Yor* . . . . . . . . . .4G **107**
Stainton. *Cumb*
    nr. Carlisle . . . . . . . . . .4E **113**
    nr. Kendal . . . . . . . . . . .1E **97**
    nr. Penrith . . . . . . . . . .2F **103**
Stainton. *Dur* . . . . . . . . . . . . .3D **104**
Stainton. *Midd* . . . . . . . . . . . .3B **106**
Stainton. *N Yor* . . . . . . . . . . . .5E **105**
Stainton. *S Yor* . . . . . . . . . . . .1C **86**
Stainton by Langworth. *Linc* . . .3H **87**
Staintondale. *N Yor* . . . . . . . . .5G **107**
Stainton le Vale. *Linc* . . . . . . . .1A **88**
Stainton with Adgarley. *Cumb* . .2B **96**
Stair. *E Ayr* . . . . . . . . . . . . . . .2D **116**
Stair. *E Ayr* . . . . . . . . . . . . . . .2D **116**
Stairhaven. *Dum* . . . . . . . . . .4H **109**
Staithes. *N Yor* . . . . . . . . . . . .3E **107**
Stakeford. *Nmbd* . . . . . . . . . . .1F **115**
Stake Pool. *Lanc* . . . . . . . . . . .5D **96**
Stakes. *Hants* . . . . . . . . . . . . .2E **17**
Stalbridge. *Dors* . . . . . . . . . . .1C **14**
Stalbridge Weston. *Dors* . . . . .1C **14**
Stalham. *Norf* . . . . . . . . . . . . .3F **79**

Stalham Green. *Norf* . . . . . . . .3F **79**
Stalisfield Green. *Kent* . . . . . . .5D **40**
Stallen. *Dors* . . . . . . . . . . . . . .1B **14**
Stallingborough. *NE Lin* . . . . . .3F **95**
Stalling Busk. *N Yor* . . . . . . . . .1B **98**
Stallington. *Staf* . . . . . . . . . . . .2D **72**
Stalmine. *Lanc* . . . . . . . . . . . .5C **96**
**Stalybridge.** *G Man* . . . . . . .1D **84**
Stambourne. *Essx* . . . . . . . . . .2H **53**
**Stamford.** *Linc* . . . . . . . . . .5H **75**
Stamford. *Nmbd* . . . . . . . . . .3G **121**
Stamford Bridge. *Ches W* . . . . .4G **83**
Stamford Bridge. *E Yor* . . . . . .4B **100**
Stamfordham. *Nmbd* . . . . . . .2D **115**
Stamperland. *E Ren* . . . . . . . .4G **127**
Stanah. *Lanc* . . . . . . . . . . . . . .5C **96**
Stanborough. *Herts* . . . . . . . . .4C **52**
Stanbridge. *C Beds* . . . . . . . . . .3H **51**
Stanbridge. *Dors* . . . . . . . . . . .2F **15**
Stanbury. *W Yor* . . . . . . . . . . .1A **92**
Stand. *N Lan* . . . . . . . . . . . . .3A **128**
Standburn. *Falk* . . . . . . . . . . .2C **128**
Standeford. *Staf* . . . . . . . . . . .5D **72**
Standen. *Kent* . . . . . . . . . . . . .1C **28**
Standen Street. *Kent* . . . . . . . .2C **28**
Standerwick. *Som* . . . . . . . . . .1D **22**
Standford. *Hants* . . . . . . . . . . .3G **25**
Standford Bridge. *Telf* . . . . . . .3B **72**
Standingstone. *Cumb* . . . . . . .5D **112**
Standish. *Glos* . . . . . . . . . . . . .5D **48**
**Standish.** *G Man* . . . . . . . . .3D **90**
Standish Lower Ground.
    *G Man* . . . . . . . . . . . . .4D **90**
Standlake. *Oxon* . . . . . . . . . . .5B **50**
Standon. *Hants* . . . . . . . . . . . .4C **24**
Standon. *Herts* . . . . . . . . . . . .3D **53**
Standon. *Staf* . . . . . . . . . . . . .2C **72**
Standon Green End. *Herts* . . . .4D **52**
Stane. *N Lan* . . . . . . . . . . . . .4B **128**
Stanecastle. *N Ayr* . . . . . . . . .1C **116**
Stanfield. *Norf* . . . . . . . . . . . .3B **78**
Stanfield. *Suff* . . . . . . . . . . . . .5G **65**
Stanford. *C Beds* . . . . . . . . . . .1B **52**
Stanford. *Kent* . . . . . . . . . . . .2F **29**
Stanford Bishop. *Here* . . . . . . .5A **60**
Stanford Bridge. *Worc* . . . . . . .4B **60**
Stanford Dingley. *W Ber* . . . . .4D **36**
Stanford in the Vale. *Oxon* . . . .2B **36**
Stanford-le-Hope. *Thur* . . . . . .2A **40**
Stanford on Avon. *Nptn* . . . . . .3C **62**
Stanford on Soar. *Notts* . . . . . .3C **74**
Stanford on Teme. *Worc* . . . . . .4B **60**
Stanford Rivers. *Essx* . . . . . . . .5F **53**
Stanfree. *Derbs* . . . . . . . . . . . .3B **86**
Stanghow. *Red C* . . . . . . . . . .3D **107**
Stanground. *Pet* . . . . . . . . . . .1B **64**
Stanhoe. *Norf* . . . . . . . . . . . . .2H **77**
Stanhope. *Dur* . . . . . . . . . . . .1C **104**
Stanhope. *Bord* . . . . . . . . . . .2D **118**
Stanion. *Nptn* . . . . . . . . . . . . .2G **63**
Stanley. *Derbs* . . . . . . . . . . . . .1B **74**
Stanley. *Dur* . . . . . . . . . . . . . .4E **115**
Stanley. *Per* . . . . . . . . . . . . . .5A **144**
Stanley. *Shrp* . . . . . . . . . . . . . .2B **60**
Stanley. *Staf* . . . . . . . . . . . . . .5D **84**
**Stanley.** *W Yor* . . . . . . . . . . .2D **92**
Stanley Common. *Derbs* . . . . . .1B **74**
Stanley Crook. *Dur* . . . . . . . . .1E **105**
Stanley Hill. *Here* . . . . . . . . . . .1B **48**
Stanlow. *Ches W* . . . . . . . . . . .3G **83**
Stanmer. *Brig* . . . . . . . . . . . . .5E **27**
**Stanmore.** *G Lon* . . . . . . . . .1C **38**
Stanmore. *Hants* . . . . . . . . . . .4C **24**
Stanmore. *W Ber* . . . . . . . . . . .4C **36**
Stannersburn. *Nmbd* . . . . . . .1A **114**
Stanningfield. *Suff* . . . . . . . . . .5A **66**
Stannington. *Nmbd* . . . . . . . .2F **115**
Stannington. *S Yor* . . . . . . . . .2H **85**
Stansbatch. *Here* . . . . . . . . . . .4F **59**
Stanshope. *Staf* . . . . . . . . . . . .5F **85**
Stanstead. *Suff* . . . . . . . . . . . .1B **54**
Stanstead Abbotts. *Herts* . . . . .4D **53**
Stansted. *Kent* . . . . . . . . . . . .4H **39**
Stansted Airport. *Essx* . . . . . . .3F **53**

Stansted Mountfitchet. *Essx* . . .3F **53**
Stanthorne. *Ches W* . . . . . . . .4A **84**
Stanton. *Derbs* . . . . . . . . . . . .4G **73**
Stanton. *Glos* . . . . . . . . . . . . .2F **49**
Stanton. *Nmbd* . . . . . . . . . . .5F **121**
Stanton. *Staf* . . . . . . . . . . . . .1F **73**
Stanton. *Suff* . . . . . . . . . . . . .3B **66**
Stanton by Bridge. *Derbs* . . . . .3A **74**
Stanton-by-Dale. *Derbs* . . . . . .2B **74**
Stanton Chare. *Suff* . . . . . . . . .3B **66**
Stanton Drew. *Bath* . . . . . . . . .5A **34**
Stanton Fitzwarren. *Swin* . . . . .2G **35**
Stanton Harcourt. *Oxon* . . . . . .5C **50**
Stanton Hill. *Notts* . . . . . . . . .4B **86**
Stanton in Peak. *Derbs* . . . . . .4G **85**
Stanton Lacy. *Shrp* . . . . . . . . .3G **59**
Stanton Long. *Shrp* . . . . . . . . .1H **59**
Stanton-on-the-Wolds. *Notts* . .2D **74**
Stanton Prior. *Bath* . . . . . . . . .5B **34**
Stanton St Bernard. *Wilts* . . . . .5F **35**
Stanton St John. *Oxon* . . . . . .5D **50**
Stanton St Quintin. *Wilts* . . . . .4E **35**
Stanton Street. *Suff* . . . . . . . . .4B **66**
Stanton under Bardon. *Leics* . . .4B **74**
Stanton upon Hine Heath.
    *Shrp* . . . . . . . . . . . . . . .3H **71**
Stanton Wick. *Bath* . . . . . . . . .5B **34**
Stanwardine in the Fields.
    *Shrp* . . . . . . . . . . . . . . .3G **71**
Stanwardine in the Wood.
    *Shrp* . . . . . . . . . . . . . . .3G **71**
Stanway. *Essx* . . . . . . . . . . . . .3C **54**
Stanway. *Glos* . . . . . . . . . . . . .2F **49**
Stanwell. *Surr* . . . . . . . . . . . . .3B **38**
Stanwell Green. *Suff* . . . . . . . .3D **66**
Stanwell Moor. *Surr* . . . . . . . . .3B **38**
Stanwick. *Nptn* . . . . . . . . . . . .3G **63**
Stanydale. *Shet* . . . . . . . . . . .6D **173**
Staoinebrig. *W Isl* . . . . . . . . . .5C **170**
Stape. *N Yor* . . . . . . . . . . . . . .5E **107**
Stapehill. *Dors* . . . . . . . . . . . .2F **15**
Stapeley. *Ches E* . . . . . . . . . . .1A **72**
Stapenhill. *Staf* . . . . . . . . . . . .3G **73**
Staple. *Kent* . . . . . . . . . . . . . .5G **41**
Staple Cross. *Devn* . . . . . . . . .4D **20**
Staplecross. *E Sus* . . . . . . . . . .3B **28**
Staplefield. *W Sus* . . . . . . . . . .3D **27**
Staple Fitzpaine. *Som* . . . . . . .1F **13**
Stapleford. *Cambs* . . . . . . . . . .5D **64**
Stapleford. *Herts* . . . . . . . . . . .4D **52**
Stapleford. *Leics* . . . . . . . . . . .4F **75**
Stapleford. *Linc* . . . . . . . . . . . .5F **87**
Stapleford. *Notts* . . . . . . . . . . .2B **74**
Stapleford. *Wilts* . . . . . . . . . . .3F **23**
Stapleford Abbotts. *Essx* . . . . .1G **39**
Stapleford Tawney. *Essx* . . . . .1G **39**
Staplegrove. *Som* . . . . . . . . . .4F **21**
Staplehay. *Som* . . . . . . . . . . . .4F **21**
Staple Hill. *S Glo* . . . . . . . . . . .4B **34**
Staplehurst. *Kent* . . . . . . . . . .1B **28**
Staplers. *IOW* . . . . . . . . . . . . .4D **16**
Stapleton. *Bris* . . . . . . . . . . . . .4B **34**
Stapleton. *Cumb* . . . . . . . . . .2G **113**
Stapleton. *Here* . . . . . . . . . . . .4F **59**
Stapleton. *Leics* . . . . . . . . . . . .1B **62**
Stapleton. *N Yor* . . . . . . . . . . .3F **105**
Stapleton. *Shrp* . . . . . . . . . . . .5G **71**
Stapleton. *Som* . . . . . . . . . . . .1E **13**
Stapley. *Som* . . . . . . . . . . . . . .1E **13**
Staploe. *Bed* . . . . . . . . . . . . . .4A **64**
Staplow. *Here* . . . . . . . . . . . . .1B **48**
Star. *Fife* . . . . . . . . . . . . . . . . .3F **137**
Star. *Pemb* . . . . . . . . . . . . . . .1G **43**
Star. *Som* . . . . . . . . . . . . . . . .1H **21**
Starbeck. *N Yor* . . . . . . . . . . . .4F **99**
Starbotton. *N Yor* . . . . . . . . . .2B **98**
Starcross. *Devn* . . . . . . . . . . . .4C **12**
Stareton. *Warw* . . . . . . . . . . . .3H **61**
Starkholmes. *Derbs* . . . . . . . . .5H **85**
Starling. *G Man* . . . . . . . . . . .3F **91**
Starling's Green. *Essx* . . . . . . . .2E **53**
Starston. *Norf* . . . . . . . . . . . . .2E **67**
Start. *Devn* . . . . . . . . . . . . . . .4E **9**
Startforth. *Dur* . . . . . . . . . . . .3D **104**
Start Hill. *Essx* . . . . . . . . . . . . .3F **53**

Startley. *Wilts* . . . . . . . . . . . . .3E **35**
Stathe. *Som* . . . . . . . . . . . . . .4G **21**
Stathern. *Leics* . . . . . . . . . . . . .2E **75**
Station Town. *Dur* . . . . . . . . . .1B **106**
Staughton Green. *Cambs* . . . . .4A **64**
Staughton Highway. *Cambs* . . .4A **64**
Staunton. *Glos*
    nr. Cheltenham . . . . . . .3C **48**
    nr. Monmouth . . . . . . . .4A **48**
Staunton in the Vale. *Notts* . . .1F **75**
Staunton on Arrow. *Here* . . . . .4F **59**
Staunton on Wye. *Here* . . . . . .1G **47**
Staveley. *Cumb* . . . . . . . . . . . .5F **103**
**Staveley.** *Derbs* . . . . . . . . . .3B **86**
Staveley. *N Yor* . . . . . . . . . . . .3F **99**
Staveley-in-Cartmel. *Cumb* . . . .1C **96**
Staverton. *Devn* . . . . . . . . . . . .2D **9**
Staverton. *Glos* . . . . . . . . . . . .3D **49**
Staverton. *Nptn* . . . . . . . . . . . .4C **62**
Staverton. *Wilts* . . . . . . . . . . . .5D **34**
Stawell. *Som* . . . . . . . . . . . . . .3G **21**
Stawley. *Som* . . . . . . . . . . . . . .4D **20**
Staxigoe. *High* . . . . . . . . . . . .3F **169**
Staxton. *N Yor* . . . . . . . . . . . .2E **101**
Staylittle. *Powy* . . . . . . . . . . . .1A **58**
Staynall. *Lanc* . . . . . . . . . . . . .5C **96**
Staythorpe. *Notts* . . . . . . . . . .5E **87**
Stean. *N Yor* . . . . . . . . . . . . . .2C **98**
Stearsby. *N Yor* . . . . . . . . . . .2A **100**
Steart. *Som* . . . . . . . . . . . . . . .2F **21**
Stebbing. *Essx* . . . . . . . . . . . . .3G **53**
Stebbing Green. *Essx* . . . . . . . .3G **53**
Stedham. *W Sus* . . . . . . . . . . .4G **25**
Steel. *Nmbd* . . . . . . . . . . . . .4C **114**
Steel Cross. *E Sus* . . . . . . . . . .2G **27**
Steelend. *Fife* . . . . . . . . . . . . .4C **136**
Steele Road. *Bord* . . . . . . . . .5H **119**
Steel Heath. *Shrp* . . . . . . . . . . .2H **71**
Steen's Bridge. *Here* . . . . . . . .5H **59**
Steep. *Hants* . . . . . . . . . . . . . .4F **25**
Steep Lane. *W Yor* . . . . . . . . . .2A **92**
Steeple. *Dors* . . . . . . . . . . . . . .4E **15**
Steeple. *Essx* . . . . . . . . . . . . . .5C **54**
Steeple Ashton. *Wilts* . . . . . . . .1E **23**
Steeple Aston. *Oxon* . . . . . . . .3C **50**
Steeple Barton. *Oxon* . . . . . . . .3C **50**
Steeple Bumpstead. *Essx* . . . . .1G **53**
Steeple Claydon. *Buck* . . . . . . .3E **51**
Steeple Gidding. *Cambs* . . . . .2A **64**
Steeple Langford. *Wilts* . . . . . .3F **23**
Steeple Morden. *Cambs* . . . . .1C **52**
Steeton. *W Yor* . . . . . . . . . . . .5C **98**
Stein. *High* . . . . . . . . . . . . . .3B **154**
Steinmanhill. *Abers* . . . . . . . .4E **161**
Stelling Minnis. *Kent* . . . . . . . .1F **29**
Stembridge. *Som* . . . . . . . . . . .4H **21**
Stemster. *High*
    nr. Halkirk . . . . . . . . . .2D **169**
    nr. Westfield . . . . . . . . .2C **168**
Stenalees. *Corn* . . . . . . . . . . . . .3E **6**
Stenhill. *Devn* . . . . . . . . . . . . .1D **12**
Stenhouse. *Edin* . . . . . . . . . . .2F **129**
**Stenhousemuir.** *Falk* . . . . . .1B **128**
Stenigot. *Linc* . . . . . . . . . . . . .2B **88**
Stenscholl. *High* . . . . . . . . . . .2D **155**
Stenso. *Orkn* . . . . . . . . . . . . .5C **172**
Stenson. *Derbs* . . . . . . . . . . . .3H **73**
Stenson Fields. *Derbs* . . . . . . . .2H **73**
Stenton. *E Lot* . . . . . . . . . . . .2C **130**
Stenwith. *Linc* . . . . . . . . . . . . .2F **75**
Steòrnabhagh. *W Isl* . . . . . . . .4G **171**
Stepaside. *Pemb* . . . . . . . . . . .4F **43**
Stepford. *Dum* . . . . . . . . . . . .1F **111**
**Stepney.** *G Lon* . . . . . . . . . . .2E **39**
Steppingley. *C Beds* . . . . . . . . .2A **52**
Stepps. *N Lan* . . . . . . . . . . . .3H **127**
Sterndale Moor. *Derbs* . . . . . . .4F **85**
Sternfield. *Suff* . . . . . . . . . . . . .4F **67**
Stert. *Wilts* . . . . . . . . . . . . . . .1F **23**
Stetchworth. *Cambs* . . . . . . . . .5F **65**
**Stevenage.** *Herts* . . . . . . . . .3C **52**
**Stevenston.** *N Ayr* . . . . . . . .5D **126**
Steventon. *Devn* . . . . . . . . . . .1F **11**
Steventon. *Hants* . . . . . . . . . . .2D **24**

Steventon—Stromeferry


Steventon. Oxon 2C 36
Steventon End. Essx 1F 53
Stevington. Bed 5G 63
Stewartby. Bed 1A 52
Stewarton. Arg 4A 122
Stewarton. E Ayr 5F 127
Stewkley. Buck 3G 51
Stewkley Dean. Buck 3G 51
Stewley. Som 1G 13
Stewton. Linc 2C 88
Steyning. W Sus 4C 26
Steynton. Pemb 4D 42
Stibb. Corn 1C 10
Stibbard. Norf 3B 78
Stibb Cross. Devn 1E 11
Stibb Green. Wilts 5H 35
Stibbington. Cambs 1H 63
Stichill. Bord 1B 120
Sticker. Corn 3D 6
Stickford. Linc 4C 88
Sticklepath. Devn 3G 11
Sticklinch. Som 3A 22
Stickling Green. Essx 2E 53
Stickney. Linc 5C 88
Stiffkey. Norf 1B 78
Stifford's Bridge. Here 1C 48
Stileway. Som 2H 21
Stillingfleet. N Yor 5H 99
Stillington. N Yor 3H 99
Stillington. Stoc T 2A 106
Stilton. Cambs 2A 64
Stinchcombe. Glos 2C 34
Stinsford. Dors 3C 14
Stiperstones. Shrp 5F 71
Stirchley. Telf 5B 72
Stirchley. W Mid 2E 61
Stirling. Abers 4H 161
**Stirling**. Stir 4G 135
Stirton. N Yor 4B 98
Stisted. Essx 3A 54
Stitchcombe. Wilts 5H 35
Stithians. Corn 5B 6
Stittenham. High 1A 158
Stivichall. W Mid 3H 61
Stixwould. Linc 4A 88
Stoak. Ches W 3G 83
Stobo. Bord 1D 118
Stobo Castle. Bord 1D 118
Stoborough. Dors 4E 15
Stoborough Green. Dors 4E 15
Stobs Castle. Bord 4H 119
Stobswood. Nmbd 5G 121
Stock. Essx 1A 40
Stockbridge. Hants 3B 24
Stockbridge. W Yor 5C 98
Stockbury. Kent 4C 40
Stockcross. W Ber 5C 36
Stockdalewath. Cumb 5E 113
Stocker's Head. Kent 5D 40
Stockerston. Leics 1F 63
Stock Green. Worc 5D 61
Stocking. Here 2B 48
Stockingford. Warw 1H 61
Stocking Green. Essx 2F 53
Stocking Pelham. Herts 3E 53
Stockland. Devn 2F 13
Stockland Bristol. Som 2F 21
Stockleigh English. Devn 2B 12
Stockleigh Pomeroy. Devn 2B 12
Stockley. Wilts 5F 35
Stocklinch. Som 1G 13
**Stockport**. G Man 2C 84
The Stocks. Kent 3D 28
**Stocksbridge**. S Yor 1G 85
Stocksfield. Nmbd 3D 114
Stockstreet. Essx 3B 54
Stockton. Here 4H 59
Stockton. Norf 1F 67
Stockton. Shrp
nr. Bridgnorth 1B 60
nr. Chirbury 5E 71
Stockton. Telf 4B 72
Stockton. Warw 4B 62
Stockton. Wilts 3E 23
Stockton Brook. Staf 5D 84
Stockton Cross. Here 4H 59
Stockton Heath. Warr 2A 84
**Stockton-on-Tees**. Stoc T 3B 106
Stockton on Teme. Worc 4B 60
Stockton-on-the-Forest. York 4A 100
Stockwell Heath. Staf 3E 73
Stock Wood. Worc 5E 61
Stockwood. Bris 5B 34
Stodmarsh. Kent 4G 41
Stody. Norf 2C 78
Stoer. High 1E 163
Stoford. Som 1A 14
Stoford. Wilts 3F 23
Stogumber. Som 3D 20
Stogursey. Som 2F 21
Stoke. Devn 4C 18
Stoke. Hants
nr. Andover 1C 24
nr. South Hayling 2F 17
Stoke. Medw 3C 40
Stoke. W Mid 3A 62
Stoke Abbott. Dors 2H 13
Stoke Albany. Nptn 2F 63
Stoke Ash. Suff 3D 66
Stoke Bardolph. Notts 1D 74
Stoke Bliss. Worc 4A 60
Stoke Bruerne. Nptn 1F 51
Stoke by Clare. Suff 1H 53
Stoke-by-Nayland. Suff 2C 54
Stoke Canon. Devn 3C 12
Stoke Charity. Hants 3C 24
Stoke Climsland. Corn 5D 10
Stoke Cross. Here 5A 60
Stoke D'Abernon. Surr 5C 38
Stoke Doyle. Nptn 2H 63
Stoke Dry. Rut 1F 63
Stoke Edith. Here 1B 48
Stoke Farthing. Wilts 4F 23
Stoke Ferry. Norf 5G 77
Stoke Fleming. Devn 4E 9
Stokeford. Dors 4D 14
Stoke Gabriel. Devn 3E 9
Stoke Gifford. S Glo 4B 34
Stoke Golding. Leics 1A 62
Stoke Goldington. Mil 1G 51
Stokeham. Notts 3E 87
Stoke Hammond. Buck 3G 51
Stoke Heath. Shrp 3A 72
Stoke Holy Cross. Norf 5E 79
Stokeinteignhead. Devn 5C 12
Stoke Lacy. Here 1B 48
Stoke Lyne. Oxon 3D 50
Stoke Mandeville. Buck 4G 51
Stokenchurch. Buck 2F 37
**Stoke Newington**. G Lon 2E 39
Stokenham. Devn 4E 9
Stoke on Tern. Shrp 3A 72
**Stoke-on-Trent**. Stoke 1C 72
Stoke Orchard. Glos 3E 49
Stoke Pero. Som 2B 20
Stoke Poges. Buck 2A 38
Stoke Prior. Here 5H 59
Stoke Prior. Worc 4D 60
Stoke Rivers. Devn 3G 19
Stoke Rochford. Linc 3G 75
Stoke Row. Oxon 3E 37
Stoke St Gregory. Som 4G 21
Stoke St Mary. Som 4F 21
Stoke St Michael. Som 2B 22
Stoke St Milborough. Shrp 2H 59
Stokesay. Shrp 2G 59
Stokesby. Norf 4G 79
Stokesley. N Yor 4C 106
Stoke sub Hamdon. Som 1H 13
Stoke Talmage. Oxon 2E 37
Stoke Town. Stoke 1C 72
Stoke Trister. Som 4C 22
Stoke Wake. Dors 2C 14
Stolford. Som 2F 21
Stondon Massey. Essx 5F 53
Stone. Buck 4F 51
Stone. Glos 2B 34
Stone. Kent 3G 39
Stone. Som 3A 22
**Stone**. Staf 2D 72
Stone. Worc 3C 60
Stonea. Cambs 1D 64
Stoneacton. Shrp 1H 59
Stone Allerton. Som 1H 21
Ston Easton. Som 1B 22
Stonebridge. N Som 1G 21
Stonebridge. Surr 1C 26
Stone Bridge Corner. Pet 5B 76
Stonebroom. Derbs 5B 86
Stonebyres Holdings. S Lan 5B 128
Stone Chair. W Yor 2B 92
Stone Cross. E Sus 5H 27
Stone Cross. Kent 2G 27
Stone-edge Batch. N Som 4H 33
Stoneferry. Hull 1D 94
Stonefield. Arg 5D 140
Stonefield. S Lan 4H 127
Stonegate. E Sus 3A 28
Stonegate. N Yor 4E 107
Stonegrave. N Yor 2A 100
Stonehall. Worc 1D 49
Stonehaugh. Nmbd 2A 114
**Stonehaven**. Abers 5F 153
Stone Heath. Staf 2D 72
Stone Hill. Kent 2E 29
Stone House. Cumb 1G 97
Stonehouse. Glos 5D 48
Stonehouse. Nmbd 4H 113
Stonehouse. S Lan 5A 128
Stone in Oxney. Kent 3D 28
Stoneleigh. Warw 3H 61
Stoneley Green. Ches E 5A 84
Stonely. Cambs 4A 64
Stonepits. Worc 5E 61
Stoner Hill. Hants 4F 25
Stonesby. Leics 3F 75
Stonesfield. Oxon 4B 50
Stones Green. Essx 3E 55
Stone Street. Kent 5G 39
Stone Street. Suff nr. Boxford 2C 54
nr. Halesworth 2F 67
Stonethwaite. Cumb 3D 102
Stoneyburn. W Lot 3C 128
Stoney Cross. Hants 1A 16
Stoneyford. Devn 2D 12
Stoneygate. Leic 5D 74
Stoneyhills. Essx 1D 40
Stoneykirk. Dum 4F 109
Stoney Middleton. Derbs 3G 85
Stoney Stanton. Leics 1B 62
Stoney Stoke. Som 3C 22
Stoney Stratton. Som 3B 22
Stoney Stretton. Shrp 5F 71
Stoneywood. Aber 2F 153
Stonham Aspal. Suff 5D 66
Stonnall. Staf 5E 73
Stonor. Oxon 3F 37
Stonton Wyville. Leics 1E 63
Stonybreck. Shet 1B 172
Stony Cross. Devn 4F 19
Stony Cross. Here
nr. Great Malvern 1C 48
nr. Leominster 4H 59
Stony Houghton. Derbs 4B 86
Stony Stratford. Mil 1F 51
Stoodleigh. Devn
nr. Barnstaple 3G 19
nr. Tiverton 1C 12
Stopham. W Sus 4B 26
Stopsley. Lutn 3B 52
Stoptide. Corn 1D 6
Storeton. Mers 2F 83
Stormontfield. Per 1D 136
Stornoway. W Isl 4G 171
Stornoway Airport. W Isl 4G 171
Storridge. Here 1C 48
Storrington. W Sus 4B 26
Storrs. Cumb 5E 103
Storth. Cumb 1D 97
Storwood. E Yor 5B 100
Stotfield. Mor 1G 159
Stotfold. C Beds 2C 52
Stottesdon. Shrp 2A 60
Stoughton. Leics 5D 74
Stoughton. Surr 5A 38
Stoughton. W Sus 1G 17
Stoul. High 4F 147
Stoulton. Worc 1E 49
**Stourbridge**. W Mid 2C 60
Stourpaine. Dors 2D 14
**Stourport-on-Severn**. Worc 3C 60
Stour Provost. Dors 4C 22
Stour Row. Dors 4D 22
Stourton. Staf 2C 60
Stourton. Warw 2A 50
Stourton. W Yor 1D 92
Stourton. Wilts 3C 22
Stourton Caundle. Dors 1C 14
Stove. Orkn 4F 172
Stove. Shet 9F 173
Stoven. Suff 2G 67
Stow. Linc
nr. Billingborough 2H 75
nr. Gainsborough 2F 87
Stow. Bord 5A 130
Stow Bardolph. Norf 5F 77
Stow Bedon. Norf 1B 66
Stowbridge. Norf 5F 77
Stow cum Quy. Cambs 4E 65
Stowe. Glos 5A 48
Stowe. Shrp 3F 59
Stowe. Staf 4F 73
Stowe-by-Chartley. Staf 3E 73
Stowell. Som 4B 22
Stowey. Bath 1A 22
Stowford. Devn
nr. Colaton Raleigh 4D 12
nr. Combe Martin 2G 19
nr. Tavistock 4E 11
Stowlangtoft. Suff 4B 66
Stow Longa. Cambs 3A 64
Stow Maries. Essx 1C 40
**Stowmarket**. Suff 5C 66
Stow-on-the-Wold. Glos 3G 49
Stowting. Kent 1F 29
Stowupland. Suff 5C 66
Straad. Arg 3B 126
**Strabane**. Derr 3C 174
Strachan. Abers 4D 152
Stradbroke. Suff 3E 67
Stradishall. Suff 5G 65
Stradsett. Norf 5F 77
Stragglethorpe. Linc 5G 87
Stragglethorpe. Notts 2D 74
Straid. S Ayr 5A 116
Straight Soley. Wilts 4B 36
Straiton. Midl 3F 129
Straiton. S Ayr 4C 116
Straloch. Per 2H 143
Stramshall. Staf 2E 73
Strang. IOM 4C 108
Strangford. Here 3A 48
**Stranraer**. Dum 3F 109
Strata Florida. Cdgn 4G 57
Stratfield Mortimer. W Ber 5E 37
Stratfield Saye. Hants 5E 37
Stratfield Turgis. Hants 1E 25
**Stratford**. G Lon 2E 39
Stratford. Worc 2D 49
Stratford St Andrew. Suff 4F 67
Stratford St Mary. Suff 2D 54
Stratford sub Castle. Wilts 3G 23
Stratford Tony. Wilts 4F 23
**Stratford-upon-Avon**. Warw 5G 61
Strath. High
nr. Gairloch 1G 155
nr. Wick 3E 169
Strathan. High
nr. Fort William 4B 148
nr. Lochinver 1E 163
nr. Tongue 2F 167
Strathan Skerray. High 2G 167
Strathaven. S Lan 5A 128
Strathblane. Stir 2G 127
Strathcanaird. High 3F 163
Strathcarron. High 4B 156
Strathcoil. Arg 5A 140
Strathdon. Abers 2A 152
Strathkinness. Fife 2G 137
Strathmashie House. High 4H 149
Strathmiglo. Fife 2E 136
Strathmore Lodge. High 4D 168
Strathpeffer. High 3G 157
Strathrannoch. High 1F 157
Strathtay. Per 3G 143
Strathvaich Lodge. High 1F 157
Strathwhillan. N Ayr 2E 123
Strathy. High
nr. Invergordon 1A 158
nr. Melvich 2A 168
Strathyre. Stir 2E 135
Stratton. Corn 2C 10
Stratton. Dors 3B 14
Stratton. Glos 5F 49
Stratton Audley. Oxon 3E 50
Stratton-on-the-Fosse. Som 1B 22
Stratton St Margaret. Swin 3G 35
Stratton St Michael. Norf 1E 66
Stratton Strawless. Norf 3E 78
Stravithie. Fife 2H 137
Stream. Som 3D 20
Streat. E Sus 4E 27
**Streatham**. G Lon 3E 39
Streatley. C Beds 3A 52
Streatley. W Ber 3D 36
Street. Corn 3C 10
Street. Lanc 4E 97
Street. N Yor 4E 107
Street. Som
nr. Chard 2G 13
**Street**. Som
nr. Glastonbury 3H 21
Street Ash. Som 1F 13
Street Dinas. Shrp 2F 71
Street End. Kent 5F 41
Street End. W Sus 3G 17
Streetgate. Tyne 4F 115
Streethay. Staf 4F 73
Streethouse. W Yor 2D 93
Streetlam. N Yor 5A 106
Street Lane. Derbs 1A 74
Streetly. W Mid 1E 61
Streetly End. Cambs 1G 53
Street on the Fosse. Som 3B 22
Strefford. Shrp 2G 59
Strelley. Notts 1C 74
Strensall. York 3A 100
Strensall Camp. York 4A 100
Stretcholt. Som 2F 21
Strete. Devn 4E 9
**Stretford**. G Man 1C 84
Stretford. Here 5H 59
Strethall. Essx 2E 53
Stretham. Cambs 3E 65
Stretton. Ches W 5G 83
Stretton. Derbs 4A 86
Stretton. Rut 4G 75
Stretton. Staf
nr. Brewood 4C 72
nr. Burton upon Trent 3G 73
Stretton. Warr 2A 84
Stretton en le Field. Leics 4H 73
Stretton Grandison. Here 1B 48
Stretton Heath. Shrp 4F 71
Stretton-on-Dunsmore. Warw 3B 62
Stretton-on-Fosse. Warw 2H 49
Stretton Sugwas. Here 1H 47
Stretton under Fosse. Warw 2B 62
Stretton Westwood. Shrp 1H 59
Strichen. Abers 3G 161
Strines. G Man 2D 84
Stringston. Som 2E 21
Strixton. Nptn 4G 63
Stroanfreggan. Dum 5F 117
Stroat. Glos 2A 34
Stromeferry. High 5A 156

Stromemore. High .....5A **156**
Stromness. Orkn .....7B **172**
Stronachie. Per .....3C **136**
Stronachlachar. Stir .....2D **134**
Stronchreggan. High .....1E **141**
Strone. Arg .....1C **126**
Strone. High
  nr. Drumnadrochit ...1H **149**
  nr. Kingussie .....3B **150**
Stronenaba. High .....5E **148**
Stronganess. Shet .....1G **173**
Stronmilchan. Arg .....1A **134**
Stronsay Airport. Orkn .....5F **172**
Strontian. High .....2C **140**
Strood. Kent .....2C **28**
**Strood**. Medw .....4B **40**
Strood Green. Surr .....1D **26**
Strood Green. W Sus
  nr. Billingshurst .....3B **26**
  nr. Horsham .....2C **26**
Strothers Dale. Nmbd .....4C **114**
**Stroud**. Glos .....5D **48**
Stroud. Hants .....4F **25**
Stroud Green. Essx .....1C **40**
Stroxton. Linc .....2G **75**
Struan. High .....5C **154**
Struan. Per .....2F **143**
Struanmore. High .....5C **154**
Strubby. Linc .....2D **88**
Strugg's Hill. Linc .....2B **76**
Strumpshaw. Norf .....5F **79**
Strutherhill. S Lan .....4A **128**
Struy. High .....5G **157**
Stryd. IOA .....2B **80**
Stryt-issa. Wrex .....1E **71**
Stuartfield. Abers .....4G **161**
**Stubbington**. Hants .....2D **16**
Stubbins. Lanc .....3F **91**
Stubble Green. Cumb .....5B **102**
Stubb's Cross. Kent .....2D **28**
Stubbs Green. Norf .....1F **67**
Stubhampton. Dors .....1E **15**
Stubton. Linc .....1F **75**
Stubwood. Staf .....2E **73**
Stuckton. Hants .....1G **15**
Studham. C Beds .....4A **52**
Studland. Dors .....4F **15**
Studley. Warw .....4E **61**
Studley. Wilts .....4E **35**
Studley Roger. N Yor .....2E **99**
Stuntney. Cambs .....3E **65**
Stunts Green. E Sus .....4H **27**
Sturbridge. Staf .....2C **72**
Sturgate. Linc .....2F **87**
Sturmer. Essx .....1G **53**
Sturminster Marshall. Dors .....2E **15**
Sturminster Newton. Dors .....1C **14**
Sturry. Kent .....4F **41**
Sturton. N Lin .....4C **94**
Sturton by Stow. Linc .....2F **87**
Sturton le Steeple. Notts .....2E **87**
Stuston. Suff .....3D **66**
Sturton. N Yor .....5G **99**
Stutton. Suff .....2E **55**
Styal. Ches E .....2C **84**
Stydd. Lanc .....1E **91**
Styrrup. Notts .....1D **86**
Suainebost. W Isl .....1H **171**
Suardail. W Isl .....4G **171**
Succoth. Abers .....5B **160**
Succoth. Arg .....3B **134**
Suckley. Worc .....5B **60**
Suckley Knowl. Worc .....5B **60**
Sudborough. Nptn .....2G **63**
Sudbourne. Suff .....5G **67**
Sudbrook. Linc .....1G **75**
Sudbrook. Mon .....3A **34**
Sudbrooke. Linc .....3H **87**
Sudbury. Derbs .....2F **73**
**Sudbury**. Suff .....1B **54**
Sudgrove. Glos .....5E **49**
Suffield. Norf .....2E **79**
Suffield. N Yor .....5G **107**
Sugnall. Staf .....2B **72**

Sugwas Pool. Here .....1H **47**
Suisnish. High .....5E **155**
Sulaisiadar. W Isl .....4H **171**
Sùlaisiadar Mòr. High .....4D **155**
Sulby. IOM .....2C **108**
Sulgrave. Nptn .....1D **50**
Sulham. W Ber .....4E **37**
Sulhamstead. W Ber .....5E **37**
Sullington. W Sus .....4B **26**
Sullom. Shet .....4E **173**
Sully. V Glam .....5E **33**
Sumburgh. Shet .....10F **173**
Sumburgh Airport. Shet .....10E **173**
Summer Bridge. N Yor .....3E **98**
Summercourt. Corn .....3C **6**
Summergangs. Hull .....1E **94**
Summer Hill. W Mid .....1D **60**
Summerhill. Aber .....3G **153**
Summerhill. Pemb .....4F **43**
Summerhouse. Darl .....3F **105**
Summersdale. W Sus .....2G **17**
Summerseat. G Man .....3F **91**
Summit. G Man .....3H **91**
**Sunbury**. Surr .....4C **38**
Sunderland. Cumb .....1C **102**
Sunderland. Lanc .....4D **96**
**Sunderland**. Tyne .....4G **115**
Sunderland Bridge. Dur .....1F **105**
Sundon Park. Lutn .....3A **52**
Sundridge. Kent .....5F **39**
Sunk Island. E Yor .....3F **95**
Sunningdale. Wind .....4A **38**
Sunninghill. Wind .....4A **38**
Sunningwell. Oxon .....5C **50**
Sunniside. Dur .....1E **105**
Sunniside. Tyne .....4F **115**
Sunny Bank. Cumb .....5D **102**
Sunny Hill. Derb .....2H **73**
Sunnyhurst. Bkbn .....2E **91**
Sunnylaw. Stir .....4G **135**
Sunnymead. Oxon .....5D **50**
Sunnyside. S Yor .....1B **86**
Sunnyside. W Sus .....2E **27**
Sunton. Wilts .....1H **23**
**Surbiton**. G Lon .....4C **38**
Surby. IOM .....4B **108**
Surfleet. Linc .....3B **76**
Surfleet Seas End. Linc .....3B **76**
Surlingham. Norf .....5F **79**
Surrex. Essx .....3B **54**
Sustead. Norf .....2D **78**
Susworth. Linc .....4B **94**
Sutcombe. Devn .....1D **10**
Suton. Norf .....1C **66**
Sutors of Cromarty. High .....2C **158**
Sutterby. Linc .....3C **88**
Sutterton. Linc .....2B **76**
Sutterton Dowdyke. Linc .....2B **76**
Sutton. Buck .....3B **38**
Sutton. Cambs .....3D **64**
Sutton. C Beds .....1C **52**
Sutton. E Sus .....5F **27**
**Sutton**. G Lon .....4D **38**
Sutton. Kent .....1H **29**
Sutton. Norf .....3F **79**
Sutton. Notts .....2E **75**
Sutton. Oxon .....5C **50**
Sutton. Pemb .....3D **42**
Sutton. Pet .....1H **63**
Sutton. Shrp
  nr. Bridgnorth .....2B **60**
  nr. Market Drayton .....2A **72**
  nr. Oswestry .....3F **71**
  nr. Shrewsbury .....4H **71**
Sutton. Som .....3B **22**
Sutton. S Yor .....3F **93**
Sutton. Staf .....3B **72**
Sutton. Suff .....1G **55**
Sutton. W Sus .....4A **26**
Sutton. Worc .....4A **60**
Sutton Abinger. Surr .....1C **26**
Sutton at Hone. Kent .....3G **39**
Sutton Bassett. Nptn .....1E **63**
Sutton Benger. Wilts .....4E **35**

Sutton Bingham. Som .....1A **14**
Sutton Bonington. Notts .....3C **74**
Sutton Bridge. Linc .....3D **76**
Sutton Cheney. Leics .....5B **74**
**Sutton Coldfield, Royal.**
  W Mid .....1F **61**
Sutton Corner. Linc .....3D **76**
Sutton Courtenay. Oxon .....2D **36**
Sutton Crosses. Linc .....3D **76**
Sutton cum Lound. Notts .....2D **86**
Sutton Gault. Cambs .....3D **64**
Sutton Grange. N Yor .....2E **99**
Sutton Green. Surr .....5B **38**
Sutton Howgrave. N Yor .....2F **99**
**Sutton in Ashfield**. Notts .....5B **86**
Sutton-in-Craven. N Yor .....5C **98**
Sutton Ings. Hull .....1E **94**
Sutton in the Elms. Leics .....1C **62**
Sutton Lane Ends. Ches E .....3D **84**
Sutton Leach. Mers .....1H **83**
Sutton Maddock. Shrp .....5B **72**
Sutton Mallet. Som .....3G **21**
Sutton Mandeville. Wilts .....4E **23**
Sutton Montis. Som .....4B **22**
Sutton on Hull. Hull .....1E **94**
Sutton on Sea. Linc .....2E **89**
Sutton-on-the-Forest. N Yor .....3H **99**
Sutton on the Hill. Derbs .....2G **73**
Sutton on Trent. Notts .....4E **87**
Sutton Poyntz. Dors .....4C **14**
Sutton St Edmund. Linc .....4C **76**
Sutton St Edmund's
  Common. Linc .....5C **76**
Sutton St James. Linc .....4C **76**
Sutton St Michael. Here .....1A **48**
Sutton St Nicholas. Here .....1A **48**
Sutton Scarsdale. Derbs .....4B **86**
Sutton Scotney. Hants .....3C **24**
Sutton-under-Brailes. Warw .....2B **50**
Sutton-under-whitestonecliffe.
  N Yor .....1G **99**
Sutton upon Derwent.
  E Yor .....5B **100**
Sutton Valence. Kent .....1C **28**
Sutton Veny. Wilts .....2E **23**
Sutton Waldron. Dors .....1D **14**
Sutton Weaver. Ches W .....3H **83**
Swaby. Linc .....3C **88**
**Swadlincote**. Derbs .....4G **73**
Swaffham. Norf .....5H **77**
Swaffham Bulbeck. Cambs .....4E **65**
Swaffham Prior. Cambs .....4E **65**
Swafield. Norf .....2E **79**
Swainby. N Yor .....4B **106**
Swainshill. Here .....1H **47**
Swainsthorpe. Norf .....5E **78**
Swainswick. Bath .....5C **34**
Swalcliffe. Oxon .....2B **50**
Swalecliffe. Kent .....4F **41**
Swallow. Linc .....4E **95**
Swallow Beck. Linc .....4G **87**
Swallowcliffe. Wilts .....4E **23**
Swallowfield. Wok .....5F **37**
Swallownest. S Yor .....2B **86**
Swampton. Hants .....1C **24**
**Swanage**. Dors .....5F **15**
Swanbister. Orkn .....7C **172**
Swanbourne. Buck .....3G **51**
Swanbridge. V Glam .....5E **33**
Swan Green. Ches W .....3B **84**
Swanland. E Yor .....2C **94**
**Swanley**. Kent .....4G **39**
Swanmore. Hants .....1D **16**
Swannington. Leics .....4B **74**
Swannington. Norf .....4D **78**
Swanpool. Linc .....3G **87**
Swanscombe. Kent .....3H **39**
**Swansea**. Swan .....3F **31**
Swan Street. Essx .....3B **54**
Swanton Abbott. Norf .....3E **79**
Swanton Morley. Norf .....4C **78**
Swanton Novers. Norf .....2C **78**
Swanton Street. Kent .....5C **40**
Swanwick. Derbs .....5B **86**

Swanwick. Hants .....2D **16**
Swanwick Green. Ches E .....1H **71**
Swarby. Linc .....1H **75**
Swardeston. Norf .....5E **78**
Swarister. Shet .....3G **173**
Swarkestone. Derbs .....3A **74**
Swarland. Nmbd .....4F **121**
Swarraton. Hants .....3D **24**
Swartha. W Yor .....5C **98**
Swarthmoor. Cumb .....2B **96**
Swaton. Linc .....2A **76**
Swavesey. Cambs .....4C **64**
Sway. Hants .....3A **16**
Swayfield. Linc .....3G **75**
Swaythling. Sotn .....1C **16**
Sweet Green. Worc .....4A **60**
Sweetham. Devn .....3B **12**
Sweetholme. Cumb .....3G **103**
Sweets. Corn .....3B **10**
Sweetshouse. Corn .....2E **7**
Swefling. Suff .....4F **67**
Swell. Som .....4G **21**
Swepstone. Leics .....4A **74**
Swerford. Oxon .....2B **50**
Swettenham. Ches E .....4C **84**
Swetton. N Yor .....2D **98**
Swffryd. Blae .....2F **33**
Swiftsden. E Sus .....3B **28**
Swilland. Suff .....5D **66**
Swillington. W Yor .....1D **93**
Swimbridge. Devn .....4G **19**
Swimbridge Newland. Devn .....3G **19**
Swinbrook. Oxon .....4A **50**
Swincliffe. N Yor .....4E **99**
Swincliffe. W Yor .....2C **92**
Swinderby. Linc .....4F **87**
Swindon. Glos .....3E **49**
Swindon. Nmbd .....5D **121**
Swindon. Staf .....1C **60**
**Swindon**. Swin .....3G **35**
Swine. E Yor .....1E **95**
Swinefleet. E Yor .....2A **94**
Swineford. S Glo .....5B **34**
Swineshead. Bed .....4H **63**
Swineshead. Linc .....1B **76**
Swineshead Bridge. Linc .....1B **76**
Swiney. High .....5E **169**
Swinford. Leics .....3C **62**
Swinford. Oxon .....5C **50**
Swingate. Notts .....1C **74**
Swingbrow. Cambs .....2C **64**
Swingfield Minnis. Kent .....1G **29**
Swingfield Street. Kent .....1G **29**
Swingleton Green. Suff .....1C **54**
Swinhill. S Lan .....5A **128**
Swinhoe. Nmbd .....2G **121**
Swinhope. Linc .....1B **88**
Swinister. Shet .....3E **173**
Swinithwaite. N Yor .....1C **98**
Swinmore Common. Here .....1B **48**
Swinscoe. Staf .....1F **73**
Swinside Hall. Bord .....3B **120**
Swinstead. Linc .....3H **75**
**Swinton**. G Man .....4F **91**
Swinton. N Yor
  nr. Malton .....2B **100**
  nr. Masham .....2E **98**
Swinton. Bord .....5E **131**
Swinton. S Yor .....1B **86**
Swithland. Leics .....4C **74**
Swordale. High .....2H **157**
Swordly. High .....2H **167**
Sworton Heath. Ches E .....2A **84**
Swyddffynnon. Cdgn .....4F **57**
Swynnerton. Staf .....2C **72**
Swyre. Dors .....4A **14**
Sycharth. Powy .....3E **70**
Sychdyn. Flin .....4E **83**
Sychnant. Powy .....3B **58**
Sychtyn. Powy .....5B **70**
Syde. Glos .....4E **49**
Sydenham. G Lon .....3E **39**
Sydenham. Oxon .....5F **51**
Sydenham. Som .....3G **21**

Sydenham Damerel. Devn .....5E **11**
Syderstone. Norf .....2H **77**
Sydling St Nicholas. Dors .....3B **14**
Sydmonton. Hants .....1C **24**
Sydney. Ches E .....5B **84**
Syerston. Notts .....1E **75**
Syke. G Man .....3G **91**
Sykehouse. S Yor .....3G **93**
Sykes. Lanc .....4F **97**
Syleham. Suff .....3E **66**
Sylen. Carm .....5F **45**
Sylfaen. Powy .....5D **70**
Symbister. Shet .....5G **173**
Symington. S Ayr .....1C **116**
Symington. S Lan .....1B **118**
Symondsbury. Dors .....3H **13**
Symonds Yat. Here .....4A **48**
Synod Inn. Cdgn .....5D **56**
Syre. High .....4G **167**
Syreford. Glos .....3F **49**
Syresham. Nptn .....1E **51**
Syston. Leics .....4D **74**
Syston. Linc .....1G **75**
Sytchampton. Worc .....4C **60**
Sywell. Nptn .....4F **63**

# T

Tabost. W Isl
  nr. Cearsiadar .....6F **171**
  nr. Suainebost .....1H **171**
Tachbrook Mallory. Warw .....4H **61**
Tackley. Oxon .....3C **50**
Tacleit. W Isl .....4D **171**
Tacolneston. Norf .....1D **66**
Tadcaster. N Yor .....5G **99**
Taddington. Derbs .....3F **85**
Taddington. Glos .....2F **49**
Taddiport. Devn .....1E **11**
**Tadley**. Hants .....5E **36**
Tadlow. Cambs .....1C **52**
Tadmarton. Oxon .....2B **50**
Tadwick. Bath .....4C **34**
**Tadworth**. Surr .....5D **38**
Tafarnaubach. Blae .....4E **46**
Tafarn-y-bwlch. Pemb .....1E **43**
Tafarn-y-Gelyn. Den .....4D **82**
Taff's Well. Rhon .....3E **33**
Tafolwern. Powy .....5A **70**
Tai-bach. Powy .....3D **70**
Tai-bach. Neat .....3A **32**
Taigh a Ghearraidh. W Isl .....1C **170**
Taigh Bhuirgh. W Isl .....8C **171**
Tain. High
  nr. Invergordon .....5E **165**
  nr. Thurso .....2E **169**
Tai-Nant. Wrex .....1E **71**
Tai'n Lon. Gwyn .....5D **80**
Tairbeart. W Isl .....8D **171**
Tairgwaith. Neat .....4H **45**
Takeley. Essx .....3F **53**
Takeley Street. Essx .....3F **53**
Talachddu. Powy .....2D **46**
Talacre. Flin .....2D **82**
Talardd. Gwyn .....3A **70**
Talaton. Devn .....3D **12**
Talbenny. Pemb .....3C **42**
Talbot Green. Rhon .....3D **32**
Taleford. Devn .....3D **12**
Talerddig. Cdgn .....5B **70**
Talgarreg. Cdgn .....5D **56**
Talgarth. Powy .....2E **47**
Talisker. High .....5C **154**
Talke. Staf .....5C **84**
Talkin. Cumb .....4G **113**
Talladale. High .....1B **156**
Talla Linnfoots. Bord .....2D **118**
Tallaminnock. S Ayr .....5C **116**
Tallarn Green. Wrex .....1G **71**
Tallentire. Cumb .....1C **102**
Talley. Carm .....2G **45**
Tallington. Linc .....5H **75**
Talmine. High .....2F **167**

Talog. Carm ....2H 43
Talsarn. Carm ....3A 46
Talsarn. Cdgn ....5E 57
Talsarnau. Gwyn ....2F 69
Talskiddy. Corn ....2D 6
Talwrn. IOA ....3D 81
Talwrn. Wrex ....1E 71
Tal-y-Bont. Cnwy ....4G 81
Tal-y-bont. Cdgn ....2F 57
Tal-y-bont. Gwyn
   nr. Bangor ....3F 81
   nr. Barmouth ....3E 69
Talybont-on-Usk. Powy ....3E 46
Tal-y-cafn. Cnwy ....3G 81
Tal-y-coed. Mon ....4H 47
Tal-y-llyn. Gwyn ....5G 69
Talyllyn. Powy ....3E 46
Talysarn. Gwyn ....5D 81
Tal-y-waenydd. Gwyn ....1F 69
Talywain. Torf ....5F 47
Tal-y-Wern. Powy ....5H 69
Tamerton Foliot. Plym ....2A 8
Tamworth. Staf ....5G 73
Tamworth Green. Linc ....1C 76
Tandlehill. Ren ....3F 127
Tandragee. Arm ....5F 175
Tandridge. Surr ....5E 39
Tanerdy. Carm ....3E 45
Tanfield. Dur ....4E 115
Tanfield Lea. Dur ....4E 115
Tangasdal. W Isl ....8B 170
Tang Hall. York ....4A 100
Tangiers. Pemb ....3D 42
Tangley. Hants ....1B 24
Tangmere. W Sus ....5A 26
Tangwick. Shet ....4D 173
Tankerness. Orkn ....7E 172
Tankersley. S Yor ....1H 85
Tankerton. Kent ....4F 41
Tan-lan. Cnwy ....4G 81
Tan-lan. Gwyn ....1F 69
Tannach. High ....4F 169
Tannadice. Ang ....3D 145
Tanner's Green. Worc ....3E 61
Tannington. Suff ....4E 67
Tannochside. N Lan ....3A 128
Tan Office Green. Suff ....5G 65
Tansley. Derbs ....5H 85
Tansley Knoll. Derbs ....4H 85
Tansor. Nptn ....1H 63
Tantobie. Dur ....4E 115
Tanton. N Yor ....3C 106
Tanvats. Linc ....4A 88
Tanworth-in-Arden. Warw ....3F 61
Tan-y-bwlch. Gwyn ....1F 69
Tan-y-fron. Cnwy ....4B 82
Tanyfron. Wrex ....5E 83
Tanygrisiau. Gwyn ....1F 69
Tan-y-groes. Cdgn ....1C 44
Tan-y-pistyll. Powy ....3C 70
Tan-yr-allt. Den ....2C 82
Taobh a Chaolais. W Isl ....7C 170
Taobh a Deas Loch Aineort.
   W Isl ....6C 170
Taobh a Ghlinne. W Isl ....6F 171
Taobh a Tuath Loch Aineort.
   W Isl ....6C 170
Taplow. Buck ....2A 38
Tapton. Derbs ....3A 86
Tarbert. Arg
   on Jura ....1E 125
   on Kintyre ....3G 125
Tarbert. W Isl ....8D 171
Tarbet. Arg ....3C 134
Tarbet. High
   nr. Mallaig ....4F 147
   nr. Scourie ....4B 166
Tarbock Green. Mers ....2G 83
Tarbolton. S Ayr ....2D 116
Tarbrax. S Lan ....4D 128
Tardebigge. Worc ....4D 61
Tarfside. Ang ....1D 145
Tarland. Abers ....3B 152
Tarleton. Lanc ....2C 90

Tarlogie. High ....5E 165
Tarlscough. Lanc ....3C 90
Tarlton. Glos ....2E 35
Tarnbrook. Lanc ....4E 97
Tarnock. Som ....1G 21
Tarns. Cumb ....5C 112
Tarporley. Ches W ....4H 83
Tarpots. Essx ....2B 40
Tarr. Som ....3E 20
Tarrant Crawford. Dors ....2E 15
Tarrant Gunville. Dors ....1E 15
Tarrant Hinton. Dors ....1E 15
Tarrant Keyneston. Dors ....2E 15
Tarrant Launceston. Dors ....2E 15
Tarrant Monkton. Dors ....2E 15
Tarrant Rawston. Dors ....2E 15
Tarrant Rushton. Dors ....2E 15
Tarrel. High ....5F 165
Tarring Neville. E Sus ....5F 27
Tarrington. Here ....1B 48
Tarsappie. Per ....1D 136
Tarscabhaig. High ....3D 147
Tarskavaig. High ....3D 147
Tarves. Abers ....5F 161
Tarvie. High ....3G 157
Tarvin. Ches W ....4G 83
Tasburgh. Norf ....1E 66
Tasley. Shrp ....1A 60
Taston. Oxon ....3B 50
Tatenhill. Staf ....3G 73
Tathall End. Mil ....1G 51
Tatham. Lanc ....3F 97
Tathwell. Linc ....2C 88
Tatling End. Buck ....2B 38
Tatsfield. Surr ....5F 39
Tattenhall. Ches W ....5G 83
Tatterford. Norf ....3A 78
Tattersett. Norf ....2H 77
Tattershall. Linc ....5B 88
Tattershall Bridge. Linc ....5A 88
Tattershall Thorpe. Linc ....5B 88
Tattingstone. Suff ....2E 55
Tattingstone White Horse.
   Suff ....2E 55
Tattle Bank. Warw ....4F 61
Tatworth. Som ....2G 13
Taunton. Som ....4F 21
Taverham. Norf ....4D 78
Taverners Green. Essx ....4F 53
Tavernspite. Pemb ....3F 43
Tavistock. Devn ....5E 11
Tavool House. Arg ....1B 132
Taw Green. Devn ....3G 11
Tawstock. Devn ....4F 19
Taxal. Derbs ....2E 85
Tayinloan. Arg ....5E 125
Taynish. Arg ....1F 125
Taynton. Glos ....3C 48
Taynton. Oxon ....4H 49
Taynuilt. Arg ....5E 141
Tayport. Fife ....1G 137
Tay Road Bridge. D'dee ....1G 137
Tayvallich. Arg ....1F 125
Tealby. Linc ....1A 88
Tealing. Ang ....5D 144
Teams. Tyne ....3F 115
Teangue. High ....3E 147
Teanna Mhachair. W Isl ....2C 170
Tebay. Cumb ....4H 103
Tebworth. C Beds ....3H 51
Tedburn St Mary. Devn ....3B 12
Teddington. Glos ....2E 49
Teddington. G Lon ....3C 38
Tedsmore. Shrp ....3F 71
Tedstone Delamere. Here ....5A 60
Tedstone Wafer. Here ....5A 60
Teesport. Red C ....2C 106
Teesside. Stoc T ....2C 106
Teeton. Nptn ....3D 62
Teffont Evias. Wilts ....3E 23
Teffont Magna. Wilts ....3E 23
Tegryn. Pemb ....1G 43
Teigh. Rut ....4F 75
Teigncombe. Devn ....4G 11

Teigngrace. Devn ....5B 12
Teignmouth. Devn ....5C 12
Telham. E Sus ....4B 28
Tellisford. Som ....1D 22
Telscombe. E Sus ....5F 27
Telscombe Cliffs. E Sus ....5E 27
Tempar. Per ....3D 142
Templand. Dum ....1B 112
Temple. Corn ....5B 10
Temple. Glas ....3G 127
Temple. Midl ....4G 129
Temple Balsall. W Mid ....3G 61
Temple Bar. Carm ....4F 45
Temple Bar. Cdgn ....5E 57
Temple Cloud. Bath ....1B 22
Templecombe. Som ....4C 22
Temple Ewell. Kent ....1G 29
Temple Grafton. Warw ....5F 61
Temple Guiting. Glos ....3F 49
Templehall. Fife ....4E 137
Temple Hirst. N Yor ....2G 93
Temple Normanton. Derbs ....4B 86
Templepatrick. Ant ....3G 175
Temple Sowerby. Cumb ....2H 103
Templeton. Devn ....1B 12
Templeton. Pemb ....3F 43
Templeton. W Ber ....5B 36
Templetown. Dur ....5E 115
Tempsford. C Beds ....5A 64
Tenandry. Per ....2G 143
Tenbury Wells. Worc ....4H 59
Tenby. Pemb ....4F 43
Tendring. Essx ....3E 55
Tendring Green. Essx ....3E 55
Tenga. Arg ....4G 139
Ten Mile Bank. Norf ....1F 65
Tenterden. Kent ....2C 28
Terfyn. Cnwy ....3B 82
Terhill. Som ....3E 21
Terling. Essx ....4A 54
Ternhill. Shrp ....2A 72
Terregles. Dum ....2G 111
Terrick. Buck ....5G 51
Terrington. N Yor ....2A 100
Terrington St Clement. Norf ....3E 77
Terrington St John. Norf ....4E 77
Terry's Green. Warw ....3F 61
Teston. Kent ....5B 40
Testwood. Hants ....1B 16
Tetbury. Glos ....2D 35
Tetbury Upton. Glos ....2D 35
Tetchill. Shrp ....2F 71
Tetcott. Devn ....3D 10
Tetford. Linc ....3C 88
Tetney. Linc ....4G 95
Tetney Lock. Linc ....4G 95
Tetsworth. Oxon ....5E 51
Tettenhall. W Mid ....5C 72
Teversal. Notts ....4B 86
Teversham. Cambs ....5D 65
Teviothead. Bord ....4G 119
Tewel. Abers ....5F 153
Tewin. Herts ....4C 52
Tewkesbury. Glos ....2D 49
Teynham. Kent ....4D 40
Teynham Street. Kent ....4D 40
Thackthwaite. Cumb ....2C 102
Thakeham. W Sus ....4C 26
Thame. Oxon ....5F 51
Thames Ditton. Surr ....4C 38
Thames Haven. Thur ....2B 40
Thamesmead. G Lon ....2F 39
Thamesport. Medw ....3C 40
Thanington Without. Kent ....5F 41
Thankerton. S Lan ....1B 118
Tharston. Norf ....1D 66
Thatcham. W Ber ....5D 36
Thatto Heath. Mers ....1H 83
Thaxted. Essx ....2G 53
Theakston. N Yor ....1F 99
Thealby. N Lin ....3B 94
Theale. Som ....2H 21
Theale. W Ber ....4E 37

Thearne. E Yor ....1D 94
Theberton. Suff ....4G 67
Theddingworth. Leics ....2D 62
Theddlethorpe All Saints.
   Linc ....2D 88
Theddlethorpe St Helen.
   Linc ....2D 89
Thelbridge Barton. Devn ....1A 12
Thelnetham. Suff ....3C 66
Thelveton. Norf ....2D 66
Thelwall. Warr ....2A 84
Themelthorpe. Norf ....3C 78
Thenford. Nptn ....1D 50
Therfield. Herts ....2D 52
Thetford. Linc ....4A 76
Thetford. Norf ....2A 66
Thethwaite. Cumb ....5E 113
Theydon Bois. Essx ....1F 39
Thick Hollins. W Yor ....3B 92
Thickwood. Wilts ....4D 34
Thimbleby. Linc ....4B 88
Thimbleby. N Yor ....5B 106
Thingwall. Mers ....2E 83
Thirlby. N Yor ....1G 99
Thirlestane. Bord ....5B 130
Thirn. N Yor ....1E 98
Thirsk. N Yor ....1G 99
Thirtleby. E Yor ....1E 95
Thistleton. Lanc ....1C 90
Thistleton. Rut ....4G 75
Thistley Green. Suff ....3F 65
Thixendale. N Yor ....3C 100
Thockrington. Nmbd ....2C 114
Tholomas Drove. Cambs ....5D 76
Tholthorpe. N Yor ....3G 99
Thomas Chapel. Pemb ....4F 43
Thomas Close. Cumb ....5F 113
Thomastown. Abers ....4E 160
Thomastown. Rhon ....3D 32
Thompson. Norf ....1B 66
Thomshill. Mor ....3G 159
Thong. Kent ....3A 40
Thongsbridge. W Yor ....4B 92
Thoralby. N Yor ....1C 98
Thoresby. Notts ....3D 86
Thoresway. Linc ....1A 88
Thorganby. Linc ....1B 88
Thorganby. N Yor ....5A 100
Thorgill. N Yor ....5E 107
Thorington. Suff ....3G 67
Thorington Street. Suff ....2D 54
Thorlby. N Yor ....4B 98
Thorley. Herts ....4E 53
Thorley Street. Herts ....4E 53
Thorley Street. IOW ....4B 16
Thormanby. N Yor ....2G 99
Thorn. Powy ....4E 59
Thornaby-on-Tees. Stoc T ....3B 106
Thornage. Norf ....2C 78
Thornborough. Buck ....2F 51
Thornborough. N Yor ....2E 99
Thornbury. Devn ....2E 11
Thornbury. Here ....5A 60
Thornbury. S Glo ....2B 34
Thornby. Cumb ....4D 112
Thornby. Nptn ....3D 62
Thorncliffe. Staf ....5E 85
Thorncombe. Dors ....2G 13
Thorncombe Street. Surr ....1A 26
Thorncote Green. C Beds ....1B 52
Thorndon. Suff ....4D 66
Thorndon Cross. Devn ....3F 11
Thorne. S Yor ....3G 93
Thornehillhead. Devn ....1E 11
Thorner. W Yor ....5F 99
Thorne St Margaret. Som ....4D 20
Thorney. Notts ....3F 87
Thorney. Pet ....5B 76
Thorney. Som ....4H 21
Thorney Hill. Hants ....3G 15
Thorney Toll. Cambs ....5C 76
Thornfalcon. Som ....4F 21
Thornford. Dors ....1B 14
Thorngrafton. Nmbd ....3A 114

Thorngrove. Som ....3G 21
Thorngumbald. E Yor ....2F 95
Thornham. Norf ....1G 77
Thornham Magna. Suff ....3D 66
Thornham Parva. Suff ....3D 66
Thornhaugh. Pet ....5H 75
Thornhill. Cphy ....3E 33
Thornhill. Cumb ....4B 102
Thornhill. Derbs ....2F 85
Thornhill. Dum ....5A 118
Thornhill. Sotn ....1C 16
Thornhill. Stir ....4F 135
Thornhill. W Yor ....3C 92
Thornhill Lees. W Yor ....3C 92
Thornhills. W Yor ....2B 92
Thornholme. E Yor ....3F 101
Thornicombe. Dors ....2D 14
Thornington. Nmbd ....1C 120
Thornley. Dur
   nr. Durham ....1A 106
   nr. Tow Law ....1E 105
Thornley Gate. Nmbd ....4B 114
Thornliebank. E Ren ....3G 127
Thornroan. Abers ....5F 161
Thorns. Suff ....5G 65
Thomsett. Derbs ....2E 85
Thornthwaite. Cumb ....2D 102
Thornthwaite. N Yor ....4D 98
Thornton. Ang ....4C 144
Thornton. Buck ....2F 51
Thornton. E Yor ....5B 100
Thornton. Fife ....4E 137
Thornton. Lanc ....5C 96
Thornton. Leics ....5B 74
Thornton. Linc ....4B 88
Thornton. Mers ....4B 90
Thornton. Midd ....3B 106
Thornton. Nmbd ....5F 131
Thornton. Pemb ....4D 42
Thornton. W Yor ....1A 92
Thornton Curtis. N Lin ....3D 94
Thorntonhall. S Lan ....4G 127
Thornton Heath. G Lon ....4E 39
Thornton Hough. Mers ....2F 83
Thornton-in-Craven. N Yor ....5B 98
Thornton in Lonsdale. N Yor ....2F 97
Thornton-le-Beans. N Yor ....5A 106
Thornton-le-Clay. N Yor ....3A 100
Thornton-le-Dale. N Yor ....1C 100
Thornton le Moor. Linc ....1H 87
Thornton-le-Moor. N Yor ....1F 99
Thornton-le-Moors. Ches W ....3G 83
Thornton-le-Street. N Yor ....1G 99
Thorntonloch. E Lot ....2D 130
Thornton Rust. N Yor ....1B 98
Thornton Steward. N Yor ....1D 98
Thornton Watlass. N Yor ....1E 99
Thornwood Common. Essx ....5E 53
Thornythwaite. Cumb ....2E 103
Thorpe. Derbs ....5F 85
Thorpe. E Yor ....5D 101
Thorpe. Linc ....2D 89
Thorpe. Norf ....1G 67
Thorpe. N Yor ....3C 98
Thorpe. Notts ....1E 75
Thorpe. Surr ....4B 38
Thorpe Abbotts. Norf ....3D 66
Thorpe Acre. Leics ....3C 74
Thorpe Arnold. Leics ....3E 75
Thorpe Audlin. W Yor ....3E 93
Thorpe Bassett. N Yor ....2C 100
Thorpe Bay. S'end ....2D 40
Thorpe by Water. Rut ....1F 63
Thorpe Common. S Yor ....1A 86
Thorpe Common. Suff ....2F 55
Thorpe Constantine. Staf ....5G 73
Thorpe End. Norf ....4E 79
Thorpe Fendike. Linc ....4D 88
Thorpe Green. Essx ....3E 55
Thorpe Green. Suff ....5B 66
Thorpe Hall. N Yor ....2H 99
Thorpe Hamlet. Norf ....5E 79

Thorpe Hesley. S Yor . . . . . . . . . .1A 86
Thorpe in Balne. S Yor . . . . . . . .3F 93
Thorpe in the Fallows. Linc . . .2G 87
Thorpe Langton. Leics . . . . . . .1E 63
Thorpe Larches. Dur . . . . . . . . .2A 106
Thorpe Latimer. Linc . . . . . . . . .1A 76
Thorpe-le-Soken. Essx . . . . . .3E 55
Thorpe le Street. E Yor . . . . .5C 100
Thorpe Malsor. Nptn . . . . . . . .3F 63
Thorpe Mandeville. Nptn . . . . .1D 50
Thorpe Market. Norf . . . . . . . . .2E 79
Thorpe Marriott. Norf . . . . . . .4D 78
Thorpe Morieux. Suff . . . . . . . . .5B 66
Thorpeness. Suff . . . . . . . . . . . .5G 67
Thorpe on the Hill. Linc . . . . .4G 87
Thorpe on the Hill. W Yor . . .2D 92
Thorpe St Andrew. Norf . . . . .5E 79
Thorpe St Peter. Linc . . . . . . .4D 89
Thorpe Salvin. S Yor . . . . . . . . .2C 86
Thorpe Satchville. Leics . . . . .4E 75
Thorpe Thewles. Stoc T . . . . .2A 106
Thorpe Tilney. Linc . . . . . . . . . .5A 88
Thorpe Underwood. N Yor . . .4G 99
Thorpe Waterville. Nptn . . . . .2H 63
Thorpe Willoughby. N Yor . . .1F 93
Thorpland. Norf . . . . . . . . . . . . .5F 77
Thorrington. Essx . . . . . . . . . . .3D 54
Thorverton. Devn . . . . . . . . . . .2C 12
Thrandeston. Suff . . . . . . . . . . .3D 66
Thrapston. Nptn . . . . . . . . . . . .3G 63
Thrashbush. N Lan . . . . . . . . . .3A 128
Threapland. Cumb . . . . . . . . . .1C 102
Threapland. N Yor . . . . . . . . . . .3B 98
Threapwood. Ches W . . . . . . . . .1G 71
Threapwood. Staf . . . . . . . . . . . .1E 73
Three Ashes. Here . . . . . . . . . . .3A 48
Three Bridges. Linc . . . . . . . . . .2D 88
Three Bridges. W Sus . . . . . . . .2D 27
Three Burrows. Corn . . . . . . . . . .4B 6
Three Chimneys. Kent . . . . . . .2C 28
Three Cocks. Powy . . . . . . . . . . .2E 47
Three Crosses. Swan . . . . . . . . .3E 31
Three Cups Corner. E Sus . . .3H 27
Threehammer Common.
    Norf . . . . . . . . . . . . . . . . . . . .3F 79
Three Holes. Norf . . . . . . . . . . . .5E 77
Threekingham. Linc . . . . . . . . . .2H 75
Three Leg Cross. E Sus . . . . . .2A 28
Three Legged Cross. Dors . . . .2F 15
Threemilestone. Corn . . . . . . . .4B 6
Three Oaks. E Sus . . . . . . . . . . .4C 28
Threlkeld. Cumb . . . . . . . . . . . .2E 102
Threshfield. N Yor . . . . . . . . . . .3B 98
Thrigby. Norf . . . . . . . . . . . . . . .4G 79
Thringarth. Dur . . . . . . . . . . . . . .2C 104
Thringstone. Leics . . . . . . . . . . .4B 74
Thrintoft. N Yor . . . . . . . . . . . . .5A 106
Thriplow. Cambs . . . . . . . . . . . . .1E 53
Throckenholt. Linc . . . . . . . . . . .5C 76
Throcking. Herts . . . . . . . . . . . . .2D 52
Throckley. Tyne . . . . . . . . . . . . .3E 115
Throckmorton. Worc . . . . . . . . .1E 49
Throop. Bour . . . . . . . . . . . . . . . .3G 15
Throphill. Nmbd . . . . . . . . . . . . .1E 115
Thropton. Nmbd . . . . . . . . . . . . .4E 121
Throsk. Stir . . . . . . . . . . . . . . . . .4A 136
Througham. Glos . . . . . . . . . . . . .5E 49
Throughgate. Dum . . . . . . . . . . .1F 111
Throwleigh. Devn . . . . . . . . . . . .3G 11
Throwley. Kent . . . . . . . . . . . . . .5D 40
Throwley Forstal. Kent . . . . . . .5D 40
Throxenby. N Yor . . . . . . . . . . .1E 101
Thrumpton. Notts . . . . . . . . . . .2C 74
Thrumster. High . . . . . . . . . . . . .4F 169
Thrunton. Nmbd . . . . . . . . . . . . .3E 121
Thrupp. Glos . . . . . . . . . . . . . . . .5D 48
Thrupp. Oxon . . . . . . . . . . . . . . .4C 50
Thrushelton. Devn . . . . . . . . . . .4E 11
Thrushgill. Lanc . . . . . . . . . . . . .3F 97
Thrussington. Leics . . . . . . . . . .4D 74
Thruxton. Hants . . . . . . . . . . . . .2A 24
Thruxton. Here . . . . . . . . . . . . . .1H 47
Thrybergh. S Yor . . . . . . . . . . . .1B 86

Thulston. Derbs . . . . . . . . . . . . . .2B 74
Thundergay. N Ayr . . . . . . . . . .5G 125
Thundersley. Essx . . . . . . . . . . .2B 40
Thundridge. Herts . . . . . . . . . . .4D 52
Thurcaston. Leics . . . . . . . . . . . .4C 74
Thurcroft. S Yor . . . . . . . . . . . . .2B 86
Thurdon. Corn . . . . . . . . . . . . . . .1C 10
Thurgarton. Norf . . . . . . . . . . . . .2D 78
Thurgarton. Notts . . . . . . . . . . .1D 74
Thurgoland. S Yor . . . . . . . . . . .4C 92
Thurlaston. Leics . . . . . . . . . . . .1C 62
Thurlaston. Warw . . . . . . . . . . .3B 62
Thurlbear. Som . . . . . . . . . . . . . .4F 21
Thurlby. Linc
    nr. Alford . . . . . . . . . . . . . . . .3D 89
    nr. Baston . . . . . . . . . . . . . .4A 76
    nr. Lincoln . . . . . . . . . . . . . .4G 87
Thurleigh. Bed . . . . . . . . . . . . . .5H 63
Thurlestone. Devn . . . . . . . . . . .4C 8
Thurloxton. Som . . . . . . . . . . . .3F 21
Thurlstone. S Yor . . . . . . . . . . .4C 92
Thurlton. Norf . . . . . . . . . . . . . . .1G 67
Thurmaston. Leics . . . . . . . . . . .5D 74
Thurnby. Leics . . . . . . . . . . . . . .5D 74
Thurne. Norf . . . . . . . . . . . . . . . .4G 79
Thurnham. Kent . . . . . . . . . . . . .5C 40
Thurning. Norf . . . . . . . . . . . . . . .3C 78
Thurning. Nptn . . . . . . . . . . . . . .2H 63
Thurnscoe. S Yor . . . . . . . . . . . .4E 93
Thursby. Cumb . . . . . . . . . . . . . .4E 113
Thursford. Norf . . . . . . . . . . . . . .2B 78
Thursford Green. Norf . . . . . . . .2B 78
Thursley. Surr . . . . . . . . . . . . . . .2A 26
Thurso. High . . . . . . . . . . . . . . . .2D 168
Thurso East. High . . . . . . . . . . .2D 168
Thurstaston. Mers . . . . . . . . . . .2E 83
Thurston. Suff . . . . . . . . . . . . . . .4B 66
Thurston End. Suff . . . . . . . . . . .5G 65
Thurstonfield. Cumb . . . . . . . . .4E 112
Thurstonland. W Yor . . . . . . . . .3B 92
Thurton. Norf . . . . . . . . . . . . . . . .5F 79
Thurvaston. Derbs
    nr. Ashbourne . . . . . . . . . . .2F 73
    nr. Derby . . . . . . . . . . . . . .2G 73
Thuxton. Norf . . . . . . . . . . . . . . .5C 78
Thwaite. Dur . . . . . . . . . . . . . . . .3D 104
Thwaite. N Yor . . . . . . . . . . . . . .5B 104
Thwaite. Suff . . . . . . . . . . . . . . . .4D 66
Thwaite Head. Cumb . . . . . . . . .5E 103
Thwaites. W Yor . . . . . . . . . . . . .5C 98
Thwaite St Mary. Norf . . . . . . .1F 67
Thwing. E Yor . . . . . . . . . . . . . . .2E 101
Tibbermore. Per . . . . . . . . . . . . .1C 136
Tibberton. Glos . . . . . . . . . . . . . .3C 48
Tibberton. Telf . . . . . . . . . . . . . .3A 72
Tibberton. Worc . . . . . . . . . . . . .5D 60
Tibenham. Norf . . . . . . . . . . . . . .2D 66
Tibshelf. Derbs . . . . . . . . . . . . . .4B 86
Tibthorpe. E Yor . . . . . . . . . . . . .4D 100
Ticehurst. E Sus . . . . . . . . . . . . .2A 28
Tichborne. Hants . . . . . . . . . . . .3D 24
Tickencote. Rut . . . . . . . . . . . . .5G 75
Tickenham. N Som . . . . . . . . . .4H 33
Tickhill. S Yor . . . . . . . . . . . . . . .1C 86
Ticklerton. Shrp . . . . . . . . . . . . .1G 59
Ticknall. Derbs . . . . . . . . . . . . . .3A 74
Tickton. E Yor . . . . . . . . . . . . . . .5E 101
Tidbury Green. W Mid . . . . . . .3F 61
Tidcombe. Wilts . . . . . . . . . . . . .1A 24
Tiddington. Oxon . . . . . . . . . . .5E 51
Tiddington. Warw . . . . . . . . . . .5G 61
Tiddleywink. Wilts . . . . . . . . . . .4D 34
Tidebrook. E Sus . . . . . . . . . . . .3H 27
Tideford. Corn . . . . . . . . . . . . . . .3H 7
Tideford Cross. Corn . . . . . . . . .2H 7
Tidenham. Glos . . . . . . . . . . . . .2A 34
Tideswell. Derbs . . . . . . . . . . . .3F 85
Tidmarsh. W Ber . . . . . . . . . . . .4E 37
Tidmington. Warw . . . . . . . . . .2A 50
Tidpit. Hants . . . . . . . . . . . . . . . .1F 15
Tidworth. Wilts . . . . . . . . . . . . . .2H 23
Tidworth Camp. Wilts . . . . . . .2H 23
Tiers Cross. Pemb . . . . . . . . . . .3D 42
Tiffield. Nptn . . . . . . . . . . . . . . .5D 62

Tifty. Abers . . . . . . . . . . . . . . . . .4E 161
Tigerton. Ang . . . . . . . . . . . . . . .2E 145
Tighnabruaich. Arg . . . . . . . . . .2A 126
Tigley. Devn . . . . . . . . . . . . . . . . .2D 8
Tilbrook. Cambs . . . . . . . . . . . . .4H 63
Tilbury. Thur . . . . . . . . . . . . . . . .3H 39
Tilbury Green. Essx . . . . . . . . . .1H 53
Tile Hill. W Mid . . . . . . . . . . . . . .3G 61
Tilehurst. Read . . . . . . . . . . . . . .4E 37
Tilford. Surr . . . . . . . . . . . . . . . . .2G 25
Tilgate Forest Row. W Sus . . .2D 26
Tillathrowie. Abers . . . . . . . . . .5B 160
Tillers Green. Glos . . . . . . . . . . .2B 48
Tillery. Abers . . . . . . . . . . . . . . . .1G 153
Tilley. Shrp . . . . . . . . . . . . . . . . . .3H 71
Tillicoultry. Clac . . . . . . . . . . . . .4B 136
Tillingham. Essx . . . . . . . . . . . . .5C 54
Tillington. Here . . . . . . . . . . . . . .1H 47
Tillington. W Sus . . . . . . . . . . . .3A 26
Tillington Common. Here . . . .1H 47
Tillybirloch. Abers . . . . . . . . . . .3D 152
Tillyfourie. Abers . . . . . . . . . . . .2D 152
Tilmanstone. Kent . . . . . . . . . . .5H 41
Tilney All Saints. Norf . . . . . . .4E 77
Tilney Fen End. Norf . . . . . . . . .4E 77
Tilney High End. Norf . . . . . . . .4E 77
Tilney St Lawrence. Norf . . . .4E 77
Tilshead. Wilts . . . . . . . . . . . . . .2F 23
Tilstock. Shrp . . . . . . . . . . . . . . .2H 71
Tilston. Ches W . . . . . . . . . . . . . .5G 83
Tilstone Fearnall. Ches W . . .4H 83
Tilsworth. C Beds . . . . . . . . . . .3H 51
Tilton on the Hill. Leics . . . . .5E 75
Tiltups End. Glos . . . . . . . . . . . .2D 34
Timberland. Linc . . . . . . . . . . . . .5A 88
Timbersbrook. Ches E . . . . . . .4C 84
Timberscombe. Som . . . . . . . . .2C 20
Timble. N Yor . . . . . . . . . . . . . . . .4D 98
Timperley. G Man . . . . . . . . . . .2B 84
Timsbury. Bath . . . . . . . . . . . . . .1B 22
Timsbury. Hants . . . . . . . . . . . . .4B 24
Timsgearraidh. W Isl . . . . . . . .4C 171
Timworth Green. Suff . . . . . . .4A 66
Tincleton. Dors . . . . . . . . . . . . . .3C 14
Tindale. Cumb . . . . . . . . . . . . . . .4H 113
Tindale Crescent. Dur . . . . . . .2F 105
Tingewick. Buck . . . . . . . . . . . . .2E 51
Tingrith. C Beds . . . . . . . . . . . . .2A 52
Tingwall. Orkn . . . . . . . . . . . . . .5D 172
Tinhay. Devn . . . . . . . . . . . . . . . .4D 11
Tinshill. W Yor . . . . . . . . . . . . . .1C 92
Tinsley. S Yor . . . . . . . . . . . . . . .1B 86
Tinsley Green. W Sus . . . . . . . .2D 27
Tintagel. Corn . . . . . . . . . . . . . . .4A 10
Tintern. Mon . . . . . . . . . . . . . . . .5A 48
Tintinhull. Som . . . . . . . . . . . . . .1H 13
Tintwistle. Derbs . . . . . . . . . . . .1E 85
Tinwald. Dum . . . . . . . . . . . . . . .1B 112
Tinwell. Rut . . . . . . . . . . . . . . . . .5H 75
Tippacott. Devn . . . . . . . . . . . . .2A 20
Tipperty. Abers . . . . . . . . . . . . .1G 153
Tipps End. Cambs . . . . . . . . . . .1E 65
Tiptoe. Hants . . . . . . . . . . . . . . .3A 16
Tipton. W Mid . . . . . . . . . . . . . . .1D 60
Tipton St John. Devn . . . . . . .3D 12
Tiptree. Essx . . . . . . . . . . . . . . . .4B 54
Tiptree Heath. Essx . . . . . . . . .4B 54
Tirabad. Powy . . . . . . . . . . . . . . .1B 46
Tircoed Forest Village. Swan .5G 45
Tiree Airport. Arg . . . . . . . . . . .4B 138
Tirinie. Per . . . . . . . . . . . . . . . . . .2F 143
Tirley. Glos . . . . . . . . . . . . . . . . . .3D 48
Tiroran. Arg . . . . . . . . . . . . . . . . .1B 132
Tir-Phil. Cphy . . . . . . . . . . . . . . .5E 47
Tirril. Cumb . . . . . . . . . . . . . . . . .2G 103
Tirryside. High . . . . . . . . . . . . . .2C 164
Tir-y-dail. Carm . . . . . . . . . . . . .4G 45
Tisbury. Wilts . . . . . . . . . . . . . . .4E 23
Tisman's Common. W Sus . . .2B 26
Tissington. Derbs . . . . . . . . . . .5F 85
Titchberry. Devn . . . . . . . . . . . . .4C 18
Titchfield. Hants . . . . . . . . . . . .2D 16
Titchmarsh. Nptn . . . . . . . . . . .3H 63

Titchwell. Norf . . . . . . . . . . . . . .1G 77
Tithby. Notts . . . . . . . . . . . . . . . .2D 74
Titley. Here . . . . . . . . . . . . . . . . .5F 59
Titlington. Nmbd . . . . . . . . . . .3E 121
Titsey. Surr . . . . . . . . . . . . . . . . . .5F 39
Titson. Corn . . . . . . . . . . . . . . . . .2C 10
Tittensor. Staf . . . . . . . . . . . . . . .2C 72
Tittleshall. Norf . . . . . . . . . . . . . .3A 78
Titton. Worc . . . . . . . . . . . . . . . . .4C 60
Tiverton. Ches W . . . . . . . . . . . .4H 83
Tiverton. Devn . . . . . . . . . . . . . .1C 12
Tivetshall St Margaret. Norf . .2D 66
Tivetshall St Mary. Norf . . . . .2D 66
Tivington. Som . . . . . . . . . . . . . .2C 20
Tixall. Staf . . . . . . . . . . . . . . . . . .3D 73
Tixover. Rut . . . . . . . . . . . . . . . . .5G 75
Toab. Orkn . . . . . . . . . . . . . . . . . .7E 172
Toab. Shet . . . . . . . . . . . . . . . . . .10E 173
Toadmoor. Derbs . . . . . . . . . . .5A 86
Tobermory. Arg . . . . . . . . . . . . .3G 139
Toberonochy. Arg . . . . . . . . . . .3E 133
Tobha Beag. W Isl . . . . . . . . . . .5C 170
Tobha Beag. W Isl . . . . . . . . . . .1E 170
Tobha Mor. W Isl . . . . . . . . . . . .5C 170
Tobhtarol. W Isl . . . . . . . . . . . . .4D 171
Tobson. W Isl . . . . . . . . . . . . . . . .4D 171
Tocabhaig. High . . . . . . . . . . . . .2E 147
Tocher. Abers . . . . . . . . . . . . . . .5D 160
Tockenham. Wilts . . . . . . . . . . .4F 35
Tockenham Wick. Wilts . . . . .3F 35
Tockholes. Bkbn . . . . . . . . . . . .2E 91
Tockington. S Glo . . . . . . . . . . .3B 34
Tockwith. N Yor . . . . . . . . . . . .4G 99
Todber. Dors . . . . . . . . . . . . . . . .4D 22
Todding. Here . . . . . . . . . . . . . . .3G 59
Toddington. C Beds . . . . . . . . .3A 52
Toddington. Glos . . . . . . . . . . . .2F 49
Todenham. Glos . . . . . . . . . . . . .2H 49
Todhills. Cumb . . . . . . . . . . . . . .3E 113
Todmorden. W Yor . . . . . . . . .2H 91
Todwick. S Yor . . . . . . . . . . . . . .2B 86
Toft. Cambs . . . . . . . . . . . . . . . . .5C 64
Toft. Linc . . . . . . . . . . . . . . . . . . .4H 75
Toft Hill. Dur . . . . . . . . . . . . . . . .2E 105
Toft Monks. Norf . . . . . . . . . . . .1G 67
Toft next Newton. Linc . . . . . .2H 87
Toftrees. Norf . . . . . . . . . . . . . . .3A 78
Tofts. High . . . . . . . . . . . . . . . . . .2F 169
Toftwood. Norf . . . . . . . . . . . . . .4B 78
Togston. Nmbd . . . . . . . . . . . . .4G 121
Tokavaig. High . . . . . . . . . . . . . .2E 147
Tokers Green. Oxon . . . . . . . . .4F 37
Tolastadh a Chaolais.
    W Isl . . . . . . . . . . . . . . . . . . .4D 171
Tolladine. Worc . . . . . . . . . . . . .5C 60
Tolland. Som . . . . . . . . . . . . . . . .3E 20
Tollard Farnham. Dors . . . . . .1E 15
Tollard Royal. Wilts . . . . . . . . .1E 15
Toll Bar. S Yor . . . . . . . . . . . . . .4F 93
Toller Fratrum. Dors . . . . . . . .3A 14
Toller Porcorum. Dors . . . . . .3A 14
Tollerton. N Yor . . . . . . . . . . . .3H 99
Tollerton. Notts . . . . . . . . . . . . .2D 74
Toller Whelme. Dors . . . . . . . .2A 14
Tollesbury. Essx . . . . . . . . . . . . .4C 54
Tolleshunt D'Arcy. Essx . . . . .4C 54
Tolleshunt Knights. Essx . . . .4C 54
Tolleshunt Major. Essx . . . . . .4C 54
Tollie. High . . . . . . . . . . . . . . . . .3H 157
Tollie Farm. High . . . . . . . . . . .1A 156
Tolm. W Isl . . . . . . . . . . . . . . . . .4G 171
Tolpuddle. Dors . . . . . . . . . . . . .3C 14
Tolstadh bho Thuath.
    W Isl . . . . . . . . . . . . . . . . . . .3H 171
Tolworth. G Lon . . . . . . . . . . . .4C 38
Tomaknock. Per . . . . . . . . . . . . .1A 136
Tomatin. High . . . . . . . . . . . . . . .1C 150
Tombuidhe. Arg . . . . . . . . . . . . .3H 133
Tomich. High
    nr. Cannich . . . . . . . . . . . .1F 149
    nr. Invergordon . . . . . . . .1B 158
    nr. Lairg . . . . . . . . . . . . . . .3D 164

Tomintoul. Mor . . . . . . . . . . . . . .2F 151
Tomnavoulin. Mor . . . . . . . . . .1G 151
Tomsléibhe. Arg . . . . . . . . . . . .5A 140
Ton. Mon . . . . . . . . . . . . . . . . . . .2G 33
Tonbridge. Kent . . . . . . . . . . . .1G 27
Tondu. B'end . . . . . . . . . . . . . . . .3B 32
Tonedale. Som . . . . . . . . . . . . . .4E 21
Tonfanau. Gwyn . . . . . . . . . . . .5E 69
Tong. Shrp . . . . . . . . . . . . . . . . . .5B 72
Tonge. Leics . . . . . . . . . . . . . . . .3B 74
Tong Forge. Shrp . . . . . . . . . . .5B 72
Tongham. Surr . . . . . . . . . . . . . .2G 25
Tongland. Dum . . . . . . . . . . . . . .4D 111
Tong Norton. Shrp . . . . . . . . . .5B 72
Tongue. High . . . . . . . . . . . . . . .3F 167
Tongue End. Linc . . . . . . . . . . .4A 76
Tongwynlais. Card . . . . . . . . . .3E 33
Tonmawr. Neat . . . . . . . . . . . . . .2B 32
Tonna. Neat . . . . . . . . . . . . . . . . .2A 32
Tonnau. Neat . . . . . . . . . . . . . . . .2A 32
Ton Pentre. Rhon . . . . . . . . . . .2C 32
Ton-Teg. Rhon . . . . . . . . . . . . . .3D 32
Tonwell. Herts . . . . . . . . . . . . . .4D 52
Tonypandy. Rhon . . . . . . . . . . .2C 32
Tonyrefail. Rhon . . . . . . . . . . . .3D 32
Toot Baldon. Oxon . . . . . . . . . .5D 50
Toot Hill. Essx . . . . . . . . . . . . . .5F 53
Toothill. Hants . . . . . . . . . . . . . .1B 16
Topcliffe. N Yor . . . . . . . . . . . . .2G 99
Topcliffe. W Yor . . . . . . . . . . . .2C 92
Topcroft. Norf . . . . . . . . . . . . . . .1E 67
Topcroft Street. Norf . . . . . . . .1E 67
Toppesfield. Essx . . . . . . . . . . .2H 53
Toppings. G Man . . . . . . . . . . .3F 91
Toprow. Norf . . . . . . . . . . . . . . . .1D 66
Topsham. Devn . . . . . . . . . . . . . .4C 12
Torbay. Torb . . . . . . . . . . . . . . . .2F 9
Torbeg. N Ayr . . . . . . . . . . . . . .3C 122
Torbothie. N Lan . . . . . . . . . . .4B 128
Torbryan. Devn . . . . . . . . . . . . . .2E 9
Torcross. Devn . . . . . . . . . . . . . .4E 9
Tore. High . . . . . . . . . . . . . . . . . .3A 158
Torgyle. High . . . . . . . . . . . . . . .2E 149
Torinturk. Arg . . . . . . . . . . . . . .3G 125
Torksey. Linc . . . . . . . . . . . . . . .3F 87
Torlum. W Isl . . . . . . . . . . . . . . .3C 170
Torlundy. High . . . . . . . . . . . . . .1F 141
Tormarton. S Glo . . . . . . . . . . .4C 34
Tormitchell. S Ayr . . . . . . . . . .5B 116
Tormore. High . . . . . . . . . . . . . .3E 147
Tormore. N Ayr . . . . . . . . . . . .2C 122
Tornagrain. High . . . . . . . . . . .4B 158
Tornaveen. Abers . . . . . . . . . . .3D 152
Torness. High . . . . . . . . . . . . . .1H 149
Toronto. Dur . . . . . . . . . . . . . . . .1E 105
Torpenhow. Cumb . . . . . . . . . .1D 102
Torphichen. W Lot . . . . . . . . . .2C 128
Torphins. Abers . . . . . . . . . . . . .3D 152
Torpoint. Corn . . . . . . . . . . . . . .3A 8
Torquay. Torb . . . . . . . . . . . . . . .2F 9
Torr. Devn . . . . . . . . . . . . . . . . . .3B 8
Torra. Arg . . . . . . . . . . . . . . . . . .4B 124
Torran. High . . . . . . . . . . . . . . . .4E 155
Torrance. E Dun . . . . . . . . . . . .2H 127
Torrans. Arg . . . . . . . . . . . . . . . .1B 132
Torranyard. N Ayr . . . . . . . . . .5E 127
Torre. Som . . . . . . . . . . . . . . . . .3D 20
Torre. Torb . . . . . . . . . . . . . . . . .2F 9
Torridon. High . . . . . . . . . . . . . .3B 156
Torrin. High . . . . . . . . . . . . . . . .1D 147
Torrisdale. Arg . . . . . . . . . . . . . .2B 122
Torrisdale. High . . . . . . . . . . . .2G 167
Torrish. High . . . . . . . . . . . . . . .2G 165
Torrisholme. Lanc . . . . . . . . . .3D 96
Torroble. High . . . . . . . . . . . . . .3C 164
Torroy. High . . . . . . . . . . . . . . . .4C 164
Torry. Aber . . . . . . . . . . . . . . . . .3G 153
Torryburn. Fife . . . . . . . . . . . . .1D 128
Torthorwald. Dum . . . . . . . . . .2B 112
Tortington. W Sus . . . . . . . . . .5B 26
Torton. Worc . . . . . . . . . . . . . . . .3C 60
Tortworth. S Glo . . . . . . . . . . .2C 34
Torvaig. High . . . . . . . . . . . . . . .4D 155
Torver. Cumb . . . . . . . . . . . . . . .5D 102
Torwood. Falk . . . . . . . . . . . . . .1B 128

Torworth. *Notts* . . . . . . . . . . . . .2D **86**
Toscaig. *High* . . . . . . . . . . . .5G **155**
Toseland. *Cambs* . . . . . . . . . .4B **64**
Tosside. *N Yor* . . . . . . . . . . . .4G **97**
Tostock. *Suff* . . . . . . . . . . . . . .4B **66**
Totaig. *High* . . . . . . . . . . . . .3A **154**
Totardor. *High* . . . . . . . . . . . .5C **154**
Tote. *High* . . . . . . . . . . . . . . . .4D **154**
Totegan. *High* . . . . . . . . . . . .2A **168**
Tothill. *Linc* . . . . . . . . . . . . . . .2D **88**
Totland. *IOW* . . . . . . . . . . . . . .4B **16**
Totley. *S Yor* . . . . . . . . . . . . . .3H **85**
Totnell. *Dors* . . . . . . . . . . . . . .2B **14**
Totnes. *Devn* . . . . . . . . . . . . . . .2E **9**
Toton. *Notts* . . . . . . . . . . . . . .2B **74**
Totronald. *Arg* . . . . . . . . . . . .3C **138**
Totscore. *High* . . . . . . . . . . . .2C **154**
**Tottenham.** *G Lon* . . . . . . . . .1E **39**
Tottenhill. *Norf* . . . . . . . . . . . .4F **77**
Tottenhill Row. *Norf* . . . . . . . .4F **77**
Totteridge. *G Lon* . . . . . . . . . .1D **38**
Totternhoe. *C Beds* . . . . . . . .3H **51**
Tottington. *G Man* . . . . . . . . .3F **91**
**Totton.** *Hants* . . . . . . . . . . . . .1B **16**
Touchen-end. *Wind* . . . . . . . .4G **37**
Toulvaddie. *High* . . . . . . . . . .5F **165**
The Towans. *Corn* . . . . . . . . . . .3C **4**
Toward. *Arg* . . . . . . . . . . . . . .3C **126**
Towcester. *Nptn* . . . . . . . . . . . .1E **51**
Townednack. *Corn* . . . . . . . . . . .3B **4**
Tower End. *Norf* . . . . . . . . . . . .4F **77**
Tower Hill. *Mers* . . . . . . . . . . .4C **90**
Tower Hill. *W Sus* . . . . . . . . . .3C **26**
Towersey. *Oxon* . . . . . . . . . . . .5F **51**
Towie. *Abers* . . . . . . . . . . . .2B **152**
Towiemore. *Mor* . . . . . . . . . .4A **160**
Tow Law. *Dur* . . . . . . . . . . . .1E **105**
The Town. *IOS* . . . . . . . . . . . . .1A **4**
Town End. *Cambs* . . . . . . . . . .1D **64**
Town End. *Cumb*
    nr. Ambleside . . . . . . .4F **103**
    nr. Kirkby Thore . . . . .2H **103**
    nr. Lindale . . . . . . . . . . .1D **96**
    nr. Newby Bridge . . . . .1C **96**
Town End. *Mers* . . . . . . . . . . . .2G **83**
Townend. *W Dun* . . . . . . . . . .2F **127**
Townfield. *Dur* . . . . . . . . . . . .5C **114**
Towngate. *Cumb* . . . . . . . . . .5G **113**
Towngate. *Linc* . . . . . . . . . . . .4A **76**
Town Green. *Lanc* . . . . . . . . . .4C **90**
Town Head. *Cumb*
    nr. Grasmere . . . . . . . .4E **103**
    nr. Great Asby . . . . . . .3H **103**
Townhead. *Cumb*
    nr. Lazonby . . . . . . . . .1G **103**
    nr. Maryport . . . . . . . .1B **102**
    nr. Ousby . . . . . . . . . . .1H **103**
Townhead. *Dum* . . . . . . . . . .5D **111**
Townhead of Greenlaw.
    *Dum* . . . . . . . . . . . . . .3E **111**
Townhill. *Fife* . . . . . . . . . . . . .1E **129**
Townhill. *Swan* . . . . . . . . . . . .3F **31**
Town Kelloe. *Dur* . . . . . . . . .1A **106**
Town Littleworth. *E Sus* . . . . .4F **27**
Town Row. *E Sus* . . . . . . . . . . .2G **27**
Towns End. *Hants* . . . . . . . . . .1D **24**
Townsend. *Herts* . . . . . . . . . . .5B **52**
Townshend. *Corn* . . . . . . . . . . . .3C **4**
Town Street. *Suff* . . . . . . . . . . .2G **65**
Town Yetholm. *Bord* . . . . . . .2C **120**
Towthorpe. *E Yor* . . . . . . . . . .3D **100**
Towthorpe. *York* . . . . . . . . . .4A **100**
Towton. *N Yor* . . . . . . . . . . . . .1E **93**
Towyn. *Cnwy* . . . . . . . . . . . . . .3B **82**
Toxteth. *Mers* . . . . . . . . . . . . .2F **83**
Toynton All Saints. *Linc* . . . . .4C **88**
Toynton Fen Side. *Linc* . . . . .4C **88**
Toynton St Peter. *Linc* . . . . . .4D **88**
Toy's Hill. *Kent* . . . . . . . . . . . .5F **39**
Trabboch. *E Ayr* . . . . . . . . . . .2D **116**
Traboe. *Corn* . . . . . . . . . . . . . . .4E **5**
Tradespark. *High* . . . . . . . . . .3C **158**
Tradespark. *Orkn* . . . . . . . . . .7D **172**
Trafford Park. *G Man* . . . . . . .1B **84**

Trallong. *Powy* . . . . . . . . . . . . .3C **46**
Y Trallwng. *Powy* . . . . . . . . . . .5E **70**
Tranent. *E Lot* . . . . . . . . . . . .2H **129**
Tranmere. *Mers* . . . . . . . . . . . .2F **83**
Trantlebeg. *High* . . . . . . . . . .3A **168**
Trantlemore. *High* . . . . . . . . .3A **168**
Tranwell. *Nmbd* . . . . . . . . . . .1E **115**
Trapp. *Carm* . . . . . . . . . . . . . . .4G **45**
Traquair. *Bord* . . . . . . . . . . . .1F **119**
Trash Green. *W Ber* . . . . . . . . .5E **37**
Trawden. *Lanc* . . . . . . . . . . . . .1H **91**
Trawscoed. *Powy* . . . . . . . . . . .2D **46**
Trawsfynydd. *Gwyn* . . . . . . . . .2G **69**
Trawsgoed. *Cdgn* . . . . . . . . . . .3F **57**
Treaddow. *Here* . . . . . . . . . . . .3A **48**
Trealaw. *Rhon* . . . . . . . . . . . . .2D **32**
Treales. *Lanc* . . . . . . . . . . . . . .1C **90**
Trearddur. *IOA* . . . . . . . . . . . .3B **80**
Treaslane. *High* . . . . . . . . . . .3C **154**
Treator. *Corn* . . . . . . . . . . . . . . .1D **6**
Trebanog. *Rhon* . . . . . . . . . . . .2D **32**
Trebanos. *Neat* . . . . . . . . . . . . .5H **45**
Trebarber. *Corn* . . . . . . . . . . . . .2C **6**
Trebartha. *Corn* . . . . . . . . . . . .5C **10**
Trebarwith. *Corn* . . . . . . . . . .4A **10**
Trebetherick. *Corn* . . . . . . . . . . .1D **6**
Treborough. *Som* . . . . . . . . . . .3D **20**
Trebudannon. *Corn* . . . . . . . . . .2C **6**
Trebullett. *Corn* . . . . . . . . . . . .5D **10**
Treburley. *Corn* . . . . . . . . . . . .5D **10**
Treburrick. *Corn* . . . . . . . . . . . . .1C **6**
Trebyan. *Corn* . . . . . . . . . . . . . . .2E **7**
Trecastle. *Powy* . . . . . . . . . . . .3B **46**
Trecenydd. *Cphy* . . . . . . . . . . .3E **33**
Trecott. *Devn* . . . . . . . . . . . . . .2G **11**
Trecwn. *Pemb* . . . . . . . . . . . . . .1D **42**
Trecynon. *Rhon* . . . . . . . . . . . .5C **46**
Tredaule. *Corn* . . . . . . . . . . . .4C **10**
Tredavoe. *Corn* . . . . . . . . . . . . . .4B **4**
Tredegar. *Blae* . . . . . . . . . . . . .5E **47**
Trederwen. *Powy* . . . . . . . . . . .4E **71**
Tredington. *Glos* . . . . . . . . . . .3E **49**
Tredington. *Warw* . . . . . . . . . .1A **50**
Tredinnick. *Corn*
    nr. Bodmin . . . . . . . . . .2F **7**
    nr. Looe . . . . . . . . . . . . .3G **7**
    nr. Padstow . . . . . . . . .1D **6**
Tredogan. *V Glam* . . . . . . . . . .5D **32**
Tredomen. *Powy* . . . . . . . . . . .2E **46**
Tredunnock. *Mon* . . . . . . . . . .2G **33**
Tredustan. *Powy* . . . . . . . . . . .2E **47**
Treen. *Corn*
    nr. Land's End . . . . . . . .4A **4**
    nr. St Ives . . . . . . . . . . . .3B **4**
Treeton. *S Yor* . . . . . . . . . . . . .2B **86**
Trefaldwyn. *Powy* . . . . . . . . . .1E **58**
Trefasser. *Pemb* . . . . . . . . . . . .1C **42**
Trefdraeth. *IOA* . . . . . . . . . . . .3D **80**
Trefdraeth. *Pemb* . . . . . . . . . .1E **43**
Trefecca. *Powy* . . . . . . . . . . . . .2E **47**
Trefechan. *Mer T* . . . . . . . . . .5D **46**
Trefeglwys. *Powy* . . . . . . . . . . .1B **58**
Trefenter. *Cdgn* . . . . . . . . . . . .4F **57**
Treffgarne. *Pemb* . . . . . . . . . .2D **42**
Treffynnon. *Flin* . . . . . . . . . . .3D **82**
Treffynnon. *Pemb* . . . . . . . . . .2C **42**
Trefil. *Blae* . . . . . . . . . . . . . . . .4E **46**
Trefilan. *Cdgn* . . . . . . . . . . . . .5E **57**
Treflach. *Shrp* . . . . . . . . . . . . .3E **71**
Trefnant. *Den* . . . . . . . . . . . . .3C **82**
Trefonen. *Shrp* . . . . . . . . . . . . .3E **71**
Trefor. *Gwyn* . . . . . . . . . . . . . .1C **68**
Trefor. *IOA* . . . . . . . . . . . . . . .2C **80**
Treforest. *Rhon* . . . . . . . . . . . .3D **32**
Trefrew. *Corn* . . . . . . . . . . . . .4A **10**
Trefriw. *Cnwy* . . . . . . . . . . . . .4G **81**
Tref-y-Clawdd. *Powy* . . . . . . . .3E **59**
Trefynwy. *Mon* . . . . . . . . . . . .4A **48**
Tregada. *Corn* . . . . . . . . . . . . .4D **10**
Tregadillett. *Corn* . . . . . . . . . .4C **10**
Tregare. *Mon* . . . . . . . . . . . . . .4H **47**
Tregaron. *Cdgn* . . . . . . . . . . . .5F **57**

Tregarth. *Gwyn* . . . . . . . . . . . . .4F **81**
Tregear. *Corn* . . . . . . . . . . . . . .3C **6**
Tregeare. *Corn* . . . . . . . . . . . . .4C **10**
Tregeiriog. *Wrex* . . . . . . . . . . .2D **70**
Tregele. *IOA* . . . . . . . . . . . . . .1C **80**
Tregeseal. *Corn* . . . . . . . . . . . . .3A **4**
Tregiskey. *Corn* . . . . . . . . . . . . .4E **6**
Tregole. *Corn* . . . . . . . . . . . . . .3B **10**
Tregolwyn. *V Glam* . . . . . . . . .4C **32**
Tregonetha. *Corn* . . . . . . . . . . . .2D **6**
Tregonhawke. *Corn* . . . . . . . . .3A **8**
Tregony. *Corn* . . . . . . . . . . . . . . .4D **6**
Tregoodwell. *Corn* . . . . . . . . .4B **10**
Tregorrick. *Corn* . . . . . . . . . . . .3E **6**
Tregoss. *Corn* . . . . . . . . . . . . . . .2D **6**
Tregowris. *Corn* . . . . . . . . . . . . .4E **5**
Tregoyd. *Powy* . . . . . . . . . . . .2E **47**
Tregrehan Mills. *Corn* . . . . . . . .3E **7**
Tre-groes. *Cdgn* . . . . . . . . . . . .1E **45**
Tregullon. *Corn* . . . . . . . . . . . . .2E **7**
Tregurrian. *Corn* . . . . . . . . . . . . .2C **6**
Tregynon. *Powy* . . . . . . . . . . . .1C **58**
Trehafod. *Rhon* . . . . . . . . . . . .2D **32**
Trehan. *Corn* . . . . . . . . . . . . . . .3A **8**
**Treharris.** *Mer T* . . . . . . . . . . .2D **32**
Treherbert. *Rhon* . . . . . . . . . . .2C **32**
Trehunist. *Corn* . . . . . . . . . . . . .2H **7**
Trekenner. *Corn* . . . . . . . . . . . .5D **10**
Treknow. *Corn* . . . . . . . . . . . .4A **10**
Trelales. *B'end* . . . . . . . . . . . . .3B **32**
Trelan. *Corn* . . . . . . . . . . . . . . . .5E **5**
Trelash. *Corn* . . . . . . . . . . . . . .3B **10**
Trelassick. *Corn* . . . . . . . . . . . . .3C **6**
Trelawnyd. *Flin* . . . . . . . . . . . .3C **82**
Trelech. *Carm* . . . . . . . . . . . . . .1G **43**
Treleddyd-fawr. *Pemb* . . . . . . .2B **42**
Trelewis. *Mer T* . . . . . . . . . . . .2E **32**
Treligga. *Corn* . . . . . . . . . . . . .4A **10**
Trelights. *Corn* . . . . . . . . . . . . . .1D **6**
Trelill. *Corn* . . . . . . . . . . . . . . .5A **10**
Trelissick. *Corn* . . . . . . . . . . . . . .5C **6**
Trellech. *Mon* . . . . . . . . . . . . .5A **48**
Trellech Grange. *Mon* . . . . . . .5H **47**
Trelogan. *Flin* . . . . . . . . . . . . .2D **82**
Trelystan. *Powy* . . . . . . . . . . . .5E **71**
Tremadog. *Gwyn* . . . . . . . . . . .1E **69**
Tremail. *Corn* . . . . . . . . . . . . . .4B **10**
Tremaine. *Corn* . . . . . . . . . . . . .1C **44**
Tremaine. *Corn* . . . . . . . . . . . .4C **10**
Tremar. *Corn* . . . . . . . . . . . . . . . .2G **7**
Trematon. *Corn* . . . . . . . . . . . . .3H **7**
Tremeirchion. *Den* . . . . . . . . . .3C **82**
Tremore. *Corn* . . . . . . . . . . . . . .2E **6**
Tremorfa. *Card* . . . . . . . . . . . . .4F **33**
Trenance. *Corn*
    nr. Newquay . . . . . . . . .2C **6**
    nr. Padstow . . . . . . . . .1D **6**
Trenarren. *Corn* . . . . . . . . . . . . .4E **7**
Trench. *Telf* . . . . . . . . . . . . . . .4A **72**
Trencreek. *Corn* . . . . . . . . . . . . .2C **6**
Trendeal. *Corn* . . . . . . . . . . . . . .3C **6**
Trenear. *Corn* . . . . . . . . . . . . . . .5A **6**
Treneglos. *Corn* . . . . . . . . . . . .4C **10**
Trenewan. *Corn* . . . . . . . . . . . . .3F **7**
Trengune. *Corn* . . . . . . . . . . . . .3B **10**
Trent. *Dors* . . . . . . . . . . . . . . .1A **14**
Trentham. *Stoke* . . . . . . . . . . .1C **72**
Trentishoe. *Devn* . . . . . . . . . . .2G **19**
Trentlock. *Derbs* . . . . . . . . . . .2B **74**
Treoes. *V Glam* . . . . . . . . . . . .4C **32**
Treorchy. *Rhon* . . . . . . . . . . . .2C **32**
Treorci. *Rhon* . . . . . . . . . . . . .2C **32**
Tre'r-ddol. *Cdgn* . . . . . . . . . . . .1F **57**
Tre'r Ilai. *Powy* . . . . . . . . . . . . .5E **71**
Trerulefoot. *Corn* . . . . . . . . . . .3H **7**
Tresaith. *Cdgn* . . . . . . . . . . . . .5B **56**
Trescott. *Staf* . . . . . . . . . . . . . .1C **60**
Trescowe. *Corn* . . . . . . . . . . . . .3C **4**
Tresham. *Glos* . . . . . . . . . . . . .2C **34**
Tresigin. *V Glam* . . . . . . . . . . .4C **32**
Tresillian. *Corn* . . . . . . . . . . . . . .4C **6**
Tresimwn. *V Glam* . . . . . . . . .4D **32**
Tresinney. *Corn* . . . . . . . . . . . .4B **10**

Treskillard. *Corn* . . . . . . . . . . . .5A **6**
Treskinnick Cross. *Corn* . . . . .3C **10**
Tresmeer. *Corn* . . . . . . . . . . . .4C **10**
Tresparrett. *Corn* . . . . . . . . . . .3B **10**
Tresparrett Posts. *Corn* . . . . . .3B **10**
Tressady. *High* . . . . . . . . . . . .3D **164**
Tressait. *Per* . . . . . . . . . . . . . .2F **143**
Tresta. *Shet*
    on Fetlar . . . . . . . . . . .2H **173**
    on Mainland . . . . . . . .6E **173**
Treswell. *Notts* . . . . . . . . . . . . .3E **87**
Treswithian. *Corn* . . . . . . . . . . .3D **4**
Tre Taliesin. *Cdgn* . . . . . . . . . .1F **57**
Trethomas. *Cphy* . . . . . . . . . . .3E **33**
Trethosa. *Corn* . . . . . . . . . . . . . .3D **6**
Trethurgy. *Corn* . . . . . . . . . . . . .3E **7**
Tretio. *Pemb* . . . . . . . . . . . . . .2B **42**
Tretire. *Here* . . . . . . . . . . . . . .3A **48**
Tretower. *Powy* . . . . . . . . . . . .3E **47**
Treuddyn. *Flin* . . . . . . . . . . . . .5E **83**
Trevadlock. *Corn* . . . . . . . . . . .5C **10**
Trevalga. *Corn* . . . . . . . . . . . . .4A **10**
Trevalyn. *Wrex* . . . . . . . . . . . . .5F **83**
Trevance. *Corn* . . . . . . . . . . . . . .1D **6**
Trevanger. *Corn* . . . . . . . . . . . . .1D **6**
Trevanson. *Corn* . . . . . . . . . . . . .1D **6**
Trevarrack. *Corn* . . . . . . . . . . . . .3B **4**
Trevarren. *Corn* . . . . . . . . . . . . . .2C **6**
Trevarrian. *Corn* . . . . . . . . . . . . .2C **6**
Trevarrick. *Corn* . . . . . . . . . . . . .4D **6**
Trevaughan. *Carm*
    nr. Carmarthen . . . . . .3E **45**
    nr. Whitland . . . . . . . .3F **43**
Treveighan. *Corn* . . . . . . . . . . .5A **10**
Trevellas. *Corn* . . . . . . . . . . . . . .3B **6**
Trevelmond. *Corn* . . . . . . . . . . . .2G **7**
Treverva. *Corn* . . . . . . . . . . . . . .5B **6**
Trevescan. *Corn* . . . . . . . . . . . . .4A **4**
Trevethin. *Torf* . . . . . . . . . . . . .5F **47**
Trevia. *Corn* . . . . . . . . . . . . . .4A **10**
Trevigro. *Corn* . . . . . . . . . . . . . .2H **7**
Trevilley. *Corn* . . . . . . . . . . . . . .4A **4**
Treviscoe. *Corn* . . . . . . . . . . . . .3D **6**
Trevivian. *Corn* . . . . . . . . . . . .4B **10**
Trevone. *Corn* . . . . . . . . . . . . . . .1C **6**
Trevor. *Wrex* . . . . . . . . . . . . . .1E **71**
Trevor Uchaf. *Den* . . . . . . . . . .1E **71**
Trew. *Corn* . . . . . . . . . . . . . . . . .4D **4**
Trewalder. *Corn* . . . . . . . . . . . .4A **10**
Trewarlett. *Corn* . . . . . . . . . . . .4D **10**
Trewarmett. *Corn* . . . . . . . . . .4A **10**
Trewassa. *Corn* . . . . . . . . . . . . .4B **10**
Treween. *Corn* . . . . . . . . . . . . .4C **10**
Trewellard. *Corn* . . . . . . . . . . . . .3A **4**
Trewen. *Corn* . . . . . . . . . . . . . .4C **10**
Trewennack. *Corn* . . . . . . . . . . . .4D **5**
Trewern. *Powy* . . . . . . . . . . . . .4E **71**
Trewetha. *Corn* . . . . . . . . . . . .5A **10**
Trewidland. *Corn* . . . . . . . . . . . .3G **7**
Trewint. *Corn* . . . . . . . . . . . . .3B **10**
Trewithian. *Corn* . . . . . . . . . . . .5C **6**
Trewoofe. *Corn* . . . . . . . . . . . . . .4A **4**
Trewoon. *Corn* . . . . . . . . . . . . . .3D **6**
Treworthal. *Corn* . . . . . . . . . . . .5C **6**
Trewyddel. *Pemb* . . . . . . . . . .1B **44**
Treyarnon. *Corn* . . . . . . . . . . . . .1C **6**
Treyford. *W Sus* . . . . . . . . . . .1G **17**
Triangle. *Staf* . . . . . . . . . . . . . .5E **73**
Triangle. *W Yor* . . . . . . . . . . . .2A **92**
Trickett's Cross. *Dors* . . . . . . .2F **15**
Trimdon. *Dur* . . . . . . . . . . . .1A **106**
Trimdon Colliery. *Dur* . . . . . .1A **106**
Trimdon Grange. *Dur* . . . . . .1A **106**
Trimingham. *Norf* . . . . . . . . . . .2E **79**
Trimley Lower Street. *Suff* . . .2F **55**
Trimley St Martin. *Suff* . . . . .2F **55**
Trimley St Mary. *Suff* . . . . . . .2F **55**
Trimpley. *Worc* . . . . . . . . . . . . .3B **60**
Trimsaran. *Carm* . . . . . . . . . . . .5E **45**
Trimstone. *Devn* . . . . . . . . . . . .2F **19**
Trinafour. *Per* . . . . . . . . . . . .2E **143**
Trinant. *Cphy* . . . . . . . . . . . . . .2F **33**
**Tring.** *Herts* . . . . . . . . . . . . . .4H **51**
Trinity. *Ang* . . . . . . . . . . . . . .2F **145**

Trinity. *Edin* . . . . . . . . . . . . .2F **129**
Trisant. *Cdgn* . . . . . . . . . . . . . .3G **57**
Triscombe. *Som* . . . . . . . . . . . . .3E **21**
Trislaig. *High* . . . . . . . . . . . . .1E **141**
Trispen. *Corn* . . . . . . . . . . . . . . .3C **6**
Tritlington. *Nmbd* . . . . . . . . . .5G **121**
Trochry. *Per* . . . . . . . . . . . . . .4G **143**
Troedrhiwdalar. *Powy* . . . . . . .5B **58**
Troedrhiwfuwch. *Cphy* . . . . . .5E **47**
Troedrhiw-gwair. *Blae* . . . . . . .5E **47**
Troedyraur. *Cdgn* . . . . . . . . . . .1D **44**
Troedyrhiw. *Mer T* . . . . . . . . .5D **46**
Trondavoe. *Shet* . . . . . . . . . . .4E **173**
Troon. *Corn* . . . . . . . . . . . . . . . .5A **6**
**Troon.** *S Ayr* . . . . . . . . . . . .1C **116**
Troqueer. *Dum* . . . . . . . . . . .2A **112**
Troston. *Suff* . . . . . . . . . . . . . .3A **66**
Trottiscliffe. *Kent* . . . . . . . . . . .4H **39**
Trotton. *W Sus* . . . . . . . . . . . .4G **25**
Troutbeck. *Cumb*
    nr. Ambleside . . . . . . .4F **103**
    nr. Penrith . . . . . . . . .2E **103**
Troutbeck Bridge. *Cumb* . . . . .4F **103**
Troway. *Derbs* . . . . . . . . . . . . . .3A **86**
**Trowbridge.** *Wilts* . . . . . . . . .1D **22**
Trowell. *Notts* . . . . . . . . . . . . . .2B **74**
Trowle Common. *Wilts* . . . . . .1D **22**
Trowley Bottom. *Herts* . . . . . .4A **52**
Trowse Newton. *Norf* . . . . . . .5E **79**
Trudoxhill. *Som* . . . . . . . . . . . .2C **22**
Trull. *Som* . . . . . . . . . . . . . . . . .4F **21**
Trumaisgearraidh. *W Isl* . . . .1D **170**
Trumpan. *High* . . . . . . . . . . .2B **154**
Trumpet. *Here* . . . . . . . . . . . . .2B **48**
Trumpington. *Cambs* . . . . . . . .5D **64**
Trumps Green. *Surr* . . . . . . . . .4A **38**
Trunch. *Norf* . . . . . . . . . . . . . . .2E **79**
Trunnah. *Lanc* . . . . . . . . . . . . .5C **96**
**Truro.** *Corn* . . . . . . . . . . . . . . . .4C **6**
Trusham. *Devn* . . . . . . . . . . . . .4B **12**
Trusley. *Derbs* . . . . . . . . . . . . . .2G **73**
Trusthorpe. *Linc* . . . . . . . . . . . .2E **89**
Tryfil. *IOA* . . . . . . . . . . . . . . . .2D **80**
Trysull. *Staf* . . . . . . . . . . . . . . . .1C **60**
Tubney. *Oxon* . . . . . . . . . . . . . .2C **36**
Tuckenhay. *Devn* . . . . . . . . . . . .3E **9**
Tuckhill. *Shrp* . . . . . . . . . . . . . .2B **60**
Tuckingmill. *Corn* . . . . . . . . . . . .4A **6**
Tuckton. *Bour* . . . . . . . . . . . . . .3G **15**
Tuddenham. *Suff* . . . . . . . . . . .3G **65**
Tuddenham St Martin. *Suff* . . . .1E **55**
Tudeley. *Kent* . . . . . . . . . . . . . .1H **27**
Tudhoe. *Dur* . . . . . . . . . . . . .1F **105**
Tudhoe Grange. *Dur* . . . . . . .1F **105**
Tudorville. *Here* . . . . . . . . . . . .3A **48**
Tudweiliog. *Gwyn* . . . . . . . . . .2B **68**
Tuesley. *Surr* . . . . . . . . . . . . . .1A **26**
Tufton. *Hants* . . . . . . . . . . . . . .2C **24**
Tufton. *Pemb* . . . . . . . . . . . . . .2E **43**
Tugby. *Leics* . . . . . . . . . . . . . . .5E **75**
Tugford. *Shrp* . . . . . . . . . . . . . .2H **59**
Tughall. *Nmbd* . . . . . . . . . . . .2G **121**
Tulchan. *Per* . . . . . . . . . . . . . .1B **136**
Tullibardine. *Per* . . . . . . . . . . .2B **136**
Tullibody. *Clac* . . . . . . . . . . . .4A **136**
Tullich. *Arg* . . . . . . . . . . . . . . .2H **133**
Tullich. *High*
    nr. Lochcarron . . . . . . .4B **156**
    nr. Tain . . . . . . . . . . . .1C **158**
Tullich. *Mor* . . . . . . . . . . . . . .4H **159**
Tullich Muir. *High* . . . . . . . . .1B **158**
Tulliemet. *Per* . . . . . . . . . . . .3G **143**
Tulloch. *Abers* . . . . . . . . . . . . .5F **161**
Tulloch. *High*
    nr. Bonar Bridge . . . .4D **164**
    nr. Fort William . . . . .5F **149**
    nr. Grantown-on-Spey
    . . . . . . . . . . . . . . . . . .2D **151**
Tulloch. *Per* . . . . . . . . . . . . . .1C **136**
Tullochgorm. *Arg* . . . . . . . . . .4G **133**
Tullybeagles Lodge. *Per* . . . .5H **143**
Tullymurdoch. *Per* . . . . . . . . . .3B **144**
Tullynessle. *Abers* . . . . . . . . . .2C **152**
Tumble. *Carm* . . . . . . . . . . . . . .4F **45**

Tumbler's Green. *Essx* ....3B 54
Tumby. *Linc* ....4B 88
Tumby Woodside. *Linc* ....5B 88
Tummel Bridge. *Per* ....3E 143
**Tunbridge Wells, Royal.**
 *Kent* ....2G 27
Tunga. *W Isl* ....4G 171
Tungate. *Norf* ....3E 79
Tunley. *Bath* ....1B 22
Tunstall. *E Yor* ....1G 95
Tunstall. *Kent* ....4C 40
Tunstall. *Lanc* ....2F 97
Tunstall. *Norf* ....5G 79
Tunstall. *N Yor* ....5F 105
Tunstall. *Staf* ....3B 72
Tunstall. *Stoke* ....5C 84
Tunstall. *Suff* ....5F 67
Tunstall. *Tyne* ....4G 115
Tunstead. *Derbs* ....3F 85
Tunstead. *Norf* ....3E 79
Tunstead Milton. *Derbs* ....2E 85
Tunworth. *Hants* ....2E 25
Tupsley. *Here* ....1A 48
Tupton. *Derbs* ....4A 86
Turfholm. *S Lan* ....1H 117
Turfmoor. *Devn* ....2F 13
Turgis Green. *Hants* ....1E 25
Turkdean. *Glos* ....4G 49
Turkey Island. *Hants* ....1D 16
Tur Langton. *Leics* ....1E 62
Turleigh. *Wilts* ....5D 34
Turlin Moor. *Pool* ....3E 15
Turnastone. *Here* ....2G 47
Turnberry. *S Ayr* ....4B 116
Turnchapel. *Plym* ....3A 8
Turnditch. *Derbs* ....1G 73
Turners Hill. *W Sus* ....2E 27
Turners Puddle. *Dors* ....3D 14
Turnford. *Herts* ....5D 52
Turnhouse. *Edin* ....2E 129
Turnworth. *Dors* ....2D 14
Turriff. *Abers* ....4E 161
Tursdale. *Dur* ....1A 106
Turton Bottoms. *Bkbn* ....3F 91
Turtory. *Mor* ....4C 160
Turves Green. *W Mid* ....3E 61
Turvey. *Bed* ....5G 63
Turville. *Buck* ....2F 37
Turville Heath. *Buck* ....2F 37
Turweston. *Buck* ....2E 50
Tushielaw. *Bord* ....3F 119
Tutbury. *Staf* ....3G 73
Tutnall. *Worc* ....3D 61
Tutshill. *Glos* ....2A 34
Tuttington. *Norf* ....3E 79
Tutts Clump. *W Ber* ....4D 36
Tutwell. *Corn* ....5D 11
Tuxford. *Notts* ....3E 87
Twatt. *Orkn* ....5B 172
Twatt. *Shet* ....6E 173
Twechar. *E Dun* ....2H 127
Tweedale. *Telf* ....5B 72
Tweedbank. *Bord* ....1H 119
Tweedmouth. *Nmbd* ....4F 131
Tweedsmuir. *Bord* ....2C 118
Twelveheads. *Corn* ....4B 6
Twemlow Green. *Ches E* ....4B 84
Twenty. *Linc* ....3A 76
Twerton. *Bath* ....5C 34
**Twickenham.** *G Lon* ....3C 38
Twigworth. *Glos* ....3D 48
Twineham. *W Sus* ....4D 26
Twinhoe. *Bath* ....1C 22
Twinstead. *Essx* ....2B 54
Twinstead Green. *Essx* ....2B 54
Twiss Green. *Warr* ....1A 84
Twiston. *Lanc* ....5H 97
Twitchen. *Devn* ....3A 20
Twitchen. *Shrp* ....3F 59
Two Bridges. *Devn* ....5G 11
Two Bridges. *Glos* ....5B 48
Two Dales. *Derbs* ....4G 85
Two Gates. *Staf* ....5G 73
Two Mile Oak. *Devn* ....2E 9

Twycross. *Leics* ....5H 73
Twyford. *Buck* ....3E 51
Twyford. *Derbs* ....3H 73
Twyford. *Dors* ....1D 14
Twyford. *Hants* ....4C 24
Twyford. *Leics* ....4E 75
Twyford. *Norf* ....3C 78
Twyford. *Wok* ....4F 37
Twyford Common. *Here* ....2A 48
Twynholm. *Dum* ....4D 110
Twyning. *Glos* ....2D 49
Twyning Green. *Glos* ....2E 49
Twynllanan. *Carm* ....3A 46
Twyn-y-Sheriff. *Mon* ....5H 47
Twywell. *Nptn* ....3G 63
Tyberton. *Here* ....2G 47
Tyburn. *W Mid* ....1F 61
Tyby. *Norf* ....3C 78
Tycroes. *Carm* ....4G 45
Tycrwyn. *Powy* ....4D 70
**Tyddewi.** *Pemb* ....2B 42
Tydd Gote. *Linc* ....4D 76
Tydd St Giles. *Cambs* ....4D 76
Tydd St Mary. *Linc* ....4D 76
Tye. *Hants* ....2F 17
Tye Green. *Essx*
 nr. Bishop's Stortford ....3F 53
 nr. Braintree ....3A 54
 nr. Saffron Walden ....2F 53
Tyersal. *W Yor* ....1B 92
Ty Issa. *Powy* ....2D 70
**Tyldesley.** *G Man* ....4E 91
Tyler Hill. *Kent* ....4F 41
Tyler's Green. *Essx* ....5F 53
Tylers Green. *Buck* ....2G 37
Tylorstown. *Rhon* ....2D 32
Tylwch. *Powy* ....2B 58
Ty Mynd. *Carm* ....4F 45
Ty-nant. *Cnwy* ....1B 70
Tyndrum. *Stir* ....5H 141
Tyneham. *Dors* ....4D 15
Tynehead. *Midl* ....4G 129
**Tynemouth.** *Tyne* ....3G 115
**Tyneside.** *Tyne* ....3F 115
**Tyne Tunnel.** *Tyne* ....3G 115
Tynewydd. *Rhon* ....2C 32
Tyninghame. *E Lot* ....2C 130
Tynron. *Dum* ....5H 117
Ty'n-y-bryn. *Rhon* ....3D 32
Ty-n-y-celyn. *Wrex* ....2D 70
Ty-n-y-cwm. *Swan* ....5G 45
Ty-n-y-ffridd. *Powy* ....2D 70
Tynygongl. *IOA* ....2E 81
Tynygraig. *Cdgn* ....4F 57
Ty'n-y-groes. *Cnwy* ....3G 81
Ty'n-yr-eithin. *Cdgn* ....4F 57
Ty-n-y-rhyd. *Powy* ....4C 70
Ty-n-y-wern. *Powy* ....3C 70
Tyrie. *Abers* ....2G 161
Tyringham. *Mil* ....1G 51
Tythecott. *Devn* ....1E 11
Tythegston. *B'end* ....4B 32
Tytherington. *Ches E* ....3D 84
Tytherington. *Som* ....2C 22
Tytherington. *S Glo* ....3B 34
Tytherington. *Wilts* ....2E 23
Tytherleigh. *Devn* ....2G 13
Tywardreath. *Corn* ....3E 7
Tywardreath Highway. *Corn* ....3E 7
Tywyn. *Cnwy* ....3G 81
Tywyn. *Gwyn* ....5E 69

## U

Uachdar. *W Isl* ....3D 170
Uags. *High* ....5G 155
Ubbeston Green. *Suff* ....3F 67
Ubley. *Bath* ....1A 22
Uckerby. *N Yor* ....4F 105
**Uckfield.** *E Sus* ....3F 27
Uckinghall. *Worc* ....2D 48
Uckington. *Glos* ....3E 49
Uckington. *Shrp* ....5H 71

Uddington. *S Lan* ....3H 127
Uddington. *S Lan* ....1A 118
Udimore. *E Sus* ....4C 28
Udny Green. *Abers* ....1F 153
Udny Station. *Abers* ....1G 153
Udston. *S Lan* ....4H 127
Udstonhead. *S Lan* ....5A 128
Uffcott. *Wilts* ....4G 35
Uffcume. *Devn* ....1D 12
Uffington. *Linc* ....5H 75
Uffington. *Oxon* ....3B 36
Uffington. *Shrp* ....4H 71
Ufford. *Pet* ....5H 75
Ufford. *Suff* ....5E 67
Ufton. *Warw* ....4A 62
Ufton Nervet. *W Ber* ....5E 37
Ugadale. *Arg* ....3B 122
Ugborough. *Devn* ....3C 8
Ugford. *Wilts* ....3F 23
Uggeshall. *Suff* ....2G 67
Ugglebarnby. *N Yor* ....4F 107
Ugley. *Essx* ....3F 53
Ugley Green. *Essx* ....3F 53
Ugthorpe. *N Yor* ....3E 107
Uidh. *W Isl* ....9B 170
Uig. *Arg* ....3C 138
Uig. *High*
 nr. Balgown ....2C 154
 nr. Dunvegan ....3A 154
Uigshader. *High* ....4D 154
Uisken. *Arg* ....2A 132
Ulbster. *High* ....4F 169
Ulcat Row. *Cumb* ....2F 103
Ulceby. *Linc* ....3D 88
Ulceby. *N Lin* ....3E 94
Ulceby Skitter. *N Lin* ....3E 94
Ulcombe. *Kent* ....1C 28
Uldale. *Cumb* ....1D 102
Uley. *Glos* ....2C 34
Ulgham. *Nmbd* ....5G 121
Ullapool. *High* ....4F 163
Ullenhall. *Warw* ....4F 61
Ulleskelf. *N Yor* ....1F 93
Ullesthorpe. *Leics* ....2C 62
Ulley. *S Yor* ....2B 86
Ullingswick. *Here* ....5H 59
Ullinish. *High* ....5C 154
Ullock. *Cumb* ....2B 102
Ulpha. *Cumb* ....5C 102
Ulrome. *E Yor* ....4F 101
Ulsta. *Shet* ....3F 173
Ulting. *Essx* ....5B 54
Ulva House. *Arg* ....5F 139
**Ulverston.** *Cumb* ....2B 96
Ulwell. *Dors* ....4F 15
Umberleigh. *Devn* ....4G 19
Unapool. *High* ....5C 166
Underbarrow. *Cumb* ....5F 103
Undercliffe. *W Yor* ....1B 92
Underdale. *Shrp* ....4H 71
Underhoull. *Shet* ....1G 173
Underriver. *Kent* ....5G 39
Under Tofts. *S Yor* ....2H 85
Underton. *Shrp* ....1A 60
Underwood. *Newp* ....3G 33
Underwood. *Notts* ....5B 86
Underwood. *Plym* ....3B 8
Undley. *Suff* ....2F 65
Undy. *Mon* ....3H 33
Union Mills. *IOM* ....4C 108
Union Street. *E Sus* ....2B 28
Unstone. *Derbs* ....3A 86
Unstone Green. *Derbs* ....3A 86
Unthank. *Cumb*
 nr. Carlisle ....5E 113
 nr. Gamblesby ....5H 113
 nr. Penrith ....1F 103
Unthank End. *Cumb* ....1F 103
Upavon. *Wilts* ....1G 23
Up Cerne. *Dors* ....2B 14
Upchurch. *Kent* ....4C 40
Upcott. *Devn* ....2F 11
Upcott. *Here* ....5F 59
Upend. *Cambs* ....5F 65

Up Exe. *Devn* ....2C 12
Upgate. *Norf* ....4D 78
Upgate Street. *Norf* ....1C 66
Uphall. *Dors* ....2A 14
Uphall. *W Lot* ....2D 128
Uphall Station. *W Lot* ....2D 128
Upham. *Devn* ....2B 12
Upham. *Hants* ....4D 24
Uphampton. *Here* ....4F 59
Uphampton. *Worc* ....4C 60
Uphill. *N Som* ....1G 21
Up Holland. *Lanc* ....4D 90
Uplawmoor. *E Ren* ....4F 127
Upleadon. *Glos* ....3C 48
Upleatham. *Red C* ....3D 106
Uplees. *Kent* ....4D 40
Uploders. *Dors* ....3A 14
Uplowman. *Devn* ....1D 12
Uplyme. *Devn* ....3G 13
Up Marden. *W Sus* ....1F 17
**Upminster.** *G Lon* ....2G 39
Up Nately. *Hants* ....1E 25
Upottery. *Devn* ....2F 13
Uppat. *High* ....3F 165
Upper Affcot. *Shrp* ....2G 59
Upper Arley. *Worc* ....2B 60
Upper Armley. *W Yor* ....1C 92
Upper Arncott. *Oxon* ....4E 50
Upper Astrop. *Nptn* ....2D 50
Upper Badcall. *High* ....4B 166
Upper Bangor. *Gwyn* ....3E 81
Upper Basildon. *W Ber* ....4D 36
Upper Batley. *W Yor* ....2C 92
Upper Beeding. *W Sus* ....4C 26
Upper Benefield. *Nptn* ....2G 63
Upper Bentley. *Worc* ....4D 61
Upper Bighouse. *High* ....3A 168
Upper Boddam. *Abers* ....5D 160
Upper Boddington. *Nptn* ....5B 62
Upper Bogside. *Mor* ....3G 159
Upper Booth. *Derbs* ....2F 85
Upper Borth. *Cdgn* ....2F 57
Upper Boyndlie. *Abers* ....2G 161
Upper Brailes. *Warw* ....1B 50
Upper Breinton. *Here* ....1H 47
Upper Broughton. *Notts* ....3D 74
Upper Brynamman. *Carm* ....4H 45
Upper Bucklebury. *W Ber* ....5D 36
Upper Bullington. *Hants* ....2C 24
Upper Burgate. *Hants* ....1G 15
Upper Caldecote. *C Beds* ....1B 52
Upper Canterton. *Hants* ....1A 16
Upper Catesby. *Nptn* ....5C 62
Upper Chapel. *Powy* ....1D 46
Upper Cheddon. *Som* ....4F 21
Upper Chicksgrove. *Wilts* ....4E 23
Upper Church Village.
 *Rhon* ....3D 32
Upper Chute. *Wilts* ....1A 24
Upper Clatford. *Hants* ....2B 24
Upper Coberley. *Glos* ....4E 49
Upper Coedcae. *Torf* ....5F 47
Upper Cound. *Shrp* ....5H 71
Upper Cudworth. *S Yor* ....4D 93
Upper Cumberworth. *W Yor* ....4C 92
Upper Cuttlehill. *Abers* ....4B 160
Upper Cwmbran. *Torf* ....2F 33
Upper Dallachy. *Mor* ....2A 160
Upper Dean. *Bed* ....4H 63
Upper Denby. *W Yor* ....4C 92
Upper Derraid. *High* ....5E 159
Upper Diabaig. *High* ....2H 155
Upper Dicker. *E Sus* ....5G 27
Upper Dinchope. *Shrp* ....2G 59
Upper Dochcarty. *High* ....2H 157
Upper Dounreay. *High* ....2B 168
Upper Dovercourt. *Essx* ....2F 55
Upper Dunsforth. *N Yor* ....3G 99
Upper Dunsley. *Herts* ....4H 51
Upper Eastern Green. *W Mid* ....2G 61
Upper Elkstone. *Staf* ....5E 85
Upper Ellastone. *Staf* ....1F 73
Upper End. *Derbs* ....3E 85

Upper Enham. *Hants* ....2B 24
Upper Farmcote. *Shrp* ....1B 60
Upper Farringdon. *Hants* ....3F 25
Upper Framilode. *Glos* ....4C 48
Upper Froyle. *Hants* ....2F 25
Upper Gills. *High* ....1F 169
Upper Glenfintaig. *High* ....5E 149
Upper Godney. *Som* ....2H 21
Upper Gravenhurst. *C Beds* ....2B 52
Upper Green. *Essx* ....2E 53
Upper Green. *W Ber* ....5B 36
Upper Green. *W Yor* ....2C 92
Upper Grove Common.
 *Here* ....3A 48
Upper Hackney. *Derbs* ....4G 85
Upper Hale. *Surr* ....2G 25
Upper Halliford. *Surr* ....4B 38
Upper Halling. *Medw* ....4A 40
Upper Hambleton. *Rut* ....5G 75
Upper Hardres Court. *Kent* ....5F 41
Upper Hardwick. *Here* ....5G 59
Upper Hartfield. *E Sus* ....2F 27
Upper Haugh. *S Yor* ....1B 86
Upper Hayton. *Shrp* ....2H 59
Upper Heath. *Shrp* ....2H 59
Upper Hellesdon. *Norf* ....4E 78
Upper Helmsley. *N Yor* ....4A 100
Upper Hengoed. *Shrp* ....2E 71
Upper Hergest. *Here* ....5E 59
Upper Heyford. *Nptn* ....5D 62
Upper Heyford. *Oxon* ....3C 50
Upper Hill. *Here* ....5G 59
Upper Hindhope. *Bord* ....4B 120
Upper Hopton. *W Yor* ....3B 92
Upper Howsell. *Worc* ....1C 48
Upper Hulme. *Staf* ....4E 85
Upper Inglesham. *Swin* ....2H 35
Upper Kilcott. *S Glo* ....3C 34
Upper Killay. *Swan* ....3E 31
Upper Kirkton. *Abers* ....5E 161
Upper Kirkton. *N Ayr* ....4C 126
Upper Knockando. *Mor* ....4F 159
Upper Knockchoilum.
 *High* ....2G 149
Upper Lambourn. *W Ber* ....3B 36
Upper Langford. *N Som* ....1H 21
Upper Langwith. *Derbs* ....4C 86
Upper Largo. *Fife* ....3G 137
Upper Latheron. *High* ....5D 169
Upper Layham. *Suff* ....1D 54
Upper Leigh. *Staf* ....2E 73
Upper Lenie. *High* ....1H 149
Upper Lochton. *Abers* ....4D 152
Upper Longdon. *Staf* ....4E 73
Upper Longwood. *Shrp* ....5A 72
Upper Lybster. *High* ....5E 169
Upper Lydbrook. *Glos* ....4B 48
Upper Lye. *Here* ....4F 59
Upper Maes-coed. *Here* ....2G 47
Upper Midway. *Derbs* ....3G 73
Uppermill. *G Man* ....4H 91
Uppermillchope. *Shrp* ....2G 59
Upper Milovaig. *High* ....4A 154
Upper Minety. *Wilts* ....2F 35
Upper Mitton. *Worc* ....3C 60
Upper Nash. *Pemb* ....4E 43
Upper Neepaback. *Shet* ....3G 173
Upper Netchwood. *Shrp* ....1A 60
Upper Nobut. *Staf* ....2E 73
Upper North Dean. *Buck* ....2G 37
Upper Norwood. *W Sus* ....4A 26
Upper Nyland. *Dors* ....4C 22
Upper Oddington. *Glos* ....3H 49
Upper Ollach. *High* ....5E 155
Upper Outwoods. *Staf* ....3G 73
Upper Padley. *Derbs* ....3G 85
Upper Pennington. *Hants* ....3B 16
Upper Poppleton. *York* ....4H 99
Upper Quinton. *Warw* ....1G 49
Upper Rissington. *Glos* ....4H 49
Upper Rochford. *Worc* ....4A 60
Upper Rusko. *Dum* ....3C 110
Upper Sandaig. *High* ....2F 147
Upper Sanday. *Orkn* ....7E 172

Upper Sapey. Here ............4A **60**
Upper Seagry. Wilts ..........3E **35**
Upper Shelton. C Beds .......1H **51**
Upper Sheringham. Norf .....1D **78**
Upper Skelmorlie. N Ayr ....3C **126**
Upper Slaughter. Glos .......3G **49**
Upper Sonachan. Arg ........1H **133**
Upper Soudley. Glos ..........4B **48**
Upper Staploe. Bed ..........5A **64**
Upper Stoke. Norf ............5E **79**
Upper Stondon. C Beds ......2B **52**
Upper Stowe. Nptn ...........5D **62**
Upper Street. Hants ..........1G **15**
Upper Street. Norf
    nr. Horning .............4F **79**
    nr. Hoveton ............4F **79**
Upper Street. Suff ............2E **55**
Upper Strensham. Worc ......2E **49**
Upper Studley. Wilts .........1D **22**
Upper Swell. Glos ............3G **49**
Upper Tankersley. S Yor ....1H **85**
Upper Tean. Staf .............2E **73**
Upperthong. W Yor ..........4B **92**
Upperthorpe. N Lin ..........4A **94**
Upper Thurnham. Lanc ......4D **96**
Upper Tillyrie. Per ...........3D **136**
Upperton. W Sus ............3A **26**
Upper Tooting. G Lon .......3D **39**
Upper Town. Derbs
    nr. Bonsall ..............5G **85**
    nr. Hognaston ..........5G **85**
Upper Town. Here ...........1A **48**
Upper Town. N Som .........5A **34**
Uppertown. Derbs ...........4H **85**
Uppertown. High ...........1F **169**
Uppertown. Nmbd ..........2B **114**
Uppertown. Orkn ...........8D **172**
Upper Tysoe. Warw .........1B **50**
Upper Upham. Wilts ........4H **35**
Upper Upnor. Medw ........3B **40**
Upper Urquhart. Fife .......3D **136**
Upper Wardall. Mil .........2F **51**
Upper Wardington. Oxon ...1C **50**
Upper Weald. Mil ..........2F **51**
Upper Weedon. Nptn .......5D **62**
Upper Wellingham. E Sus ...4F **27**
Upper Whiston. S Yor ......2B **86**
Upper Wield. Hants ........3E **25**
Upper Winchendon. Buck ...4F **51**
Upperwood. Derbs ........5G **85**
Upper Woodford. Wilts ....3G **23**
Upper Wootton. Hants .....1D **24**
Upper Wraxall. Wilts ......4D **34**
Upper Wyche. Worc .......1C **48**
Uppincott. Devn ...........2B **12**
Uppingham. Rut ...........1F **63**
Uppington. Shrp ..........5A **72**
Upsall. N Yor .............1G **99**
Upsettlington. Bord .......5E **131**
Upshire. Essx .............5E **53**
Up Somborne. Hants ......3B **24**
Upstreet. Kent ............4G **41**
Up Sydling. Dors .........2B **14**
Upthorpe. Suff ............3B **66**
Upton. Buck ..............4F **51**
Upton. Cambs ............3A **64**
Upton. Ches W ...........4G **83**
Upton. Corn
    nr. Bude ..............2C **10**
    nr. Liskeard ..........5C **10**
Upton. Cumb .............1E **102**
Upton. Devn
    nr. Honiton ..........2D **12**
    nr. Kingsbridge ......4D **8**
Upton. Dors
    nr. Poole ............3E **15**
    nr. Weymouth ........4C **14**
Upton. E Yor ............4F **101**
Upton. Hants
    nr. Andover ..........1B **24**
    nr. Southampton .....1B **16**
Upton. IOW .............3D **16**
Upton. Leics ............2F **87**

Upton. Mers .............2E **83**
Upton. Norf .............4F **79**
Upton. Nptn .............4E **62**
Upton. Notts
    nr. Retford ...........3E **87**
    nr. Southwell .........5E **87**
Upton. Oxon .............3D **36**
Upton. Pemb ............4E **43**
Upton. Pet ..............5A **76**
Upton. Slo .............3A **38**
Upton. Som
    nr. Somerton .........4H **21**
    nr. Wiveliscombe .....4C **20**
Upton. W Yor ...........5F **61**
Upton. W Yor ...........3E **93**
Upton. Wilts ...........3D **22**
Upton Bishop. Here .....3B **48**
Upton Cheyney. S Glo ...5B **34**
Upton Cressett. Shrp ...1A **60**
Upton Crews. Here .....3B **48**
Upton Cross. Corn .....5C **10**
Upton End. C Beds .....2B **52**
Upton Grey. Hants .....2E **25**
Upton Heath. Ches W ...4G **83**
Upton Hellions. Devn ...2B **12**
Upton Lovell. Wilts ....2E **23**
Upton Magna. Shrp ....4H **71**
Upton Noble. Som .....3C **22**
Upton Pyne. Devn ......3C **12**
Upton St Leonards. Glos 4D **48**
Upton Scudamore. Wilts 2D **22**
Upton Snodsbury. Worc 5D **60**
Upton upon Severn. Worc 1D **48**
Upton Warren. Worc ...4D **60**
Upwaltham. W Sus .....4A **26**
Upware. Cambs .........3E **65**
Upwell. Norf ...........5E **77**
Upwey. Dors ...........4B **14**
Upwick Green. Herts ...3E **53**
Upwood. Cambs ........2B **64**
Urafirth. Shet ..........4E **173**
Uragaig. Arg ...........4A **132**
Urchany. High ..........4C **158**
Urchfont. Wilts ........1F **23**
Urdimarsh. Here .......1A **48**
Ure. Shet ..............4D **173**
Ure Bank. N Yor ......2F **99**
Urgha. W Isl ..........8D **171**
Urlay Nook. Stoc T ....3B **106**
Urmston. G Man .......1B **84**
Urquhart. Mor ........2G **159**
Urra. N Yor ...........4C **106**
Urray. High ...........3H **157**
Usan. Ang ............3G **145**
Usborough. Dur .......5F **115**
Usk. Mon .............5G **47**
Usselby. Linc ..........1H **87**
Usworth. Tyne ........4G **115**
Utkinton. Ches W ......4H **83**
Uton. Devn ...........3B **12**
Utterby. Linc ..........1C **88**
Uttoxeter. Staf ........2E **73**
Uwchmynydd. Gwyn ...3A **68**
Uyeasound. Shet ......1G **173**
Uzmaston. Pemb .......3D **42**

Velindre. Powy ........2E **47**
Vellow. Som ..........3D **20**
Velly. Devn ...........4C **18**
Veness. Orkn .........5E **172**
Venhay. Devn .........1A **12**
Venn. Devn ...........4D **8**
Vennington. Shrp .....5F **71**
Venn Ottery. Devn ....3D **12**
Venn's Green. Here ...1A **48**
Venny Tedburn. Devn ..3B **12**
Venterdon. Corn ......5D **10**
Ventnor. IOW ........5D **16**
Vernham Dean. Hants .1B **24**
Vernham Street. Hants .1B **24**
Vernolds Common. Shrp 2G **59**
Verwood. Dors .......2F **15**
Veryan. Corn .........5D **6**
Veryan Green. Corn ...5D **6**
Vicarage. Devn .......4F **13**
Vickerstown. Cumb ...3A **96**
Victoria. Corn ........2D **6**
Vidlin. Shet ..........5F **173**
Viewpark. N Lan .....3A **128**
Vigo. W Mid .........5E **73**
Vigo Village. Kent ....4H **39**
Vinehall Street. E Sus .3B **28**
Vine's Cross. E Sus ...4G **27**
Viney Hill. Glos ......5B **48**
Virginia Water. Surr ..4A **38**
Virginstow. Devn ......3D **11**
Vobster. Som .........2C **22**
Voe. Shet
    nr. Hillside .........5F **173**
    nr. Swinister .......3E **173**
Vole. Som ............2G **21**
Vowchurch. Here .....2G **47**
Voxter. Shet ..........4E **173**
Voy. Orkn ............6B **172**
Vulcan Village. Mers ..1H **83**

## W

Waberthwaite. Cumb ...5C **102**
Wackerfield. Dur .......2E **105**
Wacton. Norf ..........1D **66**
Wadbister. Shet ........7F **173**
Wadborough. Worc .....1E **49**
Wadbrook. Devn .......2G **13**
Waddesdon. Buck ......4F **51**
Waddeton. Devn .......3E **9**
Waddicar. Mers ........1F **83**
Waddingham. Linc .....1G **87**
Waddington. Lanc .....5G **97**
Waddington. Linc .....4G **87**
Waddon. Devn .........5B **12**
Wadebridge. Corn .....1D **6**
Wadeford. Som ........1G **13**
Wadenhoe. Nptn ......2H **63**
Wadesmill. Herts ......4D **52**
Wadhurst. E Sus ......2H **27**
Wadshelf. Derbs ......3H **85**
Wadsley. S Yor ........1H **85**
Wadsley Bridge. S Yor .1H **85**
Wadswick. Wilts .......5D **34**
Wadwick. Hants .......1C **24**
Wadworth. S Yor ......1C **86**
Waen. Den
    nr. Llandymog .....4D **82**
    nr. Nantglyn .......4B **82**
Waen. Powy ..........1B **58**
Waen Fach. Powy .....4E **70**
Waen Goleugoed. Den ..3C **82**
Wag. High ............1H **165**
Wainfleet All Saints. Linc 5D **89**
Wainfleet Bank. Linc ..5D **88**
Wainfleet St Mary. Linc 5D **89**
Wainhouse Corner. Corn 3B **10**
Wainscott. Medw ......3B **40**
Wainstalls. W Yor ......2A **92**
Waitby. Cumb .........4A **104**
Waithe. Linc ..........4F **95**
Wakefield. W Yor .....2D **92**

Wakerley. Nptn ........1G **63**
Wakes Colne. Essx .....3B **54**
Walberswick. Suff ......3G **67**
Walberton. W Sus ......5A **26**
Walbottle. Tyne ........3E **115**
Walby. Cumb ...........3F **113**
Walcombe. Som ........2A **22**
Walcot. Linc ...........2H **75**
Walcot. N Lin ..........2B **94**
Walcot. Swin ...........3G **35**
Walcot. Telf ...........4H **71**
Walcot. Warw ..........5F **61**
Walcote. Leics .........2C **62**
Walcot Green. Norf .....2D **66**
Walcott. Linc ..........5A **88**
Walcott. Norf ..........2F **79**
Walden. N Yor .........1C **98**
Walden Head. N Yor ...1B **98**
Walden Stubbs. N Yor ..3F **93**
Walderslade. Medw ....4B **40**
Walderton. W Sus .....1F **17**
Walditch. Dors ........3H **13**
Waldley. Derbs ........2F **73**
Waldridge. Dur ........4F **115**
Waldringfield. Suff .....1F **55**
Waldron. E Sus ........4G **27**
Wales. S Yor ..........2B **86**
Walesby. Linc .........1A **88**
Walesby. Notts ........3D **86**
Walford. Here
    nr. Leintwardine ...3F **59**
    nr. Ross-on-Wye ...3A **48**
Walford. Shrp .........3G **71**
Walford. Staf .........2C **72**
Walford Heath. Shrp ...4G **71**
Walgherton. Ches E ....1A **72**
Walgrave. Nptn ........3F **63**
Walhampton. Hants ....3B **16**
Walkden. G Man .......4F **91**
Walker. Tyne ..........3F **115**
Walkerburn. Bord ......1F **119**
Walker Fold. Lanc .....5F **97**
Walkeringham. Notts ..1E **87**
Walkerith. Linc ........1E **87**
Walkern. Herts ........3C **52**
Walker's Green. Here ..1A **48**
Walkerville. Fife ......3E **137**
Walkerville. N Yor .....5F **105**
Walkford. Dors ........3H **15**
Walkhampton. Devn ...2B **8**
Walkington. E Yor .....1C **94**
Walkley. S Yor ........2H **85**
Walk Mill. Lanc .......1G **91**
Wall. Corn ............3D **4**
Wall. Nmbd ...........3C **114**
Wall. Staf ............5F **73**
Wallaceton. Dum ......1F **111**
Wallacetown. Shet .....6E **173**
Wallacetown. S Ayr. Ayr 2C **116**
    nr. Dailly ...........4B **116**
Wallands Park. E Sus ..4F **27**
Wallasey. Mers ........1E **83**
Wallaston Green. Pemb 4D **42**
Wallbrook. W Mid .....1D **60**
Wallcrouch. E Sus .....2A **28**
Wall End. Cumb .......1B **96**
Wallend. Medw ........3C **40**
Wall Heath. W Mid .....2C **60**
Wallingford. Oxon .....3E **36**
Wallington. G Lon .....4D **39**
Wallington. Hants ......2D **16**
Wallington. Herts .....2C **52**
Wallis. Pemb ..........2E **43**
Wallisdown. Bour ......3F **15**
Walliswood. Surr ......2C **26**
Wall Nook. Dur .......5F **115**
Walls. Shet ...........7D **173**
Wallsend. Tyne ........3G **115**
Wallsworth. Glos ......3D **48**
Wall under Heywood. Shrp 1H **59**
Wallyford. E Lot ......2G **129**
Walmer. Kent .........5H **41**
Walmer Bridge. Lanc ..2C **90**
Walmersley. G Man ...3G **91**

Walmley. W Mid ......1F **61**
Walnut Grove. Per ....1D **136**
Walpole. Suff .........3F **67**
Walpole Cross Keys. Norf 4E **77**
Walpole Gate. Norf ...4E **77**
Walpole Highway. Norf 4E **77**
Walpole Marsh. Norf ..4D **77**
Walpole St Andrew. Norf 4E **77**
Walpole St Peter. Norf 4E **77**
Walsall. W Mid ........1E **61**
Walsall Wood. W Mid ..5E **73**
Walsden. W Yor .......2H **91**
Walsgrave on Sowe.
    W Mid .............2A **62**
Walsham le Willows. Suff 3C **66**
Walshaw. G Man ......3F **91**
Walshford. N Yor ......4G **99**
Walsoken. Norf ........4D **76**
Walston. S Lan ........5D **128**
Walsworth. Herts ......2B **52**
Walter's Ash. Buck ....2G **37**
Walterston. V Glam ....4D **32**
Walterstone. Here .....3G **47**
Waltham. Kent ........1F **29**
Waltham. NE Lin ......4F **95**
Waltham Abbey. Essx ..5D **53**
Waltham Chase. Hants .1D **16**
Waltham Cross. Herts ..5D **52**
Waltham on the Wolds. Leics 3F **75**
Waltham St Lawrence. Wind 4G **37**
Walthamstow. G Lon ..2E **39**
Walton. Cumb .........3G **113**
Walton. Derbs .........4A **86**
Walton. Leics .........2C **62**
Walton. Mers .........1F **83**
Walton. Mil ...........2G **51**
Walton. Pet ...........5A **76**
Walton. Powy .........5E **59**
Walton. Som ..........3H **21**
Walton. Staf
    nr. Eccleshall ......3C **72**
    nr. Stone ..........2C **72**
Walton. Suff .........2F **55**
Walton. Telf ..........4H **71**
Walton. Warw .........5G **61**
Walton. W Yor
    nr. Wakefield ......3D **92**
    nr. Wetherby ......5G **99**
Walton Cardiff. Glos ..2E **49**
Walton East. Pemb .....2E **43**
Walton Elm. Dors ......1C **14**
Walton Highway. Norf .4D **77**
Walton in Gordano. N Som 4H **33**
Walton-le-Dale. Lanc ..2D **90**
Walton-on-Thames. Surr 4C **38**
Walton on the Hill. Surr 5D **38**
Walton-on-the-Hill. Staf 3D **72**
Walton-on-the-Naze. Essx 3F **55**
Walton on the Wolds. Leics 4C **74**
Walton-on-Trent. Derbs 4G **73**
Walton West. Pemb ....3C **42**
Walwick. Nmbd .......2C **114**
Walworth. Darl .......3F **105**
Walworth Gate. Darl ...2F **105**
Walwyn's Castle. Pemb 3C **42**
Wambrook. Som ......2F **13**
Wampool. Cumb ......4D **112**
Wanborough. Surr .....1A **26**
Wanborough. Swin .....3H **35**
Wandel. S Lan .........2B **118**
Wandsworth. G Lon ...3D **38**
Wangford. Suff
    nr. Lakenheath .....2G **65**
    nr. Southwold .....3G **67**
Wanlip. Leics ..........4C **74**
Wanlockhead. Dum ....3A **118**
Wannock. E Sus .......5G **27**
Wansford. E Yor .......4E **101**
Wansford. Pet .........1H **63**
Wanshurst Green. Kent 1B **28**
Wanstead. G Lon .......2F **39**
Wanstrow. Som ........2C **22**
Wanswell. Glos ........5B **48**

Wantage. Oxon ...3C 36
Wapley. S Glo ...4C 34
Wappenbury. Warw ...4A 62
Wappenham. Nptn ...1E 51
Warbleton. E Sus ...4H 27
Warborough. Oxon ...2D 36
Warboys. Cambs ...2C 64
Warbreck. Bkpl ...1B 90
Warbstow. Corn ...3C 10
Warburton. G Man ...2B 84
Warcop. Cumb ...3A 104
Warden. Kent ...3E 40
Warden. Nmbd ...3C 114
Ward End. W Mid ...2F 61
Ward Green. Suff ...4C 66
Ward Green Cross. Lanc ...1E 91
Wardhedges. C Beds ...2A 52
Wardhouse. Abers ...5C 160
Wardington. Oxon ...1C 50
Wardle. Ches E ...5A 84
Wardle. G Man ...3H 91
Wardley. Rut ...5F 75
Wardley. W Sus ...4G 25
Wardlow. Derbs ...3F 85
Wardsend. Ches E ...2D 84
Wardy Hill. Cambs ...2D 64
Ware. Herts ...4D 52
Ware. Kent ...4G 41
Wareham. Dors ...4E 15
Warehorne. Kent ...2D 28
Warenford. Nmbd ...2F 121
Waren Mill. Nmbd ...1F 121
Warenton. Nmbd ...1F 121
Wareside. Herts ...4D 53
Waresley. Cambs ...5B 64
Waresley. Worc ...4C 60
Warfield. Brac ...4G 37
Warfleet. Devn ...3E 9
Wargate. Linc ...2B 76
Wargrave. Wok ...4F 37
Warham. Norf ...1B 78
Waringstown. Arm ...5G 175
Wark. Nmbd
  nr. Coldstream ...1C 120
  nr. Hexham ...2B 114
Warkleigh. Devn ...4G 19
Warkton. Nptn ...3F 63
Warkworth. Nmbd ...1C 50
Warlaby. N Yor ...5A 106
Warland. W Yor ...2H 91
Warleggan. Corn ...2F 7
Warlingham. Surr ...5E 39
Warmanbie. Dum ...3C 112
Warmfield. W Yor ...2D 93
Warmingham. Ches E ...4B 84
Warminghurst. W Sus ...4C 26
Warmington. Nptn ...1H 63
Warmington. Warw ...1C 50
Warminster. Wilts ...2D 23
Warmley. S Glo ...4B 34
Warmsworth. S Yor ...4F 93
Warmwell. Dors ...4C 14
Warndon. Worc ...5C 60
Warners End. Herts ...5A 52
Warnford. Hants ...4E 24
Warnham. W Sus ...2C 26
Warningcamp. W Sus ...5B 26
Warninglid. W Sus ...3D 26
Warren. Ches E ...3C 84
Warren. Pemb ...5D 42
Warrenby. Red C ...2C 106
Warren Corner. Hants
  nr. Aldershot ...2G 25
  nr. Petersfield ...4F 25
Warrenpoint. New M ...6G 175
Warren Row. Wind ...3G 37
Warren Street. Kent ...5D 40
Warrington. Mil ...5F 63
Warrington. Warr ...2A 84
Warsash. Hants ...2C 16
Warse. High ...1F 169
Warslow. Staf ...5E 85

Warsop. Notts ...4C 86
Warsop Vale. Notts ...4C 86
Warter. E Yor ...4C 100
Warthermarske. N Yor ...2E 98
Warthill. N Yor ...4A 100
Wartling. E Sus ...5A 28
Wartnaby. Leics ...3E 74
Warton. Lanc
  nr. Carnforth ...2D 97
  nr. Freckleton ...2C 90
Warton. Nmbd ...4E 121
Warton. Warw ...5G 73
Warwick. Warw ...4G 61
Warwick Bridge. Cumb ...4F 113
Warwick-on-Eden. Cumb ...4F 113
Warwick Wold. Surr ...5E 39
Wasbister. Orkn ...4C 172
Wasdale Head. Cumb ...4C 102
Wash. Derbs ...2E 85
Washaway. Corn ...2E 7
Washbourne. Devn ...3D 9
Washbrook. Suff ...1E 54
Wash Common. W Ber ...5C 36
Washerwall. Staf ...1D 72
Washfield. Devn ...1C 12
Washford. N Yor ...4D 104
Washford Pyne. Devn ...1B 12
Washingborough. Linc ...3H 87
Washington. Tyne ...4G 115
Washington. W Sus ...4C 26
Washington Village. Tyne ...4G 115
Waskerley. Dur ...5D 114
Wasperton. Warw ...5G 61
Wasp Green. Surr ...1E 27
Wasps Nest. Linc ...4H 87
Wass. N Yor ...2H 99
Watchet. Som ...2D 20
Watchfield. Oxon ...2H 35
Watchgate. Cumb ...5G 103
Watchhill. Cumb ...5C 112
Watcombe. Torb ...2F 9
Watendlath. Cumb ...3D 102
Water. Devn ...4A 12
Water. Lanc ...2G 91
Waterbeach. Cambs ...4D 65
Waterbeach. W Sus ...2G 17
Waterbeck. Dum ...2D 112
Waterditch. Hants ...3G 15
Water End. C Beds ...2A 52
Water End. E Yor ...1A 94
Water End. Essx ...1F 53
Water End. Herts
  nr. Hatfield ...5C 52
  nr. Hemel Hempstead ...4A 52
Waterfall. Staf ...5E 85
Waterfoot. E Ren ...4G 127
Waterfoot. Lanc ...2G 91
Waterford. Herts ...4D 52
Water Fryston. W Yor ...2E 93
Waterhead. Cumb ...4E 103
Waterhead. E Ayr ...3E 117
Waterhead. S Ayr ...5C 116
Waterheads. Bord ...4F 129
Waterhouses. Dur ...5E 115
Waterhouses. Staf ...5E 85
Wateringbury. Kent ...5A 40
Waterlane. Glos ...5E 49
Waterlip. Som ...2B 22
Waterloo. Cphy ...3E 33
Waterloo. Corn ...5B 10
Waterloo. Here ...1G 47
Waterloo. High ...1E 147
Waterloo. Mers ...1F 83
Waterloo. Norf ...4E 78
Waterloo. N Lan ...4B 128
Waterloo. Pemb ...4D 42
Waterloo. Per ...5H 143
Waterloo. Pool ...3F 15
Waterloo. Shrp ...2G 71
Waterlooville. Hants ...2E 17
Watermead. Buck ...4G 51
Watermillock. Cumb ...2F 103
Water Newton. Cambs ...1A 64

Water Orton. Warw ...1F 61
Waterperry. Oxon ...5E 51
Waterrow. Som ...4D 20
Watersfield. W Sus ...4B 26
Waterside. Buck ...5H 51
Waterside. Cambs ...3F 65
Waterside. Cumb ...5D 112
Waterside. E Aymr. Ayr ...4D 116
  nr. Kilmarnock ...5F 127
Waterside. E Dun ...2H 127
Waterstein. High ...4A 154
Waterstock. Oxon ...5E 51
Waterston. Pemb ...4D 42
Water Stratford. Buck ...2E 51
Water Yeat. Cumb ...1B 96
Watford. Herts ...1C 38
Watford. Nptn ...4D 62
Wath. Cumb ...4H 103
Wath. N Yor
  nr. Pateley Bridge ...3D 98
  nr. Ripon ...2F 99
Wath Brow. Cumb ...3B 102
Wath upon Dearne. S Yor ...4E 93
Watlington. Norf ...4F 77
Watlington. Oxon ...2E 37
Watten. High ...3E 169
Wattisfield. Suff ...3C 66
Wattisham. Suff ...5C 66
Wattlesborough Heath. Shrp ...4F 71
Watton. Dors ...3H 13
Watton. E Yor ...4E 101
Watton. Norf ...5B 78
Watton at Stone. Herts ...4C 52
Wattston. N Lan ...2A 128
Wattstown. Rhon ...2D 32
Wattsville. Cphy ...2F 33
Wauldby. E Yor ...2C 94
Waulkmill. Abers ...4D 152
Waun. Powy ...4E 71
Y Waun. Wrex ...2E 71
Waunarlwydd. Swan ...3F 31
Waun Fawr. Cdgn ...2F 57
Waunfawr. Gwyn ...5E 81
Waungilwen. Carm ...1H 43
Waun-Lwyd. Blae ...5E 47
Waun y Clyn. Carm ...5E 45
Wavendon. Mil ...2H 51
Waverbridge. Cumb ...5D 112
Waverley. Surr ...2G 25
Waverton. Ches W ...4G 83
Waverton. Cumb ...5D 112
Wavertree. Mers ...2F 83
Wawne. E Yor ...1D 94
Waxham. Norf ...3G 79
Waxholme. E Yor ...2G 95
Wayford. Som ...2H 13
Way Head. Cambs ...2D 65
Waytown. Dors ...3H 13
Way Village. Devn ...1B 12
Wdig. Pemb ...1D 42
Wealdstone. G Lon ...2C 38
Weardley. W Yor ...5E 99
Weare. Som ...1H 21
Weare Giffard. Devn ...4E 19
Wearhead. Dur ...1B 104
Wearne. Som ...4H 21
Weasdale. Cumb ...4H 103
Weasenham All Saints.
  Norf ...3H 77
Weasenham St Peter. Norf ...3A 78
Weaste. Ches W ...3A 84
Weaverthorpe. N Yor ...2D 100
Webheath. Worc ...4E 61
Webton. Here ...2H 47
Wedderlairs. Abers ...5F 161
Weddington. Warw ...1A 62
Wedhampton. Wilts ...1F 23
Wedmore. Som ...2H 21
Wednesbury. W Mid ...1D 61
Wednesfield. W Mid ...5D 72
Weecar. Notts ...4F 87
Weedon. Buck ...4G 51
Weedon Bec. Nptn ...5D 62

Weedon Lois. Nptn ...1E 50
Weeford. Staf ...5F 73
Week. Devn
  nr. Barnstaple ...4F 19
  nr. Okehampton ...2G 11
  nr. South Molton ...1H 11
  nr. Totnes ...2D 9
Week. Som ...3C 20
Weeke. Devn ...2A 12
Weeke. Hants ...3C 24
Week Green. Corn ...3C 10
Weekley. Nptn ...2F 63
Week St Mary. Corn ...3C 10
Weel. E Yor ...1D 94
Weeley. Essx ...3E 55
Weeley Heath. Essx ...3E 55
Weem. Per ...4F 143
Weeping Cross. Staf ...3D 72
Weethly. Warw ...5E 61
Weeting. Norf ...2G 65
Weeton. E Yor ...2G 95
Weeton. Lanc ...1B 90
Weeton. N Yor ...5E 99
Weetwood Hall. Nmbd ...2E 121
Weir. Lanc ...2G 91
Welborne. Norf ...4C 78
Welbourn. Linc ...5G 87
Welburn. N Yor
  nr. Kirkbymoorside ...1A 100
  nr. Malton ...3B 100
Welbury. N Yor ...4A 106
Welby. Linc ...2G 75
Welches Dam. Cambs ...2D 64
Welcombe. Devn ...1C 10
Weld Bank. Lanc ...3D 90
Weldon. Nptn ...2G 63
Weldon. Nmbd ...5F 121
Welford. Nptn ...2D 62
Welford. W Ber ...4C 36
Welford-on-Avon. Warw ...5F 61
Welham. Leics ...1E 63
Welham. Notts ...2E 87
Welham Green. Herts ...5C 52
Well. Hants ...2F 25
Well. Linc ...3D 88
Well. N Yor ...1E 99
Welland. Worc ...1C 48
Wellbank. Ang ...5D 144
Well Bottom. Dors ...1E 15
Welldale. Dum ...3C 112
Wellesbourne. Warw ...5G 61
Well Hill. Kent ...4F 39
Wellhouse. W Ber ...4D 36
Welling. G Lon ...3F 39
Wellingborough. Nptn ...4F 63
Wellingham. Norf ...3A 78
Wellingore. Linc ...5G 87
Wellington. Cumb ...4B 102
Wellington. Here ...1H 47
Wellington. Som ...4E 21
Wellington. Telf ...4A 72
Wellington Heath. Here ...1C 48
Wellow. Bath ...1C 22
Wellow. IOW ...4B 16
Wellow. Notts ...4D 86
Wellpond Green. Herts ...3E 53
Wells. Som ...2A 22
Wellsborough. Leics ...5A 74
Wells Green. Ches E ...5A 84
Wells-next-the-Sea. Norf ...1B 78
Wellswood. Torb ...2F 9
Wellwood. Fife ...1D 129
Welney. Norf ...1E 65
Welsford. Devn ...4C 18
Welshampton. Shrp ...2G 71
Welsh End. Shrp ...2H 71
Welsh Frankton. Shrp ...2F 71
Welsh Hook. Pemb ...2D 42
Welsh Newton. Here ...4H 47
Welsh Newton Common.
  Here ...4A 48
Welshpool. Powy ...5E 70
Welsh St Donats. V Glam ...4D 32
Welton. Bath ...1B 22

Welton. Cumb ...5E 113
Welton. E Yor ...2C 94
Welton. Linc ...2H 87
Welton. Nptn ...4C 62
Welton Hill. Linc ...2H 87
Welton le Marsh. Linc ...4D 88
Welton le Wold. Linc ...2B 88
Welwick. E Yor ...2G 95
Welwyn. Herts ...4C 52
Welwyn Garden City. Herts ...4C 52
Wem. Shrp ...3H 71
Wembdon. Som ...3F 21
Wembley. G Lon ...2C 38
Wembury. Devn ...4B 8
Wembworthy. Devn ...2G 11
Wenallt. Cdgn ...3F 57
Wenallt. Gwyn ...1B 70
Wendens Ambo. Essx ...2F 53
Wendlebury. Oxon ...4D 50
Wendling. Norf ...4B 78
Wendover. Buck ...5G 51
Wendron. Corn ...5A 6
Wendy. Cambs ...1D 52
Wenfordbridge. Corn ...5A 10
Wenhaston. Suff ...3G 67
Wennington. Cambs ...3B 64
Wennington. G Lon ...2G 39
Wennington. Lanc ...2F 97
Wensley. Derbs ...4G 85
Wensley. N Yor ...1C 98
Wentbridge. W Yor ...3E 93
Wentnor. Shrp ...1F 59
Wentworth. Cambs ...3D 65
Wentworth. S Yor ...1A 86
Wenvoe. V Glam ...4E 32
Weobley. Here ...5G 59
Weobley Marsh. Here ...5G 59
Wepham. W Sus ...5B 26
Wereham. Norf ...5F 77
Wergs. W Mid ...5C 72
Wern. Gwyn ...1E 69
Wern. Powy
  nr. Brecon ...4E 46
  nr. Guilsfield ...4E 71
  nr. Llangadfan ...4B 70
  nr. Llanymynech ...3E 71
Wernffrwd. Swan ...3E 31
Wernyrheolydd. Mon ...4G 47
Werrington. Corn ...4D 10
Werrington. Pet ...5A 76
Werrington. Staf ...1D 72
Wervin. Ches W ...3G 83
Wesham. Lanc ...1C 90
Wessington. Derbs ...5A 86
West Aberthaw. V Glam ...5D 32
West Acre. Norf ...4G 77
West Allerdean. Nmbd ...5F 131
West Alvington. Devn ...4D 8
West Amesbury. Wilts ...2G 23
West Anstey. Devn ...4B 20
West Appleton. N Yor ...5F 105
West Ardsley. W Yor ...2C 92
West Arthurlie. E Ren ...4F 127
West Ashby. Linc ...3B 88
West Ashling. W Sus ...2G 17
West Ashton. Wilts ...1D 23
West Auckland. Dur ...2E 105
West Ayton. N Yor ...1D 101
West Bagborough. Som ...3E 21
West Bank. Hal ...2H 83
West Barkwith. Linc ...2A 88
West Barnby. N Yor ...3F 107
West Barns. E Lot ...2C 130
West Barsham. Norf ...2B 78
West Bay. Dors ...3H 13
West Beckham. Norf ...2D 78
West Bennan. N Ayr ...3D 123
West Bergholt. Essx ...3C 54
West Bexington. Dors ...4A 14
West Bilney. Norf ...4G 77
West Blackdene. Dur ...1B 104
West Blatchington. Brig ...5D 27

## Westborough—West Town

Westborough. *Linc* 1F **75**
Westbourne. *Bour* 3F **15**
Westbourne. *W Sus* 2F **17**
West Bowling. *W Yor* 1B **92**
West Brabourne. *Kent* 1E **29**
West Bradford. *Lanc* 5G **97**
West Bradley. *Som* 3A **22**
West Bretton. *W Yor* 3C **92**
**West Bridgford**. *Notts* 2C **74**
West Briggs. *Norf* 4F **77**
**West Bromwich**. *W Mid* 1E **61**
Westbrook. *Here* 1F **47**
Westbrook. *Kent* 3H **41**
Westbrook. *Wilts* 5E **35**
West Buckland. *Devn*
 nr. Barnstaple 3G **19**
 nr. Thurlestone 4C **8**
West Buckland. *Som* 4E **21**
West Burnside. *Abers* 1G **145**
West Burrafirth. *Shet* 6D **173**
West Burton. *N Yor* 1C **98**
West Burton. *W Sus* 4B **26**
Westbury. *Buck* 2E **50**
Westbury. *Shrp* 5F **71**
**Westbury**. *Wilts* 1D **22**
Westbury Leigh. *Wilts* 1D **22**
Westbury-on-Severn. *Glos* 4C **48**
Westbury on Trym. *Bris* 4A **34**
Westbury-sub-Mendip. *Som* 2A **22**
West Butsfield. *Dur* 5E **115**
West Butterwick. *N Lin* 4B **94**
Westby. *Linc* 3G **75**
West Byfleet. *Surr* 4B **38**
West Caister. *Norf* 4H **79**
West Calder. *W Lot* 3D **128**
West Camel. *Som* 4A **22**
West Carr. *N Lin* 4H **93**
West Chaldon. *Dors* 4C **14**
West Challow. *Oxon* 3B **36**
West Charleton. *Devn* 4D **8**
West Chelborough. *Dors* 2A **14**
West Chevington. *Nmbd* 5G **121**
West Chiltington. *W Sus* 4B **26**
West Chiltington Common.
 *W Sus* 4B **26**
West Chinnock. *Som* 1H **13**
West Chisenbury. *Wilts* 1G **23**
West Clandon. *Surr* 5B **38**
West Cliffe. *Kent* 1H **29**
Westcliff-on-Sea. *S'end* 2C **40**
West Clyne. *High* 3F **165**
West Coker. *Som* 1A **14**
Westcombe. *Som*
 nr. Evercreech 3B **22**
 nr. Somerton 4H **21**
West Compton. *Dors* 3A **14**
West Compton. *Som* 2A **22**
West Cornforth. *Dur* 1A **106**
Westcot. *Oxon* 3B **36**
Westcott. *Buck* 4F **51**
Westcott. *Devn* 2D **12**
Westcott. *Surr* 1C **26**
Westcott Barton. *Oxon* 3C **50**
West Cowick. *E Yor* 2G **93**
West Cranmore. *Som* 2B **22**
West Croftmore. *High* 2D **150**
West Cross. *Swan* 4F **31**
West Cullerlie. *Abers* 3E **153**
West Culvennan. *Dum* 3H **109**
West Curry. *Corn* 3C **10**
West Curthwaite. *Cumb* 5E **113**
West Dean. *W Sus* 1G **17**
West Dean. *Wilts* 4A **24**
Westdean. *E Sus* 5G **27**
West Deeping. *Linc* 5A **76**
West Derby. *Mers* 1F **83**
West Dereham. *Norf* 5F **77**
West Down. *Devn* 2F **19**
Westdowns. *Corn* 4A **10**
**West Drayton**. *G Lon* 3B **38**
West Drayton. *Notts* 3E **86**
West Dunnet. *High* 1E **169**
West Ella. *E Yor* 2D **94**
West End. *Bed* 5G **63**
West End. *Cambs* 1D **64**
West End. *Dors* 2E **15**
West End. *E Yor*
 nr. Kilham 3E **101**
 nr. Preston 1E **95**
 nr. South Cove 1C **94**
 nr. Ulrome 4F **101**
**West End**. *G Lon* 2D **39**
West End. *Hants* 1C **16**
West End. *Herts* 5C **52**
West End. *Kent* 4F **41**
West End. *Lanc* 3D **96**
West End. *Linc* 1C **76**
West End. *Norf* 4H **79**
West End. *N Som* 5H **33**
West End. *N Yor* 4D **98**
West End. *S Glo* 3C **34**
West End. *S Lan* 5C **128**
West End. *Surr* 4A **38**
West End. *Wilts* 4E **23**
West End. *Wind* 4G **37**
West End Green. *Hants* 5E **37**
Westenhanger. *Kent* 2F **29**
Wester Aberchalder. *High* 2H **149**
Wester Balgedie. *Per* 3D **136**
Wester Brae. *High* 2A **158**
Wester Culbeuchly. *Abers* 2D **160**
Westerdale. *High* 3D **168**
Westerdale. *N Yor* 4D **106**
Wester Dechmont. *W Lot* 2D **128**
Wester Fearn. *High* 5D **164**
Westerfield. *Suff* 1E **55**
Wester Galcantray. *High* 4C **158**
Westergate. *W Sus* 5A **26**
Wester Gruinards. *High* 4C **164**
Westerham. *Kent* 5F **39**
Westerleigh. *S Glo* 4C **34**
Westerloch. *High* 3F **169**
Wester Mandally. *High* 3E **149**
Wester Quarff. *Shet* 8F **173**
Wester Rarichie. *High* 1C **158**
Wester Shian. *Per* 5F **143**
Wester Skeld. *Shet* 7D **173**
Westerton. *Ang* 3F **145**
Westerton. *Dur* 1F **105**
Westerton. *W Sus* 2G **17**
Westerwick. *Shet* 7D **173**
West Farleigh. *Kent* 5B **40**
West Farndon. *Nptn* 5C **62**
West Felton. *Shrp* 3F **71**
Westfield. *Cumb* 2A **102**
Westfield. *E Sus* 4C **28**
Westfield. *High* 2C **168**
Westfield. *Norf* 5B **78**
Westfield. *N Lan* 2A **128**
Westfield. *W Lot* 2C **128**
Westfields. *Dors* 2C **14**
Westfields of Rattray. *Per* 4A **144**
West Fleetham. *Nmbd* 2F **121**
Westford. *Som* 4E **20**
West Garforth. *W Yor* 1D **93**
Westgate. *Dur* 1C **104**
Westgate. *Norf* 1B **78**
Westgate. *N Lin* 4A **94**
Westgate on Sea. *Kent* 3H **41**
West Ginge. *Oxon* 3C **36**
West Grafton. *Wilts* 5H **35**
West Green. *Hants* 1F **25**
West Grimstead. *Wilts* 4H **23**
West Grinstead. *W Sus* 3C **26**
West Haddlesey. *N Yor* 2F **93**
West Haddon. *Nptn* 3D **62**
West Hagbourne. *Oxon* 3D **36**
West Hagley. *Worc* 2D **60**
West Hall. *Cumb* 3G **113**
Westhall. *Suff* 2G **67**
West Hallam. *Derbs* 1B **74**
Westhall Terrace. *Ang* 5D **144**
West Halton. *N Lin* 2C **94**
**West Ham**. *G Lon* 2E **39**
Westham. *Dors* 5B **14**
Westham. *E Sus* 5H **27**
Westham. *Som* 2H **21**
Westhampnett. *W Sus* 2G **17**
West Handley. *Derbs* 3A **86**
West Hanney. *Oxon* 2C **36**
West Hanningfield. *Essx* 1B **40**
West Hardwick. *W Yor* 3E **93**
West Harptree. *Bath* 1A **22**
West Harting. *W Sus* 4F **25**
West Harton. *Tyne* 3G **115**
West Hatch. *Som* 4F **21**
Westhay. *Som* 2H **21**
West Head. *Norf* 5E **77**
Westhead. *Lanc* 4C **90**
West Heath. *Hants*
 nr. Basingstoke 1D **24**
 nr. Farnborough 1G **25**
West Helmsdale. *High* 2H **165**
West Hendred. *Oxon* 3C **36**
West Heogaland. *Shet* 4D **173**
West Heslerton. *N Yor* 2D **100**
West Hewish. *N Som* 5G **33**
Westhide. *Here* 1A **48**
West Hill. *Devn* 3D **12**
West Hill. *E Yor* 3F **101**
West Hill. *N Som* 4H **33**
West Hill. *W Sus* 2E **27**
Westhill. *Abers* 3F **153**
Westhill. *High* 4B **158**
West Hoathly. *W Sus* 2E **27**
West Holme. *Dors* 4D **15**
Westhope. *Here* 5G **59**
Westhope. *Shrp* 2G **59**
West Horndon. *Essx* 2H **39**
Westhorp. *Nptn* 5C **62**
Westhorpe. *Linc* 2B **76**
Westhorpe. *Suff* 4C **66**
West Horrington. *Som* 2A **22**
West Horsley. *Surr* 5B **38**
West Horton. *Nmbd* 1E **121**
West Hougham. *Kent* 1G **29**
**Westhoughton**. *G Man* 4E **91**
West Houlland. *Shet* 6D **173**
Westhouse. *N Yor* 2F **97**
Westhouses. *Derbs* 5B **86**
West Howe. *Bour* 3F **15**
Westhumble. *Surr* 5C **38**
West Huntspill. *Som* 2G **21**
West Hyde. *Herts* 1B **38**
West Hynish. *Arg* 5A **138**
West Hythe. *Kent* 2F **29**
West Ilsley. *W Ber* 3C **36**
Westing. *Shet* 1G **173**
West Keal. *Linc* 4C **88**
West Kennett. *Wilts* 5G **35**
West Kilbride. *N Ayr* 5D **126**
West Kingsdown. *Kent* 4G **39**
West Kington. *Wilts* 4D **34**
**West Kirby**. *Mers* 2E **82**
West Knapton. *N Yor* 2C **100**
West Knighton. *Dors* 4C **14**
West Knoyle. *Wilts* 3D **22**
West Kyloe. *Nmbd* 5G **131**
Westlake. *Devn* 3C **8**
West Lambrook. *Som* 1H **13**
West Langdon. *Kent* 1H **29**
West Langwell. *High* 3D **164**
West Lavington. *W Sus* 4G **25**
West Lavington. *Wilts* 1F **23**
West Layton. *N Yor* 4E **105**
West Leake. *Notts* 3C **74**
West Learmouth. *Nmbd* 1C **120**
West Leigh. *Devn* 2G **11**
Westleigh. *Devn*
 nr. Bideford 4E **19**
 nr. Tiverton 1D **12**
Westleigh. *G Man* 4E **91**
West Leith. *Herts* 4H **51**
Westleton. *Suff* 4G **67**
West Lexham. *Norf* 4H **77**
Westley. *Shrp* 5F **71**
Westley. *Suff* 4H **65**
Westley Waterless. *Cambs* 5F **65**
West Lilling. *N Yor* 3A **100**
West Lingo. *Fife* 3G **137**
Westlington. *Buck* 4F **51**
West Linton. *Bord* 4E **129**
Westlinton. *Cumb* 3E **113**
West Littleton. *S Glo* 4C **34**
West Looe. *Corn* 3G **7**
West Lulworth. *Dors* 4D **14**
West Lutton. *N Yor* 3D **100**
West Lydford. *Som* 3A **22**
West Lyng. *Som* 4G **21**
West Lynn. *Norf* 4F **77**
West Mains. *Per* 2B **136**
West Malling. *Kent* 5A **40**
West Malvern. *Worc* 1C **48**
Westmancote. *Worc* 2E **49**
West Marden. *W Sus* 1F **17**
West Markham. *Notts* 3E **86**
West Marsh. *NE Lin* 4F **95**
Westmarsh. *Kent* 4G **41**
West Marton. *N Yor* 4A **98**
West Meon. *Hants* 4E **25**
West Mersea. *Essx* 4D **54**
Westmeston. *E Sus* 4E **27**
Westmill. *Herts*
 nr. Buntingford 3D **52**
 nr. Hitchin 2B **52**
West Milton. *Dors* 3A **14**
**Westminster**. *G Lon* 3D **39**
West Molesey. *Surr* 4C **38**
West Monkton. *Som* 4F **21**
Westmoor End. *Cumb* 1B **102**
West Moors. *Dors* 2F **15**
West Morden. *Dors* 3E **15**
West Muir. *Ang* 2E **145**
Westmuir. *Ang* 3C **144**
West Murkle. *High* 2D **168**
West Ness. *N Yor* 2A **100**
Westness. *Orkn* 5C **172**
West Newton. *E Yor* 1E **95**
West Newton. *Norf* 3F **77**
West Newton. *Som* 4F **21**
Westnewton. *Cumb* 5C **112**
Westnewton. *Nmbd* 1D **120**
West Norwood. *G Lon* 3E **39**
Westoe. *Tyne* 3G **115**
West Ogwell. *Devn* 2E **9**
Weston. *Bath* 5C **34**
Weston. *Ches E*
 nr. Crewe 5B **84**
 nr. Macclesfield 3C **84**
Weston. *Devn*
 nr. Honiton 2E **13**
 nr. Sidmouth 4E **13**
Weston. *Dors*
 nr. Weymouth 5B **14**
 nr. Yeovil 2A **14**
Weston. *Hal* 2H **83**
Weston. *Hants* 4F **25**
Weston. *Here* 5F **59**
Weston. *Herts* 2C **52**
Weston. *Linc* 3B **76**
Weston. *Nptn* 1D **50**
Weston. *Notts* 4E **87**
Weston. *Shrp*
 nr. Bridgnorth 1H **59**
 nr. Knighton 3F **59**
 nr. Wem 3H **71**
Weston. *S Lan* 5D **128**
Weston. *Staf* 3D **73**
Weston. *Suff* 2G **67**
Weston. *W Ber* 4B **36**
Weston Bampfylde. *Som* 4B **22**
Weston Beggard. *Here* 1A **48**
Westonbirt. *Glos* 3D **34**
Weston by Welland. *Nptn* 1E **63**
Weston Colville. *Cambs* 5F **65**
Westoncommon. *Shrp* 3G **71**
Weston Coyney. *Stoke* 1D **72**
Weston Ditch. *Suff* 3F **65**
Weston Favell. *Nptn* 4E **63**
Weston Green. *Cambs* 5F **65**
Weston Green. *Norf* 4D **78**
Weston Heath. *Shrp* 4B **72**
Weston Hills. *Linc* 4B **76**
Weston in Arden. *Warw* 2A **62**
Westoning. *C Beds* 2A **52**
Weston in Gordano. *N Som* 4H **33**
Weston Jones. *Staf* 3B **72**
Weston Longville. *Norf* 4D **78**
Weston Lullingfields. *Shrp* 3G **71**
Weston-on-Avon. *Warw* 5F **61**
Weston-on-the-Green. *Oxon* 4D **50**
Weston-on-Trent. *Derbs* 3B **74**
Weston Patrick. *Hants* 2E **25**
Weston Rhyn. *Shrp* 2E **71**
Weston-sub-Edge. *Glos* 1G **49**
**Weston-super-Mare**.
 *N Som* 5G **33**
Weston Town. *Som* 2C **22**
Weston Turville. *Buck* 4G **51**
Weston under Lizard. *Staf* 4C **72**
Weston under Penyard. *Here* 3B **48**
Weston under Wetherley.
 *Warw* 4A **62**
Weston Underwood. *Derbs* 1G **73**
Weston Underwood. *Mil* 5F **63**
Westonzoyland. *Som* 3G **21**
West Orchard. *Dors* 1D **14**
West Overton. *Wilts* 5G **35**
Westow. *N Yor* 3B **100**
Westown. *Per* 1E **137**
West Panson. *Devn* 3D **10**
West Park. *Hart* 1B **106**
West Parley. *Dors* 3F **15**
West Peckham. *Kent* 5H **39**
West Pelton. *Dur* 4F **115**
West Pennard. *Som* 3A **22**
West Pentire. *Corn* 2B **6**
West Perry. *Cambs* 4A **64**
West Pitcorthie. *Fife* 3H **137**
West Plean. *Stir* 1B **128**
West Poringland. *Norf* 5E **79**
West Porlock. *Som* 2B **20**
Westport. *Som* 1G **13**
West Putford. *Devn* 1D **10**
West Quantoxhead. *Som* 2E **20**
Westra. *V Glam* 4E **33**
West Rainton. *Dur* 5G **115**
West Rasen. *Linc* 2H **87**
West Ravendale. *NE Lin* 1B **88**
Westray Airport. *Orkn* 2D **172**
West Raynham. *Norf* 3A **78**
Westrigg. *W Lot* 3C **128**
West Rounton. *N Yor* 4B **106**
West Row. *Suff* 3F **65**
West Rudham. *Norf* 3H **77**
West Runton. *Norf* 1D **78**
Westruther. *Bord* 4C **130**
Westry. *Cambs* 1C **64**
West Saltoun. *E Lot* 3A **130**
West Sandford. *Devn* 2B **12**
West Sandwick. *Shet* 3F **173**
West Scrafton. *N Yor* 1C **98**
Westside. *Orkn* 5C **172**
West Sleekburn. *Nmbd* 1F **115**
West Somerton. *Norf* 4G **79**
West Stafford. *Dors* 4C **14**
West Stockwith. *Notts* 1E **87**
West Stoke. *W Sus* 2G **17**
West Stonesdale. *N Yor* 4B **104**
West Stoughton. *Som* 2H **21**
West Stour. *Dors* 4C **22**
West Stourmouth. *Kent* 4G **41**
West Stow. *Suff* 3H **65**
West Stowell. *Wilts* 5G **35**
West Strathan. *High* 2F **167**
West Stratton. *Hants* 2D **24**
West Street. *Kent* 5D **40**
West Tanfield. *N Yor* 2E **99**
West Taphouse. *Corn* 2F **7**
West Tarbert. *Arg* 3G **125**
West Thirston. *Nmbd* 4F **121**
West Thorney. *W Sus* 2F **17**
West Thurrock. *Thur* 3G **39**
West Tilbury. *Thur* 3A **40**
West Tisted. *Hants* 4E **25**
West Tofts. *Norf* 1H **65**
West Torrington. *Linc* 2A **88**
West Town. *Bath* 5A **34**
West Town. *Hants* 3F **17**
West Town. *N Som* 5H **33**

West Tytherley. Hants ....4A 24
West Tytherton. Wilts ....4E 35
West View. Hart ....1B 106
Westville. Notts ....1C 74
West Walton. Norf ....4D 76
Westward. Cumb ....5D 112
Westward Ho!. Devn ....4E 19
Westwell. Kent ....1D 28
Westwell. Oxon ....5H 49
Westwell Leacon. Kent ....1D 28
West Wellow. Hants ....1A 16
West Wemyss. Fife ....4F 137
West Wick. N Som ....5G 33
Westwick. Cambs ....4D 64
Westwick. Dur ....3D 104
Westwick. Norf ....3E 79
West Wickham. Cambs ....1G 53
West Wickham. G Lon ....4E 39
West Williamston. Pemb ....4E 43
West Willoughby. Linc ....1G 75
West Winch. Norf ....4F 77
West Winterslow. Wilts ....3H 23
West Wittering. W Sus ....3F 17
West Witton. N Yor ....1C 98
Westwood. Devn ....3D 12
Westwood. Kent ....4H 41
Westwood. Pet ....5A 76
Westwood. S Lan ....4H 127
Westwood. Wilts ....1D 22
West Woodburn. Nmbd ....1B 114
West Woodhay. W Ber ....5B 36
West Woodlands. Som ....2C 22
West Woodside. Cumb ....5E 112
Westwoodside. N Lin ....1E 87
West Worldham. Hants ....3F 25
West Worlington. Devn ....1A 12
West Worthing. W Sus ....5C 26
West Wratting. Cambs ....5F 65
West Wycombe. Buck ....2G 37
West Wylam. Nmbd ....3E 115
West Yatton. Wilts ....4D 34
West Yell. Shet ....3F 173
West Youlstone. Corn ....1C 10
Wetheral. Cumb ....4F 113
Wetherby. W Yor ....5G 99
Wetherden. Suff ....4C 66
Wetheringsett. Suff ....4D 66
Wethersfield. Essx ....2H 53
Wethersta. Shet ....5E 173
Wetherup Street. Suff ....4D 66
Wetley Rocks. Staf ....1D 72
Wettenhall. Ches E ....4A 84
Wetton. Staf ....5F 85
Wetwang. E Yor ....4D 100
Wetwood. Staf ....2B 72
Wexcombe. Wilts ....1A 24
Wexham Street. Buck ....2A 38
Weybourne. Norf ....1D 78
Weybourne. Surr ....2G 25
Weybread. Suff ....2E 67
Weybridge. Surr ....4B 38
Weycroft. Devn ....3G 13
Weydale. High ....2D 168
Weyhill. Hants ....2B 24
Weymouth. Dors ....5B 14
Weythel. Powy ....5E 59
Whaddon. Buck ....2G 51
Whaddon. Cambs ....1D 52
Whaddon. Glos ....4D 48
Whaddon. Wilts ....4G 23
Whale. Cumb ....2G 103
Whaley. Derbs ....3C 86
Whaley Bridge. Derbs ....2E 85
Whaley Thorns. Derbs ....3C 86
Whalley. Lanc ....1F 91
Whalton. Nmbd ....1E 115
Whaplode. Linc ....3C 76
Whaplode Drove. Linc ....4C 76
Whaplode St Catherine.
    Linc ....3C 76
Wharfe. N Yor ....3G 97
Wharles. Lanc ....1C 90
Wharley End. C Beds ....1H 51
Wharncliffe Side. S Yor ....1G 85

Wharram-le-Street. N Yor ....3C 100
Wharton. Ches W ....4A 84
Wharton. Here ....5H 59
Whashton. N Yor ....4E 105
Whasset. Cumb ....1E 97
Whatcote. Warw ....1B 50
Whateley. Warw ....1G 61
Whatfield. Suff ....1D 54
Whatley. Som
    nr. Chard ....2G 13
    nr. Frome ....2C 22
Whatlington. E Sus ....4B 28
Whatmore. Shrp ....3A 60
Whatstandwell. Derbs ....5H 85
Whatton. Notts ....2E 75
Whauphill. Dum ....5B 110
Whaw. N Yor ....4C 104
Wheatacre. Norf ....1G 67
Wheatcroft. Derbs ....5A 86
Wheathampstead. Herts ....4B 52
Wheathill. Shrp ....2A 60
Wheatley. Devn ....3B 12
Wheatley. Hants ....2F 25
Wheatley. Oxon ....5E 50
Wheatley. S Yor ....4F 93
Wheatley. W Yor ....2A 92
Wheatley Hill. Dur ....1A 106
Wheatley Lane. Lanc ....1G 91
Wheatley Park. S Yor ....4F 93
Wheaton Aston. Staf ....4C 72
Wheatstone Park. Staf ....5C 72
Wheddon Cross. Som ....3C 20
Wheelerstreet. Surr ....1A 26
Wheelock. Ches E ....5B 84
Wheelock Heath. Ches E ....5B 84
Wheelton. Lanc ....2E 90
Wheldrake. York ....5A 100
Whelford. Glos ....2G 35
Whelpley Hill. Buck ....5H 51
Whelpo. Cumb ....1E 102
Whelston. Flin ....3E 82
Whenby. N Yor ....3A 100
Whepstead. Suff ....5H 65
Wherstead. Suff ....1E 55
Wherwell. Hants ....2B 24
Wheston. Derbs ....3F 85
Whetsted. Kent ....1A 28
Whetstone. G Lon ....1D 38
Whetstone. Leics ....1C 62
Whicham. Cumb ....1A 96
Whichford. Warw ....2B 50
Whickham. Tyne ....3F 115
Whiddon. Devn ....2E 11
Whiddon Down. Devn ....3G 11
Whigstreet. Ang ....4D 145
Whilton. Nptn ....4D 62
Whimble. Devn ....2D 10
Whimple. Devn ....3D 12
Whimpwell Green. Norf ....3F 79
Whinburgh. Norf ....5C 78
Whin Lane End. Lanc ....5C 96
Whinney Hill. Stoc T ....3A 106
Whinnyfold. Abers ....5H 161
Whippingham. IOW ....3D 16
Whipsnade. C Beds ....4A 52
Whipton. Devn ....3C 12
Whirlow. S Yor ....2H 85
Whisby. Linc ....4G 87
Whissendine. Rut ....4F 75
Whissonsett. Norf ....3B 78
Whisterfield. Ches E ....3C 84
Whistley Green. Wok ....4F 37
Whiston. Mers ....1G 83
Whiston. Nptn ....4F 63
Whiston. S Yor ....1B 86
Whiston. Staf
    nr. Cheadle ....1E 73
    nr. Penkridge ....4C 72
Whiston Cross. Shrp ....5B 72
Whiston Eaves. Staf ....1E 73
Whitacre Heath. Warw ....1G 61
Whitbeck. Cumb ....1A 96
Whitbourne. Here ....5B 60
Whitburn. Tyne ....3H 115

Whitburn. W Lot ....3C 128
Whitburn Colliery. Tyne ....3H 115
Whitby. Ches W ....3F 83
Whitby. N Yor ....3F 107
Whitbyheath. Ches W ....3F 83
Whitchester. Bord ....4D 130
Whitchurch. Bath ....5B 34
Whitchurch. Buck ....3F 51
Whitchurch. Card ....4E 33
Whitchurch. Devn ....5E 11
Whitchurch. Hants ....2C 24
Whitchurch. Here ....4A 48
Whitchurch. Pemb ....2B 42
Whitchurch. Shrp ....1H 71
Whitchurch Canonicorum.
    Dors ....3G 13
Whitchurch Hill. Oxon ....4E 37
Whitchurch-on-Thames.
    Oxon ....4E 37
Whitcombe. Dors ....4C 14
Whitcot. Shrp ....1F 59
Whitcott Keysett. Shrp ....2E 59
Whiteash Green. Essx ....2A 54
Whitebog. High ....2B 158
Whitebridge. High ....2G 149
Whitebrook. Mon ....5A 48
Whitecairns. Abers ....2G 153
Whitechapel. Lanc ....5E 97
Whitechurch. Pemb ....1F 43
White Colne. Essx ....3B 54
White Coppice. Lanc ....3E 90
White Corries. High ....3G 141
Whitecraig. E Lot ....2G 129
Whitecroft. Glos ....5B 48
White Cross. Corn ....4D 5
Whitecross. Corn ....1D 6
Whitecross. Falk ....2C 128
White End. Worc ....2C 48
Whiteface. High ....5E 164
Whitefarland. N Ayr ....5G 125
Whitefaulds. S Ayr ....4B 116
Whitefield. Dors ....3E 15
Whitefield. G Man ....4G 91
Whitefield. Som ....4D 20
Whiteford. Abers ....1E 152
Whitegate. Ches W ....4A 84
Whitehall. Devn ....1E 12
Whitehall. Hants ....1F 25
Whitehall. Orkn ....5F 172
Whitehall. W Sus ....3C 26
Whitehaven. Cumb ....3A 102
Whitehaven. Here ....3E 71
Whitehill. Hants ....3F 25
Whitehill. N Ayr ....4D 126
Whitehills. Abers ....2D 160
Whitehills. Ang ....3D 144
White Horse Common.
    Norf ....3F 79
Whitehough. Derbs ....2E 85
Whitehouse. Abers ....2D 152
Whitehouse. Arg ....3G 125
Whiteinch. Glas ....3G 127
Whitekirk. E Lot ....1B 130
White Kirkley. Dur ....1D 104
White Lackington. Dors ....3C 14
Whitelackington. Som ....1G 13
White Ladies Aston. Worc ....5D 60
White Lee. W Yor ....2C 92
Whiteley. Hants ....2D 16
Whiteley Bank. IOW ....4D 16
Whiteley Village. Surr ....4B 38
Whitemans Green. W Sus ....3E 27
White Mill. Carm ....3E 45
Whitemire. Mor ....3D 159
Whitemoor. Corn ....3D 6
Whitenap. Hants ....4B 24
White Notley. Essx ....4A 54
Whiteoak Green. Oxon ....4B 50
Whiteparish. Wilts ....4H 23
White Pit. Linc ....3C 88
Whiterashes. Abers ....1F 153
White Rocks. Here ....3H 47
White Roding. Essx ....4F 53

Whiterow. High ....4F 169
Whiterow. Mor ....3E 159
Whiteshill. Glos ....5D 48
Whiteside. Nmbd ....3A 114
Whiteside. W Lot ....3C 128
Whitesmith. E Sus ....4G 27
Whitestaunton. Som ....1F 13
White Stone. Here ....1A 48
Whitestone. Abers ....4D 152
Whitestone. Devn ....3B 12
Whitestones. Abers ....3F 161
Whitestreet Green. Suff ....2C 54
Whitewall Corner. N Yor ....2B 100
White Waltham. Wind ....4G 37
Whiteway. Glos ....4E 49
Whitewell. Lanc ....5F 97
Whitewell Bottom. Lanc ....2G 91
Whiteworks. Devn ....5G 11
Whitewreath. Mor ....3G 159
Whitfield. D'dee ....5D 144
Whitfield. Kent ....1H 29
Whitfield. Nptn ....2E 50
Whitfield. Nmbd ....4A 114
Whitfield. S Glo ....2B 34
Whitfield. Devn ....3F 13
Whitford. Flin ....3D 82
Whitgift. E Yor ....2B 94
Whitgreave. Staf ....3C 72
Whitham. Dur ....5B 110
Whiting Bay. N Ayr ....3E 123
Whitkirk. W Yor ....1D 92
Whitland. Carm ....3G 43
Whitleigh. Plym ....3A 8
Whitletts. S Ayr ....2C 116
Whitley. N Yor ....2F 93
Whitley. Wilts ....5D 35
Whitley Bay. Tyne ....2G 115
Whitley Chapel. Nmbd ....4C 114
Whitley Heath. Staf ....3C 72
Whitley Lower. W Yor ....3C 92
Whitley Thorpe. N Yor ....2F 93
Whitlock's End. W Mid ....3F 61
Whitminster. Glos ....5C 48
Whitmore. Dors ....2F 15
Whitmore. Staf ....1C 72
Whitnage. Devn ....1D 12
Whitnash. Warw ....4H 61
Whitney. Here ....1F 47
Whitrigg. Cumb
    nr. Kirkbride ....4D 112
    nr. Torpenhow ....1D 102
Whitsbury. Hants ....1G 15
Whitsome. Bord ....4E 131
Whitson. Newp ....3G 33
Whitstable. Kent ....4F 41
Whitstone. Corn ....3C 10
Whittingham. Nmbd ....3E 121
Whittingslow. Shrp ....2G 59
Whittington. Derbs ....3B 86
Whittington. Glos ....3F 49
Whittington. Lanc ....2F 97
Whittington. Norf ....1G 65
Whittington. Shrp ....2F 71
Whittington. Staf
    nr. Kinver ....2C 60
    nr. Lichfield ....5F 73
Whittington. Warw ....1G 61
Whittington. Worc ....5C 60
Whittington Barracks. Staf ....5F 73
Whittlebury. Nptn ....1E 51
Whittleford. Warw ....1H 61
Whittle-le-Woods. Lanc ....2D 90
Whittlesey. Cambs ....1B 64
Whittlesford. Cambs ....1E 53
Whittlestone Head. Bkbn ....3F 91
Whitton. N Lin ....2C 94
Whitton. Nmbd ....4E 121
Whitton. Powy ....4E 59
Whitton. Bord ....2B 120
Whitton. Shrp ....3H 59
Whitton. Stoc T ....2A 106
Whittonditch. Wilts ....4A 36
Whittonstall. Nmbd ....4D 114
Whitway. Hants ....1C 24

Whitwell. Derbs ....3C 86
Whitwell. Herts ....3B 52
Whitwell. IOW ....5D 16
Whitwell. N Yor ....5F 105
Whitwell. Rut ....5G 75
Whitwell-on-the-Hill.
    N Yor ....3B 100
Whitwick. Leics ....4B 74
Whitwood. W Yor ....2E 93
Whitworth. Lanc ....3G 91
Whixall. Shrp ....2H 71
Whixley. N Yor ....4G 99
Whoberley. W Mid ....3H 61
Whorlton. Dur ....3E 105
Whorlton. N Yor ....4B 106
Whygate. Nmbd ....2A 114
Whyle. Here ....4H 59
Whyteleafe. Surr ....5E 39
Wibdon. Glos ....2A 34
Wibtoft. Warw ....2B 62
Wichenford. Worc ....4B 60
Wichling. Kent ....5D 40
Wick. Bour ....3G 15
Wick. Devn ....2E 13
Wick. High ....3F 169
Wick. Shet
    on Mainland ....8F 173
    on Unst ....1G 173
Wick. Som
    nr. Bridgwater ....2F 21
    nr. Burnham-on-Sea ....1G 21
    nr. Somerton ....4H 21
Wick. S Glo ....4C 34
Wick. V Glam ....4C 32
Wick. W Sus ....5B 26
Wick. Wilts ....4G 23
Wick. Worc ....1E 49
Wick Airport. High ....3F 169
Wicken. Cambs ....3E 65
Wicken. Nptn ....2F 51
Wicken Bonhunt. Essx ....2E 53
Wickenby. Linc ....2H 87
Wicken Green Village.
    Norf ....2H 77
Wickersley. S Yor ....1B 86
Wicker Street Green. Suff ....1C 54
Wickford. Essx ....1B 40
Wickham. Hants ....1D 16
Wickham. W Ber ....4B 36
Wickham Bishops. Essx ....4B 54
Wickhambreaux. Kent ....5G 41
Wickhambrook. Suff ....5G 65
Wickhamford. Worc ....1F 49
Wickham Green. Suff ....4C 66
Wickham Heath. W Ber ....5C 36
Wickham Market. Suff ....5F 67
Wickhampton. Norf ....5G 79
Wickham St Paul. Essx ....2B 54
Wickham Skeith. Suff ....4C 66
Wickham Street. Suff ....4C 66
Wick Hill. Wok ....5F 37
Wicklewood. Norf ....5C 78
Wickmere. Norf ....2D 78
Wick St Lawrence. N Som ....5G 33
Wickwar. S Glo ....3C 34
Widdington. Essx ....2F 53
Widdrington. Nmbd ....5G 121
Widdrington Station.
    Nmbd ....5G 121
Widecombe in the Moor.
    Devn ....5H 11
Widegates. Corn ....3G 7
Widemouth Bay. Corn ....2C 10
Wide Open. Tyne ....2F 115
Widewall. Orkn ....8D 172
Widford. Essx ....4E 53
Widford. Herts ....4E 53
Widham. Wilts ....3F 35
Widmer End. Buck ....2G 37
Widmerpool. Notts ....3D 74
Widnes. Hal ....2H 83
Widworthy. Devn ....3F 13
Wigan. G Man ....4D 90
Wigbeth. Dors ....2F 15

Wigborough. Som ...1H 13
Wiggaton. Devn ...3E 12
Wiggenhall St Germans.
  Norf ...4E 77
Wiggenhall St Mary
  Magdalen. Norf ...4E 77
Wiggenhall St Mary the
  Virgin. Norf ...4E 77
Wiggenhall St Peter. Norf ...4E 77
Wiggens Green. Essx ...1G 53
Wigginton. Herts ...4H 51
Wigginton. Oxon ...2B 50
Wigginton. Staf ...5G 73
Wigginton. York ...4H 99
Wigglesworth. N Yor ...4H 97
Wiggonby. Cumb ...4D 112
Wiggonholt. W Sus ...4B 26
Wighill. N Yor ...5G 99
Wighton. Norf ...2B 78
Wightwick. W Mid ...1C 60
Wigley. Hants ...1B 16
Wigmore. Here ...4G 59
Wigmore. Medw ...4B 40
Wigsley. Notts ...3F 87
Wigsthorpe. Nptn ...2H 63
**Wigston.** Leics ...1D 62
Wigtoft. Linc ...2B 76
Wigton. Cumb ...5D 112
Wigtown. Dum ...4B 110
Wike. W Yor ...5F 99
Wilbarston. Nptn ...2F 63
Wilberfoss. E Yor ...4B 100
Wilburton. Cambs ...3D 65
Wilby. Norf ...2C 66
Wilby. Nptn ...4F 63
Wilby. Suff ...3E 67
Wilcot. Wilts ...5G 35
Wilcott. Shrp ...4F 71
Wilcove. Corn ...3A 8
Wildboarclough. Ches E ...4D 85
Wilden. Bed ...5H 63
Wilden. Worc ...3C 60
Wildern. Hants ...1C 16
Wilderspool. Warr ...2A 84
Wilde Street. Suff ...3G 65
Wildhern. Hants ...1B 24
Wildmanbridge. S Lan ...4B 128
Wildmoor. Worc ...3D 60
Wildsworth. Linc ...1F 87
Wildwood. Staf ...3D 72
Wilford. Nott ...2C 74
Wilkesley. Ches E ...1A 72
Wilkhaven. High ...5G 165
Wilkieston. W Lot ...3E 129
Wilksby. Linc ...4B 88
Willand. Devn ...1D 12
Willaston. Ches E ...5A 84
Willaston. Ches W ...3F 83
Willaston. IOM ...4C 108
Willen. Mil ...1G 51
Willenhall. W Mid
  nr. Coventry ...3A 62
  nr. Wolverhampton ...1D 60
Willerby. E Yor ...1D 94
Willerby. N Yor ...2E 101
Willersey. Glos ...2G 49
Willersley. Here ...1G 47
Willesborough. Kent ...1E 28
Willesborough Lees. Kent ...1E 29
**Willesden.** G Lon ...2D 38
Willesley. Wilts ...3D 34
Willett. Som ...3E 20
Willey. Shrp ...1A 60
Willey. Warw ...2B 62
Willey Green. Surr ...5A 38
Williamscot. Oxon ...1C 50
Williamsetter. Shet ...9E 173
Willian. Herts ...2C 52
Willingale. Essx ...5F 53
Willingdon. E Sus ...5G 27
Willingham. Cambs ...3D 64
Willingham by Stow. Linc ...2F 87
Willingham Green. Cambs ...5F 65
Willington. Bed ...1B 52

Willington. Derbs ...3G 73
Willington. Dur ...1E 105
Willington. Tyne ...3G 115
Willington. Warw ...2A 50
Willington Corner. Ches W ...4H 83
Willisham Tye. Suff ...5C 66
Willitoft. E Yor ...1H 93
Williton. Som ...2D 20
Willoughbridge. Staf ...1B 72
Willoughby. Linc ...3D 88
Willoughby. Warw ...4C 62
Willoughby-on-the-Wolds.
  Notts ...3D 74
Willoughby Waterleys. Leics ...1C 62
Willoughton. Linc ...1G 87
Willow Green. Worc ...5B 60
Willows Green. Essx ...4H 53
Willsbridge. S Glo ...4B 34
Willslock. Staf ...2E 73
Wilmcote. Warw ...5F 61
Wilmington. Bath ...5B 34
Wilmington. Devn ...3F 13
Wilmington. E Sus ...5G 27
Wilmington. Kent ...3G 39
Wilminstone. Devn ...5F 11
**Wilmslow.** Ches E ...2C 84
Wilnecote. Staf ...5G 73
Wilney Green. Norf ...2C 66
Wilpshire. Lanc ...1E 91
Wilsden. W Yor ...1A 92
Wilsford. Linc ...1H 75
Wilsford. Wilts
  nr. Amesbury ...3G 23
  nr. Devizes ...1F 23
Wilsill. N Yor ...3D 98
Wilsley Green. Kent ...2B 28
Wilson. Here ...3A 48
Wilson. Leics ...3B 74
Wilsontown. S Lan ...4C 128
Wilstead. Bed ...1A 52
Wilsthorpe. E Yor ...3F 101
Wilsthorpe. Linc ...4H 75
Wilstone. Herts ...4H 51
Wilton. Cumb ...3B 102
Wilton. N Yor ...1C 100
Wilton. Red C ...3C 106
Wilton. Bord ...3H 119
Wilton. Wilts
  nr. Marlborough ...5A 36
  nr. Salisbury ...3F 23
Wimbish. Essx ...2F 53
Wimbish Green. Essx ...2G 53
Wimblebury. Staf ...4E 73
**Wimbledon.** G Lon ...3D 38
Wimblington. Cambs ...1D 64
Wimboldsley. Ches W ...4A 84
**Wimborne Minster.** Dors ...2F 15
Wimborne St Giles. Dors ...1F 15
Wimbotsham. Norf ...5F 77
Wimpole. Cambs ...1D 52
Wimpstone. Warw ...1H 49
Wincanton. Som ...4C 22
Winceby. Linc ...4C 88
Wincham. Ches W ...3A 84
Winchburgh. W Lot ...2D 129
Winchcombe. Glos ...3F 49
Winchelsea. E Sus ...4D 28
Winchelsea Beach. E Sus ...4D 28
**Winchester.** Hants ...4C 24
Winchet Hill. Kent ...1B 28
Winchfield. Hants ...1F 25
Winchmore Hill. Buck ...1A 38
Winchmore Hill. G Lon ...1E 39
Wincle. Ches E ...4D 84
Windermere. Cumb ...5F 103
Winderton. Warw ...1B 50
Windhill. High ...4H 157
Windle Hill. Ches W ...3F 83
Windlesham. Surr ...4A 38
Windley. Derbs ...1H 73
Windmill. Derbs ...3F 85
Windmill Hill. E Sus ...4H 27
Windmill Hill. Som ...1G 13
Windrush. Glos ...4G 49
**Windsor.** Wind ...3A 38

Windsor Green. Suff ...5A 66
Windyedge. Abers ...4F 153
Windygates. Fife ...3F 137
Windyharbour. Ches E ...3C 84
Windyknowe. W Lot ...3C 128
Wineham. W Sus ...3D 26
Winestead. E Yor ...2G 95
Winfarthing. Norf ...2D 66
Winford. IOW ...4D 16
Winford. N Som ...5A 34
Winforton. Here ...1F 47
Winfrith Newburgh. Dors ...4D 14
Wing. Buck ...3G 51
Wing. Rut ...5F 75
Wingate. Dur ...1B 106
Wingates. G Man ...4E 91
Wingates. Nmbd ...5F 121
Wingerworth. Derbs ...4A 86
Wingfield. C Beds ...3A 52
Wingfield. Suff ...3E 67
Wingfield. Wilts ...1D 22
Wingfield Park. Derbs ...5A 86
Wingham. Kent ...5G 41
Wingmore. Kent ...1F 29
Wingrave. Buck ...4G 51
Winkburn. Notts ...5E 86
Winkfield. Brac ...3A 38
Winkfield Row. Brac ...4G 37
Winkhill. Staf ...5E 85
Winklebury. Hants ...1E 24
Winkleigh. Devn ...2G 11
Winksley. N Yor ...2E 99
Winkton. Dors ...3G 15
Winlaton. Tyne ...3E 115
Winlaton Mill. Tyne ...3E 115
Winless. High ...3F 169
Winmarleigh. Lanc ...5D 96
Winnal Common. Here ...2H 47
Winnard's Perch. Corn ...2D 6
Winnersh. Wok ...4F 37
Winnington. Ches W ...3A 84
Winnington. Staf ...2B 72
Winnothdale. Staf ...1E 73
Winscales. Cumb ...2B 102
Winscombe. N Som ...1H 21
Winsford. Ches W ...4A 84
Winsford. Som ...3C 20
Winsham. Devn ...3E 19
Winsham. Som ...2G 13
Winshill. Staf ...3G 73
Winsh-wen. Swan ...3F 31
Winskill. Cumb ...1G 103
Winslade. Hants ...2E 25
Winsley. Wilts ...5D 34
Winslow. Buck ...3F 51
Winson. Glos ...5F 49
Winson Green. W Mid ...2E 61
Winsor. Hants ...1B 16
Winster. Cumb ...5F 103
Winster. Derbs ...4G 85
Winston. Dur ...3E 105
Winston. Suff ...4D 66
Winstone. Glos ...5E 49
Winswell. Devn ...1E 11
Winterborne Clenston.
  Dors ...2D 14
Winterborne Herringston.
  Dors ...4B 14
Winterborne Houghton.
  Dors ...2D 14
Winterborne Kingston.
  Dors ...3D 14
Winterborne Monkton.
  Dors ...4B 14
Winterborne St Martin.
  Dors ...4B 14
Winterborne Stickland.
  Dors ...2D 14
Winterborne Whitechurch.
  Dors ...2D 14
Winterborne Zelston. Dors ...3D 15
Winterbourne. S Glo ...3B 34
Winterbourne. W Ber ...4C 36
Winterbourne Abbas. Dors ...3B 14

Winterbourne Bassett.
  Wilts ...4G 35
Winterbourne Dauntsey.
  Wilts ...3G 23
Winterbourne Earls. Wilts ...3G 23
Winterbourne Gunner.
  Wilts ...3G 23
Winterbourne Monkton.
  Wilts ...4G 35
Winterbourne Steepleton.
  Dors ...4B 14
Winterbourne Stoke. Wilts ...2F 23
Winterbrook. Oxon ...3E 36
Winterburn. N Yor ...4B 98
Winter Gardens. Essx ...2B 40
Winterhay Green. Som ...1G 13
Winteringham. N Lin ...2C 94
Wintersett. W Yor ...3D 93
Winterton. N Lin ...3C 94
Winterton-on-Sea. Norf ...4G 79
Winthorpe. Linc ...4E 89
Winthorpe. Notts ...5F 87
Winton. Bour ...3F 15
Winton. Cumb ...3A 104
Winton. E Sus ...5G 27
Wintringham. N Yor ...2C 100
Winwick. Cambs ...2A 64
Winwick. Nptn ...3D 62
Winwick. Warr ...1A 84
Wirksworth. Derbs ...5G 85
Wirswall. Ches E ...1H 71
**Wisbech.** Cambs ...4D 76
Wisbech St Mary. Cambs ...5D 76
Wisborough Green. W Sus ...3B 26
Wiseton. Notts ...2E 86
**Wishaw.** N Lan ...4A 128
Wishaw. Warw ...1F 61
Wisley. Surr ...5B 38
Wispington. Linc ...3B 88
Wissenden. Kent ...1D 28
Wissett. Suff ...3F 67
Wistanstow. Shrp ...2G 59
Wistanswick. Shrp ...3A 72
Wistaston. Ches E ...5A 84
Wiston. Pemb ...3E 43
Wiston. S Lan ...1B 118
Wiston. W Sus ...4C 26
Wistow. Cambs ...2B 64
Wistow. N Yor ...1F 93
Wistow. Leics ...1D 62
Wiswell. Lanc ...1F 91
Witcham. Cambs ...2D 64
Witchampton. Dors ...2E 15
Witchford. Cambs ...3E 65
**Witham.** Essx ...4B 54
Witham Friary. Som ...2C 22
Witham on the Hill. Linc ...4H 75
Witham St Hughs. Linc ...4F 87
Withcall. Linc ...2B 88
Witherenden Hill. E Sus ...3H 27
Withergate. Norf ...3E 79
Witheridge. Devn ...1B 12
Witheridge Hill. Oxon ...3E 37
Witherley. Leics ...1H 61
Withermarsh Green. Suff ...2D 54
Withern. Linc ...2D 88
Withernsea. E Yor ...2G 95
Withernwick. E Yor ...5F 101
Withersdale Street. Suff ...2E 67
Withersfield. Suff ...1G 53
Witherslack. Cumb ...1D 96
Withiel. Corn ...2D 6
Withiel Florey. Som ...3C 20
Withington. Glos ...4F 49
Withington. G Man ...1C 84
Withington. Here ...1A 48
Withington. Shrp ...4H 71
Withington. Staf ...2E 73
Withington Green. Ches E ...3C 84
Withington Marsh. Here ...1A 48
Withleigh. Devn ...1C 12
Withnell. Lanc ...2E 91
Withnell Fold. Lanc ...2E 90
Withybrook. Warw ...2B 62

Withycombe. Som ...2D 20
Withycombe Raleigh. Devn ...4D 12
Withyham. E Sus ...2F 27
Withypool. Som ...3B 20
Witley. Surr ...1A 26
Witnesham. Suff ...5D 66
**Witney.** Oxon ...4B 50
Wittering. Pet ...5H 75
Wittersham. Kent ...3C 28
Witton. Norf ...5F 79
Witton. Worc ...4C 60
Witton Bridge. Norf ...2F 79
Witton Gilbert. Dur ...5F 115
Witton-le-Wear. Dur ...1E 105
Witton Park. Dur ...1E 105
Wiveliscombe. Som ...4D 20
Wivelrod. Hants ...3E 25
Wivelsfield. E Sus ...3E 27
Wivelsfield Green. E Sus ...4E 27
Wivenhoe. Essx ...3D 54
Wiveton. Norf ...1C 78
Wix. Essx ...3E 55
Wixford. Warw ...5E 61
Wixhill. Shrp ...3H 71
Wixoe. Suff ...1H 53
Woburn. C Beds ...2H 51
Woburn Sands. Mil ...2H 51
**Woking.** Surr ...5B 38
**Wokingham.** Wok ...5G 37
Wolborough. Devn ...5B 12
Woldingham. Surr ...5E 39
Wold Newton. E Yor ...2E 101
Wold Newton. NE Lin ...1B 88
Wolferlow. Here ...4A 60
Wolferton. Norf ...3F 77
Wolfhill. Per ...5A 144
Wolf's Castle. Pemb ...2D 42
Wolfsdale. Pemb ...2D 42
Wolgarston. Staf ...4D 72
Wollaston. Nptn ...4G 63
Wollaston. Shrp ...4F 71
Wollaston. W Mid ...2C 60
Wollaton. Nott ...1C 74
Wollerton. Shrp ...2A 72
Wollescote. W Mid ...2D 60
Wolseley Bridge. Staf ...3E 73
Wolsingham. Dur ...1D 105
Wolstanton. Staf ...1C 72
Wolston. Warw ...3B 62
Wolsty. Cumb ...4C 112
Wolterton. Norf ...2D 78
Wolvercote. Oxon ...5C 50
**Wolverhampton.** W Mid ...1D 60
Wolverley. Shrp ...3G 71
Wolverley. Worc ...3C 60
Wolverton. Hants ...1D 24
Wolverton. Mil ...1G 51
Wolverton. Warw ...4G 61
Wolverton. Wilts ...3C 22
Wolverton Common. Hants ...1D 24
Wolvesnewton. Mon ...2H 33
Wolvey. Warw ...2B 62
Wolvey Heath. Warw ...2B 62
Wolviston. Stoc T ...2B 106
Womaston. Powy ...4E 59
Wombleton. N Yor ...1A 100
**Wombourne.** Staf ...1C 60
**Wombwell.** S Yor ...4D 93
Womenswold. Kent ...5G 41
Womersley. N Yor ...3F 93
Wonersh. Surr ...1B 26
Wonson. Devn ...4G 11
Wonston. Dors ...2C 14
Wonston. Hants ...3C 24
Wooburn. Buck ...2A 38
Wooburn Green. Buck ...2A 38
Wood. Pemb ...2C 42
Woodacott. Devn ...2D 11
Woodale. N Yor ...2C 98
Woodall. S Yor ...2B 86
Woodbank. Ches W ...3F 83
Woodbastwick. Norf ...4F 79
Woodbeck. Notts ...3E 87
**Woodborough.** Notts ...1D 74

Woodborough—Wythop Mill


Woodborough. *Wilts* . . . . . . . . .1G **23**
Woodbridge. *Devn* . . . . . . . . . . .3E **13**
Woodbridge. *Dors* . . . . . . . . . . .1C **14**
**Woodbridge**. *Suff* . . . . . . . . . . .1F **55**
Wood Burcote. *Nptn* . . . . . . . . . .1E **51**
Woodbury. *Devn* . . . . . . . . . . .4D **12**
Woodbury Salterton. *Devn* . . . . .4D **12**
Woodchester. *Glos* . . . . . . . . . . .5D **48**
Woodchurch. *Kent* . . . . . . . . . . .2D **28**
Woodchurch. *Mers* . . . . . . . . . . .2E **83**
Woodcock Heath. *Staf* . . . . . . . .3E **73**
Woodcombe. *Som* . . . . . . . . . . .2C **20**
Woodcote. *Oxon* . . . . . . . . . . . .3E **37**
Woodcote Green. *Worc* . . . . . . .3D **60**
Woodcott. *Hants* . . . . . . . . . . . .1C **24**
Woodcroft. *Glos* . . . . . . . . . . . .2A **34**
Woodcutts. *Dors* . . . . . . . . . . . .1E **15**
Wood Dalling. *Norf* . . . . . . . . . .3C **78**
Woodditton. *Cambs* . . . . . . . . . .5F **65**
Wood Eaton. *Staf* . . . . . . . . . . .4C **72**
Woodeaton. *Oxon* . . . . . . . . . . .4D **50**
Wood End. *Bed* . . . . . . . . . . . . .4H **63**
Wood End. *Herts* . . . . . . . . . . . .3D **52**
Wood End. *Warw*
nr. Bedworth . . . . . . . . . .2G **61**
nr. Dordon . . . . . . . . . . .1G **61**
nr. Tanworth-in-Arden . . . .3F **61**
Woodend. *Cumb* . . . . . . . . . . .5C **102**
Woodend. *Nptn* . . . . . . . . . . . . .1E **50**
Woodend. *Staf* . . . . . . . . . . . . .3F **73**
Woodend. *W Sus* . . . . . . . . . . . .2G **17**
Wood Enderby. *Linc* . . . . . . . . . .4B **88**
Woodend Green. *Essx* . . . . . . . .3F **53**
Woodfalls. *Wilts* . . . . . . . . . . . .4G **23**
Woodfield. *Oxon* . . . . . . . . . . . .3D **50**
Woodfields. *Lanc* . . . . . . . . . . . .1E **91**
Woodford. *Corn* . . . . . . . . . . . . .1C **10**
Woodford. *Devn* . . . . . . . . . . . . .3D **9**
Woodford. *Glos* . . . . . . . . . . . . .2B **34**
**Woodford**. *G Lon* . . . . . . . . . . . .1E **39**
Woodford. *G Man* . . . . . . . . . . . .2C **84**
Woodford. *Nptn* . . . . . . . . . . . . .3G **63**
Woodford. *Plym* . . . . . . . . . . . . .3B **8**
Woodford Green. *G Lon* . . . . . . .1F **39**
Woodford Halse. *Nptn* . . . . . . . .5C **62**
Woodgate. *Norf* . . . . . . . . . . . . .4C **78**
Woodgate. *W Mid* . . . . . . . . . . .2D **61**
Woodgate. *W Sus* . . . . . . . . . . .5A **26**
Woodgate. *Worc* . . . . . . . . . . . .4D **60**
**Wood Green**. *G Lon* . . . . . . . . .1D **39**
Woodgreen. *Hants* . . . . . . . . . . .1G **15**
Woodgreen. *Oxon* . . . . . . . . . . .4B **50**
Woodhall. *Inv* . . . . . . . . . . . . .2E **127**
Woodhall. *Linc* . . . . . . . . . . . . .4B **88**
Woodhall. *N Yor* . . . . . . . . . . .5C **104**
Woodhall Spa. *Linc* . . . . . . . . . .4A **88**
Woodham. *Surr* . . . . . . . . . . . . .4B **38**
Woodham Ferrers. *Essx* . . . . . . .1B **40**
Woodham Mortimer. *Essx* . . . . . .5B **54**
Woodham Walter. *Essx* . . . . . . . .5B **54**
Woodhaven. *Fife* . . . . . . . . . . .1G **137**
Wood Hayes. *W Mid* . . . . . . . . . .5D **72**
Woodhead. *Abers*
nr. Fraserburgh . . . . . . . .2G **161**
nr. Fyvie . . . . . . . . . . . .5E **161**
Woodhill. *N Som* . . . . . . . . . . . .4H **33**
Woodhill. *Shrp* . . . . . . . . . . . . .2B **60**
Woodhill. *Som* . . . . . . . . . . . . .4G **21**
Woodhorn. *Nmbd* . . . . . . . . . . .1F **115**
Woodhouse. *Leics* . . . . . . . . . . .4C **74**
Woodhouse. *S Yor* . . . . . . . . . . .2B **86**
Woodhouse. *W Yor*nr. Leeds . . . .1C **92**
nr. Normanton . . . . . . . . .2D **93**
Woodhouse Eaves. *Leics* . . . . . .4C **74**
Woodhouses. *Ches W* . . . . . . . .3H **83**
Woodhouses. *G Man*
nr. Failsworth . . . . . . . . .4H **91**
nr. Sale . . . . . . . . . . . . .1B **84**
Woodhouses. *Staf* . . . . . . . . . . .4F **73**
Woodhuish. *Devn* . . . . . . . . . . . .3F **9**
Woodhurst. *Cambs* . . . . . . . . . .3C **64**
Woodingdean. *Brig* . . . . . . . . . .5E **27**
Woodland. *Devn* . . . . . . . . . . . .2D **9**
Woodland. *Dur* . . . . . . . . . . . .2D **104**
Woodland Head. *Devn* . . . . . . . .3A **12**
Woodlands. *Abers* . . . . . . . . . .4E **153**
Woodlands. *Dors* . . . . . . . . . . . .2F **15**
Woodlands. *Hants* . . . . . . . . . . .1B **16**
Woodlands. *Kent* . . . . . . . . . . . .4G **39**
Woodlands. *N Yor* . . . . . . . . . . .4F **99**
Woodlands. *S Yor* . . . . . . . . . . .4F **93**
Woodlands Park. *Wind* . . . . . . . .4G **37**
Woodlands St Mary. *W Ber* . . . . .4B **36**
Woodlane. *Shrp* . . . . . . . . . . . .3A **72**
Woodlane. *Staf* . . . . . . . . . . . . .3F **73**
Woodleigh. *Devn* . . . . . . . . . . . .4D **8**
Woodlesford. *W Yor* . . . . . . . . .2D **92**
Woodley. *G Man* . . . . . . . . . . . .1D **84**
Woodley. *Wok* . . . . . . . . . . . . .4F **37**
Woodmancote. *Glos*
nr. Cheltenham . . . . . . . .3E **49**
nr. Cirencester . . . . . . . . .5F **49**
Woodmancote. *W Sus*
nr. Chichester . . . . . . . . .2F **17**
nr. Henfield . . . . . . . . . . .4D **26**
Woodmancote. *Worc* . . . . . . . . .1E **49**
Woodmancott. *Hants* . . . . . . . . .2D **24**
Woodmansey. *E Yor* . . . . . . . . .1D **94**
Woodmansgreen. *W Sus* . . . . . . .4G **25**
Woodmansterne. *Surr* . . . . . . . .5D **38**
Woodmanton. *Devn* . . . . . . . . . .4D **12**
Woodmill. *Staf* . . . . . . . . . . . . .3F **73**
Woodminton. *Wilts* . . . . . . . . . .4F **23**
Woodnesborough. *Kent* . . . . . . . .5H **41**
Woodnewton. *Nptn* . . . . . . . . . .1H **63**
Woodnook. *Linc* . . . . . . . . . . . .2G **75**
Wood Norton. *Norf* . . . . . . . . . .3C **78**
Woodplumpton. *Lanc* . . . . . . . . .1D **90**
Woodrising. *Norf* . . . . . . . . . . .5B **78**
Wood Row. *W Yor* . . . . . . . . . . .2D **93**
Woodrow. *Cumb* . . . . . . . . . . .5D **112**
Woodrow. *Dors*
nr. Fifehead Neville . . . . . .1C **14**
nr. Hazelbury Bryan . . . . .2C **14**
Woods Eaves. *Here* . . . . . . . . . .1F **47**
Woodseaves. *Shrp* . . . . . . . . . . .2A **72**
Woodseaves. *Staf* . . . . . . . . . . .3C **72**
Woodsend. *Wilts* . . . . . . . . . . . .4H **35**
Woodsetts. *S Yor* . . . . . . . . . . . .2C **86**
Woodsford. *Dors* . . . . . . . . . . . .3C **14**
Wood's Green. *E Sus* . . . . . . . . .2H **27**
Woodshaw. *Wilts* . . . . . . . . . . . .3F **35**
Woodside. *Aber* . . . . . . . . . . . .3G **153**
Woodside. *Brac* . . . . . . . . . . . . .3A **38**
Woodside. *Derbs* . . . . . . . . . . . .1A **74**
Woodside. *Dum* . . . . . . . . . . . .2B **112**
Woodside. *Dur* . . . . . . . . . . . . .2E **105**
Woodside. *Fife* . . . . . . . . . . . . .3G **137**
Woodside. *Herts* . . . . . . . . . . . .5C **52**
Woodside. *Per* . . . . . . . . . . . . .5B **144**
Wood Stanway. *Glos* . . . . . . . . . .2F **49**
Woodstock. *Oxon* . . . . . . . . . . . .4C **50**
Woodstock Slop. *Pemb* . . . . . . . .2E **43**
Woodston. *Pet* . . . . . . . . . . . . . .1A **64**
Wood Street. *Norf* . . . . . . . . . . .3F **79**
Wood Street Village. *Surr* . . . . . .5A **38**
Woodthorpe. *Derbs* . . . . . . . . . .3B **86**
Woodthorpe. *Leics* . . . . . . . . . .4C **74**
Woodthorpe. *Linc* . . . . . . . . . . .2D **88**
Woodthorpe. *Notts* . . . . . . . . . .1C **74**
Woodthorpe. *York* . . . . . . . . . . .5H **99**
Woodton. *Norf* . . . . . . . . . . . . .1E **67**
Woodtown. *Devn*
nr. Bideford . . . . . . . . . . .4E **19**
nr. Littleham . . . . . . . . . .4E **19**
Woodvale. *Mers* . . . . . . . . . . . . .3B **90**
Woodville. *Derbs* . . . . . . . . . . . .4H **73**
Woodwalton. *Cambs* . . . . . . . . . .2B **64**
Woodwick. *Orkn* . . . . . . . . . . . .5C **172**
Woodyates. *Dors* . . . . . . . . . . . .1F **15**
Woody Bay. *Devn* . . . . . . . . . . .2G **19**
Woofferton. *Shrp* . . . . . . . . . . .4H **59**
Wookey. *Som* . . . . . . . . . . . . . .2A **22**
Wookey Hole. *Som* . . . . . . . . . . .2A **22**
Wool. *Dors* . . . . . . . . . . . . . . .4D **14**
Woolacombe. *Devn* . . . . . . . . . . .2E **19**
Woolage Green. *Kent* . . . . . . . . .1G **29**
Woolage Village. *Kent* . . . . . . . .5G **41**
Woolaston. *Glos* . . . . . . . . . . . .2A **34**
Woolavington. *Som* . . . . . . . . . .2G **21**
Woolbeding. *W Sus* . . . . . . . . . .4G **25**
Woolcotts. *Som* . . . . . . . . . . . . .3C **20**
Wooldale. *W Yor* . . . . . . . . . . . .4B **92**
Wooler. *Nmbd* . . . . . . . . . . . . .2D **121**
Woolfardisworthy. *Devn*
nr. Bideford . . . . . . . . . .4D **18**
nr. Crediton . . . . . . . . . .2B **12**
Woolfords. *S Lan* . . . . . . . . . . .4D **128**
Woolgarston. *Dors* . . . . . . . . . . .4E **15**
Woolhampton. *W Ber* . . . . . . . . .5D **36**
Woolhope. *Here* . . . . . . . . . . . . .2B **48**
Woolland. *Dors* . . . . . . . . . . . . .2C **14**
Woollard. *Bath* . . . . . . . . . . . . .5B **34**
Woolley. *Bath* . . . . . . . . . . . . . .5C **34**
Woolley. *Cambs* . . . . . . . . . . . . .3A **64**
Woolley. *Corn* . . . . . . . . . . . . . .1C **10**
Woolley. *Derbs* . . . . . . . . . . . . .4A **86**
Woolley. *W Yor* . . . . . . . . . . . . .3D **92**
Woolley Green. *Wilts* . . . . . . . . .5D **34**
Woolmere Green. *Worc* . . . . . . . .4D **60**
Woolmer Green. *Herts* . . . . . . . .4C **52**
Woolminstone. *Som* . . . . . . . . . .2H **13**
Woolpit. *Suff* . . . . . . . . . . . . . .4B **66**
Woolridge. *Glos* . . . . . . . . . . . .3D **48**
Woolscott. *Warw* . . . . . . . . . . . .4B **62**
Woolsery. *Devn* . . . . . . . . . . . . .4D **18**
Woolsington. *Tyne* . . . . . . . . . .3E **115**
Woolstaston. *Shrp* . . . . . . . . . . .1G **59**
Woolsthorpe By Belvoir. *Linc* . . . .2F **75**
Woolsthorpe-by-
Colsterworth. *Linc* . . . . . .3G **75**
Woolston. *Devn* . . . . . . . . . . . . .4D **8**
Woolston. *Shrp*
nr. Church Stretton . . . . . .2G **59**
nr. Oswestry . . . . . . . . . . .3F **71**
Woolston. *Som* . . . . . . . . . . . . .4B **22**
Woolston. *Sotn* . . . . . . . . . . . . .1C **16**
Woolston. *Warr* . . . . . . . . . . . . .2A **84**
Woolstone. *Glos* . . . . . . . . . . . .2E **49**
Woolstone. *Oxon* . . . . . . . . . . . .3A **36**
Woolston Green. *Devn* . . . . . . . . .2D **9**
Woolton. *Mers* . . . . . . . . . . . . .2G **83**
Woolton Hill. *Hants* . . . . . . . . . .5C **36**
Woolverstone. *Suff* . . . . . . . . . .2E **55**
Woolverton. *Som* . . . . . . . . . . . .1C **22**
Woolwell. *Devn* . . . . . . . . . . . . .2B **8**
**Woolwich**. *G Lon* . . . . . . . . . . .3F **39**
Woonton. *Here*
nr. Kington . . . . . . . . . . .5F **59**
nr. Leominster . . . . . . . . .4H **59**
Wooperton. *Nmbd* . . . . . . . . . .2E **121**
Woore. *Shrp* . . . . . . . . . . . . . . .1B **72**
Wooth. *Dors* . . . . . . . . . . . . . . .3H **13**
Wooton. *Shrp* . . . . . . . . . . . . . .2B **60**
Wootton. *Bed* . . . . . . . . . . . . . .1A **52**
Wootton. *Hants* . . . . . . . . . . . . .3H **15**
Wootton. *IOW* . . . . . . . . . . . . . .3D **16**
Wootton. *Kent* . . . . . . . . . . . . .1G **29**
Wootton. *Nptn* . . . . . . . . . . . . .5E **63**
Wootton. *N Lin* . . . . . . . . . . . . .3D **94**
Wootton. *Oxon*
nr. Abingdon . . . . . . . . . .5C **50**
nr. Woodstock . . . . . . . . .4C **50**
Wootton. *Shrp*
nr. Ludlow . . . . . . . . . . .3G **59**
nr. Oswestry . . . . . . . . . .3F **71**
Wootton. *Staf*
nr. Eccleshall . . . . . . . . .3C **72**
nr. Ellastone . . . . . . . . . .1F **73**
**Wootton Bassett, Royal**.
*Wilts* . . . . . . . . . . . . . . .3F **35**
Wootton Bridge. *IOW* . . . . . . . . .3D **16**
Wootton Common. *IOW* . . . . . . .3D **16**
Wootton Courtenay. *Som* . . . . . .2C **20**
Wootton Fitzpaine. *Dors* . . . . . . .3G **13**
Wootton Rivers. *Wilts* . . . . . . . .5G **35**
Wootton St Lawrence.
*Hants* . . . . . . . . . . . . . .1D **24**
Wootton Wawen. *Warw* . . . . . . . .4F **61**
**Worcester**. *Worc* . . . . . . . . . . .5C **60**
Worcester Park. *G Lon* . . . . . . . .4D **38**
Wordsley. *W Mid* . . . . . . . . . . . .2C **60**
Worfield. *Shrp* . . . . . . . . . . . . .1B **60**
Work. *Orkn* . . . . . . . . . . . . . .6D **172**
Workhouse Green. *Suff* . . . . . . .2C **54**
**Workington**. *Cumb* . . . . . . . . .2A **102**
**Worksop**. *Notts* . . . . . . . . . . . .3C **86**
Worlaby. *N Lin* . . . . . . . . . . . . .3D **94**
World's End. *W Ber* . . . . . . . . . .4C **36**
World's End. *W Sus* . . . . . . . . . .4E **27**
Worlds End. *Hants* . . . . . . . . . . .1E **17**
Worlds End. *W Mid* . . . . . . . . . .2F **61**
Worldsend. *Shrp* . . . . . . . . . . . .1G **59**
Worle. *N Som* . . . . . . . . . . . . . .5G **33**
Worleston. *Ches E* . . . . . . . . . . .5A **84**
Worlingham. *Suff* . . . . . . . . . . .2G **67**
Worlington. *Suff* . . . . . . . . . . . .3F **65**
Worlingworth. *Suff* . . . . . . . . . .4E **67**
Wormbridge. *Here* . . . . . . . . . . .2H **47**
Wormegay. *Norf* . . . . . . . . . . . .4F **77**
Wormelow Tump. *Here* . . . . . . . .2H **47**
Wormhill. *Derbs* . . . . . . . . . . . .3F **85**
Wormingford. *Essx* . . . . . . . . . .2C **54**
Worminghall. *Buck* . . . . . . . . . .5E **51**
Wormington. *Glos* . . . . . . . . . . .2F **49**
Worminster. *Som* . . . . . . . . . . .2A **22**
Wormit. *Fife* . . . . . . . . . . . . .1F **137**
Wormleighton. *Warw* . . . . . . . . .5B **62**
Wormley. *Herts* . . . . . . . . . . . .5D **52**
Wormley. *Surr* . . . . . . . . . . . . .2A **26**
Wormshill. *Kent* . . . . . . . . . . . .5C **40**
Wormsley. *Here* . . . . . . . . . . . .1H **47**
Worplesdon. *Surr* . . . . . . . . . . .5A **38**
Worrall. *S Yor* . . . . . . . . . . . . .1H **85**
**Worsbrough**. *S Yor* . . . . . . . . .4D **92**
Worsley. *G Man* . . . . . . . . . . . . .4F **91**
Worstead. *Norf* . . . . . . . . . . . . .3F **79**
Worsthorne. *Lanc* . . . . . . . . . . .1G **91**
Worston. *Lanc* . . . . . . . . . . . . .5G **97**
Worth. *Kent* . . . . . . . . . . . . . . .5H **41**
Worth. *W Sus* . . . . . . . . . . . . . .2D **27**
Wortham. *Suff* . . . . . . . . . . . . .3C **66**
Worthen. *Shrp* . . . . . . . . . . . . .5F **71**
Worthenbury. *Wrex* . . . . . . . . . .1G **71**
Worthing. *Norf* . . . . . . . . . . . . .4B **78**
**Worthing**. *W Sus* . . . . . . . . . . .5C **26**
Worthington. *Leics* . . . . . . . . . .3B **74**
Worth Matravers. *Dors* . . . . . . .5E **15**
Worting. *Hants* . . . . . . . . . . . . .1E **24**
Wortley. *Glos* . . . . . . . . . . . . . .2C **34**
Wortley. *S Yor* . . . . . . . . . . . . .1H **85**
Wortley. *W Yor* . . . . . . . . . . . . .1C **92**
Worton. *N Yor* . . . . . . . . . . . . .1B **98**
Worton. *Wilts* . . . . . . . . . . . . . .1E **23**
Wortwell. *Norf* . . . . . . . . . . . . .2E **67**
Wotherton. *Shrp* . . . . . . . . . . . .5E **71**
Wothorpe. *Pet* . . . . . . . . . . . . .5H **75**
Wotter. *Devn* . . . . . . . . . . . . . . .2B **8**
Wotton. *Glos* . . . . . . . . . . . . . .4D **48**
Wotton. *Surr* . . . . . . . . . . . . . .1C **26**
Wotton-under-Edge. *Glos* . . . . . .2C **34**
Wotton Underwood. *Buck* . . . . . .4E **51**
Wouldham. *Kent* . . . . . . . . . . . .4B **40**
Wrabness. *Essx* . . . . . . . . . . . . .2E **55**
Wrafton. *Devn* . . . . . . . . . . . . .3E **19**
Wragby. *Linc* . . . . . . . . . . . . . .3A **88**
Wragby. *W Yor* . . . . . . . . . . . . .3E **93**
Wramplingham. *Norf* . . . . . . . . .5D **78**
Wrangbrook. *W Yor* . . . . . . . . . .3E **93**
Wrangle. *Linc* . . . . . . . . . . . . . .5D **88**
Wrangle Lowgate. *Linc* . . . . . . . .5D **88**
Wrangway. *Som* . . . . . . . . . . . . .1E **13**
Wrantage. *Som* . . . . . . . . . . . . .4G **21**
Wrawby. *N Lin* . . . . . . . . . . . . .4D **94**
Wraxall. *N Som* . . . . . . . . . . . . .4H **33**
Wraxall. *Som* . . . . . . . . . . . . . .3B **22**
Wray. *Lanc* . . . . . . . . . . . . . . . .3F **97**
Wraysbury. *Wind* . . . . . . . . . . . .3B **38**
Wrayton. *Lanc* . . . . . . . . . . . . .2F **97**
Wrea Green. *Lanc* . . . . . . . . . . .1B **90**
Wreay. *Cumb*
nr. Carlisle . . . . . . . . . . .5F **113**
nr. Penrith . . . . . . . . . . .2F **103**
Wrecclesham. *Surr* . . . . . . . . . .2G **25**
**Wrecsam**. *Wrex* . . . . . . . . . . . .5F **83**
Wrekenton. *Tyne* . . . . . . . . . . .4F **115**
Wrelton. *N Yor* . . . . . . . . . . . .1B **100**
Wrenbury. *Ches E* . . . . . . . . . . .1H **71**
Wreningham. *Norf* . . . . . . . . . . .1D **66**
Wrentham. *Suff* . . . . . . . . . . . . .2G **67**
Wrenthorpe. *W Yor* . . . . . . . . . .2D **92**
Wrentnall. *Shrp* . . . . . . . . . . . .5G **71**
Wressle. *E Yor* . . . . . . . . . . . . .1H **93**
Wressle. *N Lin* . . . . . . . . . . . . .4C **94**
Wrestlingworth. *C Beds* . . . . . . .1C **52**
Wretton. *Norf* . . . . . . . . . . . . . .1F **65**
**Wrexham**. *Wrex* . . . . . . . . . . . .5F **83**
Wreyland. *Devn* . . . . . . . . . . . . .4A **12**
Wrickton. *Shrp* . . . . . . . . . . . . .2A **60**
Wrightington Bar. *Lanc* . . . . . . .3D **90**
Wright's Green. *Essx* . . . . . . . . .4F **53**
Wrinehill. *Staf* . . . . . . . . . . . . .1B **72**
Wrington. *N Som* . . . . . . . . . . . .5H **33**
Writtle. *Essx* . . . . . . . . . . . . . .5G **53**
Wrockwardine. *Telf* . . . . . . . . . .4A **72**
Wroot. *N Lin* . . . . . . . . . . . . . .4H **93**
Wrotham. *Kent* . . . . . . . . . . . . .5H **39**
Wrotham Heath. *Kent* . . . . . . . . .5H **39**
Wroughton. *Swin* . . . . . . . . . . . .3G **35**
Wroxall. *IOW* . . . . . . . . . . . . . .4D **16**
Wroxall. *Warw* . . . . . . . . . . . . .3G **61**
Wroxeter. *Shrp* . . . . . . . . . . . . .5H **71**
Wroxham. *Norf* . . . . . . . . . . . . .4F **79**
Wroxton. *Oxon* . . . . . . . . . . . . .1C **50**
Wyaston. *Derbs* . . . . . . . . . . . . .1F **73**
Wyatt's Green. *Essx* . . . . . . . . . .1G **39**
Wybers Wood. *NE Lin* . . . . . . . . .4F **95**
Wyberton. *Linc* . . . . . . . . . . . . .1C **76**
Wyboston. *Bed* . . . . . . . . . . . . .5A **64**
Wybunbury. *Ches E* . . . . . . . . . .1A **72**
Wychbold. *Worc* . . . . . . . . . . . .4D **60**
Wych Cross. *E Sus* . . . . . . . . . . .2F **27**
Wychnor. *Staf* . . . . . . . . . . . . . .4F **73**
Wychnor Bridges. *Staf* . . . . . . . .4F **73**
Wyck. *Hants* . . . . . . . . . . . . . . .3F **25**
Wyck Hill. *Glos* . . . . . . . . . . . . .3G **49**
Wyck Rissington. *Glos* . . . . . . . .3G **49**
Wycliffe. *Dur* . . . . . . . . . . . . .3E **105**
Wycombe Marsh. *Buck* . . . . . . . .2G **37**
Yr Wyddgrug. *Flin* . . . . . . . . . . .4E **83**
Wyddial. *Herts* . . . . . . . . . . . . .2D **52**
Wye. *Kent* . . . . . . . . . . . . . . . .1E **29**
Wyesham. *Mon* . . . . . . . . . . . . .4A **48**
Wyfold. *Oxon* . . . . . . . . . . . . . .3E **37**
Wyfordby. *Leics* . . . . . . . . . . . .4E **75**
The Wyke. *Shrp* . . . . . . . . . . . . .5B **72**
Wyke. *Devn* . . . . . . . . . . . . . . .3B **12**
Wyke. *Dors* . . . . . . . . . . . . . . .4C **22**
Wyke. *Shrp* . . . . . . . . . . . . . . .5A **72**
Wyke. *Surr* . . . . . . . . . . . . . . .5A **38**
Wyke. *W Yor* . . . . . . . . . . . . . .2B **92**
Wyke Champflower. *Som* . . . . . . .3B **22**
Wykeham. *Linc* . . . . . . . . . . . . .3B **76**
Wykeham. *N Yor*
nr. Malton . . . . . . . . . . .2C **100**
nr. Scarborough . . . . . . .1D **100**
Wyken. *Shrp* . . . . . . . . . . . . . . .1B **60**
Wyken. *W Mid* . . . . . . . . . . . . .2A **62**
Wyke Regis. *Dors* . . . . . . . . . . .5B **14**
Wykey. *Shrp* . . . . . . . . . . . . . . .3F **71**
Wykin. *Leics* . . . . . . . . . . . . . . .1B **62**
Wylam. *Nmbd* . . . . . . . . . . . . .3E **115**
Wylde Green. *W Mid* . . . . . . . . . .1F **61**
Wylye. *Wilts* . . . . . . . . . . . . . . .3F **23**
Wymering. *Port* . . . . . . . . . . . . .2E **17**
Wymeswold. *Leics* . . . . . . . . . . .3D **74**
Wymington. *Bed* . . . . . . . . . . . .4G **63**
Wymondham. *Leics* . . . . . . . . . . .4F **75**
**Wymondham**. *Norf* . . . . . . . . . .5D **78**
Wyndham. *B'end* . . . . . . . . . . . .2C **32**
Wynford Eagle. *Dors* . . . . . . . . .3A **14**
Wyng. *Orkn* . . . . . . . . . . . . . .8C **172**
Wynyard Village. *Stoc T* . . . . . .2B **106**
Wyre Piddle. *Worc* . . . . . . . . . . .1E **49**
Wysall. *Notts* . . . . . . . . . . . . . .3D **74**
Wyson. *Here* . . . . . . . . . . . . . . .4H **59**
Wythall. *Worc* . . . . . . . . . . . . . .3E **61**
Wytham. *Oxon* . . . . . . . . . . . . . .5C **50**
Wythenshawe. *G Man* . . . . . . . . .2C **84**
Wythop Mill. *Cumb* . . . . . . . . .2C **102**

Wyton. *Cambs* . . . . . . . . . . . . .3B **64**
Wyton. *E Yor* . . . . . . . . . . . . . . .1E **95**
Wyverstone. *Suff* . . . . . . . . . . . .4C **66**
Wyverstone Street. *Suff* . . . . . .4C **66**
Wyville. *Linc* . . . . . . . . . . . . . . .3F **75**
Wyvis Lodge. *High* . . . . . . . . . .1G **157**

## Y

Yaddlethorpe. *N Lin* . . . . . . . .4B **94**
Yafford. *IOW* . . . . . . . . . . . . . .4C **16**
Yafforth. *N Yor* . . . . . . . . . . . .5A **106**
Yalding. *Kent* . . . . . . . . . . . . . .5A **40**
Yanley. *N Som* . . . . . . . . . . . . .5A **34**
Yanwath. *Cumb* . . . . . . . . . . . .2G **103**
Yanworth. *Glos* . . . . . . . . . . . .4F **49**
Yapham. *E Yor* . . . . . . . . . . . . .4B **100**
Yapton. *W Sus* . . . . . . . . . . . . .5A **26**
Yarburgh. *Linc* . . . . . . . . . . . . .1C **88**
Yarcombe. *Devn* . . . . . . . . . . . .2F **13**
Yarde. *Som* . . . . . . . . . . . . . . .3D **20**
Yardley. *W Mid* . . . . . . . . . . . .2F **61**
Yardley Gobion. *Nptn* . . . . . . .1F **51**
Yardley Hastings. *Nptn* . . . . . .5F **63**
Yardley Wood. *W Mid* . . . . . . .2F **61**
Yardro. *Powy* . . . . . . . . . . . . . .5E **59**
Yarhampton. *Worc* . . . . . . . . . .4B **60**
Yarkhill. *Here* . . . . . . . . . . . . . .1B **48**
Yarlet. *Staf* . . . . . . . . . . . . . . .3D **72**
Yarley. *Som* . . . . . . . . . . . . . . .2A **22**
Yarlington. *Som* . . . . . . . . . . . .4B **22**

Yarm. *Stoc T* . . . . . . . . . . . . . .3B **106**
Yarmouth. *IOW* . . . . . . . . . . . .4B **16**
Yarnbrook. *Wilts* . . . . . . . . . . .1D **22**
Yarnfield. *Staf* . . . . . . . . . . . . .2C **72**
Yarnscombe. *Devn* . . . . . . . . . .4F **19**
Yarnton. *Oxon* . . . . . . . . . . . . .4C **50**
Yarpole. *Here* . . . . . . . . . . . . . .4G **59**
Yarrow. *Nmbd* . . . . . . . . . . . . .1A **114**
Yarrow. *Bord* . . . . . . . . . . . . . .2F **119**
Yarrow. *Som* . . . . . . . . . . . . . . .2G **21**
Yarrow Feus. *Bord* . . . . . . . . . .2F **119**
Yarrow Ford. *Bord* . . . . . . . . . .1G **119**
Yarsop. *Here* . . . . . . . . . . . . . .1H **47**
Yarwell. *Nptn* . . . . . . . . . . . . . .1H **63**
Yate. *S Glo* . . . . . . . . . . . . . . . .3C **34**
Yateley. *Hants* . . . . . . . . . . . . .5G **37**
Yatesbury. *Wilts* . . . . . . . . . . . .4F **35**
Yattendon. *W Ber* . . . . . . . . . .4D **36**
Yatton. *Here*
        nr. Leominster . . . . . . .4G **59**
        nr. Ross-on-Wye . . . . . .2B **48**
Yatton. *N Som* . . . . . . . . . . . . .5H **33**
Yatton Keynell. *Wilts* . . . . . . . .4D **34**
Yaverland. *IOW* . . . . . . . . . . . .4E **16**
Yawl. *Devn* . . . . . . . . . . . . . . . .3G **13**
Yaxham. *Norf* . . . . . . . . . . . . . .4C **78**
Yaxley. *Cambs* . . . . . . . . . . . . .1A **64**
Yaxley. *Suff* . . . . . . . . . . . . . . .3D **66**
Yazor. *Here* . . . . . . . . . . . . . . .1H **47**
Yeading. *G Lon* . . . . . . . . . . . .2C **38**
Yeadon. *W Yor* . . . . . . . . . . . . .5E **98**
Yealand Conyers. *Lanc* . . . . . .2E **97**

Yealand Redmayne. *Lanc* . . . . .2E **97**
Yealand Storrs. *Lanc* . . . . . . . .2D **97**
Yealmpton. *Devn* . . . . . . . . . . . .3B **8**
Yearby. *Red C* . . . . . . . . . . . . .2D **106**
Yearngill. *Cumb* . . . . . . . . . . . .5C **112**
Yearsett. *Here* . . . . . . . . . . . . . .5B **60**
Yearsley. *N Yor* . . . . . . . . . . . . .2H **99**
Yeaton. *Shrp* . . . . . . . . . . . . . .4G **71**
Yeaveley. *Derbs* . . . . . . . . . . . . .1F **73**
Yeavering. *Nmbd* . . . . . . . . . . .1D **120**
Yedingham. *N Yor* . . . . . . . . . .2C **100**
Yeldersley Hollies. *Derbs* . . . . .1G **73**
Yelford. *Oxon* . . . . . . . . . . . . . .5B **50**
Yelland. *Devn* . . . . . . . . . . . . . .3E **19**
Yelling. *Cambs* . . . . . . . . . . . . .4B **64**
Yelsted. *Kent* . . . . . . . . . . . . . .4C **40**
Yelvertoft. *Nptn* . . . . . . . . . . . .3C **62**
Yelverton. *Devn* . . . . . . . . . . . . .2B **8**
Yelverton. *Norf* . . . . . . . . . . . . .5E **79**
Yenston. *Som* . . . . . . . . . . . . . .4C **22**
Yeoford. *Devn* . . . . . . . . . . . . . .3A **12**
Yeolmbridge. *Corn* . . . . . . . . . .4D **10**
Yeo Mill. *Devn* . . . . . . . . . . . . .4B **20**
Yeovil. *Som* . . . . . . . . . . . . . . .1A **14**
Yeovil Marsh. *Som* . . . . . . . . . .1A **14**
Yeovilton. *Som* . . . . . . . . . . . . .4A **22**
Yerbeston. *Pemb* . . . . . . . . . . .4E **43**
Yesnaby. *Orkn* . . . . . . . . . . . . .6B **172**
Yetlington. *Nmbd* . . . . . . . . . . .4E **121**
Yetminster. *Dors* . . . . . . . . . . . .1A **14**
Yett. *N Lan* . . . . . . . . . . . . . . .4A **128**
Yett. *S Ayr* . . . . . . . . . . . . . . . .2D **116**

Yettington. *Devn* . . . . . . . . . . . .4D **12**
Yetts o' Muckhart. *Clac* . . . . . .3C **136**
Yielden. *Bed* . . . . . . . . . . . . . . .4H **63**
Yieldshields. *S Lan* . . . . . . . . . .4B **128**
Yiewsley. *G Lon* . . . . . . . . . . . .2B **38**
Yinstay. *Orkn* . . . . . . . . . . . . . .6E **172**
Ynysboeth. *Rhon* . . . . . . . . . . . .2D **32**
Ynysddu. *Cphy* . . . . . . . . . . . . .2E **33**
Ynysforgan. *Swan* . . . . . . . . . . .3F **31**
Ynyshir. *Rhon* . . . . . . . . . . . . . .2D **32**
Ynyslas. *Cdgn* . . . . . . . . . . . . . .1F **57**
Ynysmaerdy. *Rhon* . . . . . . . . . .3D **32**
Ynysmeudwy. *Neat* . . . . . . . . . .5H **45**
Ynystawe. *Swan* . . . . . . . . . . . .5G **45**
Ynys-wen. *Rhon* . . . . . . . . . . . .2C **32**
Ynyswen. *Powy* . . . . . . . . . . . . .4B **46**
Ynys y Barri. *V Glam* . . . . . . . .5E **32**
Ynysybwl. *Rhon* . . . . . . . . . . . .2D **32**
Ynysymaerdy. *Neat* . . . . . . . . . .3G **31**
Yockenthwaite. *N Yor* . . . . . . . .2B **98**
Yockleton. *Shrp* . . . . . . . . . . . .4G **71**
Yokefleet. *E Yor* . . . . . . . . . . . .2B **94**
Yoker. *Glas* . . . . . . . . . . . . . . . .3G **127**
Yonder Bognie. *Abers* . . . . . . . .4C **160**
Yonderton. *Abers* . . . . . . . . . . .5G **161**
**York**. *York* . . . . . . . . . . . . . . . .4A **100**
Yorkletts. *Kent* . . . . . . . . . . . . . .4E **41**
Yorkley. *Glos* . . . . . . . . . . . . . . .5B **48**
Yorton. *Shrp* . . . . . . . . . . . . . . .3H **71**
Yorton Heath. *Shrp* . . . . . . . . . .3H **71**
Youlgreave. *Derbs* . . . . . . . . . . .4G **85**
Youlthorpe. *E Yor* . . . . . . . . . . .4B **100**

Youlton. *N Yor* . . . . . . . . . . . . .3G **99**
Young's End. *Essx* . . . . . . . . . .4H **53**
Young Wood. *Linc* . . . . . . . . . .3A **88**
Yoxall. *Staf* . . . . . . . . . . . . . . . .4F **73**
Yoxford. *Suff* . . . . . . . . . . . . . .4F **67**
Ysbyty Cynfyn. *Cdgn* . . . . . . . .3G **57**
Ysbyty Ifan. *Cnwy* . . . . . . . . . .1H **69**
Ysbyty Ystwyth. *Cdgn* . . . . . . .3G **57**
Ysceifiog. *Flin* . . . . . . . . . . . . . .3D **82**
Yspitty. *Carm* . . . . . . . . . . . . . .3E **31**
Ystalyfera. *Neat* . . . . . . . . . . . .5A **46**
Ystrad. *Rhon* . . . . . . . . . . . . . .2C **32**
Ystrad Aeron. *Cdgn* . . . . . . . . .5E **57**
Ystradfellte. *Powy* . . . . . . . . . . .4C **46**
Ystradffin. *Carm* . . . . . . . . . . . .1A **46**
Ystradgynlais. *Powy* . . . . . . . . .4A **46**
Ystradmeurig. *Cdgn* . . . . . . . . .4G **57**
Ystrad Mynach. *Cphy* . . . . . . . .2E **33**
Ystradowen. *Carm* . . . . . . . . . .4A **46**
Ystradowen. *V Glam* . . . . . . . . .4D **32**
Ystumtuen. *Cdgn* . . . . . . . . . . .3G **57**
Ythanbank. *Abers* . . . . . . . . . . .5G **161**
Ythanwells. *Abers* . . . . . . . . . . .5D **160**

## Z

Zeal Monachorum. *Devn* . . . . . .2H **11**
Zeals. *Wilts* . . . . . . . . . . . . . . . .3C **22**
Zelah. *Corn* . . . . . . . . . . . . . . . . .3C **6**
Zennor. *Corn* . . . . . . . . . . . . . . . .3B **4**
Zouch. *Notts* . . . . . . . . . . . . . . .3C **74**